Glencoe Accounting

CONCEPTS/PROCEDURES/APPLICATIONS

Donald J. Guerrieri
Norwin Senior High School
North Huntingdon, Pennsylvania

F. Barry Haber
Fayetteville State University
Fayetteville, North Carolina

William B. Hoyt
Wilton High School
Wilton, Connecticut

Robert E. Turner
McNeese State University
Lake Charles, Louisiana

GLENCOE
McGraw-Hill

New York, New York   Columbus, Ohio   Mission Hills, California   Peoria, Illinois

Donald J. Guerrieri is an accounting instructor at Norwin Senior High School, North Huntingdon, Pennsylvania. He has taught accounting at both the secondary and college levels. He also has experience working for a firm of certified public accountants Dr. Guerrieri has written numerous articles on the teaching of accounting for a variety of educational journals. He is also a program speaker at business education seminars and conferences.

F. Barry Haber is Professor of Accounting at Fayetteville State University, Fayetteville, North Carolina. Dr. Haber is a certified public accountant and is active in the American Institute of Certified Public Accountants, where he has served on the AICPA Minority Doctoral Fellows Committee. In addition to teaching accounting principles, Dr. Haber has authored three other textbooks, as well as various articles and cases in accounting.

William B. Hoyt is head of the Business Education Department at Wilton High School, Wilton, Connecticut. In addition to teaching accounting, he has been active in the development of microcomputer usage in business education courses. In this endeavor, he has taken part in panel discussions, given workshops, and written on the use of microcomputers in accounting instruction.

Robert E. Turner is the Vice President for Business Affairs at McNeese State University, Lake Charles, Louisiana. Mr. Turner has taught accounting and other business subjects at the high school and college levels. Mr. Turner has appeared on the programs of a number of business education conferences. He is also a frequent speaker at educational seminars around the country.

Library of Congress Cataloging-in-Publication Data

Glencoe accounting: concepts, procedures, applications: first-year
  course/ Donald J. Guerrieri . . . [et al.]. --3rd ed.
      p.   cm.
  Includes index
  ISBN 0-02-803617-4
  1. Accounting   I. Guerrieri, Donald J.
HF5635.G54 1995
657--dc20   93-44530
                                                          CIP

Send all inquiries to:
Glencoe/McGraw-Hill
936 Eastwind Drive
Westerville, OH 43081

ISBN 0-02-803617-4

Printed in the United States of America.

5 6 7 8 9 10 11 12 13 14 15   RRDW/MC 03 02 01 00 99 98 97 96 95

Contents

THE ACCOUNTING CYCLE FOR A MERCHANDISING BUSINESS

UNIT 3

ACCOUNTING FOR A PAYROLL SYSTEM   **414**

ACCOUNTING FOR SPECIAL PROCEDURES   **462**

ACCOUNTING FOR OTHER FORMS OF BUSINESS ORGANIZATION

Preface

"The more things change, the more they stay the same." The world of accounting is a good application of this maxim. The computer has revolutionized the generation and processing of financial records. Transactions that were formerly recorded, posted, compiled, sorted, and summarized laboriously by hand are now processed by the computer in the twinkling of an eye. Earlier critical procedures such as balancing and ruling of accounts and time-worn books of original entry such as the combination journal have been discarded or relegated to less important positions by automation. Even the language of accounting has been enlarged to include such terms as *batching, spreadsheets,* and *integrated accounting systems.*

Yet, in spite of all the changes wrought by the computer, one thing remains the same—the traditional insistence on learning the "why" as well as the "how" of accounting. To gain career success in accounting today without a sound knowledge of computer technology and familiarization with basic computerized accounting procedures would be difficult. But to gain success without a clear, conceptual knowledge of accounting—the "why" and the "how"—would be impossible.

Glencoe Accounting: Concepts/Procedures/Applications, Third Edition continues to emphasize the proven method of learning essential concepts and procedures through manual accounting, reinforced liberally with realistic applications. The sound methodology, proven practices, and solid applications of yesterday have been combined with the new approaches, contemporary procedures, and forward-looking computer technology of today to truly prepare students for tomorrow. *Glencoe Accounting* is a comprehensive instructional program thoughtfully designed to help students succeed by meeting and even anticipating the demands of the modern world of accounting.

Course Objectives

Glencoe Accounting: Concepts/Procedures/Applications, Third Edition is intended for use in a one-year introductory financial accounting course. The primary thrust of the textbook is on learning the rules and procedures of accounting for profit-motivated businesses. Learning the "how" and "why" of accounting will not only enable one to keep the accurate financial records required to produce useful business information, but will give one the capacity to *use* that financial information to make wise business decisions.

After studying this textbook and successfully completing activities in the textbook and the related working papers, students will be able to:

1. Use the basic accounting principles and procedures that are applied to accounting records kept for businesses that operate in the private enterprise economy of the United States.
2. Explain and appreciate the importance of profit in helping to ensure continued business operations.
3. Describe the three major types of business organizations in a private enterprise economy and explain how accounting procedures differ for the three.
4. Develop proficiency in the use of the computer to maintain accounting records.
5. Describe the types of on-the-job activities that are required of entry-level accounting workers.

Organization of the Textbook

Glencoe Accounting: Concepts/Procedures/Applications, Third Edition is organized in 6 units of 28 chapters. The first unit of the textbook begins with a presentation in Chapter 1 of the role of accounting in our private enterprise economy and an explanation of several important accounting assumptions. Chapter 2 introduces students to the basic accounting equation. This introduction provides students with a solid foundation on which to build their understanding of accounting theory and procedures.

The second unit of the textbook, "The Basic Accounting Cycle," takes students through a complete accounting cycle for a service business organized as a sole proprietorship. In this unit, students first learn the rules of debit and credit using T accounts and the basic accounting equation. Chapters 3 and 4 present the rules of debit and credit for the permanent accounts and for the temporary capital accounts. In Chapter 5, students learn to use a general journal to record business transactions. The general journal is preferred to other types of journals as a first learning experience because it requires students to think through the effects of transactions rather than memorizing how types of transactions are recorded. The remaining chapters in the unit complete the accounting cycle: posting to the general ledger, preparing a six-column work sheet, generating financial statements, journalizing and posting closing entries, and developing a post-closing trial balance.

Unit 3 introduces students to a merchandising business that is organized as a small, privately held corporation. Since corporations provide more than half the jobs in this country, it is important for students to be aware of the differences between accounting for a sole proprietorship and accounting for a corporation. In this unit, students will learn how to use special journals to record transactions for a merchandising business. They will complete the accounting cycle for a merchandising business by preparing a ten-column work sheet, financial statements, adjusting and closing entries, and a post-closing trial balance.

In Unit 4, students will learn how to keep payroll records, including those maintained for employees and for the employer's payroll liabilities. Students will be introduced to the changes in the social security taxes that were enacted in 1991. They will learn to apply the FICA tax deduction in two parts: (1) social security tax and (2) medicare tax.

The fifth unit comprises five chapters covering various accounting procedures that occur infrequently in many businesses. These procedures include accounting for cash funds, depreciation of plant and equipment, uncollectible accounts receivable, inventories, and notes.

Unit 6 introduces students to other forms of business organizations. In Chapter 26, students will learn about accounting for a partnership. Chapter 27 covers basic accounting procedures for publicly held corporations. In the last chapter, students are introduced to the uses of financial information for decision making. This chapter presents a few simple analyses that can be completed using the financial information reported by publicly held corporations.

Additional problems that can be used for extra and remedial practice are found in the back of the text. Enrichment chapters provide information and basic practice on the use of the combination journal and specific information and applications on accruals and deferrals.

Special Features

Glencoe Accounting is designed to promote student interest, involvement, and success through a variety of learning features.

Accounting cycle approach. The textbook utilizes a traditional accounting cycle approach to introduce students to new concepts and procedures. This step-by-step development gives students the guidance they look for and clearly demonstrates the continuity and interrelationships of the accounting process.

Chapter objectives. Clearly defined and stated objectives are provided at the beginning of each chapter to help students know exactly what they are expected to learn. The mastery of these objectives is evaluated through end-of-chapter activities, applications, and examinations.

Vocabulary emphasis. The new accounting terms defined in each chapter are listed on the first page of the chapter. This list should be used to "preview" the meaning of each term for students. Research has shown that such vocabulary "previews" help students achieve greater understanding and retention of the material in the chapter. End-of-chapter vocabulary reviews reinforce understanding of key terms. A complete glossary of accounting terms serves as a useful reference tool for students.

Clear, conversational narrative. The textbook is written in a style that is appropriate for high school students. Simple analogies make concepts meaningful for students. Abundant illustrations and numerous examples guide students through the preparation of accounting records.

Early emphasis on transaction analysis. A solid foundation in the rules of debit and credit is provided early in the textbook. Understanding the "why" of transaction analysis ensures that the "how" comes naturally.

Guided examples. These frequently used learning aids walk students through sample transactions, step by numbered step, making the "why" behind each procedure very clear.

Frequent learning reinforcement. "Check Your Learning" reinforcement activities follow major sections in every chapter to help students assume the responsibility for their own learning. "Remember" notes summarize key points and help cement important facts in students' minds. "Accounting Tips" at appropriate intervals remind students of essential practices and procedures. "Accounting Notes" inform students of interesting facts about business and the practice of accounting.

Solid end-of-chapter activities. Vocabulary reviews reinforce key accounting terms. Review questions help students expand their understanding of accounting concepts. Short activities encourage students to improve their skills in such important areas as decision making, communications, analysis, math, and human relations. A variety of exercises and problems, ranging from easy to challenging, gives students of all abilities the chance to gain practical accounting experience and to enjoy success.

Five comprehensive application activities. These "mini practice sets," at appropriate points in the textbook, require students to integrate new knowledge with learned procedures and to apply their cumulative skills. The applications may be completed manually, with the computer, or both manually and with the computer.

Computer integration. Information about computerized accounting systems is integrated into the chapter narrative, providing computer awareness and system comparisons for all students. Short vignettes, called "Focus on Computers," introduce specific aspects of computer technology. A broad range of computer activities is available on optional software: end-of-chapter problems and application activities; simulations; spreadsheets; and a microcomputer program for review, remediation, and reinforcement of key accounting principles. All such activities are completely optional. While the computer integration is provided, the use of a computer is not required for successful completion of the course.

Career orientation. Seven "Focus on Accounting Careers" vignettes provide students with a look at interesting jobs in the accounting world.

Ethics in business and accounting. Vignettes on ethical business and accounting situations, called "Focus on Ethics," are provided throughout the text. These ethical dilemmas illustrate the kinds of problems working professionals often encounter.

Acknowledgments

We wish to thank those individuals and companies that provided advice and assistance in the development of this program. We owe a debt of gratitude to thousands of teachers and students who used the previous editions of this textbook and who offered encouragement, suggestions, and advice in making a good accounting program even better.

We especially thank the Accounting Advisory Committee, composed of ten master accounting teachers from across the country, who provided excellent guidance and advice in the development and review of this program.

Finally, we wish to thank our families, colleagues, and friends who offered constant encouragement and support as we worked on the third edition.

Donald J. Guerrieri
F. Barry Haber
William B. Hoyt
Robert E. Turner

Educational Consultants and Reviewers

We wish to acknowledge the contributions of the following:

DeVon Allmaras
Longmont High School
Longmont, Colorado

Gail Blair
William Floyd High School
Mastic Beach, New York

Thelma H. Brooks
Southeast Career Center
Columbus, Ohio

Johnsie Crawford
Brandon Senior High School
Brandon, Florida

Jackie Dean
Washington High School
Washington, North Carolina

Gloria Farris
Seneca High School
Louisville, Kentucky

Trudy Formanek
Colstrip High School
Colstrip, Montana

Shirley A. Helmick
Western Hills High School
Fort Worth, Texas

Ruth Hennessy
Comeaux High School
Lafayette, Louisiana

Norma Hernandez
Galena Park I.S.D.
Galena Park, Texas

Mitch Hummel
Cocalico High School
Denver, Pennsylvania

Jerry Livingston
A.C. Jones High School
Beeville, Texas

Nancy Lord
Southeast Career Center
Columbus, Ohio

Ellen Lunden
Grand Ledge High School
Grand Ledge, Michigan

Carolyn McGraw
Lakeland High School
Lakeland, Florida

David McDonald
Rincon High School
Tucson, Arizona

John Nigro
North Haven High School
North Haven, Connecticut

JoAnne Pamer
Burbank High School
Burbank, California

Nate Rosenberg
Palo Alto High School
Palo Alto, California

Debra Saffo
Southeast Career Center
Columbus, Ohio

Michael Sailes
Carver Area High School
Chicago, Illinois

Emma Jo Spiegelberg
Laramie High School
Laramie, Wyoming

Claudia Stuvland
Rogers High School
Puyallup, Washington

Sue Thomas
Norwood High School
Norwood, Massachusetts

Carl Wenzel
Geneva High School
Geneva, New York

Frank Wood
Arrowhead High School
Hartland, Wisconsin

Eleanor A. Young
Southeast Career Center
Columbus, Ohio

UNIT 1

INTRODUCTION TO ACCOUNTING

In this first unit on accounting, you will study the role that accounting plays in the private enterprise economy of the United States. In our private enterprise economy, businesses must earn a profit if they are to continue to operate. Keeping accounting records is an important part of operating a business. Accounting records help businesses operate efficiently—and profitably—by keeping track of how much is earned and how much is spent.

Accounting is so much a part of our business lives that much of its terminology has become a part of our everyday language. Throughout this textbook, you will learn why accounting has been called the "language of business."

Chapter

ACCOUNTING IN A PRIVATE ENTERPRISE ECONOMY

Every business is somewhat like a stage production. For a play to be a success, everyone from the star to the electrician is held responsible for a task that must be performed a certain way. A stage production must run repeatedly for a certain length of time in order to make a profit. In our private enterprise economy, businesses are no different. Each business has many players, many tasks, and the need to perform successfully within certain time periods.

This textbook will describe how businesses operate in our private enterprise economy and the role accounting plays in business operations. Chapter 1 sets the stage for you to see the role accounting plays in our private enterprise economy.

Learning Objectives

When you have completed Chapter 1, you should be able to do the following:

1. Describe the three types of businesses operated to earn a profit in our private enterprise economy.
2. Discuss the three major forms of business organizations in our private enterprise economy.
3. Describe the role of accounting in our private enterprise economy.
4. Describe the variety of jobs available in accounting.
5. Recognize the major organizations that influence accounting practices.
6. Define the accounting terms introduced in this chapter.

New Terms

profit
loss
capital
service business
merchandising business
manufacturing business
sole proprietorship
partnership
corporation
charter
accounting system
business entity
going concern
fiscal period
accounting clerk
general bookkeeper
accountant
certified public accountant

The United States Private Enterprise Economy

All societies have ways of providing their members with goods and services. These ways range from very simple to very complex. The simple end of the scale is a pure barter economy: "I'll give you two bushels of corn if you give me ten chickens." In a slightly more advanced economy, the corn might be exchanged for money. The amount of money exchanged for the corn would depend on the value the owner placed on the corn and on whether the buyer could buy corn from someone else for less.

The most complex type of economy is represented by the electronic exchange of money through an electronic funds transfer system, or EFTS. With EFTS, money can be speedily transferred from one account to another, from bank account to account holder, or from one country to another. A sophisticated, computerized banking system keeps records of the amount of money transferred and to whom.

The economy of the United States is an example of a highly developed, complex economy. The United States economy is referred to as a *private enterprise economy.* In such an economy, people are free to produce the goods and services they choose. Individual buyers are free to use their money as they wish. They may choose to spend it, save it, or invest it. Since the amount of money available is limited, however, businesses must compete to attract the dollars of buyers. One measure of success in attracting dollars is the amount of profit a business earns. The amount of money earned over and above the amount spent to keep the business operating is called **profit.** Businesses that have more operating costs than earnings operate at a **loss.** In a private enterprise economy, only the businesses that consistently earn a profit will have the economic resources to continue to operate.

Businesses Operated for Profit

Groups of people get together in our economy for many different reasons, but each group is organized for some common purpose and with some common goal in mind. Some organizations are service-oriented and do not operate to earn a profit. Examples of such *not-for-profit organizations* include churches, private colleges, professional or social clubs, charitable organizations such as the United Way, and federal, state, and local governments. Other groups are business-oriented and operate to earn a profit. Both types of groups need financial information if they are to operate efficiently. In this textbook, however, you will learn about business organizations operated to earn a profit.

There are three types of businesses in our private enterprise economy that operate for profit: service businesses, merchandising businesses, and manufacturing businesses. Each type of business needs money to get started and to maintain its operations. Money is needed to buy or to make products. Money is also needed for such operating costs as rent, telephone service, and employee wages. Some of this money can be borrowed, but most of it is supplied by one or more owners of the business. The money so invested in a business by an owner is called **capital.**

Service, merchandising, and manufacturing businesses are alike in many ways, as shown in Figure 1-1 on page 4. Each business combines capital with

	Service Business	Merchandising Business	Manufacturing Business
USES:	Capital and labor	Capital and labor	Capital, labor, and materials
HAS:	Operating costs	Operating costs	Operating costs
TO:	Provide services at a fee	Buy and sell finished products	Make and sell finished products
FOR:	Profit	Profit	Profit

Figure 1-1 Types of Businesses Operated for Profit

labor, has operating costs, and hopes to make a profit. They differ from one another, however, in some basic ways. A **service business** operates to provide a needed service for a fee. Service businesses include travel agencies, beauty salons, movers, repair shops, real estate offices, and medical centers. A **merchandising business** buys finished products and resells them to individuals or other businesses. Clothing stores, new and used car dealers, supermarkets, florists, and hobby shops are all examples of merchandising businesses. A **manufacturing business,** on the other hand, buys raw materials, such as wood or iron ore, and transforms them into finished products through the use of labor and machinery. It then sells the finished products to individuals or other businesses. Manufacturing businesses range from steel makers to the corner bakery.

In the United States, businesses come in many varieties and sizes. All of these businesses need to keep accounting records to help them operate both efficiently and profitably.

Each type of business uses an accounting system to help guide the business's operations. In this accounting course, you will learn about the accounting systems used by service businesses.

Forms of Business Organization

To start a business, an owner must have a sufficient amount of money (capital) and must choose an appropriate form of business organization. With few exceptions, businesses in the United States are organized in one of three ways: as a sole proprietorship, a partnership, or a corporation.

▲ **The Sole Proprietorship**   "Sole" means "single" or "one." "Proprietor" means "owner." A **sole proprietorship,** then, is a business owned by one person. It is the oldest and most common form of business organization. It is also the simplest and easiest form of business to start. Usually, only one person invests capital in a sole proprietorship. The business may be started with little or no legal paperwork (forms and documents required by law). The success or failure of the business depends heavily on the efforts and talent of its owner. Some examples of common sole proprietorships are small neighborhood grocery stores, gift shops, and repair shops.

▲ **The Partnership**   A **partnership** is a business owned by two or more persons (called "partners") who agree to operate the business as co-owners. Business partners usually enter into a written, legal agreement. This agreement specifies the amount of money to be invested by each partner, the responsibilities of each partner, and how profits and losses are to be divided. Partnerships are often formed when the need for capital is greater than the amount of money one person can invest. Law firms, real estate offices, and "Mom and Pop" stores are frequently organized as partnerships.

▲ **The Corporation**   A **corporation** is a business organization that is recognized by law to have a life of its own. In contrast to a sole proprietorship and a partnership, a corporation must get permission to operate from the state. This legal permission is called a **charter** and gives a corporation certain rights and privileges. The charter spells out the rules under which the corporation is to operate.

Many people think that only large businesses like IBM or McDonald's are corporations. This is not always the case. Some corporations are owned and operated by a few people or by one family. Corporations often start out as sole proprietorships or partnerships. The owner(s) of a business may choose to "incorporate" to acquire the money needed to expand the business's operations. To raise this money, shares of stock are sold to hundreds or even thousands of people. These shares represent investments in the corporation. Shareholders, who are also called stockholders, are, therefore, the legal owners of a corporation.

Whatever their form of organization, all businesses share common financial characteristics and methods of recording and reporting the transactions that occur during the operation of the business.

The Role of Accounting

Accounting plays a very important role in our private enterprise system because its function is to process financial information and to report on profits and losses. An **accounting system** is the process of recording and reporting financial events, or transactions. The steps involved in an accounting system are illustrated in Figure 1-2.

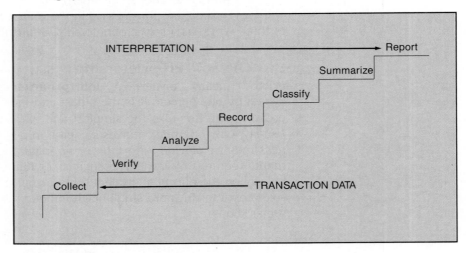

Figure 1-2 Steps in an Accounting System

As you can see, the first step in the process is to collect and verify the financial information for transactions. Each event or transaction having a financial impact on the business must be analyzed and recorded. The recorded information is then classified to make it more useful. After the information has been recorded and classified, it is summarized and presented in the form of accounting reports or statements. Examples of financial reports commonly prepared by accountants are presented in Figure 1-3. Accountants interpret the reports by looking for relationships and trends to help make the information more meaningful to the reader. Accounting is often called the "language of business" because it is a standard means of communicating financial information in a form that is clearly understood by all those interested in the operations and financial condition of a business.

The information in accounting reports has a wide audience. The owner of a business uses financial information to make decisions that affect day-to-day operations. People or institutions who loan money to a business use financial information to determine whether the business will be able to repay loans. Local, state, and federal governments may want to see financial records to determine whether a business is paying the proper amount of taxes. Finally, people who are thinking of investing money in a business want to know whether they can expect a return on their investments.

The Basis of an Accounting System

Accounting consists of many rules and procedures. These rules (or principles) and procedures guide the setting up and maintaining of financial records. Each business sets up its accounting system according to its specific needs, but all businesses follow the same basic rules and procedures.

Eastgate Furniture Corporation
Income Statement for Year Ended December 31, 19 --

Revenue from sales:
Gross sales			$650,000
Less: Sales returns and allowances		$ 1,500	
Sales discounts		4,500	6,000
Net sales			$644,000

Cost of goods sold:
Merchandise inventory, Jan. 1, 19-- .....
Purchases ....
Less: Purchases returns and allowances .
Purchases discounts ....
Net purchases ....
Add freight in ....
Cost of goods purchased ....
Goods available for sale ....
Merchandise inventory, Dec. 31, 19--.....
Cost of goods sold ....

Gross profit from sales ....

Operating expenses:
Selling expenses:
Sales salaries expense ....
Rent expense, selling space ....
Advertising expense ....
Store supplies expense ....
Depreciation expense, store equipment .
Total selling expenses ....
General and administrative expenses:
Office salaries expense ....
Rent expense, office space ....
Insurance expense ....
Office supplies expense ....
Depreciation expense, office equipment .
Total general and admin. expenses ..
Total operating expenses ....

Income from operations
Less income taxes expense ....
Net income

Eastgate Furniture Corporation
Balance Sheet, December 31, 19 --

Assets

Current assets:
Cash	$38,900	
Accounts receivable	9,900	
Merchandise inventory	23,000	
Prepaid expenses	4,400	
Total current assets		$ 76,200

Plant and equipment:
Office equipment	$14,000		
Less accumulated depreciation	1,050	$12,950	
Store equipment	$27,550		
Less accumulated depreciation	4,600	22,950	
Total plant and equipment			35,900
Total assets			$112,100

Liabilities

Current liabilities:
Accounts payable	$ 4,000	
Income taxes payable	2,100	
Total current liabilities		$ 6,100

Stockholders' Equity

Common stock, $5 par value, 4,000 shares authorized and outstanding	$20,000	
Retained earnings	86,000	
Total stockholders' equity		106,000
Total liab. and stockholders' equity		$112,100

Figure 1-3 Accounting Reports

An assumption is something taken for granted as true. When we go to a play, we assume that the show will be as advertised, that the actors can be heard by the audience, and that they are all speaking a language we understand. If our assumptions are wrong, the play will be disappointing or make no sense. Business "audiences" also must be able to make assumptions.

Accounting is based on four assumptions about business operations. These assumptions underlie all reports and are summarized by the terms "business entity," "going concern," "unit of measure," and "time period."

▲ **Business Entity**   A **business entity** is an organization that exists independently of its owner's personal holdings. This means that accounting records contain only the financial information related to the business. The business owner's personal financial activities or other investments are not included in the reports of the business. For example, the personal residence of a business owner, valued at $75,000, is not reported in the accounting records of the business. Buildings owned by the business, however, are included in its financial records and reports.

▲ **Going Concern**   In accounting, it is assumed that a business will continue to operate in the future. In other words, a business is said to be a **going concern.** Financial reports are prepared on the assumption that the business will operate long enough to carry out its operations and meet future obligations. That assumption is why a business might report that its long-term debts of $100,000 must be paid in the year 2010.

▲ **Unit of Measure**   The effects of business transactions are measured in money amounts. In the United States, the monetary unit of measure is the dollar. For accounting records, the dollar is assumed to have a fixed buying power. In other words, the effects of inflation or deflation are not reflected in the financial records of a business. Everything is recorded at cost. For example, a business purchased an office building for $150,000. The office building might now cost $180,000 to replace due to inflation. In the accounting records, however, the building would be listed at its original cost of $150,000.

▲ **Time Period**   Accounting reports are prepared for a specific period of time. A period of time covered by an accounting report is referred to as a **fiscal period.**   The fiscal period can cover any period of time—such as one month or three months—but the most common period is one year.

Accounting and the Computer

Before the invention of calculators and computers, all business transactions were recorded by hand. Now the computer performs routine record-keeping tasks and prepares reports that sometimes took accounting workers months to summarize manually. The computer is ideally suited to accounting work, and accountants were among the earliest users to recognize its practical applications. Found only in large businesses at first, computers are now commonplace. Microcomputers give even one-person businesses the option of using a computerized accounting system.

In today's business world, it is becoming increasingly important for accounting workers to be familiar with computerized accounting.

Regardless of how or whether a business uses computers, the nature of accounting remains the same. Information may be recorded in a manual accounting system and a computerized accounting system in different ways, but the same financial reports will result. The rules and principles that you learn from this textbook will apply to both manual and computerized accounting systems.

Career Opportunities in Accounting

According to the *Occupational Outlook Handbook,* the number of jobs for bookkeeping and accounting workers is expected to increase substantially during the 1990s. Although the jobs will require varying amounts of education and experience, most of the jobs will fall into the categories of accounting clerk, general bookkeeper, or accountant. Let's take a look at the requirements of these jobs and their roles in business.

Accounting Clerk

Most entry-level jobs in accounting are clerical. The people who hold these jobs are generally called **accounting clerks.** According to the *Dictionary of Occupational Titles,* an accounting clerk does "routine computing, calculating, and posting of financial, statistical, and other numerical data, manually or by machine, to maintain accounting records and to record details of business transactions."

The job of an accounting clerk varies with the size of the company. In a small business, the clerk might handle most of the business's recordkeeping tasks. In a large company, clerks might specialize in one part of the accounting system. Minimum requirements for most accounting clerk positions are graduation from high school and one or two years of accounting courses. More and more employers want workers who can handle computerized accounting tasks. Some of the entry-level clerical jobs that you see in want ads call for accounting clerks in these categories: payroll, accounts receivable, accounts payable, general ledger, cash, inventory, and purchasing.

General Bookkeeper

Many small- or medium-sized businesses employ only one person to keep their accounting records. This person is usually called a **general bookkeeper.** In addition to processing and recording all the information from a company's transactions, a general bookkeeper often calculates wages and prepares checks for the payment of those wages. In companies with several accounting clerks, a general bookkeeper will often also be a supervisor.

Education requirements vary with the size of the company and the complexity of its accounting system. A general bookkeeper may or may not be required to have a four-year college degree in accounting. Experience or an associate's degree in accounting is sometimes enough to fulfill the job's requirements.

Accountant

The term **accountant** describes a fairly broad range of jobs. In general, an accountant is expected to make choices and decisions about the design of accounting systems and to prepare and explain financial reports. An accountant may also supervise the work of accounting clerks who perform routine recordkeeping functions.

Many accountants enter the field with either a bachelor's or a master's degree in accounting. It is not unusual, however, for accountants to have started at entry-level positions and studied for their degrees while on the job. Although accountants work in every kind of business, their work can be divided into four major categories: public accounting, managerial accounting, not-for-profit accounting, and teaching.

▲ **Public Accounting**   Public accountants provide services to clients on a fee basis. Like medicine and law, public accounting requires a license, or certification by the state. To become a **certified public accountant,** or CPA, an accountant must pass a rigorous examination on accounting theory, accounting practices, auditing, and business law. CPAs provide a variety of services to their clients. They often prepare income tax returns and give financial advice about the operation of a business.

▲ **Managerial Accounting**   Unlike public accounting, *managerial accounting* takes place only inside a business firm. A managerial accountant may determine the cost of products, prepare budgets and tax returns, and provide financial information to the business's managers. By passing an examination similar to the CPA's, a managerial accountant may receive a Certificate in Management Accounting (CMA). A CMA, however, is not a license to practice and does not allow the accountant to perform services for the general public.

▲ **Not-for-Profit Accounting**   Groups that provide services to the general public and do not operate to make money are called not-for-profit organizations. Not-for-profit organizations include universities, churches, government agencies, and most hospitals. Although these organizations do not have profit as their main goal, they still require accounting services. They are concerned with the efficient use of the resources available to them. Not-for-profit accountants specialize in accounting for these organizations.

▲ **Teaching Accounting**   The field of education offers many opportunities for people with degrees and experience in accounting. High schools, colleges, and universities offer a wide variety of accounting courses that require qualified instructors.

Organizations that Influence Accounting Practice

In the United States, four groups have had a major impact on accounting practice. The four groups are the American Institute of Certified Public Accountants, the Financial Accounting Standards Board, the Securities and Exchange Commission, and the Internal Revenue Service.

The American Institute of Certified Public Accountants

The American Institute of Certified Public Accountants (AICPA) is a professional association. Its members are certified public accountants in public practice, business and industry, education, and government. The Institute's main concern has been the development of standards of professional practice for its members. Although the AICPA no longer issues official statements on accounting standards, it still has a strong influence.

Financial Accounting Standards Board

The Financial Accounting Standards Board (FASB) was established in 1973 to develop financial accounting standards for businesses and not-for-profit organizations. The FASB is authorized to issue two publications: *Statements of Financial Accounting Standards* and *Interpretations.* The *Statements* and *Interpretations* help in preparing and auditing financial reports.

Securities and Exchange Commission

The Securities and Exchange Commission (SEC) was established by Congress in 1934 to regulate the sale of stock certificates to the general public. The SEC was also given broad authority to regulate and control accounting and other information distributed by corporations. The SEC, however, has generally relied on the accounting profession to perform these functions. In only a few cases has the SEC exerted its legal power by disagreeing with a position taken by the AICPA or the FASB.

Internal Revenue Service

The Internal Revenue Service (IRS) has a widespread impact on many aspects of our economy. The IRS is charged with the collection of federal taxes, the enforcement of tax regulations, and the interpretation of tax laws relating to particular businesses or situations. Through these functions, the IRS has a direct effect on tax-related aspects of accounting.

Other Influences

Several other organizations continue to influence accounting practices and standards. The National Council on Governmental Accounting (NCGA) develops and interprets principles of accounting and financial reporting for state and local governments. The American Accounting Association (AAA), an organization of accounting professors and certified public accountants, is concerned with developing accounting standards. The Institute of Management Accountants is concerned with accounting for management purposes.

Summary of Key Points

1. In the United States private enterprise economy, businesses are concerned with earning a profit. Businesses that do not earn a profit over a period of time will not be able to continue operating.

2. The three types of businesses organized to earn a profit are service businesses, merchandising businesses, and manufacturing businesses.
3. The three major forms of business organization found in the United States are the sole proprietorship, the partnership, and the corporation.
4. Accounting is a systematic process of recording and reporting the financial information resulting from business transactions.
5. Accounting information is used by a wide variety of people to make decisions about how well or how poorly a business is operating.
6. Computers have affected the speed with which accounting is performed, but their use has not altered the basic accounting system.
7. There is a wide variety of jobs available in bookkeeping and accounting. The number of job openings in this area is expected to increase in the next decade.
8. Accounting practices are influenced and regulated by such groups as the AICPA, FASB, SEC, and IRS.

Review and Applications

Building Your Accounting Vocabulary

In your own words, write the definitions of each of the following accounting terms. Use complete sentences for your definitions.

accountant
accounting clerk
accounting system
business entity
capital
certified public
  accountant
charter

corporation
fiscal period
general bookkeeper
going concern
loss
manufacturing
  business

merchandising
  business
partnership
profit
service business
sole proprietorship

Reviewing Your Accounting Knowledge

1. The United States economy is referred to as a private enterprise economy. What is the major characteristic of our private enterprise economy?
2. What is one measure of business success?
3. What is the major difference between a merchandising business and a manufacturing business?
4. List the main difference between a partnership and a corporation.
5. What is the basic function of an accounting system?
6. Who are the users of accounting information?
7. List and briefly explain the four assumptions about business operations on which accounting is based.
8. What are some of the duties of an accounting clerk?
9. What are the four possible career areas in the field of accounting?
10. What organizations influence accounting as it is practiced in the United States?

Improving Your Decision-Making Skills

One way to make a decision is to follow a step-by-step pattern that is called the decision-making process. The steps in this process are

1. Face the problem (recognize the need for a decision).
2. Get information about the problem.
3. List alternative ways of dealing with the problem.
4. Evaluate the alternatives.
5. Reach a decision.
6. Act on the decision.

Suppose you are trying to decide whether a career in accounting is right for you. Using the steps in the decision-making process, describe the actions you would take at each step. Be specific about information you would need and where you would get it.

Applying Accounting Procedures

Exercise 1-1 Understanding Business and Accounting Terms

Instructions: Number a sheet of paper from 1 to 10. Write the word or words from the list below that best matches each numbered statement.

accounting reports
dollar
electronic funds transfer system
managerial accounting
not-for-profit organization

organization
partners
private enterprise economy
shareholders
stock

1. An economy in which people are free to produce the goods or services they choose
2. An organization that is service-oriented and that does not operate to earn a profit
3. The legal owners of a corporation
4. The end results of an accounting system
5. The unit of measure for financial information in the United States
6. Co-owners of a business
7. Shares of ownership in a corporation
8. A system that provides financial information to interested persons within an organization
9. A computerized system for transferring funds
10. A group of people who come together with a common goal in mind

Exercise 1-2 Using Financial Information

Instructions: Give one or more reasons why each of the following would be interested in the financial reports of the Pacific Company, a fishing fleet.

1. James Taylor is looking for an investment in which he can make a profit, even if a little risk is involved.
2. Rita Hays, the local union agent, is preparing the bargaining position for employee wage increases.
3. Diane Hauser, a buyer for a fish market, is seeking a new supplier from which to buy fresh fish.
4. Mark Siebert, a credit manager, has been asked to approve a loan for the Pacific Company.
5. Jill Mercer, a retired widow, is looking for an investment that will provide a steady income for her retirement years.

Exercise 1-3 Exploring Accounting Careers

Instructions: Read the following paragraph and assume that you are Lee Harms. On a sheet of paper, write what you think Lee's response would be.

A CAREER DAY MEETING

Two accounting students, Richard Cummings and Nancy Purcell, were discussing whether they should become accountants. They met Lee Harms, a CPA, at a career day meeting and asked her what types of employment opportunities they might find in accounting.

Exercise 1-4   Describing Types of Businesses

Instructions: On a sheet of paper, indicate whether each of the following businesses is a service business, a merchandising business, or a manufacturing business.

1. International Business Machines (IBM)
2. J. C. Penney Co., Inc.
3. Glendale Medical Center
4. Avis Rent-a-Car
5. Ford Motor Company
6. The Chase Manhattan Bank
7. Ace Hardware Stores
8. Michigan City Animal Hospital
9. Apple Computer, Inc.
10. K Mart Discount Department Store
11. Prudential Insurance Company of America
12. Bethlehem Steel Corporation

*A*utomation:
A Business's Life Support System

In today's business world, time and money are precious resources. Wise decision making can help control spending and productivity. To this end, one of the wisest decisions management can make is to automate.

Small businesses have discovered that computers can help them in a big way. Consider these cases.

The estimator in a family-owned metal fabricating shop in the Midwest wrote his own computer program to help him prepare price estimates. He keys in the quantity and size of material, and the program prepares the estimate. By hand, estimates take 15 to 20 *minutes;* the electronic estimates take 15 to 20 *seconds.* Not only are the computer estimates faster—they're also more accurate.

A property management company oversees 65 properties, some of which are shopping centers. The work is done with just 4 bookkeepers, 8 property managers, and a network of computers. Without automation, the company president estimates they'd need 20 bookkeepers instead of 4 and 24 property managers instead of 8. The company saves over $400,000 a year in payroll costs alone. The company president says that savings is the difference between profit and bankruptcy.

Big businesses can save even more. Commercial banks move about $300 billion every day in international electronic funds transfers. The cost of a single international transfer is $10 to $12 if done on paper. Done electronically, the cost drops to about $2 per transfer.

Government agencies save time and money through automation, too. The U.S. Forest Service says that, since it automated, its environmental impact statements take 39% less time to prepare.

Buying or sending gifts over long distances is easy today with the help of computers.

Timber sales contracts take 27% less time. A study revealed that automation saved the Forestry Service $125 million in 1985.

To business owners, the question is not, "*Should* I automate?" Rather the question is, "How long will I survive without it?"

Chapter 2

BUSINESS TRANSACTIONS AND THE BASIC ACCOUNTING EQUATION

In Chapter 1 you learned that accounting has been called the "language of business." Accounting provides financial information that is essential for the success of any business. Accounting provides that financial information to a wide variety of users: owners, managers, employees, investors, and so on.

In this chapter, you will begin to learn some of the language of accounting. You'll learn about the basic accounting equation—the foundation of accounting. This equation expresses the relationship between property and the rights or claims to that property.

Learning Objectives

When you have completed Chapter 2, you should be able to do the following:

1. Describe the relationship between property and property rights.
2. Explain the meaning of "equity" as it is used in accounting.
3. List the parts of the basic accounting equation and define each part.
4. Show how various business transactions affect the basic accounting equation.
5. Check the balance of the basic accounting equation after a business transaction has been analyzed and recorded.
6. Define the accounting terms introduced in this chapter.

New Terms

property
property rights
credit
creditor
assets
equity
owner's equity
liabilities
basic accounting equation
business transaction
account
accounts receivable
accounts payable
capital
on account
revenue
expense
withdrawal

Property and Property Rights

The right to own property is basic to our private enterprise system. **Property** is anything of value that is owned or controlled. When you own an item of property, you have a legal right to that item. When you have control over an item, you have the right only to the use of the item. For example, you own a pair of skis you have bought. If you had rented the skis for a weekend instead of buying them, you would have control of the skis. You would have the right to use the skis for the weekend, but you would not own them. As you can see from this example, you can have certain rights, or claims, to the items that you either own or control.

When you purchase property, you acquire certain rights, or financial claims to that property.

Businesses also own and control property. One of the purposes of accounting is to provide financial information about property and a business's rights to that property. In accounting, property and property rights are measured in dollar amounts. Dollar amounts measure both the cost of the property and the **property rights,** or financial claims, to the property. For example, if you had paid $100 cash to buy the skis mentioned above, you would have a property right or financial claim of $100 to those skis. This relationship between property and property rights is shown in the equation that follows:

PROPERTY (COST)	=	PROPERTY RIGHTS (FINANCIAL CLAIMS)
Skis	=	Your Claim to Skis
$100	=	$100

When you buy property with cash, you acquire all of the property rights (financial claims) to that property at the time of purchase. What happens, however, when you buy property on credit? What happens to the financial claim when you don't pay for the property right away?

When you buy property and agree to pay for it later, you are buying on **credit.** The business or person selling you the property on credit is called a **creditor.** A creditor can be any person or business to which you owe money. When you buy property on credit, you do not have the only financial claim to the property. You share the financial claim to that property with your creditor. For example, suppose you want to buy a pair of ski boots that costs $150, but you have only $75. A store agrees to sell you the boots on credit. You pay the store $75 and sign an agreement to pay the remaining $75 over the next three months. Since you owe the store (the creditor) $75, you share the financial claim to the boots with the creditor. The creditor's financial claim to the ski boots is $75 and your claim is $75. The combined claims equal the cost of the property (the boots). Your purchase of the ski boots can be expressed in terms of the equation PROPERTY = PROPERTY RIGHTS.

PROPERTY =	PROPERTY RIGHTS		
Ski Boots	= Creditor's Financial Claim	+	Owner's Financial Claim
$150	= $75	+	$75

As you can see, two (or more) people can have financial claims to the same property. The total financial claims always equal the total cost of the property. Before you read any further, answer the following questions to check your understanding of the relationship between property and property rights.

Check Your Learning

The equation below shows the relationship between property and its corresponding financial claims. Use the equation to answer the questions that follow. (Use notebook paper if you want to write your answer.)

Property = Creditor's Financial Claim + Owner's Financial Claim

1. What are the missing dollar amounts in each equation?
   a. Property (?) = Creditor's Claim ($1,000) + Owner's Claim ($6,000)
   b. Property ($2,000) = Creditor's Claim ($500) + Owner's Claim (?)
   c. Property ($30,000) = Creditor's Claim (?) + Owner's Claim ($22,000)
2. What is the amount of a creditor's claim to a radio if the radio cost $75 and the owner has paid $35 on it?
3. What is the amount of the owner's claim to a baseball glove if the glove cost $32 and the amount still owed is $12?
4. What was the cost of an automobile if the owner has a $3,000 claim and a creditor has an $11,000 claim?

The answers to these questions can be found in the answers section at the back of this book. Compare your answers to the answers for this activity. If you missed the answer to a question, find out why. Go back to the appropriate section of the chapter and study the material related to the answer you may have missed.

Financial Claims in Accounting

As you learned in Chapter 1, every business is considered a separate entity. In other words, the property of a business is separate from the personal property of its owner(s). The accounting records of a business are kept only for transactions affecting the business itself. The owner's personal financial transactions are not a part of the business's records. For example, if the owner buys a car for her or his personal use, that car would not be recorded as property of the business.

In accounting, the property or items of value owned by a business are referred to as **assets.** Some examples of assets are cash, office equipment, manufacturing equipment, buildings, and land. There is also an accounting term for the financial claims to these assets. The total financial claims to the assets, or property, of a business are referred to as **equity.** If you have a financial claim to property, you are said to have equity in that property. Let's explore the meaning of this term.

Suppose Book Ends, a small bookstore, has just bought a new building for its operations. The building cost $45,000 and Book Ends made a cash down payment of $15,000 to the seller of the building. A local bank loaned the store the remaining $30,000. Both the book store and the bank now have financial claims to the building. As creditor, the bank has equity in the building equal to its investment of $30,000. Book Ends has equity equal to its down payment of $15,000. Over the years, as Book Ends repays the loan, its equity will increase. As less money is owed, the equity of the creditor (the bank) will decrease. When the loan is completely repaid, the creditor's financial claim will be canceled. In other words, the owner's equity will then equal the cost of the building. Book Ends will both own and control the property and will, therefore, have full property rights to it.

As you can see from this example, equity is simply the claims—of both creditor(s) and owner(s)—to the assets of a business. In accounting, there are separate terms for owner's claims and creditor's claims. The owner's claims to the assets of the business are called **owner's equity.** Owner's equity is measured by the dollar amount of the owner's claims to the total assets of the business.

The creditor's claims to the assets of the business are called **liabilities.** Liabilities are the debts of a business. They are measured by the amount of money owed by a business to its creditors. The relationship between assets and total equities—liabilities plus owner's equity—can be shown in the **basic accounting equation,** which is

ASSETS = LIABILITIES + OWNER'S EQUITY

Figure 2-1 shows the basic accounting equation applied to the example of Book Ends and the bank that gave it a loan. Notice that assets equal the combined claims to those assets.

R — E — M — E — M — B — E — R

Total equities includes both the creditor's claims and the owner's claims.

| ASSETS | = | | EQUITIES | |

| $45,000 Building | | $30,000 Loan | | $15,000 Investment |

Property	=	Creditor's Claim	+	Owner's Claim
$45,000		$30,000		$15,000
ASSETS	=	LIABILITIES	+	OWNER'S EQUITY

Figure 2-1   The Basic Accounting Equation

Before you go on to learn about business transactions, do the Check Your Learning activity that follows to check your understanding of the basic accounting equation.

Check Your Learning

Use the basic accounting equation to answer these questions. (If you want to write your answers, use notebook paper.)

1. If a business has invested $50,000 in an asset that cost $75,000, what is the amount of its liability?

2. In accounting, there are two kinds of equity: ___?___ and owner's equity.

3. If a business has liabilities of $60,000 and assets of $218,000, what is the amount of owner's equity?

Compare your answers to those in the answers section. Re-read the preceding part of the chapter to find the correct answers to any questions that you may have missed.

Business Transactions

A **business transaction** is an economic event that causes a change in assets, liabilities, or owner's equity. Business transactions involve the buying, selling, or exchange of goods and services. Some businesses have hundreds, or even thousands, of business transactions every day. When a business transaction occurs, the financial position of the business changes. The change is reflected in the accounting system of the business as an increase or decrease in assets, liabilities, or owner's equity. Let's look at an example.

If a business buys a typewriter and pays cash for it, the amount of cash the business has is decreased. At the same time, the business has increased its equipment. In an accounting system, the increases and decreases caused by business transactions are recorded in specific accounts. An **account,** then, is a record of the increases or decreases in and the balance for a specific item such as cash or equipment.

Accounts represent things in the real world, such as money invested in a business, office furniture, or money owed to a creditor. For example, an account for office furniture represents the dollar cost of all the office furniture bought by the business.

Each business sets up its accounts and its accounting system according to its needs. There is no standard number of accounts a business should use. Some businesses have only a few accounts, while others have hundreds. Regardless of the number of accounts a business has, all its accounts may be classified as either assets, liabilities, or owner's equity. The following account titles are but a few examples of the types of accounts a business can have:

ASSETS	=	LIABILITIES	+	OWNER'S EQUITY
Cash in Bank		Accounts Payable		Paul Howard, Capital
Accounts Receivable				
Office Furniture				
Equipment				

Some of these account titles need more explanation. The second asset account listed is Accounts Receivable. **Accounts receivable** is the total amount of money to be received in the future for goods or services sold on credit. Accounts receivable is an asset because it represents something owned: a business's claim to the assets of another person or another business. It represents a future value that eventually will bring cash into the business. When the business eventually receives payment in cash, the claim will be canceled.

The liability account listed is Accounts Payable. **Accounts payable** is the amount of money owed, or payable, to a business's creditors. It is a future obligation requiring the payment of cash or services to another person or business. Finally, note that the owner's equity account in a business is identified by the owner's name followed by a comma and the word "Capital." **Capital** refers to the dollar amount of the owner's investment in the business.

ACCOUNTING *Notes*
The word *capital* has its roots in the Latin word *capitalis*, meaning "property." *Capital* first meant "main." Later the term came to stand for a person's wealth, which was the main source of a person's importance.

Effects of Business Transactions on the Basic Accounting Equation

When a business transaction occurs, an accounting clerk analyzes the transaction to see how it affects each part of the basic accounting equation. As an accounting clerk, you must select the information in a transaction that indicates any change in assets, liabilities, or owner's equity. You will find it easy to analyze the effects of a transaction if you follow the steps that are listed:

1. Identify the accounts affected.
2. Classify the accounts affected (asset, liability, or owner's equity).
3. Determine the amount of increase or decrease for each account affected.
4. Make sure the basic accounting equation remains in balance.

The business transactions that follow are examples of transactions that occur often in most businesses. To help you learn about various kinds of transactions, these examples are categorized as follows: (1) investments by the owner, (2) cash transactions, (3) credit transactions, (4) revenue and expense transactions, and (5) withdrawals by the owner.

Investments by the Owner

Paul Howard has decided to start a word processing service business. He plans to call the business WordService.

Business Transactions 1 and 2 concern investments made in the business by the owner. Transaction 1 is a cash investment; Transaction 2 is an investment of equipment.

Business Transaction 1: The owner of WordService, Paul Howard, deposited $20,000 in a bank checking account under the name of WordService.

Analysis:
1. Identify the accounts affected.

   Every transaction will affect at least two accounts. You can determine the accounts affected by analyzing the transaction to see which accounts are being changed. Here are the accounts used by WordService.

ASSETS	=	LIABILITIES	+	OWNER'S EQUITY
Cash in Bank		Accounts Payable		Paul Howard, Capital
Accounts Receivable				
Office Furniture				
Equipment				

   Now look at Transaction 1 again. The business has received cash. Cash transactions are summarized in the account entitled Cash in Bank. Paul Howard is investing his personal funds in the business. An owner's investments in the business are summarized in the account called Paul Howard, Capital.
2. Classify the accounts affected.

   Cash in Bank is an asset account. Paul Howard, Capital is an owner's equity account.
3. Determine the amount of increase or decrease for each account affected.

   Cash in Bank is increased by $20,000. Paul Howard, Capital is increased by $20,000.
4. Make sure the basic accounting equation remains in balance.

	ASSETS	=	LIABILITIES	+	OWNER'S EQUITY
	Cash in Bank				Paul Howard, Capital
Trans. 1	+$20,000				+$20,000
Balance	$20,000	=	0	+	$20,000

   The asset account Cash in Bank totals $20,000. Liabilities plus owner's equity also total $20,000. The basic accounting equation remains in balance.

R — E — M — E — M — B — E — R

Each transaction affects at least two accounts.

Business Transaction 2: *The owner, Paul Howard, invested an electric typewriter worth $300 in the business.*

Analysis:

1. Identify the accounts affected.

   The business has received an electric typewriter. Since a typewriter is equipment, the account Equipment is affected. Paul Howard has invested a personal asset in the business, so the account Paul Howard, Capital is also affected.

2. Classify the accounts affected.

   Equipment is an asset account and Paul Howard, Capital is an owner's equity account.

3. Determine the amount of increase or decrease for each account affected.

   Equipment is increased by $300. Paul Howard, Capital is increased by $300.

4. Make sure the basic accounting equation remains in balance.

	ASSETS		= LIABILITIES	+	OWNER'S EQUITY
	Cash in Bank	Equipment			Paul Howard, Capital
Prev. Bal.	$20,000	0	0		$20,000
Trans. 2		+$300		+	300
Balance	$20,000 +	$300	= 0	+	$20,300

The asset accounts Cash in Bank and Equipment total $20,300. Liabilities and owner's equity total $20,300, so the basic accounting equation is in balance.

Cash Payment Transactions

Transaction 3 is an example of a transaction in which an asset is purchased for cash. Any asset that is purchased for cash will be recorded as in this transaction. In similar transactions, the account title will change, depending upon the asset bought.

Business Transaction 3: *WordService issued a $4,000 check for the purchase of a microcomputer.*

Analysis:

1. Identify the accounts affected.

   The business has purchased a microcomputer. The Equipment account is used to summarize transactions involving any type of equipment. Since the business has paid out cash for the microcomputer, the account Cash in Bank is affected. (Payments made by check are always treated as cash payments and are summarized in the Cash in Bank account.)

2. Classify the accounts affected.

   Equipment and Cash in Bank are both asset accounts.

3. Determine the amount of increase or decrease for each account affected.

   Equipment is increased by $4,000. The account Cash in Bank is decreased by $4,000.

4. Make sure the basic accounting equation remains in balance.

	ASSETS		= LIABILITIES	+ OWNER'S EQUITY
	Cash in Bank	Equipment		Paul Howard, Capital
Prev. Bal.	$20,000	$ 300	0	$20,300
Trans. 3	− 4,000	+ 4,000		
Balance	$16,000 +	$4,300 =	0	+ $20,300

Transaction 3 affected only the assets side of the equation. WordService exchanged one asset (cash) for another asset (equipment). The total assets remain at $20,300. Liabilities plus owner's equity total $20,300, so the equation remains in balance.

Credit Transactions

Now that you have learned about cash transactions, let's look at how the use of credit affects the basic accounting equation. When a business buys on credit, it is often said to be buying **on account.** In the next three transactions, you will learn about a purchase on account, a payment on account, and a sale on account.

Business Transaction 4: *WordService bought office furniture on account from Office Interiors for $3,000.*

Analysis:
1. Identify the accounts affected.
   WordService has received additional property (office furniture), so the account Office Furniture is affected. The business has promised to pay for the office furniture at a later time. This promise to pay is a liability of WordService, therefore, the Accounts Payable account is affected.
2. Classify the accounts affected.
   Office Furniture is an asset account and Accounts Payable is a liability account.
3. Determine the amount of increase or decrease for each account affected.
   Office Furniture is increased by $3,000. Accounts Payable is also increased by $3,000.
4. Make sure the basic accounting equation remains in balance.

	ASSETS			= LIABILITIES	+ OWNER'S EQUITY
	Cash in Bank	Office Furniture	Equipment	Accounts Payable	Paul Howard, Capital
Prev. Bal.	$16,000	0	$4,300	0	$20,300
Trans. 4		+$3,000		+$3,000	
Balance	$16,000 +	$3,000 +	$4,300	= $3,000	+ $20,300

Assets now total $23,300. Liabilities plus owner's equity also total $23,300, so the equation remains in balance.

Business Transaction 5: *WordService issued a check for $1,000 in partial payment of the amount owed to its creditor, Office Interiors.*

Analysis:
1. Identify the accounts affected.
   The payment decreased the total amount owed to the creditor, so Accounts Payable is affected. A check was given in payment, so the account Cash in Bank is affected.
2. Classify the accounts affected.
   Accounts Payable is a liability account, while Cash in Bank is an asset account.
3. Determine the amount of increase or decrease for each account affected.
   Accounts Payable is decreased by $1,000. Cash in Bank is also decreased by $1,000.
4. Make sure the basic accounting equation remains in balance.

	ASSETS			= LIABILITIES +	OWNER'S EQUITY
	Cash in Bank	Office Furniture	Equipment	Accounts Payable	Paul Howard, Capital
Prev. Bal.	$16,000	$3,000	$4,300	$3,000	$20,300
Trans. 5	− 1,000			− 1,000	
Balance	$15,000 +	$3,000	+ $4,300	= $2,000	+ $20,300

The asset accounts total $22,300, and liabilities plus owner's equity total $22,300, so the equation is in balance.

Business Transaction 6: *WordService sold the electric typewriter for $300 on account.*

Analysis:
1. Identify the accounts affected.
   Since WordService has agreed to receive payment for the typewriter at a later time, the Accounts Receivable account is affected. The business sold equipment, so the account Equipment is also affected.
2. Classify the accounts affected.
   Accounts Receivable is an asset account, as is Equipment.
3. Determine the amount of increase or decrease for each account affected.
   Accounts Receivable is increased by $300. Equipment is decreased by $300.
4. Make sure the basic accounting equation remains in balance.

	ASSETS				= LIABILITIES +	OWNER'S EQUITY
	Cash in Bank	Accounts Receivable	Office Furniture	Equipment	Accounts Payable	Paul Howard, Capital
Prev. Bal.	$15,000	0	$3,000	$4,300	$2,000	$20,300
Trans. 6		+$300		− 300		
Balance	$15,000 +	$300	+ $3,000	+ $4,000	= $2,000	+ $20,300

The four asset accounts total $22,300. Liabilities plus owner's equity total $22,300, so the equation is in balance.

Before you go on to the next transaction, do the following activity to check your understanding of the transactions you have studied so far.

Check Your Learning

Use these accounts to analyze the business transactions of Swift Delivery Service.

ASSETS	=	LIABILITIES	+	OWNER'S EQUITY
Cash in Bank		Accounts Payable		Jan Swift, Capital
Accounts Receivable				
Office Furniture				
Delivery Equipment				

Identify the accounts affected by each transaction and the amount of increase or decrease for each account. Make sure the basic accounting equation is in balance after each transaction. Set up your transactions as shown for Transaction 6.

1. To get the business started, the owner, Jan Swift, deposited $30,000 in a checking account under the name of Swift Delivery Service.
2. The owner also invested a desk and chair valued at $700.
3. Swift Delivery Service issued a check for $10,000 for the purchase of delivery equipment.
4. The business bought office furniture on account for $5,000 from Eastern Furniture Company.
5. The old desk and chair invested by the owner were sold on account for $700.
6. Swift Delivery Service wrote a check for $2,000 in partial payment of the amount owed to a creditor.

Compare your answers to those in the answers section. Re-read the preceding part of the chapter to find the correct answers to any questions you may have missed.

Revenue and Expense Transactions

Most businesses have to earn profits to survive. In addition, business owners expect a return on their investment in a business. The most common way for a business to provide a return for its owner(s) is by selling goods and services. Income earned from the sale of goods and services is called **revenue.** Examples of revenue are fees earned for services performed and income earned from the sale of merchandise. Revenue increases owner's equity because it increases the business's assets.

In order to operate, most businesses must also buy goods and services. These goods and services are routine needs of the business (much as we need food, clothing, and shelter to keep ourselves operating). An **expense** is any price paid for goods and services used to operate a business. Examples of business expenses are rent, utility bills, and newspaper advertising. Expenses decrease owner's equity because they decrease the business's assets or increase liabilities.

Business Transaction 7: *WordService wrote a check for $500 to pay the rent for the month.*

Analysis:
1. **Identify the accounts affected.**
   WordService is receiving the use of a building it rents. Since rent is an expense, and expenses decrease owner's equity, the account Paul Howard, Capital is affected. The business is paying out cash for the use of the building, so Cash in Bank is affected.
2. **Classify the accounts affected.**
   Paul Howard, Capital is an owner's equity account. Cash in Bank is an asset account.
3. **Determine the amount of increase or decrease for each account affected.**
   Paul Howard, Capital is decreased by $500. Cash in Bank is decreased by $500.
4. **Make sure the basic accounting equation remains in balance.**

	ASSETS				= LIABILITIES +	OWNER'S EQUITY
	Cash in Bank	Accounts Receivable	Office Furniture	Equipment	Accounts Payable	Paul Howard, Capital
Prev. Bal.	$15,000	$300	$3,000	$4,000	$2,000	$20,300
Trans. 7	− 500					− 500
Balance	$14,500 +	$300	+ $3,000	+ $4,000	= $2,000	+ $19,800

The assets total $21,800. Liabilities and owner's equity total $21,800, so the equation remains in balance.

Business Transaction 8: *WordService received a check for $1,200 from a customer for preparing a report.*

Analysis:
1. **Identify the accounts affected.**
   WordService has received cash, so Cash in Bank is affected. The payment is revenue to WordService. Revenue increases owner's equity, so Paul Howard, Capital is also affected.
2. **Classify the accounts affected.**
   Cash in Bank is an asset account; Paul Howard, Capital is an owner's equity account.
3. **Determine the amount of increase or decrease for each account affected.**
   Cash in Bank is increased by $1,200. Paul Howard, Capital is also increased by $1,200.
4. **Make sure the basic accounting equation remains in balance.**

	ASSETS				= LIABILITIES +	OWNER'S EQUITY
	Cash in Bank	Accounts Receivable	Office Furniture	Equipment	Accounts Payable	Paul Howard, Capital
Prev. Bal.	$14,500	$300	$3,000	$4,000	$2,000	$19,800
Trans. 8	+ 1,200					+ 1,200
Balance	$15,700 +	$300	+ $3,000	+ $4,000	= $2,000	+ $21,000

The total assets equal the total of liabilities plus owner's equity: $23,000. The equation remains in balance.

UNIT 1   Introduction to Accounting

Business owners and accounting workers today can quickly and easily determine account balances when business transaction data are stored in computer memory.

Withdrawals by the Owner

Generally, if a business earns revenue, the owner will take cash or other assets from the business for personal use. This transaction is called a **withdrawal.** Withdrawals are often made in anticipation of future profits. Many new small-business owners get into financial trouble because they "withdraw" without realizing that they must have more profits than withdrawals if they are to keep their businesses operating.

When business assets are decreased because of a withdrawal by the owner, the owner's financial claim to the business's assets is also decreased. A withdrawal decreases both assets and owner's equity. Look at Transaction 9 to see how a withdrawal affects the basic accounting equation.

Business Transaction 9: Paul Howard withdrew $400 from the business for his personal use.

Analysis:
1. Identify the accounts affected.
   A withdrawal decreases the owner's claim to the business's assets, so Paul Howard, Capital is affected. Cash has been paid out, so the Cash in Bank account is affected.
2. Classify the accounts affected.
   Paul Howard, Capital is an owner's equity account. Cash in Bank is an asset account.
3. Determine the amount of increase or decrease for each account affected.
   Paul Howard, Capital is decreased by $400. Cash in Bank is decreased by $400.

4. Make sure the basic accounting equation remains in balance.

	ASSETS				= LIABILITIES +	OWNER'S EQUITY
	Cash in Bank	Accounts Receivable	Office Furniture	Equipment	Accounts Payable	Paul Howard, Capital
Prev. Bal.	$15,700	$300	$3,000	$4,000	$2,000	$21,000
Trans. 9	– 400					– 400
Balance	$15,300 +	$300 +	$3,000 +	$4,000 =	$2,000 +	$20,600

The total assets equal $22,600. Liabilities plus owner's equity are $22,600, so the equation remains in balance.

Before you go on to the end-of-chapter activities, do the following activity to check your understanding of the analysis of business transactions.

Check Your Learning

Use the accounts of Swift Delivery Service to analyze these business transactions. The previous balance for each is shown following the account title.

ASSETS	= LIABILITIES	+ OWNER'S EQUITY
Cash in Bank, $18,000	Accounts Payable	Jan Swift, Capital
Accounts Receivable, $700	$3,000	$30,700
Office Furniture, $5,000		
Delivery Equipment, $10,000		

Identify the accounts affected by each transaction and the amount of the increase or decrease for each acccount. Make sure the basic accounting equation is in balance after each transaction.

1. Paid $50 for advertising in the local newspaper.
2. Received $1,000 as payment for delivery services.
3. Wrote a $600 check for the month's rent.
4. Jan Swift withdrew $800 for her personal use.
5. Received $200 on account from the person who had purchased the old office furniture.

Compare your answers to those in the answers section. Re-read the preceding part of the chapter to find the correct answers to any questions you may have missed.

Using a Computer in Accounting

As you have just learned, each business transaction changes one or more parts of the basic accounting equation. The changes in the equation were summarized as increases or decreases in accounts. A simple worksheet was used to illustrate the various changes in the accounts. This worksheet, called a *spreadsheet,* is used in accounting to perform financial calculations and to record transactions.

An electronic spreadsheet can be used by an accounting clerk to record the same changes. The accounting clerk can use a computer to show the effects of business transactions on the basic accounting equation quickly and accurately. If the computer is programmed properly, all the accounting clerk must do is determine (1) the accounts affected, (2) the amounts involved, and (3) whether the accounts are being increased or decreased. Once that data are entered, the computer will automatically calculate the new account balances and determine whether the equation is in balance. Figure 2-2 illustrates how the transactions you just studied would be prepared on a computer spreadsheet.

	A	B	C D	E F	G H	I J	K L
		Cash in Bank +	Accts. Rec. +	Off. Furn. +	Equip. =	Accts. Pay. +	P. Howard, Capital
1							
2							
3							
4	1	20000					20000
5	Balance	20000 +	0 +	0 +	0 =	0 +	20000
6	2				300		300
7	Balance	20000 +	0 +	0 +	300 =	0 +	20300
8	3	-4000			4000		
9	Balance	16000 +	0 +	0 +	4300 =		20300
10	4			3000		3000	
11	Balance	16000 +	0 +	3000 +	4300 =	3000 +	20300
12	5	-1000				-1000	
13	Balance	15000 +	0 +	3000 +	4300 =	2000 +	20300
14	6	300			-300		
15	Balance	15000 +	300 +	3000 +	4000 =	2000 +	20300
16	7	-500					-500
17	Balance	14500 +	300 +	3000 +	4000 =	2000 +	19800
18	8	1200					1200
19	Balance	15700 +	300 +	3000 +	4000 =	2000 +	21000
20	9	-400					-400
21	Balance	15300 +	300 +	3000 +	4000 =	2000 +	20600
22							
23							

Figure 2-2 A Computerized Spreadsheet

Summary of Key Points

1. For all property that is owned or controlled, there are corresponding financial claims equal to the cost of the property.
2. The accounting term for a financial claim to a business's assets is *equity.*
3. The relationship between total assets and total equities is shown in the basic accounting equation: Assets = Liabilities + Owner's Equity.
4. Each business transaction changes one or more parts of the basic accounting equation.
5. When a business buys on account, the amounts owed are called accounts payable. When a business sells on account, the total amounts owed to the business are called accounts receivable.
6. Businesses must earn revenue to provide a return on the owner's investment and to allow the business to continue its operations. Revenue increases the owner's equity in the business.
7. The costs of items used in the operation of a business are called expenses. Expenses decrease the owner's equity in the business.
8. Withdrawals decrease the owner's financial claim.

Review and Applications

Building Your Accounting Vocabulary

In your own words, write a definition for each of the following accounting terms. Use complete sentences.

account
accounts payable
accounts receivable
assets
basic accounting
   equation
business transaction

capital
credit
creditor
equity
expense
liabilities
on account

owner's equity
property
property rights
revenue
withdrawal

Reviewing Your Accounting Knowledge

1. What is the relationship between property and property rights?
2. Why are a business's assets separate from the owner's personal assets?
3. List five examples of business assets. Explain why they are business assets rather than personal assets.
4. Name two types of equity in a business, and explain what each type represents. Give an example of each.
5. Why are accounts used in an accounting system?
6. Explain the difference between accounts receivable and accounts payable.
7. Why are at least two accounts affected by each business transaction?
8. What steps should you follow in analyzing a business transaction?
9. How can you determine if the basic accounting equation is in balance?
10. Why is it important for a business to earn revenue?
11. Explain the difference between revenue and expenses.
12. Why does the withdrawal of cash by the owner for personal use decrease owner's equity?

Improving Your Decision-Making Skills

Liberty Fashions, a manufacturing company, was started by Helen Baker as a sole proprietorship. The company needs to expand its plant facilities at an estimated cost of $125,000. Helen does not have the money needed herself. What should she do now? Remember to follow the decision-making process you used in Chapter 1.

Applying Accounting Procedures

Exercise 2-1   Balancing the Accounting Equation

Determine the missing dollar amounts in each equation at the top of the next page. Use either the form in your workbook or plain paper and write in the missing amounts for each question mark.

ASSETS	=	LIABILITIES	+	OWNER'S EQUITY
1. $17,000	=	$7,000	+	?
2. $10,000	=	?	+	$ 7,000
3. ?	=	$9,000	+	$17,000
4. $ 8,000	=	$2,000	+	?
5. ?	=	$6,000	+	$20,000

Exercise 2-2   Classifying Accounts

All accounts belong in one of the following classifications: Asset, Liability, Owner's Equity.

Instructions: For each of the following accounts, indicate the classification in which it belongs.

1. John Jones, Capital
2. Cash in Bank
3. Accounts Receivable
4. Accounts Payable
5. Computer Equipment

6. Calculator
7. Delivery Trucks
8. Building
9. Land
10. Typewriter

Exercise 2-3   Completing the Accounting Equation

The following accounts are used in a business owned and operated by Mike Murray.

Instructions: Look at the following list of accounts and determine the missing amount for each of the question marks.

ASSETS		=	LIABILITIES	+	OWNER'S EQUITY
Cash in Bank	$4,500	=	Accounts Payable ?	+	Mike Murray, Capital $9,250
Accounts Receivable	1,350				
Office Equipment	5,000				
	?				

Problem 2-1   Classifying Accounts within the Accounting Equation

Listed below, in alphabetical order, are the account titles and account balances for a business owned by Larry Hicks.

Accounts Payable	$7,000	Equipment	$12,000
Accounts Receivable	$2,000	Larry Hicks, Capital	$15,000
Cash in Bank	$5,000	Office Equipment	$ 3,000

Instructions: Using these account titles and balances,
(1) List and total the assets of the business.
(2) Determine the amount owed by the business.
(3) Give the amount of the owner's equity in the business.
(4) Determine whether the basic accounting equation is in balance for this business.

Problem 2-2   Determining Increases and Decreases in Accounts

Listed at the top of the next page are the account titles used by A-1 Carpet Cleaners.

	ASSETS	=	LIABILITIES	+	OWNER'S EQUITY
	Cash in Bank		Accounts Payable		Kay Gentry, Capital
	Accounts Receivable				
	Cleaning Equipment				
	Office Equipment				

Instructions: Use a form similar to the one that follows. For each transaction that follows:

(1) Identify the accounts affected.

(2) Classify the accounts.

(3) Determine the amount of the increase (+) or decrease (−) for each account affected.

The first transaction is completed as an example.

Trans.	Accounts Affected	Classification	Amount of Increase (+) or Decrease (−)
1	Cash in Bank Kay Gentry, Capital	Asset Owner's Equity	+$25,000 +$25,000

Transactions:

1. Kay Gentry, the owner, invested $25,000 cash in the business.

2. Bought cleaning equipment with cash, $12,000.

3. Purchased $2,500 worth of office equipment on account.

4. Wrote a check for the monthly rent, $800.

5. Received cash for services performed, $1,000.

6. The owner withdrew $600 cash from the business for personal use.

Problem 2-3   Determining the Effects of Transactions on the Accounting Equation

After becoming a CPA, Tony LaBato decided to start an accounting business.

Instructions: Use a form similar to the one that follows. For each of the following transactions:

(1) Identify the accounts affected, using the account titles on the form.

(2) Determine the amount of the increase or decrease for each account.

(3) Write the amount of the increase (+) or decrease (−) in the space under each account affected.

(4) On the following line, write the new balance for each account.

	ASSETS				=	LIABILITIES	+	OWNER'S EQUITY
Trans.	Cash in Bank	Accts. Rec.	Office Equip.	Acctg. Supplies	=	Accounts Payable	+	Tony LaBato, Capital
1	+$10,000							+$10,000

Transactions:

1. Tony LaBato began the business by depositing $10,000 in a checking account at the Lakeside National Bank in the name of the business, Tony LaBato, CPA.

Transactions:

2. Bought accounting supplies for cash, $250.
3. Issued a check for $900 for the monthly rent on the office.
4. Bought $6,000 worth of new office equipment on account for use in the business.
5. Received $700 cash for accounting services performed for a customer.
6. Issued a $2,000 check to the creditor as partial payment for the office equipment purchased on account.
7. Performed accounting services and agreed to be paid for them later, $500.

SPREADSHEET

PROBLEM

Problem 2-4   Determining the Effects of Business Transactions on the Accounting Equation

Andrea Hunt has decided to go into business for herself as a professional photographer.

Instructions: Use a form similar to the one below. For each of the following transactions:

(1) Identify the accounts affected.
(2) Write the amount of the increase (+) or decrease (−) in the space provided on the form.
(3) Determine the new balance for each account.

	ASSETS					=	LIABILITIES	+	OWNER'S EQUITY
Trans.	Cash in Bank	Accts. Rec.	Camera Equip.	Photo Supplies	Office Equip.	=	Accounts Payable	+	Andrea Hunt, Capital

Transactions:

1. Ms. Hunt, the owner, opened a checking account for the business by depositing $60,000 of her personal funds.
2. Paid the monthly rent of $3,000.
3. Bought supplies for developing photographs by writing a check for $300.
4. Bought $24,000 worth of camera equipment for cash.
5. Purchased office equipment on account for $4,000.
6. Received payment for photography services, $2,500.
7. Andrea Hunt invested an electric typewriter, which was valued at $450, in the business.
8. Withdrew $3,000 cash from the business for personal use.
9. Wrote a check to a creditor as partial payment on account, $2,000.
10. Took wedding photographs and agreed to accept payment later, $1,200.

Problem 2-5   Describing Business Transactions

The transactions for Oglesby Electrical Repair Service that follow are shown as they would appear in the basic accounting equation. In your own words, describe what has happened in each transaction. Transaction 1 is completed as an example.

Example:

1. The owner invested $30,000 in the business.

Trans.	Cash in Bank	Accts. Rec.	Office Equip.	Repair Tools	=	Accounts Payable	+	Jane Oglesby, Capital
1	+$30,000							+$30,000
2	−$ 2,000		+$2,000					
3				+$8,000		+$8,000		
4	+$ 700							+$ 700
5		+$500						+$ 500
6			+$ 200					+$ 200
7	−$ 3,000					−$3,000		
8		+$200	−$ 200					
9	+$ 500	−$500						
10	−$ 1,000							−$ 1,000

CHALLENGE

PROBLEM

Problem 2-6   Completing the Accounting Equation

Look at the following account titles and balances for a business owned by Fran Henry. Determine the missing amount for each of the question marks. Use the form in your workbook or plain paper and write in the missing amounts.

	ASSETS			=	LIABILITIES	+	OWNER'S EQUITY
	Cash in Bank	Accounts Receivable	Business Equipment	=	Accounts Payable	+	Fran Henry, Capital
1.	$5,000 ?	$ 2,000	$ 1,000		$ 500		$ 7,500
2.	$ 3,000	$ 9,000	$6,000 ?		$2,000		$16,000
3.	$ 8,000	$ 1,000	$10,000		? $4,000		$15,000
4.	$ 4,000	? $10,000	$ 4,000		$1,000		$17,000
5.	$ 9,000	$ 7,000	$ 6,000		$5,000		? $17,000
6.	$10,000	$14,000	? $12,000		$6,000		$32,000
7.	$ 6,000	$ 4,000	$10,000		? $5,000		$15,000
8.	? $4,000	$ 5,000	$ 9,000		$1,000		$17,000 ?

In #8, total assets are $18,000.

*A*ccounting:
A Mobile Profession

Accountants have been around for a long time. As early as 3600 B.C., priests in Babylonia kept accounts on clay tablets. In today's economic era, there are well over a million accountants in the United States. In spite of this, there simply are not enough accountants and accounting workers to go around.

A bachelor's degree with a major in accounting can lead to a variety of career choices. Today's accounting positions offer attractive salaries and are more challenging than ever before.

Public accountants offer professional services to the public for a fee. These services include tax preparation, auditing, management, consulting, and general accounting. To become a certified public accountant (CPA), you must pass a rigorous, state-administered examination in accounting theory and practice, auditing, and business law. Many public accountants leave the field to take high-level positions with clients.

Managerial accountants perform accounting functions for businesses. They might specialize in corporate taxes, operations, budgeting, investing, or internal auditing. Managerial accountants provide critical information for corporate executives and take active roles in long-range planning. Like the CPA, the managerial accountant can take an examination to become a certified management accountant (CMA). Managerial accountants are in a good position to learn about all aspects of a business's operations. As a result, many work their way into top management positions.

Not-for-profit accountants work for hospitals, school districts, colleges, or government agencies. They can be general accountants, auditors, controllers, bank examiners, or even IRS or FBI agents. Like accountants who work for profit-mak-

Positions in accounting are expected to increase faster than average through the 1990s.

ing businesses, these accountants offer consulting and other services to ensure the successful financial operation of the organization. Not-for-profit accounting, particularly in government, offers high job security, an important consideration for many people.

Today, accounting is more than simply balancing debits and credits. It may even be a stepping-stone to that corner office.

UNIT 2

THE BASIC ACCOUNTING CYCLE

All businesses keep financial records. In Unit 2 you will learn how business transactions affect the financial records of a business. Learning to analyze business transactions correctly is the first step toward learning accounting. You will then learn how to record those transactions in the business's accounting records. The business used in the examples in this unit is a sole proprietorship. The business, called Global Travel Agency, provides travel services to its customers. After studying the chapters in this unit, you will have learned how to keep accounting records through a complete accounting cycle.

GLOBAL TRAVEL AGENCY
Chart of Accounts

ASSETS	101	Cash in Bank
	105	Accounts Receivable—Burton Co.
	110	Accounts Receivable—Greer's Market
	120	Computer Equipment
	130	Office Equipment
LIABILITIES	201	Accounts Payable—City News
	205	Accounts Payable—Modern Office Suppliers
OWNER'S EQUITY	301	Jan Harter, Capital
	305	Jan Harter, Withdrawals
	310	Income Summary
REVENUE	401	Fees
EXPENSES	501	Advertising Expense
	510	Maintenance Expense
	520	Rent Expense
	530	Utilities Expense

Chapter  3

ANALYZING TRANSACTIONS AFFECTING ASSETS, LIABILITIES, AND OWNER'S EQUITY

In Chapter 2, you learned that there is a relationship between property and the financial claims to that property. In accounting, this relationship is expressed by the basic accounting equation. You also learned that each business transaction causes a change in the basic accounting equation. This change is reflected as an increase or a decrease in assets, liabilities, or owner's equity. Even though a change does occur, the basic accounting equation remains in balance.

In this chapter, you will learn the rules of debit and credit for asset, liability, and owner's equity accounts. These rules state how increases and decreases are to be recorded. You will then learn to apply these rules as you analyze typical business transactions.

As you study Chapter 3, always keep in mind the basic accounting equation that follows:

ASSETS = LIABILITIES + OWNER'S EQUITY.

Learning Objectives

When you have completed Chapter 3, you should be able to do the following:

1. List and apply the rules of debit and credit for asset, liability, and owner's equity accounts.
2. Use T accounts to analyze a business transaction into its debit and credit parts.
3. Determine the balances of the accounts affected by a business transaction.
4. Define the accounting terms introduced in this chapter.

New Terms

double-entry accounting
T account
debit
credit
balance side

The Basis of an Accounting System

You learned in Chapter 2 that every business transaction affects at least two accounts. When you recorded the dollar amount of a transaction in one account, you recorded that same amount in another account. You did this to keep the sides of the basic accounting equation equal, or in balance. In entering the transaction amount twice, you were using a "double-entry" system of recordkeeping.

In accounting, the financial recordkeeping system in which each business transaction affects at least two accounts is called **double-entry accounting.** Double-entry accounting forms the basis for the accounting concepts and procedures that you will study in this textbook. Although you will mainly study manual accounting systems, the rules of double-entry accounting apply as well to computerized accounting systems. In other words, whether you are keeping accounting records by writing information on accounting stationery or by entering information into a computer, the resulting reports are the same.

The T Account

In Chapter 2, you used the basic accounting equation to analyze business transactions. This method works well when a business has only a few accounts. It becomes awkward, however, when a business has several accounts and many transactions to analyze. A more efficient and convenient tool is the T account. The **T account,** so called because of its T shape, is used to show the increase or decrease in an account caused by a transaction. Accountants use T accounts to analyze the parts of a transaction.

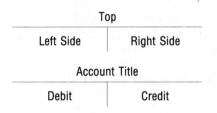

As you can see from the illustration, a T account has a top, a left side, and a right side. On the top of the T is the title of an account. The left side of the T is always used for debit amounts. A **debit** then is an amount entered on the *left* side of the T account. The right side of the T account is always used for credit amounts. A **credit** is an amount entered on the *right* side of the T account. The words "debit" and "credit" are simply the accountant's terms for "left" and "right." Remember, *debit = left side* and *credit = right side.*

The Rules of Debit and Credit

Debits and credits are used to record the increases and decreases in each account affected by a business transaction. Under the double-entry system, for each debit entry made in one account, a credit of an equal amount must be made in another account. The rules of debit and credit vary according to whether an account is classified as an asset, a liability, or an owner's equity account. Let's look first at the rules of debit and credit for accounts classified as assets.

Rules for Asset Accounts

There are three rules of debit and credit for asset accounts:

1. An asset account is increased (+) on the debit side.
2. An asset account is decreased (−) on the credit side.
3. The normal balance for an asset account is a debit balance.

We can illustrate these rules using T accounts and the basic accounting equation. Look at the left-hand side of the equation below.

ASSETS = LIABILITIES + OWNER'S EQUITY

Asset Accounts	
Debit	Credit
+	−
Increase Side	Decrease Side
Balance Side	

For asset accounts, the *increase* side is the debit (left) side of the T account. The *decrease* side is the credit (right) side of the T account. Notice the + and − signs. These signs are used to indicate the increase and decrease sides of the account. They do not mean the same thing as "debit" and "credit."

Each classification of account also has a specific side that is its normal balance side. This **balance side** is always the same as the side used to record increases to the account. Since the increase side of an asset account is always the debit side, asset accounts have a normal debit balance. The word "normal" used here means "usual." For example, in the normal course of business, total increases to assets are larger than total decreases. You would expect an asset account, then, to have a normal debit balance.

We can summarize the rules of debit and credit for asset accounts by using a T account.

Asset Accounts	
Debit	Credit
+	−
1 Increase Side	2 Decrease Side
3 Balance Side	

Rule 1: Asset accounts are increased by debits.
Rule 2: Asset accounts are decreased by credits.
Rule 3: The normal balance for asset accounts is a debit balance.

Let's apply these rules now to an actual asset account. Look at the entries in the T account below for Cash in Bank.

Cash in Bank	
Debit	Credit
+	−
$200	$ 70
150	40
$350	$110
Balance, $240	

The increases in the account are recorded on the left, or debit, side. The decreases in the account are recorded on the right, or credit, side. Total debits equal $350 ($200 + $150). Total credits equal $110 ($70 + $40). To find the balance, subtract total credits from total debits ($350 − $110). The debit balance is $240.

The normal balance side of any account is the same as the side used to increase that account.

Before you go any further, do the activity below to see if you understand the rules of debit and credit for asset accounts.

Check Your Learning

Answer these questions using the rules of debit and credit for asset accounts.

1. Asset accounts are increased on the left, or ___?___ , side.
2. Asset accounts are decreased on the right, or ___?___ , side.
3. The normal balance for asset accounts is a ___?___ balance.
4. On notebook paper, draw a T account for the asset account Office Equipment. Enter debits of $2,000 and $1,500. Enter a credit of $500. What is the balance, and on what side of the T account is it shown?

Compare your answers to those in the answers section. Re-read the preceding part of the chapter to find the correct answers to any questions you may have missed.

Rules for Liability and Owner's Equity Accounts

The rules for liability accounts and owner's equity accounts—specifically, the owner's capital account—are listed below:

1. The liability and capital accounts are increased (+) on the credit side.
2. The liability and capital accounts are decreased (−) on the debit side.
3. The normal balance for the liability and capital accounts is a credit balance.

Let's look again at the T accounts within the basic accounting equation, particularly those on the right-hand side. How do the T accounts for the liability and capital accounts differ from the T account for assets?

ASSETS		=	LIABILITIES		+	OWNER'S EQUITY	
Asset Accounts		=	Liability Accounts		+	Capital Account	
Debit	Credit		Debit	Credit		Debit	Credit
+	−		−	+		−	+
Increase Side	Decrease Side		Decrease Side	Increase Side		Decrease Side	Increase Side
Balance Side				Balance Side			Balance Side

The debit side of all three accounts is still on the left side of the T account, and the credit side of all three types of accounts remains on the right. Notice, however, that the increase (+) and decrease (−) sides of the liability and capital accounts are the opposite of those for assets. This is because accounts classified as liabilities and owner's equity are on the opposite side of the equation from accounts classified as assets. As a result, debit and credit rules on one side of the equation—and the T accounts within it—are mirror images of those on the other side.

We can summarize the rules of debit and credit for liability accounts and the owner's capital account by using a T account.

Liabilities and Capital

Debit	Credit
−	+
2 Decrease Side	1 Increase Side
	3 Balance Side

Rule 1: Liability and capital accounts are increased by credits.

Rule 2: Liability and capital accounts are decreased by debits.

Rule 3: The normal balance for liability and capital accounts is a credit balance.

Let's apply these rules now to actual accounts. First, look at the entries in the T account below for the liability account Accounts Payable.

Accounts Payable

Debit	Credit
−	+
$100	$200
75	175
$175	$375
	Balance, $200

The increases in the account are recorded on the right, or credit, side. The decreases in the account are recorded on the left, or debit, side. Total credits equal $375 ($200 + $175); total debits equal $175 ($100 + $75). To find the balance, subtract the total debits from the total credits ($375 − $175). The credit balance is $200.

Now look at the entries in the T account below for the owner's equity account Jan Harter, Capital. Remember, the rules of debit and credit for the capital account are the same as for a liability account.

Jan Harter, Capital

Debit	Credit
−	+
$350	$1,500
200	2,500
$550	$4,000
	Balance, $3,450

Increases to capital are recorded on the right, or credit, side of the account. Decreases are recorded on the left, or debit, side. The capital account has a normal credit balance. If you subtract the total debits from the total credits ($4,000 − $550), you have a credit balance of $3,450.

Summary of the Rules of Debit and Credit

Let's summarize the rules of debit and credit in terms of the basic accounting equation and T accounts.

ASSETS		=	LIABILITIES		+	OWNER'S EQUITY	
Asset Accounts		=	Liability Accounts		+	Capital Account	
Debit	Credit		Debit	Credit		Debit	Credit
+	−		−	+		−	+
Increase Side	Decrease Side		Decrease Side	Increase Side		Decrease Side	Increase Side
Balance Side				Balance Side			Balance Side

Asset accounts are increased on the debit side and decreased on the credit side. The normal balance for an asset account is a debit. Liability and capital accounts are increased on the credit side and decreased on the debit side. The normal balance for liability and capital accounts is a credit.

Before you read any further, complete the following activity to see if you understand the rules of debit and credit for liability and capital accounts.

Check Your Learning

Answer these questions using the rules of debit and credit for liabilities and capital.

1. Liability and capital accounts are increased on the ____?____ side.
2. Liability and capital accounts are decreased on the ____?____ side.
3. The normal balance side for liability and capital accounts is the ____?____.
4. On notebook paper, draw a T account for the liability account Accounts Payable. Enter debits of $600, $200, and $400. Enter credits of $700, $500, and $300. What is the amount of the balance, and on what side of the T account is it shown?
5. Draw a T account for the account Patrick Vance, Capital. Enter debits of $1,500 and $700. Enter credits of $9,000, $3,000, and $1,500. What is the amount of the balance, and on what side of the T account is it shown?

Compare your answers to those in the answers section. Re-read the preceding part of the chapter to find the correct answers to any questions you may have missed.

Applying the Rules of Debit and Credit

Now that you are familiar with the rules of debit and credit for asset, liability, and capital accounts, the next step is to apply those rules to the analysis of business transactions. When analyzing business transactions, you should ask yourself these six questions:

1. Which accounts are affected?
2. What is the classification of each account?
3. Is each account increased or decreased?
4. Which account is debited, and for what amount?
5. Which account is credited, and for what amount?
6. What is the complete entry?

R — E — M — E — M — B — E — R

Debits are used to	Credits are used to
1. Increase (+) assets.	1. Decrease (−) assets.
2. Decrease (−) liabilities.	2. Increase (+) liabilities.
3. Decrease (−) owner's capital.	3. Increase (+) owner's capital.

The business transactions that follow are for Global Travel Agency. Global Travel Agency is a small business that provides travel services to individuals and businesses. Global Travel is owned and operated as a sole proprietorship by Jan Harter. Jan has set up her accounting system to include the following asset, liability, and owner's equity accounts.

ASSETS	LIABILITIES	OWNER'S EQUITY
Cash in Bank	Accounts Payable	Jan Harter, Capital
Accounts Receivable		
Computer Equipment		
Office Equipment		

These accounts will be used to analyze several business transactions.

Business Transaction 1: *On October 1, Jan Harter took $25,000 from personal savings and deposited that amount to open a business checking account in the name of Global Travel Agency.*

1. Which accounts are affected?
The accounts affected are Cash in Bank and Jan Harter, Capital.
2. What is the classification of each account?
Cash in Bank is an asset account, and Jan Harter, Capital is an owner's equity account.
3. Is each account increased or decreased?
Cash in Bank is increased because the owner, Jan Harter, has deposited cash in the business checking account. Jan Harter, Capital is also increased because the owner's financial claim to the assets of the business has increased.
4. Which account is debited, and for what amount?

Cash in Bank	
Debit	Credit
+	−
$25,000	
Balance, $25,000	

Cash in Bank is an asset account. Increases in assets are recorded as debits. Cash in Bank is, therefore, debited for $25,000. Since this is an asset account, the normal balance is a debit balance.

5. Which account is credited, and for what amount?

Jan Harter, Capital	
Debit	Credit
−	+
	$25,000
	Balance, $25,000

Jan Harter, Capital is an owner's equity account. Increases in the owner's capital account are recorded as credits. Jan Harter, Capital is, therefore, credited for $25,000. The normal balance for the owner's capital account is a credit balance.

6. What is the complete entry?
Remember that in the double-entry system, each transaction affects at least two accounts. Cash in Bank is debited for $25,000 and Jan Harter, Capital is credited for $25,000. You can see from the T accounts on page 48 that the amount of the debit equals the amount of the credit.

Jan Harter must analyze each business transaction carefully to determine the accounts affected.

Cash in Bank		Jan Harter, Capital	
Debit	Credit	Debit	Credit
+	−	−	+
$25,000			$25,000

R E M E M B E R

In the double-entry accounting system, total debits must equal total credits in each business transaction.

Business Transaction 2: On October 2, Global Travel Agency issued Check 101 for $8,000 to buy a microcomputer system from Info-Systems, Inc.

1. Which accounts are affected?
Computer Equipment and Cash in Bank are affected.
2. What is the classification of each account?
Computer Equipment and Cash in Bank are both asset accounts.
3. Is each account increased or decreased?
Computer Equipment is increased because the purchase of the microcomputer increased the assets of the business. Cash in Bank is decreased because the business paid out cash.
4. Which account is debited and for what amount?

Computer Equipment	
Debit	Credit
+	−
$8,000	
Balance, $8,000	

Computer Equipment is an asset account. Increases in assets are recorded as debits. Computer Equipment is, therefore, debited for $8,000.

5. Which account is credited, and for what amount?

$25,000
− 8,000
$17,000

Cash in Bank	
Debit	Credit
+	−
$25,000	$8,000
Balance, $17,000	

Cash in Bank is also an asset account. Since decreases in asset accounts are recorded as credits, Cash in Bank is credited for $8,000.

6. What is the complete entry?
Computer Equipment is debited for $8,000 and Cash in Bank is credited for $8,000. The debit entry is equal to the credit entry.

Computer Equipment		Cash in Bank	
Debit	Credit	Debit	Credit
+	−	+	−
$8,000			$8,000

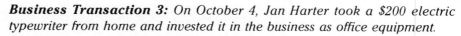

Business Transaction 3: *On October 4, Jan Harter took a $200 electric typewriter from home and invested it in the business as office equipment.*

1. Which accounts are affected?
   Office Equipment and Jan Harter, Capital are affected.
2. What is the classification of each account?
   Office Equipment is an asset account. Jan Harter, Capital is an owner's equity account.
3. Is each account increased or decreased?
   The investment of the typewriter increased the assets owned by the business. Office Equipment is thus increased. Since the typewriter is an investment by the owner of personal property, Jan Harter, Capital is also increased.
4. Which account is debited, and for what amount?

Office Equipment	
Debit	Credit
+	−
$200	
Balance, $200	

Office Equipment is an asset account. Since increases in assets are recorded as debits, Office Equipment is debited for $200.

5. Which account is credited and for what amount?

	Jan Harter, Capital	
	Debit	Credit
	−	+
$25,000		$25,000
+ 200		200
$25,200		Balance, $25,200

Jan Harter, Capital is an owner's equity account. Increases in owner's equity are recorded as credits. Jan Harter, Capital is credited for $200.

6. What is the complete entry?
   Office Equipment is debited for $200 and Jan Harter, Capital is credited for the same amount. These amounts are shown in the T accounts below. The amount of the debit equals the amount of the credit.

Office Equipment			Jan Harter, Capital	
Debit	Credit		Debit	Credit
+	−		−	+
$200				$200

Business Transaction 4: *On October 9, Global Travel bought a new electronic typewriter on account for $1,500 from Modern Office Suppliers.*

1. Which accounts are affected?
   Office Equipment and Accounts Payable are affected. Remember, an item bought on account (on credit) is to be paid for in the future. The amount owed for the purchase is recorded in Accounts Payable until actual payment is made.

Many different types of items are purchased for use in a business's operations, such as a microcomputer or even a car.

2. What is the classification of each account?

Office Equipment is an asset account and Accounts Payable is a liability account.

3. Is each account increased or decreased?

Each account is increased. Office Equipment is increased because property is being acquired. Accounts Payable is increased because the business owes money on account.

4. Which account is debited, and for what amount?

Office Equipment	
Debit	Credit
+	−
$ 200	
1,500	
Balance, $1,700	

$ 200
+1,500
$1,700

Office Equipment is debited for $1,500. Office Equipment is an asset account, and increases in assets are recorded as debits.

5. Which account is credited, and for what amount?

Accounts Payable	
Debit	Credit
−	+
	$1,500
	Balance, $1,500

Accounts Payable is a liability account. Increases in liability accounts are recorded as credits. The amount of the credit is $1,500.

6. What is the complete entry?

Office Equipment is debited for $1,500 and Accounts Payable is credited for $1,500. The changes caused by this transaction are summarized in the T accounts on the next page.

Office Equipment		Accounts Payable	
Debit	Credit	Debit	Credit
+	−	−	+
$1,500			$1,500

Business Transaction 5: *On October 11, Global Travel sold the electric typewriter on account to Greer's Market for $200.*

1. Which accounts are affected?
   Accounts Receivable and Office Equipment are affected.
2. What is the classification of each account?
   Both Accounts Receivable and Office Equipment are asset accounts.
3. Is each account increased or decreased?
   Money that is to be received in the future increases Accounts Receivable. The sale of the typewriter decreases Office Equipment.
4. Which account is debited, and for what amount?

Accounts Receivable	
Debit	Credit
+	−
$200	
Balance, $200	

Increases in assets are recorded as debits. Accounts Receivable is an asset account, so it is debited for $200.

5. Which account is credited, and for what amount?

	Office Equipment	
	Debit	Credit
$ 200	+	−
+1,500	$ 200	$200
− 200	1,500	
$1,500	Balance, $1,500	

Decreases in assets are recorded as credits. Office Equipment is an asset account, so it is credited for $200.

6. What is the complete entry?
   Accounts Receivable is debited for $200 and Office Equipment is credited for the same amount. The debit amount equals the credit amount.

Accounts Receivable		Office Equipment	
Debit	Credit	Debit	Credit
+	−	+	−
$200			$200

Business Transaction 6: *On October 14, Global Travel mailed Check 102 for $750 as a partial payment to Modern Office Suppliers (for the $1,500 electronic typewriter bought in Transaction 4).*

1. Which accounts are affected?
   The accounts affected are Accounts Payable and Cash in Bank.

2. What is the classification of each account?

Accounts Payable is a liability account and Cash in Bank is an asset account.

3. Is each account increased or decreased?

The partial payment of a debt reduces the business's liability. There is a decrease, therefore, in Accounts Payable. Making a payment by check decreases the balance in Cash in Bank.

4. Which account is debited, and for what amount?

	Accounts Payable	
	Debit	Credit
$1,500	−	+
− 750	$750	$1,500
$ 750		Balance, $750

Decreases in liabilities are recorded as debits. Since Accounts Payable is a liability account, it is decreased. The amount of the decrease is the amount of the partial payment, $750.

5. Which account is credited, and for what amount?

	Cash in Bank	
	Debit	Credit
$25,000	+	−
− 8,000	$25,000	$8,000
− 750		750
$16,250	Balance, $16,250	

Decreases in assets are recorded as credits. Since Cash in Bank is an asset account, it is credited for $750, the amount of the check.

6. What is the complete entry?

Accounts Payable is debited for $750 and Cash in Bank is credited for the same amount. As you can see, the amount of the debit equals the amount of the credit.

Accounts Payable			Cash in Bank	
Debit	Credit		Debit	Credit
−	+		+	−
$750				$750

Business Transaction 7: On October 26, Global Travel received and deposited a check for $200 from Greer's Market. This is full payment for the electric typewriter that was sold on account on October 9.

1. Which accounts are affected?

Cash in Bank and Accounts Receivable are affected.

2. What is the classification of each account?

Cash in Bank and Accounts Receivable are both asset accounts.

3. Is each account increased or decreased?

Cash in Bank is increased by the receipt and deposit of the check. Accounts Receivable is decreased because the money Global Travel was to receive is now being paid.

4. Which account is debited, and for what amount?

	Cash in Bank		Cash in Bank is debited for $200.
$25,000	Debit	Credit	
− 8,000	+	−	
− 750	$25,000	$8,000	
+ 200	200	750	
$16,450	Balance, $16,450		

5. Which account is credited, and for what amount?

	Accounts Receivable		Accounts Receivable is decreased, so it is credited for $200.
	Debit	Credit	
$200	+	−	
−200	$200	$200	
$ 0	Balance, $0		

6. What is the complete entry?
Cash in Bank is debited for $200 and Accounts Receivable is credited for $200. The amount of the debit equals the amount of the credit.

Cash in Bank		Accounts Receivable	
Debit	Credit	Debit	Credit
+	−	+	−
$200			$200

Summary of Key Points

1. Double-entry accounting is a system of recordkeeping in which each business transaction affects at least two accounts.
2. The T account is a tool for analyzing the debit and credit parts of a business transaction.
3. The top of the T is used for the account title; debits are entered on the left side of the T; credits, on the right.
4. Every account has an increase side and a decrease side.
5. For asset accounts, the increase side is the debit side and the decrease side is the credit side.
6. The normal balance for an asset account is a debit balance.
7. For liability accounts and the owner's capital account, the increase side is the credit side and the decrease side is the debit side.
8. The normal balance for both liability and capital accounts is a credit balance.
9. In double-entry accounting, the amount of the debit must equal the amount of the credit.

Review and Applications

Building Your Accounting Vocabulary

Using your own words, write a definition of each of the following accounting terms. Use complete sentences for your definitions.

balance side   double-entry
credit   accounting
debit   T account

Reviewing Your Accounting Knowledge

1. Why is a transaction amount entered in at least two accounts?
2. Would double-entry accounting be used in a computerized accounting system? Why or why not?
3. Why do accountants use T accounts?
4. Name the three basic parts of a T account.
5. What is the left side of a T account called? the right side?
6. State briefly the rules of debit and credit for increasing and decreasing: (a) asset accounts, (b) liability accounts, (c) owner's capital account.
7. What is the normal balance side of asset accounts? liability accounts? the owner's capital account?
8. Classify the following accounts.
    a. Office Equipment   e. Cash in Bank
    b. Delivery Truck   f. Lee Jones, Capital
    c. Accounts Receivable   g. Office Supplies
    d. Store Supplies   h. Accounts Payable
9. Explain briefly what is meant by each of the following phrases.
    a. A debit of $100 to Cash in Bank.
    b. A credit balance.
    c. A credit of $500 to Accounts Payable.
    d. A debit balance.
10. What are the six questions that should be answered whenever a business transaction is analyzed?

Improving Your Math Skills

Calculators and computers do a lot of number crunching for us today, but it is still important to know your numbers if you plan to work in accounting. Complete the exercises that follow to check your skills.

1. Identify each place value in this number: 1,495.885.
2. Round the following numbers to the nearest hundredth.
    (a) 0.578   (c) 1.9001   (e) 10.38601
    (b) 4.89182   (d) 70.475   (f) 583.70121
3. Write the following amounts in words.
    (a) $2.00   (c) $31.56   (e) $1,492.61
    (b) $0.50   (d) $387.81   (f) $21.65

Applying Accounting Procedures

Exercise 3-1   Applying the Rules of Debit and Credit

Shultz's Speedy Delivery uses the following accounts.

Cash in Bank   Office Equipment   Accounts Payable
Accounts Receivable   Delivery Van   A. Schultz, Capital

Instructions: Use a form similar to the one below. For each account,
(1) Classify the account as an asset, liability, or owner's equity account.
(2) Indicate whether the increase side is a debit or a credit.
(3) Indicate whether the decrease side is a debit or a credit.
(4) Indicate whether the account has a normal debit or credit balance.

Account Title	Account Classification	Increase Side	Decrease Side	Normal Balance
Cash in Bank	Asset	Debit	Credit	Debit

Exercise 3-2   Identifying Accounts Affected by Transactions

Shirley Adams uses the following accounts in her business.

Cash in Bank   Office Furniture   Accounts Payable
Accounts Receivable   Office Supplies   Shirley Adams, Capital
Office Equipment

Instructions: For each of the following transactions,
(1) Indicate the two accounts affected.
(2) Indicate whether each account is debited or credited.

Transactions:
1. Sold an unneeded office typewriter to Jay's Department Store on account.
2. Purchased a computer on credit, promising to pay for it within 60 days.
3. Shirley Adams brought a filing cabinet from home and invested it in the business (office furniture).
4. Bought office supplies for cash.

Exercise 3-3   Identifying Increases and Decreases in Accounts

Alice Roberts uses the following accounts in her business.

Cash in Bank   Office Equipment   Accounts Payable
Accounts Receivable   Office Furniture   Alice Roberts, Capital

Instructions: Analyze each of the following transactions using the format shown below. Explain the debit, then the credit.

Example:
On June 2, Alice Roberts invested $5,000 of her own money into a business called Roberts Employment Agency.

a. The asset Cash in Bank is increased. Increases in assets are recorded as debits.
b. The owner's equity account Alice Roberts, Capital is increased. Increases in the capital account are recorded as credits.

Transactions:

1. Sold an unneeded office desk (office furniture) for $750 cash.
2. Bought a used computer from Computer, Inc., on account for $2,500.
3. Paid $750 on account to Computer, Inc.

Problem 3-1   Using T Accounts to Analyze Transactions

Norman Rocky decided to start his own business. He plans to use the following accounts.

Cash in Bank	Fishing Equipment	Accounts Payable
Accounts Receivable	Boat	Norman Rocky, Capital

Instructions: For each transaction,

(1) Determine which two accounts are affected.
(2) Prepare two T accounts for the accounts identified in Instruction #1.
(3) Enter the debit and credit amounts in the T accounts.

Transactions:

1. Norman Rocky invested $40,000 cash in a business called Rocky's Charter Service.
2. Bought a fishing boat on account for $27,000 from Charter Boats, Inc.
3. Norman Rocky invested his personal fishing equipment, valued at $3,750.
4. Rocky's purchased new fishing equipment for $7,500 cash.
5. Rocky's Charter Service sold some of the old fishing equipment on account to Fish & Bait Charters for $1,200.

Problem 3-2   Analyzing Transactions into Debit and Credit Parts

Abraham Schultz completed the following transactions soon after opening Schultz's Speedy Delivery.

Instructions:

(1) Prepare a T account for each account listed in Exercise 3-1.
(2) Analyze and record each of the business transactions using the appropriate T accounts. Identify each transaction by number.
(3) After recording all transactions, write the word "Balance" on the normal balance side of each T account. Then compute and record the balance for each account.

Transactions:

1. Mr. Schultz invested $45,000 cash in his business.
2. Bought a van on account for $8,500 to use for deliveries.
3. Purchased an office lamp for $85, Check 100.
4. Mr. Schultz invested a typewriter worth $200 in the business.
5. Made a $3,000 payment on the van bought on account, Check 101.
6. Sold the old typewriter on account for $200.
7. Bought a new typewriter for $1,500, Check 102.
8. Received a $100 payment for the typewriter sold on account.

Problem 3-3   Analyzing Transactions into Debit and Credit Parts

Helen Marquez owns a dog grooming business. The accounts she uses to record and report business transactions are listed on page 57.

Cash in Bank   Grooming Equipment Accounts Payable
Accounts Receivable Store Equipment   Helen Marquez, Capital
Grooming Supplies

Instructions:
(1) Prepare a T account for each account listed above.
(2) Analyze and record each business transaction in the appropriate T accounts. Identify each transaction by number.
(3) After recording all transactions, compute and record the account balance on the normal balance side of each T account.
(4) Add the balances of those accounts with normal debit balances.
(5) Add the balances of those accounts with normal credit balances.
(6) Compare the two totals. Are they the same?

Transactions:
1. Helen Marquez invested $53,250 from savings into the business.
2. Bought grooming supplies for $550, Check 1000.
3. Bought grooming equipment on account from Dogs & Cats, Inc., for $2,675.
4. Ms. Marquez invested a dog drying lamp, value $150, in the business.
5. Bought a cash register for the store on account from Able Store Equipment for $1,250.
6. Sold the drying lamp on credit for $150.
7. Paid $500 on account to Able Store Equipment, Check 1001.
8. Purchased display shelves for the store for $650, Check 1002.
9. Paid $1,250 on account to Dogs & Cats, Inc., Check 1003.
10. Bought grooming supplies for $175, Check 1004.

Problem 3-4 ˙ Analyzing Transactions

Bob Hamilton completed the following transactions soon after opening his business, Your Cleaning Shop.

Cash in Bank   Office Equipment   Accounts Payable
Accounts Receivable Cleaning Equipment Bob Hamilton, Capital
Cleaning Supplies

Instructions:
(1) Prepare a T account for each account used by Your Cleaning Shop.
(2) Analyze and enter each transaction in the appropriate T accounts.
(3) After recording all transactions, compute and record each balance.
(4) Make a list of the asset accounts and their balances.
(5) Add the asset account balances.
(6) Make a list of the liability and owner's equity accounts and balances.
(7) Add the liability and owner's equity account balances.
(8) Compare the totals. Are the totals the same?

Transactions:
1. Mr. Hamilton invested $10,000 of his personal savings in the business.
2. Bought cleaning supplies on account for $750 from Jack's Cleaning.
3. Bought an office desk for $175, Check 1001.
4. Mr. Hamilton invested his $100 calculator in the business.
5. Purchased a new carpet cleaning machine on account for $1,000 from Acme Industrial Equipment.

6. Bought a used typewriter for $195, Check 1002.
7. Made a $350 payment to Jack's Cleaning for the supplies purchased earlier, Check 1003.
8. Sold the old calculator on account for $100.
9. Paid Acme Industrial Equipment $500 on account, Check 1004.
10. Bought carpet spray for $35, Check 1005.

CHALLENGE **Problem 3-5   Analyzing Transactions Recorded in T Accounts**

PROBLEM

Mary McColly owns and operates a word processing service. The T accounts that follow summarize several business transactions that occurred during May.

Instructions: Use a form similar to the one below. For each transaction,
(1) Identify the account debited and record the account title in the appropriate column.
(2) Indicate whether the account debited is being increased or decreased.
(3) Identify the account credited and write the account title in the appropriate column.
(4) Indicate whether the account credited is being increased or decreased.
(5) Write a short description of the transaction.

Trans. No.	Account Debited	Increase (I) or Decrease (D)	Account Credited	Increase (I) or Decrease (D)	Description
1	Cash in Bank	I	Mary McColly, Capital	I	Mary McColly invested $15,000 in the business

Cash in Bank

Debit +		Credit −	
(1) $15,000		(4) $1,225	
(9) 225		(6) 900	
		(7) 95	
		(8) 2,000	

Accounts Receivable

Debit +	Credit −
(5) $225	(9) $225

Office Equipment

Debit +		Credit −	
(2) $ 225		(5) $225	
(3) 8,000			
(4) 1,225			

Office Furniture

Debit +	Credit −
(6) $900	
(10) 145	

Office Supplies

Debit +	Credit −
(7) $95	

Accounts Payable

Debit −	Credit +
(8) $2,000	(3) $8,000
	(10) 145

Mary McColly, Capital

Debit −	Credit +
	(1) $15,000
	(2) 225

U.S. Forestry Service Fights Fires with *Computers?*

We've all heard that "only you can prevent a forest fire." When a fire does start, however, it takes the U.S. Forestry Service to put it out. Around 1980, fire management specialists in the Forestry Service were determined to roll back soaring fire-fighting costs. To help them, they enlisted a brigade of computers. "Models" were developed to predict how fires spread and how different fire-fighting methods worked. These models were then entered into hand-held computers that fire fighters could carry with them.

By entering information about weather, wind speed, and terrain, fire fighters can determine how a particular fire will spread. The presence of a river or of strong winds makes a big difference in how fast a fire spreads. When fire fighters know how a fire will spread, they can then use computers to select the best tactics to control it. They'll also have a good idea of how many fire fighters and how much equipment will be needed to get the job done. Getting the jump on a fire means controlling it faster, and controlling the costs of fire management.

How well do the computers perform? Experts predict that, in one year alone, the new technology saved the Forestry Service $10 million. In that year, one major fire in Idaho cost less than $400,000 to put out. Without the aid of computers, experts say, the cost could have exceeded $3 million. One technology consultant estimates that the Forestry Service will see a 4900% return on its investment in computer technology over a five-year period.

Computers aren't as cuddly as Smokey the Bear. If they can help save our tax dollars and preserve our forests, however, Smokey may have to share the limelight.

Computers help the U.S. Forestry Service manage the nation's forests.

ANALYZING TRANSACTIONS AFFECTING REVENUE, EXPENSES, AND WITHDRAWALS

Learning Objectives

When you have completed Chapter 4, you should be able to do the following:

1. Explain the difference between permanent accounts and temporary capital accounts.
2. List and apply the rules of debit and credit for revenue, expense, and withdrawals accounts.
3. Use the six-step method to analyze business transactions affecting revenue, expense, and withdrawals accounts.
4. Test a series of transactions for equality of debits and credits.
5. Define the accounting terms introduced in this chapter.

In Chapter 3, you learned the rules of debit and credit for accounts classified as assets, liabilities, and owner's equity. As you applied these rules of debit and credit, you saw that accounting is based upon a double-entry system: For every debit, there is an equal credit. You also learned that the T account is a tool used by accountants to analyze the effects of each business transaction on specific accounts. In other words, you saw how a debit in one account was always offset by an equal credit in another account.

In Chapter 4, you will learn about the temporary capital accounts for revenue, expenses, and withdrawals. You will then learn about the rules of debit and credit for revenue, expense, and withdrawals accounts. You will also learn how to apply these rules to analyze the effects of business transactions involving these accounts.

New | Terms

temporary capital accounts
permanent accounts
revenue principle

The Need for Specific Accounting Information

No pilot would take off in a plane equipped with only a speedometer and a gas gauge. These two instruments, although necessary, do not give all the kinds of information needed to keep such a complex machine on course and operating smoothly. Operating a business is a bit like operating a plane. Certain information is needed to keep the business on course. In this chapter, we will take a close look at three types of accounts that provide information about how well the business is doing. These accounts are the revenue, expense, and withdrawals accounts.

The Relationship of Revenue, Expenses, and Withdrawals to Owner's Capital

You learned earlier that the owner's capital account shows the amount of the owner's investment, or equity, in a business. Owner's capital can be increased or decreased, however, by transactions other than owner's investments. For example, the revenue, or income, earned by the business increases owner's capital. Expenses and withdrawals decrease owner's capital.

Revenue, expenses, and withdrawals could be recorded as increases or decreases in the capital account. This method, however, makes finding specific information about these items difficult. A more efficient way to record information about revenue, expenses, and withdrawals is to set up separate accounts for each of these items. By looking at the amounts recorded in the revenue and expense accounts, the owner can tell at a glance whether revenue and expenses are increasing or decreasing. Such information helps the business owner decide, for example, whether some expenses need to be cut to save money.

Temporary Capital Accounts

The revenue, expense, and withdrawals accounts are called **temporary capital accounts.** Temporary capital accounts start each new accounting period with zero balances. That is, the amounts in these accounts are not carried forward from one accounting period to another. Temporary accounts are not temporary in the sense that they are used for a short time and then discarded. They continue to be used in the accounting system, but the amounts recorded in them accumulate for only *one* accounting period. At the end of that period, the balances in the temporary accounts are transferred to the owner's capital account. (The procedure for moving these amounts to the capital account is discussed in Chapter 9.)

Let's use the temporary account Utilities Expense as an example. During an accounting period, utility costs for such items as electricity and telephones are recorded in Utilities Expense. By using this separate account, the owner can see at a glance how much money is being spent on this type of expense. The amounts accumulate in the account during the accounting period. At the end of the period, the total is transferred to the owner's capital account and subtracted from the balance of that account. (As you recall, expenses decrease owner's capital.) Utilities Expense, then, starts the next accounting period with a zero balance — ready to accumulate that period's costs.

Maintenance expense might include the costs of repairing equipment, painting, or taking care of the grounds around the office.

Permanent Accounts

In contrast to the temporary accounts, the owner's capital account is a permanent account. Assets and liabilities are also permanent accounts. **Permanent accounts** are continuous from one accounting period to the next. That is, at the end of an accounting period, the balances in these accounts are carried forward to the next period.

The permanent accounts report balances on hand or amounts owed on a regular basis. They show the day-to-day changes in assets, liabilities, and owner's capital. For example, during an accounting period many increases and decreases are recorded in the Cash in Bank account. The balance in this account reports the amount of cash on hand (in the bank) at any given time. At the end of the accounting period, the ending balance in this account becomes the beginning balance for the next accounting period. In other words, this account—and all other permanent accounts—continues from one accounting period to the next.

The Rules of Debit and Credit for Temporary Capital Accounts

In Chapter 3, you learned the rules of debit and credit for the asset, liability, and owner's capital accounts. In this chapter, we will continue the rules of debit and credit, this time for revenue, expense, and withdrawals accounts. Before looking at these rules, let's review quickly the basic accounting equation with T accounts showing the rules of debit and credit for assets, liabilities, and owner's capital.

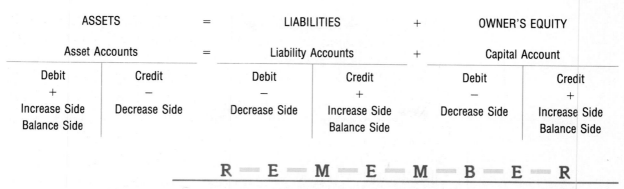

ASSETS		=	LIABILITIES		+	OWNER'S EQUITY	
Asset Accounts		=	Liability Accounts		+	Capital Account	
Debit	Credit		Debit	Credit		Debit	Credit
+	−		−	+		−	+
Increase Side	Decrease Side		Decrease Side	Increase Side		Decrease Side	Increase Side
Balance Side				Balance Side			Balance Side

R — E — M — E — M — B — E — R

The normal balance for assets is a debit balance. The normal balance for liabilities and owner's capital is a credit balance.

Now let's look at the rules of debit and credit for accounts classified as revenue.

Rules for Revenue Accounts

Accounts set up to record business income are classified as revenue accounts. The following rules of debit and credit apply to revenue accounts:

1. A revenue account is increased (+) on the credit side.
2. A revenue account is decreased (−) on the debit side.
3. The normal balance for a revenue account is a credit balance.

Revenue earned from selling goods or services increases owner's capital. The relationship of the revenue account to the owner's capital account is shown by the T accounts in Figure 4-1. Can you explain why the T account for revenue is used to represent the credit (right) side of the capital account?

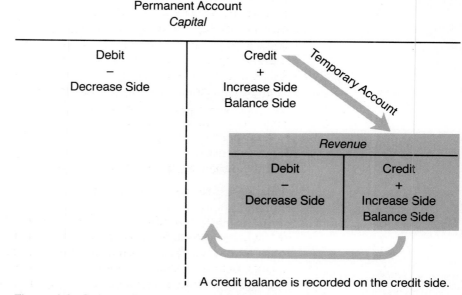

Figure 4-1 Rules of Debit and Credit for Revenue Accounts

The credit side of the capital account is used to increase that account. Since revenue increases capital, the revenue account is used to represent the credit side of the capital account.

We can summarize the rules of debit and credit for revenue accounts with a T account.

Revenue Accounts	
Debit	Credit
−	+
2 Decrease Side	1 Increase Side
	3 Balance Side

Rule 1: Revenue accounts are increased by credits.

Rule 2: Revenue accounts are decreased by debits.

Rule 3: The normal balance for revenue accounts is a credit balance.

Let's apply these rules of debit and credit to an actual revenue account. Look at the entries in the following T account for the revenue account called Fees.

Fees	
Debit	Credit
−	+
$200	$ 500
	1,000
	2,000
	Balance, $3,300

The increases to revenue are recorded on the right, or credit, side of the T account. The decreases to revenue are recorded on the left, or debit, side. To find the balance, subtract total debits ($200) from total credits ($500 + $1,000 + $2,000 = $3,500). You get a balance of $3,300 on the credit side, the normal balance side for a revenue account.

R E M E M B E R

The normal balance side of any account is the same as the side used to increase that account.

Rules for Expense Accounts

Accounts that are set up to record the costs of goods and services used by the business are classified as expense accounts. Within an expense account itself, the following rules of debit and credit apply:

1. An expense account is increased (+) on the debit side.
2. An expense account is decreased (−) on the credit side.
3. The normal balance for an expense account is a debit balance.

Expenses are the costs of doing business. Expenses decrease owner's capital. Expenses, therefore, have the opposite effect from that of revenue on the owner's capital account. Look at the T accounts in Figure 4-2. Can you explain why the T account for expenses is used to represent the debit (left) side of the capital account?

Decreases in capital are shown on the debit side of that account. Since expenses decrease capital, expense accounts are used to represent the debit side of the owner's capital account.

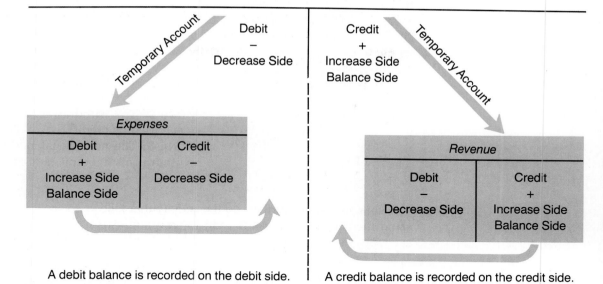

Permanent Account
Capital

	Debit	Credit	
Temporary Account	−	+	Temporary Account
	Decrease Side	Increase Side	
		Balance Side	

Expenses

Debit	Credit
+	−
Increase Side	Decrease Side
Balance Side	

Revenue

Debit	Credit
−	+
Decrease Side	Increase Side
	Balance Side

A debit balance is recorded on the debit side.   A credit balance is recorded on the credit side.

Figure 4-2   Rules of Debit and Credit for Expense Accounts

Let's use a T account to summarize the rules of debit and credit for expense accounts.

Expense Accounts

Debit	Credit
+	−
1 Increase Side	2 Decrease Side
3 Balance Side	

Rule 1: Expense accounts are increased by debits.
Rule 2: Expense accounts are decreased by credits.
Rule 3: The normal balance for expense accounts is a debit balance.

Now look at the entries recorded in the following T account for the expense account entitled Advertising Expense.

Advertising Expense

Debit	Credit
+	−
$400	$125
200	
Balance, $475	

The increases to the expense account are recorded on the left, or debit, side of the T account. The decreases to the account are recorded on the right, or credit, side of the T account. When total credits ($125) are subtracted from total debits ($600), there is a balance of $475 on the debit side, which is the normal balance side for expense accounts.

R — E — M — E — M — B — E — R

The normal balance of a revenue account is a credit. The normal balance for an expense account is a debit.

Rules for the Withdrawals Account

A withdrawal is an amount of money or an asset taken out of the business by the owner. Since withdrawals do not occur as frequently as expenses, no separate classification is used for the withdrawals account. Rather, it is classified as a temporary owner's equity account. Withdrawals decrease capital, so the rules of debit and credit are the same as for expense accounts.

Withdrawals Account	
Debit	Credit
+	−
1 Increase Side	2 Decrease Side
3 Balance Side	

Rule 1: The withdrawals account is increased by debits.

Rule 2: The withdrawals account is decreased by credits.

Rule 3: The normal balance for the withdrawals account is a debit balance.

Before you go any further, do the activity that follows to see if you understand the rules of debit and credit for revenue, expense, and withdrawals accounts.

Check Your Learning

Answer these questions about revenue, expense, and withdrawals accounts.

1. What is the normal balance side of any account?
2. What effect does a debit have on an expense account?
3. What is the normal balance for a revenue account?
4. What effect does a credit have on a revenue account?
5. What is the normal balance for an expense account?
6. What effect does a credit have on a withdrawals account?
7. What is the normal balance for a withdrawals account?

Compare your answers to those in the answers section. Re-read the preceding part of the chapter to find the correct answers to any questions you may have missed.

Summarizing the Rules of Debit and Credit

Revenue represents the increase side of the capital account. As a result, revenue accounts are increased on the credit side and decreased on the debit side. The normal balance for revenue accounts is a credit balance. The rules of debit and credit for expense and withdrawals accounts are opposite the rules for revenue accounts. Expenses and withdrawals represent the decrease side of the capital account. Expense and withdrawals accounts then are increased on the debit side and decreased on the credit side. The normal balance for expense and withdrawals accounts is a debit balance. These basic accounting relationships are shown in the T accounts in Figure 4-3.

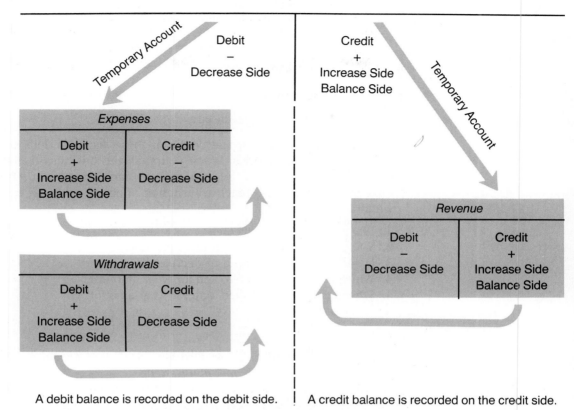

Figure 4-3   Rules of Debit and Credit for Temporary Capital Accounts

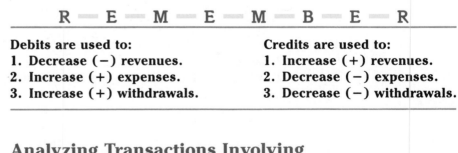

Debits are used to:	Credits are used to:
1. Decrease (−) revenues.	1. Increase (+) revenues.
2. Increase (+) expenses.	2. Decrease (−) expenses.
3. Increase (+) withdrawals.	3. Decrease (−) withdrawals.

Analyzing Transactions Involving Revenue, Expenses, and Withdrawals

The Global Travel Agency transactions in Chapter 3 dealt with asset and liability accounts and with the owner's equity account Jan Harter, Capital. To keep track of revenue, expenses, and withdrawals, Jan Harter has expanded the number of accounts used by the business. The following list shows all the account titles used by Global Travel. As you can see, the accounts have been classified as assets, liabilities, owner's equity, revenue, and expenses. The accounts have also been numbered so that they can be easily and quickly located.

ASSETS
101 Cash in Bank
105 Accounts Receivable
120 Computer Equipment
130 Office Equipment

LIABILITIES
201 Accounts Payable

OWNER'S EQUITY
301 Jan Harter, Capital
305 Jan Harter, Withdrawals

REVENUE
401 Fees

EXPENSES
501 Advertising Expense
505 Maintenance Expense
510 Rent Expense
515 Utilities Expense

Using the rules of debit and credit for these accounts, let's analyze several business transactions. When you analyzed business transactions in Chapter 3, you asked six questions about each transaction. These same questions also apply to each transaction affecting revenue, expenses, or withdrawals.

1. Which accounts are affected?
2. What is the classification of each account?
3. Is each account increased or decreased?
4. Which account is debited, and for what amount?
5. Which account is credited, and for what amount?
6. What is the complete entry?

Business Transaction 8: *On October 15, Global Travel Agency mailed Check 103 for $550 to pay the month's rent.*

1. Which accounts are affected?
   The accounts affected are Rent Expense and Cash in Bank.
2. What is the classification of each account?
   Rent Expense is an expense account. Cash in Bank is an asset account.
3. Is each account increased or decreased?
   The payment of rent increases the business's costs, so Rent Expense is increased. The writing of a check reduces cash, so Cash in Bank is decreased.
4. Which account is debited, and for what amount?

Rent Expense	
Debit	Credit
+	−
$550	
Balance, $550	

Increases in expense accounts are recorded as debits. Rent Expense, therefore, is debited for $550.

5. Which account is credited, and for what amount?

Cash in Bank	
Debit	Credit
+	−
$16,450	$550
Balance, $15,900	

Decreases in assets are recorded as credits. Cash in Bank is, therefore, credited for $550.

6. What is the complete entry?

Rent Expense is debited for $550 and Cash in Bank is credited for $550. Remember, in the double-entry system, the debit amount of a transaction must equal the credit amount.

Rent Expense			Cash in Bank	
Debit	Credit		Debit	Credit
+	−		+	−
$550				$550

R E M E M B E R

Expenses decrease owner's capital. As a result, increases to expenses are recorded as debits and the normal balance of an expense account is a debit balance.

Business Transaction 9: On October 16, Jan Harter bought a $75 advertisement on account from City News.

1. Which accounts are affected?

Advertising Expense and Accounts Payable are affected.

2. What is the classification of each account?

Advertising Expense is an expense account; Accounts Payable is a liability account.

3. Is each account increased or decreased?

Buying advertising adds to expenses, so Advertising Expense is increased. Accounts Payable is increased because the amount the business owes is increased.

4. Which account is debited, and for what amount?

Advertising Expense	
Debit	Credit
+	−
$75	
Balance, $75	

Increases in expenses are recorded as debits. Advertising Expense is being increased by $75 and is, therefore, debited for that amount.

5. Which account is credited, and for what amount?

Accounts Payable	
Debit	Credit
−	+
	$750
	75
	Balance, $825

Increases in liabilities are recorded as credits. Accounts Payable is a liability and is, therefore, credited for the amount of the increase, $75.

6. What is the complete entry?

Advertising Expense is debited for $75 and Accounts Payable is credited for $75.

Advertising Expense			Accounts Payable	
Debit	Credit		Debit	Credit
+	−		−	+
$75				$75

Business Transaction 10: *On October 18, Jan Harter completed travel plans requested by the Sims Corporation. She received $1,200 as payment for her services.*

1. Which accounts are affected?

Cash in Bank and Fees are affected.

2. What is the classification of each account?

Cash in Bank is an asset account and Fees is a revenue account.

3. Is each account increased or decreased?

Money received increases Cash in Bank. Fees received for services completed add to revenue, so the revenue account Fees is increased.

4. Which account is debited and for what amount?

Cash in Bank	
Debit	Credit
+	−
$16,450	$550
1,200	
Balance, $17,100	

Increases in assets are recorded as debits. The asset account Cash in Bank is debited for $1,200.

5. Which account is credited, and for what amount?

Fees	
Debit	Credit
−	+
	$1,200
	Balance, $1,200

Increases in revenue are recorded as credits. The revenue account Fees is credited for $1,200.

6. What is the complete entry?

Cash in Bank is debited for $1,200 and Fees is credited for the same amount.

Cash in Bank			Fees	
Debit	Credit		Debit	Credit
+	−		−	+
$1,200				$1,200

Global Travel Agency earns revenue by providing travel services to various customers.

Business Transaction 11: *On October 20, Jan Harter completed travel plans for a customer. She billed the customer $450 for the work.*

1. Which accounts are affected?
   The customer has not yet paid for the job, so Accounts Receivable is affected. Fees is also affected.
2. What is the classification of each account?
   Accounts Receivable is classified as an asset account. Fees is a revenue account.
3. Is each account increased or decreased?
   Money to be received in the future increases Accounts Receivable. Accounts Receivable is, therefore, increased. Money to be received for a job is revenue, so Fees is increased. For accounting purposes, revenue is recognized and recorded on the date it is earned even if cash has not been received on that date. This is known as the **revenue principle.**
4. Which account is debited, and for what amount?

Accounts Receivable	
Debit	Credit
+	−
$450	
Balance, $450	

Increases in assets are recorded as debits. The asset account Accounts Receivable is debited for $450.

5. Which account is credited, and for what amount?

Fees	
Debit	Credit
−	+
	$1,200
	450
	Balance, $1,650

Increases in revenue are recorded as credits. The revenue account Fees is credited for $450.

6. What is the complete entry?
Accounts Receivable is debited for $450 and Fees is credited for $450.

Accounts Receivable		Fees	
Debit	Credit	Debit	Credit
+	−	−	+
$450			$450

Business Transaction 12: On October 28, Global Travel Agency paid a $125 telephone bill with Check 104.

1. Which accounts are affected?
The cost of telephone service used by the business is an expense. The account Utilities Expense is affected. ("Utilities" are electricity, gas, heat, telephone service, and water.) Cash in Bank is also affected.
2. What is the classification of each account?
Utilities Expense is an expense account. Cash in Bank is an asset account.
3. Is each account increased or decreased?
The payment of a telephone bill increases expenses, so Utilities Expense is increased. The writing of a check reduces the amount of cash in the bank, so Cash in Bank is decreased.
4. Which account is debited, and for what amount?

Utilities Expense	
Debit	Credit
+	−
$125	
Balance, $125	

Increases in expenses are recorded as debits. Utilities Expense is debited for $125.

5. Which account is credited, and for what amount?

Cash in Bank	
Debit	Credit
+	−
$16,450	$550
1,200	125
Balance, $16,975	

Decreases in assets are recorded as credits. Cash in Bank is credited for $125.

6. What is the complete entry?
Utilities Expense is debited for $125 and Cash in Bank is credited for the same amount.

Utilities Expense		Cash in Bank	
Debit	Credit	Debit	Credit
+	−	+	−
$125			$125

UNIT 2   The Basic Accounting Cycle

Business Transaction 13: *On October 29, Jan Harter wrote Check 105 for $450 to have the office repainted.*

1. Which accounts are affected?

Repainting is a cost of maintaining the office, so the Maintenance Expense account is affected. Cash in Bank is also affected since cash is being paid out.

2. What is the classification of each account?

Maintenance Expense is an expense account. Cash in Bank is an asset account.

3. Is each account increased or decreased?

Maintenance Expense is increased and Cash in Bank is decreased.

4. Which account is debited, and for what amount?

Maintenance Expense	
Debit	Credit
+	–
$450	
Balance, $450	

Increases in expenses are recorded as debits. Maintenance Expense is, therefore, debited for $450.

5. Which account is credited, and for what amount?

Cash in Bank	
Debit	Credit
+	–
$16,450	$550
1,200	125
	450
Balance, $16,525	

Decreases in assets are recorded as credits. Cash in Bank is, therefore, credited for $450.

6. What is the complete entry?

Maintenance Expense is debited for $450 and Cash in Bank is credited for $450.

Maintenance Expense			Cash in Bank	
Debit	Credit		Debit	Credit
+	–		+	–
$450				$450

Business Transaction 14: *On October 31, Jan Harter withdrew $400 cash for personal use by writing Check 106.*

1. Which accounts are affected?

Money taken out of the business by the owner is recorded in the withdrawals account. The accounts affected, therefore, are Jan Harter, Withdrawals and Cash in Bank.

2. What is the classification of each account?

Jan Harter, Withdrawals is classified as a temporary owner's equity account. Cash in Bank is an asset account.

3. Is each account increased or decreased?

Jan Harter, Withdrawals is used to accumulate amounts taken out of the business by the owner. The amount of money withdrawn by the owner increases the account, so Jan Harter, Withdrawals is increased. The writing of a check decreases Cash in Bank.

4. Which account is debited, and for what amount?

Jan Harter, Withdrawals	
Debit	Credit
+	−
$400	
Balance, $400	

Increases in withdrawals are recorded as debits. Jan Harter, Withdrawals is, therefore, debited for $400.

5. Which account is credited, and for what amount?

Cash in Bank	
Debit	Credit
+	−
$16,450	$550
1,200	125
	450
	400
Balance, $16,125	

Decreases in assets are recorded as credits. Cash in Bank is, therefore, credited for $400.

6. What is the complete entry?

Jan Harter, Withdrawals is debited for $400 and Cash in Bank is credited for $400.

Jan Harter, Withdrawals			Cash in Bank	
Debit	Credit		Debit	Credit
+	−		+	−
$400				$400

R — E — M — E — M — B — E — R

Amounts taken out of the business decrease owner's capital. Therefore, increases in the withdrawals account are recorded as debits.

Before continuing, complete the following activity to check your understanding of how to analyze transactions involving revenue, expenses, and withdrawals.

Analyze this transaction using the six-step method you used in this chapter.

On March 1, J & L Enterprises mailed Check 107 for $2,000 to pay the month's rent.

1. Which accounts are affected?
2. What is the classification of each account?
3. Is each account increased or decreased?
4. Which account is debited, and for what amount?
5. Which account is credited, and for what amount?
6. What is the complete entry? Show in T account form.

Compare your answers to those in the answers section. Re-read the preceding part of the chapter to find the correct answers to any questions that you may have missed.

Summary of the Rules of Debit and Credit

The rules of debit and credit for the permanent accounts—assets, liabilities, and the owner's capital account—are summarized below using T accounts and the basic accounting equation.

| ASSETS | = | LIABILITIES | + | OWNER'S EQUITY |

| Asset Accounts | = | Liability Accounts | + | Capital Account |

| Debit
+
Increase Side
Balance Side | Credit
−
Decrease Side | Debit
−
Decrease Side | Credit
+
Increase Side
Balance Side | Debit
−
Decrease Side | Credit
+
Increase Side
Balance Side |

Assets have **DEBIT BALANCES.**

Equities (liabilities and capital) have **CREDIT BALANCES.**

The rules of debit and credit for the temporary capital accounts—expenses, revenue, and the owner's withdrawals account—can also be summarized using T accounts.

TEMPORARY CAPITAL ACCOUNTS

| Withdrawals | | Expenses | | Revenue | |

| Debit
+
Increase Side
Balance Side | Credit
−
Decrease Side | Debit
+
Increase Side
Balance Side | Credit
−
Decrease Side | Debit
−
Decrease Side | Credit
+
Increase Side
Balance Side |

Testing for the Equality of Debits and Credits

In a double-entry accounting system, correct analysis and recording of business transactions should result in total debits being equal to total credits. Testing for the equality of total debits and credits is one way of finding out whether you have made any errors in recording transaction amounts. To test for the equality of total debits and credits, follow these steps:

1. Make a list of the account titles used by the business.
2. Opposite each account title, list the final or current balance of the account. Use two columns, one for debit balances and one for credit.
3. Add each amount column.

If you have recorded all the amounts correctly, the total of the debit column will equal the total of the credit column. The test for equality of debits and credits for the transactions in Chapters 3 and 4 shows that total debits are equal to total credits, so the accounting system is in balance.

ACCOUNT TITLE	DEBIT BALANCES	CREDIT BALANCES
Cash in Bank	$16,125	
Accounts Receivable	450	
Computer Equipment	8,000	
Office Equipment	1,500	
Accounts Payable		$ 825
Jan Harter, Capital		25,200
Jan Harter, Withdrawals	400	
Fees		1,650
Advertising Expense	75	
Maintenance Expense	450	
Rent Expense	550	
Utilities Expense	125	
Totals	$27,675	$27,675

Summary of Key Points

1. The accounts used by a business can be separated into permanent accounts and temporary capital accounts. Permanent accounts have balances that carry over from one accounting period to the next. Temporary capital accounts start each new accounting period with a zero balance.
2. Revenue, expense, and withdrawals accounts are temporary capital accounts; they are extensions of the owner's capital account.
3. Revenue accounts temporarily substitute for the credit side of the owner's capital account.
4. For revenue accounts, the increase side is the credit side and the decrease side is the debit side. The normal balance is a credit balance.
5. Expense and withdrawals accounts temporarily substitute for the debit side of the owner's capital account.
6. For expense and withdrawals accounts, the increase side is the debit side and the decrease side is the credit side. The normal balance for expense and withdrawals accounts is a debit balance.

4 Review and Applications

Building Your Accounting Vocabulary

In your own words, write the definition of each of the following accounting terms. Use complete sentences for your definitions.

permanent accounts   temporary capital
revenue principle   accounts

Reviewing Your Accounting Knowledge

1. Why are temporary capital accounts used?
2. What is the difference between a temporary capital account and a permanent account? Give three examples of each type of account.
3. State briefly the rules of debit and credit for increasing and decreasing: (a) revenue accounts, (b) expense accounts, (c) withdrawals account.
4. List the normal balance side of: (a) revenue accounts, (b) expense accounts, (c) withdrawals account, (d) asset accounts, (e) liability accounts, (f) the owner's capital account.
5. Why does a revenue account serve as a temporary substitute for the credit side of the owner's capital account?
6. What effect does a revenue transaction have on owner's capital?
7. Explain why the expense accounts serve as a temporary substitute for the debit side of the owner's capital account.
8. What effect does an expense transaction have on owner's capital?
9. How is a withdrawal different from an expense? How are they the same?
10. How would you test for the equality of debits and credits?

Improving Your Analysis Skills

The basic accounting equation is a simple mathematical equation: $A = L + OE$. The equation can be expanded to include revenue and expenses: $A = L + OE + R - E$. As with any equation, the parts can be rearranged to solve for different amounts. For example, to determine the amount of liabilities when assets and owner's equity are known, the equation becomes $L = A - OE$. Use the basic or expanded equation to find the amounts below.

1. Assets = $22,420; liabilities = $6,408
2. Liabilities = $9,470; revenue = $14,100; expenses = $7,000; owner's equity = $15,000
3. Assets = $18,400; liabilities = $4,900; revenue = $8,500; expenses = $2,300
4. Assets = $19,840; owner's equity = $12,400
5. Revenue = $22,500; liabilities = $12,880; expenses = $8,750; owner's equity = $15,000

Applying Accounting Procedures

Exercise 4-1 Applying the Rules of Debit and Credit

Edward Palmer uses the following accounts in his flying service business.

Cash in Bank	Edward Palmer,	Advertising Expense
Accounts Receivable	Capital	Food Expense
Airplanes	Edward Palmer,	Fuel and Oil Expense
Accounts Payable	Withdrawals	Repairs Expense
	Flying Fees	

Instructions: Use a form similar to the one that follows. For each account,
(1) Classify the account as an asset, liability, owner's equity, revenue, or expense account.
(2) Indicate whether the increase side is a debit or a credit.
(3) Indicate whether the decrease side is a debit or a credit.
(4) Indicate whether the account has a normal debit balance or a normal credit balance.
The first account is completed as an example.

Account Title	Account Classification	Increase Side	Decrease Side	Normal Balance
Cash in Bank	Asset	Debit	Credit	Debit

Exercise 4-2 Identifying Accounts Affected by Transactions

John Albers uses the following accounts in his business.

Cash in Bank	John Albers, Capital	Advertising Expense
Accounts Receivable	John Albers,	Rent Expense
Office Equipment	Withdrawals	Utilities Expense
Accounts Payable	Service Fees	

Instructions: For each of the following transactions,
(1) Identify the two accounts affected.
(2) Indicate whether each account is debited or credited.

Transactions:

1. Paid the electric bill for the month of July.
2. Billed a customer for services provided on account.
3. John Albers took cash from the business for his personal use.
4. Issued Check 567 to pay for a recent advertisement.

Exercise 4-3 Identifying Increases and Decreases in Accounts

The following accounts are used by Roy Jenny in his business, the Easy Rider Driving School.

Cash in Bank	Accounts Payable	Advertising Expense
Accounts Receivable	Roy Jenny, Capital	Gas and Oil Expense
Office Equipment	Roy Jenny, Withdrawals	Maintenance Expense
Cars	Instruction Fees	Utilities Expense

Instructions: Analyze each of the following transactions using the format shown below. Explain the debit, then the credit.

Example:

On June 11, Roy Jenny paid the office cleaning bill of $100.

a. The expense account Maintenance Expense is increased. Increases in expenses are recorded as debits.

b. The asset account Cash in Bank is decreased. Decreases in assets are recorded as credits.

Transactions:

1. On April 3, Roy Jenny withdrew $500 from his business for his own use, Check 768.
2. On April 8, the business received $1,200 cash in instruction fees from various customers.
3. On April 12, the telephone bill of $85 was paid by issuing Check 769.

Problem 4-1   Using T Accounts To Analyze Transactions

Esther Wills plans to open her own law office. She will use the following accounts.

Cash in Bank	Esther Wills, Capital	Rent Expense
Accounts Receivable	Esther Wills,	Repairs Expense
Office Equipment	Withdrawals	Utilities Expense
Accounts Payable	Legal Fees	

Instructions: For each transaction,

(1) Determine which two accounts are affected.
(2) Prepare two T accounts for the accounts identified in Instruction #1.
(3) Enter the amount of the debit and the amount of the credit in the T accounts.

Transactions:

1. On May 7, Esther Wills received a check for $1,675 for professional legal services.
2. On May 12, Esther Wills paid the monthly rent of $450 by writing Check 100.
3. On May 15, Esther Wills withdrew $250 for her personal use, Check 101.
4. On May 29, Esther Wills had the business's computer repaired at a cost of $245 and was given until next month to pay.

Problem 4-2   Analyzing Transactions into Debit and Credit Parts

Edward Palmer completed the transactions that follow soon after opening the Palmer Flying Service.

Instructions:

(1) Prepare a T account for each account listed in Exercise 4-1.
(2) Enter a balance of $15,000 in the Cash in Bank account; also enter a balance of $15,000 in the Edward Palmer, Capital account.
(3) Analyze and record each business transaction, using the appropriate T accounts. Identify each transaction by number.

(4) After all the transactions have been recorded, write the word "Balance" on the normal balance side of each account.

(5) Compute and record the balance for each account.

Transactions:

1. Purchased an airplane for $12,700, Check 1001.
2. Wrote Check 1002 for fuel for the airplane, $125.
3. Received $1,850 cash for charter flight services.
4. Paid $150 (Check 1003) for in-flight lunches.
5. Placed an ad in the newspaper for $75 and agreed to pay for it later.
6. Edward Palmer withdrew $150 for personal use, Check 1004.
7. Provided flight services on account, $775.
8. Paid for plane repairs by writing Check 1005 for $325.
9. Refueled the airplane at a cost of $115, Check 1006.
10. Purchased in-flight lunches for $75, Check 1007.
11. Received $225 on account from a charge customer.

Problem 4-3 Analyzing Transactions into Debit and Credit Parts

Marna Ritter operates Ritter's Cycle Rental Service. She uses the following accounts to record and summarize her business transactions.

Cash in Bank	M. Ritter, Capital	Equipment Repairs
Accounts Receivable	M. Ritter, Withdrawals	Expense
Bike Equipment	Rental Fees	Rent Expense
Accounts Payable		Utilities Expense

Instructions:

(1) Prepare a T account for each account used by the business.

(2) Analyze and record each of the following transactions using the appropriate T accounts. Identify each transaction by number.

(3) After recording all transactions, compute and record the account balance on the normal balance side of each T account.

(4) Test for the equality of debits and credits.

Transactions:

1. Marna Ritter invested $12,000 cash in her new business.
2. Bought five new touring bikes on account for $3,750.
3. Allowed a group to charge bike rental fees in the amount of $750.
4. Had three bikes repaired at a cost of $123, Check 1.
5. Wrote Check 2 to pay the electric bill of $95.
6. Received $225 for bike rental fees.
7. Paid the $225 rent for the month, Check 3.
8. Paid $1,750 toward the touring bikes bought on account, Check 4.
9. Marna Ritter withdrew $250 cash for personal use, Check 5.
10. Received bike rental fees of $250.

Problem 4-4 Analyzing Transactions

Juanita Nash owns the Hi-Style Images beauty salon. She plans to use the following accounts for recording and reporting business transactions.

Cash in Bank	Accounts Payable	Styling Fees
Accounts Receivable	Juanita Nash, Capital	Rent Expense
Salon Supplies	Juanita Nash,	Utilities Expense
Equipment	Withdrawals	Wages Expense

Instructions:

(1) Prepare a T account for each account listed above.
(2) Analyze and record each transaction using the appropriate T accounts. Identify each transaction by number.
(3) After recording all transactions, compute a balance for each account.
(4) Test for the equality of debits and credits.

Transactions:

1. Juanita Nash invested $17,500 cash in Hi-Style Images.
2. Bought equipment on account from Salon Products, Inc., for $2,400.
3. Bought salon supplies from Beauty Aids on account for $75.
4. Paid the rent for the month of $150, Check 1.
5. Wrote Check 2 to pay a part-time hair stylist $65.
6. Sent a bill for $67 to Pines Nursing Home for hair cuts and shampoos completed for patients at the home.
7. Deposited the daily receipts from styling services, $233.
8. Paid the gas and electric bill of $125, Check 3.
9. Sent Check 4 for $75 to Beauty Aids as payment on account.
10. Ms. Nash withdrew $150 for her personal use, Check 5.
11. Paid the part-time hair stylist $45, Check 6.
12. Mary Jones, a customer, charged a $25 hair set to her account.
13. Deposited daily receipts of $264 in the bank.

CHALLENGE Problem 4-5   Completing the Accounting Equation

PROBLEM

With the addition of temporary capital accounts, the basic accounting equation can be expanded as follows:

Assets = Liabilities + Owner's Equity − Withdrawals + Revenue − Expenses

Instructions: Using this formula, determine the missing amounts for each of the question marks below. Use the form in your workbook or plain paper. The first one is completed as an example.

	Assets =	Liabilities +	Owner's Equity	− Withdrawals +	Revenue −	Expenses
1.	$64,400	$8,200	$56,300	$ 500	$10,000	$ 9,600
2.	$22,150	525	18,800	1,200	12,100	?
3.	17,500	75	21,650	?	4,115	3,250
4.	49,450	?	47,840	1,500	20,300	17,610
5.	21,900	1,150	20,005	950	?	16,570
6.	72,640	2,790	?	10,750	67,908	39,749
7.	?	1,988	41,194	6,196	52,210	42,597
8.	50,780	1,493	64,110	16,050	?	29,986
9.	?	3,840	61,774	?	40,163	21,637

(Expenses plus withdrawals equal $27,749.)

| 10. | 64,070 | ? | 49,102 | 4,875 | 53,166 | ? |

(Total owner's equity after adding revenue and subtracting expenses and withdrawals is $50,643.)

*S*oftware Piracy: A Matter of Ethics?

You've just bought a new integrated software program. On the disk package, a formidable license agreement in small type sets forth your rights and obligations as the licensee of this program. At the heart of the agreement is the copyright statement. Federal *copyright laws* protect literary and artistic works from unauthorized use. The Software Protection Act of 1980 allows the owner of software to make one backup copy of the original disk in case the original is damaged, lost, or doesn't work.

Your friend has a deal for you. If you let him copy your backup disks and manual, he'll pay you half of what the program originally cost you. What a break! It took you many hours at the department store to earn the money to buy it, and you certainly could use that extra money.

How much could that little transaction between friends hurt a multimillion dollar software company?

One survey estimates that for every disk that's sold, ten are stolen. The Software Publishers Association estimates that over $1 billion a year is lost to software pirates. Software development is costly. It requires talented people and expensive equipment. When consumers don't respect the company's copyright protection, the law-abiding buyer helps pay the price. To help offset the company's losses from piracy, you paid more for the program at the store. If there weren't software pirates, your software probably would have cost much less.

It's not very likely that the software company will discover this violation of trust. Software publishers haven't yet come up with a solution to stop software piracy, but consumers can. When we refuse to participate in these illegal acts and honor

Piracy has become a serious problem for developers and sellers of software.

our purchase agreements, we demonstrate our respect for the creativity of the developers and acknowledge the investment that the company has made in bringing these innovative ideas to us.

In the end, isn't it really a question of ethics?

Chapter 5

RECORDING TRANSACTIONS IN A GENERAL JOURNAL

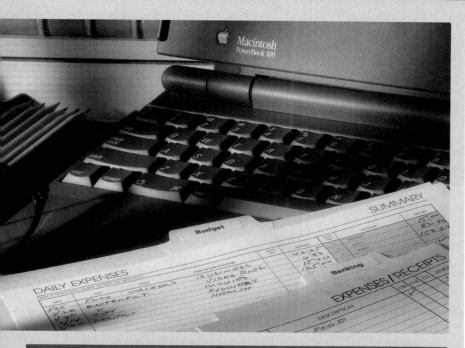

In earlier chapters, you learned to use the accounting equation and T accounts to analyze business transactions. You also studied the rules of debit and credit for asset, liability, owner's equity, revenue, and expense accounts. In this chapter, you will learn how to record information about business transactions in a journal.

In this chapter, you will follow step-by-step procedures for journalizing the transactions you have analyzed in previous chapters. These procedures are very important in ensuring accurate accounting records because they reduce the chance of error. Since errors do occasionally occur, however, you will be shown a procedure for correcting them.

In this chapter, you will also learn more about the chart of accounts, a formal listing of the accounts used in a business's accounting system.

Learning Objectives

When you have completed Chapter 5, you should be able to do the following:

1. Describe the first three steps in the accounting cycle.
2. Explain why source documents are created and give several examples of source documents.
3. Explain the need for journalizing.
4. Describe the steps followed to make a general journal entry.
5. Make accurate entries for business transactions in a general journal.
6. Correct errors in general journal entries.
7. Explain the purpose and use of a chart of accounts.
8. Define the accounting terms introduced in this chapter.

New Terms

accounting cycle
source document
invoice
receipt
memorandum
check stub
journal
journalizing
manual accounting system
computerized accounting system
general journal
chart of accounts
liquidity

The Accounting Cycle

Accounting records are kept and then summarized for a certain period of time called a *fiscal period*. A fiscal period may be for any length of time, such as a month or even a quarter of a year. Most businesses, however, use a year as their fiscal period. The year does not have to be a calendar year; that is, from January 1 to December 31. Many businesses start their fiscal periods in months other than January. For example, many department stores have fiscal periods that begin February 1 and end January 31. Other businesses may have fiscal periods that begin July 1 and end June 30 of the following calendar year.

The fiscal period of a business is separated into activities that help the business keep its accounting records in an orderly fashion. These activities are called the **accounting cycle.** The steps in the accounting cycle are

1. Collect source documents and verify the financial information on them.
2. Analyze business transactions into their debit and credit parts.
3. Record the debit and credit parts of each business transaction in a journal.
4. Post each journal entry to the ledger accounts.
5. Prepare a trial balance.
6. Prepare a work sheet to summarize the financial information for the accounting period.
7. Prepare the financial statements.
8. Record and post the closing entries.
9. Prepare a post-closing trial balance.

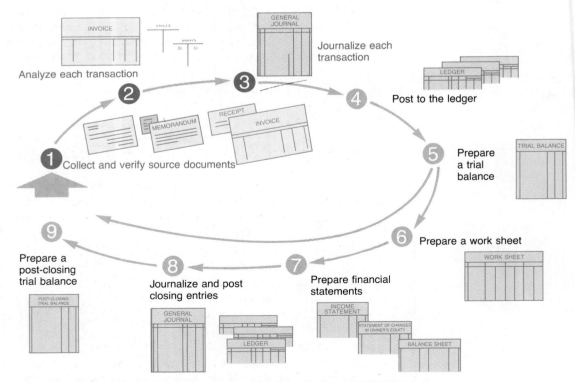

Figure 5-1 Steps in the Accounting Cycle, with Steps 1, 2, and 3 Highlighted

The steps in the accounting cycle are shown in Figure 5-1. In this chapter, you will read about and use Steps 1, 2, and 3. Each of the remaining chapters in this unit will cover at least one more step in the accounting cycle. After studying Chapters 3 through 9, you will have completed the accounting cycle for a service business organized as a sole proprietorship. The business used in these chapters is Global Travel Agency, which you first read about in Chapter 3. Now let's look at the first step in the accounting cycle: collecting source documents and verifying the information on them.

Step 1: Collecting and Verifying Source Documents

Most business transactions take place during the daily operations of a business. When a business transaction occurs, a paper is prepared as evidence of that transaction. This paper is called a **source document.** The source documents for business transactions are sent regularly to the accounting clerk for use in keeping the business's accounting records. The accounting clerk begins the accounting cycle by collecting and verifying the source documents. The accounting clerk checks the accuracy of the documents first. One way is to verify the arithmetic on the source documents.

There are several types of source documents, which may be prepared in different ways. Some source documents are written by hand. Others may be prepared by machine or by computer. The type of source document prepared as a record of a transaction depends upon the nature of the transaction. Some commonly used source documents are (1) invoices, (2) receipts, (3) memorandums, and (4) check stubs.

An **invoice** is a form that lists specific information about a business transaction involving the buying or selling of an item. The invoice includes such information as the date of the transaction and the quantity, description, and cost of each item. For example, if Global Travel buys a new typewriter, the invoice prepared as a record of the transaction would include the information shown on the invoice in Figure 5-2 on page 86.

A **receipt** is a form prepared as a record of cash received by a business. For example, when Global Travel receives payment for a service completed for a client, a receipt is prepared to indicate the date the payment was received, the name of the person or business from whom the payment was received, and the amount of the payment. An example of a receipt is shown in Figure 5-2.

A **memorandum** is a brief message that is usually written to describe a transaction that takes place within a business. A memorandum like that shown in Figure 5-2 may also be prepared if no other source document exists for the business transaction.

A **check stub** is the part remaining in the business's checkbook after a check has been torn out. The check stub lists the same information that appears on a check: the date a check was written, the person or business to whom the check was written, and the amount of the check (see Figure 5-2). The check stub also shows the balance in the checking account before and after each check is written.

A business also receives bills for other items or services such as electricity, water, or telephones. One example is a utility bill, such as the one shown in Figure 5-2. This bill shows the charge for telephone service for the month of October.

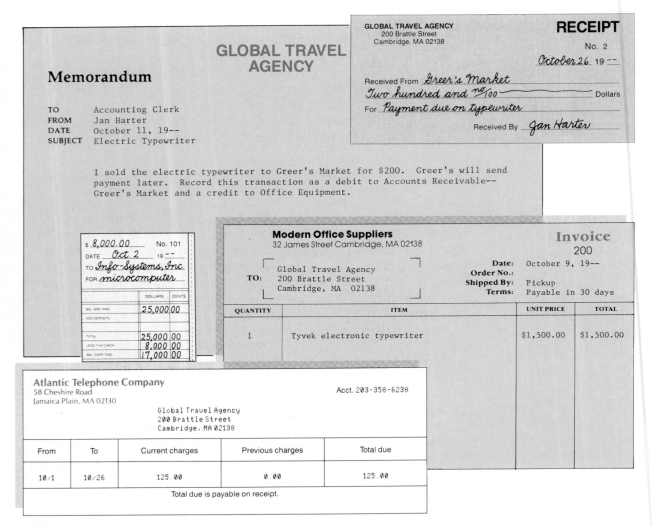

Figure 5-2 Examples of Source Documents

Step 2: Analyzing Business Transactions

After collecting and verifying source documents, the accounting clerk performs the second step in the accounting cycle. This is analyzing the information on the source documents to determine their debit and credit parts.

You have already learned how to analyze business transactions using the rules of debit and credit. When you first learned to analyze transactions, you were given a description of each transaction, such as the one that follows: Global Travel Agency bought a microcomputer for $8,000 and issued Check 101 in payment.

In real life, the accounting clerk must look at a source document to determine what has occurred during a business transaction. There is not enough space in this textbook to show you the source documents for all the transactions that you will study. As a result, you will continue to analyze descriptions of business transactions. You should remember, however, that source documents are evidence of business transactions, and they are the basis for the information recorded in the accounting system.

Step 3: Recording Business Transactions in a Journal

The third step in the accounting cycle is to record the debit and credit parts of each business transaction in a journal. A **journal** is a chronological record of a business's transactions. The process of recording these business transactions in a journal is called **journalizing.** Keeping a journal can be compared to keeping a diary in which all important events are written. The journal contains the most important information relating to a business transaction. It is the only place in which the complete details, including both the debit and credit parts of the transaction, are recorded. For this reason, the journal is often called a *record or "book" of original entry.*

Without accurate financial records, a business cannot keep track of either how well or how poorly it is doing. It cannot operate efficiently or, in the long run, profitably. A company without records, and a system for keeping them, is like a spaceship without an instrument panel and monitoring system. It cannot reach its destination if its operators receive no feedback.

Keeping accurate financial records begins with the recording of information from business transactions. The recording of such information is a part of each business's accounting system. Some businesses use a **manual accounting system** in which information is recorded by hand. Other businesses have a **computerized accounting system** in which information is recorded by entering it into a computer. Although some small businesses still use a manual accounting system, many use a computerized one. Large businesses rely almost entirely on computerized accounting systems because they must process vast amounts of financial information quickly.

Although computerized accounting systems are becoming more and more common for all businesses, understanding manual systems serves as background for understanding computerized systems. A basic procedure in a manual accounting system is the recording of daily business transactions in a journal.

The General Journal

Many kinds of journals are used in business. One of the most common is the general journal. As its name suggests, the **general journal** is an all-purpose journal in which all of a business's transactions may be recorded. The general journal you will be using throughout the accounting cycle for Global Travel, shown in Figure 5-3 on page 88, has two amount columns. The first amount column in the journal is used to record debit amounts. The second amount column is used to record credit amounts.

Each entry made in the general journal includes the following information, entered in this order:

1. The date of the transaction.
2. The title of the account debited.
3. The amount of the debit.
4. The title of the account credited.
5. The amount of the credit.
6. A brief reference to the source document for the transaction or an explanation of the entry.

The preceding information must be entered for each transaction that you journalize. Look at the general journal shown in Figure 5-3 to find where each kind of information should be entered.

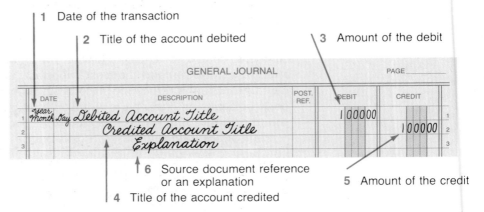

1 Date of the transaction

2 Title of the account debited

3 Amount of the debit

6 Source document reference or an explanation

5 Amount of the credit

4 Title of the account credited

Figure 5-3 Two-Column General Journal

Before reading any further, complete the following activity to check your understanding of the material covering the first three steps of the accounting cycle.

Check Your Learning

Write your answers to the questions below on notebook paper.

1. A period of time into which a business separates its accounting records is called a(n) __?__ .
2. The accounting __?__ includes all the activities that help a business keep its accounting records during its __?__ .
3. Papers prepared as records of business transactions are called __?__ .
4. An all-purpose journal in which all of a business's transactions can be recorded is the __?__ .

Compare your answers to those in the answers section. Re-read the preceding part of the chapter to find the correct answers to any questions you may have missed.

Journalizing Business Transactions

In Chapters 3 and 4, you learned a six-step method for analyzing business transactions. The steps are the answers to these questions:

1. Which accounts are affected?
2. What is the classification of each account?
3. Is each account increased or decreased?
4. Which account is debited, and for what amount?
5. Which account is credited, and for what amount?
6. What is the complete entry?

Continue to use these steps to determine the debit and credit parts of each journal entry. You may also want to use T accounts to help you analyze transactions. After analyzing many transactions, you will find that you need these tools less and less to determine the debit and credit parts of a journal entry.

Business Transaction 1: *On October 1, Jan Harter took $25,000 from personal savings and deposited that amount to open a business checking account in the name of Global Travel Agency, Memorandum 1.*

1. Which accounts are affected? The accounts affected are Cash in Bank and Jan Harter, Capital.
2. What is the classification of each account? Cash in Bank is an asset account, and Jan Harter, Capital is an owner's equity account.
3. Is each account increased or decreased? Both are increased.
4. Which account is debited, and for what amount?

Cash in Bank	
Dr.	Cr.
+	−
$25,000	

Using T accounts to show the effects of this transaction, we can see that Cash in Bank is debited for $25,000 since increases to asset accounts are recorded as debits.

5. Which account is credited, and for what amount?

Jan Harter, Capital	
Dr.	Cr.
−	+
	$25,000

Increases to the capital account are recorded as credits, so Jan Harter, Capital is credited for $25,000.

6. What is the complete entry? The complete entry for this transaction is shown in the general journal illustrated in Figure 5-4 on page 90. Be sure you understand how to journalize this transaction before you go on to Business Transaction 2.

Look again at the journal page shown in Figure 5-4. Notice that in the upper, right-hand corner there is a line for the page number. Journal pages are numbered in consecutive order; that is, 1, 2, 3, and so on. When you fill one page with journal entries, go on to the next page. Be sure to number each new page before you make any more journal entries.

R — E — M — E — M — B — E — R

Six types of information must be entered in the general journal for each transaction: the date, the title of the account to be debited, the amount of the debit, the title of the account to be credited, the amount of the credit, and a reference to the source document or a brief explanation.

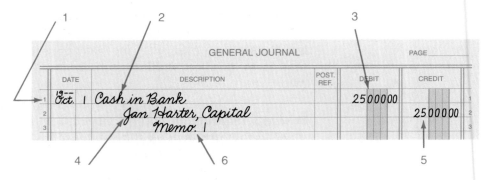

1. Enter the date of the transaction first. Note that the year and the month are written in the left side of the date section. The day is written in the right side. The year is written only once for all the journal entries on a page unless it changes. The day of each transaction is always entered, even when it is the same as the preceding transaction.

2. Write the title of the account to be debited at the extreme left of the Description column.

3. Write the amount of the debit in the Debit column. Do not use commas or decimals when entering amounts in a journal. If the amount is a whole number, enter zeroes in the cents part of the column.

4. Write the title of the account to be credited about 1/2 inch from the left edge of the Description column. Do not skip a line between the title of the account debited and the title of the account credited.

5. Write the amount of the credit in the Credit column.

6. Write the source document reference for the transaction on the line under the title of the account credited. Indent about 1 inch from the left edge of the Description column when writing the source document reference.

Figure 5-4 General Journal Entry for Business Transaction 1

Business Transaction 2: *On October 2, Global Travel Agency issued Check 101 for $8,000 to buy a microcomputer system from Info-Systems, Inc.*

1. Which accounts are affected? The accounts affected are Computer Equipment and Cash in Bank.
2. What is the classification of each account? Both are asset accounts.
3. Is each account increased or decreased? Computer Equipment is increased. Cash in Bank is decreased.
4. Which account is debited, and for what amount?

Computer Equipment	
Dr.	Cr.
+	−
$8,000	

Increases to asset accounts are recorded as debits, so Computer Equipment is debited for $8,000.

5. Which account is credited, and for what amount?

Cash in Bank	
Dr.	Cr.
+	−
	$8,000

Decreases to asset accounts are recorded as credits, so Cash in Bank is credited for $8,000.

6. What is the complete entry? The complete entry is shown in the general journal that follows. Note that there is no blank line between the journal entries.

	DATE	DESCRIPTION	POST. REF.	DEBIT	CREDIT	
1	19-- Oct. 1	*Cash in Bank*		25 00 00 0		1
2		*Jan Harter, Capital*			25 00 00 0	2
3		*Memo. 1*				3
4	2	*Computer Equipment*		8 00 00 0		4
5		*Cash in Bank*			8 00 00 0	5
6		*Check 101*				6

GENERAL JOURNAL   PAGE __1__

Before going on to the next transaction, complete the activity that follows to check your understanding of how to make an entry in the general journal.

Check
Your Learning

Use a sheet of notebook paper to answer these questions about this transaction.

Today's date is September 14. The accounting clerk for Keeton Storage Co. is journalizing transactions. On September 12, Keeton issued Check 424 to Miami Office Supplies for the cash purchase of letterhead stationery. The amount of the check was $125.

1. Which date should be recorded in the journal entry for this transaction?
2. What is the title of the account to be debited and the amount of the debit?
3. What is the title of the account to be credited and the amount of the credit?
4. What is the source document reference or the explanation?

Compare your answers to those in the answers section. Re-read the preceding part of the chapter to find the correct answers to any questions you may have missed.

After analyzing a number of transactions, the rules of debit and credit will become second nature to you. Remember when you first learned to play a sport? You had to concentrate to remember how to do even simple actions. Learning to analyze business transactions is the same as learning anything else: the more you do it, the easier it gets.

Let's look now at the remaining transactions Global Travel completed during the month of October.

Business Transaction 3: *On October 4, Jan Harter took a $200 electric typewriter from home and invested it in the business as office equipment, Memorandum 2.*

In this transaction, the owner is investing personal property in the business. The two accounts affected are Office Equipment and Jan Harter, Capital. Both accounts are increased by the transaction. The increase in office equipment is recorded as a debit to Office Equipment. The increase in owner's equity is recorded as a credit to Jan Harter, Capital. This transaction is shown in the following journal entry.

		GENERAL JOURNAL			PAGE 1	
	DATE	DESCRIPTION	POST. REF.	DEBIT	CREDIT	
7	4	Office Equipment		20000		7
8		Jan Harter, Capital			20000	8
9		Memo. 2				9

Business Transaction 4: *On October 9, Global Travel bought a new electronic typewriter on account for $1,500 from Modern Office Suppliers, Invoice 200.*

With this transaction, Global Travel has increased its office equipment in return for money to be paid later to Modern Office Suppliers. Money owed to a creditor is recorded as an account payable. To keep the amounts owed to different creditors separate, Global Travel uses Accounts Payable followed by the creditor's name as the account title. The title of the account used to record this transaction then is Accounts Payable — Modern Office Suppliers. When making the journal entry, you may have to abbreviate the title to fit it all on one line. An acceptable abbreviation is Accts. Pay. — Modern Off. Supp. or AP — Modern Office Suppliers.

This transaction increases an asset and also increases a liability. As you recall, debits increase asset accounts and credits increase liability accounts. The journal entry for this transaction follows.

		GENERAL JOURNAL			PAGE 1	
	DATE	DESCRIPTION	POST. REF.	DEBIT	CREDIT	
10	9	Office Equipment		150000		10
11		Accts. Pay. – Modern Off. Supp.			150000	11
12		Invoice 200				12

Business Transaction 5: *On October 11, Global Travel sold the electric typewriter on account to Greer's Market for $200, Memorandum 3.*

With this transaction, Global Travel has increased one asset account and decreased another. Accounts Receivable is increased because Greer's Market now owes Global Travel $200. Increases to assets are recorded as debits, so Accounts Receivable is debited for $200. The title of the account used to record money owed by Greer's Market is Accounts Receivable — Greer's Market. This title may be abbreviated as Accts. Rec. — Greer's Market or as AR — Greer's Market to fit it on one line of the journal. The journal entry for this transaction follows.

	GENERAL JOURNAL			PAGE __1__

	DATE	DESCRIPTION	POST. REF.	DEBIT	CREDIT	
13	11	Accts. Rec. – Greer's Market		2 0 0 00		13
14		Office Equipment			2 0 0 00	14
15		Memo 3				15

Business Transaction 6: *On October 14, Global Travel mailed Check 102 for $750 as a partial payment to Modern Office Suppliers.*

This partial payment decreases the amount of money owed to Modern Office Suppliers, an account payable. Decreases to the liability account Accounts Payable are recorded as debits. Accounts Payable—Modern Office Suppliers is then debited for $750. The payment also decreases cash, so Cash in Bank is credited for $750. The complete journal entry follows.

	GENERAL JOURNAL			PAGE __1__

	DATE	DESCRIPTION	POST. REF.	DEBIT	CREDIT	
16	14	Accts. Pay. – Modern Off. Supp.		7 5 0 00		16
17		Cash in Bank			7 5 0 00	17
18		Check 102				18

Business Transaction 7: *On October 15, Global Travel mailed Check 103 for $550 to pay the month's rent.*

With this transaction, Global Travel increased its expenses. Increases to an expense account are recorded as debits. The account Rent Expense is debited for $550. The payment of the rent decreased the asset account Cash in Bank. Decreases to assets are recorded as credits. Cash in Bank is, therefore, credited for $550. The journal entry for this transaction follows.

	GENERAL JOURNAL			PAGE __1__

	DATE	DESCRIPTION	POST. REF.	DEBIT	CREDIT	
19	15	Rent Expense		5 5 0 00		19
20		Cash in Bank			5 5 0 00	20
21		Check 103				21

Business Transaction 8: *On October 16, Jan Harter bought an advertisement on account from City News for $75, Invoice 129.*

The purchase of the ad has increased the expense account Advertising Expense. An increase to an expense account is recorded as a debit. Advertising Expense is debited for $75. Buying the ad on account has also increased Global Travel's liabilities. An increase to a liability account is recorded as a credit. To keep this transaction separate from other accounts payable transactions, the account title Accounts Payable—City News is used. Accounts Payable—City News is, therefore, credited for $75. The journal entry for this transaction appears at the top of page 94.

GENERAL JOURNAL   PAGE 1

	DATE	DESCRIPTION	POST. REF.	DEBIT	CREDIT	
22	16	Advertising Expense		75 00		22
23		Accts Payable - City News			75 00	23
24		Invoice 129				24

Business Transaction 9: *On October 18, Global Travel completed travel plans for the Sims Corporation and received $1,200 as payment, Receipt 1.*

This transaction increases the asset account Cash in Bank. Increases to asset accounts are recorded as debits, so Cash in Bank is debited for $1,200. Fees earned for a service completed for a customer increase the revenue account Fees. Increases to a revenue account are recorded as credits, so Fees is credited for $1,200. The journal entry for this transaction follows.

GENERAL JOURNAL   PAGE 1

	DATE	DESCRIPTION	POST. REF.	DEBIT	CREDIT	
25	18	Cash in Bank		1 200 00		25
26		Fees			1 200 00	26
27		Receipt 1				27

Business Transaction 10: *On October 20, Jan Harter completed travel plans for Burton Co. She billed Burton $450 for the work, Invoice 1000.*

In this transaction, Global Travel has provided a service for money to be received in the future. The account Accounts Receivable is thus increased. The asset account Accounts Receivable — Burton Co. is debited for $450. Revenue for Global Travel has also increased, so the revenue account Fees is credited for $450. The journal entry for this transaction follows.

GENERAL JOURNAL   PAGE 1

	DATE	DESCRIPTION	POST. REF.	DEBIT	CREDIT	
28	20	Accts. Receivable –Burton Company		450 00		28
29		Fees			450 00	29
30		Invoice 1000				30

Business Transaction 11: *On October 26, Global Travel received and deposited a check for $200 from Greer's Market, Receipt 2.*

The deposit of the check in the business's checking account increases the asset account Cash in Bank. Asset accounts are increased by debits, so Cash in Bank is debited for $200. The receipt of money owed to Global Travel decreases the asset account Accounts Receivable. Accounts Receivable— Greer's Market is, therefore, credited for $200. The complete journal entry follows.

GENERAL JOURNAL PAGE 1

	DATE	DESCRIPTION	POST. REF.	DEBIT	CREDIT	
31	26	Cash in Bank		2000 00		31
32		Accts. Rec. – Greer's Market			2000 00	32
33		Receipt 2				33

Business Transaction 12: *On October 28, Global Travel paid a $125 telephone bill with Check 104.*

The payment of the telephone bill increases the expense account Utilities Expense. Expense accounts are increased by debits, so Utilities Expense is debited for $125. This payment decreases Global Travel's cash, so Cash in Bank is decreased by a credit of $125. The complete journal entry follows.

GENERAL JOURNAL PAGE 1

	DATE	DESCRIPTION	POST. REF.	DEBIT	CREDIT	
34	28	Utilities Expense		125 00		34
35		Cash in Bank			125 00	35
36		Check 104				36

R — E — M — E — M — B — E — R

Every business transaction requires a debit and a credit entry. In a general journal, the debit part of the entry is made first. The credit part of the entry is entered next, and then the source document reference is written.

Business Transaction 13: *On October 29, Jan Harter wrote Check 105 for $450 to have the office repainted.*

The cost of having the office repainted is an expense to Global Travel. The expense account Maintenance Expense is thus increased with a debit of $450. The payment of the expense decreases the amount of cash, so Cash in Bank is credited for $450. The complete journal entry follows.

GENERAL JOURNAL PAGE 2

	DATE	DESCRIPTION	POST. REF.	DEBIT	CREDIT	
1	19-- Oct. 29	Maintenance Expense		450 00		1
2		Cash in Bank			450 00	2
3		Check 105				3

Business Transaction 14: *On October 31, Jan Harter withdrew $400 cash for her personal use by writing Check 106.*

In this transaction, the owner is taking an asset out of the business (cash) for personal use. The withdrawals account is used to record such amounts.

The withdrawals account is increased by debits, so Jan Harter, Withdrawals is debited for $400. The business's cash is decreased by the withdrawal, so Cash in Bank is credited for $400. The complete journal entry follows.

	GENERAL JOURNAL				PAGE 2
DATE	DESCRIPTION	POST. REF.	DEBIT	CREDIT	
4	31 *Jan Harter, Withdrawals*		400 00		4
5	*Cash in Bank*			400 00	5
6	*Check 106*				6

Correcting Errors in Journal Entries

Occasionally, errors in journalizing do occur. When an error is discovered, it must be corrected. Note, however, that *an error should never be erased.* An erasure looks suspicious. It might be seen as an attempt to cover up a mistake or, worse, to cheat or to change the accounting records.

If you find an error in a journal entry shortly after journalizing, the error is easy to correct. Use a ruler to draw a horizontal line through the entire incorrect item and write the correct information above the crossed-out error. A correction for an incorrect amount is shown in the journal below.

		GENERAL JOURNAL				PAGE 1
	DATE	DESCRIPTION	POST. REF.	DEBIT	CREDIT	
1	19-- Oct. 1	*Cash in Bank*		25 000 00 ~~52 000 00~~		1
2		*Jan Harter, Capital*			25 000 00 ~~52 000 00~~	2
3		*Memo. 1*				3

A correction for an incorrect account title is shown below.

		GENERAL JOURNAL				PAGE 1
	DATE	DESCRIPTION	POST. REF.	DEBIT	CREDIT	
1	19-- Oct. 1	*Cash in Bank* ~~*Office Equipment*~~		25 000 00		1
2		*Jan Harter, Capital*			25 000 00	2
3		*Memo. 1*				3

Recording Transactions in a Computerized Accounting System

Journalizing business transactions is basically the same whether a business uses a manual accounting system or a computerized accounting system. A journal entry recorded in a computer contains the same six types of information: the date, the title of the account debited, the debit amount, the title of the account credited, the credit amount, and the source document reference or explanation of the transaction. Figure 5-5 shows how Global Travel Agency's business transactions would appear in a computerized accounting system.

```
                    GENERAL JOURNAL                    Page   1

        DATE                 DESCRIPTION              DEBIT      CREDIT

        19XX
        Oct.  1  Cash in Bank                       25000.00
                    Jan Harter. Capital                       25000.00
                    Memo. 1
              2  Computer Equipment                  8000.00
                    Cash in Bank                               8000.00
                    Check 101
              4  Office Equipment                     200.00
                    Jan Harter. Capital                         200.00
                    Memo. 2
              9  Office Equipment                    1500.00
                    Accts. Pay.--Modern Off. Supp.             1500.00
                    Invoice 200
             11  Accts. Rec.--Greer's Market          200.00
                    Office Equipment                            200.00
                    Memo. 3
             14  Accts. Pay.--Modern Off. Supp.       750.00
                    Cash in Bank                                750.00
                    Check 102
             15  Rent Expense                         550.00
                    Cash in Bank                                550.00
                    Check 103
             16  Advertising Expense                   75.00
                    Accts. Pay.--City News                       75.00
                    Invoice 129
             18  Cash in Bank                        1200.00
                    Fees                                       1200.00
                    Receipt 1
             20  Accts. Rec.--Burton Company          450.00
                    Fees                                        450.00
                    Invoice 1000
             26  Cash in Bank                         200.00
                    Accts. Rec.--Greer's Market                 200.00
                    Receipt 2
             28  Utilities Expense                    125.00
                    Cash in Bank                                125.00
                    Check 104
             29  Maintenance Expense                  450.00
                    Cash in Bank                                450.00
                    Check 105
             31  Jan Harter. Withdrawals              400.00
                    Cash in Bank                                400.00
                    Check 106
```

Figure 5-5 General Journal Entries in a Computerized Accounting System

Check Your Learning

Use Figure 5-5 to answer the following questions. Write your answers on a sheet of notebook paper.

1. What account was debited in the October 16 transaction?
2. How many entries affected the Cash in Bank account during October?
3. What was the source document for the October 4 transaction?
4. On what date was a check written to pay the monthly rent?
5. How many entries affected the Fees account during October?
6. Describe the transaction recorded on October 20.

Compare your answers to those in the answers section.

At the touch of a button, an accounting worker can obtain printed copies of journal transactions.

The Chart of Accounts

In Chapter 3, you were shown a list of accounts used by Global Travel Agency. An "official" list of all the accounts used for journalizing a business's transactions is called a **chart of accounts.** Look at the chart of accounts in Figure 5-6. As you can see, each account is listed in the chart of accounts first by classification and then by account number.

You will also see in the chart of accounts an account you have not yet used, the Income Summary account. This account is used only at the end of the fiscal period when the balances in the temporary capital accounts are transferred to the owner's capital account. This process will be explained in detail in Chapter 9.

The Order of Accounts

In accounting, it is traditional to list accounts in the chart of accounts according to certain rules. Asset accounts are listed according to their liquidity. **Liquidity** refers to the ease with which an asset can be converted to cash. The accounts that can be most easily converted to cash are listed first. In the chart of accounts, Cash in Bank is the most "liquid" asset, so it is listed first. Since it is assumed that money owed to the business—accounts receivable—will soon be paid, Accounts Receivable accounts are listed next. The other asset accounts are then listed according to the next easiest to convert to cash, and so on. The accounts within each of the remaining classifications are listed in alphabetical order.

The Numbering of Accounts

An account number identifies an account much as a Dewey Decimal number identifies the location of a library book or a ZIP Code identifies the location of an address. Account numbers may have two, three, four, or more

Global Travel Agency
Chart of Accounts

ASSETS (100-199)
101   Cash in Bank
105   Accounts Receivable—Burton Co.
110   Accounts Receivable—Greer's Market
120   Computer Equipment
130   Office Equipment

LIABILITIES (200-299)
201   Accounts Payable—City News
205   Accounts Payable—Modern Office Suppliers

OWNER'S EQUITY (300-399)
301   Jan Harter, Capital
305   Jan Harter, Withdrawals
310   Income Summary

REVENUE (400-499)
401   Fees

EXPENSES (500-599)
501   Advertising Expense
510   Maintenance Expense
520   Rent Expense
530   Utilities Expense

Figure 5-6   Global Travel Agency's Chart of Accounts

digits. The number of digits used varies with the needs of the business. In this textbook, we will use three-digit numbers for accounts.

Think of each account number as a code. Each digit in the code has a special meaning. The first digit in an account number tells you the classification of an account. Asset accounts begin with the number 1; liability accounts, 2; owner's equity accounts, 3; revenue accounts, 4; and expense accounts, 5. The accounts are "filed" according to their classification. That is, the asset accounts appear first, the liability accounts appear second, and so on.

The second and third digits in the account number tell you the position of an account within its classification. For example, in Global Travel's chart of accounts, Cash in Bank has the number 101. The "01" tells you that the Cash in Bank account is the first asset account.

In an accounting system using three-digit account numbers, there can be up to ninety-nine accounts within each classification.

Assets	100-199
Liabilities	200-299
Owner's Equity	300-399
Revenue	400-499
Expenses	500-599

Look again at the account numbers in the chart of accounts for Global Travel (Figure 5-6). The account numbers are not consecutive. The "gap" between numbers allows a business to add other accounts as needed and still keep all the accounts properly ordered. Now that you know how accounts are numbered and organized, do the following activity.

Check Your Learning

Write your answers to each of these questions on notebook paper.

1. What is the classification of each of the following accounts?
   a. Accounts Receivable—Martinez Company
   b. Cash in Bank
   c. B. Watson, Capital
   d. Miscellaneous Expense
   e. Membership Fees
   f. Accounts Payable—Podaski Co.
   g. Maintenance Expense
2. List the above accounts in the order in which they would be listed on a chart of accounts.
3. For each of the accounts in #1, list the first digit in the account number.

Compare your answers to those in the answers section. Re-read the preceding part of the chapter to find the correct answers to any questions you may have missed.

Summary of Key Points

1. Each business keeps its accounting records for a certain period of time called a fiscal period. A fiscal period can be any length of time, but most businesses use a year as their fiscal period.
2. The activities involved in keeping accounting records during a fiscal period make up the accounting cycle for a business.
3. The first step in the accounting cycle is to collect and verify source documents. Source documents are business papers prepared as evidence of business transactions.
4. The second step in the accounting cycle is to analyze the business transactions into their debit and credit parts.
5. Entering information from a business transaction in a journal is the third step in the accounting cycle. Each journal entry contains the date of the transaction, the title of the account debited, the amount of the debit, the title of the account credited, the amount of the credit, and a source document reference or brief explanation of the transaction.
6. If an error is made in a journal entry, a correction must be made. An account title or an amount is often the part of the journal entry that is incorrect. To correct either of these errors, use a ruler to draw a line through the incorrect part of the entry. Then write the correct information above the line.
7. Each business has a chart of accounts listing the accounts used in its accounting system by classification, account number, and account title.
8. Asset accounts are listed on the chart of accounts in the order of liquidity. Liquidity is the ease with which an asset can be converted to cash. The accounts in the other classifications are listed in alphabetical order.

Review and Applications

Building Your Accounting Vocabulary

In your own words, write the definition of each of the following accounting terms. Use complete sentences for your definitions.

accounting cycle
chart of accounts
check stub
computerized
  accounting system

general journal
invoice
journal
journalizing
liquidity

manual accounting
  system
memorandum
receipt
source document

Reviewing Your Accounting Knowledge

1. What is meant by the term "fiscal period"?
2. List the nine steps of the accounting cycle.
3. What is the purpose of a source document?
4. List four source documents and explain when each is used.
5. Why is a journal often called a record or book of original entry?
6. Why is it important for businesses to keep accurate financial records?
7. How are the two amount columns of the general journal used to record dollar amounts?
8. What information is included in each general journal entry?
9. What procedure is used for correcting an error in a journal entry?
10. What two rules are followed in listing accounts in the chart of accounts?
11. What is the meaning of each digit in an account number?

Improving Your Decision-Making Skills

Miguel Ortega is planning to start his own bicycle repair shop, using the garage of his home as his place of business. Miguel has saved $7,000 to buy tools and equipment and get his business started. He also knows that he should have an accounting system for his new business. He has asked for your help in planning the accounting system. Can you suggest some titles for the accounts that Miguel will need in his accounting system?

Applying Accounting Procedures

Exercise 5-1   Analyzing Business Transactions

Patti Fair recently started a day care center. She uses the following accounts to record business transactions.

Cash in Bank
Accounts Receivable—Tiny Tots Nursery
Office Furniture
Delivery Van
Accounts Payable—Acme Truck Service
Patti Fair, Capital

Patti Fair, Withdrawals
Day Care Fees
Rent Expense
Utilities Expense
Van Expense

Instructions: Use a form similar to the one that follows. For each transaction,

(1) Determine which accounts are affected.

(2) Classify each account.

(3) Determine whether the accounts are being increased or decreased.

(4) Indicate which account is debited and which account is credited in the general journal entry. The first transaction is completed as an example.

Trans.	Account Title	Account Classification	Account Increase	Decrease	General Journal Debit	Credit
1	Delivery Van	Asset	✔		✔	
	Cash in Bank	Asset		✔		✔

Transactions:

1. Bought a delivery van for cash.

2. Paid the telephone bill for the month.

3. Received cash from customers for day care services.

4. Patti Fair withdrew cash from the business for personal use.

5. Billed Tiny Tots Nursery for services provided.

6. Patti Fair invested a desk and chair in the business.

Exercise 5-2   Correcting Errors in Journal Entries

After journalizing several business transactions, the accounting clerk for Blake's discovered that errors had been made.

Instructions: Use the following information to correct the general journal transactions illustrated in the working papers accompanying this textbook.

1. On July 2, the debit should have been made to Office Supplies.

2. The amounts of the July 3 transaction should have been $300.

Exercise 5-3   Numbering Accounts

The list that follows describes the location of accounts used by Fit-Right Shoe Repairs.

Instructions: Use a form similar to the one that follows. For each account,

(1) Write the account description.

(2) Indicate an account number that would probably be assigned to the account. The first account is completed as an example.

Location of Account	Account Number
1. The first asset account	101

1. The first asset account

2. The first liability account

3. The owner's capital account

4. The first revenue account

5. The first expense account

6. The owner's withdrawals account

7. The second asset account
8. The second expense account
9. The third asset account
10. The second liability account
11. The third expense account
12. The fourth asset account

COMPUTER

PROBLEM

Problem 5-1   Preparing a Chart of Accounts

The accountant for the Northwood Insurance Agency recommends the following accounts be used in recording transactions for the company.

210	Accounts Payable—BMI, Inc.	510	Rent Expense
105	Office Supplies	401	Commissions
501	Advertising Expense	110	Office Equipment
305	William Bair, Withdrawals	215	Accounts Payable—Fleming Co.
101	Cash in Bank	505	Office Expense
120	Office Furniture	301	William Bair, Capital
310	Income Summary		

Instructions: Prepare a chart of accounts for the Northwood Insurance Agency. Refer to Figure 5-6 on page 99 as an example.
(1) Write the heading, including the company name and the title "Chart of Accounts."
(2) List the assets including each account number and account title.
(3) List the liabilities including each account number and title.
(4) List the owner's equity accounts including the account number and title.
(5) List the revenue account by account number and title.
(6) List the expenses with each account number and title.

Problem 5-2   Recording General Journal Transactions

Dan Decaro, an architect, owns and operates an architectural firm called Decaro and Co., Architects. The following accounts are needed to journalize the business's transactions.

Cash in Bank	Dan Decaro, Withdrawals
Accounts Receivable—Modern Builders	Professional Fees
Office Furniture	Equipment Rental Expense
Office Equipment	Salary Expense
Accounts Payable—Office Suppliers	Utilities Expense
Dan Decaro, Capital	

Instructions: Record the transactions that follow on page 1 of a general journal. For each transaction,
(1) Enter the date. Use the current year.
(2) Enter the title of the account debited.
(3) Enter the amount of the debit.
(4) Enter the title of the account credited.
(5) Enter the amount of the credit.
(6) Enter a source document reference.

Transactions:
Apr. 1   Wrote Check 410 for the secretary's salary, $270.
       3   Bought a $900 desk on account from Office Suppliers, Invoice 320.
       5   Received $500 for preparing house plans for a client, Receipt 10.

Apr. 7 Wrote Check 411 to pay the electric bill of $110.
11 Billed a client, Modern Builders, $1,700 for drawing up office plans, Invoice 462.
12 Dan Decaro withdrew $325 for personal use, Check 412.
14 Bought a desk calculator from Dante Business Equipment Co. for $300, Check 413.
16 Wrote Check 414 for $450 to Office Suppliers in partial payment of the amount owed.
25 Received $850 from Modern Builders on account, Receipt 11.
30 Paid Office Equipment Leasing Co. $75 for the rental of an electronic typewriter, Check 415.

SPREADSHEET

PROBLEM

Problem 5-3   Recording General Journal Transactions

Ellen Day operates Phoenix Computer Center, which provides computer services to small businesses. The following accounts are used to record Phoenix Computer Center's business transactions.

Cash in Bank	Ellen Day, Capital
Accounts Receivable — Connare Co.	Ellen Day, Withdrawals
Computer Equipment	Service Fees
Office Equipment	Advertising Expense
Accounts Payable — Star Systems	Rent Expense

Instructions: Record the transactions that follow on page 1 of a general journal.

June 1 Ellen Day invested $12,000 in the business, Memorandum 1.
5 Purchased $5,000 worth of computer equipment from Star Systems on account, Invoice 1632.
8 Received $1,600 for computer services completed for a customer, Receipt 101.
10 Paid the *Village Bulletin* $75 for running an ad, Check 101.
13 Ellen Day withdrew $300 for personal use, Check 102.
17 Billed the Connare Co. $700 for computer services, Invoice 102.
18 Paid Star Systems $2,500 as part payment on account, Check 103.
20 Ellen Day invested an electric typewriter valued at $350 in the business, Memorandum 2.
22 Wrote Check 104 for $600 to Shadyside Realty for the rent.
24 Paid Star Systems the remaining $2,500 owed, Check 105.
28 Received a $700 check from Connare Co. in full payment of its account, Receipt 102.

COMPUTER

PROBLEM

Problem 5-4   Recording General Journal Transactions

Frank Palmer, a certified public accountant, owns and operates a public accounting office called Palmer Associates, CPAs. The following accounts are used to journalize the business's transactions.

101	Cash in Bank	301	Frank Palmer, Capital
110	Accounts Receivable — Lisa Logan	305	Frank Palmer, Withdrawals
120	Computer Equipment	401	Fees
130	Office Furniture & Equipment	505	Maintenance Expense
210	Accounts Payable — Comp Systems, Inc.	545	Rent Expense
		570	Salaries Expense
220	Accounts Payable — Premier Processors	580	Utilities Expense

Instructions: Record the following transactions on general journal page 7.

Mar. 2 Received $125 for preparing a client's tax return, Receipt 300.

3 Frank Palmer invested a desk, chair, and lamp, valued at $270, in the business, Memorandum 63.

5 Completed accounting work for Lisa Logan and billed her $1,600, Invoice A12.

9 Wrote Check 711 for $150 for the secretary's salary.

11 Frank Palmer withdrew $380 for personal use, Check 712.

14 Purchased a microcomputer, monitor, and printer for $2,600 from Comp Systems, Inc., on account, Invoice 911.

16 Paid the monthly rent of $400 by issuing Check 713.

18 Wrote Check 714 to Leone & Sons for painting the office, $290.

21 Received $3,600 for completing an audit for a client, Receipt 301.

25 Paid the $70 electric bill, Check 715.

28 Purchased on credit an additional disk drive for the computer from Premier Processors for $540, Invoice C457.

31 Received a check from Lisa Logan for $1,600 to apply on her account, Receipt 302.

CHALLENGE **Problem 5-5 Recording General Journal Transactions**

PROBLEM

Doug Hawk opened Hawk's Heating and Air Conditioning on November 1. The following accounts are used to record the business's transactions.

Cash in Bank
Accounts Receivable—Carley Cole
Accounts Receivable—Lee Industries
Truck
Tools
Office Equipment
Accounts Payable—First National Bank

Accounts Payable—Lock-On Tool Co.
Doug Hawk, Capital
Doug Hawk, Withdrawals
Repair Revenue
Rent Expense
Utilities Expense

Instructions: Record the following transactions on page 1 of a general journal.

Nov. 1 Doug Hawk began business by investing the following assets in the business: Cash, $1,500; truck, $3,000; tools, $1,300; and office equipment, $200; Memorandum 101.

2 Paid the rent on the shop space, $400, Check 211.

4 Purchased a calculator from Marlo Equipment Co. for $150 by writing Check 212.

6 Completed repair work and received $600, Receipt 1001.

8 Bought $450 worth of tools on account from Lock-On Tool Co., Invoice 7872.

10 Doug Hawk withdrew $175 from the business for personal use, Check 213.

12 Completed $550 in repair work for Carley Cole on account, Invoice 10.

19 Received a check for $225 from Carley Cole to apply on account, Receipt 1002.

25 Wrote Check 214 to Lock-On Tool Co. for $450.

30 Completed repair work for $850 for Lee Industries. Accepted $425 cash (Receipt 1003) and a promise from Lee Industries to pay the balance in 30 days (Invoice 11).

Passwords to Computer Security

Before the computer revolution, companies kept highly sensitive and confidential data under lock and key. In today's world of electronic data management, the computer's hard disk is the "file cabinet" and the "key" is a password.

Sometimes it is difficult to convince employees that a password is a security protection device. It's not uncommon to find a password taped to the computer. ("But I keep forgetting it!") Nor is it uncommon to hear a shared password shouted across a crowded office. ("Hey, Clare, run that password by me one more time.") Sometimes employees make a password so obvious that anyone would guess it. ("I know! I'll use my initials. No one knows my middle name." Oh, sure. Check the company phone directory!)

Passwords should be easy to remember, but hard to decode. They should be known to one person only. When several people share a computer, a company may want to add an extra protection product or method to the password system. Here are some devices companies can use.

• When the user logs on, *biometric devices* compare the user's fingerprints to those stored in its memory.

• *Key-reading devices* check a special identification card before allowing a user access to computer facilities.

• With *graphics passwords*, the computer screen might display, for example, a car. The user must then point to three parts in the correct sequence before gaining access to the system.

• A person calling in to a computer system may be connected to a *port protection device*, which requires the person to enter a password. If the password matches one in the device's memory, the caller is connected to the computer system. If it does not, the telephone call is terminated.

With the growing importance of computers, businesses are becoming more conscious of security.

• *Encryption* changes the text into an unrecognizable form through character substitution or transposition. For example, GEORGE would be HFP-SHF by simply substituting for each letter the letter that follows it in the alphabet. A caller who doesn't know the encryption scheme can't read the data.

If confidentiality isn't respected or security is lax, the last word may be TOOLATE.

Chapter 6

POSTING JOURNAL ENTRIES TO GENERAL LEDGER ACCOUNTS

In Chapter 5, you learned how to analyze business transactions and enter those transactions in a general journal. The general journal is an all-purpose journal in which the details of a business's transactions are recorded. These details include the date, the accounts affected, the debit and credit amounts, and a source document reference.

After the information about a business's transactions has been journalized, that information is transferred to the specific accounts affected by each transaction. The process of transferring this information is called posting. Posting is the fourth step in the accounting cycle.

After posting has been completed, the balances of all the accounts must be proved to make sure the accounting system is still in balance. This is done by preparing a trial balance, the fifth step in the accounting cycle.

Learning Objectives

When you have completed Chapter 6, you should be able to do the following:

1. Describe the steps followed in the posting process.
2. Accurately post business transactions from a general journal to the accounts in the ledger.
3. Prepare a trial balance.
4. Record correcting entries in the general journal.
5. Define the accounting terms introduced in this chapter.

New Terms

posting
trial balance
ledger
ledger account form
proving the ledger
transposition error
slide
correcting entry

The Fourth and Fifth Steps
in the Accounting Cycle

Earlier, we referred to the general journal as a sort of business diary in which all of a business's transactions are recorded. You cannot, however, easily see the increases and decreases taking place in the business's accounts by looking at these journal entries. To provide a clear picture of how each account is affected by a business transaction, the information in a journal entry must be recorded in the accounts themselves. The process of transferring the information in a journal entry to an individual account is called **posting.** The purpose of posting is to show the effects of business transactions on the business's accounts.

After posting has been completed, a trial balance is prepared. A **trial balance** is a proof of the equality of total debits and total credits. As you can see in Figure 6-1, posting is the fourth step in the accounting cycle. Preparing a trial balance is the fifth step in the accounting cycle.

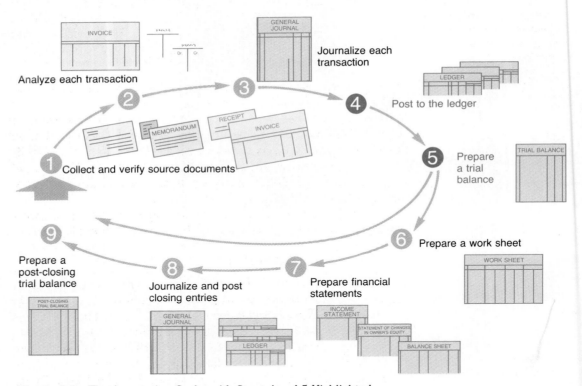

Figure 6-1 The Accounting Cycle, with Steps 4 and 5 Highlighted

The General Ledger

In a manual accounting system, the accounts used by a business are kept on separate pages or cards. These pages or cards are kept together in a book or file called a **ledger.** In a computerized accounting system, accounts are kept on magnetic tapes or disks, but the accounts as a group are

A company's general ledger accounts may be maintained on separate sheets in a ledger book.

still referred to as the ledger, or the ledger accounts. In either system, the ledger is often called a *general ledger*.

Posting to the ledger accounts creates a record of the effects of business transactions on each account used by a business. After journal entries have been posted, a business owner or manager can look at a specific account and easily find its current balance. If, for example, Jan Harter wants to know how much money Global Travel has in its bank account, she can simply look at the balance of the Cash in Bank account.

Before journal entries can be posted, however, all the accounts used in a business's accounting system must be opened in the ledger.

The Four-Column Ledger Account Form

In a manual accounting system, the accounting stationery used to record financial information about specific accounts is a **ledger account form.** There are several common ledger account forms. These forms — as well as other accounting stationery — are usually described by the number of amount columns they have. In other words, the number of columns refers only to those columns on the forms in which dollar amounts are recorded. For example, the ledger account form used for Global Travel's accounts is a four-column account form.

The four-column account form has spaces to enter certain information such as the account title, the account number, the date, an explanation of the entry, and the posting reference. It also has four columns in which to record dollar amounts. Look at the four-column account form shown in Figure 6-2 on page 110. Notice the four amount columns: the debit column, the credit column, the debit balance column, and the credit balance column. The first two amount columns are used to enter debit and credit amounts from journal entries. The last two amount columns are used to enter the new account balance after a journal entry has been posted. Which balance column is used depends on the type of account. For example, the balance of an account having a normal debit balance—such as an asset or expense account—is entered in the debit balance column. The balance of an account having a normal credit balance—such as a liability or revenue account—is entered in the credit balance column. The balance column shows the current balance in the account. The ledger account balances, therefore, are kept up to date.

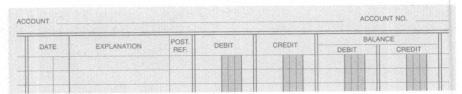

Figure 6-2   Four-Column Ledger Account Form

Opening Accounts in the Ledger

Before journal entries can be posted to the accounts in the ledger, an account must be opened for each account that appears on the chart of accounts. There are two steps to opening an account: (1) writing the account title on the account form and (2) writing the account number on the account form. Each account form will hold several entries, so it is not necessary to write the account title and number again until the first page is filled and a new page is needed. The accounts opened for Global Travel Agency's first three asset accounts are shown in Figure 6-3 as an example.

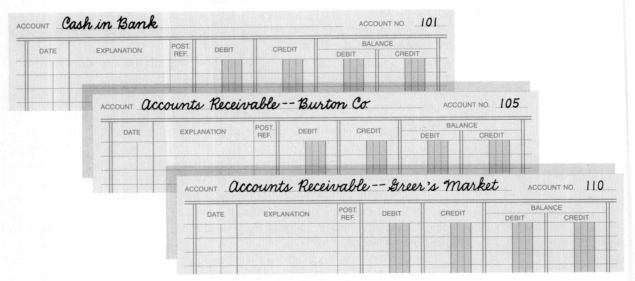

Figure 6-3   Opened General Ledger Accounts

In a computerized accounting system, the procedure is similar. An account is opened by entering the account title and number for each account on the chart of accounts. Computerized accounting systems vary, but all of them require that such information as the account numbers and titles be entered into the computer files.

The Posting Process

How often posting occurs depends on the size of a business, the number of its transactions, and whether posting is done manually or by computer. Large businesses must post daily to keep their accounts up to date. Smaller businesses may be able to post weekly or even monthly. The posting process remains the same, though, regardless of how often it is done.

As in journalizing a transaction, posting to the accounts is completed from left to right. Let's look at the first journal entry for Global Travel to be posted to a ledger account.

Global Travel's first transaction affected two accounts: Cash in Bank and Jan Harter, Capital. The information in the journal entry for this transaction is transferred item by item from the journal to each of the accounts affected. As you read about each step in the posting process, refer to Figure 6-4.

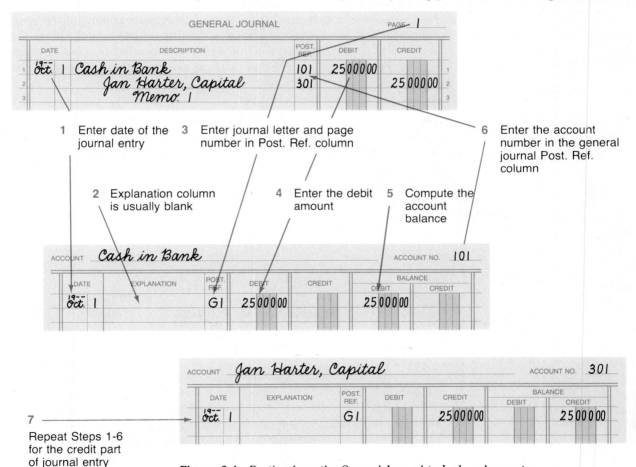

1 Enter date of the journal entry

2 Explanation column is usually blank

3 Enter journal letter and page number in Post. Ref. column

4 Enter the debit amount

5 Compute the account balance

6 Enter the account number in the general journal Post. Ref. column

7 ——— Repeat Steps 1-6 for the credit part of journal entry

Figure 6-4 Posting from the General Journal to Ledger Accounts

1. Write the date of the journal entry in the Date column of the account debited. Use the date of the journal entry, not the date on which the posting is done. Write the year and month in the left side of the Date column. It is not necessary to write the year and month for other postings to the same account unless one or both change. The day, however, is always entered.

2. The Explanation column is usually left blank on the ledger account. Some businesses use this space to write in the source document number.
3. In the Posting Reference (Post. Ref.) column, write a letter for the journal from which the entry is being posted and the page number on which the journal entry is recorded. Use the letter "G" for the general journal.
4. Enter the debit amount in the Debit column of the ledger account.
5. Compute and record the new account balance in the appropriate balance column. Every amount posted will either increase or decrease the balance of that account. Remember that asset, withdrawals, and expense accounts have normal debit balances. Liability, owner's capital, and revenue accounts have normal credit balances.
6. Return to the journal and record the number of the account to which you just posted the debit part of the journal entry. Write the account number in the Posting Reference column on the same line as the debit entry.

   This step in the posting process is very important. The notation in the Posting Reference column of the journal tells anyone looking at the journal that an entry has been posted. The posting reference also shows the account to which the entry was posted. If the posting process is interrupted, perhaps by a telephone call, the posting reference signals the point at which posting stopped.
7. Repeat steps 1-6 for the credit part of the journal entry.

Before reading further, complete the following activity.

Check Your Learning

Use the following journal entry to answer these questions.

GENERAL JOURNAL					PAGE 6

	DATE	DESCRIPTION	POST. REF.	DEBIT	CREDIT	
1	19-- June 6	Accounts Payable-Monroe Products		1 00000		1
2		Cash in Bank			1 00000	2
3		Check 610				3

1. Assume that the ledger accounts have been opened. What is the first item of information that will be transferred to a ledger account?
2. What is the title of the first ledger account to which you will post?
3. If Accounts Payable—Monroe Products has a current balance (before posting) of $1,250, what will the balance be after this journal entry has been posted? Does this account have a debit balance or a credit balance?
4. If the accounts to which this entry will be posted are numbered 101 and 210, which number will be written in the Posting Reference column of the journal after the credit part of the entry has been posted?

Compare your answers to those in the answers section. Re-read the preceding part of the chapter to find answers to any questions you may have missed.

The journal entries made in Chapter 5 for Global Travel's business transactions are shown in Figure 6-5. The postings made to the general ledger accounts from these entries are shown in Figure 6-6 on pages 114-115. Study these illustrations to check your understanding of the posting process.

	DATE	DESCRIPTION	POST. REF.	DEBIT	CREDIT	
		GENERAL JOURNAL			PAGE 1	
1	19-- Oct. 1	Cash in Bank	101	2500000		1
2		Jan Harter, Capital	301		2500000	2
3		Memo. 1				3
4	2	Computer Equipment	120	800000		4
5		Cash in Bank	101		800000	5
6		Check 101				6
7	4	Office Equipment	130	20000		7
8		Jan Harter, Capital	301		20000	8
9		Memo. 2				9
10	9	Office Equipment	130	150000		10
11		Accts. Pay.-Modern Off. Supp.	205		150000	11
12		Invoice 200				12
13	11	Accts. Rec.-Greer's Market	110	20000		13
14		Office Equipment	130		20000	14
15		Memo. 3				15
16	14	Accts. Pay.-Modern Off. Supp.	205	75000		16
17		Cash in Bank	101		75000	17
18		Check 102				18
19	15	Rent Expense	520	55000		19
20		Cash in Bank	101		55000	20
21		Check 103				21
22	16	Advertising Expense	501	7500		22
23		Accts. Payable – City News	201		7500	23
24		Invoice 129				24
25	18	Cash in Bank	101	120000		25
26		Fees	401		120000	26
27		Receipt 1				27
28	20	Accts. Rec.- Burton Company	105	45000		28
29		Fees	401		45000	29
30		Invoice 1000				30
31	26	Cash in Bank	101	20000		31
32		Accts. Rec.- Greer's Market	110		20000	32
33		Receipt 2				33
34	28	Utilities Expense	530	12500		34
35		Cash in Bank	101		12500	35
36		Check 104				36

	DATE	DESCRIPTION	POST. REF.	DEBIT	CREDIT	
		GENERAL JOURNAL			PAGE 2	
1	19-- Oct 29	Maintenance Expense	510	45000		1
2		Cash in Bank	101		45000	2
3		Check 105				3
4	31	Jan Harter, Withdrawals	305	40000		4
5		Cash in Bank	101		40000	5
6		Check 106				6

Figure 6-5 General Journal Entries for October Business Transactions

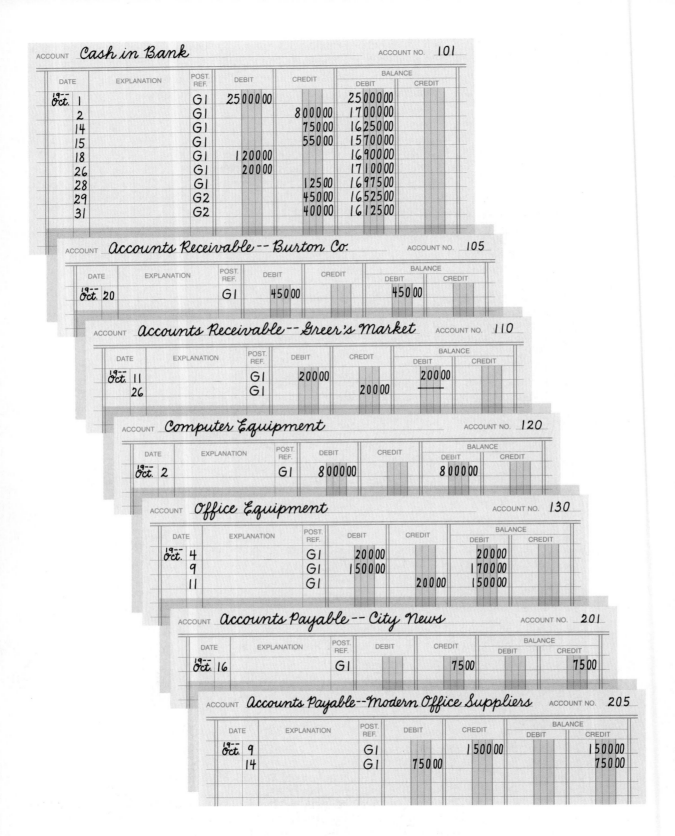

Figure 6-6 Postings to General Ledger Accounts for the Month of October

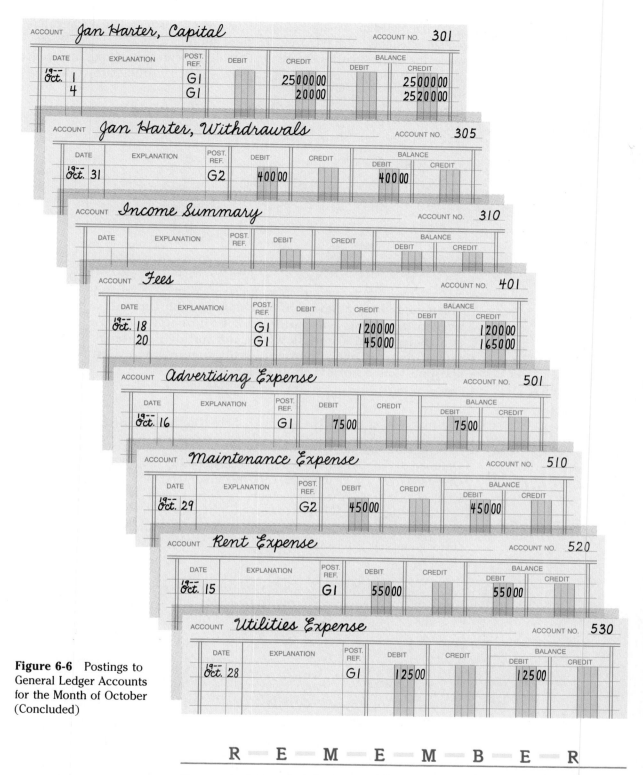

Figure 6-6 Postings to General Ledger Accounts for the Month of October (Concluded)

R—E—M—E—M—B—E—R

For every journal entry, you will post to at least two ledger accounts. You will post to one account for the debit part of the entry and then to another account for the credit part.

A ledger account usually has space for several postings. Often, blank lines remain after the journal entries for the month have been posted. To save space, the journal entries for the next month are entered on the same ledger page. Both the new month and day are entered in the Date column, as shown below.

ACCOUNT Cash in Bank					ACCOUNT NO. 101	
DATE	EXPLANATION	POST. REF.	DEBIT	CREDIT	BALANCE DEBIT	BALANCE CREDIT
19-- Oct. 1		G1	25000 00		25000 00	
31		G2		400 00	16125 00	
Nov. 1		G2		50 00	16075 00	

R — E — M — E — M — B — E — R

When computing a new account balance, debit amounts are added to accounts having a normal debit balance. Credit amounts are subtracted from accounts with a normal debit balance. Likewise, credit amounts are added and debit amounts are subtracted from accounts with a normal credit balance.

Showing a Zero Balance in a Ledger Account

Sometimes a ledger account will have a zero balance. For example, on October 11, Global Travel sold an old typewriter for $200 on account to Greer's Market. On October 26, Greer's Market paid for the typewriter in full with a $200 check. When the October 26 journal entry is posted, the account Accounts Receivable—Greer's Market will have a zero balance. Look at the ledger account below. The dash across the debit balance column means that the account has a zero balance.

ACCOUNT Accounts Receivable – Greer's Market					ACCOUNT NO. 110	
DATE	EXPLANATION	POST. REF.	DEBIT	CREDIT	BALANCE DEBIT	BALANCE CREDIT
19-- Oct. 11		G1	200 00		200 00	
26		G1		200 00	—	

Opening an Account with a Balance

When the first page of an account is filled, a second page must be opened. To transfer information from one page of an account to the next, follow these steps:

1. Write the account title at the top of the new page.
2. Enter the account number.
3. Enter the complete date (year, month, and day) of the *last* entry on the previous account page.

4. Write the word "Balance" in the Explanation column of the new account page.
5. Place a check mark (✔) in the Posting Reference column to show that the amount entered on this line is not being posted from a journal.
6. Enter the amount of the balance in the appropriate balance column of the new page.

The following illustration shows an example of an entry made to open an account with a balance.

ACCOUNT Cash in Bank					ACCOUNT NO. 101	
DATE	EXPLANATION	POST. REF.	DEBIT	CREDIT	BALANCE DEBIT	CREDIT
19-- Nov. 15	Balance	✔			26 470 00	

Posting in a Computerized Accounting System

In a computerized accounting system, the posting process is completed automatically by the computer. After entering the journal entries into the computer, the computer operator simply instructs the computer to post the entries to the accounts stored in the computer files. After posting has been completed, the operator can obtain a trial balance to prove the equality of total debits and credits.

Before continuing, complete the following activity to check your understanding of the posting process.

Check Your Learning

Write your answers to these questions on a sheet of notebook paper.

1. What is recorded in the Posting Reference column of a ledger account?
2. Cash in Bank has a balance of $4,350. If a credit of $150 is posted to the account, what is the new balance of Cash in Bank?
3. What does a dash in a Balance column of a ledger account indicate?
4. When is a check mark entered in the Posting Reference column of a ledger account?
5. You are opening a new page for Accounts Payable—Apex Systems. In which column would you enter the balance of $1,650?

Compare your answers with those in the answers section. Re-read the preceding part of the chapter to find the correct answers to any questions you may have missed.

Proving the Equality of the Ledger

After the journal entries have been posted to the accounts in the general ledger, the total of all the debit balances should equal the total of all the credit balances. Adding all the debit balances and all the credit balances and then comparing the two totals to see whether they are equal is called **proving the ledger.**

In earlier chapters, you proved the equality of total debits and credits simply by listing each account title and its balance and then adding all the debit balances and all the credit balances. This proof of the equality of total debits and credits is called a trial balance. As you recall, preparing a trial balance is the fifth step in the accounting cycle. The trial balance for Global Travel Agency for the month of October is shown in Figure 6-7.

Global Travel Agency
Trial Balance
October 31, 19--

	Debit	Credit
Cash in Bank	16 125 00	
Accts. Rec. – Burton Co.	450 00	
Accts. Rec. – Greer's Market		
Computer Equipment	8 000 00	
Office Equipment	1 500 00	
Accts. Pay. – City News		75 00
Accts. Pay. – Modern Office Suppliers		750 00
Jan Harter, Capital		25 200 00
Jan Harter, Withdrawals	400 00	
Income Summary		
Fees Income		1 650 00
Advertising Expense	75 00	
Maintenance Expense	450 00	
Rent Expense	550 00	
Utilities Expense	125 00	
Totals	27 675 00	27 675 00

Figure 6-7 Trial Balance

Notice that this trial balance has been prepared on two-column accounting stationery. All of the debit balances are entered in the first amount column and all of the credit balances are entered in the second amount column. A trial balance may also be handwritten on plain paper, typed, or prepared on a computer.

If the total debits equal the total credits on the trial balance, the ledger has been proved. If the two amounts are not equal, an error has been made either in journalizing or posting. You must find the error and correct it before continuing with the next step in the accounting cycle.

Finding Errors

Most trial balance errors can be located easily and quickly by following these steps:

1. Re-add the trial balance columns. One or both of the columns may have been added incorrectly.
2. Determine the amount that you are out of balance by finding the difference between the trial balance debit and credit columns. If the difference

between the columns is 10, 100, 1,000, and so on, you have probably made an addition error. Suppose, for example, you have a debit column total of $35,245 and a credit column total of $35,345. The difference between the debit and credit columns is $100. Re-add the columns to find the error.

3. If the columns are added correctly, divide the column difference by 9. For example, suppose the difference between two totals is $27. That number is evenly divisible by 9 (27 ÷ 9 = 3). If the difference between the columns is evenly divisible by 9, you may have made a transposition error. A **transposition error** results when two numbers are accidentally reversed. If you have written the amount $325 as $352, for example, you have made a transposition error.

   A difference divisible by 9 may also indicate a slide error. A **slide** occurs when a decimal point is moved by mistake. For example, if you write $1,800 as either $180 or $18,000, you have made a slide error.

   To find the error, check the trial balance amounts against the balances in the general ledger accounts to make sure you have copied the balances correctly.

4. Check to make sure that you have not omitted one of the general ledger accounts. Look in the general ledger for an account balance equal to the amount of the column difference. For example, if the difference between the two columns is $725, look in the general ledger for an account having a balance of $725.

5. If all the general ledger accounts and their balances have been included in the trial balance, one of the account balances may be recorded in the wrong column. To find out if this is the case, divide the difference between the column totals by 2. For example, suppose that the difference between the two columns is $300; that amount divided by 2 is $150. Look in the debit and credit columns for an account balance matching this amount. Check to see whether a balance of $150 was entered in the wrong column.

6. If you still have not found the error, recompute the balance in each ledger account. You may have made an addition or subtraction error.

7. Finally, check the postings to verify that the correct amounts were posted from the journal entries. Check to make sure that the amounts were posted to the correct amount columns.

Correcting Entries

Accounting workers understand very well the truth in the saying, "To err is human. . . ." When mistakes are made in accounting, one rule applies: *Never erase an error.* Erasures look suspicious. Honest mistakes should be honestly corrected.

The method for correcting an error depends on when the error is found. You learned in Chapter 5 that when an error in a journal entry is discovered *before* posting, it may be corrected by drawing a single line through the incorrect item and writing the correction directly above. However, when an error in a journal entry is discovered *after* posting, the correction is made by a **correcting entry.**

On November 15, Global Travel's accountant found an error in a journal entry made on November 2. A $100 check written to pay the electric bill had been journalized and posted to the Maintenance Expense account by mistake. The original journal entry is shown below in T-account form.

Maintenance Expense		Cash in Bank	
Dr.	Cr.	Dr.	Cr.
+	−	+	−
$100			$100

The T accounts below show how the transaction *should* have been recorded.

Utilities Expense		Cash in Bank	
Dr.	Cr.	Dr.	Cr.
+	−	+	−
$100			$100

As you can see, the $100 credit to Cash in Bank was correct. The error is in the debit part of the November 2 transaction. Maintenance Expense was incorrectly debited for $100. To correct the error, it must now be credited for that same amount. Utilities Expense should have been debited for $100. To correct the error, it is debited now.

The accountant wrote Memorandum 70 to notify the accounting clerk of the mistake. The correcting entry, recorded in the general journal, is shown below.

GENERAL JOURNAL   PAGE 3

	DATE	DESCRIPTION	POST. REF.	DEBIT	CREDIT	
1	19-- Nov. 15	Utilities Expense		100 00		1
2		Maintenance Expense			100 00	2
3		Memo. 70				3

Posting a correcting entry is similar to any other posting. In the Explanation column of the ledger accounts, however, the words "Correcting Entry" are written. The illustration below and at the top of page 121 shows how the correcting entry was posted to the Maintenance Expense and Utilities Expense accounts.

ACCOUNT Maintenance Expense   ACCOUNT NO. 510

DATE	EXPLANATION	POST. REF.	DEBIT	CREDIT	BALANCE DEBIT	BALANCE CREDIT
19-- Oct. 29		G2			450 00	
Nov. 2		G2	100 00		550 00	
15	Correcting Entry	G3		100 00	450 00	

UNIT 2   The Basic Accounting Cycle

| | ACCOUNT | Utilities Expense | | | | | ACCOUNT NO. | 530 |

DATE	EXPLANATION	POST. REF.	DEBIT	CREDIT	BALANCE DEBIT	CREDIT
19-- Oct. 28		G1	125 00		125 00	
nov. 15	Correcting Entry	G3	100 00		225 00	

Summary of Key Points

1. Posting is the fourth step in the accounting cycle. It is the process of transferring the information in a journal entry to the specific accounts in the ledger affected by that entry.
2. The accounts used by a business are kept in the ledger. In a manual accounting system, the ledger accounts are kept on pages or cards. In a computerized accounting system, the accounts are stored on magnetic tapes or disks.
3. The accounts in the ledger must be opened before posting can begin. An account is opened by writing the account title and its number at the top of the ledger account form.
4. A four-column ledger account form has four amount columns: one for a debit entry, one for a credit entry, one for a debit balance, and one for a credit balance.
5. After posting has been completed, the equality of the ledger must be proved. A proof of the equality of total debits and credits is called a trial balance. Preparing a trial balance is the fifth step in the accounting cycle.
6. The most common errors made in accounting records are addition or subtraction errors, transpositions, slides, omissions, and incorrect debiting or crediting.
7. Errors discovered after a transaction has been journalized and posted must be corrected by a correcting entry recorded in the general journal.

Review and Applications

Building Your Accounting Vocabulary

In your own words, write the definition of each of the following accounting terms. Use complete sentences for your definitions.

correcting entry
ledger
ledger account form

posting
proving the ledger
slide

transposition error
trial balance

Reviewing Your Accounting Knowledge

1. What is the purpose of posting?
2. In what way can the information posted in the ledger accounts be helpful to the business owner?
3. What two steps are required to open a ledger account?
4. What determines the frequency of posting?
5. List the steps followed in posting.
6. What two things does the posting reference in a journal indicate?
7. How is a zero balance indicated in a ledger account?
8. List the steps you should follow to open the second page of a ledger account.
9. What steps would you follow to locate a trial balance error?
10. How should an accounting clerk correct an incorrect journal entry that has not yet been posted?
11. How should an accounting clerk correct a transaction that has been incorrectly journalized and posted?

Improving Your Communications Skills

Often the way we say things has a big impact on how our listeners respond to us. Angry words can bring an equally angry response, and no real communication will have taken place. Communication occurs when one person is able to express an idea in words and tone that are heard *and understood* in the way the speaker intended. See if you can identify why communication did not take place in the following examples. How would you have said things differently?

1. *Supervisor:* (Angrily) "You're late again, Wiley. If you're not here on time every day from now on, you're out of a job."
   Employee: "Aw, man. Get off my back. I'm tryin' as hard as I can."
2. *First Person:* "I'm tired of you always making the decisions on our projects. You never listen to what I want to do."
   Second Person: Well, you don't have to work with me anymore. I'll find someone else."

Applying Accounting Procedures

Exercise 6-1 Posting to Ledger Accounts

Kati Karl operates an alterations business called Kati's Custom Alterations. Listed below are several transactions that took place during the fiscal period.

Instructions: Use a form similar to the one that follows. For each transaction below,

(1) Enter the title of the account affected (indicated in parentheses at the end of the transaction) on the form.

(2) Indicate whether the transaction amount would be posted to the debit column or the credit column of the ledger account.

(3) Indicate in which balance column (debit or credit) the new account balance would be recorded. The first transaction is given as an example.

Transactions:

1. Paid the telephone bill. (Utilities Expense)
2. Received cash for altering a coat for a customer. (Alterations Revenue)
3. Purchased thread, paying cash. (Supplies)
4. Ms. Karl withdrew cash from the business. (Kati Karl, Withdrawals)
5. Paid a creditor a portion of the amount owed. (Accounts Payable—ALCO, Inc.)
6. Received cash from Alvin Jones on account. (Accounts Receivable—A. Jones)

| | | | | Balance | |
Trans.	Account Affected	Debit	Credit	Debit	Credit
1	Utilities Expense	✔		✔	

Exercise 6-2 Determining Account Balances

The transactions that follow affect the account Accounts Receivable—Pat Downey.

Instructions:

(1) Open the ledger account by writing in the account title and account number, 115.

(2) Record the account balance of $350 as of June 1 of the current year.

(3) Post the following transactions to the ledger account. All of the transactions were recorded on general journal page 1.

Transactions:

June 2 Received $200 from Pat Downey on account.
     5 Completed services for Pat Downey and billed her $70.
     21 Received a check for $220 from Pat Downey.
     29 Sent Invoice 417 to Pat Downey for services completed, $90.

Exercise 6-3 Correcting Errors

Several errors are described below. Use a form similar to the one that follows. For each error,

(1) Determine whether the error will affect the totals of the trial balance.

(2) Indicate whether the error requires a correcting entry. The first one has been completed as an example.

Error	Does Error Affect Trial Balance Totals?	Correcting Entry Required?
1	Yes	No

Errors:
1. A $50 debit was not posted to the Office Supplies account.
2. A $200 purchase of store equipment was journalized and posted to Store Supplies.
3. A $30 job completed for Sarah James was recorded and posted to James Scott's account.
4. A $500 check received as payment for services was journalized and posted to the capital account.
5. A $69 debit to the withdrawals account was posted as $96.
6. A $100 debit to Cash in Bank was posted as $10.
7. After posting a $75 credit to a creditor's account, the account balance was incorrectly calculated.
8. A $25 debit to the Store Supplies account was posted as a credit.

Problem 6-1   Posting General Journal Transactions

Giles Gilbert, an orthodontist, operates Gilbert's Dental Services. The accounts used by the business have been opened and are included in the working papers accompanying this textbook. The general journal entries for the September business transactions are also included in the working papers.

Instructions: Post the transactions recorded in the general journal to the accounts in the general ledger.

Problem 6-2   Preparing a Trial Balance

Instructions: Use the general ledger accounts from Problem 6-1 to prepare a trial balance for the month ended September 30.

Problem 6-3   Journalizing and Posting
Business Transactions

You will need the general ledger from Problem 6-1 to complete this problem. During the month of October, Gilbert's Dental Services completed the transactions that follow.

Instructions:
(1) Journalize the transactions on page 2 of the general journal.
(2) Post the journal entries to the same general ledger accounts used in Problem 6-1.
(3) Prove the accuracy of the ledger by preparing a trial balance. Compare the totals to be certain they are in agreement.

Transactions:
Oct. 1   Bought several chairs and tables for the waiting room for $560, issuing Check 104.

Oct. 3 Received a $490 check from Rod McCune on account, Receipt 103.
5 Issued Check 105 for $1,350 to Dental Distributors on account.
8 Sarah Ashley sent a check for $375 to apply on her account, Receipt 104.
10 Giles Gilbert withdrew $600 from the business, Check 106.
15 Purchased $480 worth of dental supplies for cash, Check 107.
17 Bought dental equipment costing $1,300 from Dental Distributors on account, Invoice AB629.
20 Paid the electric bill for the month of $180, Check 108.
22 Completed dental work for several patients receiving $3,330, Receipts 105-108.
25 Giles Gilbert invested an office desk, valued at $75, in the business, Memorandum 3.
31 Completed dental services for Rod McCune and billed him $300, Invoice 102.

COMPUTER PROBLEM

Problem 6-4 Journalizing and Posting Business Transactions

Chris Courtney started a business to provide legal services to the community. The chart of accounts for Chris Courtney, Attorney at Law, is as follows.

ASSETS
101 Cash in Bank
105 Accounts Receivable — Jenny Simms
110 Legal Supplies
120 Professional Library
125 Office Furniture

LIABILITIES
201 Accounts Payable — Office Interiors

OWNER'S EQUITY
301 Chris Courtney, Capital
305 Chris Courtney, Withdrawals
310 Income Summary

REVENUE
401 Legal Fees

EXPENSES
501 Salaries Expense

Instructions:

(1) Open an account in the general ledger for each account in the chart of accounts.
(2) Record the February transactions on page 1 of the general journal.
(3) Post each journal entry to the appropriate accounts in the ledger.
(4) Prove the ledger by preparing a trial balance.

Transactions:

Feb. 1 Chris Courtney invested $5,000 in the business, Memorandum 1.
3 Invested law books valued at $1,200 in the business, Memorandum 2.
5 Issued Check 101 for $300 for the purchase of legal supplies.
7 Bought a desk, chair, and table on account for $1,800 from Office Interiors, Invoice LX201.
9 Completed legal work for Jenny Simms on account, $400, Invoice 100.
12 Paid Office Interiors $900 on account, Check 102.
15 Issued Check 103 for $200 to pay the office secretary's salary.
18 Chris Courtney withdrew $500 cash from the business, Check 104.
20 Completed legal work for a client and received $800 cash, Receipt 100.

Feb. 24 Wrote Check 105 for $400 to Office Interiors on account.
    26 Received a check for $100 from Jenny Simms, Receipt 101.
    28 Chris Courtney took home $15 worth of supplies for personal use, Memorandum 3.

CHALLENGE

PROBLEM

Problem 6-5   Recording and Posting Correcting Entries

An auditor reviewed the accounting records of Lopez's Chiropractic Service. The auditor wrote a memo, outlined below, about a number of errors discovered in the June records. The general journal for June and a portion of the general ledger are included in the working papers.

Instructions:

(1) Record whatever correcting entries are required on general journal page 22. Some errors will not require correcting entries, but will require a general ledger correction. Use Memorandum 50 as the source document for all correcting entries and June 30 as the date.

(2) Post all correcting entries to the appropriate general ledger accounts.

Errors:

June 3 The purchase was for store supplies.
     7 A $200 payment to a creditor, Vicki Dash, was not posted to the account.
     9 The Furniture and Fixtures account should have been debited for $500.
   13 Trina Lopez withdrew $1,200 from the business for personal use.
   17 Cash totaling $2,000 was received for professional services completed for patients.
   19 A $75 receipt from Suzanne Sharpe was posted as $57.
   27 Trina Lopez invested an additional $3,000 in the business.

*A*ccounting Clerks: Patient, Persistent, Good with Figures

If you have these qualities—along with a high school diploma—clerical accounting could be in your future.

In today's work force, there are about two million clerical accounting workers—also known as accounting clerks or bookkeepers. Their tasks vary widely depending upon the size of the company that employs them. Generally speaking, accounting clerks are responsible for maintaining accurate records for all financial transactions (journalizing and posting) and preparing material for reports that measure the company's financial position or reports that facilitate corporate decision making.

In small companies, clerical accounting workers perform many of the steps in the accounting cycle: analyzing and recording business transactions, posting to ledgers, preparing a trial balance. They might also perform a wide variety of other accounting tasks: computing payrolls, writing checks to pay bills, making deposits to the business's checking account, reconciling bank statements, handling telephone inquiries about orders and bills, preparing statements for customers, placing orders for supplies or equipment, maintaining records of merchandise purchased and sold, and being responsible for change or petty cash funds.

In larger companies, there may be many accounting clerks. Since there are more people to perform basic accounting tasks, the accounting clerks tend to specialize. For example, an accounting clerk might only handle activities involving the purchase of items used or sold by the business. Other specialized clerical accounting positions include cash clerk, payroll clerk, accounts receivable or accounts payable clerk.

Clerical accounting workers perform a wide variety of tasks.

In today's business world, many companies use computers to process and maintain their accounting records. Even smaller businesses have access to microcomputers. Be sure, then, that you can add this line to your resume: Can perform accounting tasks on a computer.

Mini Practice Set

APPLICATION ACTIVITY 1

Setting Up Accounting Records for a Sole Proprietorship

You have just completed your study of the first five steps in the accounting cycle. Now you will have the opportunity to apply what you have learned by setting up the accounting records for Jack Hires, Attorney at Law. The accounting stationery needed to complete this activity is included in the working papers accompanying this textbook.

When you have completed this activity, you will have done the following:

1. Analyzed business transactions.
2. Used the general journal to journalize business transactions.
3. Posted journal entries to the general ledger accounts.
4. Prepared a trial balance.

Jack Hires, Attorney at Law

Jack Hires, Attorney at Law, is organized as a sole proprietorship. The business is fully owned and operated by Jack Hires. The firm provides a wide range of legal services to local businesses and to individuals who live in the community. These services include criminal defense, personal injury, family law, bankruptcy, and general practice. Revenue earned by the firm is in the form of professional fees.

Chart of Accounts

The chart of accounts for Jack Hires, Attorney at Law, follows.

JACK HIRES, ATTORNEY AT LAW
Chart of Accounts

	101	Cash in Bank
	105	Accounts Receivable — Andrew Hospital
	110	Accounts Receivable — Indiana Trucking
ASSETS	115	Accounts Receivable — Sunshine Products
	130	Office Supplies
	135	Office Equipment
	140	Office Furniture
	145	Professional Library
LIABILITIES	205	Accounts Payable — Legal Services, Inc.
	210	Accounts Payable — Office Systems
OWNER'S EQUITY	301	Jack Hires, Capital
	305	Jack Hires, Withdrawals
REVENUE	401	Professional Fees
	505	Professional Expenses
EXPENSES	510	Rent Expense
	515	Utilities Expense

Business Transactions

Jack Hires, Attorney at Law, began business operations on May 1 of this year. During the month of May, the business completed the transactions that follow.

Instructions: Use the accounting stationery in the working papers accompanying this textbook to complete this activity.

(1) Open a general ledger account for each account in the chart of accounts.
(2) Analyze each business transaction.
(3) Enter each business transaction in the general journal. Begin on journal page 1.
(4) Post each journal entry to the appropriate accounts in the general ledger.
(5) Prove the general ledger by preparing a trial balance.

Transactions:

May 1 Jack Hires invested $30,000 in the business by opening a checking account in the name of the business at City National Bank, Memorandum 1.
2 Bought a computer for the office for $3,500, Check 101.
2 Issued Check 102 for $125 for the purchase of office supplies.
3 Bought office furniture for $2,700 on account from Office Systems, Invoice 457.
7 Mr. Hires invested his personal law library worth $2,350 in the business, Memorandum 2.
9 Received $675 from Mr. and Mrs. James Market for representing them in court, Receipt 101.
11 Completed legal work for Andrew Hospital and agreed to be paid later, Invoice 101 for $750.
12 Bought additional law books on account from Legal Services, Inc., Invoice 876, $1,325.
14 Wrote Check 103 for $118 to pay the electric bill.
15 Jack Hires withdrew $500 for personal expenses, Check 104.
17 Completed legal services on account for Sunshine Products, Invoice 102, $1,250.
18 Bought a filing cabinet (office equipment) for $275, Check 105.
19 Received a check for $600 as payment legal services provided to a client, Receipt 102.
20 Provided legal services on account to Indiana Trucking, Invoice 103 for $600.
21 Prepared Receipt 103 for $625 received on account from Sunshine Products.
22 Paid the telephone bill of $145, Check 106.
25 Sent Check 107 for $1,350 to Office Systems as payment on account.
26 Received $245 for legal services, Receipt 104.
27 Paid the annual dues for membership in the American Bar Association, $350, Check 108.
30 Wrote Check 109 for the monthly rent, $750.
30 Withdrew $500 for personal expenses, Check 110.

Chapter

PREPARING A SIX-COLUMN WORK SHEET

Learning Objectives

When you have completed Chapter 7, you should be able to do the following:

1. Explain the purpose of the work sheet.
2. Describe the parts of a six-column work sheet.
3. Prepare a six-column work sheet.
4. Calculate net income and net loss amounts.
5. Define the accounting terms introduced in this chapter.

In Chapter 6, you learned how to prepare a trial balance. At the end of a fiscal period, however, the owner of a business needs more information than a list of the account balances. The owner needs to know the business's financial position. In other words, has the business earned revenue greater than its expenses? Have expenses for the period increased or decreased? Has the business grown during the period?

The answers to such questions are found by preparing end-of-fiscal-period reports. Preparing a work sheet is the activity that begins the end-of-fiscal-period work. In this chapter, you will see how the work sheet is used to organize the information that has been recorded in the general ledger accounts during the fiscal period. You will also learn how to calculate the net income or the net loss for the fiscal period.

New   Terms

work sheet
ruling
matching principle
net income
net loss

The Sixth Step of the Accounting Cycle

The length of a fiscal period varies from one company to another. The maximum period covered by the accounting cycle, however, is one year. The first five steps of the accounting cycle are performed frequently during the cycle. The last four steps—preparing a work sheet, preparing financial statements, journalizing and posting closing entries, and preparing a post-closing trial balance—complete the accounting cycle. These steps begin the end-of-fiscal-period work. As you can see in Figure 7-1, this work begins with the sixth step of the accounting cycle: preparing a work sheet.

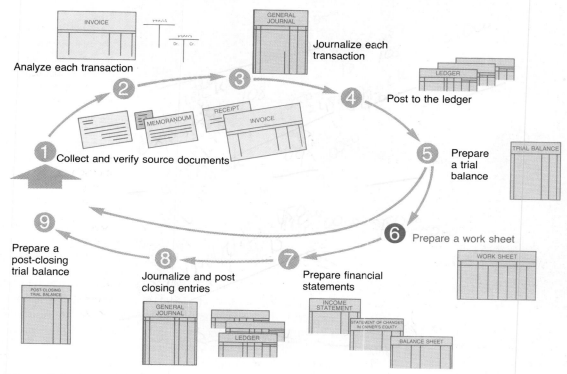

Figure 7-1   Steps in the Accounting Cycle, with Step 6 Highlighted

A **work sheet** is just what its name implies—a working paper used to collect information from the ledger accounts on one sheet of paper. Like the T account, the work sheet is a tool used by the accountant. The work sheet pulls together all the information needed to prepare the financial statements and complete the other end-of-fiscal-period activities.

Preparing a Work Sheet

A work sheet is prepared in pencil on standard multi-column accounting paper. The paper comes in several sizes and is usually printed without column headings. Blank spaces for column headings allow accounting clerks to write in headings needed by a particular business. The Global Travel Agency work sheet uses a six-column format with the column headings already filled in.

The work sheet is an accounting tool. Accountants use it to gather, on one document, all of the information needed to prepare end-of-period reports.

The Global Travel work sheet has five sections: (1) the heading, (2) the Account Title section, (3) the Trial Balance section, (4) the Income Statement section, and (5) the Balance Sheet section. The Account Title section includes a column for the account number and a column for the account name. Find each of these parts on the work sheet shown in Figure 7-2.

The Trial Balance, Income Statement, and Balance Sheet sections each have debit and credit amount columns. The six amount columns give this work sheet its name: the six-column work sheet.

			Global Travel Agency			
			Work Sheet			
			For the Month Ended October 31, 19--			
ACCT. NO.	ACCOUNT NAME	TRIAL BALANCE		INCOME STATEMENT		BALANCE SHEET	
		DEBIT	CREDIT	DEBIT	CREDIT	DEBIT	CREDIT
1							
2							

Figure 7-2   Six-Column Work Sheet

The Heading

The heading of a work sheet is made up of three kinds of information, each centered on its own line. The heading includes

1. The name of the business.
2. The name of the accounting form.
3. The fiscal period covered by the work sheet.

It is easy to remember the function of the lines in the heading. Each line answers a "W" question: the name of the business (Who?), the name of the accounting form being prepared (What?), and the fiscal period covered (When?). Notice how these elements are positioned on the work sheet in Figure 7-2. Follow this format when preparing the heading of any work sheet.

The Account Title and Trial Balance Sections

Information for the Account Title and Trial Balance sections is taken from the general ledger accounts. In Chapter 6, as the fifth step of the accounting cycle, you prepared a trial balance by listing the account titles and their final balances. A trial balance can be prepared at any time during the fiscal period to prove the general ledger. When a trial balance is prepared at the end of a fiscal period, though, it is prepared as a part of the work sheet.

Look at the work sheet in Figure 7-3. The account numbers, titles, and balances were taken from Global Travel's general ledger. The account numbers and titles are listed on the work sheet in the same order as they appear in the general ledger. As you recall, asset accounts are placed first. After assets come the liability, owner's equity, revenue, and expense accounts. *All the general ledger accounts are listed on the work sheet, even those having a zero balance.* All the accounts are listed to avoid accidentally omitting an account and to ensure that the work sheet contains all the accounts needed to prepare the financial reports.

Global Travel Agency
Work Sheet
For the Month Ended October 31, 19--

ACCT. NO.	ACCOUNT NAME	TRIAL BALANCE		INCOME STATEMENT		BALANCE SHEET	
		DEBIT	CREDIT	DEBIT	CREDIT	DEBIT	CREDIT
101	Cash in Bank	16125 00					
105	Accts. Rec. - Burton Co.	450 00					
110	Accts. Rec. - Greer's Market	—					
120	Computer Equipment	8000 00					
130	Office Equipment	1500 00					
201	Accts. Pay. - City News		75 00				
205	Accts. Pay. - Mod. Off. Supp.		750 00				
301	Jan Harter, Capital		25200 00				
305	Jan Harter, Withdrawals	400 00					
310	Income Summary	—					
401	Fees		1650 00				
501	Advertising Expense	75 00					
510	Maintenance Expense	450 00					
520	Rent Expense	550 00					
530	Utilities Expense	125 00					

Figure 7-3 Work Sheet with Account Titles and Trial Balance Amounts

R E M E M B E R

On the work sheet, be sure to enter the number, title, and final balance of every account that appears in the general ledger.

The final balance for each account is entered in the Trial Balance section in the column that corresponds to its normal balance side. In other words, the final balances of accounts with normal debit balances are entered in the Trial Balance debit column. The final balances for accounts with normal credit balances are entered in the Trial Balance credit column. If an account has a zero balance at the end of the period, a dash is entered in the normal balance column. Notice in Figure 7-3 that a dash was entered in the Trial Balance debit column for Accounts Receivable—Greer's Market. Dashes were also recorded in the Trial Balance debit *and* credit columns for Income Summary. Income Summary does not have a normal balance side. You'll learn more about this account in Chapter 9.

Ruling and Totaling the Trial Balance Section

Ruling means "drawing a line." In accounting, a single rule drawn under a column of amounts means that the entries above the rule are to be added or subtracted. After all account titles and their balances have been entered on the work sheet, a single line is drawn under the last entry and across the entire Trial Balance section as shown in Figure 7-4. The debit and credit columns are now ready for totaling. If the ledger is in balance, the total debits will equal the total credits. Look again at Figure 7-4. The totals match, with each column totaling $27,675.00. Since total debits equal total credits, a double rule is drawn across both amount columns just beneath the totals, as shown in Figure 7-4. This double rule means that the amounts just above are totals and that no other entries will be made in the Trial Balance columns.

If the total debits do not equal the total credits, an error has been made. The error must be found and corrected before the work sheet can be completed. Procedures for locating errors were discussed in Chapter 6.

Global Travel Agency
Work Sheet
For the Month Ended October 31, 19--

	ACCT. NO.	ACCOUNT NAME	TRIAL BALANCE DEBIT	TRIAL BALANCE CREDIT	INCOME STATEMENT DEBIT	INCOME STATEMENT CREDIT	BALANCE SHEET DEBIT	BALANCE SHEET CREDIT	
1	101	Cash in Bank	16 125 00						1
2	105	Accts. Rec.-Burton Co.	450 00						2
3	110	Accts. Rec.-Greer's Market	—						3
4	120	Computer Equipment	8 000 00						4
5	130	Office Equipment	1 500 00						5
6	201	Accts. Pay.-City News		75 00					6
7	205	Accts. Pay.-Mod. Off. Supp.		750 00					7
8	301	Jan Harter, Capital		25 200 00					8
9	305	Jan Harter, Withdrawals	400 00						9
10	310	Income Summary		—					10
11	401	Fees		1 650 00					11
12	501	Advertising Expense	75 00						12
13	510	Maintenance Expense	450 00						13
14	520	Rent Expense	550 00						14
15	530	Utilities Expense	125 00						15
16			27 675 00	27 675 00					16

Figure 7-4 Work Sheet with Trial Balance Section Completed

Before you read about the Income Statement and Balance Sheet sections of the work sheet, complete the following activity.

Check Your Learning

The Balance Sheet Section

The Balance Sheet section of the work sheet contains the balances of the asset, liability, and owner's equity accounts. As a result, these accounts are called the "balance sheet accounts." Once the Trial Balance section has been proved, the next step is to *extend,* or transfer, the amounts to the Balance Sheet section. In other words, the Trial Balance amounts for the asset, liability, and owner's equity accounts are simply copied to the appropriate Balance Sheet amount columns. Start on line 1 and extend each account balance in order. Debit amounts are extended to the Balance Sheet debit column, credit amounts to the Balance Sheet credit column. The work sheet in Figure 7-5 shows the balances extended to the Balance Sheet section.

Global Travel Agency
Work Sheet
For the Month Ended October 31, 19--

	ACCT. NO.	ACCOUNT NAME	TRIAL BALANCE		INCOME STATEMENT		BALANCE SHEET		
			DEBIT	CREDIT	DEBIT	CREDIT	DEBIT	CREDIT	
1	101	Cash in Bank	16125 00				16125 00		1
2	105	Accts. Rec.– Burton Co.	450 00				450 00		2
3	110	Accts. Rec.– Greer's Market	—				—		3
4	120	Computer Equipment	8000 00				8000 00		4
5	130	Office Equipment	1500 00				1500 00		5
6	201	Accts. Pay.– City News		75 00				75 00	6
7	205	Accts. Pay.– Mod. Off. Supp.		750 00				750 00	7
8	301	Jan Harter, Capital		25200 00				25200 00	8
9	305	Jan Harter, Withdrawals	400 00				400 00		9
10	310	Income Summary	—	—					10
11	401	Fees		1650 00					11
12	501	Advertising Expense	75 00						12
13	510	Maintenance Expense	450 00						13
14	520	Rent Expense	550 00						14
15	530	Utilities Expense	125 00						15
16			27675 00	27675 00					16

Figure 7-5   Work Sheet with Trial Balance Amounts Extended to Balance Sheet Section

The next step in completing the work sheet is to extend the account balances to the Income Statement section.

The Income Statement Section

The Income Statement section of the work sheet contains the balances of the revenue and expense accounts. These accounts are listed on the work sheet after the asset, liability, and owner's equity accounts. They are extended to the Income Statement section *after* the accounts are extended to the Balance Sheet section. Revenue accounts have a normal credit balance. The account balances for revenue accounts are, therefore, extended to the credit column of the Income Statement section. Since expense accounts have a normal debit balance, account balances for expenses are extended to the Income Statement debit column. Notice the amounts in the debit and credit columns of the Income Statement section in Figure 7-6.

Global Travel Agency
Work Sheet
For the Month Ended October 31, 19--

	ACCT. NO.	ACCOUNT NAME	TRIAL BALANCE DEBIT	TRIAL BALANCE CREDIT	INCOME STATEMENT DEBIT	INCOME STATEMENT CREDIT	BALANCE SHEET DEBIT	BALANCE SHEET CREDIT	
1	101	Cash in Bank	16 125 00				16 125 00		1
2	105	Accts. Rec. – Burton Co.	450 00				450 00		2
3	110	Accts. Rec. – Greer's Market	—				—		3
4	120	Computer Equipment	8 000 00				8 000 00		4
5	130	Office Equipment	1 500 00				1 500 00		5
6	201	Accts. Pay.– City News		75 00				75 00	6
7	205	Accts. Pay.– Mod. Off. Supp.		750 00				750 00	7
8	301	Jan Harter, Capital		25 200 00				25 200 00	8
9	305	Jan Harter, Withdrawals	400 00				400 00		9
10	310	Income Summary							10
11	401	Fees		1 650 00		1 650 00			11
12	501	Advertising Expense	75 00		75 00				12
13	510	Maintenance Expense	450 00		450 00				13
14	520	Rent Expense	550 00		550 00				14
15	530	Utilities Expense	125 00		125 00				15
16			27 675 00	27 675 00					16

Figure 7-6 Work Sheet with Trial Balance Amounts Extended to Income Statement Section

Totaling the Income Statement and Balance Sheet Sections

After all the amounts in the Trial Balance section have been extended to the Balance Sheet and Income Statement sections, those sections are totaled. As in the Trial Balance section, a single rule is drawn across the four debit and credit columns to indicate that the columns are ready to be added. Look now at Figure 7-7 on page 137. After the four columns are totaled, notice that the debit and credit columns in each section are *not* equal. Unlike the Trial Balance debit and credit totals, the column totals in these two sections will not be equal until the net income or net loss for the fiscal period is added.

Showing Net Income on the Work Sheet

Businesses must spend money to provide goods and services for customers and to pay the costs of operating the business. The costs of operating a business (such as telephone bills and rent) are expenses. In

UNIT 2 The Basic Accounting Cycle

Global Travel Agency
Work Sheet
For the Month Ended October 31, 19--

	ACCT. NO.	ACCOUNT NAME	TRIAL BALANCE		INCOME STATEMENT		BALANCE SHEET		
			DEBIT	CREDIT	DEBIT	CREDIT	DEBIT	CREDIT	
1	101	Cash in Bank	16 125 00				16 125 00		1
2	105	Accts. Rec. - Burton Co.	450 00				450 00		2
3	110	Accts. Rec. - Greer's Market	—				—		3
4	120	Computer Equipment	8 000 00				8 000 00		4
5	130	Office Equipment	1 500 00				1 500 00		5
6	201	Accts. Pay.-City News		75 00				75 00	6
7	205	Accts. Pay.-Mod. Off. Supp.		750 00				750 00	7
8	301	Jan Harter, Capital		25 200 00				25 200 00	8
9	305	Jan Harter, Withdrawals	400 00				400 00		9
10	310	Income Summary							10
11	401	Fees		1 650 00		1 650 00			11
12	501	Advertising Expense	75 00		75 00				12
13	510	Maintenance Expense	450 00		450 00				13
14	520	Rent Expense	550 00		550 00				14
15	530	Utilities Expense	125 00		125 00				15
16			27 675 00	27 675 00	1 200 00	1 650 00	26 475 00	26 025 00	16
17									17

Figure 7-7 Work Sheet with Income Statement and Balance Sheet Sections Totaled

accounting, expenses are always matched against revenue for the same period. This is referred to as the **matching principle.** Matching the expenses of a period to the revenue earned during the same period provides a more reliable measure of profit. Matching expenses to revenue provides information on the cost (expense) of producing revenue for the period. This information helps the business owner or manager make decisions about such things as whether expenses are too high compared to the amount of revenue those expenses produced.

The Income Statement section of the work sheet includes both the revenue and the expenses for the fiscal period. After the columns have been totaled, total expenses (the debit column total) are subtracted from total revenue (the credit column total) to find the net income. **Net income** is the amount left after expenses for the period have been subtracted from revenue for the period. Global Travel Agency has a net income of $450.00 for the month of October.

$1,650.00
−1,200.00
$ 450.00

The amount of the net income must also be reflected in the Balance Sheet section of the work sheet. Remember, revenue and expense accounts are temporary capital accounts. Both revenue and expenses affect capital. Revenue increases capital, while expenses decrease capital. A net income, therefore, increases capital since total revenue is greater than total expenses. During the fiscal period, revenue and expense amounts are recorded in the temporary capital accounts set up for this purpose. At the end of the fiscal period, the net income — the difference between total revenue and total expenses — is transferred to the owner's capital account. Since the capital account is increased by credits, the amount of the net income is shown on the work sheet as an addition to the total of the Balance Sheet *credit* column.

$26,475.00
−26,025.00
$ 450.00

To check the accuracy of the net income amount, subtract the total of the Balance Sheet credit column from the total of the Balance Sheet debit column. Your answer should equal the amount of the net income. If the two amounts match, enter the net income on the work sheet. If the amounts do not match, an error has been made. That error must be found and corrected. Check to be sure that all amounts have been extended correctly from the Trial Balance section and that the totals of all columns were added correctly.

To record the net income on the work sheet, follow these steps:

1. Skip a line after the last account title and then write the words "Net Income" in the Account Name column.   **A**
2. On the same line, enter the net income amount in the Income Statement debit column.   **B**
3. On the same line, enter the net income amount in the Balance Sheet credit column.   **C**

Look at the partial work sheet shown in Figure 7-8 to see how net income is recorded.

Global Travel Agency
Work Sheet
For the Month Ended October 31, 19‑‑

ACCT. NO.	ACCOUNT NAME	TRIAL BALANCE DEBIT	TRIAL BALANCE CREDIT	INCOME STATEMENT DEBIT	INCOME STATEMENT CREDIT	BALANCE SHEET DEBIT	BALANCE SHEET CREDIT	
401	Fees		1 650 00		1 650 00			11
501	Advertising Expense	75 00		75 00				12
510	Maintenance Expense	450 00		450 00				13
520	Rent Expense	550 00		550 00				14
530	Utilities Expense	125 00		125 00				15
		2 767 5 00	2 767 5 00	1 200 00	1 650 00	26 475 00	26 025 00	16
A	Net Income			**B** 450 00			**C** 450 00	17

Figure 7-8   Partial Work Sheet Showing Net Income

Completing the Work Sheet

To complete the Income Statement and Balance Sheet sections, follow these steps. The completed work sheet for Global Travel is shown in Figure 7-9 on page 139.

1. Draw a single rule across all four columns on the line under the net income amount.   **D**
2. Add the net income amount to the previous total of the Income Statement debit column. Enter the new total and bring down the total of the Income Statement credit column to the same line. Total debits should equal total credits.   **E**
3. Repeat this process for the Balance Sheet section. Again, the total debit amount should equal the total credit amount.   **F**
4. Draw a double rule under the column totals and across all four columns. The double rule indicates that the debit and credit columns are equal and that no more amounts are to be entered in these columns.   **G**

Showing a Net Loss on the Work Sheet

When total expenses are greater than total revenue, a **net loss** occurs. A net loss decreases owner's equity. This decrease is shown as a debit to the capital account. When a net loss occurs, the Income Statement debit column

Figure 7-9 — Global Travel Agency Work Sheet

Global Travel Agency
Work Sheet
For the Month Ended October 31, 19--

	ACCT. NO.	ACCOUNT NAME	TRIAL BALANCE DEBIT	TRIAL BALANCE CREDIT	INCOME STATEMENT DEBIT	INCOME STATEMENT CREDIT	BALANCE SHEET DEBIT	BALANCE SHEET CREDIT	
1	101	Cash in Bank	16 125 00				16 125 00		1
2	105	Accts. Rec. – Burton Co.	450 00				450 00		2
3	110	Accts. Rec. – Greer's Market							3
4	120	Computer Equipment	8 000 00				8 000 00		4
5	130	Office Equipment	1 500 00				1 500 00		5
6	201	Accts. Pay. – City News		75 00				75 00	6
7	205	Accts. Pay. – Mod. Off. Supp.		750 00				750 00	7
8	301	Jan Harter, Capital		25 200 00				25 200 00	8
9	305	Jan Harter, Withdrawals	400 00				400 00		9
10	310	Income Summary							10
11	401	Fees		1 650 00		1 650 00			11
12	501	Advertising Expense	75 00		75 00				12
13	510	Maintenance Expense	450 00		450 00				13
14	520	Rent Expense	550 00		550 00				14
15	530	Utilities Expense	125 00		125 00				15
16			27 675 00	27 675 00	1 200 00	1 650 00	26 475 00	26 025 00	16
17	A	Net Income			B 450 00			C 450 00	17
18					G 1 650 00	1 650 00	26 475 00	26 475 00	18
19									19
20									20

D (single rule markers) E F (arrows indicating net income carry)

Figure 7-9 Completed Work Sheet

$4,132.00
−3,904.00
$ 228.00

total (total expenses) is greater than the Income Statement credit column total (total revenue). The partial work sheet in Figure 7-10 shows a net loss. Expenses exceed revenue by $228.00.

To enter a net loss on the work sheet, follow the same general procedure as for entering net income:

1. Skip a line after the last account title and write the words "Net Loss" in the Account Name column.   A
2. On the same line, enter the net loss amount in the *credit* column of the Income Statement section.   B   Enter this same amount in the *debit* column of the Balance Sheet section.   C   (Remember to check the accuracy of the net loss amount by subtracting the Balance Sheet debit total from the Balance Sheet credit total. The difference should be the same as the amount of the net loss.)
3. Draw a single rule across all four columns.   D
4. Add the net loss amount to the previous totals and enter the new totals. Bring down the totals of the other two columns.   E   Draw a double rule under the column totals across all four columns.   F

Figure 7-10 — Partial Work Sheet

			DEBIT	CREDIT	DEBIT	CREDIT	DEBIT	CREDIT	
13	510	Maintenance Expense	1 600 00		1 600 00				13
14	520	Rent Expense	1 400 00		1 400 00				14
15	530	Utilities Expense	525 00		525 00				15
16			5 824 100	5 824 100	4 132 00	3 904 00	3 124 200	3 147 000	16
17	A	Net Loss				B 228 00	C 228 00		17 D
18					E 4 132 00	4 132 00	3 147 000	3 147 000	18 F
19									19
20									20

Figure 7-10 Partial Work Sheet Showing a Net Loss

A *net income* amount is recorded in the debit column of the Income Statement section and in the credit column of the Balance Sheet section. A *net loss* amount is recorded in the credit column of the Income Statement section and in the debit column of the Balance Sheet section.

Check Your Learning

Answer these questions about the Income Statement and Balance Sheet sections of the work sheet.

1. Balances from the Trial Balance section of the work sheet are extended first to the ___?___ section.
2. The difference between total revenue and total expenses is ___?___ .
3. When the Balance Sheet debit and credit columns are first totaled, the totals are not equal. The totals are not equal because the amount of the net income or net loss for the period is not reflected in the ___?___ account.
4. If the difference between the Income Statement debit and credit totals does not match the difference between the Balance Sheet debit and credit totals, what should you do to find the error?

Compare your answers to those in the answers section. Re-read the preceding part of the chapter to find the correct answers to any questions you may have missed.

A Review of the Steps in Preparing a Six-Column Work Sheet

Follow these steps—in order—when preparing a six-column work sheet:

1. Write the heading on the work sheet.
2. In the Account Title and Trial Balance sections, list all account numbers and titles and each account balance from the general ledger.
3. Prove the equality of total debits and total credits in the Trial Balance section.
4. Extend the amounts of the Trial Balance section to the appropriate Balance Sheet and Income Statement columns.
5. Total the columns in the Income Statement and Balance Sheet sections.
6. Determine the amount of the net income or the net loss for the fiscal period.
7. Enter the amount of the net income or the net loss in the appropriate columns in the Income Statement and Balance Sheet sections.
8. Total and rule the Income Statement and Balance Sheet sections.

Summary of Key Points

1. The preparation of a work sheet is the sixth step in the accounting cycle.
2. A work sheet is prepared to pull together all the information needed to complete the end-of-fiscal-period work.
3. The Trial Balance section of the work sheet is completed first. The Income Statement and Balance Sheet sections cannot be completed until the debit and credit totals in the Trial Balance section are equal.
4. Amounts are extended from the Trial Balance section to the Balance Sheet section and then to the Income Statement section.
5. The work sheet is used to calculate the net income or net loss for the fiscal period. Net income results when revenue is greater than the expenses. A net loss results when expenses are greater than revenue.

Review and Applications

Building Your Accounting Vocabulary

In your own words, write the definition of each of the following accounting terms. Use complete sentences for your definitions.

matching principle   net loss   work sheet
net income   ruling

Reviewing Your Accounting Knowledge

1. Explain why a work sheet is prepared.
2. Name and briefly describe the five parts of a six-column work sheet.
3. In what order are the account titles listed on the work sheet?
4. Why are all accounts, including those with zero balances, listed on the work sheet?
5. What does the Trial Balance section of the work sheet prove when it has been totaled and ruled?
6. Which account balances are extended to the Balance Sheet section of the work sheet?
7. Which account balances are extended to the Income Statement section of the work sheet?
8. Why is the matching principle important?
9. Explain how net income and net loss are recorded on the work sheet.
10. What does a double rule on the work sheet indicate?

Improving Your Math Skills

Many types of work require you to convert fractions into decimals and vice versa. Practice your skills at converting decimals and fractions in the following problems.

Convert the following fractions into decimals.

1. $\frac{1}{2}$ 2. $\frac{1}{5}$ 3. $\frac{1}{3}$
4. $\frac{4}{5}$ 5. $\frac{7}{8}$ 6. $\frac{3}{10}$

Convert the following decimals into fractions.

7. 0.889   8. 0.60   9. 0.375
10. 0.25   11. 0.667   12. 0.75

Applying Accounting Procedures

Exercise 7-1   Entering Account Balances on the Work Sheet

The following accounts appear in the Account Title section of the work sheet.

Store Equipment
Rent Expense
Service Fees
Accounts Payable — Panters Supply
Vincent Lee, Capital

Advertising Expense
Accounts Receivable — John Long
Vincent Lee, Withdrawals
Maintenance Expense
Office Supplies

Instructions: Use a form similar to the one that follows. For each account,
(1) Classify the account.
(2) Use a check mark to indicate whether the account balance will be entered in the debit or the credit column of the Trial Balance section of the work sheet. The first account is shown as an example.

Account Title	Account Classification	Trial Balance	
		Debit	Credit
Store Equipment	Asset	✔	

Exercise 7-2 Extending Amounts

Instructions: Use the same account titles listed in Exercise 7-1. On a form similar to the one that follows, indicate to which column on the work sheet the account balance will be extended. The first account has been completed as an example.

Account Title	Income Statement		Balance Sheet	
	Debit	Credit	Debit	Credit
Store Equipment			✔	

Exercise 7-3 Calculating Net Income or Net Loss

The totals of the Income Statement debit and credit columns of several different work sheets are listed below. Calculate the amount of the net income or net loss for each set of work sheet amounts.

	Income Statement	
	Debit	Credit
1.	$2,342.00	$1,814.00
2.	914.00	1,173.00
3.	1,795.00	1,424.00
4.	6,933.00	8,256.00
5.	9,125.00	7,258.00
6.	1,182.00	2,089.00

Problem 7-1 Preparing a Six-Column Work Sheet

The final balances in the ledger accounts of the Snowbird Playhouse for the fiscal period ended September 30 appear on page 144.

		Debit Balances	Credit Balances
101	Cash in Bank	$7,469.00	
105	Stage Equipment	8,396.00	
110	Concession Equipment	5,340.00	
205	Accounts Payable—Atlas, Inc.		$ 1,920.00
210	Accounts Payable—King Co.		834.00
301	Sue Wellen, Capital		13,760.00
305	Sue Wellen, Withdrawals	1,200.00	
310	Income Summary		
401	Ticket Revenue		17,663.00
501	Advertising Expense	3,405.00	
505	Maintenance Expense	1,483.00	
510	Rent Expense	4,500.00	
515	Utilities Expense	2,384.00	

Instructions: Using the preceding account titles and balances, prepare a work sheet for the month ended September 30.

(1) Write the heading on the work sheet.

(2) List all of the account numbers, account titles, and each account balance in the Trial Balance section.

(3) Total and rule the Trial Balance section. (Remember, the two totals must equal before you can continue the work sheet.)

(4) Extend the amounts to the Balance Sheet section.

(5) Extend the amounts to the Income Statement section.

(6) Total the amount columns in the Income Statement and Balance Sheet sections.

(7) Enter the amount of net income or net loss in the appropriate columns in the Income Statement and Balance Sheet sections.

(8) Total and rule the Income Statement and Balance Sheet sections.

Problem 7-2   Preparing a Six-Column Work Sheet

The ledger for the Four Star Travel Center shows the following account balances on June 30, the end of the fiscal period.

101	Cash in Bank	$10,589.00
105	Accounts Receivable—Frank Perkins	476.00
110	Accounts Receivable—Judy Mudre	385.00
115	Office Equipment	15,395.00
120	Computer Equipment	7,459.00
125	Office Furniture	2,486.00
201	Accounts Payable—Turner Co.	4,396.00
205	Accounts Payable—Spencer Corp.	2,840.00
210	Accounts Payable—LKH Co.	1,036.00
301	Karen Hart, Capital	27,500.00
305	Karen Hart, Withdrawals	2,500.00
310	Income Summary	
401	Commissions Revenue	14,957.00
501	Advertising Expense	3,940.00
505	Entertainment Expense	1,836.00
510	Miscellaneous Expense	924.00
515	Rent Expense	3,500.00
520	Utilities Expense	1,239.00

Instructions: Using the preceding account numbers, account titles, and balances, prepare a work sheet for the Four Star Travel Center. The Center operates on a three-month fiscal period.

SPREADSHEET

PROBLEM

Problem 7-3 Preparing a Six-Column Work Sheet

The final balances in the ledger of the Tower Movie Theatre at the end of November are as follows.

101	Cash in Bank	$13,394.50
105	Accounts Receivable—Kline, Inc.	357.00
110	Concession Equipment	9,305.75
115	Projection Equipment	4,395.00
120	Office Equipment	5,497.58
125	Office Furniture	1,385.70
205	Accounts Payable—K & D Supply	3,945.65
210	Accounts Payable—Janson Co.	2,846.90
215	Accounts Payable—Top Movie, Inc.	1,923.00
301	Pat Morganstern, Capital	30,426.48
305	Pat Morganstern, Withdrawals	2,500.00
310	Income Summary	
401	Admissions Revenue	11,596.00
405	Concession Revenue	4,496.00
501	Advertising Expense	3,675.00
505	Maintenance Expense	2,658.55
510	Miscellaneous Expense	864.59
515	Rent Expense	7,500.00
520	Telephone Expense	753.96
525	Utilities Expense	2,946.40

until it sleeps

Instructions: Prepare a work sheet for the month ended November 30 for the Tower Movie Theatre.

CHALLENGE

PROBLEM

Problem 7-4 Locating and Correcting Work Sheet Errors

A-1 Computer Repair Co.'s work sheet for the month ended September 30 appears in the working papers. The Trial Balance section of the work sheet has been completed, and the total debits and total credits are equal. The amounts have also been extended to the Balance Sheet and Income Statement sections. Unfortunately, as the amounts were extended, several errors were made.

Instructions:

(1) Locate and correct all errors in the Income Statement and Balance Sheet sections. Cross out incorrect amounts and write the correct amount above the crossed-out amount or in the correct column.

(2) Complete the work sheet and determine the net income or net loss for the month.

CHALLENGE

Problem 7-5 Completing the Work Sheet

The work sheet for Matt's Cleaning Service appears on page 146. Several amounts have been deleted from various columns.

Instructions: Calculate all missing amounts and complete the work sheet.

PROBLEM

Matt's Cleaning Service
Work Sheet
For the Month Ended March 31, 19--

ACCT. NO.	ACCOUNT NAME	TRIAL BALANCE		INCOME STATEMENT		BALANCE SHEET		
		DEBIT	CREDIT	DEBIT	CREDIT	DEBIT	CREDIT	
101	Cash in Bank	1486240				1486240		1
105	Accts. Rec.-Lynn Tarok	271491				271491		2
110	Accts. Rec.-Jeffrey Holden					160400		3
115	Office Furniture	988140						4
120	Office Equipment					301745		5
125	Computer Equipment							6
130	Delivery Equipment					914650		7
201	Accts. Pay.-Peterson Supply		601319				601319	8
205	Accts. Pay.-Atlas Co.							9
210	Accts. Pay.-New Mark, Inc.		568309				568309	10
301	Jason Stone, Capital						3245000	11
305	Jason Stone, Withdrawals	200000						12
310	Income Summary							13
401	Commissions Revenue		1431980		1431980			14
501	Advertising Expense	360500		360500				15
505	Entertainment Expense			39491				16
510	Maintenance Expense			183140				17
515	Miscellaneous Expense	43265						18
520	Rent Expense			500000				19
525	Utilities Expense	21324		21324				20
								21
	Net Income			284260				22
							5108145	23

146

Planning for Disasters

Sarah was feeling proud of herself. After weeks of entering accounting data into her company's computer, she expected to reach the end of her project by the end of the day. As she was opening up the document for the final data entry, she accidentally wiped out everything. There were no backup disks. Disaster #1: Data Loss.

Greg, bookkeeper for *The Good Earth Gardeners*, got a promotion—to another company. No one else knew the system. Disaster #2: Personnel Loss.

Carlos's restaurant on the Florida Keys managed to bear the brunt of the hurricane. The building was still standing, but it was standing in several feet of water. The computer was inoperable and inaccessible. Disaster #3: Site Loss.

In the age of computer data management, companies need to ask themselves these questions: Have we assessed the short-term and long-term effects of data or computer loss? Do we have contingency plans? Is the plan in writing and has it been communicated to all who share the system?

For starters, here are some guidelines for disaster planning:
- Install computer locks and passwords.
- Always make backup disks of important data. How often data is saved should be measured by how much the company can afford to lose.
- Keep a fireproof safe on the premises or elsewhere for storing backup records.
- Appoint a security administrator who's responsible for communicating risks and alternative procedures, and reviewing them regularly with users.
- Keep an inventory of all hardware and software—and a list of suppliers that can supply and install compatible systems quickly. Establish alternative sites.
- Use surge protectors to safeguard against sudden electrical surges.

Proper planning may mean the difference between continuing operations or going out of business if a disaster strikes.

- Train personnel in order to minimize software errors.

Whether the computer disaster results from a fire or flood, theft, vandalism, power failure, or employee absenteeism, a company needs to plan for the worse case—because according to Murphy's Law, "If anything can go wrong, it will."

Chapter 8

PREPARING FINANCIAL STATEMENTS FOR A SOLE PROPRIETORSHIP

At the end of a fiscal period, financial reports are prepared to show the effects of business transactions for the period. In Chapter 7, you learned how to prepare a work sheet to summarize the financial information needed to prepare the financial reports. In this chapter, you will learn how to prepare those reports: namely, the income statement, the statement of changes in owner's equity, and the balance sheet.

Financial reports are prepared to give the business owner information on how successfully the business is operating. By comparing current financial reports with those from previous fiscal periods, the owner can make more informed decisions about how to run the business.

Learning Objectives

When you have completed Chapter 8, you should be able to do the following:

1. Explain the purpose of the income statement.
2. Prepare an income statement.
3. Explain the purpose of the statement of changes in owner's equity.
4. Prepare a statement of changes in owner's equity.
5. Explain the purpose of a balance sheet.
6. Prepare a balance sheet in report form.
7. Define the accounting terms introduced in this chapter.

New Terms

financial statements
income statement
statement of changes in
  owner's equity
balance sheet
report form

The Seventh Step of the Accounting Cycle

To operate a business profitably, a business owner needs to have up-to-date financial information. Financial statements are prepared to provide such information. **Financial statements** are reports prepared to summarize the changes resulting from business transactions that have occurred during a fiscal period. As you can see from Figure 8-1, the preparation of financial statements is the seventh step in the accounting cycle. By analyzing these statements, a business owner can tell whether the business is on course, experiencing some difficulty, or headed for serious trouble.

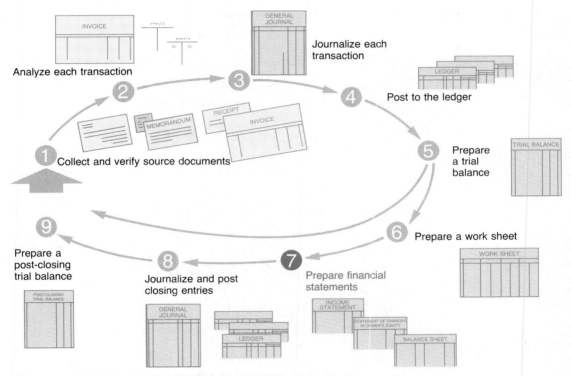

Figure 8-1   The Accounting Cycle, with Step 7 Highlighted

Comparing information shown on the financial statements for different fiscal periods helps owners spot trends that indicate the "health" of a business. Are total assets or total liabilities increasing or decreasing? Is owner's equity increasing or decreasing? Is net income increasing or decreasing? If there is a net loss, is it a one-time occurrence or has it been going on for some time? If owner's equity and net income have decreased, or if the business has shown a net loss, an owner must find out the cause and try to correct the problem. Any business that shows losses over several reporting periods is in trouble, often severe trouble.

The primary financial statements prepared for a sole proprietorship are the income statement and the balance sheet. A third statement, the statement of changes in owner's equity, is also often prepared. Let's look now at how these reports are prepared and the information that is shown on each of them.

The Income Statement

The **income statement** reports the net income or net loss for the fiscal period it covers. As you recall from Chapter 7, net income or net loss is the difference between total revenue and total expenses. The main purpose of the income statement is to provide a report of the revenue earned and the expenses incurred over a specific period of time. For this reason, it is sometimes called a "profit-and-loss statement" or an "earnings statement."

The income statement may be handwritten, typed, or prepared on a computer. Since it is a formal report, the income statement is prepared in ink if it is done by hand. The income statement contains the following sections: (1) the heading, (2) the revenue for the period, (3) the expenses for the period, and (4) the net income or net loss for the period.

The Heading

Like the work sheet heading, the heading of an income statement has three parts, which answer the questions who? what? when? The parts of the heading are as follows:

1. The name of the business (who?).
2. The name of the report (what?).
3. The period covered (when?).

The heading for Global Travel Agency's income statement is shown in Figure 8-2. Notice that each line of the heading is centered on the stationery.

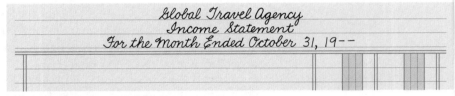

Figure 8-2 The Heading for an Income Statement

When preparing an income statement, be sure to follow the wording, capitalization, and punctuation shown in Figure 8-2. The wording of the date line is especially important. The reporting period on the income statement must be clearly identified. The reporting period covered by the income statement is the entire fiscal period. The net income (or loss) reported on the income statement is the profit (or loss) for the entire fiscal period.

The wording of the date line will vary from business to business. For Global Travel, the reporting period is one month. The heading, therefore, reads "For the Month Ended October 31, 19—." For a three-month period, the heading would read "For the Quarter Ended March 31, 19—." The date line for an income statement covering a full year would read "For the Year Ended June 30, 19—."

A business must be consistent in the fiscal period it uses as the basis for its financial reports. Owners want to be able to compare the data on financial statements from one fiscal period to the next. This is difficult to do if one statement covers a period of, say, one month while another covers a period of six months.

Owners use the information on financial statements to help them make more informed business decisions.

The Revenue Section

After the heading has been completed, the revenue earned for the period is entered on the income statement. This information is taken from the Income Statement section of the work sheet. Look at the income statement for Global Travel Agency shown in Figure 8-3 on page 152. The Income Statement section of the work sheet has been included to show you the source of the information used in preparing the income statement.

The income statement for Global Travel Agency is prepared on standard accounting stationery having a column for account titles and two amount columns. The two amount columns, however, are *not* used for debit and credit entries. Rather, they are used to separate individual account balances from totals. The first amount column is used to enter the balances of the individual revenue and expense accounts. The second amount column is used to enter totals: total revenue, total expenses, and net income (or net loss).

Refer to Figure 8-3 as you read the procedures for preparing an income statement:

1. Write the classification "Revenue:" on the first line at the left side of the form.   A
2. Enter the titles of the accounts classified as revenue accounts. Enter the account titles beginning on the second line, indented about a half inch from the left edge of the column.   B
3. Enter the balance of the revenue account(s)—in this case, the balance of the Fees account. Since Global Travel has only one revenue account, total revenue is the same as the balance of the one revenue account. The balance is thus written in the second, or totals, column.   C

Global Travel Agency
Work Sheet
For the Month Ended October 31, 19--

ACCT. NO.	ACCOUNT NAME	TRIAL BALANCE DEBIT	TRIAL BALANCE CREDIT	INCOME STATEMENT DEBIT	INCOME STATEMENT CREDIT	BALANCE SHEET DEBIT	BALANCE SHEET CREDIT	
101	Cash in Bank	16 125 00				16 125 00		1
105	Accts. Rec.- Burton Co.	450 00				450 00		2
110	Accts. Rec.- Greer's Market	—				—		3
120	Computer Equipment	8 000 00				8 000 00		4
130	Office Equipment	1 500 00				1 500 00		5
201	Accts. Pay.- City News		75 00				75 00	6
205	Accts. Pay.- Mod. Off. Supp.		750 00				750 00	7
301	Jan Harter, Capital		25 200 00				25 200 00	8
305	Jan Harter, Withdrawals	400 00				400 00		9
310	Income Summary	—						10
401	Fees		1 650 00		1 650 00			11
501	Advertising Expense	75 00		75 00				12
510	Maintenance Expense	450 00		450 00				13
520	Rent Expense	550 00		550 00				14
530	Utilities Expense	125 00		125 00				15
		27 675 00	27 675 00	1 200 00	1 650 00	26 475 00	26 025 00	16
	Net Income			450 00			450 00	17
				1 650 00	1 650 00	26 475 00	26 475 00	18

Global Travel Agency
Income Statement
For the Month Ended October 31, 19--

Revenue: A			
B. Fees		1 650 00	C
Expenses: D			
Advertising Expense	75 00		
Maintenance Expense	450 00		
E Rent Expense	550 00		E
Utilities Expense F	125 00		
Total Expenses G		H 1 200 00	I
Net Income K		J 450 00	L

Figure 8-3 Preparing an Income Statement

Global Travel uses only one revenue account, Fees. Many businesses, however, have more than one revenue account, with a separate account for each different source of revenue. For example, a tennis club might have such revenue accounts as Membership Fees, Court Rental Fees, and Instruction Fees.

If a business has more than one revenue account, the individual account balances are entered in the first amount column. The total revenue is then written on a separate line in the second amount column. Figure 8-4 on page 153 illustrates the revenue section for a business that has more than one revenue account. Notice that the words "Total Revenue" are indented about one inch from the left edge of the form.

R E M E M B E R

The information needed to prepare the income statement is taken from the Income Statement section of the work sheet.

Revenue:		
Membership Fees	1000000	
Service Fees	350000	
Total Revenue		1350000

Figure 8-4 Income Statement with More Than One Revenue Account

ACCOUNTING **Tips**
To lessen the chance of error, write all numbers clearly. Be especially careful with numbers that look alike. For example, do not write 4's that look like 9's or 3's that look like 8's.

The Expenses Section

After total revenue has been entered, the expenses incurred during the period must be reported. The expense account titles and the balances shown in the Income Statement section of the work sheet are used to prepare this section of the income statement. The listing of expenses on the income statement is shown in Figure 8-3 on page 152. Refer to this illustration as you read the instructions that follow:

1. On the line following the entry for total revenue, write the classification "Expenses:" at the left side of the form.   **D**
2. Write the titles of the expense accounts, indented half an inch, in the order they appear on the work sheet. Since there are several expense accounts, enter the individual balances in the first amount column.   **E**
3. Draw a single rule under the last expense account balance.   **F**
4. Write the words "Total Expenses" on the line following the last expense account title, indented about one inch.   **G**
5. Add the balances for all the expense accounts. Write the total expense amount in the second amount column, one line below the last expense account balance.   **H**

The Net Income Section

After the amount of total expenses has been entered in the second amount column, the net income is entered. A net income, remember, occurs when total revenue is greater than total expenses.

1. Draw a single rule under the total expenses amount.   **I**
2. Subtract the total expenses from the total revenue to find net income. Enter the amount of the net income in the second amount column under total expenses.   **J**
3. On the same line in the wide column, write the words "Net Income" at the left edge of the form.   **K**
4. If the amount of net income matches the amount shown on the work sheet, draw a double rule under the net income amount.   **L**   The income statement is now complete.

If the amount of net income shown on the work sheet and the amount shown on the income statement do not agree, an error has been made. Since the work sheet has been balanced and ruled, it is safe to assume that the error has occurred while preparing the income statement. An account balance may have been omitted or entered on the income statement incorrectly, or an error in addition or subtraction may have been made. The error must be found and corrected before the income statement can be completed (double ruled).

Showing a Net Loss

If the total expenses are greater than the total revenue for the period, the result is a net loss. To determine the amount of net loss, subtract total revenue from total expenses. Enter the amount in the second amount column under total expenses. Write the words "Net Loss" on the same line at the left edge of the form. An illustration of how to report a net loss is shown in Figure 8-5.

Revenue:		
Fees		2765 00
Expenses:		
Advertising Expense	750 00	
Maintenance Expense	295 00	
Miscellaneous Expense	164 00	
Rent Expense	1400 00	
Utilities Expense	393 00	
Total Expenses		3002 00
Net Loss		237 00

Figure 8-5   Income Statement Showing a Net Loss

R E M E M B E R

The net income or net loss amount reported on the income statement must match the amount calculated on the work sheet.

Before reading about the statement of changes in owner's equity, complete the following activity to check your understanding of the income statement.

Check Your Learning

Answer these questions about the income statement. Write your answers on notebook paper.

1. What are the three "W" questions answered by the heading of the income statement?
2. What is the date line for an income statement prepared for the three months of April, May, and June?
3. The first amount column on the income statement is used to report ____?____ . The second amount column on the income statement is used to report ____?____ .
4. If expenses for a period are $19,351 and revenue is $19,587, does the business have a net income or a net loss? What is the amount of net income or net loss?

Compare your answers to those in the answers section. Re-read the preceding part of the chapter to find the correct answers to any questions you may have missed.

The Statement of Changes in Owner's Equity

One of the most important things an owner wants to know is whether her or his equity in the business has increased or decreased during the fiscal period. Increases in owner's equity mean *increases* in assets, which in turn means the business has grown. Decreases in owner's equity mean *decreases* in assets and in turn a reduction in the size of the business.

During the period, transactions involving investments by the owner are recorded in the capital account. However, transactions affecting revenue, expenses, and withdrawals are recorded in separate accounts. At the end of the period, a financial statement is prepared to summarize the effects on the capital account of the various business transactions that occurred during the period. This statement is called the **statement of changes in owner's equity.**

The statement of changes in owner's equity is completed as a supporting document for the balance sheet. The information needed to prepare this statement is found in three places: the work sheet, the income statement, and the capital account in the general ledger. Look at Figure 8-6 below to see the statement of changes in owner's equity prepared by Global Travel Agency for the month ended October 31.

Global Travel Agency
Statement of Changes in Owner's Equity
For the Month Ended October 31, 19---

		B	
Beginning Capital, October 1, 19-- A		B ------	
C Add: Investment	D	25200 00	
Net Income	E	450 00	
Total Increase in Capital			F 25 650 00
Subtotal			G 25 650 00
Less: Withdrawals			H 400 00
Ending Capital, October 31, 19-- I			J 25 250 00

Figure 8-6 Statement of Changes in Owner's Equity

The statement shows the changes in capital from the beginning of the fiscal period through the end of the period. As a result, the heading of the statement is similar to that for the income statement.

Follow these steps to complete the statement of changes in owner's equity:

1. On the first line, write the words "Beginning Capital," followed by the first day of the fiscal period. For Global Travel, that date is October 1, 19—. **A**

2. In the second amount column, enter the balance of the capital account at the beginning of the fiscal period. The source of this information is the capital account in the general ledger. Since Global Travel began operations during this fiscal period, there is no beginning capital balance. Enter a dash in the second amount column. **B**

3. Next, enter the *increases* to the capital account, namely, investments by the owner and net income. First, write the word "Add:" at the left side of the form. **C**

The first addition would be any investments by the owner during the period. This information is found in the capital account in the general ledger. Jan Harter, the owner of Global Travel, invested a total of $25,200 in the business in the month of October. Write "Investment" following the word "Add." Enter the amount of the investment in the first amount column. **D**

On the next line, write the words "Net Income." Enter the amount of the net income—taken from the income statement—in the first amount column. Draw a single rule under the investment and net income amounts. **E**

4. Write the words "Total Increase in Capital" on the next line at the left edge of the form. Add the total investments and net income amounts and enter the total in the second amount column. Then draw a single rule under the amount. **F**

5. Write "Subtotal" on the next line, at the left edge of the form. Add the amounts for beginning capital and total increase in capital. Enter the total in the second amount column. **G** Since Global Travel did not have a beginning capital balance, this amount is the same as the total increase in capital amount.

6. The next section of the statement lists the *decreases* to the capital account: withdrawals and net loss. Since Global Travel did not have a net loss for the period, write the words "Less: Withdrawals" at the left edge of the account title column. Enter the amount of withdrawals for the period (taken from the work sheet) in the second amount column. Then draw a single rule under the amount. **H**

7. On the next line, write the words "Ending Capital," followed by the last day of the fiscal period. **I**

8. Subtract the withdrawals amount from the subtotal to determine the new, ending balance of the capital account. Finally, draw a double rule below the ending capital amount. **J**

The statement of changes in owner's equity is now complete. The ending capital balance determined on this statement will be used in preparing the balance sheet.

A statement of changes in owner's equity for an ongoing business that had a net loss for the period is shown in Figure 8-7. Notice that the investment by the owner increases the capital account, while the withdrawals and net loss decrease the capital account.

Beginning Capital, May 1, 19--		46300 00
Add: Investment		1000 00
Subtotal		47300 00
Less: Withdrawals	2100 00	
Net Loss	675 00	
Total Decrease in Capital		2775 00
Ending Capital, May 31, 19--		44525 00

Figure 8-7 Statement of Changes in Owner's Equity Showing a Net Loss

Before reading about the preparation of the balance sheet, complete the following activity to check your understanding of the statement of changes in owner's equity.

Check Your Learning

Answer the following questions about the statement of changes in owner's equity. Write your answers on notebook paper.

1. The statement of changes in owner's equity is prepared to reflect the changes in the __?__ from the beginning of the period to the end.
2. The wording in the date line for the statement of changes in owner's equity is the same as that used for the __?__ .
3. If the owner invested $20,000 during the period covered by this statement, and net income was $3,200, the ending balance in the capital account is __?__ .
4. The information on the statement of changes in owner's equity is used in preparing the __?__ .

Compare your answers to those in the answers section. Re-read the preceding part of the chapter to find the correct answers to any questions you may have missed.

The Balance Sheet

The **balance sheet** is a report of the final balances in all the asset, liability, and owner's equity accounts at the end of the fiscal period. These accounts, you'll remember, are the permanent accounts. The main purpose of the balance sheet is to provide a record of the business's assets and a summary of the claims (of both creditors and owners) against those assets *on a specific date.* In other words, the balance sheet states the financial position of a business at a specific point in time. It pinpoints what a business owns, owes, and is worth. For this reason, the balance sheet is sometimes called a "position statement."

Like the income statement and the statement of changes in owner's equity, the balance sheet may be handwritten, typed, or prepared by computer. A handwritten balance sheet is prepared in ink since it is a formal record.

The balance sheet prepared by Global Travel Agency is prepared in report form. In **report form,** the classifications of balance sheet accounts are shown one under the other.

The balance sheet is prepared from the information in the Balance Sheet section of the work sheet and from the statement of changes in owner's equity. Let's look now at the sections of the balance sheet: (1) the heading, (2) the assets section, and (3) the liabilities and owner's equity sections.

The Heading

Like the heading of the income statement, the heading of the balance sheet answers the questions who? what? when? The heading includes

1. The name of the business (who?).
2. The name of the financial statement (what?).
3. The date of the balance sheet (when?).

As you recall, the income statement reports the amount of net income (or net loss) for the complete fiscal period. Unlike the income statement, the balance sheet refers to only one day in the fiscal period, usually the last day. The amounts shown on the balance sheet are the balances in the accounts as of that day. Look at the headings in Figure 8-8 to see the difference between the date lines on the income statement and on the balance sheet.

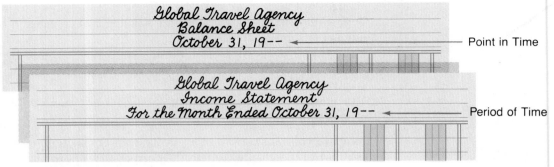

Figure 8-8 Headings of Financial Statements

The Assets Section

Refer to Figure 8-9 on page 159 as you read the procedures for preparing the balance sheet. The work sheet and statement of changes in owner's equity have been included in the illustration to show the sources of the information used to prepare the balance sheet.

1. Write the word "Assets" in the center of the first line.   **A**
2. Next, enter the asset account titles and their balances. The account titles and balances are listed on the balance sheet in the same order as they appear in the Balance Sheet section of the work sheet. Enter the individual account balances in the first amount column. Then draw a single rule under the last account balance.   **B**
3. On the next line, write the words "Total Assets," indented about half an inch. Add the individual balances and enter the total assets amount in the second amount column.   **C**

Do *not* draw a double rule under the total at this time. The double rule is not entered until the Liabilities and Owner's Equity sections have been completed and are shown to be equal to total assets.

The Liabilities and Owner's Equity Sections

The information for the Liabilities and Owner's Equity sections is taken from the work sheet *and* from the statement of changes in owner's equity. To complete these sections of the balance sheet, follow these steps:

1. Skip one line and then write the heading "Liabilities," centered.   **D**
2. List the liability account titles and their balances, using the same order as they appear in the Balance Sheet section of the work sheet. Enter the account balances in the first amount column. Draw a single rule under the last account balance.   **E**
3. On the next line, write the words "Total Liabilities," indented about half an inch. Total the individual balances and enter the total liabilities amount in the second amount column.   **F**

4. Skip a line and write the heading "Owner's Equity," centering it on the line. **G**

5. Write the title of the capital account and enter its balance in the second amount column. The balance is the amount of the ending balance shown on the statement of changes in owner's equity. **H**

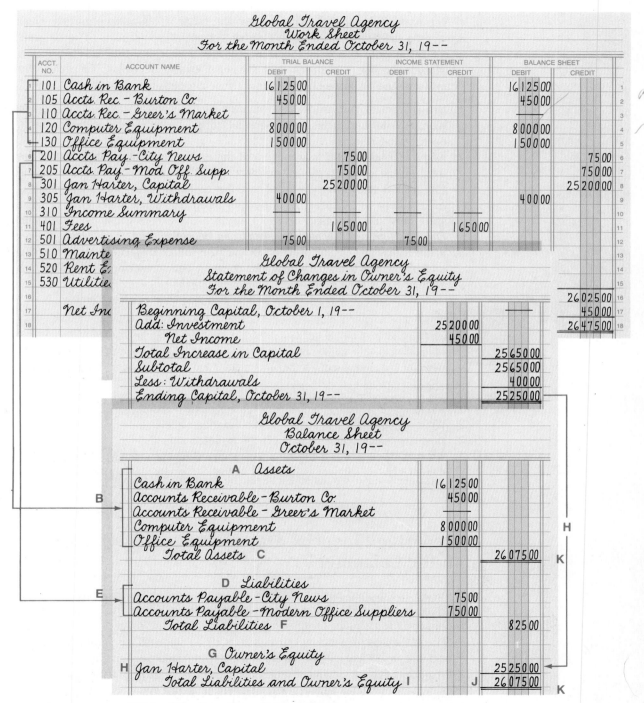

Global Travel Agency
Work Sheet
For the Month Ended October 31, 19--

ACCT. NO.	ACCOUNT NAME	TRIAL BALANCE DEBIT	TRIAL BALANCE CREDIT	INCOME STATEMENT DEBIT	INCOME STATEMENT CREDIT	BALANCE SHEET DEBIT	BALANCE SHEET CREDIT	
101	Cash in Bank	16125 00				16125 00		1
105	Accts. Rec. - Burton Co.	450 00				450 00		2
110	Accts. Rec. - Greer's Market	—				—		3
120	Computer Equipment	8000 00				8000 00		4
130	Office Equipment	1500 00				1500 00		5
201	Accts. Pay.-City News		75 00				75 00	6
205	Accts. Pay.- Mod. Off. Supp.		750 00				750 00	7
301	Jan Harter, Capital		25200 00				25200 00	8
305	Jan Harter, Withdrawals	400 00				400 00		9
310	Income Summary			—	—			10
401	Fees		1650 00		1650 00			11
501	Advertising Expense	75 00		75 00				12
510	Mainte							13
520	Rent E							14
530	Utilitie							15
							26025 00	16
	Net In						450 00	17
							26475 00	18

Global Travel Agency
Statement of Changes in Owner's Equity
For the Month Ended October 31, 19--

Beginning Capital, October 1, 19--			—
Add: Investment	25200 00		
Net Income	450 00		
Total Increase in Capital		25650 00	
Subtotal		25650 00	
Less: Withdrawals		400 00	
Ending Capital, October 31, 19--		25250 00	

Global Travel Agency
Balance Sheet
October 31, 19--

	A Assets		
	Cash in Bank	16125 00	
B	Accounts Receivable - Burton Co.	450 00	
	Accounts Receivable - Greer's Market	—	
	Computer Equipment	8000 00	
	Office Equipment	1500 00	
	Total Assets **C**		26075 00	**K**
	D Liabilities		
E	Accounts Payable - City News	75 00	
	Accounts Payable - Modern Office Suppliers	750 00	
	Total Liabilities **F**		825 00
	G Owner's Equity		
H	Jan Harter, Capital		25250 00
	Total Liabilities and Owner's Equity **I**	**J**	26075 00	**K**

Figure 8-9 Preparing a Balance Sheet

Use the balance calculated on the statement of changes in owner's equity for the balance of the capital account on the balance sheet.

Proving the Equality of the Balance Sheet

You learned in earlier chapters that the basic accounting equation must always be in balance in a double-entry system of accounting. The balance sheet represents the basic accounting equation; thus, the Assets section must balance the Liabilities and Owner's Equity sections. To prove the equality of the balance sheet, follow these procedures:

1. Draw a single rule under the balance of the capital account. Write the words "Total Liabilities and Owner's Equity," indented about half an inch, on the next line.   **I**
2. Add the total liabilities amount and the ending capital balance. Enter the total in the second amount column.   **J**   This total must agree with the total assets amount. If the totals are not equal, an error has been made — most likely in transferring amounts from the work sheet or from the statement of changes in owner's equity. Any errors must be found and corrected before the balance sheet can be completed.
3. If the totals are equal, draw a double rule under the total assets amount *and* under the total liabilities and owner's equity amount.   **K**   The balance sheet is now complete.

Check Your Learning

Answer these questions about Figure 8-9, shown on page 159, using notebook paper.

1. What is the wording used in the date line of the balance sheet?
2. What are the three sections of the balance sheet?
3. How are the accounts listed on the balance sheet?
4. What is the source of the balance reported for Jan Harter, Capital?

Compare your answers to those in the answers section.

Preparing Financial Statements on the Computer

As we mentioned earlier, financial statements may be handwritten, typewritten, or prepared using a computer. Regardless of how they are prepared, the information shown on the statements remains the same.

The balance sheet shown in Figure 8-10 on page 161 is an example of a report prepared with a computer. In a computerized accounting system, the information for preparing financial statements is stored in the computer files. When financial reports are needed, it is not necessary to prepare a work sheet since all the information from business transactions is already

```
                    Global Travel Agency
                       Balance Sheet
                      October 31, 19--

                          Assets
Cash in Bank                              16125.00
Accts. Rec.--Burton Co.                     450.00
Accts. Rec.--Greer's Market                   0.00
Computer Equipment                         8000.00
Office Equipment                           1500.00
                                          _____
     Total Assets                                    26075.00
                                                     =========


                        Liabilities
Accts. Pay.--City News                       75.00
Accts. Pay.--Modern Office Suppliers        750.00
                                          _____
     Total Liabilities                                 825.00

                       Owner's Equity
Jan Harter, Capital                                  25250.00

     Total Liabilities and Owner's Equity            26075.00
                                                     =========
```

Figure 8-10 Balance Sheet Prepared by Computer

stored in the computer. The computer operator simply gives a command indicating the reports needed. The computer calculates the net income or net loss and adjusts the capital account to correctly report any changes that have occurred during the period. Obviously, the information in the computer files must be kept up to date through regular journal entries or the reports generated from that information will not be accurate.

Summary of Key Points

1. The preparation of financial reports is the seventh step in the accounting cycle. The primary reports are the income statement and the balance sheet. The statement of changes in owner's equity is also often prepared.
2. The income statement reports the net income or net loss for the period. Net income or net loss is the difference between total revenue and total expenses over a specific period of time.
3. The statement of changes in owner's equity summarizes the effects of the period's business transactions on the capital account.
4. The balance sheet reports the final balances of asset, liability, and owner's equity accounts at the end of the fiscal period.
5. The work sheet is the source of information for preparing the income statement. The statement of changes in owner's equity is prepared from the work sheet, the income statement, and the capital account in the general ledger. The balance sheet is prepared from the work sheet and the statement of changes in owner's equity.
6. Financial reports may be handwritten on accounting stationery, typewritten, or prepared using a computer. If prepared by hand, the reports are written in ink.

Review and Applications

Building Your Accounting Vocabulary

In your own words, write the definition of each of the following accounting terms. Use complete sentences for your definitions.

balance sheet   income statement   statement of changes
financial statements   report form   in owner's equity

Reviewing Your Accounting Knowledge

1. Why are financial statements prepared?
2. What is the purpose of the income statement?
3. What other names can be given to an income statement?
4. Why does a business need to be consistent in the fiscal period it uses as the basis for its financial reports?
5. What is the source of information used to prepare the income statement?
6. What is the purpose of the statement of changes in owner's equity?
7. What are the sources of information used to prepare the statement of changes in owner's equity?
8. What is the purpose of the balance sheet?
9. What are the sources of the information needed to prepare the balance sheet?
10. How does the date in the heading of a balance sheet differ from the date in the heading of an income statement and a statement of changes in owner's equity?
11. Which financial statement represents the basic accounting equation?

Improving Your Decision-Making Skills

Anna Choi is the accounting clerk for George Damaris, owner of Colonial Bakery. For several months, Anna has tried to convince George to install a computer. Anna believes that a computer would save time, especially when financial statements are being prepared. She has explained to George that all of the information for preparing financial statements can be stored in the computer files. Then, when the financial statements are needed, it is not necessary to prepare a work sheet. George believes that a computer will cost too much money. He also believes that if just one mistake is made in entering an amount, the financial statements will not provide a true picture of the business. What would you say to convince George that a computer should be installed for use in the business?

Applying Accounting Procedures

Exercise 8-1   Reporting Accounts on Financial Statements

The following list contains some of the account titles from the general ledger of the Winter Theater.

Accounts Payable—Boyden Company
Accounts Payable—Gail's Supplies
Accounts Receivable—Clinton Co.
Accounts Receivable—King Company
Admissions Revenue
Advertising Expense
Cash in Bank

Clem Winter, Capital
Clem Winter, Withdrawals
Concession Revenue
Miscellaneous Expense
Office Furniture
Projection Equipment
Rent Expense

Instructions: Use a form similar to the one that follows. For each account listed,

(1) Write the classification of the account.

(2) Use a check mark to indicate whether the account balance will be entered in the Trial Balance debit or credit column of the work sheet.

(3) Use a check mark to indicate on which financial statement (income statement or balance sheet) the account will appear. The first account is shown as an example.

Account Title	Account Classification	Trial Balance		Financial Statements	
		Debit	Credit	Income Statement	Balance Sheet
Accounts Payable— Boyden Co.	Liability		✔		✔

Exercise 8-2   Determining Ending Capital Amounts

The financial data affecting the capital accounts for several different businesses is summarized below.

Instructions: Use the form in your working papers or plain paper. Determine the ending capital balance for each business.

	Beginning Capital	Investments	Revenue	Expenses	Withdrawals
1.	$40,000	$ 500	$ 5,800	$3,400	$ 600
2.	24,075	0	14,980	6,240	900
3.	19,800	1,000	6,450	6,980	0
4.	0	26,410	5,920	4,790	200
5.	6,415	0	4,420	3,975	800
6.	20,870	1,200	12,980	9,240	1,200

Problem 8-1   Preparing an Income Statement

The work sheet for Matira's Delivery Service for the month ended April 30, 19—, appears on page 164.

Instructions: Using the work sheet, prepare an income statement for Matira's Delivery Service.

Problem 8-2   Preparing a Statement of Changes in Owner's Equity

Instructions: Using the work sheet for Matira's Delivery Service and the income statement prepared in Problem 8-1, prepare a statement of changes in owner's equity. Pat Matira made an additional investment in the business of $500 during the period.

Matira's Delivery Service
Work Sheet
For the Month Ended April 30, 19--

ACCT. NO.	ACCOUNT NAME	TRIAL BALANCE DEBIT	TRIAL BALANCE CREDIT	INCOME STATEMENT DEBIT	INCOME STATEMENT CREDIT	BALANCE SHEET DEBIT	BALANCE SHEET CREDIT	
101	Cash in Bank	5391 00				5391 00		1
104	Accts. Rec.-J. Lincoln	423 00				423 00		2
106	Accts. Rec.-A. Jones	914 00				914 00		3
110	Office Equipment	2806 00				2806 00		4
115	Computer Equipment	6482 00				6482 00		5
120	Delivery Equipment	12361 00				12361 00		6
205	Accts. Pay.-Modern Supp.		4618 00				4618 00	7
210	Accts. Pay.-A&L Forms		2394 00				2394 00	8
301	Pat Matira, Capital		19589 00				19589 00	9
302	Pat Matira, Withdrawals	1500 00				1500 00		10
303	Income Summary							11
401	Delivery Fees		9309 00		9309 00			12
501	Advertising Expense	1852 00		1852 00				13
505	Delivery Expense	931 00		931 00				14
510	Miscellaneous Expense	246 00		246 00				15
515	Rent Expense	2400 00		2400 00				16
520	Utility Expense	604 00		604 00				17
		35910 00	35910 00	6033 00	9309 00	29877 00	26601 00	18
	Net Income			3276 00			3276 00	19
				9309 00	9309 00	29877 00	29877 00	20

Problem 8-3   Preparing a Balance Sheet

Instructions: Using the work sheet for Matira's Delivery Service and the statement of changes in owner's equity prepared in Problem 8-2, prepare a balance sheet in report form.

Problem 8-4   Preparing Financial Statements

The trial balance for the Joker Amusement Center has been prepared. It is included on the work sheet in the working papers accompanying this textbook.

Instructions:

(1) Complete the work sheet.

(2) Prepare an income statement for the quarter ended March 31.

(3) Prepare a statement of changes in owner's equity. Ken Graf made no additional investments during the period.

(4) Prepare a balance sheet in report form.

COMPUTER

PROBLEM

Problem 8-5   Preparing Financial Statements

The general ledger accounts for Jenkins Caterers follow. The balance in each account at the end of the fiscal period is also given.

101	Cash in Bank	$ 3,956
110	Accounts Receivable—Brian Doonan	1,328
114	Accounts Receivable—Fran Ullman	1,204
120	Catering Supplies	1,968
125	Office Equipment	10,957
130	Delivery Equipment	8,396

210	Accounts Payable—Adams Supply	3,976
215	Accounts Payable—Graham Co.	2,946
220	Accounts Payable—King Supply	1,285
301	Judy Jenkins, Capital	22,336
302	Judy Jenkins, Withdrawals	1,900
303	Income Summary	
401	Catering Revenue	4,989
403	Party Revenue	1,420
505	Advertising Expense	934
510	Delivery Expense	803
520	Maintenance Expense	1,483
525	Miscellaneous Expense	748
530	Rent Expense	1,850
535	Repair Expense	589
540	Utility Expense	836

Handwritten: 9869 6033 3276

Instructions:

(1) Prepare a work sheet for the month ended October 31.

(2) Prepare an income statement for the period.

(3) Prepare a statement of changes in owner's equity. Judy Jenkins made an additional investment of $1,000 during the period.

(4) Prepare a balance sheet.

CHALLENGE
PROBLEM

Problem 8-6   Preparing a Statement of Changes in Owner's Equity

You are the accounting clerk at the Raintree Company. The financial statements for the month of November have already been prepared. Unfortunately, the statement of changes in owner's equity was damaged when someone accidentally spilled a cup of coffee. Mary Fienwald, the accountant, has asked you to reconstruct that statement. Ms. Fienwald reminded you that the owner, Tyler Best, made an additional investment of $4,000 and withdrew $1,500 during the period.

Instructions: Use the balance sheet and income statement shown below and on page 166 to prepare a new statement of changes in owner's equity.

Raintree Company
Balance Sheet
November 30, 19--

Assets		
Cash in Bank	8297 00	
Accounts Receivable – Lester Maltese	693 00	
Accounts Receivable – Brian Cropp	478 00	
Store Equipment	16204 00	
Video Equipment	24869 00	
Total Assets		50541 00
Liabilities		
Accounts Payable – C & L Amusements	4013 00	
Accounts Payable – Gotham Company	3192 00	
Total Liabilities		7205 00
Owner's Equity		
Tyler Best, Capital		43336 00
Total Liabilities and Owner's Equity		50541 00

Raintree Company
Income Statement
For the Month Ended November 30, 19--

Revenue:			
Concession Revenue	1 930 00		
Game Revenue	8 295 00		
Total Revenue		10 225 00	
Expenses:			
Advertising Expense	1 854 00		
Miscellaneous Expense	831 00		
Rent Expense	2 350 00		
Utility Expense	752 00		
Total Expenses		5 787 00	
Net Income		4 438 00	

CHALLENGE

PROBLEM

Problem 8-7   Interpreting Financial Information

You are applying for a job with Foran Tree Service. The job includes preparing financial statements. In order to determine your ability to do the job, the owner, Carl Foran, has given you the following information.

At the beginning of the last fiscal period, the account Carl Foran, Capital had a balance of $46,105. At the end of the period, the account showed a balance of $49,386. During the period, Mr. Foran made an additional investment of $2,000 and had withdrawals of $500. The revenue for the period was $13,248.

Instructions: Use the stationery provided in the workbook or plain paper. Based on the information just given, determine the total expenses for the period.

*F*inancial Report or Financial Repair?

Anyone who has ever applied for a bank loan has probably noticed as they prepare to sign the application, the formula line: "This is a true and accurate statement of financial dealings, and that knowingly making false statements on such a form is a crime." Following this warning is a description of the penalties which include fines or imprisonment or both. Perhaps some people might be anxious before they sign, hoping they have not left anything out of the application. Most people, however, would not *knowingly* misrepresent themselves, would they?

Imagine you find yourself in the following situation. Your Uncle Henry, whom you are very fond of, has been running a small restaurant for five years. Unfortunately, it has not been very profitable. Your uncle has been doing his own bookkeeping, but admits that he knows little about the formalities of it all. He decides that to move his restaurant "out of the red," he needs a loan so that he can expand and remodel his restaurant. Since Uncle Henry knows you are good with numbers and are taking some accounting classes, he asks you to look over the books and make an accounting report that he can present at the bank. Knowing how desperately your uncle wants and needs his business to succeed, you agree.

As you go over the books, however, you have a growing conviction that no bank will give your uncle the loan. As you stare at the numbers and agonize over telling your uncle, you notice that by rearranging the numbers just a little bit, your Uncle Henry's business could look a little more promising. After all, you rationalize, once the loan goes through and your uncle makes the planned improvements, business is bound to pick up. The bank does not need to know how things are now,

Most people at sometime in their life run into a situation in which it is difficult to decide between "right" and "wrong".

they just need to know that the loan will be repaid. After all, the amount of money your uncle needs is not really that much. . . .

What is the ethical dilemma in this case? What course of action would you choose? Perhaps for you the situation is a clear choice between right and wrong. Most people, however, run into situations in which it is difficult to decide what is "right" and what is "wrong." Commonly known as *situation ethics*, choosing what is right and wrong in a particular set of circumstances can lead to stress and anxiety, especially if something that you know is wrong under most circumstances suddenly seems okay. The best way to make an ethical decision, one that you can stand by and still live with yourself, is to outline all your options and choose one that does not compromise your beliefs.

In Uncle Henry's case, for example, you could more closely examine the possibility of his success by taking customer surveys, studying successful neighborhood restaurants, and then incorporating the findings into a business plan. This business plan could be submitted with an accurate financial report to help convince the bank to loan your uncle the money.

Chapter 9

COMPLETING THE ACCOUNTING CYCLE FOR A SOLE PROPRIETORSHIP

In Chapter 8, you learned how to prepare the end-of-period financial statements for a sole proprietorship service business. The income statement reports the business's revenue, expenses, and net income or net loss for a fiscal period. The statement of changes in owner's equity summarizes the effects of the business transactions for the period on the owner's capital account. The balance sheet reports the financial position of the business as of the end of the fiscal period.

In this chapter, you will complete the accounting cycle for Global Travel Agency. The accounting cycle is completed by journalizing the closing entries and preparing a post-closing trial balance.

Learning Objectives

When you have completed Chapter 9, you should be able to do the following:

1. Explain why the temporary capital accounts are closed at the end of the fiscal period.
2. Explain the purpose of the Income Summary account.
3. Explain the relationship between the Income Summary account and the capital account.
4. Analyze and journalize closing entries.
5. Post closing entries to accounts in the general ledger.
6. Prepare a post-closing trial balance.
7. Define the accounting terms introduced in this chapter.

New Terms

closing entries
post-closing trial balance
Income Summary account
compound entry

The Eighth and Ninth Steps in the Accounting Cycle

During a fiscal period, the temporary capital accounts are used to record transactions involving revenue, expenses, and withdrawals. At the end of the period, the balances in these accounts are transferred to the capital account to summarize the changes in owner's equity and to bring that account up to date.

The balances in the temporary capital accounts are transferred by recording a series of closing entries. **Closing entries** are journal entries made to close out, or reduce to zero, the balances in the temporary capital accounts and to transfer the net income or net loss for the period to the capital account.

After the closing entries have been journalized and posted, a trial balance is prepared to prove the equality of the general ledger after the closing process. The trial balance prepared after closing is called a **post-closing trial balance.** As you can see in Figure 9-1, the closing process and the post-closing trial balance complete the accounting cycle.

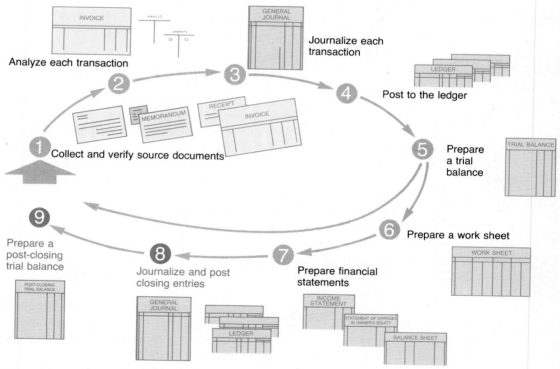

Figure 9-1 The Accounting Cycle, with Steps 8 and 9 Highlighted

The Closing Process

Preparing financial records for the start of another fiscal period is a little like keeping the records for a basketball team. Although individual and team scores are kept and tallied at the end of every game, each new game starts with a score of zero. Similarly, although entries are recorded in the accounts during the fiscal period, the temporary capital accounts start each new fiscal period with zero balances.

In Chapter 8, you learned how to prepare an income statement. The income statement, you'll remember, reports the net income or net loss for *one accounting period.* The statement is prepared from information recorded and accumulated in the revenue and expense accounts. At the end of the period, then, the revenue and expense accounts must be closed or cleared because their balances apply to only one fiscal period. Closing entries are prepared to reduce the balances in the revenue and expense accounts to zero, thus preparing them for use during the next fiscal period.

Closing entries are also used to transfer the net income or net loss for the period to the capital account. Earlier you learned how to calculate the net income or loss on the work sheet. The net income or loss is then reported on the income statement and reflected in the ending balance of the capital account reported on the balance sheet. This ending capital balance is calculated on the statement of changes in owner's equity. No journal entries have yet been recorded to update the balance of the capital account in the general ledger. For example, the balance for Jan Harter, Capital shown on the work sheet is $25,200. The balance for Jan Harter, Capital reported on the balance sheet is $25,250. These two amounts are different because the withdrawals and the net income for the period have not yet been recorded in the capital account in the general ledger. This is done during the closing process.

The Income Summary Account

Before the closing entries are journalized and posted, there is no single account in the general ledger that shows the revenue and expenses for the fiscal period. This information appears in the balances of the individual revenue and expense accounts, but it is not shown in any one account in the general ledger.

There is, however, one general ledger account that, up to this point, has not been used. That is the Income Summary account. The **Income Summary account** is used to accumulate and summarize the revenue and expenses for the period. The account, then, serves as a simple income statement in the ledger. That is, the balance of the account equals the net income or net loss for the fiscal period.

Income Summary	
Dr.	Cr.
Expense Account Balances	Revenue Account Balances

Look at the T account for Income Summary. Expenses, which have debit balances, are transferred as debits to Income Summary. Revenues, which have credit balances, are transferred as credits to Income Summary.

Look back at the chart of accounts for Global Travel on page 40. You will notice that Income Summary is located in the owner's equity section of the general ledger. It is located there because of its relationship to the owner's capital account. Remember, revenue and expenses actually represent increases and decreases to owner's equity. The balance of Income Summary (the net income or net loss for the period) must be transferred to the capital account at the end of the closing process.

Like the withdrawals account, Income Summary is a temporary capital account. Income Summary is quite different, however, from the other temporary capital accounts. First, Income Summary is used only at the end of the fiscal period. It is used only to summarize the balances from the revenue and expense accounts. Second, Income Summary does not have a normal balance, which means that it does not have an increase side or a decrease side. The debit and credit sides of the account are simply used to summarize the period's revenue and expenses. If the business has a net income, Income Summary will have a credit balance because the revenue recorded on the credit side will exceed the expenses recorded on the debit side. If the business has a net loss, the account will have a debit balance because the expenses recorded on the debit side will exceed the revenue recorded on the credit side.

Journalizing the Closing Entries

Four separate journal entries are prepared to close the temporary capital accounts for Global Travel. They include

1. The balance of the revenue account is transferred to the credit side of the Income Summary account.
2. The expense account balances are transferred to the debit side of the Income Summary account.
3. The balance of the Income Summary account is transferred to the capital account (net income to the credit side; net loss to the debit side).
4. The balance of the withdrawals account is transferred to the debit side of the capital account.

The work sheet is the source of the information for the closing entries.

Closing the Balance of the Revenue Account into Income Summary

The first step in the closing procedure is to transfer the balance of the revenue account to Income Summary. The account balance for the revenue account is taken from the Income Statement section of the work sheet. Global Travel has only one revenue account, Fees, so the accounts affected by this first closing entry are Fees and Income Summary.

The balance for Fees shown on the work sheet is $1,650. To close Fees, the balance must be reduced to zero. Since Fees has a credit balance of $1,650, a debit of $1,650 to that account will result in a balance of zero. The closing entry for revenue is therefore a debit of $1,650 to Fees and a credit of $1,650 to Income Summary. This closing entry reduces the balance of the Fees account to zero and transfers the amount of total income to the Income Summary account.

Fees		Income Summary	
Dr.	Cr.	Dr.	Cr.
−	+		
Clo. $1,650	Bal. $1,650		Clo. $1,650

The journal entry to close the revenue account into Income Summary is shown in Figure 9-2. To record the closing entry in the general journal:

	GENERAL JOURNAL			PAGE 3	
DATE	DESCRIPTION	POST. REF.	DEBIT	CREDIT	
	Closing Entries				1
19-- Oct. 31	*Fees*		1650 00		2
	Income Summary			1650 00	3

Figure 9-2   Closing the Revenue Account

1. Write the words "Closing Entries" in the center of the Description column. If you are recording the closing entries on a journal page that contains other entries, skip a line after the last entry. If you begin the closing entries on a new journal page, write the heading "Closing Entries" on the first line. This heading is the explanation for *all* the closing entries.
2. Enter the date (the last day of the fiscal period) in the Date column.
3. Enter the title of the account(s) debited and the amount of the debit.
4. Enter the title of the account credited and the amount of the credit.

Closing the Balances of the Expense Accounts into Income Summary

The second closing entry is made to transfer the balances of the expense accounts into Income Summary. The balances of the expense accounts are taken from the Income Statement section of the work sheet. The expense accounts used by Global Travel are Advertising Expense, Maintenance Expense, Rent Expense, and Utilities Expense.

Look at the T accounts that follow. Each expense account must be credited for the amount of its debit balance. (It is not necessary to use a separate closing entry for each expense account.) Income Summary then is debited for the total amount of expenses, $1,200.

Income Summary		Advertising Expense		Maintenance Expense	
Dr.	Cr.	Dr. +	Cr. −	Dr. +	Cr. −
Clo. $1,200	Clo. $1,650	Bal. $75	Clo. $75	Bal. $450	Clo. $450

Rent Expense		Utilities Expense	
Dr. +	Cr. −	Dr. +	Cr. −
Bal. $550	Clo. $550	Bal. $125	Clo. $125

The journal entry to close the expense accounts appears in Figure 9-3.

Look again at the second closing entry. You will notice that it has one debit and four credits. A journal entry having two or more debits or two or more credits is called a **compound entry.** The compound entry saves both space and posting time. For example, each expense account could have been closed into Income Summary separately. That, however, would have required four entries, and postings, to Income Summary instead of one.

GENERAL JOURNAL				PAGE __3__
DATE	DESCRIPTION	POST. REF.	DEBIT	CREDIT
	Closing Entries			1
31	*Income Summary*		1 2 0 0 00	4
	Advertising Expense			7 5 00 5
	Maintenance Expense			4 5 0 00 6
	Rent Expense			5 5 0 00 7
	Utilities Expense			1 2 5 00 8

Figure 9-3 Closing the Expense Accounts

R E M E M B E R

To close revenue accounts, debit each revenue account for the amount of its credit balance. Credit Income Summary for the amount of total revenue. To close expense accounts, debit Income Summary for the amount of total expenses. Credit each expense account for the amount of its debit balance.

Before going on, complete the following activity to make certain you understand how to close the revenue and expense accounts.

Check Your Learning

Write your answers to these questions on a sheet of paper.

1. A closing entry must be made for the account Ticket Revenue, which has a balance of $6,000.
   a. What is the title of the account debited?
   b. What is the title of the account credited?
   c. What is the amount of the debit? the credit?
2. A business has three expense accounts: Gas and Oil Expense (balance, $700), Miscellaneous Expense (balance, $600), and Utilities Expense (balance, $1,800). The end of the business's fiscal period is June 30.
   a. The date of the journal entry to close these accounts is ___?___ .
   b. The account debited is ___?___ .
   c. The amount of the debit is ___?___ .
   d. The accounts credited are ___?___ .
   e. The amounts of the credits are ___?___ .

Compare your answers to those in the answers section. Re-read the preceding part of the chapter to find the answers to any questions you missed.

Closing the Balance of the Income Summary Account into Capital

The next journal entry is made to close the balance of the Income Summary account into the capital account. After closing the revenue and expense accounts, Income Summary has a credit balance of $450. This balance is the amount of the net income for the period. It is the same amount that was calculated on the work sheet.

The first part of this closing entry is a debit of $450 to Income Summary. As you can see from the following T account, a debit of $450 to Income Summary reduces the balance of that account to zero. The amount of net income must be closed into the owner's capital account, so the second part of this closing entry is a credit of $450 to Jan Harter, Capital.

Income Summary		Jan Harter, Capital	
Dr.	Cr.	Dr.	Cr.
		−	+
Clo. $1,200	Clo. $1,650		Bal. $25,200
Clo. 450			Clo. 450

The journal entry to close the balance of Income Summary (the net income for the period) into the capital account is illustrated in Figure 9-4.

	GENERAL JOURNAL			PAGE 3	
DATE	DESCRIPTION	POST. REF.	DEBIT	CREDIT	
9	31 Income Summary		450 00		9
10	Jan Harter, Capital			450 00	10

Figure 9-4 Closing the Income Summary Account

If a business reports a net loss for the period, Income Summary would have a debit balance. The third closing entry, then, would be a debit to the capital account and a credit to Income Summary for the amount of the net loss. This situation is shown in Figure 9-5.

	GENERAL JOURNAL			PAGE 3	
DATE	DESCRIPTION	POST. REF.	DEBIT	CREDIT	
9	31 Jan Harter, Capital		250 00		9
10	Income Summary			250 00	10

Figure 9-5 Closing Income Summary for the Amount of Net Loss

Closing the Balance of the Withdrawals Account into Capital

The last closing entry made is to close the balance of the withdrawals account into capital. As you recall, withdrawals decrease owner's equity. The balance of the withdrawals account must be transferred to the capital account at the end of the period to show the decrease it causes in owner's equity. To close the withdrawals account, the amount of its balance—taken from the Balance Sheet section of the work sheet—is debited to capital. The withdrawals account is credited for the same amount to reduce its balance to zero. Jan Harter, Capital, therefore, is debited for $400, and Jan Harter, Withdrawals is credited for $400.

Jan Harter, Capital			Jan Harter, Withdrawals	
Dr.	Cr.		Dr.	Cr.
–	+		+	–
Clo. $400	Bal. $25,200		Bal. $400	Clo. $400
	450			

This journal entry is shown in Figure 9-6.

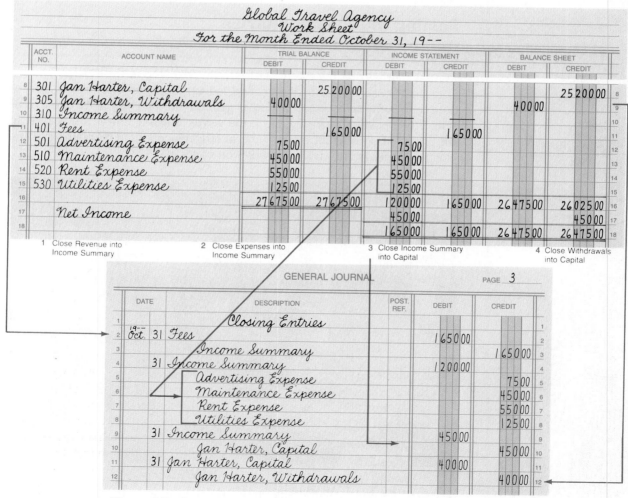

GENERAL JOURNAL PAGE 3

	DATE	DESCRIPTION	POST. REF.	DEBIT	CREDIT	
11	31	Jan Harter, Capital		400 00		11
12		Jan Harter, Withdrawals			400 00	12

Figure 9-6 Closing the Withdrawals Account

The work sheet and the journal entries made to close the temporary capital accounts for Global Travel are shown in Figure 9-7.

Global Travel Agency
Work Sheet
For the Month Ended October 31, 19--

	ACCT. NO.	ACCOUNT NAME	TRIAL BALANCE DEBIT	TRIAL BALANCE CREDIT	INCOME STATEMENT DEBIT	INCOME STATEMENT CREDIT	BALANCE SHEET DEBIT	BALANCE SHEET CREDIT	
8	301	Jan Harter, Capital		25 200 00				25 200 00	8
9	305	Jan Harter, Withdrawals	400 00				400 00		9
10	310	Income Summary							10
11	401	Fees		1 650 00		1 650 00			11
12	501	Advertising Expense	75 00		75 00				12
13	510	Maintenance Expense	450 00		450 00				13
14	520	Rent Expense	550 00		550 00				14
15	530	Utilities Expense	125 00		125 00				15
16			2 767 500	2 767 500	1 200 00	1 650 00	2 647 500	2 602 500	16
17		Net Income			450 00			450 00	17
18					1 650 00	1 650 00	2 647 500	2 647 500	18

1 Close Revenue into Income Summary

2 Close Expenses into Income Summary

3 Close Income Summary into Capital

4 Close Withdrawals into Capital

GENERAL JOURNAL PAGE 3

	DATE	DESCRIPTION	POST. REF.	DEBIT	CREDIT	
1		Closing Entries				1
2	19-- Oct. 31	Fees		1 650 00		2
3		Income Summary			1 650 00	3
4	31	Income Summary		1 200 00		4
5		Advertising Expense			75 00	5
6		Maintenance Expense			450 00	6
7		Rent Expense			550 00	7
8		Utilities Expense			125 00	8
9	31	Income Summary		450 00		9
10		Jan Harter, Capital			450 00	10
11	31	Jan Harter, Capital		400 00		11
12		Jan Harter, Withdrawals			400 00	12

Figure 9-7 Journalizing the Closing Entries

CHAPTER 9 Completing the Accounting Cycle for a Sole Proprietorship

Before you read any further, complete the following activity to check your understanding of closing entries.

Check Your Learning

Use notebook paper and answer these questions about Figure 9-7.

1. What is the source of information for the closing entries?
2. How many expense accounts are affected by the closing entries?
3. Which account serves as a "clearinghouse" during the closing process?
4. In the third closing entry, is the capital account being increased or decreased?
5. How many closing entries affect the Income Summary account?

Compare your answers to those in the answers section. Re-read the preceding part of the chapter to find the correct answers to any questions you may have missed.

Posting the Closing Entries to the General Ledger

After journalizing the closing entries, the next step in the closing process is to post those entries to the general ledger accounts. The posting procedure here is the same as for any other general journal entry, with one exception. When posting a closing entry, the words "Closing Entry" are written in the Explanation column of the general ledger account. The posting of the closing entries is shown in Figure 9-8 on pages 177-178.

Closing entries divide the accounting activities of one fiscal period from those of another. This process provides financial data with which the owner or manager can evaluate the business's success.

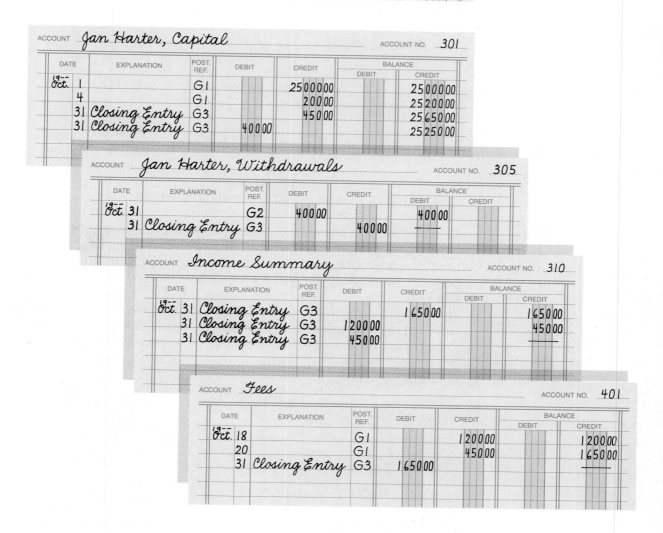

Figure 9-8 Closing Entries Posted to the General Ledger

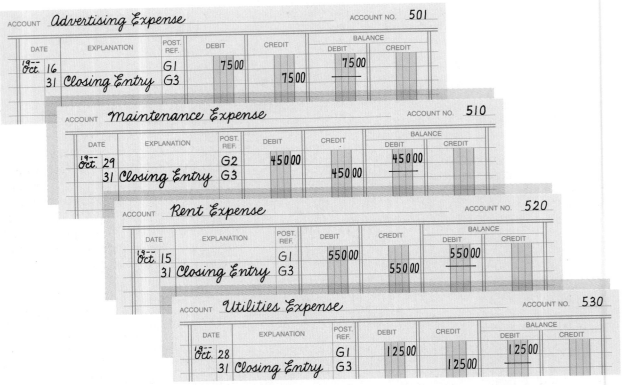

Figure 9-8 Closing Entries Posted to the General Ledger (Continued)

Preparing a Post-Closing Trial Balance

Preparing the post-closing trial balance is the last step in the accounting cycle. This trial balance is prepared to make sure the total debits in the ledger accounts are equal to total credits after the closing entries have been posted. The post-closing trial balance for Global Travel Agency is shown in Figure 9-9.

Notice that the only accounts and balances listed on the post-closing trial balance are the permanent accounts of the business. After the closing process, only permanent accounts have balances. Temporary capital accounts

Global Travel Agency		
Post-Closing Trial Balance		
October 31, 19--		
Cash in Bank	16 125 00	
Accounts Receivable – Burton Co.	450 00	
Computer Equipment	8 000 00	
Office Equipment	1 500 00	
Accounts Payable – City News		75 00
Accounts Payable – Modern Office Suppliers		750 00
Jan Harter, Capital		25 250 00
Total	26 075 00	26 075 00

Figure 9-9 Post-Closing Trial Balance

have zero balances, so there is no need to list those accounts on the post-closing trial balance.

The Computer and Closing Entries

The closing entries we just discussed were prepared manually. In a computerized accounting system, closing entries may be completed entirely by the computer. A command from the computer operator instructs the computer to close the general ledger. The computer will close the temporary capital accounts, determine the amount of net income or net loss, and update the owner's capital account. After the closing is complete, the operator can instruct the computer to prepare a post-closing trial balance. The post-closing trial balance prepared by the computer lets the accounting clerk know that the temporary capital accounts have zero balances. A computer-prepared post-closing trial balance is illustrated in Figure 9-10.

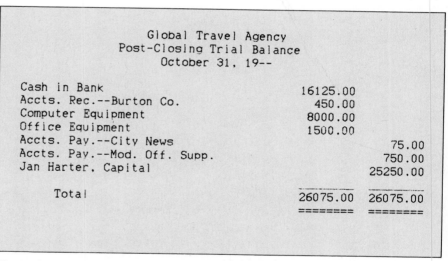

Figure 9-10   Post-Closing Trial Balance Prepared by Computer

You have now completed an accounting cycle for a service business organized as a sole proprietorship.

Summary of Key Points

1. The eighth and ninth steps in the accounting cycle are to record and post the closing entries and to prepare a post-closing trial balance. These steps complete the accounting cycle.
2. Closing is the process of transferring the balances in the temporary capital accounts to the capital account. The work sheet is the source of the balances of the temporary capital accounts.

3. Only temporary capital accounts are closed. The asset, liability, and owner's capital account are never closed.

4. The first closing entry transfers the balance of the revenue account(s) into Income Summary. The balances of the expense accounts are then closed into Income Summary. The balance of the Income Summary account (the net income or net loss for the period) is then closed into the capital account. The last closing entry transfers the balance of the withdrawals account into the capital account.

5. After the closing entries have been journalized, they are posted to the general ledger. A post-closing trial balance is then prepared to test the equality of total debits and credits in the ledger.

Review and Applications

Building Your Accounting Vocabulary

In your own words, write the definition of each of the following accounting terms. Use complete sentences for your definitions.

closing entries
compound entry

Income Summary
account

post-closing trial
balance

Reviewing Your Accounting Knowledge

1. Why are the temporary capital accounts closed at the end of the fiscal period?
2. What is the purpose of the Income Summary account?
3. Explain the relationship between the Income Summary account and the capital account.
4. How is the Income Summary account different from the other temporary capital accounts?
5. List the steps involved in closing the temporary capital accounts.
6. What is the source of information for the closing entries?
7. How does the closing procedure for a net loss differ from the closing procedure for a net income?
8. In what way is the posting procedure for closing entries different from the posting procedure for other general journal entries?
9. What is the purpose of preparing a post-closing trial balance?
10. Why do only the balances of permanent accounts appear on the post-closing trial balance?

Improving Your Human Relations Skills

Recently Elena, a new employee, was assigned to work with you on several important projects in your office. You have found that Elena is not very well organized and often has to redo her part of an assignment. As a result of her poor work, you have already missed your first deadline.

1. What should you say to Elena?
2. How would you explain this problem to your supervisor?
3. What can be done to make sure you do not miss future deadlines?

Applying Accounting Procedures

Exercise 9-1   Understanding the Accounting Cycle

The nine steps in the accounting cycle are listed at the top of page 182, but not in the proper order.

Instructions: Rearrange these steps in the order in which they would be completed by a business during an accounting period. Use the form in the workbook or plain paper. Place a number (from 1 to 9) on the line preceding the step.

a. Complete the work sheet.
b. Analyze business transactions.
c. Prepare a post-closing trial balance.
d. Journalize and post the closing entries.
e. Collect and verify data on source documents.
f. Prepare a trial balance.
g. Post each entry to the general ledger.
h. Journalize business transactions.
i. Prepare the financial statements.

Exercise 9-2 Determining Accounts Affected by Closing Entries

The following list contains some of the accounts used by the Living Well Health Spa.

Accounts Payable—The Fitness Shop
Accounts Receivable—Linda Brown
Advertising Expense
Cash in Bank
Exercise Class Revenue
Exercise Equipment
Income Summary
Laundry Equipment
Maintenance Expense

Membership Fees
Miscellaneous Expense
Office Furniture
Rent Expense
Repair Tools
Ted Chapman, Capital
Ted Chapman, Withdrawals
Utilities Expense

Instructions: Use a form similar to the one that follows. For each account,
(1) Indicate the statement on which each account is reported by writing "Balance Sheet" or "Income Statement" in the space provided.
(2) In the next column, use "Yes" or "No" to indicate whether the account is closed.
(3) In the last column, use "Yes" or "No" to indicate whether the account is included in the post-closing trial balance. The first account is shown as an example.

Account Title	Financial Statement	Is the account affected by a closing entry?	Does the account appear on the post-closing trial balance?
Accounts Payable— The Fitness Shop	Balance Sheet	No	Yes

Problem 9-1 Preparing Closing Entries

A portion of the work sheet for Holmes Accounting Service for the period ended September 30 appears on page 183.

Instructions: Using the information from the work sheet, prepare the journal entries to close the temporary capital accounts. Use journal page 7.
(1) Record the closing entry for the revenue account.
(2) Record the closing entry for the expense accounts.
(3) Record the closing entry for the Income Summary account.
(4) Record the closing entry for the withdrawals account.

	ACCT. NO.	ACCOUNT NAME	INCOME STATEMENT DEBIT	INCOME STATEMENT CREDIT	BALANCE SHEET DEBIT	BALANCE SHEET CREDIT	
1	101	Cash in Bank			7000 00		1
2	105	Accts. Rec. – Betty Foley			3000 00		2
3	115	Office Equipment			12000 00		3
4	120	Accounting Library			6000 00		4
5	201	Accts. Pay. – Ron Williams				900 00	5
6	301	Robert Holmes, Capital				19775 00	6
7	305	Robert Holmes, Withdrawals			2350 00		7
8	310	Income Summary	———	———			8
9	401	Accounting Fees		15865 00			9
10	501	Entertainment Expense	3400 00				10
11	510	Miscellaneous Expense	560 00				11
12	520	Rent Expense	1000 00				12
13	530	Utilities Expense	1230 00				13
14			6190 00	15865 00	30350 00	20675 00	14
15		Net Income	9675 00			9675 00	15
16			15865 00	15865 00	30350 00	30350 00	16

Problem 9-2   Preparing a Post-Closing Trial Balance

Shown below are the accounts of Carrier's Repair Shop on June 30 after the closing entries have been journalized and posted.

Cash in Bank	
Dr.	Cr.
+	−
$8,000	

Accounts Receivable— Kathy Clarke	
Dr.	Cr.
+	−
$875	

Accounts Receivable— Malcolm, Inc.	
Dr.	Cr.
+	−
$5,050	

Accounts Receivable— James Moreaux	
Dr.	Cr.
+	−
$1,275	

Shop Equipment	
Dr.	Cr.
+	−
$6,000	

Tools	
Dr.	Cr.
+	−
$9,000	

Accounts Payable— Beste Tool & Die Co.	
Dr.	Cr.
−	+
	$1,000

Accounts Payable— Oliver Equipment	
Dr.	Cr.
−	+
	$2,500

J. C. Carrier, Capital	
Dr.	Cr.
−	+
$1,500	$21,000
	7,200

J. C. Carrier, Withdrawals	
Dr.	Cr.
+	−
$1,500	$1,500

Income Summary	
Dr.	Cr.
$7,800	$15,000
7,200	

Repair Revenue	
Dr.	Cr.
−	+
$15,000	$15,000

(handwritten notes near Repair Revenue: 28,200 / 1500 / 28,700)

Rent Expense	
Dr.	Cr.
+	−
$5,000	$5,000

Utilities Expense	
Dr.	Cr.
+	−
$2,800	$2,800

Instructions: Use the information in the T accounts to prepare the June 30 post-closing trial balance for Carrier's Repair Shop.

Problem 9-3 Journalizing Closing Entries

The following account titles and balances appeared on the work sheet for Whitman Contractors. The work sheet was for the month ended July 31.

	Income Statement		Balance Sheet	
	Debit	Credit	Debit	Credit
Cash in Bank			9,300	
Accounts Receivable—Projean Co.			3,000	
Accounts Receivable—Ford Bakery			10,000	
Office Equipment			8,000	
Construction Equipment			60,000	
Accounts Payable—Joseph's Elec.				5,000
Accounts Payable—Moran Cement Co.				1,500
Accounts Payable—Stoll Bldg. Supp.				15,000
C. Whitman, Capital				64,500
C. Whitman, Withdrawals			7,000	
Income Summary				
Construction Revenue	2	20,000		
Advertising Expense	1,700			
Gas and Oil Expense	4,300			
Miscellaneous Expense	700			
Repairs Expense	1,200			
Utilities Expense	800			
	9,700			

Instructions: Using the above information, record the closing entries for Whitman Contractors. Use general journal page 11.

Problem 9-4 Posting Closing Entries and Preparing a Post-Closing Trial Balance

Instructions: Use the closing entries prepared in Problem 9-3 to complete this problem.

(1) Post the closing entries recorded in Problem 9-3 to the appropriate general ledger accounts. The general ledger accounts for Whitman Contractors are included in the working papers accompanying this textbook.

(2) Prepare a post-closing trial balance.

COMPUTER
PROBLEM

Problem 9-5 Completing End-of-Period Activities

At the end of April, the general ledger for Tsung Management Company shows the following account balances.

110	Cash in Bank	$12,000	220	Accounts Payable— The Computer Shop	$15,500
120	Accounts Receivable— Hatter Company	3,000	301	Alan Tsung, Capital	54,675
130	Accounts Receivable— Jackson Co.	900	302	Alan Tsung, Withdrawals	4,000
140	Accounts Receivable— Zest Realty Co.	1,800	303	Income Summary	
			401	Management Fees	9,600
150	Office Supplies	500	510	Advertising Expense	1,000
160	Office Equipment	13,000	520	Miscellaneous Expense	400
170	Computer Equipment	42,000	530	Rent Expense	1,200
210	Accounts Payable— Fox Office Supply	400	540	Utilities Expense	375

Instructions: Using the preceding account titles and balances,

(1) Prepare the six-column work sheet. The period covered is one month.

(2) Prepare the financial statements. Alan Tsung made an investment of $10,000 during the month.

(3) Record the closing entries on page 12 of a general journal.

(4) Post the closing entries.

(5) Prepare a post-closing trial balance.

CHALLENGE

PROBLEM

Problem 9-6   Correcting Errors in the Closing Entries

The work sheet and financial statements for Bennett Company for the month of November have been completed. They show that during this one-month period,

a. The net income for the period was $1,800.

b. The owner, Dale Bennett, made an additional investment of $5,000.

c. Dale Bennett withdrew $2,000.

d. The November 30 balance of Dale Bennett, Capital that appeared on the work sheet was $30,000.

e. Expenses for the month were as follows: Advertising Expense, $900; Miscellaneous Expense, $300; Rent Expense, $1,400; and Utilities Expense, $600.

The closing entries for the month were entered in the general journal as shown below.

		GENERAL JOURNAL			PAGE 14
	DATE	DESCRIPTION	POST. REF.	DEBIT	CREDIT
1		*Closing Entries*			
2	19-- Nov 30	Fees		5 000 00	
3		Income Summary			5 000 00
4	30	Income Summary		3 200 00	
5		Advertising Expense			900 00
6		Miscellaneous Expense			300 00
7		Rent Expense			1 400 00
8		Utilities Expense			600 00
9	30	Income Summary		30 000 00	
10		Dale Bennett, Capital			30 000 00
11	30	Dale Bennett, Capital		2 000 00	
12		Dale Bennett, Withdrawals			2 000 00

Instructions: Based on these closing entries, answer the following questions.

(1) What error has been made in recording the closing entries?

(2) After posting the entries shown, will Income Summary have a debit or a credit balance?

(3) After posting these entries, what will the balance of the capital account be?

(4) What *should* the balance of Dale Bennett, Capital be?

(5) Why does the additional investment of $5,000 *not* appear in the closing entries?

Make corrections in the journal entries in your working papers.

*C*omputers in Sports: New Angles on the Winning Performance

When mere hundredths of inches, seconds, or points separate winning performances from second-place finishes, coaches of world-class athletes are adopting state-of-the-art coaching assistants: computers.

At the U.S. Olympic Committee sports science lab in Colorado Springs, Colorado, researchers videotape an athlete's performance. They then process and digitize the performance frame by frame to create multidimensional images that can be analyzed from different angles. The analysis can point out flaws in the athlete's technique that might not otherwise be noticed. The computer can even be told to look for a specific flaw and highlight it throughout the analysis.

This $35,000 motion-analysis system was created by Phillip Cheetham, a former Olympic gymnast from Australia. Cheetham withdrew from competition as the result of an injury. His injury led him to develop another system used by the U.S. Olympic Committee to analyze how gymnastic injuries can be prevented.

Young Tom Eldredge, junior world figure-skating champion, believes motion-analysis helped him become one of only a dozen figure skaters in the United States to perform a triple-axel (three and a half revolutions in the air).

As this technology becomes more widely used, will world records fall even faster? Will athletes be able to leap higher and longer, run faster, score more perfect 10s than ever before? How much does technique contribute to the winning performance? How much is the result of conditioning, training, body type, and the competitive spirit?

Computer analysis of the serve may improve this tennis player's performance.

Chapter 10

CASH CONTROL AND BANKING ACTIVITIES

An important part of the record-keeping for any business involves the records kept on the cash received and paid out. Cash is a business's most liquid asset. It is the asset needing the greatest protection, to prevent its loss or waste.

In this chapter, you will learn about the controls businesses use to protect their cash. One of the most commonly used controls is a checking account. The use of a checking account not only helps protect cash but also provides a separate record of cash transactions.

Learning Objectives

When you have completed Chapter 10, you should be able to do the following:

1. Describe the internal controls used to protect cash.
2. Describe the forms used to open and use a checking account.
3. Accurately record information on check stubs.
4. Prepare a check correctly.
5. Reconcile a bank statement.
6. Journalize and post entries relating to bank service charges.
7. Define the terms introduced in this chapter.

New Terms

internal controls
external controls
checking account
check
depositor
signature card
deposit slip
endorsement
restrictive endorsement
payee
drawer
drawee
voiding a check
bank statement
canceled checks
reconciling the bank statement
outstanding checks
outstanding deposits
bank service charge
stop payment order
NSF check
electronic funds transfer
    system (EFTS)

One way a business can control, or protect, its cash is by making all payments by check and depositing all cash received in a bank account.

Protecting Cash

In any business, ready cash (bills, coins, and checks) is used daily for a large number of transactions. A business receives cash in return for its goods or services. It pays out cash to purchase goods and services or to pay its expenses.

You learned in an earlier chapter that cash is a business's most liquid asset. It is important to protect that asset from loss, waste, theft, forgery, and embezzlement. Cash can be protected through internal controls and external controls. **Internal controls** refer to those steps the business takes to protect cash and other assets. For example, internal controls may include

1. Limiting the number of persons handling cash.
2. Separating accounting tasks involving cash (such as, not allowing the person who handles cash receipts and cash payments to also keep the accounting records showing the amounts received or paid out).
3. Bonding (insuring) employees who handle cash or cash records.
4. Using a safe or a cash register.
5. Depositing cash receipts in the bank daily.
6. Using checks to make all cash payments.

External controls are those controls provided outside the business. For example, banks maintain controls to protect the funds deposited by their customers. These controls include verifying the accuracy of signatures on checks and maintaining records of the transfer of money into and out of each customer's checking account.

Opening a Checking Account

A **checking account** is a bank account that allows a bank customer to deposit cash and to write checks against the account balance. A **check** is a written order from a depositor telling the bank to pay a stated amount of cash to the person or business named on the check. A **depositor** is a person or business that has cash on deposit in a bank. To open a checking account, a business owner must fill out a signature card and deposit cash in the bank.

A **signature card** contains the signature(s) of the person(s) authorized to write checks on the bank account. The signature card is kept on file by the bank so that it can be matched against signed checks presented for payment. The use of a signature card helps protect both the account holder and the bank against checks with forged signatures.

The signature card signed by Jan Harter to open the checking account for Global Travel Agency is shown in Figure 10-1.

ACCOUNTING *Notes*

Modern banking began in Italy over 500 years ago. Our word *bank* comes from the Italian word *banco*, meaning "bench." Why? In early times, Italian bankers set up benches along the streets to do business.

ACCT. NO. __303443__

ACCT. TYPE: ☑ CKG. ☐ SAV. ☐ C.R.
☐ OTHER _____
NO. SIGNATURES REQUIRED __1__
SOC. SEC. NO. OR TAXPAYER I.D. NO.

ACCOUNT NAME *Global Travel Agency*

SIGNATURE *Jan Harter*

1 _____ SIGNATURE

2 _____ SIGNATURE

THE INDIVIDUALS WHO HAVE SIGNED ABOVE ARE AUTHORIZED TO USE THIS ACCOUNT ACCORDING TO THE RULES AND REGULATIONS THAT APPLY TO IT **AND** ANY SPECIAL INSTRUCTIONS ON FILE WITH THE BANK. EACH PERSON WHO SIGNS ACKNOWLEDGES THAT THESE RULES AND REGULATIONS HAVE BEEN RECEIVED AND AGREES TO THEIR TERMS. EACH PERSON ALSO AUTHORIZES THE BANK TO REQUEST A CONSUMER REPORT FROM ANY CONSUMER REPORTING AGENCY.

FOR BANK USE

IDENTIFICATION PRESENTED *Mass. State License*

COMMENTS *Sole Proprietorship - travel agency*

ACCOUNT ADDRESS *200 Brattle Street, Cambridge, MA 02138*

HOME PHONE *258-4512*   BUSINESS PHONE *258-2020*

☑ NEW ACCOUNT   ☐ CAPTION CHANGE   ☐ NEW SIGNATURE   ☐ ADDITIONAL SIGNATURE

☐ INDIVIDUAL   ☐ JOINT   ☐ CORPORATE   ☑ BUSINESS   ☐ FIDUCIARY

☐ OTHER _____

NCPS   OPENED BY *GLC*   BRANCH

DATE OPENED OR CHANGED *10/1*   AMOUNT DEPOSITED $ *25,000.00*

Figure 10-1 Checking Account Signature Card

CHAPTER 10   Cash Control and Banking Activities

189

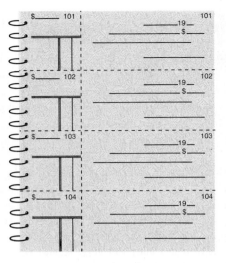

When a depositor opens a checking account, checks are printed for the sole use of that depositor. Printed checks are packaged together in *checkbooks*. The checkbook chosen by Jan Harter is typical of those used by businesses. It looks like a spiral-bound notebook. Its pages are made up of detachable checks attached to check stubs. Each check — and its stub — is numbered in sequence. Prenumbered checks help a business keep track of every check that is written. Using checks with printed numbers is an important part of the internal control of cash.

In addition to the check number, each check is printed with the business's account number and an American Bankers Association (ABA) number. The ABA number is the fractional number printed in the upper right corner of a check, just below the check number. The ABA number is a code that identifies exactly where a check comes from. For example, look at the ABA number on the check in Figure 10-2.

Figure 10-2 Printed Check

The part of the number above the line and to the left of the hyphen stands for the city or state in which the bank is located. The number to the right of the hyphen indicates the specific bank on which the check is written. The number below the line is a code for the Federal Reserve district in which the bank is located.

The ABA number was developed to speed the sorting of checks by hand. An updated version of the ABA number is also printed on the bottom of each check for use in electronic sorting. The ABA number, the depositor's account number, and perhaps the check number are printed at the bottom of the check in a special ink and typeface. These specially printed numbers are referred to as MICR (*m*agnetic *i*nk *c*haracter *r*ecognition) numbers. Can you identify the MICR number on the check in Figure 10-2?

Making Deposits to a Checking Account

A business should make regular deposits to protect the currency and checks it receives. Most businesses make daily deposits. A **deposit slip** is a bank form on which the currency (bills and coins) and checks to be deposited are listed. The deposit slip, also called a deposit ticket, gives both the depositor and the bank a detailed record of a deposit. Most banks provide their depositors with deposit slips on which the depositor's name, address, and account number are printed. A deposit slip for Global Travel Agency is shown in Figure 10-3. To complete a deposit slip, follow these steps:

1. Write the date on the Date line.
2. On the Cash line, list the total amount of bills and coins being deposited.
3. List checks separately by their ABA numbers. If many checks are being deposited, list the checks by amount on a calculator tape and attach the tape to the deposit slip. On the first Checks line, write "See tape listing," followed by the total amount of the checks.
4. Total the cash and checks, and write the total amount being deposited on the Total line.

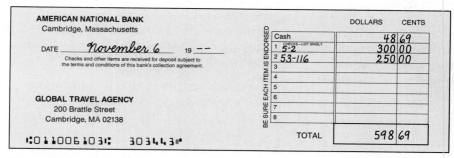

Figure 10-3 Deposit Slip

The deposit slip and the cash and checks being deposited are handed to a bank teller. Checks should be arranged in the order listed on the deposit slip. The teller verifies the deposit and gives the depositor a receipt. The deposit receipt may be a stamped and initialed (by the teller) copy of the deposit slip or a machine-printed form.

R E M E M B E R

On the deposit slip, list checks being deposited by their ABA numbers.

Endorsing Checks

When a business receives a check in payment for a product or service, it acquires the right to that check. The check is a form of property. To deposit the check in a checking account, the depositor endorses the check to transfer its ownership to the bank. An **endorsement** is an authorized signature that is written or stamped on the back of a check.

The endorsement on the check represents a promise to pay. For example, suppose the bank cannot collect the amount of the check from the account

FOR DEPOSIT ONLY IN

Global Travel
Agency

Acct. 303443

Figure 10-4 Restrictive Endorsement

Figure 10-5 Recording a Deposit in the Checkbook

on which the check is written. The endorsement of the depositor authorizes the bank to deduct the amount of the check from the depositor's account. The depositor, of course, can go back to the person or business that wrote the check to collect payment on it.

Types of endorsements vary, but most businesses use restrictive endorsements. A **restrictive endorsement** restricts, or limits, how a check may be handled. To protect checks from being cashed by anyone else, Global Travel Agency stamps a restrictive endorsement on each check as soon as it is received. For example, by writing "For Deposit Only" as part of its endorsement, Global Travel limits any other use of the check. A typical restrictive endorsement is shown in Figure 10-4.

Recording Deposits in the Checkbook

The check stubs in the checkbook are a duplicate record of the Cash in Bank account. That is, the completed stubs contain the records of all checking account transactions: withdrawals, deposits, and bank service charges.

To record a deposit in the checkbook, follow these procedures:

1. Enter the date of the deposit on the Add Deposits line of the next unused check stub.
2. Enter the total amount of the deposit on the same line in the amount column.
3. Add the deposit amount to the amount on the Balance Brought Forward line. The result is the new checkbook balance. Enter the new balance on the Total line.

The check stub in Figure 10-5 illustrates how deposits are recorded in Global Travel Agency's checkbook.

Writing Checks

Writing checks is a simple procedure governed by a few important rules. These rules must be followed to ensure correct recordkeeping and proper handling of the money represented by the check.

First, *always write checks in ink.* Typewritten checks are also acceptable. Checks written in pencil are *not* acceptable. Checks typed or written in ink are difficult to change, while those written in pencil may be easily altered.

Next, always complete the check stub *before* writing the check. Following this procedure reduces the chance of forgetting to complete the stub. After the check is removed from the checkbook, the stub serves as a permanent record of the check.

Completing the Check Stub

Global Travel's check stub is divided into two parts. The upper half summarizes the details of the cash payment transaction. The lower half is a record of the effects of the transaction on the checking account. It contains the balance before the transaction, any current deposits, the transaction amount, and the balance after the transaction. To complete the check stub, follow these steps:

The following check stub (No. 104):

	$125.00	No. 104

DATE Oct. 28 19 – –
TO Bay State Bell
FOR Telephone bill

	DOLLARS	CENTS
BAL. BRO. FWD.	15,700	00
ADD DEPOSITS Oct. 18	1,200	00
Oct. 26	200	00
TOTAL	17,100	00
LESS THIS CHECK	125	00
BAL. CARR. FWD.	16,975	00

Stub No. 105:

	$	No. 105

DATE ___ 19 ___
TO ___
FOR ___

	DOLLARS	CENTS
BAL. BRO. FWD.	16,975	00
ADD DEPOSITS		
TOTAL		
LESS THIS CHECK		
BAL. CARR. FWD.		

1. In the upper half of the stub, enter the amount of the check, the date, the name of the payee (on the To line), and the purpose of the check (on the For line). A **payee** is the person or business to whom a check is written.
2. If you have not already done so, enter the total balance on the Total line on the bottom half of the stub.
3. Enter the amount of the check on the line marked "Less This Check." This amount must be the same as the amount shown on the first line in the upper half of the stub.
4. Subtract the check amount from the total balance. Enter the new balance on the line marked "Balance Carried Forward."
5. Enter the new balance on the first line of the *next* check stub on the line labeled "Balance Brought Forward."

R E M E M B E R

Always complete the check stub *before* you write a check.

Filling Out the Check

After you have completed the check stub, write the check following the steps below. Remember to write the check in ink so that it cannot easily be changed.

1. Write the date on which the check is being issued.
2. Write the payee's name on the line marked "Pay To the Order Of." Start the payee's name as far left as possible.
3. Enter the amount of the check in numbers. Write clearly and begin the first number as close to the printed dollar sign as possible.
4. On the next line, write the dollar amount of the check *in words*. Start at the left edge of the line. Write any cents amount as a fraction. Draw a line from the cents fraction to the word "Dollars."
5. Sign the check. Only an authorized person—one who has signed the signature card for that account—may sign a check. The person who signs a check is the **drawer.** The bank on which the check is written is called the **drawee.**

The checkbook is now ready for the next transaction. A completed check and its stub are shown in Figure 10-6.

Figure 10-6 Completed Check and Stub

Some businesses use a check-writing machine when preparing a check. A check writer perforates the amount of the check in words on the Dollars line. These perforations protect a check from alteration, since the holes in the check are almost impossible to alter.

Voiding a Check

As a rule, if an error is made while writing a check, that check is not used. Corrected checks are not used because the corrections might look suspicious to banks. Instead, the incorrect check is marked "Void" and a new check is prepared. Writing the word "Void" in large letters across the front of a check (in ink) is known as **voiding a check.** When a check is voided, the stub is also voided.

The business needs to account for each check used, so a voided check is never destroyed. It is kept and filed in the business's records. One means of filing a voided check is to fold it and staple it to its check stub. A special file can also be set up for voided checks.

Before reading any further, complete the following activity to check your understanding of the information that appears on a check.

Check Your Learning

Study the check below and then answer the questions that follow. Write your answers on notebook paper.

1. The payee of this check is ___?___ .
2. The drawer is ___?___ , and the drawee is ___?___ .
3. The number in the upper right corner, $\frac{5\text{-}3421}{110}$, is the ___?___ number.
4. The number 293111 at the bottom of the check is the ___?___ number.

Compare your answers to those in the answers section. Re-read the preceding part of the chapter to find the correct answers to any questions you may have missed.

Proving Cash

The balance in the Cash in Bank account in the general ledger is regularly compared with the balance in the checkbook. If all cash receipts have been deposited, all cash payments made by check, and all transactions journalized and posted, the Cash in Bank account balance should agree with the checkbook balance. Comparing these two cash balances regularly is part of the internal control of cash. Some businesses prove cash daily or weekly, while others prove cash on a monthly basis.

If the Cash in Bank balance does not agree with the checkbook balance, and the trial balance has been proved, the error is probably in the checkbook. A checkbook error is usually the result of: (1) faulty addition or subtraction, (2) failure to record a deposit or a check, or (3) a mistake in copying the balance brought forward amount.

If an error has been made in the checkbook, the proper place to enter the correction is on the next unused stub. For example, suppose Check 22 for $84.60 has been recorded on the check stub as $48.60. The error is found when cash is proved. By this time, several other checks have been written, so the next unused check stub is 31. In this case, the amount of the error ($84.60 − 48.60 = $36.00) should be subtracted from the balance brought forward amount on check stub 31. A note is written on check stub 22 to indicate that the error has been corrected on check stub 31.

The Bank Statement

A **bank statement** is an itemized record of all the transactions occurring in a depositor's account over a given period, usually a month. Typical bank statements include the following information: (1) the checking account

It is important to reconcile the bank statement to ensure that the business's cash records and the bank's records agree.

balance at the beginning of the period, (2) a list of all deposits made by the business during the period, (3) a list of all checks paid by the bank, (4) a list of any other deductions from the depositor's account, and (5) the checking account balance at the end of the period. Find each of these items on Global Travel Agency's bank statement in Figure 10-7 below.

When a bank sends a statement to a depositor, it also returns the checks paid by the bank and deducted from the depositor's account. These returned checks are called **canceled checks.** Canceled checks are stamped or marked with the word "Paid" and the date of payment.

Upon receiving the bank statement, a business should promptly check the statement against its checkbook. The process of determining any differences between the balance shown on the bank statement and the checkbook balance is called **reconciling the bank statement.** The ending balance on the bank statement seldom agrees with the balance in the checkbook. There are several reasons for this.

There is frequently a two- or three-day delay between the preparation and delivery of a bank statement. During that delay, the business may have written additional checks. Often, checks written in one statement period do not reach the bank for payment until the next period. A deposit made when the statement is being prepared may not be listed on the statement. Finally, the depositor does not know about some bank transactions, such as service charges, until the statement is received.

STATEMENT

Global Travel Agency 200 Brattle Street Cambridge, MA 02138	**ACCOUNT NUMBER** 303443 **DATE OF STATEMENT** 10/30/--

PREVIOUS BALANCE	CHECKS AND CHARGES	NO. OF DEPOSITS	NO. OF CHECKS	DEPOSITS AND CREDITS	BALANCE AT THIS DATE
00.00	9,433.00	3	4	26,400.00	16,967.00

CHECKS AND OTHER CHARGES		DEPOSITS AND OTHER CREDITS	DATE	BALANCE
		25,000.00	10/1	25,000.00
8,000.00			10/4	17,000.00
750.00	550.00		10/16	15,700.00
		1,200.00	10/18	16,900.00
		200.00	10/26	17,100.00
8.00S	125.00		10/30	16,967.00

PLEASE EXAMINE YOUR STATEMENT AT ONCE. IF NO ERROR IS REPORTED IN 10 DAYS THE ACCOUNT WILL BE CONSIDERED CORRECT AND VOUCHERS GENUINE. ALL ITEMS ARE CREDITED SUBJECT TO FINAL PAYMENT.

C = Certified Check   T = Ticket Debit or Credit   S = Service Charge   L = List   CR = Overdraft   R = Returned Check

Figure 10-7 Bank Statement

The three situations most frequently causing differences between the bank statement balance and the checkbook balance involve outstanding checks, outstanding deposits, and bank service charges.

Outstanding Checks and Deposits

In banking terms, the word "outstanding" simply means "not yet received." **Outstanding checks,** therefore, are checks that have been written but not yet presented to the bank for payment. **Outstanding deposits** are deposits that have been made and recorded in the checkbook but that do not appear on the bank statement.

Bank Service Charges

The statement balance will also reflect any service charges made by the bank during the statement period. A **bank service charge** is a fee charged by the bank for maintaining bank records and for processing bank statement items for the depositor. This charge varies from bank to bank, but it is frequently based on the number of checks and deposits handled during the month or the balance kept in the depositor's account. The bank subtracts the service charge from the depositor's account and then notifies the depositor of the amount of the charge on the bank statement.

The checkbook balance must be adjusted to show the amount of the bank service charge. One way to adjust the balance in the checkbook is shown on the stub. The words "Less: Service Charge" are written on the line above the Total line. Next, the amount of the service charge is entered in the amount column—preceded by a minus sign. The balance is then recalculated and entered on the Total line.

R E M E M B E R

Before reconciling the bank statement, record in the checkbook any bank service charges or other deductions listed on the bank statement.

Reconciling a Bank Statement

Promptly reconciling the bank statement is a good way to guard against disorderly cash records or cash loss. Banks expect to be notified immediately of any error on the statement. Failure to do so within the time noted on the statement releases the bank from any responsibility for the error.

Most banks provide a form on the back of the bank statement for use in reconciling the bank statement. The reconciliation form for Global Travel's bank statement is shown in Figure 10-8 on page 198. This form documents the differences between the bank balance and the checkbook balance. Follow these steps when reconciling a bank statement:

1. Arrange the canceled checks in numerical order. Compare the canceled checks with those listed on the statement and with the stubs. As you find matching checks and stubs, place a check mark beside the check amount on the bank statement and on the check stub. Then list on the reconciliation form, by number and amount, all the stubs without check marks. These are the outstanding checks.

BANK RECONCILIATION FORM

PLEASE EXAMINE YOUR STATEMENT AT ONCE. ANY
DISCREPANCY SHOULD BE REPORTED TO THE BANK
IMMEDIATELY.

1. Record any transactions appearing on this statement but not
   listed in your checkbook.
2. List any checks still outstanding in the space provided to the
   right.

	CHECKS OUTSTANDING	
Number	**Amount**	
105	450	00
106	400	00

3. Enter the balance shown on this statement here.

    16,967 00

4. Enter deposits recorded in your checkbook but not shown on this statement.

    ———

5. Total Lines 3 and 4 and enter here.

    16,967 00

6. Enter total checks outstanding here.

    850 00

7. Subtract Line 6 from Line 5. This adjusted bank balance should agree with your checkbook balance.

    16,117 00

| TOTAL | 850 | 00 |

Figure 10-8 Bank Reconciliation

2. Enter the ending balance shown on the bank statement.
3. Compare deposits listed on the bank statement to deposits listed in the checkbook. Enter the total of any outstanding deposits on the reconciliation form. Add this total to the bank statement balance and enter the amount on the form.
4. Subtract the total of the outstanding checks from the amount calculated in Step 3. The result is the adjusted bank balance.
5. Compare the adjusted bank balance to the adjusted checkbook balance. The two amounts should match.

If the adjusted bank balance does not match the adjusted checkbook balance, the error must be found and corrected. If the bank has made an error on the bank statement, notify the bank immediately. It is more likely, however, that the error is in the checkbook. Check the addition and subtraction on the check stubs to be sure they are correct.

When the adjusted balances match, the bank statement has been reconciled. The bank fees shown on the bank statement must then be recorded in the accounting records of the business. Before you read about the recording of bank service charges, complete the following Check Your Learning activity.

R—E—M—E—M—B—E—R

If you are having problems reconciling a bank statement, double check for any outstanding checks or outstanding deposits that you may not have included in your calculations.

Check Your Learning

Valleyview Rental Center received its bank statement on April 27. The balance in the checkbook on April 27 is $2,944.20. The checking account balance shown on the statement is $3,085.95. A deposit of $345.00 was made on April 26, and on April 27 of $290.00. The service charge for the month was $5.25. Valleyview has these four outstanding checks:

Check 344	$202.00	Check 350	$ 25.00
Check 346	55.00	Check 351	500.00

1. What is the amount of the adjusted checkbook balance?
2. What is the amount of outstanding deposits?
3. What is the total amount of outstanding checks?
4. What is the amount of the adjusted bank balance?
5. Does the adjusted bank balance match the adjusted checkbook balance?

Compare your answers to those in the answers section. Re-read the preceding part of the chapter to find the answers to any questions you missed.

Recording Bank Service Charges

Like any other business, banks charge fees for their services. To the depositor, a service charge is an expense that must be recorded in the accounting records. Bank service charges are often recorded in the account Miscellaneous Expense. Since expenses decrease owner's equity, Miscellaneous Expense is debited for the amount of the service charge. Cash in Bank is also decreased by the amount of the service charge, so that account is credited. Remember, the amount of the service charge has already been deducted from the depositor's account, so it is not necessary to write a check for this expense. The journal entry for this transaction is shown in Figure 10-9. The bank statement is the source document for recording the bank service charge.

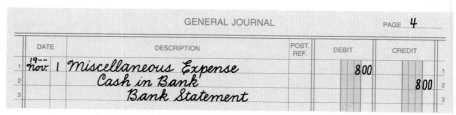

Figure 10-9 General Journal Entry for Bank Service Charge

Special Banking Procedures

Checks are usually written or received and deposited without any problems. A business, however, may not want its bank to pay a check that it has written and sent out. A business may also receive a check from a customer who does not have enough money to cover the amount of the check.

Stopping Payment on a Check

Occasionally, a drawer will ask the bank (drawee) not to honor, or pay, a check. A **stop payment order** is a demand by the depositor that the bank not honor a certain check. The depositor must issue a stop payment order *before* the check has been presented to the bank for payment. Usually, the depositor must complete and sign a written stop payment order.

When payment is stopped on a check, the accounting clerk writes the words "Stopped Payment" on the appropriate check stub. The clerk must then *add* the amount of the stopped check to the current balance in the checkbook (on the next unused check stub). If appropriate, the accounting clerk then issues a new check.

Most banks charge a fee for stopping payment on a check. When this occurs, the amount of the fee must be subtracted from the checkbook balance and recorded in the business's accounting records. Most businesses record the amount of the fee as an expense in the Miscellaneous Expense account. The journal entry is similar to that made for the bank service charge.

Recording NSF Checks

An **NSF check** is one returned by the bank because there are *not* sufficient funds in the drawer's checking account to cover the amount of the check. For example, suppose Global Travel received and deposited a check from a customer. If the customer does not have enough money in the bank to cover the check, the check will be returned to Global Travel. Global Travel will notify the customer that the check was returned by the bank. The customer must then deposit enough money in the bank to cover the check or find another means of paying its bill.

When the bank returns the NSF check to Global Travel, it deducts the amount of the check from Global Travel's checking account. Global Travel must then subtract the amount of the check from its checkbook balance.

A journal entry must also be made to record the return of the NSF check. Since the check represents payment for an amount owed to Global Travel, the amount of the check is recorded as an account receivable. Cash in Bank was originally debited for the amount of the check, so that account is now credited for the same amount. The journal entry is shown in Figure 10-10.

	DATE	DESCRIPTION	POST. REF.	DEBIT	CREDIT	
14	18	Accts. Rec. — Burton Company		450 00		14
15		Cash in Bank			450 00	15
16		NSF Check				16

GENERAL JOURNAL   PAGE ___

Figure 10-10 Recording the Return of an NSF Check

Electronic Funds Transfer System

As you learned earlier, when a bank sends a statement to a depositor, it also returns the checks paid by the bank. Let's look at the route a check follows from the time it is written until it is returned with the bank statement.

1. Global Travel Agency writes Check 103 to Abrams Real Estate for $550 for the month's rent.
2. Abrams Real Estate deposits the check in its acccount at the First National Bank.
3. First National Bank increases the balance in Abrams' checking account by $550.
4. First National Bank sends the $550 check to American National Bank, Global Travel Agency's bank, for collection.
5. American National Bank sends the First National Bank $550 and deducts this amount from Global Travel's account.
6. The paid check is returned to Global Travel Agency by American National Bank with the monthly bank statement.

As you can see, the exchange of checks and funds is a routine procedure. Since the number of checks written each day is in the millions, this transferring of funds from one bank to another is quite a job if handled manually. Today, banks use the electronic funds transfer system (EFTS) to handle the details of exchanging funds. The **electronic funds transfer system** enables banks to transfer funds from the account of one depositor to the account of another quickly and accurately without the immediate exchange of checks.

The full development of the electronic funds transfer system is not now being used because the general public does not wish to move to a system that is completely checkless.

Summary of Key Points

1. The use of a checking account is an important way for a business to protect cash. The checking account also serves as a duplicate record of all cash transactions.
2. Deposit slips are prepared when cash and checks are deposited in a bank account. Copies of deposit slips should be kept as proof of deposits.
3. Checks must be endorsed before they can be deposited. Most businesses stamp a restrictive endorsement on checks as soon as they are received. A restrictive endorsement limits how a check may be handled. The restrictive endorsement helps protect the checks received by a business from misuse.
4. Correctly written checks and accurate check stubs help prevent the loss of cash through carelessness or fraud.
5. As a part of its control of cash, a business regularly proves cash by comparing the Cash in Bank balance to the checkbook balance and finding the reason for any differences between the two amounts.
6. A bank statement is sent to each depositor, usually once a month. A bank statement should be reconciled promptly upon receipt. Any errors found on the bank statement must be reported to the bank immediately.
7. Bank service charges are recorded in the checkbook to keep the checkbook balance up to date.
8. After the bank statement has been reconciled, the service charges reported on the bank statement are journalized and then posted to the appropriate accounts.

Review and Applications

Building Your Accounting Vocabulary

In your own words, write the definition of each of the following accounting terms. Use complete sentences for your definitions.

bank service charge
bank statement
canceled checks
check
checking account
deposit slip
depositor
drawee
drawer

electronic funds
    transfer system
endorsement
external controls
internal controls
NSF check
outstanding check
outstanding deposit
payee

reconciling the bank
    statement
restrictive
    endorsement
signature card
stop payment order
voiding a check

Reviewing Your Accounting Knowledge

1. Explain why it is important for businesses to protect their cash.
2. What internal controls can a business use to protect its cash?
3. What external controls can a business use to protect its cash?
4. Describe the types of forms that are needed to open and use a checking account.
5. What is the purpose of a check endorsement?
6. Why should you always complete the check stub *before* writing the check?
7. What information does a bank statement contain?
8. List the steps followed in reconciling a bank statement.
9. Explain how bank service charges and NSF checks are recorded in the accounting records of a business.
10. How is the bank service charge recorded in the checkbook?

Improving Your Analysis Skills

Maria Varga and John Wills are cashiers for Bacon Construction Co. Both Maria and John are responsible for receiving and paying out cash and are authorized to sign checks for the company. Maria is supposed to record all cash transactions in the company's accounting records, although John often helps. What is wrong with the cash control policies followed by Bacon Construction Co.? What suggestions can you make for improving these policies?

Applying Accounting Procedures

Exercise 10-1   Preparing a Deposit Slip

On August 14, Loretta Harper, owner of Harper Limousine Service, deposited the following items in the business's checking account.

Cash: $784.29

Checks: Charles Ling, drawn on American Bank of Commerce, Dallas, ABA No. 32-7091; $39.44

Keith Lopez, drawn on People's Bank, Baton Rouge, ABA No. 84-268; $249.82

Marjorie Luke, drawn on Horizon Federal Savings and Loan, Shreveport, ABA No. 84-6249; $846.19

Instructions: Using this information, complete a deposit slip.

Exercise 10-2   Writing a Check

Carey Video Rentals received a bill from Northeast Telephone for $214.80 for September telephone services.

Instructions: Prepare Check 41 to pay the telephone bill. Use October 12 as the date and sign your name as drawer.

Exercise 10-3   Recording Deposits in the Checkbook

On January 20, Jon Preston, owner of Preston Fitness Center, deposited $1,434.86 in the business's checking account.

Instructions: Record this deposit on check stub 44 in Preston Fitness Center's checkbook.

Exercise 10-4   Recording Bank Service Charges in the Checkbook

The December bank statement for the Century Advertising Agency listed a bank service charge of $19.80.

Instructions: Record this service charge in the checkbook on check stub 24.

Problem 10-1   Handling Deposits

On February 4, Stanford Mott, owner of Mott Furniture Rental, deposited the following items in the company's checking account at the First National Bank in Ocala, Florida.

Cash: Currency, $374.00; Coins, $7.42

Checks: Bob Warner, drawn on Consumers Bank, Ocala, ABA No. 63-706; $64.98

Joan Walkman, drawn on Sun Bank, Gainesville, ABA No. 63-699; $349.81

Ernesto Garcia, drawn on Progressive Savings and Loan, Tampa, ABA No. 63-710; $29.44

Instructions:

(1) Endorse the checks with a restrictive endorsement. Use the name "Mott Furniture Rental."

(2) Fill out a deposit slip. Use the ABA number to identify each check.

(3) Record the deposit in the checkbook on check stub 651.

Problem 10-2   Maintaining the Checkbook

As the accounting clerk for Currie Construction, you write and sign checks and make deposits. The current checkbook balance, shown on check stub 104, is $3,486.29.

Instructions: For each transaction,

(1) Record the necessary information on the check stub. Determine the new balance and carry the balance forward.

(2) Write checks where requested. Sign your name as drawer.

Transactions:

Mar. 3 Issued Check 104 for $868.45 to Custom Construction for construction supplies.

3 Deposited $601.35 in the checking account.

6 Purchased building materials for cash by issuing Check 105 for $299.60 to Cunningham Lumber.

7 Paid Laverne Brothers $1,000.00 for completing a painting job, Check 106.

10 Made a deposit of $342.80 in the checking account.

10 Wrote Check 107 to Union Utilities for the February electric bill of $175.50.

Problem 10-3   Reconciling the Bank Statement

On May 31, George Fister, the accountant for Anco Financial Services, received the bank statement dated May 30. After comparing the company's checkbook with the bank statement, George found

1. The checkbook balance on May 31 was $960.
2. The ending bank statement balance was $1,380.
3. The bank statement showed a service charge of $10.
4. A deposit of $405 was made on May 30 but did not appear on the bank statement.
5. Check 468 for $529 and Check 472 for $306 were outstanding.

Instructions:

(1) Record the bank service charge in the checkbook.

(2) Reconcile the bank statement for Anco Financial Services.

(3) Journalize the entry for the bank service charge in the general journal.

(4) Post the bank service charge to the appropriate general ledger accounts.

SPREADSHEET

PROBLEM

Problem 10-4   Reconciling the Bank Statement

On July 31, June Hankins, owner of Hankins Photography Studio, received a bank statement dated July 30. After she compared the company's checkbook records with the bank statement, June found

1. The checkbook had a balance of $2,551.34.
2. The bank statement showed a balance of $2,272.36.
3. The statement showed a bank service charge of $20.00.
4. A check from Ted Koonce for $62.44 that was deposited on July 18 was returned by the bank. There was no fee for handling the NSF check.
5. A deposit of $672.48 made on July 30 did not appear on the July bank statement.
6. These checks are outstanding:

Check 172 for $126.84   Check 183 for $192.80
Check 181 for $ 87.66   Check 187 for $ 68.64

Instructions: Using the preceding information,

(1) Record the service charge and the NSF check in the checkbook.
(2) Reconcile the bank statement for Hankins Photography Studio.
(3) Journalize the service charge and the NSF check on page 7 of a general journal.
(4) Post the journal entries to the appropriate general ledger accounts.

CHALLENGE **Problem 10-5   Reconciling the Bank Statement
Using the T Account Form**

PROBLEM   On February 20, the Northam Computer Service Co. received its bank statement dated February 18. After examining it and the checkbook, these facts were determined.

1. The checkbook balance on February 20 was $880.84.
2. The ending bank balance was $344.58.
3. There was a service charge of $14.00 for the month.
4. The following checks were outstanding:

Check 164	$ 88.41	Check 171	$129.88
Check 169	69.34	Check 173	14.25

5. A $68.42 check from Tom McCrary that was deposited on February 13 was returned by the bank for insufficient funds. The bank charged Northam's account $7.00 for handling the NSF check. No journal entry has yet been made for the NSF check.
6. A deposit of $938.72 made on February 9 does not appear on the bank statement.
7. A check for $200.00 made out to Fontenot, Inc., was lost in the mail and has never been cashed. A stop payment order, which cost $10.00, was issued on February 15. No new check has yet been issued.

Instructions: Reconcile the bank statement. Using the T account form in the working papers, list changes to the bank statement balance on the left side and changes to the checkbook balance on the right side.

Pocketing Differences

Christine recently got a job at the neighborhood grocery store as a cashier. She planned to use the money she earned to help pay for college. She enjoyed talking to people as she checked out their purchases, and she worked hard to become one of the fastest cashiers in the store.

Because she was quick, she had a large number of customers go through her aisle each day, and she took in a fair percentage of the day's earnings. Occasionally, when she totaled her receipts and cash at the end of her shift, she found herself either a little short or a little over. If she was a little short, of course, she reported the discrepancy to the manager according to the store's policy. Often if she was a little over, however, she kept the difference for her "college fund." She knew some of the other cashiers did the same thing. Since she had not heard of anyone getting into trouble over the matter, she assumed that management indulgently overlooked the practice.

Employees sometimes overlook the ethical implications of taking small items from their work place.

One day as Christine was totaling up the day's transactions, she found she was over by $34.50. Whenever she had an excess in cash before, it had only been a few dollars. As she again counted the cash in her drawer, she noticed that she had a $50 bill mixed in with the $20 bills. Usually she placed the rare $50 or $100 bill under the checks. Christine wondered if she could have taken a $50 bill from a customer and, assuming it was a $20 bill, given incorrect change.

What is Christine's ethical dilemma? The $34.50 would be a nice bonus, but what if the customer realized his or her mistake and returned to the store? If she reports the difference to the manager, what if the manager asks about other discrepancies that Christine has had? What should Christine do?

Often employees do not think of the ethical implications of taking small amounts of money or small items such as pens or note pads from the work place, but do realize the ethical aspects of taking home something more costly. Christine did not deliberate much over pocketing a dollar or two. A company pen costs about that much, and many employees take home pens without giving it a second thought. Christine's $34.50 difference, however, forced her to stop and think, and led her back to her earlier actions with smaller amounts of cash. Often, by deciding ahead of time what your own ethical stand on such issues will be, you can act consistently and ethically each time such a situation occurs.

Completing the Accounting Cycle for a Sole Proprietorship

You have just completed your study of the accounting cycle and the banking activities for a service business organized as a sole proprietorship. Now you will have the opportunity to apply what you have learned as you work through the accounting cycle for Jenny's Gymnastic Academy.

When you have completed this activity, you will have done the following:

1. Analyzed business transactions.
2. Journalized business transactions in the general journal.
3. Posted journal entries to the general ledger accoutns.
4. Prepared a trial balance and a work sheet.
5. Prepared financial statements.
6. Journalized and posted the closing entries.
7. Prepared a post-closing trial balance.
8. Prepared a reconciliation of the bank statement and recorded any bank service charges.

Jenny's Gymnastic Academy

Jenny's Gymnastic Academy is owned and managed by Jennifer Rachael. The business is organized as a sole proprietorship. The academy provides gymnastic programs for children ages 4-18. The business earns revenue from membership fees and fees charged for special classes.

Chart of Accounts

The chart of accounts for Jenny's Gymnastic Academy appears at the top of the next page.

Business Transactions

Jenny's Gymnastic Academy began business operations on March 1 of this year. During the month of March, the business completed the transactions that follow.

Instructions: Use the accounting stationery in the working papers accompanying this textbook to complete this activity.

(1) Open a general ledger account for each account in the chart of accounts.
(2) Analyze each business transaction.
(3) Enter each business transaction in the general journal. Begin on journal page 1.
(4) Post each journal entry to the appropriate accounts in the general ledger.

JENNY'S GYMNASTIC ACADEMY
Chart of Accounts

	101	Cash in Bank
	105	Accounts Receivable—Sally Chapin
	110	Accounts Receivable—Carla DiSario
	115	Accounts Receivable—George McGarty
ASSETS	120	Accounts Receivable—Joyce Torres
	130	Office Supplies
	135	Office Furniture
	140	Office Equipment
	145	Gymnastic Equipment
	205	Accounts Payable—Custom Designs
LIABILITIES	210	Accounts Payable—The Gym House
	215	Accounts Payable—T & N Equipment
	301	Jennifer Rachael, Capital
OWNER'S EQUITY	305	Jennifer Rachael, Withdrawals
	310	Income Summary
REVENUE	401	Membership Fees
	405	Class Fees
	505	Maintenance Expense
EXPENSES	510	Miscellaneous Expense
	515	Rent Expense
	525	Utilities Expense

(5) Reconcile the bank statement that was received on March 31. The statement is dated March 30.
   a. The checkbook has a current balance of $19,580.00.
   b. The bank statement shows a balance of $19,831.00.
   c. The bank service charge is $15.00.
   d. A deposit of $140.00 made on March 30 does not appear on the bank statement.
   e. These checks are outstanding: Check 112 for $106.00 and Check 113 for $300.00.
(6) Make any necessary adjustments to the checkbook balance.
(7) Journalize and post the entry for the bank service charge.
(8) Prepare a trial balance and then complete the work sheet.
(9) Prepare an income statement.
(10) Prepare a statement of changes in owner's equity.
(11) Prepare a balance sheet.
(12) Journalize and post the closing entries.
(13) Prepare a post-closing trial balance.

Transactions:

Mar. 1 Jennifer Rachael invested $25,000 in Jenny's Gymnastic Academy, Memorandum 1, by opening a business checking account.
   2 Bought a cash register (office equipment) for $525, Check 101.
   2 Purchased $73 in office supplies and issued Check 102.

Mar. 3 Received Invoice 2348 from Custom Designs for office furniture bought on account, $2,680.

4 Jennifer Rachael invested a used typewriter worth $135 in the business, Memorandum 2.

5 Purchased gymnastic equipment for $3,924, Check 103.

5 Received $950 for membership fees, Receipt 1.

6 Bought $8,495 of gymnastic equipment on account from The Gym House, Invoice 395.

8 Carla DiSario completed two classes, $36, Invoice 101, to be paid later.

9 Wrote Check 104 for $850 for the March rent.

10 Charged George McGarty $175 for special classes, on account, Invoice 102.

10 Received Invoice 5495 for a $2,375 microcomputer system bought on account from T & N Equipment.

11 Prepared Receipt 2 for $695 in membership fees received.

13 Received $36 from Carla DiSario on account, Receipt 3.

14 Sent Check 105 for $200 to The Gym House on account.

14 Jennifer Rachael invested $800 worth of gymnastic equipment in the business, Memorandum 3.

15 Wrote Check 106 for $750 to repaint a section of the gym.

16 Completed classes totaling $250 with Joyce Torres, Invoice 103, on account.

18 Jennifer Rachael withdrew $500 for personal use, Check 107.

19 Sent Check 108 for the electric bill of $183.

20 Received a check from George McGarty for $75 to apply on his account, Receipt 4.

21 Issued Check 109 for $45 for stamps (Miscellaneous Expense).

22 Received membership fees, Receipt 5 for $550.

24 Sent Check 110 for $500 to Custom Designs on account.

25 Paid $85 for the cleaning of the office, Check 111.

26 Completed classes with Sally Chapin, $185, to be paid later, Invoice 104.

27 Paid the $106 electric bill, Check 112.

28 Sold a piece of gymnastic equipment to another gym for $175 cash, Receipt 6.

30 Paid T & N Equipment $300 on account, Check 113.

30 Received $140 on account from Joyce Torres, Receipt 7.

31 Bought additional office supplies on account for $227 from T & N Equipment, Invoice 5643.

UNIT 3

THE ACCOUNTING CYCLE FOR A MERCHANDISING BUSINESS

In this unit, you will learn how to keep the accounting records for a business that sells merchandise to its customers. The business we will use in our examples in this unit is organized as a corporation. You will study the complete accounting cycle for a merchandising business called Champion Building Products, Inc. The accounting cycle for a merchandising business that is organized as a corporation is very much like that for the service business organized as a sole proprietorship that you studied in Unit 2.

BUILDING PRODUCTS, INC.

CHAMPION BUILDING PRODUCTS, INC.
Chart of Accounts

ASSETS	101	Cash in Bank
	105	Accounts Receivable
	110	Merchandise Inventory
	115	Supplies
	120	Prepaid Insurance
	150	Delivery Equipment
	155	Store Equipment
LIABILITIES	201	Accounts Payable
	205	Federal Income Tax Payable
	210	Sales Tax Payable
STOCKHOLDERS' EQUITY	301	Capital Stock
	305	Retained Earnings
	310	Income Summary
REVENUE	401	Sales
	405	Sales Discounts
	410	Sales Returns and Allowances
COST OF MERCHANDISE	501	Purchases
	505	Transportation In
	510	Purchases Discounts
	515	Purchases Returns and Allowances
EXPENSES	601	Advertising Expense
	605	Bank Card Fees Expense
	610	Delivery Expense
	615	Insurance Expense
	620	Maintenance Expense
	625	Miscellaneous Expense
	630	Rent Expense
	635	Salaries Expense
	640	Supplies Expense
	645	Utilities Expense
	650	Federal Income Tax Expense

Accounts Receivable Subsidiary Ledger	*Accounts Payable Subsidiary Ledger*
Amy Anderson	Aluminum Plus, Inc.
Shawn Flannery	Center City Supply
Gateway School District	Custom Doors, Inc.
Greensburg School District	Key Paint Company
Norwin School District	Starks Lumber Co.
Pelco Construction Co.	Viking Motors
St. Clair Roofing Co.	Wilson Electric, Inc.
Lisa Whitmore	

Chapter 11

ACCOUNTING FOR SALES ON ACCOUNT

In Unit 2, you learned to classify, record, and report accounting information for businesses that provided a service to their customers. In this unit, you will learn about a different type of business—one that sells merchandise to its customers.

As a business grows, the volume of its transactions increases and a more efficient system for recording transactions is needed. Special journals provide that more efficient system. Transactions that are similar are recorded in one journal.

In this chapter, you will study the sales journal and related records used to keep track of sales on account.

Learning Objectives

When you have completed Chapter 11, you should be able to do the following:

1. Explain the difference between a service business and a merchandising business.
2. Identify the special journals and explain how they are used in a merchandising business.
3. Record sales of merchandise on account in a multicolumn sales journal.
4. Post from the sales journal to customer accounts in the accounts receivable subsidiary ledger.
5. Foot, prove, and total the sales journal at the end of the month and post column totals to the general ledger.
6. Define the accounting terms introduced in this chapter.

New Terms

merchandising business
retailer
wholesaler
merchandise
inventory
sale on account
charge customer
credit card
sales slip
sales tax
credit terms
special journals
sales journal
accounts receivable subsidiary
  ledger
subsidiary ledger
controlling account
footing

Accounting for a Merchandising Business

A **merchandising business** buys goods—such as books, clothing, or furniture—and then sells those goods to customers for a profit. Most merchandising businesses operate either as retailers or as wholesalers, although there are many businesses that do both. A **retailer** is a business that sells to the final user; that is, to you as the consumer. Retailers include clothing stores, record shops, and automobile dealerships. A **wholesaler** is a business that sells to retailers. Electrical supply companies, automobile parts distributors, and food supply companies are all wholesalers.

In the chapters in Unit 3, you will study the accounting cycle for a merchandising business called Champion Building Products, Inc. Champion Building Products is a retail business that sells building materials and home improvement products. The chart of accounts for Champion Building Products is shown on page 212. Looking at this chart of accounts, you will notice several new accounts used by a merchandising business. As you study the accounting cycle for a merchandising business, you will learn how each of these accounts is used to record merchandising transactions. Some of the accounts in the chart of accounts are related to the fact that Champion Building Products is organized as a corporation. Let's introduce you now to the accounts Merchandise Inventory and Sales.

Merchandise Inventory

A merchandising business earns a profit by buying goods from a wholesaler or a manufacturing business and then selling these goods to its customers. The goods bought for resale to customers are called **merchandise.** The items of merchandise the business has in stock are referred to as **inventory.** At the beginning of each fiscal period, the amount of merchandise in stock is represented by the debit balance in the account Merchandise Inventory. Merchandise Inventory is an asset account.

Merchandise Inventory	
Dr.	Cr.
+	−
Increase Side	Decrease Side
Balance Side	

During business operations, the merchandise in stock will be sold and new items will be bought to replace the ones sold. Separate accounts, however, are used to record the sale of merchandise and the purchase of new merchandise.

Sales

Sales	
Dr.	Cr.
−	+
Decrease Side	Increase Side
	Balance Side

When a retail merchandising business sells goods to a customer, the amount of the merchandise sold is recorded in an account entitled Sales. Sales is the revenue account used by a merchandising business. As in other revenue accounts, increases to Sales are recorded as credits and decreases are recorded as debits. Sales may be either for cash or on account. Either type of transaction is recorded as a credit to Sales.

Sales on Account

In a merchandising firm, the most frequent type of transaction is the sale of merchandise. Some businesses sell only on a cash-and-carry basis. Others sell only on credit. Most sell on both a cash basis and a credit basis. In this chapter, you will learn about the sale of merchandise on credit.

The sale of goods that will be paid for later is called a **sale on account.** The customer to whom a sale on account is made is a **charge customer.** Some businesses issue **credit cards** to their charge customers. A credit card, imprinted with the customer's name and account number, entitles a charge customer to charge merchandise.

The Sales Slip

A **sales slip** is a form that lists the details of a sale: the date of the sale, the name of the customer, and the description, quantity, and price of the items sold. The description may be the physical details (such as "red wool socks"), a stock number, or both. A sales slip is usually prepared in multiple copies. The customer receives the original of the sales slip as proof of purchase. The number of copies kept by the business varies with its needs. A copy always goes to the accounting department. It is the business's record of the transaction and the source document for the journal entry.

Just as prenumbered checks help businesses keep track of every check written, prenumbered sales slips help them keep track of all sales made on account. Champion Building Products uses prenumbered sales slips printed with its name and address. Champion's sales slip is shown in Figure 11-1.

CHAMPION BUILDING PRODUCTS, INC.				
601 Mt. Lebanon Road				
Pittsburgh, PA 15230				
Date *December 1* 19 — —			No. 80	
SOLD TO	AMY ANDERSON 103 WOODSTONE DRIVE LAUGHLINTOWN, PA 15655			

Clerk	Cash	Charge	Terms	
FJK		✓	*n/30*	

Qty.	Description	Unit Price	Amount	
1	*Steel (white) door*	350.00	350	00
2	*Storm windows*	70.00	140	00
1	*Package insulation*	10.00	10	00
		Sub Total	500	00
		Sales Tax	30	00
Thank You!		Total	530	00

Figure 11-1
Champion Building Products' Sales Slip

Notice that the final amount on the sales slip is not simply the total cost of the items sold. A sales tax has been figured into the total.

The Sales Tax

Most states and some cities tax the retail sale of goods and services. This tax is called a **sales tax.** Taxable items vary from state to state, as do sales tax rates. The sales tax rate is usually stated as a percentage of the sale, such as 5%. Champion is located in a state with a 6% sales tax rate.

The sales tax is paid by the customer and collected by the business, which acts as the collection agent for the government. (Any governing body can levy taxes. Since, however, most sales taxes are levied by state governments, from now on we will refer to the taxing body as the state.) At the time of the sale, the business adds the amount of the tax to the selling price of the goods. Periodically, the business sends the collected sales taxes to the state. Until the state is paid, however, the sales taxes collected from customers represent a liability of the business. The business keeps a record of the sales tax owed to the state in the liability account Sales Tax Payable.

The amount of the sales tax is found by multiplying the total selling price of the merchandise by the sales tax rate. In the sales slip in Figure 11-1, for example, Amy Anderson bought $500 worth of merchandise. To find the sales tax, the sales clerk multiplied $500 by 6% (.06). The sales tax on the $500 sale was $30. The total transaction amount then was $530.

Not all sales of retail merchandise are taxed. In most states, sales made to government agencies, such as schools, are not taxed. For example, on December 5, Champion sold $1,240.50 worth of merchandise on account to the Norwin School District. Since schools are tax exempt, no sales tax was added to the amount of the sale.

Credit Terms

On the sales slip in Figure 11-1, there is a space to indicate the credit terms of the sale. **Credit terms** set out the time allowed for payment. The credit terms for the sale to Amy Anderson are *n/30*. The "n" stands for the *net,* or total, amount of the sale. The "30" stands for the number of days the customer has to pay for the merchandise. Amy Anderson must pay Champion the $530 within 30 days of December 1, or by December 31.

Analyzing Sales on Account

In the first part of this book, you recorded business transactions for Global Travel Agency, a service business organized as a sole proprietorship. When Global Travel completed travel arrangements and billed the customer, the accounts affected by the transaction were Accounts Receivable and Fees. Let's now look at how a revenue transaction involving a sale on account is recorded for a merchandising business.

December 1: *Sold merchandise on account to Amy Anderson for $500.00 plus sales tax of $30.00, Sales Slip 80.*

Three accounts are affected by this transaction: Sales, Sales Tax Payable, and Accounts Receivable. Sales is the revenue account used by a merchandising business. It is being increased, so it is credited. The amount of the credit is $500.00, the total amount of merchandise sold. The liability account Sales Tax Payable is being increased since Champion owes sales tax to the state. Sales Tax Payable is credited for $30.00. The asset account Accounts Receivable is being increased, so it is debited. The amount of the debit is $530.00, the total amount to be received from Amy Anderson.

This transaction is shown below in T-account form.

Accounts Receivable		Sales		Sales Tax Payable	
Dr.	Cr.	Dr.	Cr.	Dr.	Cr.
+	−	−	+	−	+
$530.00			$500.00		$30.00

When recording transactions involving sales on account, remember that the amount recorded as a debit to Accounts Receivable includes *both* the cost of the merchandise *and* the sales tax.

Before you learn how to record a sale on account, do the following activity.

Check Your Learning

Use notebook paper to write your answers to these questions.

1. The revenue account for a merchandising business is ___?___ .
2. A(n) ___?___ lists the details of a sale and is the source document for the journal entry.
3. Sales Tax Payable is classified as a(n) ___?___ account.
4. ___?___ list the amount of time a charge customer has to pay for a purchase.
5. Record the following transaction in T-account form: Sold merchandise on account to John Lowell for $50.00 plus $3.00 sales tax, Sales Slip 141.

Compare your answers to those in the answers section. Re-read the preceding part of the chapter to find the answers to any questions you may have missed.

Using Special Journals in an Accounting System

A merchandising business could choose to record all sales of merchandise on account in a general journal. As an example, let's look at three sales transactions for Champion Building Products.

December 1: *Sold merchandise on account to Amy Anderson for $500.00, plus $30.00 sales tax, Sales Slip 80.*

December 3: *Sold merchandise on account to Pelco Construction Co. for $380.00, plus $22.80 sales tax, Sales Slip 81.*

December 5: *Sold merchandise on account to Norwin School District for $1,240.50, Sales Slip 82.*

Look at Figure 11-2. You can see that there is a great deal of repetition in the journal entries and in the postings. These three sales on account required three journal entries (11 lines), three postings to Accounts Receivable accounts, two postings to Sales Tax Payable, and three postings to Sales. If

GENERAL JOURNAL   PAGE 20

	DATE	DESCRIPTION	POST. REF.	DEBIT	CREDIT	
1	19-- Dec. 1	Accts. Receivable—Amy Anderson	103	530 00		1
2		Sales	401		500 00	2
3		Sales Tax Payable	210		30 00	3
4		Sales Slip 80				4
5	3	Accts. Rec.—Pelco Construction Co.	109	402 80		5
6		Sales	401		380 00	6
7		Sales Tax Payable	210		22 80	7
8		Sales Slip 81				8
9	5	Accts. Rec.—Norwin School District	106	1240 50		9
10		Sales	401		1240 50	10
11		Sales Slip 82				11
12						12

ACCOUNT Accounts Receivable—Amy Anderson   ACCOUNT NO. 103

DATE	EXPLANATION	POST. REF.	DEBIT	CREDIT	BALANCE DEBIT	BALANCE CREDIT
19-- Dec. 1		G20	530 00		530 00	

ACCOUNT Accounts Receivable—Norwin School District   ACCOUNT NO. 106

DATE	EXPLANATION	POST. REF.	DEBIT	CREDIT	BALANCE DEBIT	BALANCE CREDIT
19-- Dec. 5		G20	1240 50		1240 50	

ACCOUNT Accounts Receivable—Pelco Construction Co.   ACCOUNT NO. 109

DATE	EXPLANATION	POST. REF.	DEBIT	CREDIT	BALANCE DEBIT	BALANCE CREDIT
19-- Dec. 3		G20	402 80		402 80	

ACCOUNT Sales Tax Payable   ACCOUNT NO. 210

DATE	EXPLANATION	POST. REF.	DEBIT	CREDIT	BALANCE DEBIT	BALANCE CREDIT
19-- Dec. 1		G20		30 00		30 00
3		G20		22 80		52 80

ACCOUNT Sales   ACCOUNT NO. 401

DATE	EXPLANATION	POST. REF.	DEBIT	CREDIT	BALANCE DEBIT	BALANCE CREDIT
19-- Dec. 1		G20		500 00		500 00
3		G20		380 00		880 00
5		G20		1240 50		2120 50

Figure 11-2   Sales Transactions Recorded in a General Journal

it took only three cre̶ ̶s to generate all this, what would result from fifty credit sales? a hun ̶d? several hundred? Obviously, a business having many sales on account needs a system for journalizing and posting that is less time consuming. For a merchandising business having a large number of transactions, a more efficient accounting system involves the use of special journals.

Special journals are multicolumn journals that have columns reserved for the recording of specific types of transactions. Special journals simplify the journalizing and posting process. In most cases, the details of a transaction can be recorded on one line rather than the three or four lines needed for a general journal entry. Each special journal has special amount columns reserved for recording debits and credits to the general ledger accounts named in the column headings.

Four common special journals are the sales journal, the cash receipts journal, the purchases journal, and the cash payments journal.

1. The sales journal is used to record sales of merchandise on account.
2. The cash receipts journal is used to record all cash received by the business.
3. The purchases journal is used to record the purchase on account of any item—whether merchandise or supplies and equipment used in operating the business.
4. The cash payments journal is used to record all payments of cash. Since most businesses pay by check, all checks written are recorded in the cash payments journal.

The general journal is also needed in an accounting system using special journals. The general journal is used to record any transactions that do not fit into the special journals. Now let's look at how to record sales on account in a sales journal.

The Sales Journal

A **sales journal** is a special journal used to record only the sale of merchandise on account. Cash sales of merchandise are recorded in a special journal called a cash receipts journal. You will learn about the cash receipts journal in Chapter 12.

The sales journal used by Champion Building Products is shown in Figure 11-3. Like the general journal, the sales journal has a space for the page number and columns for the date and the posting reference. There is a separate column in which to record the sales slip number and a column in which to record the name of the charge customer. There are also three special amount columns.

			SALES JOURNAL			PAGE
DATE	SALES SLIP NO.	CUSTOMER'S ACCOUNT DEBITED	POST. REF.	SALES CREDIT	SALES TAX PAYABLE CREDIT	ACCOUNTS RECEIVABLE DEBIT

Figure 11-3 Sales Journal

The Sales Credit column is used to record the amount of the merchandise sold on account. Sales Tax Payable Credit column is used to record the amount of tax for a sale on account. The Accounts Receivable Debit column is used to record the total amount to be received from a customer for a sale on account. As you can see, the column headings indicate the general ledger accounts that are being debited and credited.

Journalizing Sales on Account

The information for Champion's first sale on account in December is as follows.

December 1: *Sold merchandise on account to Amy Anderson for $500.00 plus $30.00 sales tax, Sales Slip 80.*

The sales slip for this transaction appears in Figure 11-1 on page 215. To journalize the transaction in the sales journal, follow these steps. The sales journal entry for this transaction is shown in Figure 11-4.

1. Enter the sales slip date in the Date column.
2. Enter the sales slip number in the Sales Slip No. column.
3. Enter the name of the charge customer in the Customer's Account Debited column.
4. Enter the total selling price of the merchandise sold in the Sales Credit column. (This is the amount shown in the subtotal box of the sales slip.)
5. Enter the amount of the sales tax in the Sales Tax Payable Credit column.
6. Enter the total amount to be received from the charge customer in the Accounts Receivable Debit column. (This is the amount shown in the total box of the sales slip.)

		SALES JOURNAL				PAGE 12
DATE	SALES SLIP NO.	CUSTOMER'S ACCOUNT DEBITED	POST. REF.	SALES CREDIT	SALES TAX PAYABLE CREDIT	ACCOUNTS RECEIVABLE DEBIT
19-- Dec. 1	80	Amy Anderson		500 00	30 00	530 00
1	2	3		4	5	6

Figure 11-4 Recording a Sale on Account in the Sales Journal

You learned earlier that sales taxes are not imposed on sales of merchandise to government agencies. The next transaction involves such a sale.

December 5: *Sold merchandise on account to Norwin School District for $1,240.50, Sales Slip 82.*

There are only five steps involved in journalizing this transaction. The first four steps are the same as those for the sale on account to Amy Anderson. Step 5 is as follows:

5. Skip the Sales Tax Payable Credit column. Enter the total amount to be received from the customer in the Accounts Receivable Debit column.

For those sales that do not include a sales tax, the amounts entered in the Sales Credit column and in the Accounts Receivable Debit column are the same. This transaction is shown in Figure 11-5.

		SALES JOURNAL			PAGE 12	

	DATE	SALES SLIP NO.	CUSTOMER'S ACCOUNT DEBITED	POST. REF.	SALES CREDIT	SALES TAX PAYABLE CREDIT	ACCOUNTS RECEIVABLE DEBIT	
1	19-- Dec. 1	80	Amy Anderson		500 00	30 00	530 00	1
2	3	81	Pelco Construction Co.		380 00	22 80	402 80	2
3	5	82	Norwin School District		1 240 50		1 240 50	3
4								4
5	1	2	3		4		5	5

Figure 11-5   Recording a Sale Without Sales Tax in the Sales Journal

The Accounts Receivable Ledger

After a sale on account is journalized, it is posted to the customer's Accounts Receivable account. Businesses with only a few charge customers usually include an Accounts Receivable account for each customer in the general ledger. Large businesses, however, with many charge customers usually set up a separate ledger that contains accounts for all charge customers. This ledger is the **accounts receivable subsidiary ledger.** A **subsidiary ledger** is a ledger, or book, that is summarized in a controlling account in the general ledger. The accounts receivable subsidiary ledger is summarized in the Accounts Receivable account in the general ledger. Accounts Receivable is a **controlling account** because its balance must equal the total of all the account balances in the subsidiary ledger. The balance of Accounts Receivable thus serves as a control on the accuracy of the balances in the accounts receivable subsidiary ledger after posting.

The Accounts Receivable Subsidiary Ledger Form

The accounts receivable subsidiary ledger form used by Champion Building Products is shown in Figure 11-6.

Name						
Address						

DATE	EXPLANATION	POST. REF.	DEBIT	CREDIT	BALANCE

Figure 11-6   Subsidiary Ledger Account Form

Champion's subsidiary ledger account form has lines at the top for the name and address of the customer. In a manual accounting system, subsidiary ledger accounts are arranged in alphabetical order. They are not usually numbered. In a computerized system, however, each charge customer is assigned a specific account number.

Almost all companies that sell on credit keep an individual accounts receivable record for each customer. Most companies place these customer accounts in a separate accounts receivable subsidiary ledger.

Notice that the subsidiary ledger form has only three amount columns. The Debit and Credit columns are used to record increases and decreases to the customer's account, as on a general ledger account form. The subsidiary ledger form, however, has only one Balance column. Since the Accounts Receivable controlling account is an asset, customer accounts in the accounts receivable subsidiary ledger will normally always have debit balances.

Posting to the Accounts Receivable Subsidiary Ledger

To be certain that the balances in customers' accounts are always current, sales journal transactions are posted to the accounts receivable subsidiary ledger daily. To post a transaction from the sales journal to the customer's subsidiary ledger account, follow the steps on page 223. Refer to Figure 11-7, which shows the posting to Amy Anderson's account, as you read these steps.

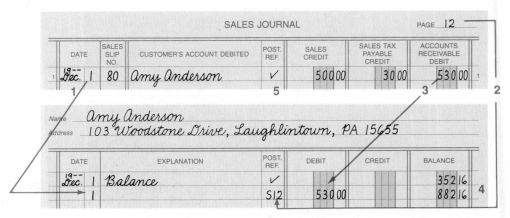

Figure 11-7 Posting a Sales Journal Entry to the Accounts Receivable Subsidiary Ledger

1. Enter the date of the transaction in the Date column of the subsidiary ledger account. Be sure to use the same date as in the journal entry.
2. Enter the letter of the journal and the page number on which the transaction was recorded in the Posting Reference column of the subsidiary ledger account. "S" is the letter used for the sales journal.
3. In the Debit column of the subsidiary ledger form, enter the total amount to be received from the customer, as recorded in the Accounts Receivable Debit column.

Prev. Bal.	$352.16
Debit	530.00
New Bal.	$882.16

4. Compute the new balance and enter it in the Balance column. To find the new balance, add the amount in the Debit column to the previous balance amount.
5. Return to the sales journal and enter a check mark (✔)in the Posting Reference column. The check mark indicates that this transaction has been posted to the accounts receivable subsidiary ledger. Champion Building Products uses a manual accounting system, so its subsidiary ledger accounts are not numbered. In a computerized accounting system, the customer's account number, rather than a check mark, would be entered in the Posting Reference column.

R E M E M B E R

When posting from a special journal, post information moving from left to right across the ledger form. By following this procedure, you are less likely to forget to enter all the information from the journal entry.

Before you learn how to complete the sales journal, do the following activity to check your understanding of the sales journal and the accounts receivable subsidiary ledger.

Check Your Learning

Use notebook paper to write your answers to these questions.

1. What type of transaction is recorded in the sales journal?
2. What does a check mark in the Posting Reference column of the sales journal indicate?
3. How often are sales journal entries posted to the accounts receivable subsidiary ledger?
4. What is a controlling account?
5. How does an accounts receivable subsidiary ledger account form differ from a general ledger account form?

Compare your answers to those in the answers section. Re-read the preceding part of the chapter to find the answers to any questions you may have missed.

Completing the Sales Journal

 All special journals have special amount columns in which debits and credits to frequently used accounts are recorded. The special amount columns in the sales journal are the Sales Credit, the Sales Tax Payable Credit, and the Accounts Receivable Debit columns. By recording transactions in these special columns, the accounting clerk can simply post the *column totals* to the general ledger accounts instead of posting each entry separately. Only three postings need to be made to the general ledger from the sales journal.

R E M E M B E R

The major characteristic of a special journal is that it saves time in posting.

Footing, Proving, Totaling, and Ruling the Sales Journal

Before amounts can be posted to the general ledger, the accounting clerk must calculate and verify the column totals. Here is the procedure for doing so. Use ink for all steps *except* Step 2.

1. Draw a single rule across the three amount columns, just below the last transaction.
2. Foot the amount columns. A **footing** is a column total written in small pencil figures. A footing must be verified. It is written in pencil so that it can be easily corrected if a mistake is discovered.
3. On a sheet of paper, test for the equality of debits and credits. The total of the debit column should equal the total of the two credit columns.

ACCOUNTING **Tips**
To lessen the risk of error, use a calculator, preferably one that prints out a tape to use in checking your work. Always clear the machine first.

Debit Column		Credit Columns	
Accounts Receivable	$13,328.45	Sales Tax Payable	$ 543.45
		Sales	12,785.00
Total	$13,328.45	Total	$13,328.45

4. In the Date column on the line below the single rule, enter the date on which the journal is being totaled.
5. On the same line in the Customer's Account Debited column, enter the word "Totals."
6. Enter the column totals — in ink — just below the footings.
7. Double-rule the three amount columns. A double rule, as you know, indicates that the totals have been verified.

The totaled and ruled sales journal for Champion Building Products is shown in Figure 11-8 on page 225.

After the sales journal has been footed, proved, totaled, and ruled, the column totals are posted to the general ledger.

SALES JOURNAL

PAGE 12

	DATE	SALES SLIP NO.	CUSTOMER'S ACCOUNT DEBITED	POST. REF.	SALES CREDIT	SALES TAX PAYABLE CREDIT	ACCOUNTS RECEIVABLE DEBIT	
1	19-- Dec. 1	80	Amy Anderson	✓	500 00	30 00	530 00	1
2	3	81	Pelco Construction Co.	✓	380 00	22 80	402 80	2
3	5	82	Norwin School District	✓	1240 50		1240 50	3
4	9	83	Lisa Whitmore	✓	60 00	3 60	63 60	4
5	11	84	St. Clair Roofing Co.	✓	3500 00	210 00	3710 00	5
6	13	85	Shawn Flannery	✓	75 00	4 50	79 50	6
7	15	86	Norwin School District	✓	1320 00		1320 00	7
8	17	87	Gateway School District	✓	750 00		750 00	8
9	21	88	Shawn Flannery	✓	230 00	13 80	243 80	9
10	22	89	Greensburg School Dist.	✓	417 00		417 00	10
11	24	90	Pelco Construction Co.	✓	112 00	6 72	118 72	11
12	27	91	St. Clair Roofing Co.	✓	1700 00	102 00	1802 00	12
13	28	92	Amy Anderson	✓	420 50	25 23	445 73	13
14	29	93	Lisa Whitmore	✓	130 00	7 80	137 80	14
15	30	94	St. Clair Roofing Co.	✓	1950 00	117 00	2067 00	15
16	31		Totals		12785 00	543 45	13328 45	16
17	4		5					17

Figure 11-8 Totaled and Ruled Sales Journal

R E M E M B E R

Use a pencil when first totaling the columns. If an error is made in adding the columns, penciled numbers are much easier to correct.

Posting the Total of the Sales Credit Column

The procedure for posting the total of the Sales Credit column to the Sales account in the general ledger is as follows. Refer to Figure 11-9 as you read the steps on page 226.

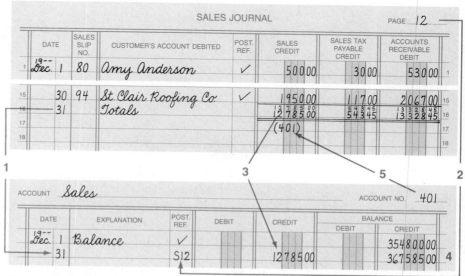

Figure 11-9 Posting the Sales Credit Total to the General Ledger Account

1. In the Date column of the Sales account in the general ledger, enter the date.
2. Enter the sales journal page number in the Posting Reference column. Remember to begin with the letter "S."
3. In the Credit column, enter the total from the Sales Credit column of the sales journal.

$354,800.00
+ 12,785.00
$367,585.00

4. Compute the new balance and enter it in the Credit Balance column. To determine the new balance, add the amount entered in the Credit column to the previous balance.
5. Return to the sales journal and enter the Sales account number — in parentheses — below the double rule in the Sales Credit column. This indicates that the column total has been posted to the general ledger account.

Posting the Total of the Sales Tax Payable Credit Column

The next total to be posted to the general ledger is that of the Sales Tax Payable Credit column. The steps in posting are listed below. The posting made to the general ledger account is shown in Figure 11-10.

1. In the Date column of the Sales Tax Payable account, enter the date.
2. Enter the sales journal page number in the Posting Reference column.

$ 852.15
+ 543.45
$1,395.60

3. In the Credit column, enter the total from the Sales Tax Payable Credit column of the sales journal.
4. Compute the new balance and enter it in the Credit Balance column.
5. Return to the sales journal and enter the Sales Tax Payable account number — in parentheses — below the double rule in the Sales Tax Payable Credit column.

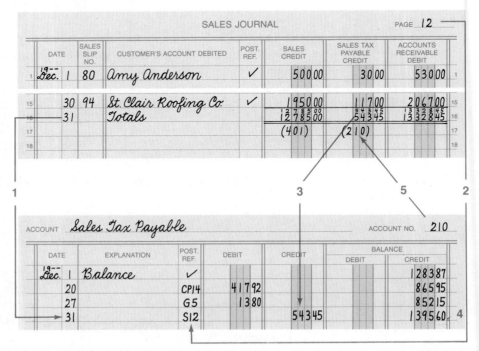

Figure 11-10 Posting the Sales Tax Payable Credit Total to the General Ledger Account

UNIT 3   The Accounting Cycle for a Merchandising Business

An account number in parentheses placed under a column total means that the column total has been posted to the general ledger account whose number is shown.

Posting the Total of the Accounts Receivable Debit Column

The last column of the sales journal to be posted to the general ledger is the Accounts Receivable Debit column. To complete the posting, follow the steps listed below. Refer to Figure 11-11 as you read these steps.

1. In the Date column of the Accounts Receivable account, enter the date.
2. Enter the sales journal page number in the Posting Reference column.
3. In the Debit column, enter the total from the Accounts Receivable Debit column of the sales journal.
4. Compute the new balance and enter it in the Debit Balance column.
5. Return to the sales journal and enter the account number of the Accounts Receivable account — in parentheses — below the double rule in the Accounts Receivable Debit column.

$ 9,380.36
+13,328.45
$22,708.81

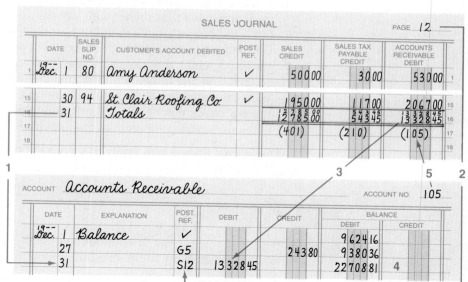

Figure 11-11 Posting the Accounts Receivable Debit Total to the General Ledger Account

Proving the Sales Journal at the End of a Page

The sales journal, like all special journals, is totaled and proved at the end of every month. Sometimes, however, a business has so many transactions in one month that it is impossible to fit them all on one journal page. When this occurs, the journal page is totaled and ruled before entries are recorded on the next page.

Follow the steps on page 228 to record the totals and carry them forward to the next page. These steps are illustrated in Figure 11-12 on page 228.

SALES JOURNAL

PAGE 12

	DATE	SALES SLIP NO.	CUSTOMER'S ACCOUNT DEBITED	POST. REF.	SALES CREDIT	SALES TAX PAYABLE CREDIT	ACCOUNTS RECEIVABLE DEBIT	
18	19-- Jan. 1	95	Norwin School District	✓	300 00		300 00	18
32	23	109	Lisa Whitmore	✓	120 00	7 20	127 20	32
33	24	110	Shawn Flannery	✓	180 00	10 80	190 80	33
34	24		Carried Forward	✓	3 150 00	189 00	3 339 00	34

SALES JOURNAL

PAGE 13

	DATE	SALES SLIP NO.	CUSTOMER'S ACCOUNT DEBITED	POST. REF.	SALES CREDIT	SALES TAX PAYABLE CREDIT	ACCOUNTS RECEIVABLE DEBIT	
1	19-- Jan. 24		Brought Forward	✓	3 150 00	189 00	3 339 00	1

Figure 11-12 Proving the Sales Journal at the End of a Page

1. Foot the amount columns and prove the equality of debits and credits.
2. Enter the date of the *last* transaction in the Date column.
3. In the Customer's Account Debited column, write "Carried Forward."
4. Place a check mark (✔) in the Posting Reference column. This check mark indicates that these totals are not to be posted.
5. Enter the column totals in ink.
6. On the next journal page, enter the new page number.
7. On line 1, enter the complete date (year, month, and day) in the Date column. Use the same date as on the last line of the previous page.
8. Write "Brought Forward" in the Customer's Account Debited column.
9. Place a check mark (✔) in the Posting Reference column.
10. Enter the column totals from the previous page on line 1.

The journal page is now ready to record the next transaction. These same steps would be followed for any special journal.

Check Your Learning

Write your answers to these questions on a sheet of paper.

1. How many column totals in the sales journal are posted to general ledger accounts at the end of the month?
2. Why are the amount columns in the sales journal footed at the end of the month?
3. How would you indicate that the total of the Sales Credit column has been posted to the general ledger account?
4. Is the total posted to the Accounts Receivable account from the sales journal entered in the Debit or Credit column?
5. When the column totals in the sales journal are carried forward to a new page, what is entered in the Posting Reference column?

Compare your answers to those in the answers section. Re-read the preceding part of the chapter to find the answers to any questions you missed.

UNIT 3   The Accounting Cycle for a Merchandising Business

Using the Computer to Record and Post Sales on Account

Many businesses today use computerized accounting systems to keep their records of sales on account. In a computerized accounting system, each charge customer is assigned an account number. Every time a sale on account is made, the customer's account number is written or imprinted on the sales slip, which is the source document for entering sales information into the computer.

In a computerized system, the accounts receivable subsidiary ledger is stored in the computer's memory. Information about a particular account is called out of memory or is added to the account using the customer's account number. In most computerized accounting systems, entries made to a customer's account are automatically posted to the controlling account. The balance in Accounts Receivable is, therefore, always up to date. Examples of computer-generated general and subsidiary ledger accounts related to sales on account are shown in Figure 11-13.

```
                    Champion Building Products, Inc.
                           General Ledger

            Account 105 Accounts Receivable

                                        Post.
    Date                                Ref.    Debit      Credit

    12/01 Beginning Balance                     9624.16
    12/27                                 G5                243.80
    12/31                                S12    13328.45
    12/31 Ending Balance                        22708.81


               Accounts Receivable Subsidiary Ledger

            Account 805 Amy Anderson

                                        Post.
    Date                                Ref.    Debit      Credit

    12/01 Beginning Balance                     352.16
    12/01 Sales Slip 80                  S12    530.00
    12/28 Sales Slip 92                  S12    445.73
    12/31 Ending Balance                        1327.89


            Account 835 Pelco Construction Co.

                                        Post.
    Date                                Ref.    Debit      Credit

    12/01 Beginning Balance                     3890.70
    12/03 Sales Slip 81                  S12    402.80
    12/24 Sales Slip 90                  S12    118.72
    12/31 Ending Balance                        4412.22
```

Figure 11-13 Computer-Generated General Ledger Accounts

Summary of Key Points

1. Retail firms buy merchandise to sell at a profit to consumers. Two of the accounts used by merchandising businesses are Merchandise Inventory and Sales.
2. A sales slip, prepared in multiple copies, lists the details of a sale on account. It is the source document for the journal entry.
3. Most states and some cities tax the retail sale of goods. Businesses collect these sales taxes and record them as a liability until they are paid to the state.
4. Special journals are used by businesses having a great many business transactions. The most common special journals are the sales journal, the cash receipts journal, the purchases journal, and the cash payments journal.
5. A sales journal is used to record all sales of merchandise on account.
6. The accounts receivable subsidiary ledger contains an account for each charge customer. The controlling account for this ledger is the Accounts Receivable account.
7. The individual amounts in the Accounts Receivable Debit column are posted daily to customer accounts in the accounts receivable subsidiary ledger.
8. At the end of the month, the totals of the special amount columns in the sales journal are posted to the accounts named in the column headings.
9. In a computerized accounting system, charge customers are assigned account numbers. The subsidiary ledger is stored in the computer's memory. All entries made to a customer's account are automatically posted to the controlling account in the general ledger.

11 Review and Applications

Building Your Accounting Vocabulary

In your own words, write the definition of each of the following accounting terms. Use complete sentences for your definitions.

accounts receivable
    subsidiary ledger
charge customer
controlling account
credit card
credit terms
footing

inventory
merchandise
merchandising
    business
retailer
sale on account

sales journal
sales slip
sales tax
special journal
subsidiary ledger
wholesaler

Reviewing Your Accounting Knowledge

1. How does a merchandising business differ from a service business?
2. What is the difference between a wholesaler and a retailer?
3. Classify the following accounts: Merchandise Inventory, Sales, and Sales Tax Payable.
4. What is the source document for recording sales on account in the sales journal?
5. What information is shown on a sales slip?
6. How does a merchandising business act as a collection agency for the state government?
7. What three accounts are affected by a sale on account?
8. When are special journals used in an accounting system?
9. Name and describe four commonly used special journals.
10. When are sales journal transactions posted to the accounts receivable subsidiary ledger?
11. Describe the procedure for totaling and proving the sales journal at the end of the month.
12. Describe the procedure for totaling and proving the sales journal at the end of a page.

Improving Your Math Skills

Percentages are used frequently in business. Sales taxes, discounts, interest rates, and income tax rates are just a few examples of the percentages used. Accountants especially must be able to calculate percentages with ease. Check your skill in using percentages by completing the following problems.

1. $6\frac{1}{2}\%$ of $1,185
2. 33% of $21,982
3. 12% of $2,400

4. $5\frac{1}{2}\%$ of $67.90
5. $7\frac{1}{4}\%$ of $2,000
6. $9\frac{3}{4}\%$ of $34,400

7. 122% of $8,920
8. $825 is ?% of $9,400
9. $441 is 6% of ?

Applying Accounting Procedures

Exercise 11-1   Computing Total Sales

Casey's Corner made the following sales on account during November. The state sales tax rate is 6%.

Sales Slip No.	Amount of Merchandise Sold	Sales Slip No.	Amount of Merchandise Sold
201	$300.00	207	80.00
202	95.00	208	400.00
203	150.00	209	40.00
204	30.00	210	115.00
205	500.00	211	310.00
206	225.00	212	750.00

Instructions: Use a form similar to the one that follows. For each transaction,

(1) Write the number of the sales slip in the first column.

(2) Write the total amount of merchandise sold in the Sales column.

(3) Compute the amount of the sales tax and enter it in the Sales Tax Payable column.

(4) Calculate the total amount of the sale and enter it in the Accounts Receivable column. The first transaction is completed as an example.

Sales Slip Number	Sales	Sales Tax Payable	Accounts Receivable
201	$300.00	$18.00	$318.00

Exercise 11-2   Identifying Special Journals

Instructions: Use a form similar to the one that follows. For each of the following transactions, identify the journal in which each transaction would be recorded by placing a check mark in the appropriate column. The first transaction is completed as an example.

Trans.	Sales Journal	Cash Receipts Journal	Purchases Journal	Cash Payments Journal	General Journal
1			✔		

Transactions:

1. Bought merchandise on account.
2. Received a payment from a charge customer.
3. Sold merchandise on credit.
4. Paid the utility bill for the month.
5. Received cash for merchandise sold.
6. Bought merchandise for cash.
7. Bought supplies on account.
8. Paid for merchandise purchased on account.
9. Bought store equipment and agreed to pay for it later.
10. Sold office equipment on account.
11. Recorded a correcting entry.

Exercise 11-3 Labeling Column Headings for the Sales Journal

Instructions: In the sales journal given below, label all the column headings.

SALES JOURNAL   Page____

Exercise 11-4 Opening a Customer Account

On March 17, Jim Jackson, 160 Grove Street, Pittsburgh, PA 15230, opened a charge account at Avon Home Center. On the same day, he purchased on account an electric garage door opener for $110.00 plus sales tax of $6.60. Avon Home Center recorded the transaction on sales journal page 4.

Instructions: Open an account in the accounts receivable subsidiary ledger for Jim Jackson. Then record the amount of the sale in the account.

Problem 11-1 Recording Transactions in a Sales Journal

The 1776 Shop is a retail merchandising store specializing in eighteenth century furniture. During the month of October, it had the following charge sales.

Instructions: Record the charge sales for the month of October on sales journal page 10.

Transactions:

Oct. 1 Sold a curio cabinet to Laura Todd for $190.00 plus a sales tax of $6.65, Sales Slip 606.

5 Sold to Harry Long an early American rocker for $180.00 plus a sales tax of $6.30, Sales Slip 607.

7 Sold a country quilt rack to Martha Adams, $37.00 plus sales tax of $1.30, Sales Slip 608.

10 Sold Alex Hamilton a spindle magazine rack for $44.00 plus $1.54 sales tax, Sales Slip 609.

15 Sold a coat tree to Laura Todd, for $48.00, sales tax $1.68, Sales Slip 610.

18 Sold a butler's cart to Alex Hamilton for $107.00 plus $3.75 sales tax, Sales Slip 611.

23 Sold Martha Adams a colonial arm chair, $63.00 plus sales tax of $2.21, Sales Slip 612.

25 Sold a wall mirror to Harry Long for $82.00, plus $2.87 sales tax, Sales Slip 613.

30 Sold to Martha Adams for $27.00 plus a sales tax of $0.95 a log storage rack, Sales Slip 614.

31 Sold a $13.00 fireplace popcorn popper to Laura Todd, sales tax $0.46, Sales Slip 615.

Problem 11-2 Posting to the Accounts Receivable Subsidiary Ledger

You will need the sales journal completed in Problem 11-1 for this problem.

Instructions: Using three-column account forms, post each entry in the sales journal to the individual accounts in the accounts receivable ledger. The opened customer accounts are included in the working papers.

Problem 11-3 Posting Column Totals to the General Ledger

Towne Auto Parts had the following sales on account during September.

Instructions:

(1) Record each transaction on page 12 of the sales journal.

(2) Foot, prove, total, and rule the sales journal.

(3) Post the totals from the sales journal to the general ledger accounts.

Transactions:

Sept. 1 Sold a heavy-duty car battery to Roxanne Stein for $70.00, plus sales tax of $4.20, Sales Slip 425.

3 Sold David Fink a truck bumper, $205.00 plus $12.30 sales tax, Sales Slip 426.

5 Sold to Lakeside Township Municipality $480.00 in welding equipment, no sales tax, Sales Slip 427.

8 Sold to Oklahoma City School District $375.00 in van parts, no sales tax, Sales Slip 428.

10 Sold a case of automobile wax to the Auto Spa for $150.00 plus sales tax of $9.00, Sales Slip 429.

12 Sold $120.00 in auto parts, plus $7.20 sales tax, to Jax Auto Body Shop, Sales Slip 430.

15 Sold to David Fink $110.00 in auto parts, plus $6.60 sales tax, Sales Slip 431.

17 Sold $420.00 in bus parts to Oklahoma City School District, no sales tax, Sales Slip 432.

19 Sold to the Auto Spa $200.00 in waxes and cleaners, sales tax $12.00, Sales Slip 433.

21 Sold $45.00 in automobile accessories to Roxanne Stein, $2.70 sales tax, Sales Slip 434.

27 Sold to Jax Auto Body Shop $85.00 worth of paints and thinners, sales tax $5.10, Sales Slip 435.

30 Sold $190.00 in parts and equipment to Lakeside Township Municipality, no sales tax, Sales Slip 436.

Problem 11-4 Proving the Sales Journal
at the End of a Page

Johnson the Florist sells flowers on a retail basis. Although most of its sales are for cash, some charge sales are also made. The sales tax rate is 3%. The first eight transactions in February have already been recorded. The following transactions are the remaining charge sales for February.

Instructions:

(1) Record the first four transactions on page 20 of the sales journal.

(2) Foot, prove, and total the sales journal at the end of page 20.

(3) Carry forward the column totals to page 21.

(4) Record the remaining transactions in the sales journal.

(5) Foot, prove, and total the sales journal at the end of February.

Transactions:

Feb. 15 Sold "Bear Balloons" to Cindy Adams, $15.00 plus sales tax of $0.45, Sales Slip 119.

17 Sold wall wreaths to the First National Bank for $220.00, sales tax $6.60, Sales Slip 120.

18 Sold to Lynn Dunmire a bouquet of flowers for $32.00 plus $0.96 sales tax, Sales Slip 121.

20 Sold a "Pick-Me-Up" basket to Larry Farina for $26.50 plus sales tax of $0.80, Sales Slip 122.

22 Sold Marcia Macko a potted plant for $8.90 plus $0.27 sales tax, Sales Slip 123.

23 Sold a miniature rose bush to Wes Wertz, $7.80 plus sales tax of $0.23, Sales Slip 124.

24 Sold to Peggy Zelno a $28.00 floral wreath, sales tax $0.84, Sales Slip 125.

25 Sold Edward Bollinger one dozen long-stemmed roses, $18.00 plus $0.54 sales tax, Sales Slip 126.

26 Sold "Bear Balloons" to Holly Mills for $15.00, plus sales tax of $0.45, Sales Slip 127.

28 Sold a $55.00 door wreath to Betty Thomas, sales tax $1.65, Sales Slip 128.

COMPUTER

PROBLEM

Problem 11-5   Recording and Posting Sales Transactions

The Pro Athlete, a retail sports supply store, has the following balances in the accounts receivable subsidiary ledger and the general ledger.

General Ledger (Partial)

Account Number		Account Balance
105	Accounts Receivable	$ 2,243.60
210	Sales Tax Payable	190.50
401	Sales	13,480.75

Accounts Receivable Subsidiary Ledger

Account Number		Account Balance
805	Arlington Heights High School, 3895 La Coste Boulevard, Arlington, TX 76107	$ 1,500.00
825	Bobbi Jo Gates, 350 Canyon Road, Houston, TX 77002	75.80
840	Jennifer Hope, 202 Casa View Drive, Abilene, TX 79604	110.50
860	Joseph Montoya, 1201 Blossom Lane, Dallas, TX 75221	248.90
870	Lou Ann Simmons, 1442 Cottonwood Road, Ft. Worth, TX 76101	308.40

Instructions:

(1) Open the three accounts in the general ledger and record the June 1 balances.

(2) Open the five accounts in the accounts receivable subsidiary ledger and record the June 1 balances.

(3) Record the following transactions on page 6 of the sales journal.

(4) Post each transaction to the accounts receivable subsidiary ledger.

(5) Foot, prove, total, and rule the sales journal.

(6) Post the column totals to the general ledger.

Transactions:

June 1 Sold a tent to Jennifer Hope for $120.00 plus sales tax of $6.30, Sales Slip 555.

3 Sold Joseph Montoya a $350.00 set of golf clubs, sales tax $18.38, Sales Slip 556.

7 Sold to Bobbi Jo Gates jogging shoes and a warm-up suit, $105.00 plus $5.51 sales tax, Sales Slip 557.

9 Sold a graphite racquetball racquet for $90.00 plus sales tax of $4.73 to Lou Ann Simmons, Sales Slip 558.

11 Sold Jennifer Hope an aerobic suit, $52.00 plus $2.73 sales tax, Sales Slip 559.

13 Sold football helmets to Arlington Heights High School, total $3,200.00, Sales Slip 560.

15 Sold a backpack and hiking boots, totaling $115.00 plus $6.04 sales tax, to Bobbi Jo Gates, Sales Slip 561.

18 Sold to Joseph Montoya a $230.00 crossbow and arrows, sales tax $12.08, Sales Slip 562.

21 Sold a racquetball gear bag to Lou Ann Simmons for $24.00, sales tax $1.26, Sales Slip 563.

24 Sold a $130.00 pacer exercise bicycle to Jennifer Hope, plus $6.83 sales tax, Sales Slip 564.

27 Sold a Maxi Gympac to Arlington Heights High School for $700.00, Sales Slip 565.

30 Sold Joseph Montoya a fishing tackle box, $21.00 plus $1.10 sales tax, Sales Slip 566.

CHALLENGE

PROBLEM

Problem 11-6 Locating and Correcting Errors in the Sales Journal

The Todaro Company posts transactions to the subsidiary ledger on a weekly basis. Before posting, however, the accounting supervisor checks all sales slips against the data entered in the sales journal. In April, a number of errors were discovered. You were asked to make the corrections.

Instructions:

(1) Compare each transaction described below with the sales journal entry. (The Todaro Company is located in a state with a 6% sales tax.)

(2) Correct any incorrect data.

(3) Foot, prove, total, and rule the sales journal.

Transactions:

Apr. 25 Suzette Simons purchased merchandise, $330.00, Sales Slip 3100.

25 On Sales Slip 3101, John Joyce bought $450.00 worth of merchandise.

26 Sold merchandise to Fred Woodburn on account, $170.00, Sales Slip 3102.

26 Sales Slip 3103, Carl Frost charged merchandise costing $200.00.

27 Bob Cummins purchased merchandise on account, $80.00, Sales Slip 3104.

28 Sold John Joyce merchandise on account, $30.00, Sales Slip 3105.

29 Sales Slip 3106, sold to Bob Cummins $425.00 of merchandise.

29 Carl Frost charged merchandise totaling $110.00, Sales Slip 3107.

30 Sold to Suzette Simons, Sales Slip 3108, merchandise, $90.00.

30 Sold merchandise to Fred Woodburn, $160.00, Sales Slip 3109.

*T*oday's CPA

Do you have a flair for working with numbers? Do you like interpreting facts and solving problems? If you do, you might want to consider a career as a certified public accountant. These professionals offer accounting advice and assistance to the public for a fee.

To become a certified public accountant (CPA), you'll need a bachelor's degree, a passing grade on a two-and-a-half day examination, plus a certificate from a state accountancy board. In 48 states, the board also requires an additional 40 hours of continuing education classwork a year. And, while not a written requirement, computer literacy is indispensable.

Over 300,000 CPAs practice in this country. Every year, about 10,000 new CPAs enter the field. Some are self-employed, but the majority work for accounting firms. Over half of the accountants entering the profession today are women.

CPAs have traditionally worked in the fields of taxation and auditing. Tax accountants prepare tax returns for their clients. Auditors verify the accuracy of financial statements prepared by business accountants.

Tax laws are becoming more demanding and small businesses are growing, and because of this, the demand for certified public accountants is increasing. This consumer demand is moving CPAs toward fields such as financial planning, computer auditing, tax law, or consulting services. In addition to being experts in accounting, CPAs may also need to be experts in a particular industry. CPAs who perform consulting services are increasingly being asked to participate in long-range planning, to give advice on marketing plans, to implement and evaluate computer systems, or to evaluate management personnel for promotion.

Today's CPAs play leading roles in a wide variety of industries.

Today's challenging business environment and computer technology are redefining the CPA profession. Public accounting firms that march to this different drummer are moving toward specialization. While this trend may require different employee qualifications, it can also present new opportunities to those of you who wish to enter the field in the coming years.

Chapter

ACCOUNTING FOR CASH RECEIPTS

In Chapter 11, you learned that many businesses record their business transactions in special journals. These journals streamline the journalizing and posting process through the use of special amount columns. The totals of the special amount columns are posted to the general ledger accounts at the end of the month.

In the last chapter, you were introduced to the first special journal, the sales journal. In this chapter, you will learn how to record various kinds of cash receipts in another special journal, a six-column cash receipts journal. You will also learn how to post from this journal to the general ledger and to the accounts receivable subsidiary ledger.

Learning Objectives

When you have completed Chapter 12, you should be able to do the following:

1. Journalize cash received by a business in a cash receipts journal.
2. Post from the cash receipts journal to the accounts receivable subsidiary ledger and to the general ledger.
3. Foot, prove, total, and rule a cash receipts journal.
4. Post column totals from the cash receipts journal to the general ledger.
5. Prepare a schedule of accounts receivable.
6. Define the accounting terms introduced in this chapter.

New   Terms

cash receipt
receipt
cash sale
bank card
cash discount
contra account
cash receipts journal
schedule of accounts
    receivable

Kinds of Cash Receipts

The cash received by a business is referred to as a **cash receipt.** The three most common sources of cash for a merchandising business are cash received from charge customers, cash sales, and bank card sales. Cash is also received, though much less frequently, from such transactions as the sale of an asset other than merchandise. Let's look at how these four kinds of cash receipts are handled.

Cash from Charge Customers

When a business receives a payment on account from a charge customer, that payment must be recorded. The business does so by first preparing a receipt. A **receipt,** shown in Figure 12-1, is a form that serves as a record of cash received.

Like sales slips, receipts are prenumbered and may be prepared in multiple copies. Champion Building Products prepares a receipt as the source document for the journal entry of the transaction.

Figure 12-1   Receipt for Cash Received from a Charge Customer

As you can see, the receipt lists the date the cash was received, the customer's name, the amount received, and an explanation of the transaction.

Cash Sales

A **cash sale** is a transaction in which a business receives full payment for the merchandise sold *at the time of the sale.* The proof of sale and the source document generated by this type of transaction differ from those for a sale on account.

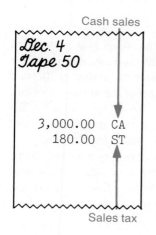

Most retailers use a cash register to record (or "register") cash sales. Instead of using preprinted sales slips, records of cash sales are made on two rolls of tape inside the cash register. When a cash sale occurs, the details of the sale are printed on the two tapes at the same time. One tape is fed outside the machine, torn off, and handed to the customer as a receipt. The other tape remains in the register.

At the end of the day, the cash register is totaled and cleared. The total cash sales for the day and the total sales taxes collected on those sales are listed on the cash register tape. The tape also shows the total charge sales for the day. A proof is usually prepared to show that the amount of cash in the cash register equals the amount of cash sales recorded on the cash register tape. The proof and the tape are sent to the accounting clerk, who uses

Most retail merchandising stores today accept bank cards and, of course, cash in payment for merchandise sold.

the tape as the source document for the journal entry to record the day's cash sales.

Bank Card Sales

Many businesses today allow customers to use bank cards to buy merchandise. A **bank card** is a credit card issued by a bank and honored by many businesses. Bank cards are a sort of "super credit card" since they are accepted by many different businesses. The most widely used bank cards in North America are VISA® and MasterCard®.

Bank card sales are processed differently from a store's regular charge card sales. It is important to remember that a bank card holder has an account with the bank that issued the card, not with the business or businesses where the card is used. The bank pays the business and the bank card customer pays the bank. The business receives cash from the bank soon after it deposits its bank card sales slips. The business does not have to wait until the bank collects from the card holder. Bank card sales, therefore, are recorded as though they were cash sales.

When a bank card sale occurs, the sales clerk at Champion Building Products completes a multicopy bank card sales slip. The sales slip is inserted into the cash register, which records the details of the sale on both the sales slip and the cash register tape. When the cash register is totaled at the end of the day, the total bank card sales and the sales taxes for those sales are listed on the cash register tape. Since the cash register tape includes the bank card sales, those sales are included on the daily cash proof. Bank card sales are journalized from the same tape as the cash sales for the day.

Champion deposits all bank card sales slips in its checking account, using a special deposit slip. In its records, Champion treats deposits of bank card sales the same as cash deposits. There is, however, often a three- to four-day delay before the amount of the deposit is credited to Champion's checking

Bank card sales

Dec. 4
Tape 50

700.00 BCS
42.00   ST

Sales tax

account. This delay occurs because Champion's bank must collect from the other banks that issued the bank cards used by Champion's customers.

R E M E M B E R

The bank card holder has an account with the bank that issued the card, not with the business or businesses where the card is used.

Other Cash Receipts

Most of the cash receipts of a merchandising business result from the sale of merchandise. Cash may also be received from other transactions such as the sale of other assets or a loan from a bank. These types of cash transactions occur infrequently in most merchandising businesses.

When such transactions do occur, a receipt is prepared to indicate the source of the cash received. This receipt is similar to that prepared for cash received from a charge customer. All the information needed for the journal entry, however, is listed on the explanation line.

Cash Discounts

To encourage customers to pay promptly, some merchandising businesses offer a cash discount to their charge customers. A **cash discount** is the amount a customer can deduct if the merchandise is paid for within a certain time. A cash discount is an advantage to both buyer and seller. The buyer gets merchandise at a reduced cost; the seller receives cash quickly.

Businesses do not automatically offer cash discounts to all their customers. Some businesses may offer cash discounts only to their business customers. Champion offers a cash discount only to certain charge customers who buy merchandise in large quantities. Its credit terms for such customers are stated as *2/10, n/30.* This means that the customer can deduct 2% of the cost of the merchandise if it pays for the merchandise within 10 days of the sale date. Otherwise, the net (full) amount must be paid within 30 days. A cash discount, then, decreases the amount the business actually receives from the sale. Let's look at an example.

On December 5, Champion sold $1,240.50 worth of merchandise on account to the Norwin School District. In the sales journal, this transaction was recorded as a $1,240.50 credit to Sales and a $1,240.50 debit to Accounts Receivable. If Norwin pays within 10 days (by December 15), Champion will actually receive only $1,215.69, or the original price less the cash discount of $24.81 ($1,240.50 × 2%). Which accounts are involved in this cash receipt transaction?

Net amount	$1,240.50
Discount	− 24.81
Amount received	$1,215.69

Cash in Bank would be debited for $1,215.69, the amount of cash actually received. Accounts Receivable would be credited for the full $1,240.50 because the customer has paid for the merchandise that was sold. What happens to the discount amount?

The $24.81 discount could be debited to the Sales account since Champion will receive less revenue from this transaction than originally recorded. Instead, a separate account is used to have a complete record of all discounts taken by customers. The discount amount is entered in an account called Sales Discounts.

As you know, the normal balance side of the Sales account is the credit side. A cash discount, however, reduces the revenue earned from sales. The normal balance side of the Sales Discounts account, then, is the *debit* side.

Sales			Sales Discounts	
Dr.	Cr.		Dr.	Cr.
–	+		+	–
Decrease Side	Increase Side		Increase Side	Decrease Side
	Balance Side		Balance Side	

Accounts such as Sales Discounts are called contra accounts. A **contra account** is an account whose balance is a decrease in (is "*contra*ry to") another account's balance.

When the sale is made, a business does not know whether a charge customer will take advantage of the cash discount. A cash discount, therefore, can be recorded only when the customer actually pays for the merchandise within the time allowed. If sales taxes were paid, the discount is calculated on the amount of the merchandise sold, before taxes are added.

R E M E M B E R

Sales Discounts is a contra revenue account. Its normal balance is a debit balance.

Before going any further, do the following activity to check your understanding of the material you have just studied.

Check Your Learning

Write your answers to these questions on notebook paper.

1. What is the source document for the journal entry to record cash received from a charge customer? for a cash sale? for a bank card sale?
2. What is the normal balance side of the Sales Discounts account? Why?
3. The Phone Center's credit terms are 3/15, n/30. On April 2, it sold $3,500 worth of merchandise to a charge customer. The customer paid for the merchandise on April 8, taking advantage of the discount. What was the discount amount? How much cash was received?

Compare your answers to those in the answers section. Re-read the preceding part of the chapter to find the correct answers to any questions you may have missed.

The Cash Receipts Journal

As you already know, when a business has a great many transactions, it can save time by using special journals. One special journal used is the sales journal; another is the cash receipts journal.

The **cash receipts journal** is a special journal used to record all transactions in which cash is received. The number of special amount columns varies, depending upon a business's needs. Every transaction recorded in the journal, however, requires a debit to the Cash in Bank account. The cash receipts journal, therefore, always includes a Cash in Bank Debit column.

The cash receipts journal used by Champion Building Products is shown in Figure 12-2. In addition to the date, source document, account title, and posting reference columns, it contains six amount columns. The General Credit column is used to record credits to accounts for which there is no special column. The amount of merchandise sold in cash and bank card sales is recorded in the Sales Credit column. The sales taxes collected for cash and bank card sales are entered in the Sales Tax Payable Credit column. The Accounts Receivable Credit column is used to record payments from charge customers. The Sales Discounts Debit column is used to record the amount of any cash discount taken by a charge customer. The Cash in Bank Debit column is used to record the amount of cash actually received.

CASH RECEIPTS JOURNAL

PAGE ______

	DATE	DOC. NO.	ACCOUNT TITLE	POST. REF.	GENERAL CREDIT	SALES CREDIT	SALES TAX PAYABLE CREDIT	ACCOUNTS RECEIVABLE CREDIT	SALES DISCOUNTS DEBIT	CASH IN BANK DEBIT	
1											1
2											2

Figure 12-2 Cash Receipts Journal

The entries in the Accounts Receivable Credit column are posted individually during the month to charge customers' accounts in the accounts receivable subsidiary ledger. The entries in the General Credit column are posted individually during the month to the general ledger accounts. At the end of the month, the totals of all the special amount columns are posted to the general ledger accounts named in the column headings.

Journalizing Cash Receipts

Now let's look at how various types of cash receipt transactions are recorded in the cash receipts journal.

Journalizing Cash from Charge Customers

Champion's first cash receipt transaction for December is cash received from a charge customer. The source document for this transaction is the receipt in Figure 12-1 on page 239.

December 1: *Received $79.30 from Lisa Whitmore on account, Receipt 301.*

The accounts affected by this transaction are Cash in Bank and Accounts Receivable. Since Cash in Bank is being increased, it is debited for the amount of cash received, $79.30. Champion Building Products now expects to receive less money, so Accounts Receivable is being decreased. It is credited for $79.30.

The entry for this transaction is shown in Figure 12-3. Follow these steps when journalizing cash received from charge customers:

1. Enter the date of the receipt in the Date column.
2. Enter the receipt number in the Document Number column. Write the letter "R" (for receipt) in front of the receipt number.
3. Enter the name of the charge customer in the Account Title column.
4. Enter the amount received in the Accounts Receivable Credit column.
5. Enter the amount of cash received in the Cash in Bank Debit column.

The Posting Reference column will be completed when this entry is posted to the customer's account in the accounts receivable subsidiary ledger.

		CASH RECEIPTS JOURNAL								PAGE 14	
DATE	DOC. NO.	ACCOUNT TITLE	POST. REF.	GENERAL CREDIT	SALES CREDIT	SALES TAX PAYABLE CREDIT	ACCOUNTS RECEIVABLE CREDIT	SALES DISCOUNTS DEBIT	CASH IN BANK DEBIT		
19-- Dec. 1	R301	Lisa Whitmore					79 30		79 30		1
1	2	3					4		5		2

Figure 12-3   Recording Cash Received from a Charge Customer in the Cash Receipts Journal

Journalizing Cash Received on Account, Less a Cash Discount

The second cash receipt transaction involves a cash discount.

December 2: *Received $1,166.20 from Greensburg School District in payment of Sales Slip 72 for $1,190.00, less the discount of $23.80, Receipt 302.*

The accounts affected are Cash in Bank, Sales Discounts, and Accounts Receivable. Cash in Bank is being increased, so it is debited for $1,166.20, the amount of cash actually received. The Sales Discounts account is being increased. It is debited for $23.80, the amount of the cash discount. Payments on account from charge customers decrease Accounts Receivable. That account is credited for the *entire* amount of the original transaction, $1,190.00.

Follow these steps when journalizing cash receipts involving a cash discount. The journal entry for this transaction is shown on line 2 of Figure 12-4.

1. Enter the date of the receipt in the Date column.
2. Enter the receipt number in the Document Number column.
3. Enter the name of the charge customer in the Account Title column.

4. Enter the amount of the original transaction in the Accounts Receivable Credit column.
5. Enter the cash discount amount in the Sales Discounts Debit column.
6. Enter the actual amount of cash received in the Cash in Bank Debit column.

	DATE	DOC. NO.	ACCOUNT TITLE	POST. REF.	GENERAL CREDIT	SALES CREDIT	SALES TAX PAYABLE CREDIT	ACCOUNTS RECEIVABLE CREDIT	SALES DISCOUNTS DEBIT	CASH IN BANK DEBIT	
1	19-- Dec. 1	R301	Lisa Whitmore					79 30		79 30	1
2	2	R302	Greensburg School Dist.					1190 00	23 80	1166 20	2
3	4	T50	Cash Sales	—		3000 00	180 00			3180 00	3
4	4	T50	Bank Card Sales	—		700 00	42 00			742 00	4
5	6	R303	Store Equipment		50 00					50 00	5

CASH RECEIPTS JOURNAL — PAGE 14

Figure 12-4 Recording Transactions in the Cash Receipts Journal

R E M E M B E R

When journalizing a cash receipt transaction with a sales discount, be sure to credit Accounts Receivable for the total amount of the original sales transaction.

Journalizing Cash Sales

As a rule, businesses journalize cash sales and make cash deposits daily. In this chapter, however, we will assume that Champion Building Products records its cash sales every two weeks.

December 4: Sold merchandise for $3,000.00 cash, plus $180.00 sales taxes, Tape 50.

The accounts affected by this transaction are Cash in Bank, Sales, and Sales Tax Payable. Cash in Bank is being increased. It is debited for $3,180.00, the cash received for the merchandise sold ($3,000.00) plus the sales taxes collected ($180.00). Sales is also being increased. It is credited for $3,000.00, the amount of merchandise sold. Sales Tax Payable is being increased since more money is now owed to the state. It is credited for $180.00.

The journal entry for this transaction is shown in Figure 12-4, line 3. The source document for the transaction is the cash register tape shown on page 239.

1. Enter the date written on the cash register tape in the Date column.
2. Enter the number of the tape in the Document Number column. Place a "T" (for tape) before the number.
3. Enter the words "Cash Sales" in the Account Title column.
4. Enter a dash in the Posting Reference column. The amounts recorded for cash sales are posted as part of the column totals at the end of the

month. The dash indicates that the entry is not posted individually to the general ledger accounts.

5. Enter the amount of merchandise sold in the Sales Credit column.
6. Enter the amount of sales taxes collected in the Sales Tax Payable Credit column.
7. Enter the total cash received in the Cash in Bank Debit column.

Journalizing Bank Card Sales

How often a business records bank card sales and deposits its bank card sales slips depends on the number of bank card sales it has. In this textbook, we will assume that Champion Building Products processes bank card sales every two weeks.

We mentioned earlier that a bank card sale is a form of cash sale. As you learn how to journalize bank card sales, notice the similarities between the two entries.

December 4: *Had bank card sales of $700.00, plus $42.00 sales taxes, Tape 50.*

The accounts affected are Cash in Bank, Sales, and Sales Tax Payable. Since the business receives cash when the bank card sales slips are deposited, Cash in Bank is being increased. It is debited for $742.00, the amount of merchandise sold ($700.00) plus the sales taxes on that merchandise ($42.00). Sales is also being increased. It is credited for $700.00, the total of the merchandise sold. Sales Tax Payable is being increased; it is credited for $42.00.

The journal entry for this transaction is shown in Figure 12-4, line 4. The source document for the entry is the cash register tape illustrated on page 240.

1. Enter the date of the cash register tape in the Date column.
2. Enter the number of the tape in the Document Number column. Remember to record a "T" before the number.
3. Enter the words "Bank Card Sales" in the Account Title column.
4. Enter a dash in the Posting Reference column. The bank card sales amounts are also posted to the general ledger as part of the column totals.
5. Enter the amount of merchandise sold in the Sales Credit column.
6. Enter the amount of sales taxes collected in the Sales Tax Payable Credit column.
7. Enter the total cash received in the Cash in Bank Debit column.

Journalizing Other Cash Receipts

Occasionally, a business will receive cash from a transaction that does not involve the sale of merchandise. However, since the business is receiving cash, the transaction is still entered in the cash receipts journal.

December 6: *Received $50.00 cash from Mandy Owens, an employee, for shelving no longer used by the business, Receipt 303.*

According to Bankcard Holders of America, there are more than 800 million charge cards and bank cards in use today.

The accounts affected are Cash in Bank and Store Equipment. Cash in Bank is being increased by the amount received for the shelving, so it is debited for $50.00. Since Champion no longer owns the shelving, Store Equipment is being decreased and is credited for $50.00.

The journal entry for this transaction is shown on line 5 of Figure 12-4 on page 245.

1. Enter the date of the receipt in the Date column.
2. Enter the receipt number in the Document Number column.
3. Enter the title of the account credited in the Account Title column.
4. Enter the amount of the credit in the General Credit column. The General Credit column is used whenever the credit part of the entry cannot be entered in any other special amount column.
5. Enter the amount of cash received in the Cash in Bank Debit column.

Before you go any further, do the following activity to check your understanding of the material you have just studied.

Check Your Learning

Use notebook paper to write your answers to the questions about the following cash receipt transactions of Horizon Leather Goods.

1. On July 3, received $75.00 on account from Brooke Powell, Receipt 311. What should be entered in the Document Number column of the cash receipts journal?
2. On July 6, received $25.00 cash from Paul Robbins for a filing cabinet no longer used by the company, Receipt 312. In which column would the $25.00 credit be entered?
3. Cash sales for the week ended July 7 were $1,790.00, plus $89.50 in sales taxes, Tape 41. What amount should be recorded in the Sales Credit column?
4. Bank card sales for the week ended July 7 were $1,225.00, plus sales taxes of $61.25, Tape 41. How would you show that these amounts are not posted individually to the general ledger?
5. On July 10, received $923.44 on account from Stylecraft, Inc., in payment of Sales Slip 247 for $952.00, less a 3% cash discount of $28.56, Receipt 313. What amount should be recorded in the Cash in Bank Debit column?

Compare your answers to those in the answers section. Re-read the preceding part of the chapter to find the correct answers to any questions you may have missed.

Posting from the Cash Receipts Journal

During the month, two kinds of postings are made from the cash receipts journal. Cash receipts from charge customers are posted to the customer accounts in the accounts receivable subsidiary ledger. Entries in the General Credit column relating to cash receipts are posted to the appropriate general ledger accounts.

Posting to the Accounts Receivable Subsidiary Ledger

The amounts entered in the Accounts Receivable Credit column are posted to the accounts receivable subsidiary ledger daily. This ensures that customer accounts are always up to date.

To post a cash receipt transaction to an account in the accounts receivable subsidiary ledger, follow these steps. Refer to Figure 12-5 as you read the steps.

1. Enter the date of the transaction in the Date column of the subsidiary ledger account.
2. Enter the letter of the journal and the page number on which the entry is recorded in the Posting Reference column. Use the letters "CR" for the cash receipts journal.
3. In the Credit column, enter the amount shown in the Accounts Receivable Credit column.
4. Compute the new balance and enter it in the Balance column. If the account has a zero balance, draw a line through the Balance column.
5. Return to the cash receipts journal and enter a check mark in the Posting Reference column.

Prev. Bal. $79.30
Credit   −79.30
New Bal. $ 0.00

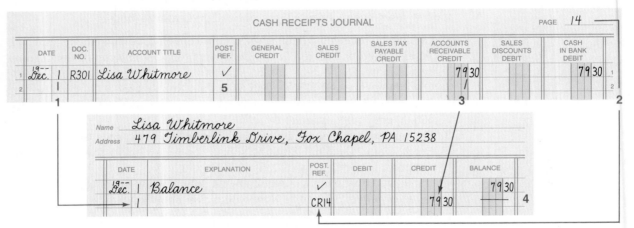

Figure 12-5 Posting from the Cash Receipts Journal to the Accounts Receivable Subsidiary Ledger

Follow these steps for all transactions that must be posted to the accounts receivable subsidiary ledger. Figure 12-6, on pages 249-250, shows the complete accounts receivable subsidiary ledger after all the entries in the cash receipts journal have been posted. Notice that the accounts include entries from both the sales journal and the cash receipts journal.

R E M E M B E R

When posting from the cash receipts journal to the accounts receivable subsidiary ledger, be sure to post the amount recorded in the Accounts Receivable Credit column.

UNIT 3   The Accounting Cycle for a Merchandising Business

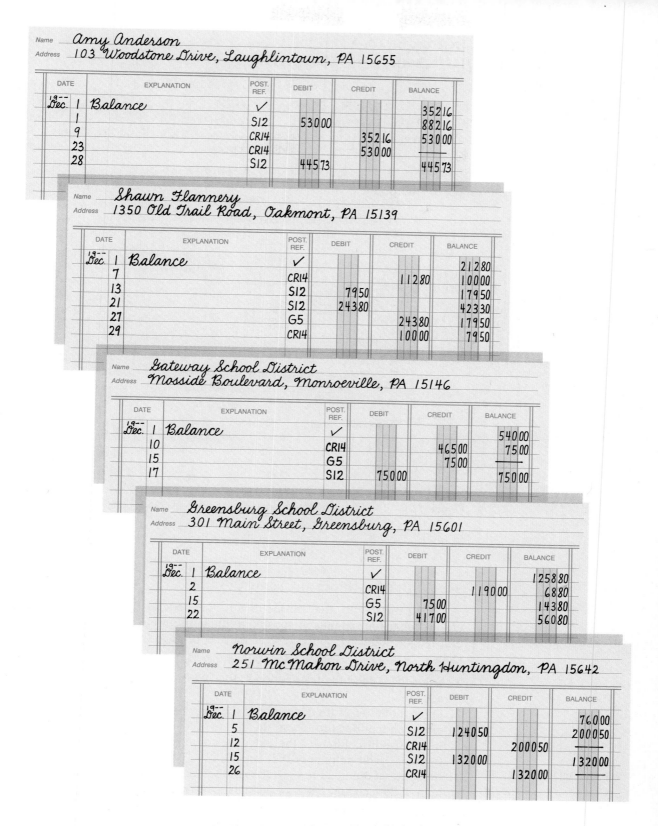

Figure 12-6 The Completed Accounts Receivable Subsidiary Ledger

DATE	EXPLANATION	POST. REF.	DEBIT	CREDIT	BALANCE
19-- Dec. 1	Balance	✓			3890 70
3		S12	402 80		4293 50
15		CR14		3890 70	402 80
24		S12	118 72		521 52

Name   *St. Clair Roofing Co.*
Address   *12 Mulberry Hill Road, Latrobe, PA 15650*

DATE	EXPLANATION	POST. REF.	DEBIT	CREDIT	BALANCE
19-- Dec. 1	Balance	✓			2530 40
10		CR14		2530 40	—
11		S12	3710 00		3710 00
21		CR14		3710 00	—
27		S12	1802 00		1802 00
30		S12	2067 00		3869 00

Name   *Lisa Whitmore*
Address   *479 Timberlink Drive, Fox Chapel, PA 15238*

DATE	EXPLANATION	POST. REF.	DEBIT	CREDIT	BALANCE
19-- Dec. 1	Balance	✓			79 30
1		CR14		79 30	—
9		S12	63 60		63 60
19		CR14		63 60	—
29		S12	137 80		137 80

Figure 12-6 The Completed Accounts Receivable Subsidiary Ledger (Concluded)

Posting the General Credit Column

During the month, the transactions in the General Credit column of the cash receipts journal must be posted to the appropriate accounts in the general ledger. Refer to Figure 12-7 at the top of page 251 as you read these steps.

1. Enter the date of the transaction in the Date column of the general ledger account.
2. Enter the letter of the journal and the page number in the Posting Reference column. Be sure to use the letters "CR."
3. In the Credit column of the ledger account, enter the amount from the General Credit column of the journal.
4. Compute and enter the new account balance in the proper Balance column. If the account has a zero balance, draw a line through the appropriate Balance column.
5. Return to the cash receipts journal and enter the general ledger account number in the Posting Reference column.

Prev. Bal.	$26,277.45
Credit	− 50.00
New Bal.	$26,227.45

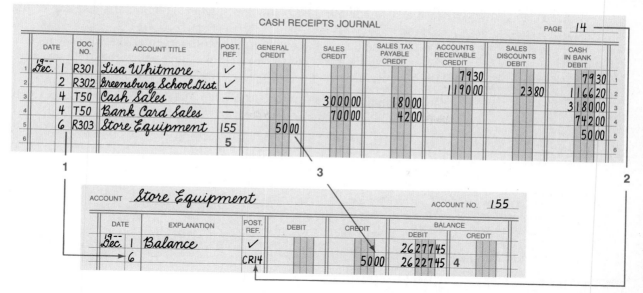

Figure 12-7 Posting from the General Credit Column of the Cash Receipts Journal

The cash receipts journal entry for the December 6 transaction is now complete. All transactions recorded in the General Credit column are posted in the same manner.

Completing the Cash Receipts Journal

As with the sales journal, the cash receipts journal must be footed, proved, totaled, and ruled at the end of the month. The totals of the special amount columns are then posted to the general ledger.

In a manual accounting system, these end-of-the-month tasks are completed by accounting clerks. In a computerized system, the computer can simply be instructed to total the journal and post the data stored in the system.

Totaling, Proving, and Ruling the Cash Receipts Journal

To complete the cash receipts journal, follow the procedures on this page and on page 252:

1. Draw a single rule across the six amount columns, just below the last transaction.
2. Foot the columns.
3. Test for the equality of debits and credits.

Debit Columns		
Sales Discounts	$	180.11
Cash in Bank		26,627.35
		_____
		$26,807.46

Credit Columns		
General	$	75.00
Sales		9,800.00
Sales Tax Payable		588.00
Accounts Receivable		16,344.46
		_____
		$26,807.46

4. In the Date column, just below the single rule, enter the last day of the month.
5. On the same line in the Account Title column, enter the word "Totals."
6. Enter the verified column totals — in ink — just below the footings.
7. Double-rule the amount columns.

The completed journal page is shown in Figure 12-8. The column totals can now be posted to the general ledger.

CASH RECEIPTS JOURNAL PAGE _____

	DATE	DOC. NO.	ACCOUNT TITLE	POST. REF.	GENERAL CREDIT	SALES CREDIT	SALES TAX PAYABLE CREDIT	ACCOUNTS RECEIVABLE CREDIT	SALES DISCOUNTS DEBIT	CASH IN BANK DEBIT	
1	19-- Dec 1	R301	Lisa Whitmore	✓				79 30		79 30	1
2	2	R302	Greensburg School Dist.	✓				1190 00	23 80	1166 20	2
3	4	T50	Cash Sales	—		3000 00	180 00			3180 00	3
4	4	T50	Bank Card Sales	—		700 00	42 00			742 00	4
5	6	R303	Store Equipment	155	50 00					50 00	5
6	7	R304	Shawn Flannery	✓				112 80		112 80	6
7	9	R305	Amy Anderson	✓				352 16		352 16	7
8	10	R306	Gateway School Dist.	✓				465 00	9 30	455 70	8
9	10	R307	St. Clair Roofing Co.	✓				2530 40	47 74	2482 66	9
10	12	R308	Norwin School District	✓				2000 50		2000 50	10
11	15	R309	Pelco Construction Co.	✓				3890 70		3890 70	11
12	16	R310	Supplies	115	25 00					25 00	12
13	18	T51	Cash Sales	—		2500 00	150 00			2650 00	13
14	18	T51	Bank Card Sales	—		400 00	24 00			424 00	14
15	19	R311	Lisa Whitmore	✓				63 60		63 60	15
16	21	R312	St. Clair Roofing Co.	✓				3710 00	70 00	3640 00	16
17	23	R313	Amy Anderson	✓				530 00		530 00	17
18	26	R314	Norwin School District	✓				1320 00	26 40	1293 60	18
19	29	R315	Shawn Flannery	✓				100 00		100 00	19
20	31	T52	Cash Sales	—		2700 00	162 00			2862 00	20
21	31	T52	Bank Card Sales	—		500 00	30 00			530 00	21
22	31		Totals		75 00 / 75 00	9800 00 / 9800 00	588 00 / 588 00	16344 46 / 16344 46	177 24 / 177 24	26630 22 / 26630 22	22

Figure 12-8 Totaled Cash Receipts Journal

R — E — M — E — M — B — E — R

Column totals are written in pencil first. Verified totals are written in ink.

Posting Column Totals to the General Ledger

There are six amount columns in the cash receipts journal used by Champion Building Products. Only five of the column totals, however, are posted to the general ledger. The total of the General Credit column is *not* posted. The entries in this column have already been posted to the general ledger accounts. To indicate that the total of this column is not posted, place a check mark in parentheses below the double rule in the General Credit column.

As shown in Figure 12-9, the totals of the other five amount columns are posted to the general ledger accounts named in the column headings. The column heading indicates whether the amount is to be posted to the Debit

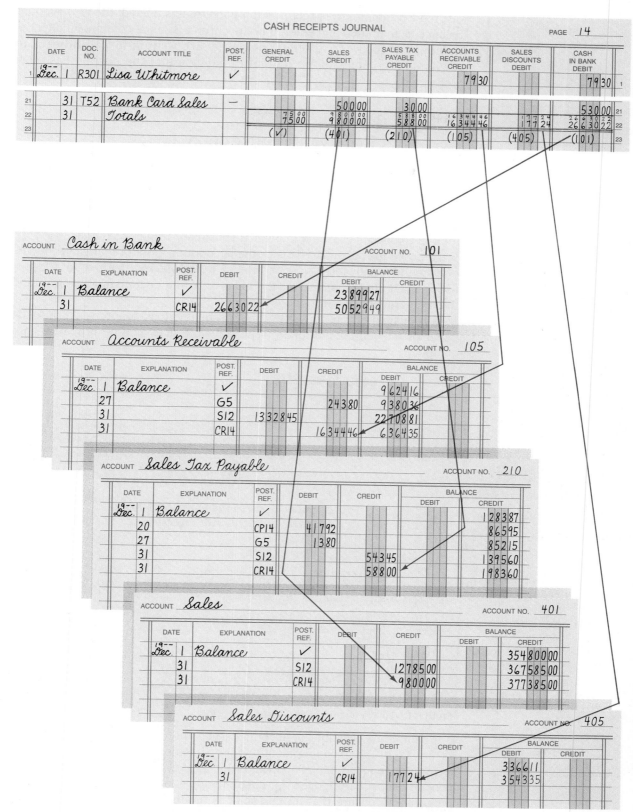

Figure 12-9 Posting Column Totals from the Cash Receipts Journal

or Credit column of the account. After each total is posted, the new account balance is computed and entered in the correct Balance column. Finally, the numbers of the general ledger accounts are written in parentheses in the amount columns of the journal to indicate that the posting has been completed.

Proving the Accounts Receivable Subsidiary Ledger

The Accounts Receivable account is the controlling account for the accounts receivable subsidiary ledger. That is, it summarizes all the customer accounts in the subsidiary ledger. At the end of the month, after the posting has been completed, the balance of Accounts Receivable should equal the total of the balances of the individual subsidiary ledger accounts.

To prove the subsidiary ledger, the accounting clerk prepares a schedule of accounts receivable. A **schedule of accounts receivable** is a report listing each charge customer, the balance in the customer's account, and the total amount due from all customers.

In a manual accounting system, the schedule may be prepared on plain paper or accounting stationery. The schedule may also be prepared on a computer.

ACCOUNTING **Tips**
When tracking an error, start at the end and work backward.
1. Re-add the balances in the schedule of accounts receivable.
2. Check the balances against the subsidiary ledger accounts.
3. Verify each customer's account balance.
4. Check the postings from the sales and cash receipts journals.
5. Verify the balance of the Accounts Receivable account.
6. Check the totals posted from the sales and cash receipts journals.

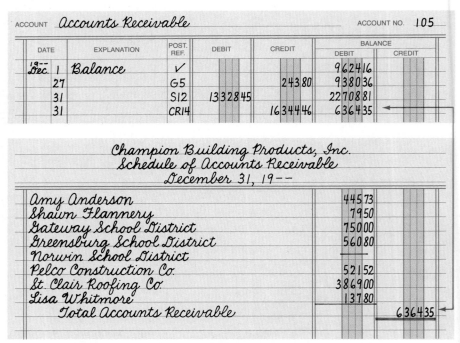

Figure 12-10 Schedule of Accounts Receivable

Champion's schedule of accounts receivable for December is shown in Figure 12-10. The heading identifies the statement and the date. Customer accounts are listed in alphabetical order, as they appear in the accounts receivable subsidiary ledger. All customers are listed, even those with zero balances, to ensure that no customer is omitted by mistake. According to the schedule, the total amount to be received from all customers is

$6,364.35. As you can see, this total matches the balance of the Accounts Receivable account in the general ledger. The accounts receivable subsidiary ledger has, therefore, been proved.

Using the Computer with Accounts Receivable Transactions

In a computerized accounting system, transactions affecting accounts receivable are handled much like other transactions. The information for each transaction is entered into the computer. When instructed to do so, the computer will post the transaction amounts to the general ledger controlling account and to the subsidiary ledger accounts. The subsidiary ledger accounts and the controlling account are then always up to date.

Many businesses then use the stored data to prepare and send statements of account to their charge customers. A *statement of account* summarizes the transactions affecting a charge customer's account over a period of time. The statement usually lists the customer's previous balance, all charge sales made, and any payments or other decreases to the account balance. A statement of account is usually prepared for a one-month period.

Many customers, particularly those who have not been offered cash discounts, wait to receive a statement of account before sending a payment check. Other customers only use the statement of account as a means of verifying their own records.

CHAMPION BUILDING PRODUCTS, INC.
601 Mt. Lebanon Road
Pittsburgh, PA 15230

STATEMENT OF ACCOUNT

TO: Amy Anderson
103 Woodstone Drive
Laughlintown, PA 15655

CLOSING DATE	PAYMENT DUE DATE	PREVIOUS BALANCE	NEW BALANCE
12/31/--	01/20/--	352.16	445.73

DATE	DESCRIPTION	AMOUNT
12/01	PURCHASE	530.00
12/09	PAYMENT -- THANK YOU	352.16-
12/23	PAYMENT -- THANK YOU	530.00-
12/28	PURCHASE	445.73

PREVIOUS BALANCE	NEW PURCHASES	PAYMENTS	NEW BALANCE
352.16	975.73	882.16	445.73

Figure 12-11   Computer-Generated Statement of Account

A statement of account that might be prepared by Champion Building Products, Inc., is illustrated in Figure 12-11. Compare this statement with the information listed in Amy Anderson's subsidiary ledger account in Figure 12-6.

Summary of Key Points

1. The cash received by a business is first recorded on receipts and cash register tapes. These receipts and tapes are the source documents for the journal entries.
2. Bank card sales are recorded as though they were cash sales.
3. Some merchandising businesses give cash discounts to customers for paying their bills early. A customer who takes advantage of a cash discount may deduct a certain percentage of the cost of merchandise if it pays the bill within the discount period.
4. The Sales Discounts account is used to record the amount of any cash discounts taken by charge customers. It is referred to as a contra account because it reduces the balance of the Sales account.
5. The cash receipts journal is a special journal used to record all cash received by a business.
6. The cash receipts journal contains special amount columns for transactions that occur frequently. Credit amounts that cannot be entered in a special amount column are entered in the General Credit column.
7. Transactions are posted from the cash receipts journal to the accounts receivable subsidiary ledger daily. Transactions entered in the General Credit column are posted periodically during the month.
8. Column totals from the cash receipts journal are posted at the end of each month.
9. A schedule of accounts receivable lists all charge customers, their ending balances, and the total amount due from all customers. The total of the schedule of accounts receivable must match the balance of the Accounts Receivable account.

Review and Applications

Building Your Accounting Vocabulary

In your own words, write the definition of each of the following accounting terms. Use complete sentences for your definitions.

bank card
cash discount
cash receipt

cash receipts journal
cash sale
contra account

receipt
schedule of accounts
  receivable

Reviewing Your Accounting Knowledge

1. What are the source documents for transactions recorded in the cash receipts journal?
2. Why are bank card sales considered to be a form of cash sale?
3. Give an example of a cash receipt that a merchandising business might have that did not result from the sale of merchandise.
4. Why would a business offer a cash discount to its customers?
5. What is the normal balance side of the Sales Discounts account?
6. Why does a cash receipts journal always have a Cash in Bank Debit column?
7. What accounts are affected when a business receives a payment from a charge customer who has taken advantage of a cash discount?
8. What are the two kinds of postings made from the cash receipts journal during the month?
9. When are amounts in the Accounts Receivable Credit column of the cash receipts journal posted to the accounts receivable subsidiary ledger?
10. Why is a check mark in parentheses placed below the double rule in the General Credit column of the cash receipts journal?
11. What is the purpose of preparing a schedule of accounts receivable?

Improving Your Communications Skills

Words that are similar in meaning are called *synonyms*. Using synonyms adds variety to communications. However, if your reader doesn't understand the word you use, you are not communicating. For this reason, it is usually a good idea to use familiar language in business writing. Rewrite each of the following sentences, supplying a synonym for the word in italics.

1. Some of the points that were raised during the meeting did not seem *germane*.
2. Please *expedite* the processing of these invoices.
3. To complete the report, it was necessary for Rosa to *procure* a copy of the monthly sales figures.
4. Andrew did a *prodigious* amount of work in a very short time.
5. The memo *aggrandized* the number of customer complaints.

Applying Accounting Procedures

Exercise 12-1 Completing a Receipt Form

On December 15, The Rug Center received a check from the Barker Co. The $382.20 check was in payment of Sales Slip 493 for $390.00, less a 2% discount.

Instructions: Prepare a receipt for this cash receipt. The receipt is included in your working papers. Sign your name on the Received By line.

Exercise 12-2 Computing Cash Discounts

Expo Communications received the payments shown below for sales made on account. The companies that were offered cash discounts all paid within the discount period.

	Sale Amount	Credit Terms
1.	$4,600.00	2/10, n/30
2.	1,500.00	n/30
3.	2,760.00	1/10, n/30
4.	3,800.00	3/15, n/30
5.	450.30	n/30
6.	777.40	2/15, n/30
7.	1,362.75	2/10, n/30

Instructions: Use a form similar to the one that follows. For each sale amount,

(1) Indicate the credit terms for the sale in the second column.
(2) Compute the amount of the cash discount, if any.
(3) Determine the amount of cash actually received. The first payment has been completed as an example.

Sale Amount	Credit Terms	Cash Discount Amount	Amount of Cash Received
$4,600.00	2/10, n/30	$92.00	$4,508.00

Exercise 12-3 Analyzing Cash Receipt Transactions

Instructions: Listed below are several cash receipt transactions. Use a form similar to the one that follows. For each transaction, indicate in which columns of the cash receipts journal the transaction amounts should be recorded. The first transaction is given as an example.

Trans.	General Credit	Sales Credit	Sales Tax Payable Credit	Accounts Receivable Credit	Sales Discounts Debit	Cash in Bank Debit
1	✔					✔

Transactions:

1. Sold an old typewriter to an employee for $100.00 cash.
2. Recorded $2,500.00 in cash sales for the week plus $100.00 in sales taxes.
3. Received $50.00 on account from A. C. Reynolds.

4. Recorded the week's bank card sales of $800.00 plus $32.00 sales tax.

5. Received $245.00 from the Porter Company in payment of merchandise purchased on account for $250.00, less a 2% cash discount.

6. As a favor to a neighboring business, sold office supplies for $25.00 cash.

SPREADSHEET

PROBLEM

Problem 12-1   Recording Transactions in the Cash Receipts Journal

ColorCraft Mart, a retail merchandising store, had the following transactions during the month of November.

Instructions: Record the cash receipts for November on page 11 of the cash receipts journal.

Transactions:

Nov. 1   Received a check for $100.00 from Johanna Ambrose on account, Receipt 300.

   3   Richard Perry sent a $40.00 check to apply on his account, Receipt 301.

   8   Received a check from Rachel Quinn for $269.50 as payment for a purchase of $275.00, less a 2% cash discount of $5.50, Receipt 302.

   9   As a favor to Hoffman Realty, sold three reams of duplicating paper (office supplies) for $18.00, Receipt 303.

   10   Prepared Receipt 304 for a $60.00 check from David Dinsmore on account.

   12   Farrah Fletcher sent a check for $245.00 in payment of Sales Slip 1163 for $250.00 less a cash discount of $5.00, Receipt 305.

   15   Cash sales for the first two weeks amounted to $1,150.00, plus sales taxes of $57.50, Tape 48.

   15   Bank card sales for the period were $475.00, plus $23.75 in sales taxes, Tape 48.

   15   Received a $125.00 check on account from Stephen Walsh, Receipt 306.

   16   Richard Perry sent his check for $80.00 to apply on his account, Receipt 307.

   18   A check for $70.00 was received from Johanna Ambrose on account, Receipt 308.

   20   David Dinsmore sent a $110.00 check to apply to his account, Receipt 309.

   22   Received a check for $30.00 from Stephen Walsh to apply on his account, Receipt 310.

   24   Sold an old typewriter (office equipment) to an employee for $45.00, Receipt 311.

   26   A check for $65.00 was received on account from David Dinsmore, Receipt 312.

   30   Cash sales for the period totaled $1,400.00, plus $70.00 sales taxes, Tape 49.

   30   Bank card sales were $500.00 plus sales taxes of $25.00, Tape 49.

Problem 12-2   Posting from the Cash Receipts Journal

You will need the cash receipts journal prepared in Problem 12-1 to complete this problem.

Instructions:

(1) Post the individual amounts from the Accounts Receivable Credit column to the customers' accounts in the accounts receivable subsidiary ledger. The opened customer accounts are included in the working papers accompanying this textbook.

(2) Post the individual amounts from the General Credit column to the appropriate accounts in the general ledger.

(3) Foot, prove, total, and rule the cash receipts journal.

(4) Post the column totals to the general ledger accounts named in the column headings.

Problem 12-3 Journalizing and Posting Cash Receipts Transactions

The Country Peddler, a retail merchandising store, uses special journals and an accounts receivable subsidiary ledger for recording business transactions. The accounts receivable subsidiary ledger and a portion of the general ledger are included in the working papers. The current account balances are recorded in the accounts. During the month of July, the Country Peddler had the cash receipts transactions that follow.

Instructions:

(1) Record the transactions in the cash receipts journal. Use page 7.

(2) Post the individual amounts from the Accounts Receivable Credit column to the customers' accounts in the accounts receivable subsidiary ledger.

(3) Post the individual amounts in the General Credit column to the general ledger accounts.

(4) Foot, prove, total, and rule the cash receipts journal.

(5) Post the column totals to the general ledger accounts named in the column headings.

(6) Prepare a schedule of accounts receivable.

Transactions:

July 1 Charlotte Cole sent a check for $50.00 to apply on her account, Receipt 401.

3 Received cash on account from Kelly O'Brien, $75.00, Receipt 402.

5 A $25.00 check was received from Jedd Girard to apply on his account, Receipt 403.

6 Received a check for $291.00 from Joseph Zider in payment of a sales slip for $300.00, less a 3% cash discount, Receipt 404.

7 Sold $15.00 worth of supplies, as a favor, to Lou's Pharmacy, Receipt 405.

8 Charlotte Cole, a charge customer, sent a $20.00 check as payment on her account, Receipt 406.

10 Received a check for $352.80 from Pat Eagleson in payment for merchandise totaling $360.00, less a 2% cash discount, Receipt 407.

11 Jedd Girard sent a check for $80.00, on account, Receipt 408.

13 A $60.00 check was received from Kelly O'Brien as a payment on account, Receipt 409.

15 Dana Vella, a charge customer, sent a $75.00 check, Receipt 410.

15 Recorded cash sales of $1,000.00, plus $60.00 in sales taxes, Tape 102.

15 Bank card sales totaled $350.00, plus $21.00 sales taxes, Tape 102.
20 Sold a duplicating machine (office equipment) for $125.00, Receipt 411.
23 A $70.00 check was received from Jedd Girard, Receipt 412.
24 Sold two reams of paper for $12.00, as a favor to Bill Davies, Receipt 413.
25 Kelly O'Brien sent a check for $45.00 as a payment on her account, Receipt 414.
26 A $35.00 check was received from Charlotte Cole, Receipt 415.
28 Dana Vella sent an $85.00 check, on account, Receipt 416.
31 Recorded cash sales of $1,500.00 plus $90.00 in sales taxes, Tape 103.
31 Bank card sales for the period were $600.00, plus $36.00 sales taxes, Tape 103.

COMPUTER
PROBLEM

Problem 12-4   Recording and Posting Sales and Cash Receipt Transactions

On April 1, Pennwood Paints, a merchandising distributor of paints and paint products, has the following balances in its accounts receivable subsidiary ledger and general ledger.

General Ledger (Partial)

Account Number		Account Balance
101	Cash in Bank	$3,000.00
105	Accounts Receivable	5,826.33
110	Supplies	175.00
115	Office Equipment	1,200.00
210	Sales Tax Payable	326.50
401	Sales	9,984.45
405	Sales Discounts	47.52

Accounts Receivable Subsidiary Ledger

Account Number		Account Balance
820	James Coletti, 114 Putnam St., San Francisco, CA 94101	$ 479.56
832	Norma Fury, 5654 Beach St., San Francisco, CA 94101	350.60
840	Heritage Racquet Club, 890 Fremont Blvd., Monterey, CA 93940	2,684.16
846	Myra Kristan, 386 Bay St., Santa Cruz, CA 95060	150.75
860	O'Mara Enterprises, 547 University Ave., Berkeley, CA 94704	1,890.36
890	Nick Pomeroy, 103 Prospect Ave., Santa Clara, CA 95050	270.90

NICK POMEROY acct. #890 !!

Instructions:

(1) Open the general ledger accounts and record the April 1 balances.
(2) Open the customer accounts in the accounts receivable subsidiary ledger and record the April 1 balances.
(3) Record the April transactions in the sales and cash receipts journals. Use page 4 for each journal.
(4) Post the individual amounts from the two journals to the accounts receivable subsidiary ledger on a daily basis. Post the amounts in the

General Credit column of the cash receipts journal to the general ledger accounts daily.

(5) Foot, prove, total, and rule the journals.

(6) Post the column totals in the journals to the general ledger. Post the sales journal totals first.

(7) Prepare a schedule of accounts receivable.

Transactions:

Apr. 1 Received a check for $2,633.52 from Heritage Racquet Club in full payment of their account of $2,684.16, less a 2% cash discount of $50.64, Receipt 150.

2 Sold $200.00 worth of merchandise to Nick Pomeroy, plus sales taxes of $12.00, Sales Slip 401.

3 Norma Fury sent us a check for $350.60 in full payment of her account, Receipt 151.

5 Received a check for $75.00 from Myra Kristan to apply on account, Receipt 152.

6 O'Mara Enterprises sent a $1,854.69 check in full payment of Sales Slip 391 for $1,890.36, less a 2% discount of $35.67, Receipt 153.

7 Sold merchandise on account to Norma Fury for $415.00 plus $24.90 sales taxes, Sales Slip 402.

8 Sold to James Coletti on account, $310.00 in merchandise, sales taxes $18.60, Sales Slip 403.

9 Myra Kristan bought $175.00 worth of merchandise on account, sales tax $10.50, Sales Slip 404.

10 Cash sales for the first part of the month were $1,850.00 plus sales taxes of $111.00, Tape 20.

10 Bank card sales totaled $670.00 plus $40.20 sales taxes, Tape 20.

11 Sold $950.00 in merchandise on account to Heritage Racquet Club, $57.00 sales taxes, Sales Slip 405.

12 Sold $10.00 in memo pads (supplies), as a favor, for cash, Receipt 154.

13 James Coletti sent a check for $479.56 in payment of Sales Slip 397, Receipt 155.

14 Sold to O'Mara Enterprises on account $1,200.00 in merchandise, plus sales taxes of $72.00, Sales Slip 406.

15 Received a $270.90 check from Nick Pomeroy to apply on his account, Receipt 156.

16 Norma Fury sent a check to apply on her account, Receipt 157 for $125.00.

18 Sold an old typewriter to Doug Jones, an employee, for $60.00, Receipt 158.

19 Sold to James Coletti merchandise totaling $140.00, $8.40 sales taxes, on account, Sales Slip 407.

21 Received a check for $988.00 from Heritage Racquet Club in full payment of Sales Slip 405 for $1,007.00, less a 2% cash discount of $19.00, Receipt 159.

22 Recorded Receipt 160 for a check from James Coletti for $328.60, on account.

23 Received a check for $160.00 from Nick Pomeroy on account, Receipt 161.

25   Sold to Myra Kristan $215.00 worth of merchandise on account, sales taxes $12.90, Sales Slip 408.

26   Sold merchandise totaling $150.00 to Nick Pomeroy on account, sales tax $9.00, Sales Slip 409.

27   Received a check for $1,236.00 from O'Mara Enterprises in payment of Sales Slip 406 for $1,272.00 less a 3% cash discount of $36.00, Receipt 162.

28   Sold $770.00 in merchandise to Heritage Racquet Club on account, sales taxes of $46.20, Sales Slip 410.

29   Sold on account to O'Mara Enterprises $1,300.00 worth of merchandise, plus $78.00 sales taxes, Sales Slip 411.

29   Sold $80.00 in merchandise on account, plus $4.80 sales tax, to James Coletti, Sales Slip 412.

30   Cash sales for the period were $1,790.00, plus sales taxes of $107.40, Tape 21.

30   The amount of bank card sales was $530.00, plus $31.80 sales taxes, Tape 21.

CHALLENGE

PROBLEM

Problem 12-5   Analyzing Sales and Cash Receipt Errors

The Grenon Lumberyard uses special journals to record sales on account and cash receipts. During the past month, an accounting clerk made each of the errors described below. Explain how each error might be discovered.

1. A sale on account was journalized correctly but posted to the Credit column of the customer's account.

2. A sale of some office supplies for $36.00 cash was correctly recorded in the cash receipts journal but posted to the Office Supplies account as a debit of $36.00.

3. Made an addition error in totaling the Cash in Bank Debit column of the cash receipts journal.

4. A sale on account to Paul Forest was recorded correctly in the sales journal but posted to the account of Pauline Fredericks.

5. Made a subtraction error in determining the balance of a customer's account.

6. Recorded the sale of an old piece of office equipment in the Sales Credit column of the cash receipts journal.

7. A sale on account for $125.00 plus $6.25 sales tax was recorded in the sales journal as a debit of $125.00 to Accounts Receivable, a credit of $6.25 to Sales Tax Payable, and a credit of $131.25 to Sales.

8. The total of the Sales Tax Payable Credit column was posted to the Accounts Receivable account in the general ledger.

9. Recorded a cash receipt from a charge customer but forgot to post the amount to the customer's account.

10. Sold merchandise on account to a charge customer but forgot to include the amount of the sales tax in the sales journal entry.

*B*ar Codes:
An Idea on the Fast Track

*A*t the grocery store checkout, the cashier whisks the label on a jar, box, or bag across a window. There's a flash and a beep, and a price appears on the cash register screen faster than human fingers could key in $2.43.

What you didn't see was the lightning-fast transfer of information between the cash register and the store's computer.

• A scanner uses a bright light to "read" the bar code, the striped symbols on the product label. The stripes represent the manufacturer and the product. (Numbers below the bars also represent the manufacturer and the product.)

• The pattern is decoded into data and sent to the computer.

• The computer "looks up" the price and sends it back to the cash register. The computer also updates the store's inventory for the product.

Supermarkets were the first to use bar code technology in the early 1970s, resulting in faster order processing, a detailed receipt of purchases, and far fewer errors. Now bar codes are turning up everywhere.

• The U.S. Postal Service uses bar codes to speed up mail sorting and routing.

• Hospitals match bar codes printed on patients' wristbands with codes on prescription drug labels to make sure the right medicine goes to the right patient.

• Airlines hope to cut down on lost luggage by using bar codes on claim checks and luggage tags and matching them to aircraft.

• Hand-held scanners attached to video cassette recorders allow users to program their VCRs by running the scanners over bar-coded listings printed in the TV schedule.

• State judicial systems use bar codes to monitor cases and work loads. Bar-coded files and docu-

Scanning bar codes on merchandise speeds up the checkout process and helps the store keep an up-to-date inventory.

ments are scanned each time they're used. A central computer stores the information and prepares a weekly analysis of the entire judicial system.

• Courier and delivery companies use bar codes to track packages.

Yes, the beep goes on!

Chapter 13

ACCOUNTING FOR PURCHASES ON ACCOUNT

In the last two chapters, you have learned that businesses use special journals to record transactions that are alike and occur often. Special journals help accountants avoid accounting traffic jams. They channel incoming data into appropriate "lanes" and are a shortcut for much of the data headed for the general ledger.

The special journals you have studied so far cover only part of the daily flow of transactions. The sales and cash receipts journals are used for merchandise *leaving* the business. Merchandise and other items used to operate the business must also *enter* the business.

In this chapter, you'll learn about another special journal: the purchases journal. You will also learn about the subsidiary ledger used by businesses having large numbers of creditors.

Learning Objectives

When you have completed Chapter 13, you should be able to do the following:

1. Describe the procedures for processing a purchase on account.
2. Explain the use of the Purchases account.
3. Journalize a purchase on account in a purchases journal.
4. Post from the purchases journal to the accounts payable subsidiary ledger and to the general ledger.
5. Define the accounting terms introduced in this chapter.

New Terms

purchase requisition
purchase order
packing slip
invoice
processing stamp
purchase discount
discount period
Purchases account
cost of merchandise
purchases journal
tickler file
due date
accounts payable subsidiary
   ledger

Purchasing Items Needed by a Business

Businesses buy as well as sell. This is true at every level of business—from the corner grocery store to a giant international corporation. Regardless of its type, size, or purpose, a business needs supplies and equipment to operate. All businesses need such things as paper, pencils, pens, and other items for their employees' use. They also need various types of furniture and equipment—from desks, to typewriters, to cash registers, to delivery vans. Retail businesses need shopping bags for customers, sales slips, and cash register tapes. Retail businesses must also buy merchandise to resell to their customers. Although these items may be bought on a cash basis, they are usually bought on account.

The purchase of supplies, equipment, and merchandise can be divided into four stages: requesting the needed items, ordering from a supplier, verifying items received, and processing the supplier's bill. Let's take a look at each of these stages.

Requesting Needed Items

When equipment or supplies are needed or when the inventory of merchandise on hand becomes low, the person or department in charge of purchasing must be notified. In a small business, the owner does all the buying. In a large business, a separate purchasing department usually buys items for the entire company.

Most businesses require that a request for items to be purchased be in writing. A **purchase requisition** is a written request that a certain item or items be ordered. Like many business documents, a purchase requisition is usually a prenumbered, multicopy form.

A purchase requisition includes the quantity, description, and stock number of each item requested. A requisition may cover several different items. The form usually lists the date the requested items are needed and may have a space for the suggested supplier. The original of the completed form is sent to the purchasing department or the purchasing agent. One copy is kept by the person making the request. Figure 13-1 shows the purchase requisition form used by Champion Building Products.

PURCHASE REQUISITION		
	NO. 9421	
FOR DEPARTMENT Home Improvements	DATE Nov. 12, 19--	
NOTIFY Betty Connor ON DELIVERY	DATE WANTED Dec. 5, 19--	
QUANTITY	DESCRIPTION	STOCK NO.
4 gal.	Exterior paint, white	94682
4 gal.	Exterior paint, gray	94788
6 gal.	Exterior paint, brown	94281
6 gal.	Exterior paint, beige	94666
6 gal.	Exterior paint, peach	94711
ORDER FROM Key Paint Company	APPROVED BY Paul Andrews	
	PURCHASING AGENT	

Figure 13-1 A Typical Purchase Requisition

Placing an Order with a Supplier

After a purchase requisition is approved, a purchase order is prepared. A **purchase order** is a written offer to a supplier to buy certain items. Much of the information on the purchase order is taken directly from the purchase requisition. Other information may be obtained from the supplier's catalog. The purchase order contains the quantity, description, unit price, and total cost of each item being ordered. The *unit price* is the cost of a single item or of the smallest quantity—such as a dozen—in which an item can be bought. The purchase order also contains the supplier's name and address, the date the items are needed, and, perhaps, the method of shipping.

Look at the purchase order prepared by Champion Building Products in Figure 13-2. Like the purchase requisition, the purchase order is a prenumbered, multicopy form. The original of the purchase order is sent to the supplier from whom the items are being ordered. One copy of the purchase order may be sent to the department requesting the items. Another copy is kept by the purchasing department.

CHAMPION BUILDING PRODUCTS, INC.   Purchase Order
601 Mt. Lebanon Road
Pittsburgh, PA 15230

No.   9784

To
Key Paint Company
1714 Peak Road
Cleveland, OH 44109

Date: November 15, 19--
Date Needed: December 5, 19--

Quantity	Item	Unit Price	Total
4 gal.	Exterior paint: white, # 94682	$6.98	$ 27.92
4 gal.	Exterior paint: gray, #94788	6.98	27.92
6 gal.	Exterior paint: brown, #94281	6.98	41.88
6 gal.	Exterior paint: beige, #94666	6.98	41.88
6 gal.	Exterior paint: peach, #94711	6.98	41.88
	TOTAL		$181.48

Figure 13-2   A Typical Purchase Order

Note that a purchase order is only an *offer* to buy items. Until the items ordered are actually received, the buyer does not know whether or not the supplier has accepted the offer and shipped the items. A supplier may not be able to fill the purchase order because an item is out of stock or has been discontinued. The mailing of a purchase order, therefore, does not require a journal entry.

It is important to verify the packing slip to ensure that the business received the exact items and quantities ordered.

Verifying the Items Received

A supplier accepts a purchase order by shipping the items requested and billing the buyer for the items shipped. When an order is shipped to a buyer, a packing slip is included with the order. A **packing slip** is a form that lists the items included in the shipment.

When a shipment is received, it is immediately unpacked and checked against the quantities and items listed on the packing slip. If the contents of the shipment do not agree with those listed on the packing slip—in quantity or type of item—a notation about the mistake is made on the packing slip. The packing slip is then sent to the accounting department to be checked against both the purchase order and the supplier's bill. Checking a shipment of items against the packing slip and the purchase order is important to avoid costly mistakes. A buyer does not have to pay for items not ordered, not received, or received but damaged.

Processing the Supplier's Bill

When items are shipped to a buyer, the supplier prepares a bill called an invoice. An **invoice** lists the credit terms and the quantity, description, unit price, and total cost of the items shipped to the buyer. The invoice may also list the buyer's purchase order number and method of shipment.

Invoices are sent directly to the buyer's accounting department, where an accounting clerk uses a date stamp to indicate when the invoice was received. Next, the accounting clerk checks each detail on the invoice against the verified packing slip and the purchase order. This is done to make sure that Champion is billed for only the quantities and items actually ordered and received.

Once verified, the invoice becomes the source document for a journal entry. Before the invoice is recorded, however, the accounting clerk adds a processing stamp on the invoice. A **processing stamp** is just what the words indicate. It is a stamp placed on an invoice that outlines a set of steps to be followed in processing the invoice for payment. The information on the processing stamp includes: (1) the date the invoice is to be paid; (2) the discount amount, if any; (3) the amount to be paid (the net amount of the invoice less the discount); and (4) the check number. The accounting clerk completes the first three lines on the stamp at the time the invoice is received. The check number is entered later—when the check is issued.

Look at the invoice in Figure 13-3. Notice that a date has been stamped on the invoice to show when Champion received it. Notice, also, the processing stamp information.

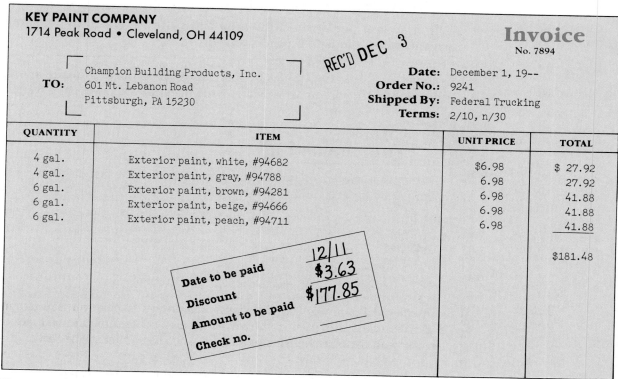

Figure 13-3   An Invoice

Purchase Discounts

Suppliers often offer credit customers a cash discount for early payment. From the buyer's point of view, this discount for early payment is a **purchase discount.** A purchase discount is calculated in the same way a sales discount was calculated in Chapter 12.

For example, Champion Building Products purchased $181.48 worth of merchandise on account from Key Paint Company. The invoice, dated December 1 and shown in Figure 13-3, lists credit terms of 2/10, n/30. If Champion pays for the merchandise within 10 days of the invoice date, it may deduct 2% from the total of the invoice. Those 10 days are referred to as the discount period. A **discount period** is the period of time within which an invoice must be paid if a discount is to be taken. If Champion does not pay for the merchandise within the discount period, it must pay the net, or total, amount within 30 days.

The discount amount is found by multiplying the invoice total by the discount percent. The discount amount is then subtracted from the invoice total to determine the actual amount to be paid. As you can see, by paying on or before December 11 (December 1 + 10 days), Champion can save $3.63.

Invoice Total	$181.48	Invoice Total	$181.48
Discount Percent	× .02	Discount Amount	− 3.63
Discount Amount	$ 3.63	Amount to be Paid	$177.85

R E M E M B E R

The discount period is calculated from the date the invoice was prepared, not the date it was received.

Before you learn how to analyze purchases on account, do the following activity to check your understanding of the material you have just covered.

Check Your Learning

Write your answers on notebook paper. Determine the last day of the discount period for each of the invoices below.

	Invoice Date	Terms
1.	May 14	2/10, n/30
2.	June 17	2/15, n/30
3.	July 28	1/10, n/30
4.	September 22	3/10, n/60

Assume that you work for a business that always takes advantage of purchase discounts. For each of the invoices below, determine the last day of the discount period, the discount amount, and the amount to be paid.

	Invoice Date	Invoice Total	Terms
5.	October 27	$3,500	2/10, n/30
6.	November 28	$ 600	3/15, n/30
7.	March 5	$ 952	2/15, n/30
8.	August 19	$7,255	2/15, n/30

Compare your answers to those in the answers section. Re-read the preceding part of the chapter to find the answers to any questions you missed.

The Purchases Account

Most of the purchases on account made by a merchandising business are for merchandise to be resold to customers. Since a merchandising business earns revenue by selling merchandise, it is important that the business keep a record of the cost of that merchandise. In Chapter 11, you learned that a merchandising business uses a separate account to record the sale of merchandise. Likewise, when a merchandising business buys new goods to replace those sold to customers, it uses a separate account. The cost of new merchandise is recorded in the **Purchases account.** The balance in this account shows the cost of merchandise purchased during a fiscal period.

You learned in earlier chapters that revenue and expense accounts are temporary equity accounts. The Purchases account is also a temporary equity account. It is classified as a **cost of merchandise** account. The cost of merchandise is just what the words indicate. It is the actual cost to the business of the merchandise sold to customers.

Purchases	
Dr.	Cr.
+	−
Increase Side	Decrease Side
Balance Side	

Merchandise that is purchased for resale is a cost of doing business. Like expenses, the cost of purchases decreases owner's or stockholders' equity. The Purchases account, therefore, follows the same rules of debit and credit as expense accounts. That is, Purchases is increased by debits and decreased by credits. The normal balance of the Purchases account is a debit balance.

R E M E M B E R

The amount of merchandise bought during the period is recorded in the Purchases account. Purchases is classified as a cost of merchandise account.

The Purchases Journal

You learned earlier that when a business has similar transactions that occur often, it is easier to record those transactions in a special journal. The **purchases journal** is a special journal used to record all transactions in which items are bought on account. The purchases journal used by Champion Building Products appears in Figure 13-4. Like the sales and cash receipts journals, the purchases journal has special amount columns for recording purchases transactions that occur frequently.

	DATE	INVOICE NO.	CREDITOR'S ACCOUNT CREDITED	POST. REF.	ACCOUNTS PAYABLE CREDIT	PURCHASES DEBIT	GENERAL			
							ACCOUNT DEBITED	POST. REF.	DEBIT	
1										1
2										2

Figure 13-4 The Purchases Journal

As you already know, a liability is created whenever a business purchases items on account. Regardless of what is bought, a purchase on account always requires a credit to the Accounts Payable account. The purchases journal, therefore, always includes an Accounts Payable Credit column.

The debit columns in the purchases journal are used to record two different types of purchases on account. We mentioned earlier that most of the purchases on account a business makes are for merchandise to be resold to customers. Since merchandise bought on account is recorded in the Purchases account, the purchases journal includes a Purchases Debit column. The total of this column is posted as a debit to the Purchases account in the general ledger at the end of each month.

The General Debit column is used to record purchases of all other items on account. Examples of items that would be recorded in the General Debit column are purchases of supplies or equipment on account. Each amount recorded in the General Debit column is posted directly to the general ledger account named in the General Account Debited column.

R E M E M B E R

Every purchase on account results in either a debit to the Purchases account (for merchandise bought on account) or a debit to a general ledger account (for all purchases other than merchandise). Accounts Payable is always credited for a purchase on account.

Journalizing Purchases on Account

After an invoice has been verified by the accounting clerk, the purchase is recorded in the purchases journal.

Recording the Purchase of Merchandise on Account

Champion's first purchase on account in December involves a purchase of merchandise on account. The source document for this transaction is the invoice in Figure 13-3 on page 269.

December 3: *Received Invoice 7894 from Key Paint Company for merchandise purchased on account, $181.48.*

Purchases

Dr.	Cr.
+	−
$181.48	

Accounts Payable

Dr.	Cr.
−	+
	$181.48

The accounts affected by this transaction are Purchases and Accounts Payable. The Purchases account is debited whenever any merchandise is bought for resale to customers. In this transaction, Purchases is debited for $181.48. Accounts Payable is increased since Champion now owes more money to its creditors. It is credited for $181.48.

The recording of this transaction in the purchases journal is shown in Figure 13-5. Refer to this illustration as you read these steps.

1. Enter the date in the Date column. Use the date Champion *received* the invoice, not the date the invoice was prepared.
2. Enter the number of the creditor's invoice in the Invoice No. column.
3. Enter the creditor's name in the Creditor's Account Credited column.
4. Enter the *total* of the invoice in the Accounts Payable Credit column.

5. For a purchase of merchandise on account, enter the total amount of the invoice in the Purchases Debit column.

				PURCHASES JOURNAL					PAGE 12	
	DATE	INVOICE NO.	CREDITOR'S ACCOUNT CREDITED	POST. REF.	ACCOUNTS PAYABLE CREDIT	PURCHASES DEBIT	GENERAL			
							ACCOUNT DEBITED	POST. REF.	DEBIT	
1	19-- Dec. 3	7894	Key Paint Company		181 48	181 48				1
2	1	2	3		4	5				2

Figure 13-5 Recording the Purchase of Merchandise on Account in the Purchases Journal

R E M E M B E R

The purchase of merchandise on account is recorded as a debit to Purchases and a credit to Accounts Payable.

After the invoice from Key Paint Company has been journalized, it is placed in a tickler file. A **tickler file** is a file that contains a folder for each day of the month. Invoices are placed in the folders according to their **due dates,** the dates that they must be paid. For example, an invoice due on December 11 would be placed in the folder marked "11."

R E M E M B E R

The due date is the date on which an invoice must be paid.

Journalizing Other Purchases on Account

Champion Building Products does not purchase supplies and other items on account often enough to set up special columns in the purchases journal. When such purchases do occur, they are recorded in the General Debit column of the purchases journal.

December 12: *Received Invoice 3417, dated December 10, from Center City Supply for supplies bought on account, $362.60, terms n/30.*

The accounts affected by this transaction are Supplies and Accounts Payable. The asset account Supplies is being increased, so it is debited for the amount of the purchase, $362.60. Champion now owes Center City Supply for the supplies purchased on account, so Accounts Payable is also being increased. Accounts Payable is credited for $362.60.

Supplies		Accounts Payable	
Dr.	Cr.	Dr.	Cr.
+	−	−	+
$362.60			$362.60

CHAPTER 13 Accounting for Purchases on Account

The journal entry for this transaction is shown in Figure 13-6, line 4. Refer to this illustration as you read the steps that follow:

1. Enter the date the invoice was received in the Date column.
2. Enter the invoice number in the Invoice No. column.
3. Enter the creditor's name in the Creditor's Account Credited column.
4. Enter the total of the invoice in the Accounts Payable Credit column.
5. Since there is no special amount column for supplies, write the title of the general ledger account being debited in the General Account Debited column.
6. Enter the total amount of the invoice in the General Debit column.

After journalizing the invoice, the accounting clerk places it in the tickler file. Center City Supply does not offer its credit customers a cash discount. "January 9" had, therefore, been recorded on the processing stamp on the invoice. The accounting clerk placed this invoice in the folder marked "9" to indicate the bill is to be paid on January 9.

						PURCHASES JOURNAL					PAGE 12	
									GENERAL			
	DATE	INVOICE NO.	CREDITOR'S ACCOUNT CREDITED	POST. REF.	ACCOUNTS PAYABLE CREDIT	PURCHASES DEBIT		ACCOUNT DEBITED	POST. REF.	DEBIT		
1	Dec. 3	7894	Key Paint Company		1 81 48	1 81 48						1
2	6	204C	Starks Lumber Co.		3 495 66	3 495 66						2
3	9	2419	Aluminum Plus, Inc.		7 842 98	7 842 98						3
4	12	3417	Center City Supply		362 60			Supplies		362 60		4
5	1	2	3		4			5		6		5

Figure 13-6 Recording the Purchase of Supplies on Account in the Purchases Journal

Before you learn how to post from the purchases journal, do the following activity to check your understanding of the material you have just studied.

Check Your Learning

Use notebook paper to write your answers to these questions.

1. In what account is the cost of merchandise purchased for resale to customers recorded?
2. Does the cost of merchandise increase or decrease owner's (stockholders') equity?
3. Increases to the Purchases account are recorded as ___?___ while decreases to the Purchases account are recorded as ___?___ .
4. If merchandise is purchased on account, its cost is recorded as a debit to ___?___ and a credit to ___?___ .
5. Store equipment bought on account is recorded as a debit to ___?___ and a credit to ___?___ .
6. What types of purchases are recorded in the General Debit column of the purchases journal?

Compare your answers to those in the answers section. Re-read the preceding part of the chapter to find the answers to any questions you missed.

Businesses that make many purchases on account may prepare weekly, or even daily, printouts of the invoices that must be paid.

The Accounts Payable Subsidiary Ledger

In Chapters 11 and 12, you learned that when a business has many charge customers it is more efficient to set up a subsidiary ledger for those customers. Likewise, when a business has many creditors, it is more efficient to set up a subsidiary ledger for those creditors. The **accounts payable subsidiary ledger** is a ledger that contains accounts for all creditors and the amount that is owed to each. The individual creditors' accounts in the accounts payable subsidiary ledger are summarized in the general ledger controlling account Accounts Payable. The balance of the Accounts Payable controlling account and the total of all the account balances in the accounts payable subsidiary ledger must agree after all posting has been completed.

In a manual accounting system, creditors' accounts in the accounts payable subsidiary ledger do not have account numbers. Instead, the accounts are arranged in alphabetical order. In a computerized accounting system, each creditor is assigned an account number.

The ledger account form used for the accounts payable subsidiary ledger is the same form that is used for the accounts receivable subsidiary ledger. An accounts payable subsidiary ledger account is shown in Figure 13-7 on page 276. As you can see, the subsidiary ledger account form has lines at the top for the creditor's name and address.

In the accounts payable subsidiary ledger, the Debit column of the ledger account form is used to record decreases to the creditor's account. Any payments on account are recorded in the Debit column. The Credit column is used to record increases to the creditor's account. All purchases on account are recorded in the Credit column. The Balance column is used to record the total, up-to-date amount that is owed to the creditor. Since Accounts Payable is a liability account, suppliers' accounts in the accounts payable subsidiary ledger will normally have credit balances.

Posting from the Purchases Journal

After a transaction has been journalized, it must be posted. All the transactions in the purchases journal must be posted to the creditors' accounts in the accounts payable subsidiary ledger. In addition, the purchases of items other than merchandise must be posted to the appropriate general ledger accounts.

Posting to the Accounts Payable Subsidiary Ledger

Each transaction in the purchases journal is a purchase on account that must be posted to the accounts payable subsidiary ledger. The entry is posted as a credit to the account listed in the Creditor's Account Credited column. Transactions are posted daily to the accounts payable subsidiary ledger.

The first entry that must be posted involves the Key Paint Company account. Refer to Figure 13-7 as you read the steps that follow:

1. In the Date column of the subsidiary ledger account, enter the date of the transaction.
2. In the Posting Reference column, record the letter of the journal and the page number on which the transaction was recorded. "P" is the letter used for the purchases journal.
3. In the Credit column, enter the amount of the purchase as recorded in the Accounts Payable Credit column.

Prev. Bal. $1,835.12
Credit   +   181.48
New Bal. $2,016.60

4. Compute the new balance. To do this, add the amount in the Credit column to the previous balance amount. Enter the new balance in the Balance column.
5. Return to the purchases journal and place a check mark (✔) in the *first* Posting Reference column (following the Creditor's Account Credited column).

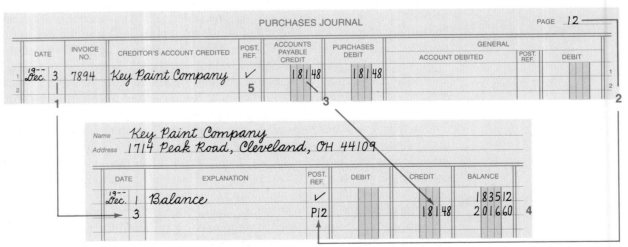

Figure 13-7   Posting from the Purchases Journal to the Accounts Payable Subsidiary Ledger

The first entry in the purchases journal has now been posted to the accounts payable subsidiary ledger. Follow the steps above whenever you post a purchase on account to the accounts payable subsidiary ledger.

UNIT 3   The Accounting Cycle for a Merchandising Business

Creditor accounts in the accounts payable subsidiary ledger normally have credit balances.

Posting from the General Debit Column

During the month, the accounting clerk also posts the transactions recorded in the General Debit column of the purchases journal. The transactions in this column are posted to the general ledger accounts named in the General Account Debited column. The first transaction to be posted involves the Supplies account.

The posting of this transaction is shown in Figure 13-8. Refer to Figure 13-8 as you read the steps that follow:

1. In the Date column of the general ledger account, enter the date of the transaction.
2. In the Posting Reference column, record the journal and page number of the transaction. Be sure to use the letter "P."
3. In the Debit column of the ledger account, enter the amount recorded in the General Debit column.
4. Compute and record the new balance in the Debit Balance column.
5. Return to the purchases journal and place the general ledger account number in the General Posting Reference column (following the General Account Debited column).

Prev. Bal. $5,074.40
Debit   + 362.60
New Bal. $5,437.00

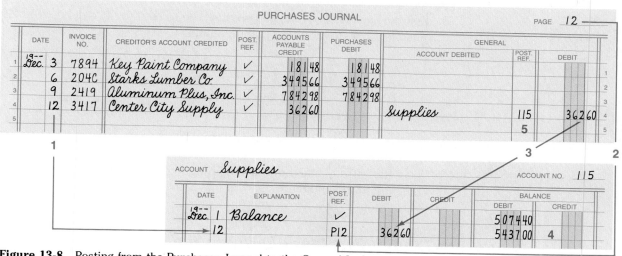

Figure 13-8   Posting from the Purchases Journal to the General Ledger

Completing the Purchases Journal

As you recall, a special journal eliminates the many postings to certain accounts by setting up special amount columns to represent those accounts. At the end of the month, the totals of these special columns are posted to the appropriate accounts in the general ledger. In the purchases journal, column totals are posted to the Accounts Payable and Purchases accounts.

Totaling, Proving, and Ruling the Purchases Journal

At the end of the month, the accounting clerk totals the purchases journal. The steps followed are the same as those for totaling the sales and the cash receipts journals. Refer to the purchases journal in Figure 13-9 as you read the steps that follow.

PURCHASES JOURNAL   PAGE 12

	DATE	INVOICE NO.	CREDITOR'S ACCOUNT CREDITED	POST. REF.	ACCOUNTS PAYABLE CREDIT	PURCHASES DEBIT	GENERAL ACCOUNT DEBITED	POST. REF.	GENERAL DEBIT	
1	Dec. 3	7894	Key Paint Company	✓	181 48	181 48				1
2	6	204C	Starks Lumber Co.	✓	3495 66	3495 66				2
3	9	2419	Aluminum Plus, Inc.	✓	7842 98	7842 98				3
4	12	3417	Center City Supply	✓	362 60		Supplies	115	362 60	4
5	15	11162	Viking Motors	✓	1200 00		Delivery Equipment	150	1200 00	5
6	22	295C	Starks Lumber Co.	✓	1008 36	1008 36				6
7	24	4681	Wilson Electric, Inc.	✓	5680 04	5680 04				7
8	28	11193	Viking Motors	✓	125 95		Store Equipment	155	125 95	8
9	29	2498	Aluminum Plus, Inc.	✓	3600 00	3600 00				9
10	31	349	Custom Doors, Inc	✓	640 00	640 00	← 1 →		2	10
11	31		Totals		24137 07	22448 52			1688 55	11
12	4		5				← 7 →		6	12

Figure 13-9 The Completed Purchases Journal

1. Draw a single rule under the three amount columns: Accounts Payable Credit, Purchases Debit, and General Debit.
2. Foot each amount column.
3. Test the equality of debits and credits. The total of the two debit columns must equal the total of the credit column.

Debit Columns		Credit Column	
Purchases	$22,448.52	Accounts Payable	$24,137.07
General	1,688.55		
	$24,137.07		$24,137.07

4. In the Date column, on the line below the single rule, enter the last day of the month.
5. Write the word "Totals" in the Creditor's Account Credited column.
6. Enter the three column totals — in ink — just below the footings.
7. Draw a double rule across the three amount columns.

Posting the Special Column Totals of the Purchases Journal

After the purchases journal has been totaled and ruled, the accounting clerk posts the totals of the Accounts Payable Credit column and the Purchases Debit column to the general ledger accounts. The new account balances for each account are calculated an entered in the appropriate Balance column. The posting of these column totals is shown in Figure 13-10 on page 279.

After posting each column total, the accounting clerk places the account number to which the amount was posted, in parentheses, just below the double rule in the column. The total of the General Debit column is not posted because the individual amounts were posted during the month.

A check mark (ν), therefore, is placed in parentheses below the double rule in the General Debit column.

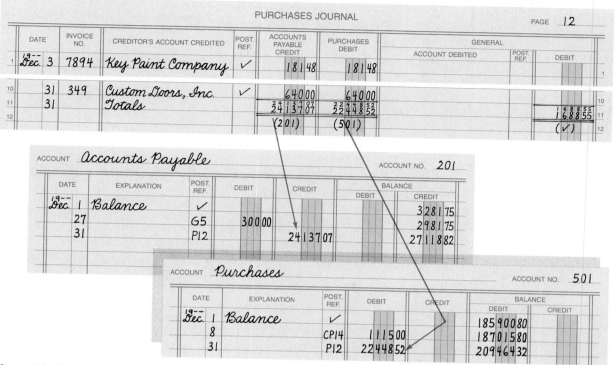

Figure 13-10 Posting Column Totals from the Purchases Journal to the General Ledger

Handling Purchases on Account in a Computerized Accounting System

You have just learned the manual method for recording entries for purchases on account, posting to subsidiary ledgers, and proving the totals of the purchases journal. A computerized system processes purchases on account in a manner similar to a manual system.

In a computerized accounting system, a number of purchase transactions are often grouped for processing. The transactions may be grouped daily, weekly, or biweekly. Each group of invoices is known as a *batch*. Each batch of transactions is assigned a *batch number*. Batch numbers are assigned in consecutive order. For example, Batch 121 might be assigned to the group of transactions for the first working week in December and Batch 122 for the second working week.

In a computerized system, each creditor has its own account number. The account number assigned to a business from which goods and services are bought on account is called a *vendor number*.

The batch number and the vendor number—as well as the account numbers for the accounts being debited and credited—are recorded on the processing stamp on each invoice. The information on the processing stamp is then entered into the computer through a keyboard terminal or perhaps an optical scanner. The computer prints a summary of the batched transactions. This summary, which looks much like the purchases journal, is shown in Figure 13-11. The summary is compared with batch proof information to determine if the accounting data was entered accurately. The computer calculates daily account balances and prints out any reports needed. All this is done with speed and accuracy that are not possible in a manual accounting system.

```
                PURCHASES  JOURNAL                  PAGE   12

        INV.  CREDITOR'S ACCOUNT  ACCTS. PAY. PURCHASES G.L.    G.L.
  DATE  NO.      CREDITED           CREDIT      DEBIT   ACT#   DEBIT

  12/03  7894 Key Paint Co.            181.48    181.48
  12/06  204c Starks Lumber Co.       3495.66   3495.66
  12/09  2419 Aluminum Plus, Inc.     7842.98   7842.98
  12/12  3417 Center City Supply       362.60             115   362.60
  12/15 11162 Viking Motors           1200.00             150  1200.00
  12/22  295c Starks Lumber Co.       1008.36   1008.36
  12/24  4681 Wilson Electric, Inc.   5680.04   5680.04
  12/28 11193 Viking Motors            125.95             155   125.95
  12/29  2498 Aluminum Plus, Inc.     3600.00   3600.00
  12/31   349 Custom Doors, Inc.       640.00    640.00
                                     --------  --------        -------
          TOTALS                     24137.07  22448.52        1688.55
                                     ========  ========        =======
```

Figure 13-11   Computerized Purchases Journal

Complete the following activity to check your understanding of the material you've just covered.

Check Your Learning

Use notebook paper to write your answers to these questions about this transaction.

On December 15, the Johnston Company received Invoice 29761, dated December 12, from Sung International Imports for merchandise bought on account for $600, terms 2/10, n/30.

1. The date of the entry in the purchases journal to record this transaction is ___?___ .
2. The creditor's account credited in the purchases journal is ___?___ .
3. The amount of this transaction, $600, is entered in the ___?___ column and the ___?___ column of the purchases journal.
4. This transaction is posted to the ___?___ subsidiary ledger.
5. After this transaction has been posted to the creditor's account, a ___?___ is placed in Post. Ref. column of the purchases journal.
6. At the end of the month, the totals of the ___?___ column and the ___?___ column are posted to the ___?___ .
7. To indicate that a special column total has been posted, the ___?___ is written in parentheses under each column total.

Compare your answers to those in the answers section. Re-read the preceding part of the chapter to find the correct answers to any questions you may have missed.

Summary of Key Points

1. Four documents involved in a purchase on account are: purchase requisition, purchase order, packing slip, and invoice. The purchase requisition is a request to order goods; the purchase order is an offer to buy goods; and the packing slip is a list of the goods shipped. An invoice lists the quantity, description, unit price, and total cost of the items shipped to the buyer. It must be checked against the purchase order and the packing slip before the purchase may be recorded.

2. When an invoice is received by the accounting department, a processing stamp is placed on the invoice. The information on the processing stamp includes: (a) the date the invoice is to be paid; (b) the discount amount, if any; (c) the amount to be paid (the total of the invoice less any discount); and (d) the check number.

3. Some suppliers offer a cash discount to their credit customers for early payment. Buyers refer to this discount as a purchase discount.

4. The Purchases account is used by merchandising businesses to record the cost of merchandise purchased during the fiscal period. Purchases is classified as a cost of merchandise account. The rules of debit and credit for Purchases are the same as those for expense accounts.

5. The purchases journal is a special journal used to record all purchases on account made by a merchandising business. The source document for a purchases journal entry is an invoice.

6. The purchases journal contains special amount columns for credits to Accounts Payable and debits to Purchases. Debit amounts that cannot be entered in a special column are entered in the General Debit column.

7. Journalized invoices are filed according to their due dates in a tickler file. A tickler file contains a folder for each day of the month.

8. The accounts payable subsidiary ledger contains an account for each creditor. The total of the account balances in the accounts payable subsidiary ledger must match the balance of the Accounts Payable controlling account in the general ledger.

9. Transactions are posted from the purchases journal to the accounts payable subsidiary ledger daily. Transactions entered in the General Debit column are posted periodically during the month.

10. The totals of the special amount columns in the purchases journal are posted to the general ledger at the end of each month.

Review and Applications

Building Your Accounting Vocabulary

In your own words, write the definition of each of the following accounting terms. Use complete sentences for your definitions.

accounts payable
  subsidiary ledger
cost of merchandise
discount period
due date

invoice
packing slip
processing stamp
purchase discount
purchase order

purchase requisition
Purchases account
purchases journal
tickler file

Reviewing Your Accounting Knowledge

1. Why is an invoice checked against both the purchase order and the packing slip?
2. What information is included on a processing stamp?
3. Why would a supplier give a cash discount to its credit customers?
4. Which account is used only to record the cost of merchandise bought for resale?
5. What are the two special amount columns in a purchases journal?
6. Which account is always credited when items are bought on account?
7. When a store buys on account shelves for displaying merchandise, in which column of the purchases journal is the debit amount of the transaction recorded?
8. How are invoices filed in a tickler file?
9. Do accounts in the accounts payable subsidiary ledger have normal debit balances or credit balances? Why?
10. What two types of postings from the purchases journal are completed during the month?
11. Why is the total of the General Debit column in the purchases journal not posted?

Improving Your Human Relations Skills

Two weeks ago you took a part-time job as an accounting clerk at the Brandeis Company. Bryan Thomas is a co-worker who sits at the desk next to yours. One day at the afternoon break, Bryan told you that your co-workers were concerned with your work habits. He said that all the other employees took an extra five minutes at break time. And, no one in the office worries about completing work on time. If the work is not finished on time, it can be finished later and overtime will be paid. Bryan suggested that you conform to the work habits of your co-workers.

1. What do you think about Bryan's suggestion?
2. What would you say to Bryan about his suggestion?

Applying Accounting Procedures

Exercise 13-1   Determining Due Dates and Discount Amounts

Jason's Appliance Center frequently purchases merchandise on account. When invoices are received, a processing stamp is placed on the invoice indicating the due date, the amount of any discount, and the amount to be paid. The following invoices were received during August.

	Invoice Number	Invoice Date	Credit Terms	Amount of Invoice
1.	24574	August 5	2/10, n/30	$3,000.00
2.	530992	August 7	3/10, n/30	5,550.00
3.	211145	August 12	2/15, n/60	729.95
4.	45679	August 16	n/45	345.67
5.	34120	August 23	2/10, n/30	1,526.50
6.	00985	August 27	n/30	700.00

Instructions: Use a form similar to the one that follows. The first invoice has been completed as an example. For each invoice,

(1) Determine the due date. Assume that Jason's always pays invoices within the discount period.

(2) Compute the discount amount, if any.

(3) Compute the amount that is to be paid.

Invoice Number	Invoice Date	Credit Terms	Invoice Amount	Due Date	Discount Amount	Amount to be Paid
24574	Aug. 5	2/10, n/30	$3,000.00	Aug. 15	$60.00	$2,940.00

Exercise 13-2   Analyzing Purchases on Account

Listed below are several transactions of the South Shore Home Improvement Center.

Instructions:

(1) Open T accounts and record the April 1 balances for the following accounts: Office Supplies, $157.30; Store Equipment, $21,945.00; Accounts Payable, $1,354.50; and Purchases, $31,416.45.

(2) Record each of the following transactions in the T accounts.

(3) Determine the ending balance for each account.

Transactions:

Apr. 4   Purchased 13 boxes of wallpapering kits on account from the Enloe Corp., $700.00, Invoice 1248.

   7   Purchased a new cash register on account from Honeycutt Office Equipment, Invoice 384 for $1,200.00.

   12   Received Invoice 891 from Lopez Stationers for copy machine paper bought on account, $200.00.

   15   Bought 15 cartons of paint in assorted colors on account from Day Glow, Inc., for $3,400.00, Invoice 2847.

   30   Received a bill from W & R Company for typewriter ribbons and erasing tapes purchased on account for $250.00, Invoice 8469.

Exercise 13-3 Understanding the Steps
in the Purchasing Process

Listed below are the steps that Martinez Bicycles follows when it purchases items on account. The steps, however, are not listed in the order they occur.

Instructions: Use the form provided in the working papers. Place a number from 1 to 8 on the line to the left of each step to indicate when that step would be completed.

- Record information on processing stamp.
- Prepare purchase order.
- Receive and verify invoice.
- Place invoice in tickler file.
- Prepare purchase requisition.
- Record invoice in purchases journal.
- Post transaction to accounts payable subsidiary ledger.
- Receive order and verify packing slip.

Problem 13-1 Journalizing Purchases on Account

The Swan Music Center uses a purchases journal to record its purchases on account.

Instructions: Record the following transactions on page 4 of a purchases journal.

Transactions:

Jan. 3 Purchased merchandise on account from the Brass Corp. for $577.50, Invoice 2312.

   5 Received Invoice 78934 from Hankins Sheet Music for merchandise bought on account, $478.98.

   8 Bought $124.50 worth of supplies on account from Rosemont Office Supplies, Invoice 9876.

  12 Purchased merchandise on account from Weber Drums, Invoice 777 for $390.65.

  18 Anderson Equipment sent Invoice 44456 for $1,567.88 for office equipment purchased on account.

  24 Bought on account from Parsons, Inc., merchandise costing $900.00, Invoice 6743.

  26 Received an invoice for merchandise bought on account from Brass Corp., $789.25, Invoice 2468.

  29 Received Invoice 9888 from Rosemont Office Supplies for supplies bought on account, $200.00.

  31 Bought merchandise on account, $2,890.50, from Weber Drums, Invoice 804.

Problem 13-2 Posting from the Purchases Journal

Use the purchases journal prepared in Problem 13-1 to complete this problem. The opened general ledger accounts and the accounts payable subsidiary ledger appear in the working papers accompanying this textbook.

Instructions:

(1) Post amounts from the Accounts Payable Credit column to the creditors' accounts in the accounts payable subsidiary ledger.

(2) Post the transactions in the General Debit column to the general ledger accounts.

(3) Foot, prove, total, and rule the purchases journal.

(4) Post the totals of the special columns to the general ledger accounts.

Problem 13-3   Journalizing and Posting Purchases on Account

Frank's Book Nook uses a purchases journal to record its purchases on account. The opened accounts for the general ledger and the accounts payable subsidiary ledger appear in the working papers.

Instructions:

(1) Record the following transactions on page 8 of the purchases journal. The first few transactions in November were recorded on journal page 7.

(2) Post the transactions from the purchases journal to the accounts payable subsidiary ledger.

(3) Post the amounts in the General Debit column to the general ledger.

(4) Foot, prove, total, and rule the purchases journal.

(5) Post the totals of the special columns to the general ledger.

Transactions:

Nov. 6   Purchased merchandise on account from Redstone Publishers, $1,458.00, Invoice 2020.

8   Bought supplies on account from Central Supply for $420.24, Invoice 8091.

9   Received Invoice 3987 for merchandise purchased on account from All South Circulation Co., $240.80.

10   Bought $295.20 worth of merchandise on account from Redstone Publishers, Invoice 2093.

12   Wakefield, Inc., sent Invoice 7428 for merchandise purchased on account, $250.30.

19   Purchased on account from Lake Equipment display shelves for the store, $2,946.80, Invoice 6311.

24   Received an invoice for merchandise bought on account from Longview Publications, $1,700.00, Invoice 9009.

27   Purchased $2,900.50 worth of merchandise on account from Wakefield, Inc., Invoice 7583.

30   Received Invoice 8173 for $250.00 for supplies purchased on account from Central Supply.

COMPUTER

PROBLEM

Problem 13-4   Recording and Posting Purchases Transactions

On August 1, Modern Furniture, Inc., a retail merchandising business, had the following balances in the accounts payable subsidiary ledger and in the general ledger.

General Ledger (Partial)

Account Number		Account Balance
120	Office Supplies	$ 845.25
140	Office Furniture	2,013.95
145	Office Equipment	1,369.45
150	Store Equipment	3,496.00
155	Delivery Equipment	0.00
201	Accounts Payable	5,099.70
501	Purchases	146,592.75

Accounts Payable Subsidiary Ledger

Account Number		Account Balance
910	Davis Business Center, 1066 Morris Blvd., St. Louis, MO 63104	$ 214.90
920	Eaves Office Products, 4277 Memorial Dr., Decatur, GA 30032	0.00
927	Forey, Inc., 90 South 9th St., Minneapolis, MN 55402	1,675.00
935	Hillman Brothers, Inc., 500 Texas Ave., Dallas, TX 75245	2,495.00
941	Jackson & Sons, Inc., 200 E. Broad St., Richmond, VA 23219	0.00
960	R & S Copiers, 700 Market St., St. Louis, MO 63101	714.80
980	Tom's Auto City, 5000 Delmar Blvd., St. Louis, MO 63112	0.00

Instructions:

(1) Open the general ledger accounts and record the August 1 balances.

(2) Open the accounts in the accounts payable subsidiary ledger and record the August 1 balances.

(3) Record the following transactions on purchases journal page 14.

(4) Post daily to the accounts payable subsidiary ledger and the general ledger.

(5) Total, prove, and rule the purchases journal.

(6) Post the totals of the special amount columns.

Transactions:

Aug. 1 Bought office equipment on account from Davis Business Center, $85.00, Invoice 804.

3 Jackson & Sons sent Invoice 2808 for $2,000.00 for merchandise purchased on account.

6 Received Invoice 1236 for office supplies purchased on account from Eaves Office Products, $600.00.

8 Bought on account from Hillman Brothers, Inc., merchandise costing $2,825.64, Invoice 3727.

10 Purchased a new delivery van on account from Tom's Auto City, Invoice 944 for $5,400.00.

16 Bought merchandise on account from Jackson & Sons, $540.00, Invoice 2847.

20 Received Invoice 1253 for $400.00 from Eaves Office Products for a new chair for the office.

25 Received from Jackson & Sons Invoice 2944 for $9,000.00 for merchandise purchased on account.

27 Purchased merchandise from Hillman Brothers, Inc., on account, $3,460.00, Invoice 3844.

29 Bought merchandise on account from Forey, Inc., Invoice 2074, $2,200.00.

30 Received Invoice 2999 from R & S Copiers for a copy machine bought on account for $780.00.

31 Purchased file folders on account for $84.00 from Eaves Office Products, Invoice 1301.

Problem 13-5 Analyzing Errors in the Purchases Journal

The purchases journal for the month of May for Home Hardware Center appears in the working papers. After all amounts, including the column totals, had been posted, an error was discovered: On May 29, Home Hardware purchased a new keyboard for the office computer from the Arnold Company, Invoice 1468.

Instructions: Answer the following questions regarding this error.

(1) What is the error?

(2) Which account *should* have been debited?

(3) Why did the totals of the debit columns and the credit column still prove equal?

(4) Will the balance in the accounts payable subsidiary ledger agree with the balance in the controlling account in the general ledger? Why or why not?

(5) What would the column totals have been if the entry had been made correctly?

(6) How would you correct this error?

*H*ardware and Software: Buying Smart

Let's pretend. You own a small, home-based, start-up business in custom designing and silk-screening T-shirts. It's called "Ts for You." In the past six months, you've sold 2,000 shirts. All this just by running two ads in the local newspaper and by talking to friends.

A week ago, you decided to mail a letter to some local businesses. Since then the phone has been ringing off the hook. And there are labels to type, inventory to track, customer lists to develop, supplies to order.

Time to automate! How do you start?

The Computer and Accessories. Choosing and buying a computer is an important decision. You need to take time to do your homework and make intelligent choices.

- Go to the library and check the consumer reports.
- Seek out users who have needs similar to yours. Find out what equipment they have and how satisfied they are.
- Go to a reputable computer store. Ask a *lot* of questions. Try out the equipment. Find out about servicing.
- Shop for a good price.
- Don't be ambitious, but also don't underestimate your growing needs.
- If you decide to upgrade in the future, how easy will it be with the equipment you've chosen?

The Software. No matter what your needs are, there's probably a software package that will fit those needs.

- Make a list of the tasks you want to accomplish. Do you need a special-purpose program or an integrated one?
- Check software directories, magazines, and software databases at your library for reviews and information.
- Read the sales literature and ask your computer

Determine your computer needs first. Then consider such factors as memory, software, and price.

store or distributor for demonstrations. Is it easy to use?
- Check the age of the product. Has it been updated? How recently?
- Again, shop for a good price.

Not everyone needs a computer, just as not everyone needs a car. More and more, however, computers are becoming an essential part of business life. As with other products, it is important to buy the right product for the job.

Chapter 14

ACCOUNTING FOR CASH PAYMENTS

You have now learned how to use the sales, cash receipts, and purchases journals to record business transactions. You have also learned how two subsidiary ledgers—the accounts receivable and accounts payable subsidiary ledgers—make an accounting system more efficient.

In this chapter, you will learn about a fourth special journal: the cash payments journal. Many business transactions involve the payment of cash. Creditors' invoices must be paid, expenses such as rent and utilities must be met, and various types of assets must be purchased. As a business's cash payments increase, a special journal for recording those payments becomes necessary.

You'll also learn how to determine whether the balance of the Cash in Bank account agrees with the business's checkbook records.

Learning Objectives

When you have completed Chapter 14, you should be able to do the following:

1. Journalize various cash payments in a cash payments journal.
2. Post from the cash payments journal to the accounts payable subsidiary ledger and the general ledger.
3. Total, prove, and rule the cash payments journal.
4. Post special amount column totals to the general ledger.
5. Prepare a schedule of accounts payable.
6. Prove cash.
7. Define the accounting terms introduced in this chapter.

New Terms

- premium
- FOB destination
- FOB shipping point
- bank card fee
- cash payments journal
- schedule of accounts payable
- proving cash

The Management and Control of Cash

If cash is the lifeblood of a business, the accounting department is its heart. All cash entering or leaving a business must at some time be pumped through the accounting department. If it is not, cash loss occurs. Earlier chapters have discussed various ways to guard against cash loss, particularly the use of a bank account in which to deposit all cash receipts.

Cash receipts, however, account for only half of the cash system. Procedures must also be set up and followed for managing cash payments. All cash payments should be authorized. Each authorization should be supported by an approved source document, such as an invoice. All payments should be made by prenumbered check. Checks should be signed only by an authorized person. Finally, every spoiled check should be accounted for, marked "Void," and filed in sequence.

Kinds of Cash Payments

A business makes many different cash payments every month. Merchandising businesses, for example, routinely pay out cash for the purchase of supplies, equipment, and merchandise. In addition, payments are made for expenses and to creditors.

At Champion Building Products, all cash payments are made by check. When a cash payment is to be made, the details are first recorded on the check stub. (The check stub becomes the source document for the journal entry to record the cash payment.) A check is then prepared and signed by an authorized person.

$ 1,500.00		No. 1211
DATE *Dec. 1*		19 – –
TO *Keystone Ins. Co.*		
FOR *6-mo. ins policy*		
	DOLLARS	CENTS
BAL. BRO. FWD.	26,267	49
ADD DEPOSITS		
TOTAL	26,267	49
LESS THIS CHECK	1,500	00
BAL. CARR. FWD.	24,767	49

Cash Purchases

In Chapter 13, you learned that a business often buys merchandise, supplies, and equipment on account. Sometimes these items, particularly supplies, are bought with cash instead of on credit.

Insurance protection is also purchased for cash. Like families, businesses buy insurance to protect themselves against losses from theft, fire, or flood. Insurance policies can be bought for varying lengths of time, such as six months or one year. The amount paid for insurance is called the **premium.** A premium is paid in advance at the beginning of the insurance period. The asset account used to record the premium is called Prepaid Insurance. Prepaid Insurance is an asset account because insurance protection represents a benefit to a company if an insured loss occurs.

Cash Payments of Expenses

In accounting, expenses are the costs of goods or services used to operate a business. Rent, utilities, advertising, and salaries are examples of expenses. Most expenses are billed and paid monthly. Businesses routinely write checks to pay for these expenses when they are incurred.

It is good cash management not to pay invoices before they are due. Cash is an important asset and should be held until the last moment.

Cash Payments for Items Bought on Account

When a business buys on account, it receives an invoice (bill) from the supplier. The credit terms on the invoice indicate when it is to be paid. After the invoice is journalized, the invoice is filed by its due date in a tickler file.

One of the daily tasks of an accounting clerk is to process invoices for payment. Each day, the clerk removes the invoices due for payment from the tickler file. Checks are then prepared, signed by an authorized person, and mailed to creditors.

The amount of the check written in payment of an invoice depends on the credit terms. In Chapter 13, you learned that businesses often take advantage of purchase discounts offered by suppliers.

For example, Champion Building Products purchased $181.48 worth of merchandise on account from Key Paint Company. When the invoice was received, it was recorded as a $181.48 debit to Purchases and a $181.48 credit to Accounts Payable. The invoice, dated December 1, listed credit terms of 2/10, n/30. If Champion pays for the merchandise on or before December 11, it may deduct 2% from the total of the invoice, or $3.63.

When the invoice is paid on December 11, Champion will debit Accounts Payable for the full $181.48 since it is paying for the merchandise purchased on account. Cash in Bank will be credited for $177.85, the actual amount of the check being written. Where should the amount of the purchase discount be recorded?

A purchase discount decreases the cost of merchandise bought on account. The discount, then, could be recorded as a credit to Purchases. Accountants prefer, however, to set up a separate account called Purchases Discounts. Purchases Discounts is classified as a cost of merchandise account. It is also a contra account; its normal balance is "contrary to" that of

Purchases			Purchases Discounts	
Dr.	Cr.		Dr.	Cr.
+	−		−	+
Increase Side	Decrease Side		Decrease Side	Increase Side
Balance Side				Balance Side

the Purchases account. As you know, Purchases has a normal debit balance. The normal balance side of Purchases Discounts, therefore, is the credit side.

Taking advantage of all purchase discounts is good business practice. Over a period of time, such discounts can add up to a sizable reduction in costs.

R — E — M — E — M — B — E — R

Purchases Discounts is a contra cost of merchandise account. It has a normal credit balance.

Other Cash Payments

When a company buys merchandise from a supplier, there is often a charge for shipping the goods. This shipping charge may be paid by either the buyer or the supplier. Who pays depends on the terms of the purchase.

Shipping terms are stated as either FOB destination or FOB shipping point. "FOB" stands for "free on board." **FOB destination** means that the supplier pays the shipping cost to the buyer's destination or location. **FOB shipping point** means that the buyer pays the shipping charge from the supplier's shipping point.

A shipping charge is considered an additional cost of the merchandise purchased for resale. As such, the shipping charge could be debited to the Purchases account. That account would then reflect two costs, the cost of the merchandise itself and the shipping costs paid by the buyer. However, most accountants prefer to have a separate record of shipping charges. The account set up to handle these charges is Transportation In. Transportation In is classified as a cost of merchandise account.

Transportation In	
Dr.	Cr.
+	−
Increase Side	Decrease Side
Balance Side	

Like purchases of merchandise, shipping charges are a cost of doing business. The Transportation In account thus follows the same rules of debit and credit as expense accounts. That is, Transportation In is increased by debits and decreased by credits. The account has a normal debit balance.

If the shipping terms are FOB shipping point, the transporting company gives the freight bill directly to the buyer at delivery. Usually, the buyer must pay the freight bill before it can take possession of the merchandise. In other words, although suppliers do not necessarily require on-the-spot payment, shippers do. The business writes a check for the amount of the shipping charges and records that amount as a debit to the Transportation In account.

Cash Decreases for Bank Service Charges and Bank Card Fees

Most banks charge a monthly fee for servicing a business's checking account. Since checking account service charges occur only once a month and involve a small amount of money, they are usually debited to the Miscellaneous Expense account.

Champion's bank also charges a fee for handling bank card sales slips. This **bank card fee** is usually based on the total dollar volume of the bank card sales processed. The fee is stated as a percentage of the total bank card sales. The percentage rate varies from bank to bank. Accountants usually record the amount of the fee in an expense account entitled Bank Card Fees Expense.

Both amounts are automatically deducted from the business's checking account and appear on the monthly bank statement. No checks are involved, even though Cash in Bank is decreased. These two decreases are expenses and must be recorded as deductions to Cash in Bank. The bank statement is the source document for the journal entry.

Before you learn how to journalize cash payment transactions, do the following activity to check your understanding of the material you have just studied.

Check Your Learning

Write your answers to these questions on notebook paper.

1. What is the amount paid for insurance called?
2. What is the source document for most cash payments?
3. What is the normal balance of Purchases Discounts?
4. Why is it good business practice to take advantage of purchase discounts?
5. Does a purchase discount increase or decrease the cost of merchandise?

Compare your answers to those in the answers section. Re-read the preceding part of the chapter to find the correct answers to any questions you may have missed.

The Cash Payments Journal

So far, you have studied three special journals: the sales journal, the cash receipts journal, and the purchases journal. The cash payments journal is the fourth and last special journal.

The **cash payments journal** is a special journal used to record all transactions in which cash is paid out or decreased. These transactions include payments to creditors for items bought on account, cash purchases of merchandise and other assets, payments for various expenses, and cash decreases for bank service charges and bank card fees. The source documents for the journal entries are the check stubs and the bank statement.

The cash payments journal used by Champion Building Products is shown in Figure 14-1. The first four columns are for the date, the source document number, the title of the account, and the posting reference. The number of amount columns differs from business to business. Champion's journal has four amount columns.

The General Debit column is used for debits to all general ledger accounts for which there is no special column. The Accounts Payable Debit column is used to record all decreases to accounts in the accounts payable subsidiary ledger and to the Accounts Payable account. The Purchases Discounts Credit column is used to enter the amount of any purchase discount taken by Champion. Every transaction recorded in the cash payments journal involves a decrease to Cash in Bank. The cash payments journal, therefore, always has a Cash in Bank Credit column.

Figure 14-1 Cash Payments Journal

The entries in the General Debit column are posted individually to the general ledger during the month. At the end of the month, the totals of the three special amount columns are posted to the general ledger accounts named in the column headings.

R — E — M — E — M — B — E — R

The cash payments journal is used to record all transactions that decrease Cash in Bank.

Journalizing Cash Payments

The six transactions that follow are typical of those recorded in the cash payments journal. Notice that each transaction results in a credit to Cash in Bank.

Journalizing Cash Purchases

A business may buy many things for cash. Here are two examples.

December 1: *Paid $1,500.00 to Keystone Insurance Co. for the premium on a six-month insurance policy, Check 1211.*

Two asset accounts are affected by this transaction: Prepaid Insurance and Cash in Bank. In this transaction, Prepaid Insurance is being increased. It is debited for $1,500.00, the amount of the premium. Cash in Bank is being decreased and is credited for $1,500.00.

	Prepaid Insurance		Cash in Bank	
	Dr.	Cr.	Dr.	Cr.
	+	−	+	−
	$1,500.00			$1,500.00

To journalize the cash payment for the purchase of an asset, follow these steps. This journal entry is shown in Figure 14-2.

	DATE	DOC. NO.	ACCOUNT TITLE	POST. REF.	GENERAL DEBIT	ACCOUNTS PAYABLE DEBIT	PURCHASES DISCOUNTS CREDIT	CASH IN BANK CREDIT	
1	Dec. 1	1211	Prepaid Insurance		1500 00			1500 00	1
2	1	2	3		4			5	2

CASH PAYMENTS JOURNAL   PAGE 14

Figure 14-2 Recording a Cash Purchase in the Cash Payments Journal

1. Enter the date in the Date column of the cash payments journal.
2. Enter the number of the check in the Document Number column.
3. Enter the title of the account being debited in the Account Title column.
4. Enter the amount of the debit in the General Debit column.
5. Enter the amount of the credit in the Cash in Bank Credit column.

Merchandise for resale is usually purchased on account and, thus, recorded in the purchases journal. A business may, however, also buy merchandise for cash. In this case, the transaction is recorded in the cash payments journal.

December 2: *Purchased merchandise from Starks Lumber Co. for $1,115.00 cash, Check 1212.*

The accounts affected by this transaction are Purchases and Cash in Bank. Purchases is being increased because Champion has bought additional merchandise. It is debited for $1,115.00. The merchandise was purchased for cash, so Cash in Bank is being decreased. That account is credited for $1,115.00.

	Purchases		Cash in Bank	
	Dr.	Cr.	Dr.	Cr.
	+	−	+	−
	$1,115.00			$1,115.00

To record the purchase of merchandise for cash, follow the steps listed below. The journal entry is shown in Figure 14-3, line 2, on the next page.

1. Enter the date in the Date column.
2. Enter the number of the check issued for the payment in the Document Number column.
3. Enter the title of the account debited in the Account Title column.
4. Enter the amount of the purchase in the General Debit column.
5. Enter the amount of the check in the Cash in Bank Credit column.

	DATE	DOC. NO.	ACCOUNT TITLE	POST. REF.	GENERAL DEBIT	ACCOUNTS PAYABLE DEBIT	PURCHASES DISCOUNTS CREDIT	CASH IN BANK CREDIT	
1	Dec. 1	1211	Prepaid Insurance		1 500 00			1 500 00	1
2	2	1212	Purchases		1 115 00			1 115 00	2
3	2	1213	Rent Expense		1 250 00			1 250 00	3
4	3	1214	Key Paint Company			1 835 12	36 70	1 798 42	4
14	25	1224	Center City Supply			85 91		85 91	14
15	26	1225	Transportation In		554 37			554 37	15
16	31	1226	Salaries Expense		7 000 00			7 000 00	16
17	31	—	Miscellaneous Expense		5 50			5 50	17
18	31	—	Bank Card Fees Expense		87 65			87 65	18

Figure 14-3   Journalizing Transactions in the Cash Payments Journal

R E M E M B E R

Purchases is debited whenever merchandise to be resold to customers is bought — whether the purchase is for cash or on account.

Journalizing Cash Payments of Expenses

Expenses are generally paid — by check — when they are incurred.

December 2: *Paid $1,250.00 to Berenson Realty for the December rent, Check 1213.*

Rent Expense and Cash in Bank are affected by this transaction. Rent Expense is being increased. It is, therefore, debited for $1,250.00. Cash in Bank is being decreased, so it is credited for $1,250.00.

Rent Expense		Cash in Bank	
Dr.	Cr.	Dr.	Cr.
+	−	+	−
$1,250.00			$1,250.00

The journal entry to record this transaction is shown in Figure 14-3, line 3. Refer to this illustration as you read these steps describing how to record the cash payment of an expense.

1. Enter the date in the Date column.
2. Enter the check number in the Document Number column.
3. Enter the name of the account being debited in Account Title column.
4. Enter the amount of the expense in the General Debit column.
5. Enter the amount of the check in the Cash in Bank Credit column.

Journalizing Payments on Account

On the due date of an invoice for merchandise or other items purchased on account, the accounting clerk prepares a check in payment. Frequently, the cash payment involves a purchase discount.

December 3: *Paid $1,798.42 to Key Paint Company for merchandise purchased on account, $1,835.12 less a discount of $36.70, Check 1214.*

The accounts affected by this transaction are Accounts Payable, Purchases Discounts, and Cash in Bank. Accounts Payable is being decreased by the payment to the creditor. It is debited for $1,835.12, the amount of the original purchase. Purchases Discounts is being increased because Champion is taking advantage of the discount offered by Key Paint. It is credited for $36.70. Cash in Bank is being decreased. It is credited for $1,798.42, the amount of cash actually paid out.

Accounts Payable		Purchases Discounts		Cash in Bank	
Dr.	Cr.	Dr.	Cr.	Dr.	Cr.
−	+	−	+	+	−
$1,835.12			$36.70		$1,798.42

This transaction is shown in the cash payments journal in Figure 14-3, line 4. Refer to this illustration as you read the following steps:

1. Enter the date in the Date column.
2. Enter the number of the check issued for the payment in the Document Number column.
3. Enter the creditor's name in the Account Title column.
4. Enter the amount of the debit in the Accounts Payable Debit column. (This is the same amount as the original purchase.)
5. Enter the amount of the purchase discount in the Purchases Discounts Credit column.
6. Enter the amount of the check in the Cash in Bank Credit column.

After the cash payment is journalized, the accounting clerk places the number of the check on the invoice's processing stamp, on the line marked "Check No." The paid invoice is then filed.

Businesses are not always able to take advantage of discounts offered by suppliers. In other instances, the supplier may not offer a discount at all. When this occurs, the check is written for the amount of the original purchase. Such a cash payment is illustrated in Figure 14-3, line 14.

Journalizing Other Cash Payments

Checks are also written to pay for shipping charges when merchandise is sent FOB shipping point.

December 26: *Issued Check 1225 for $554.37 to Fast Delivery Co. for shipping charges on merchandise bought from Aluminum Plus, Inc.*

The accounts affected by this transaction are Transportation In and Cash in Bank. The Transportation In account, remember, is used to record shipping charges on merchandise purchased from suppliers. Transportation In is being increased. It is, therefore, debited for $554.37. Cash in Bank is being decreased and is credited for $554.37.

If shipping terms are FOB destination, the shipping charges are already built into the cost of the merchandise.

Transportation In		Cash in Bank	
Dr.	Cr.	Dr.	Cr.
+	−	+	−
$554.37			$554.37

To record a cash payment for shipping charges, follow the steps below. The journal entry is shown on line 15 of Figure 14-3 on page 296.

1. Enter the date in the Date column.
2. Enter the number of the check issued for the payment in the Document Number column.
3. Enter the title of the account being debited in the Account Title column.
4. Enter the amount of the shipping costs in the General Debit column.
5. Enter the amount of the check in the Cash in Bank Credit column.

R — E — M — E — M — B — E — R

The word "General" in the column heading of a special journal refers to the general ledger. The account named in the Account Title column is the general ledger account affected by the transaction.

Journalizing Bank Charges

Bank service charges and bank card fees are automatically deducted from Champion's checking account. Champion does not write a check for these two expenses. Since they result in decreases to Cash in Bank, the transactions are recorded in Champion's cash payments journal.

▲ **Journalizing Checking Account Service Charges**   On Champion's December bank statement, the bank included a $5.50 service charge. After the accounting clerk reconciled the bank statement, the service charge was recorded in the cash payments journal.

December 31: *Recorded the bank service charge of $5.50, December bank statement.*

The two accounts affected by this transaction are Miscellaneous Expense and Cash in Bank. Miscellaneous Expense is being increased because of the bank service charge. The account is debited for $5.50. The service charge reduces the checking account balance; therefore, Cash in Bank is being decreased. That account is credited for $5.50.

ACCOUNTING **Notes**
Service charges may not seem too high if you consider that it costs a financial institution between 10 cents and 30 cents to process each check.

Miscellaneous Expense			Cash in Bank	
Dr.	Cr.		Dr.	Cr.
+	−		+	−
$5.50				$5.50

To record the bank service charge, follow these steps. The journal entry is shown on line 17 of Figure 14-3 on page 296.

1. Enter the date in the Date column.
2. Enter a dash in the Document Number column. This indicates that a check was not written for this transaction.
3. Enter the title of the account debited in the Account Title column.
4. Enter the amount of the service charge in the General Debit column.
5. Enter the amount of the cash decrease in the Cash in Bank Credit column.

▲ **Journalizing Bank Card Fees**   Most banks charge a fee for handling a business's bank card sales. Champion's bank charges a fee of 5% of the total bank card sales. During the time covered by the December bank statement, the bank processed $1,753.00 in bank card sales for Champion. The bank card fee was, therefore, $87.65 ($1,753.00 × .05). The fee was listed on the bank statement as a deduction from the checking account balance. This decrease in cash is recorded in the cash payments journal.

December 31: *Recorded the bank card fee of $87.65, December bank statement.*

The accounts affected by this transaction are Bank Card Fees Expense and Cash in Bank. Since Bank Card Fees Expense is being increased, it is debited for $87.65. Cash in Bank is credited for the same amount.

Bank Card Fees Expense			Cash in Bank	
Dr.	Cr.		Dr.	Cr.
+	−		+	−
$87.65				$87.65

To journalize the bank card fee, follow the same steps as in recording the bank service charge. Bank Card Fees Expense, however, is entered in the

Account Title column of the cash payments journal. This journal entry is illustrated on line 18 of Figure 14-3 on page 296.

After the bank charges have been recorded, they must also be entered in the checkbook records. One way to adjust the balance on the check stub is shown on the stub. The deposit heading is crossed out, and the words "Bank Statement" written in its place. The accounting clerk adds the two bank charges and enters the total of $93.15 ($87.65 + $5.50) in the Amount column. A minus sign is also entered to show that the amount is to be subtracted from the balance brought forward.

$		No. 1227	
DATE		19	
TO			
FOR			
		DOLLARS	CENTS
BAL. BRO. FED. *Bk Stmt*		22,277	27
ADD DEPOSITS		− 93	15
TOTAL		22,184	12
LESS THIS CHECK			
BAL. CARR. FWD.			

Posting from the Cash Payments Journal

After cash payments have been journalized, they are posted. Payments on account are posted to the creditors' accounts in the accounts payable subsidiary ledger. Entries in the General Debit column are posted to the named accounts in the general ledger.

Posting to the Accounts Payable Subsidiary Ledger

To keep creditors' accounts current, amounts in the Accounts Payable Debit column are posted daily. The first Champion entry to be posted to the accounts payable subsidiary ledger is the December 3 payment to Key Paint Company.

To post an entry from the cash payments journal to the accounts payable subsidiary ledger, follow the steps below. Refer to Figure 14-4 as you read these steps.

1. Enter the date of the transaction in the Date column of the creditor's account.
2. In the ledger account's Posting Reference column, enter the letter of the journal and the page number on which the entry appears. "CP" are the letters for the cash payments journal.
3. In the Debit column, enter the amount recorded in the Accounts Payable Debit column of the journal.

Prev. Bal.	$2,016.60
Debit	−1,835.12
New Bal.	$ 181.48

4. Compute the new balance and enter it in the Balance column. If the account now has a zero balance, draw a line through the Balance column.
5. Return to the cash payments journal and enter a check mark (✔) in the Posting Reference column.

R E M E M B E R

The individual amounts in the Accounts Payable Debit column are posted daily to the creditors' accounts in the accounts payable subsidiary ledger.

	DATE	DOC. NO.	ACCOUNT TITLE	POST. REF.	GENERAL DEBIT	ACCOUNTS PAYABLE DEBIT	PURCHASES DISCOUNTS CREDIT	CASH IN BANK CREDIT	
1	Dec. 1	1211	Prepaid Insurance	120	1500 00			1500 00	1
2	2	1212	Purchases	501	1115 00			1115 00	2
3	2	1213	Rent Expense	630	1250 00			1250 00	3
4	3	1214	Key Paint Company	✓		1835 12	36 70	1798 42	4

Name Key Paint Company
Address 1714 Peak Road, Cleveland, OH 44109

DATE	EXPLANATION	POST. REF.	DEBIT	CREDIT	BALANCE
Dec. 1	Balance	✓			1835 12
3		P12		181 48	2016 60
3		CP14	1835 12		181 48

Figure 14-4 Posting from the Cash Payments Journal to the Accounts Payable Subsidiary Ledger

All other payments on account are posted to creditors' accounts in the subsidiary ledger in the same manner. Figure 14-5 on pages 302-303 shows the complete accounts payable subsidiary ledger after all postings have been completed. Notice that the accounts contain entries from both the purchases journal and the cash payments journal.

Before continuing, do the following activity.

Check Your Learning

Use Figure 14-5 to answer these questions. Write your answers on a separate sheet of paper.

1. How many creditors does Champion Building Products have?
2. How much was owed to Aluminum Plus, Inc., on December 1?
3. How much was paid on account to Custom Doors, Inc., during December?
4. How many times during December did Champion purchase items on account from Key Paint Company?
5. How much was owed to Starks Lumber Co. on December 31?
6. Did Champion make a payment to Viking Motors during December?
7. In what journal was the December 28 transaction involving Wilson Electric, Inc., recorded?
8. How many postings were made to the accounts payable subsidiary ledger from the cash payments journal during December?

Compare your answers to those in the answers section. Re-read the preceding part of the chapter to find the correct answers to any questions you may have missed.

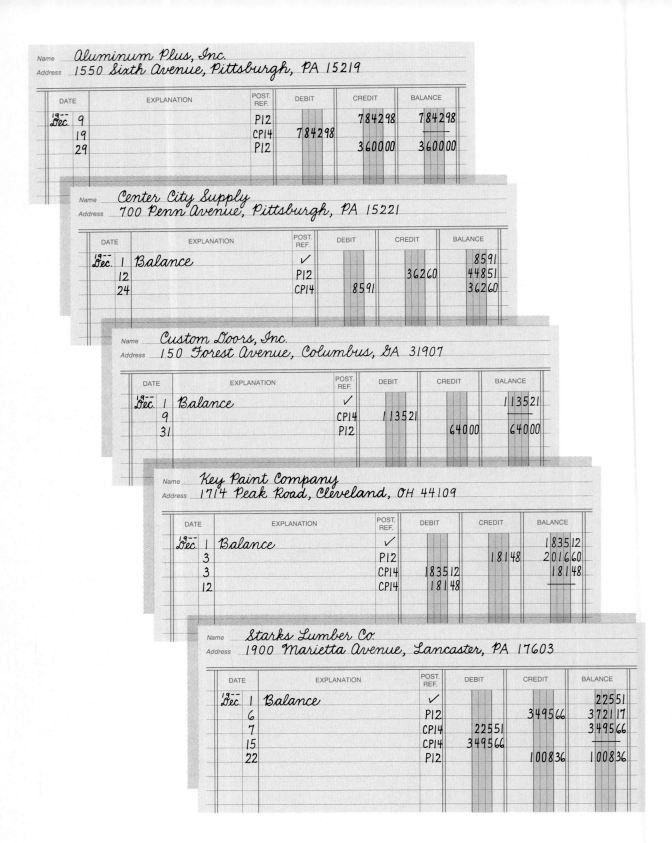

Figure 14-5 The Completed Accounts Payable Subsidiary Ledger

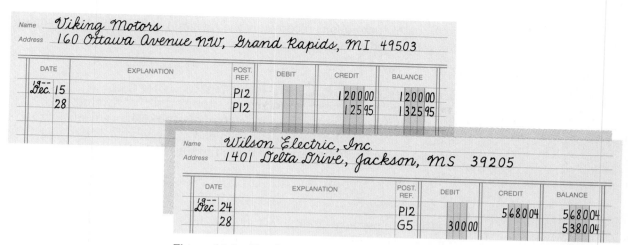

Figure 14-5   The Completed Accounts Payable Subsidiary Ledger (Concluded)

Posting from the General Debit Column

Periodically during the month, the transactions in the General Debit column are posted to the appropriate general ledger accounts. The first December transaction in the General Debit column is the Prepaid Insurance transaction on December 1.

To post an entry from the cash payments journal to the general ledger, follow these steps. Refer to Figure 14-6 as you read the steps.

1. Enter the date of the transaction in the Date column of the general ledger account.
2. Enter the letter of the journal and the page number on which the transaction appears in the account's Posting Reference column. Be sure to use the letters "CP."
3. In the Debit column, enter the amount from the General Debit column of the journal.
4. Compute the new balance and enter it in the appropriate Balance column. (Since there is no previous balance, enter the amount recorded in the Debit column in the Debit Balance column.)
5. Return to the cash payments journal and enter the account number in the Posting Reference column.

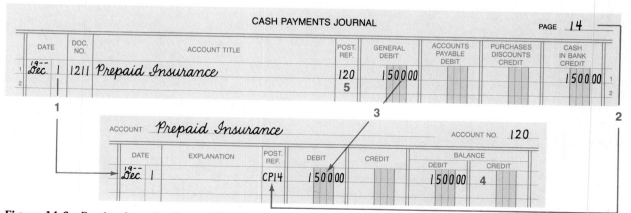

Figure 14-6   Posting from the General Debit Column of the Cash Payments Journal

All other transactions recorded in the General Debit column are posted to the general ledger accounts in the same way.

Completing the Cash Payments Journal

As with the three preceding special journals, the cash payments journal is footed, proved, totaled, and ruled at the end of the month. The totals of the special amount columns are then posted to the general ledger accounts.

Totaling, Proving, and Ruling the Cash Payments Journal

The cash payments journal is totaled following the same procedures used for the other special journals. Before the journal can be ruled, the accounting clerk must prove the equality of debits and credits. The total of the debit columns must equal the total of the credit columns.

Debit Columns		Credit Columns	
General	$14,730.44	Purchases Discounts	$ 294.31
Accounts Payable	14,801.87	Cash in Bank	29,238.00
	$29,532.31		$29,532.31

The cash payments journal can now be double-ruled, as shown in Figure 14-7.

CASH PAYMENTS JOURNAL   PAGE 14

	DATE	DOC. NO.	ACCOUNT TITLE	POST. REF.	GENERAL DEBIT	ACCOUNTS PAYABLE DEBIT	PURCHASES DISCOUNTS CREDIT	CASH IN BANK CREDIT	
1	19-- Dec. 1	1211	Prepaid Insurance	120	1500 00			1500 00	1
2	2	1212	Purchases	501	1115 00			1115 00	2
3	2	1213	Rent Expense	630	1250 00			1250 00	3
4	3	1214	Key Paint Company	✓		1835 12	36 70	1798 42	4
5	7	1215	Starks Lumber Co.	✓		225 51	4 51	221 00	5
6	9	1216	Custom Doors, Inc.	✓		1135 21	22 70	1112 51	6
7	12	1217	Key Paint Company	✓		181 48	3 63	177 85	7
8	15	1218	Utilities Expense	645	225 00			225 00	8
9	15	1219	Supplies	115	137 50			137 50	9
10	15	1220	Starks Lumber Co.	✓		3495 66	69 91	3425 75	10
11	15	1221	Federal Income Tax Expense	650	2437 50			2437 50	11
12	19	1222	Aluminum Plus, Inc.	✓		7842 98	156 86	7686 12	12
13	20	1223	Sales Tax Payable	210	417 92			417 92	13
14	24	1224	Center City Supply	✓		85 91		85 91	14
15	26	1225	Transportation In	505	554 37			554 37	15
16	31	1226	Salaries Expense	635	7000 00			7000 00	16
17	31	—	Miscellaneous Expense	625	5 50			5 50	17
18	31	—	Bank Card Fees Expense	605	87 65			87 65	18
19	31		Totals		14730 44	14801 87	294 31	29238 00	19

Figure 14-7   The Completed Cash Payments Journal

R — E — M — E — M — B — E — R

Columns are first footed in pencil. Verified totals are then written in ink.

Posting Column Totals to the General Ledger

At the end of the month, the total of each special amount column is posted to the general ledger account named in the column heading. In the cash payments journal, column totals are posted to Accounts Payable, Purchases Discounts, and Cash in Bank. Figure 14-8 shows the posting of the three column totals to the general ledger accounts. Note that the account numbers for the three accounts are written in parentheses in the appropriate columns.

The total of the General Debit column is not posted. Each entry in that column has already been posted to a specific general ledger account. A check mark is, therefore, entered below the double rule in the General Debit column.

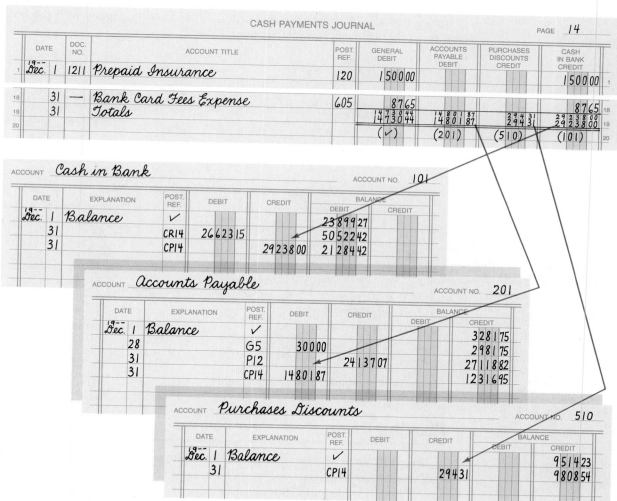

Figure 14-8 Posting Column Totals from the Cash Payments Journal

---

R E M E M B E R

To show that column totals are not posted, place a check mark in parentheses (✓) below the double rule.

Proving the Accounts Payable Subsidiary Ledger

After the column totals have been posted, the accounting clerk prepares a **schedule of accounts payable.** This schedule lists all creditors in the accounts payable ledger, the balance in each account, and the total amount still owed to creditors. The accounts payable subsidiary ledger is proved when the total of the schedule of accounts payable agrees with the balance of the Accounts Payable account. Accounts Payable, you will remember, is the controlling account for the accounts payable subsidiary ledger.

Champion's schedule of accounts payable for December is shown in Figure 14-9. As in the schedule of accounts receivable, the accounts are listed in alphabetical order. All creditors are listed, even those with zero balances. Notice that the total listed on the schedule, $12,316.95, agrees with the balance of the Accounts Payable account.

ACCOUNT	Accounts Payable						ACCOUNT NO.	201	
DATE	EXPLANATION	POST. REF.	DEBIT	CREDIT		BALANCE			
						DEBIT		CREDIT	
19-- Dec. 1	Balance	✓						3281 75	
28		G5	300 00					2981 75	
31		P12		2413707				2711882	
31		CP14	1480187					1231695	←

Champion Building Products, Inc. Schedule of Accounts Payable December 31, 19--		
Aluminum Plus, Inc.	3 600 00	
Center City Supply	362 60	
Custom Doors, Inc.	640 00	
Key Paint Company	—	
Starks Lumber Co.	100836	
Viking Motors	132595	
Wilson Electric, Inc.	538004	
Total Accounts Payable		1231695 ←

Figure 14-9   Schedule of Accounts Payable

Proving Cash

Proving cash is the process of determining whether the amounts of cash recorded in a business's accounting records and in its checkbook agree. Ideally a business should prove cash each day. When a business uses special journals, however, the Cash in Bank account in the general ledger is not updated daily. Postings to the Cash in Bank account are not made until the end of the month. For many businesses, then, proving cash is done at the end of the month. The cash proof may be prepared on plain paper, on accounting stationery, or on a special cash proof form. The cash proof prepared by Champion's accounting clerk, shown in Figure 14-10, was prepared on two-column accounting stationery. To prove cash, follow the steps on page 307.

Champion Building Products, Inc.
Cash Proof
December 31, 19--

Beginning Cash in Bank balance		23 899 27
Plus: Cash receipts for the month		26 623 15
Subtotal		50 522 42
Less: Cash payments for the month		29 238 00
Ending Cash in Bank balance		21 284 42
Check stub balance		21 284 42

Figure 14-10 Cash Proof

1. On the first line, record the beginning balance of Cash in Bank according to the general ledger account.
2. Add the total cash received during the month. This is the total of the Cash in Bank Debit column of the cash receipts journal.
3. From the subtotal, subtract the cash payments for the month. This is the total of the Cash in Bank Credit column of the cash payments journal.
4. Compare this figure against the balance shown on the last check stub in the checkbook. If the ending balance of Cash in Bank and the balance on the check stub match, cash is proved.

The ending balance of Cash in Bank is $21,284.42. Since the balance shown on the last check stub is also $21,284.42, cash has been proved.
Now do the following activity.

Check Your Learning

Write your answers to these questions on notebook paper.

1. The total of the Purchases Discounts Credit column is posted to the ____?____ account in the general ledger.
2. Amounts in the General Debit column of the cash payments journal are posted to ____?____ .
3. The Accounts Payable Debit column total is posted to the ____?____ account in the general ledger.
4. The Cash in Bank Credit column total is posted to the ____?____ account in the general ledger.
5. The accounts payable subsidiary ledger is proved when the total of the creditors' account balances agrees with the balance of the ____?____ account in the ____?____ ledger.
6. If the beginning Cash in Bank balance is $15,000, cash receipts for the month are $10,000, and cash payments for the month are $20,000, what is the ending Cash in Bank balance? If the checkbook balance is $5,000, has cash been proved?

Compare your answers to those in the answers section. Re-read the preceding part of the chapter to find the correct answers to any questions you may have missed.

Summary of Key Points

1. Good internal controls require that all cash payments be authorized, all payments be made by check, and all checks be signed by an authorized person.
2. The premium paid for insurance coverage is debited to the asset account Prepaid Insurance.
3. Suppliers may offer cash discounts to encourage their credit customers to pay promptly. The buyer calls this a purchase discount. It is a deduction from the cost of merchandise purchased and is recorded in the Purchases Discounts account. Purchases Discounts is a contra account that reduces the balance of the cost of merchandise account Purchases.
4. The cost of shipping charges for merchandise purchased from suppliers is considered an additional cost of merchandise. The cost of shipping charges is debited to the Transportation In account, which appears in the cost of merchandise section of the chart of accounts.
5. Banks charge fees for handling a business's checking account and for processing its bank card sales. These fees are automatically deducted from the business's checking account. Since the fees decrease Cash in Bank, they are recorded in the cash payments journal. The service charge and the bank card fee must also be deducted from the business's checkbook records.
6. The cash payments journal is a special journal used to record all transactions in which cash is paid out. The source documents for the journal entry are check stubs and the bank statement.
7. Transactions are posted from the cash payments journal to the accounts payable ledger daily. Transactions entered in the General Debit column are posted periodically during the month.
8. A schedule of accounts payable is a list of all creditors, the amount owed to each, and the total amount owed to all creditors. The total of the schedule of accounts payable must agree with the balance of the Accounts Payable controlling account.
9. At the end of the month, cash is proved by determining whether the balance of Cash in Bank according to the accounting records agrees with the balance shown in the checkbook.

Review and Applications

Building Your Accounting Vocabulary

In your own words, write the definition of each of the following accounting terms. Use complete sentences for your definitions.

bank card fee
cash payments
  journal

FOB destination
FOB shipping point
premium

proving cash
schedule of accounts
  payable

Reviewing Your Accounting Knowledge

1. List five procedures that a business should use to control its cash payments.
2. Why are shipping charges an additional cost of merchandise purchased for resale?
3. Classify the following accounts: Prepaid Insurance, Purchases Discounts, Transportation In.
4. On what amount is the bank card fee based?
5. To which accounts are bank service charges and bank card fees debited?
6. What kinds of transactions are recorded in the cash payments journal?
7. What information can you get from the accounts payable subsidiary ledger that cannot be found in the Accounts Payable controlling account?
8. When are transactions in the cash payments journal posted to the accounts payable subsidiary ledger? To the general ledger?
9. Is the balance of the Accounts Payable account in the general ledger always equal to the total of its subsidiary ledger? Explain.
10. Why is a schedule of accounts payable important?
11. List the steps followed to prove cash at the end of the month.

Improving Your Decision-Making Skills

Decision making is involved whenever you have to determine which of several tasks you should complete first. This process is known as *setting priorities*.

Paula Blake is an accounting clerk for the Hudson Company. When she arrived at work on Monday, September 14, she found the following tasks awaiting her. Read through the list and decide in which order *you* would complete the tasks.

1. File ten paid invoices in the creditors' files.
2. Prepare checks for three invoices with due dates of September 15.
3. Prepare a report for the supervisor listing the suppliers from whom the company purchases merchandise and the credit terms offered by each supplier. The report is needed for a meeting on Tuesday morning.
4. Open and sort the morning's mail.
5. Journalize and post the day's cash payments.
6. Reconcile the bank statement, which arrived this morning.

Applying Accounting Procedures

Exercise 14-1 Entering Amounts in the Cash Payments Journal

Listed below are several transactions of Modern Home Draperies that took place during the first week of July.

Instructions: Use a chart similar to the one that follows. For each transaction, indicate in which columns of the cash payments journal the transaction amounts would be recorded. The first transaction has been completed as an example.

Trans.	General Debit	Accounts Payable Debit	Purchases Discounts Credit	Cash in Bank Credit
1	✔			✔

Transactions:

1. Issued Check 342 to Reid Real Estate for the July rent.
2. Issued Check 343 to French Designs in payment of Invoice 20711 less a 2% discount.
3. Bought office supplies from Marks Corp., Check 344.
4. Wrote Check 345 for freight charges on merchandise bought from the Hayes Company.
5. Purchased merchandise for cash from the Wood Company, Check 346.
6. Recorded the bank service charge, June bank statement.
7. Recorded the bank card fee, June bank statement.

Exercise 14-2 Preparing a Schedule of Accounts Payable

The accounts payable ledger of The Corner Book Store included the accounts that follow.

Carswell Magazines	$1,157.20	Barker Publications	$ 186.35
Petrocelli Publishing	5,611.90	Ridgewood, Inc.	2,630.25
Beardsley Equipment	3,868.00	Jenkins Supplies	419.38

Instructions:

(1) Prepare a schedule of accounts payable for August.
(2) If the balance of the Accounts Payable account is $13,873.08, has the subsidiary ledger been proved?

Exercise 14-3 Proving Cash

On November 30, the total of the Cash in Bank Credit column of the cash payments journal is $19,975.12. The total of the Cash in Bank Debit column of the cash receipts journal is $20,956.47. The balance on check stub 1533 is $8,277.98.

Instructions: Use the space provided in the working papers. Prove cash for November. The balance of Cash in Bank on November 1 was $7,296.63.

Problem 14-1 Journalizing Cash Payments Transactions

Owens Office Supply Co., a retail merchandising business, makes all cash payments by check and uses a multicolumn cash payments journal.

Instructions: Record the following transactions on page 8 of the cash payments journal.

Transactions:

July 1   Paid cash for a new $700.00 desk for the office, Check 497.

     2   Issued Check 498 to Able Realty to pay the July rent, $400.00.

     7   Bought $298.00 worth of office supplies for cash, Check 499.

   10   Issued Check 500 for $808.50 to Moore Paper Co. in payment of Invoice 798 for $825.00, less a 2% discount of $16.50.

   12   Prepared Check 501 for $921.50 in payment of AAA Envelope Co.'s Invoice 684 for $950.00, less a 3% discount of $28.50.

   14   Paid Sam's, Inc., $490.00 for Invoice 2478 for $500.00, less a $10.00 discount, Check 502.

   20   Paid the AAA Envelope Co. $600.00 on account, Check 503.

   22   Issued Check 504 for $8,820.00 to Crawford Paper Products in payment of Invoice 3-729 for $9,000.00, less a 2% discount of $180.00.

   26   Wrote Check 505 to Interstate Transit for shipping charges on merchandise purchased from Crawford Paper Products, $89.90.

   26   Purchased merchandise for cash, $629.00, Check 506.

   28   Paid Sam's, Inc., $254.80 for Invoice 2498 for $260.00, less a 2% discount of $5.20, Check 507.

   29   Sent Check 508 for $428.60 to Moore Paper Co. in payment of Invoice 868.

   30   Issued Check 509 in the amount of $372.40 to Crawford Paper Products for Invoice 3-800, $380.00 less $7.60 discount.

   31   Prepared Check 510 for $1,500.00 for salaries for the month.

Problem 14-2   Posting Transactions from the

You will need the cash payments journal from Problem 14-1 to complete this problem. The opened general ledger and accounts payable subsidiary ledger for Owens Office Supply Co. appear in the working papers accompanying this textbook.

Instructions:

(1) Post the amounts in the Accounts Payable Debit column to the creditors' accounts in the accounts payable subsidiary ledger.

(2) Post the amounts in the General Debit column to the accounts in the general ledger.

(3) Foot, prove, total, and rule the cash payments journal.

(4) Post the column totals to the general ledger.

(5) Prepare a schedule of accounts payable.

Problem 14-3   Recording Cash Payment Transactions

The Four Seasons Shop uses special journals and subsidiary ledgers to record its business transactions. The opened general ledger and accounts payable subsidiary ledger are included in the working papers.

Instructions:

(1) Record the following transactions in the cash payments journal, page 9.

(2) Post the transactions to the accounts payable subsidiary ledger and to the general ledger daily.

(3) Total, prove, and rule the cash payments journal at the end of the month.

(4) Post the column totals to the general ledger.

(5) Prepare a schedule of accounts payable.

(6) Prove cash. The beginning Cash in Bank balance was $8,941.62. Total cash receipts for the month were $32,146.80. The balance shown on check stub 201 is $21,508.77.

Transactions:

May 2   Issued Check 185 to Lake Developers for the May rent of $800.00.

3   Paid Brown Carpet Co. $4,753.00 for Invoice 2416 totaling $4,900.00, less the 3% discount of $147.00, Check 186.

5   Purchased $900.00 worth of merchandise from Materials Unlimited for cash, Check 187.

9   Paid the monthly telephone bill of $149.25, Check 188.

9   Sent Check 189 to Jane Aday, Inc., $1,212.50, for Invoice 296-P for $1,250.00 less a 3% discount of $37.50.

11   Issued Check 190 for office supplies costing $362.49.

14   Paid the electric bill for the month, $128.47, Check 191.

14   Sent Check 192 for $900.00 to Williams Company to apply on account.

16   Issued Check 193 to Brigg's Brothers, Inc., for $3,492.00 in full payment of Invoice 3498 for $3,600.00 less a $108.00 discount.

17   Paid Invoice 2741 from Central Manufacturing Corp., $1,200.00 less a discount of $24.00, Check 194 for $1,176.00.

18   Purchased stamps (Miscellaneous Expense), $25.00, Check 195.

22   Paid $1,800.00 for a one-year general liability insurance policy, Check 196.

24   Purchased merchandise for $2,600.00 cash, Check 197.

26   Sent Check 198 to Jane Aday, Inc., for $774.40. The check was in payment of Invoice 389-P for $798.35, less a 3% discount of $23.95.

29   Purchased office supplies for cash, Check 199 for $128.40.

30   Recorded the bank service charge of $15.00, May bank statement.

30   The bank card fee for the month was $63.14, May bank statement.

31   Sent Check 200 for $300.00 to Brown Carpet Co. to apply on account.

COMPUTER

PROBLEM

Problem 14-4   Processing Purchases and Cash Payments Transactions

The Concord Department Store uses special journals and subsidiary ledgers to record its business transactions. On October 1, the store had the following balances in its general ledger and accounts payable subsidiary ledger accounts.

General Ledger (Partial)

Account Number		Account Balance
101	Cash in Bank	$12,241.65
120	Prepaid Insurance	0.00
125	Supplies	1,400.00
140	Office Equipment	6,450.00
201	Accounts Payable	2,990.00
501	Purchases	60,198.00
505	Transportation In	1,577.00

510	Purchases Discounts	1,200.00
605	Bank Card Fees Expense	684.19
620	Miscellaneous Expense	415.75
625	Rent Expense	10,800.00
635	Utilities Expense	1,959.25

Accounts Payable Subsidiary Ledger

Account Number		Account Balance
910	Belleview Company, 1145 Belvedere Avenue, Baltimore, MD 21239	$ 90.00
915	BKP Kitchen Products, 100 First Avenue, Kitty Hawk, NC 27949	1,400.00
935	Loup Corporation, 301 Joppa Road, Baltimore, MD 21204	0.00
937	Love's Women's Wear, 72 Rockaway Boulevard, Brooklyn, NY 11212	0.00
970	Randolph Linens, 601 Brattle Street, Randolph, MA 02368	0.00
978	Richmond Designs, 1722 Monument Avenue, Richmond, VA 23220	1,500.00

Instructions:

(1) Open the accounts and enter beginning balances in Concord Department Store's general ledger.

(2) Open the creditors' accounts in the accounts payable subsidiary ledger and record the beginning balances.

(3) Record the following transactions in the purchases journal (page 9) and the cash payments journal (page 10). For some transactions, you will have to determine the amount of the discount (if any) and the amount of the check written.

(4) Post to the accounts payable ledger daily from the purchases and cash payments journals.

(5) Post the entries in the General columns of the purchases and cash payments journals on a daily basis.

(6) At the end of October, the total of the Cash in Bank Debit column of the cash receipts journal, page 12, was $15,261.80. Post this total to the Cash in Bank account.

(7) Total the purchases journal and the cash payments journal.

(8) Post the column totals to the general ledger. Post the purchases journal totals first.

(9) Prepare a schedule of accounts payable.

(10) Prove cash. The balance shown on check stub 502 is $11,208.53.

Transactions:

Oct. 1 Purchased merchandise on account from BKP Kitchen Products, $2,000.00, Invoice K-691 dated Sept. 28, terms 3/15, n/30.

2 Issued Check 488 for $1,200.00 to Lyons Real Estate for the October rent.

4 Wrote Check 489 for $1,470.00 to Richmond Designs in payment of Invoice 78942 for $1,500.00, less a $30.00 discount.

7 Paid BKP Kitchen Products $1,400.00 on account, Check 490.

8 Sent Check 491 for $90.00 to the Belleview Company on account.

11 Issued Check 492 for $1,940.00 to BKP Kitchen Products in payment of Invoice K-691 for $2,000.00, less a discount of $60.00.

12 Paid the monthly telephone bill of $214.87, Check 493.

12 Purchased merchandise for cash from the Belleview Company, $1,945.60, Check 494.

13 Issued Check 495 to Tidewater Insurance Co. for a one-year fire insurance policy, $950.00.

14 Bought office equipment on account from Loup Corp., $5,300.00, Invoice K-4444 dated Oct. 10, terms n/30.

16 Issued Check 496 for $75.00 for carpet cleaning (Miscellaneous Expense).

18 Bought $120.00 worth of supplies from Loup Corp. on account, Invoice K-4462 dated Oct. 16, terms n/30.

20 Received Invoice 4215, dated Oct. 18 with terms of 2/20, n/60, from Love's Women's Wear for $945.20 worth of merchandise purchased on account.

20 Wrote Check 497 for $25.00 for freight charges on merchandise bought from Love's Women's Wear.

21 Purchased merchandise from Randolph Linens on account for $3,480.00, Invoice CP422 dated Oct. 18, terms 2/15, n/30.

21 Bought $3,200.00 worth of merchandise on account from Richmond Designs, Invoice 79211 dated Oct. 19, terms 3/10, n/30.

23 Paid the $321.00 electric bill, Check 498.

24 Received Invoice 2832 dated Oct. 22, terms 2/10, n/30, for merchandise purchased on account from Belleview Company, $800.00.

25 Bought merchandise on account from Randolph Linens for $1,684.25, Invoice CP478 dated Oct. 24, terms 2/15, n/30.

26 Paid cash for office supplies, $50.00, Check 499.

27 Sent Check 500 to Richmond Designs in full payment of Invoice 79211, less the discount.

28 Recorded the monthly bank service charge of $25.00, October bank statement.

28 Recorded the $74.05 bank card fee, October bank statement.

28 Bought merchandise totaling $600.00 from Randolph Linens on account, Invoice CP500 dated Oct. 27, terms 2/15, n/30.

30 Sent Check 501 to Randolph Linens in full payment of Invoice CP422, less the discount.

31 Purchased merchandise on account from BKP Kitchen Products for $1,346.80, Invoice K788 dated Oct. 29, terms 3/15, n/30.

CHALLENGE

PROBLEM

Problem 14-5   Examining the Cash Payments Journal

The completed cash payments journal of The Piece Goods Shop for the month of April appears on page 315. Some amounts and other information have been deleted from the journal.

Instructions: Fill in the missing information and complete the journal. The chart of accounts for The Piece Goods Shop includes the following accounts.

101	Cash in Bank	510	Purchases Discounts
115	Prepaid Insurance	605	Bank Card Fees Expense
120	Office Supplies	630	Miscellaneous Expense
201	Accounts Payable	650	Rent Expense
501	Purchases	660	Utilities Expense
505	Transportation In		

	DATE	DOC. NO.	ACCOUNT TITLE	POST. REF.	GENERAL DEBIT	ACCOUNTS PAYABLE DEBIT	PURCHASES DISCOUNTS CREDIT	CASH IN BANK CREDIT	
1	19-- Apr. 2	176	Rent Expense	650	750 00			750 00	1
2	3	177	Utilities Expense	660	167 50			167 50	2
3	5	178	Baker Curtains, Inc.	✓		250 00		250 00	3
4	9			501				788 50	4
5	9	180	Office Supplies		209 50				5
6	11	181	Andrews Fabrics	✓			22 50	727 50	6
7	13	182	Warneford, Inc.	✓		875 00		875 00	7
8	13	183	Buckeye Manufacturing	✓		1500 00	30 00	1470 00	8
9	16	184	Utilities Expense	660	87 50			87 50	9
10	17	185	First Avenue Fabrics			2430 00	48 60		10
11	18	186		630	23 00			23 00	11
12	19	187	Purchases		2133 20			2133 20	12
13	23	188	Prepaid Insurance	115					13
14	25	189	Andrews Fabrics	✓		1181 75		1146 30	14
15	27	190	Baker Curtains, Inc.	✓			42 66		15
16	30		Office Supplies	120	535 50			535 50	16
17	30	—	Miscellaneous Expense	630	10 00				17
18	30		Bank Card Fees Expense	605	59 00				18
19					6163 70				19
20					6163 70			15104 44	20

*C*redit Managers Take Risks in Stride

If you're challenged by risk-taking and you feel you've got pretty good judgment, read on. This could be the career for you.

In today's economy, money is more than a measure of value for goods and services. It's also a tradeable commodity. From country to country, business to business, business to consumer, extending credit can make or break a business—and the credit manager's judgment and instincts can make the difference. No risk means no gain. The successful business makes credit available in order to expand its market share and increase its profits. Some bad debts (uncollectible accounts) are inevitable; keeping the bad debts to a minimum is the real challenge.

Any business that lends money or extends credit employs a credit manager: banks; credit bureaus; mortgage, finance, or investment companies; brokerages; department stores; businesses. The credit manager is the person who directs or coordinates activities of workers engaged in conducting credit investigations. He or she reviews and evaluates applications and data gathered by the staff, and rejects or approves the applications. Essentially, it's the credit manager's responsibility to determine whether a business or an individual is a good credit risk.

In businesses, credit managers are often accountants. Banks and other lending institutions hire college graduates with degrees in accounting and business. Once these employees complete a bank-officer trainee program and gain experience, their responsibilities grow.

In larger companies, credit management is subdivided into financial analysis and credit analysis. These positions require an advanced background in accounting and more experience. Few colleges offer training in credit management, so candidates

The ability to minimize risks is an essential skill for a credit manager.

often seek advanced training at the Credit Research Foundation or the National Association of Credit Management.

A day in the life of a credit manager presents opportunities to exercise critical assessments of a client's character and credibility, the economic climate, and the terms of repayment. The employer is banking on the fact that he or she won't make too many mistakes.

Chapter 15

RECORDING GENERAL JOURNAL TRANSACTIONS

Learning Objectives

When you have completed Chapter 15, you should be able to do the following:

1. Explain the purpose of debit and credit memorandums.
2. Journalize transactions involving sales returns and allowances.
3. Journalize transactions involving purchases returns and allowances.
4. Journalize correcting entries.
5. Define the accounting terms introduced in this chapter.

In Chapters 11 through 14, you learned how to record business transactions in four special journals. Each special journal is designed to handle a specific kind of business transaction: sales of merchandise on account, the cash received by a business, the purchase of merchandise and other assets on account, and all cash payments or decreases to cash.

There are, however, some transactions that do not fit into one of these four categories. As a result, these transactions cannot be recorded in one of the special journals. They are instead recorded in the general journal, which you first learned about in Chapter 5.

In this chapter, you will learn how the general journal fits into an accounting system using special journals. You will also learn about the kinds of business transactions that are recorded in it.

New Terms

sales return
sales allowance
credit memorandum
debit memorandum
purchases return
purchases allowance

Handling Business Transactions that Occur Infrequently

A business designs its special journals to handle particular kinds of transactions that occur frequently, usually daily. Any transaction that cannot be recorded in a special journal is recorded in the general journal. Examples of transactions that would be recorded in a general journal include sales returns and allowances, purchases returns and allowances, and correcting entries. These general journal entries will be explained in this chapter.

Sales Returns and Allowances

All merchandising businesses expect to have some customers who are not satisfied with their purchases. The reasons for dissatisfaction vary. An item may be damaged or defective. The color or size may be incorrect. Perhaps the customer made a mistake and bought the wrong item. Whatever the reason, merchants usually allow dissatisfied customers to return merchandise. Any merchandise returned for full credit or a cash refund is called a **sales return.**

Sometimes a customer discovers that merchandise is damaged or defective but still usable. When this happens, the merchant may reduce the sales price for the damaged merchandise. This price reduction granted by a business for damaged goods kept by the customer is called a **sales allowance.**

Many merchandising businesses have separate departments to handle customer returns of merchandise.

UNIT 3   The Accounting Cycle for a Merchandising Business

If the sales return or sales allowance occurs on a charge sale, the business usually prepares a credit memorandum. A **credit memorandum** is a form that lists the details of a sales return or sales allowance. It is called a "credit" memorandum because the charge customer's account will be *credited* for (or decreased by) the amount of the return or allowance.

The credit memorandum, or credit memo, used by Champion Building Products is shown in Figure 15-1. This credit memo was prepared when Shawn Flannery returned merchandise he had bought on credit on December 21. Notice that the credit memo includes a description of the returned item, the reason for the return, and the amount to be credited to Shawn Flannery's account. Champion's credit memo also includes spaces for the date and sales slip number of the original sale. Notice too that the total on the credit memo includes the sales tax charged on the original sale.

CHAMPION BUILDING PRODUCTS, INC.	CREDIT MEMORANDUM			NO. 124

601 Mt. Lebanon Road
Pittsburgh, PA 15230

ORIGINAL SALES DATE	ORIGINAL SALES SLIP	APPROVAL		
12/21	#76	J.R.	X	MDSE RET

Date: *December 27, 19--*

Name: *Shawn Flannery*

Address: *1350 Old Trail Road*
Oakmont, PA 15139

QTY	DESCRIPTION	AMOUNT
1 bx	Flooring materials	230 00

Reason for return *wrong color*

The total shown at the right will be credited to your account.

SUB TOTAL	230 00
SALES TAX	13 80
TOTAL	243 80

Shawn Flannery
Customer Signature

Figure 15-1 Credit Memorandum

The same form would have been used had Shawn Flannery been given a sales allowance. Of course, the amount credited to his account would have been less. Any credit granted for an allowance is the difference between the original sales price and the reduced price.

Champion's credit memos are prenumbered and prepared in duplicate. The original is given or sent to the customer. The copy kept by the business is the source document for the journal entry to record the transaction.

The Sales Returns and Allowances Account

Sales returns and sales allowances decrease the total revenue earned by a business. This decrease, however, is not recorded in the Sales account. Instead, a separate account called Sales Returns and Allowances is used. (Sales discounts, you'll remember, are also treated separately.) Sales Returns and Allowances summarizes the total amount of returns and allowances for damaged, defective, or otherwise unsatisfactory merchandise. Separating sales returns and allowances from Sales is efficient. There are, however, other reasons for having a separate account.

With a separate account for returns and allowances, Sales always represents the gross, or total, revenue for the period. Having a separate account for sales returns and allowances allows management to better monitor customer dissatisfaction. The balance in the account may also signal merchandising problems. If the monthly balance of Sales Returns and Allowances is large in comparison to the balance of the Sales account, steps should be taken to discover why and to correct the cause. For example, management would want to know if any one supplier is responsible for a large number of returns, if returns and allowances are mainly from one department, or if merchandise is being mishandled inside the company.

Like Sales Discounts, Sales Returns and Allowances is classified as a contra revenue account. As a contra account, its balance decreases the balance of the revenue account Sales. Since the normal balance side of Sales is the credit side, the normal balance side of Sales Returns and Allowances is the debit side. This relationship is shown in the T accounts.

Sales		Sales Returns and Allowances	
Dr.	Cr.	Dr.	Cr.
−	+	+	−
Decrease Side	Increase Side	Increase Side	Decrease Side
	Balance Side	Balance Side	

R — E — M — E — M — B — E — R

The balance of a contra account decreases the balance of its related account. The normal balance side of any contra account, therefore, is always opposite the normal balance side of the account it decreases.

Analyzing Sales Returns and Allowances Transactions

On December 21, Champion sold merchandise on account to Shawn Flannery for $230.00 plus sales tax of $13.80. The transaction was recorded in the sales journal and posted to the customer's account in the accounts receivable subsidiary ledger. The December 21 transaction is shown below in T-account form.

GENERAL LEDGER

Accounts Receivable		Sales Tax Payable	
Dr.	Cr.	Dr.	Cr.
+	−	−	+
$243.80			$13.80

SUBSIDIARY LEDGER

Sales		Shawn Flannery	
Dr.	Cr.	Dr.	Cr.
−	+	+	−
	$230.00	$243.80	

On December 27, Shawn Flannery returned the merchandise purchased on account for full credit. The credit memo shown in Figure 15-1 was prepared by Champion for this transaction.

December 27: Issued Credit Memo 124 to Shawn Flannery for the return of merchandise purchased on account, $230.00 plus $13.80 sales tax.

The accounts affected by this transaction are Sales Returns and Allowances, Sales Tax Payable, and Accounts Receivable in the general ledger and the accounts receivable subsidiary ledger account Shawn Flannery.

The Sales Returns and Allowances account is being increased since the amount of merchandise returned by customers has increased. It is, therefore, debited for $230.00, the original sales price of the merchandise. Since the merchandise sold and taxed earlier has been returned, Champion no longer owes the state the sales tax on the December 21 sale. Sales Tax Payable, then, is being decreased. It is debited for $13.80. Accounts Receivable is also being decreased because Champion no longer expects to receive cash from Shawn Flannery. It is credited for $243.80, the original sales price of the returned merchandise ($230.00) plus the sales tax ($13.80). Accounts Receivable is the controlling account for the accounts receivable subsidiary ledger. If the controlling account is being credited, one of the accounts in the subsidiary ledger must also be credited. That account is Shawn Flannery. Since Accounts Receivable was credited for $243.80, the Shawn Flannery account is also credited for $243.80.

GENERAL LEDGER

Accounts Receivable			Sales Tax Payable	
Dr.	Cr.		Dr.	Cr.
+	−		−	+
$243.80	$243.80		$13.80	$13.80

Sales Returns and Allowances			**SUBSIDIARY LEDGER**	
			Shawn Flannery	
Dr.	Cr.		Dr.	Cr.
+	−		+	−
$230.00			$243.80	$243.80

As you can see from the T accounts, the December 27 sales return transaction has, in effect, "wiped out" the earlier journal entry recording the sale to Shawn Flannery.

Journalizing Sales Returns and Allowances Transactions

Champion's special journals are not designed to handle returns of merchandise sold on account. The entry, therefore, is recorded in the general journal, as shown in Figure 15-2 on page 322.

Look at the third line of the journal entry. Since a general ledger controlling account and a subsidiary ledger account are affected by this transaction, both Accounts Receivable and Shawn Flannery are written on the same line in the Description column. The two account titles are separated by a diagonal line.

Notice also that a diagonal line was entered in the Posting Reference column. The diagonal line indicates that the amount (the $243.80 credit) is to be posted to *two* places. The amount will be posted *first* to the Accounts Receivable controlling account in the general ledger and *then* to the Shawn Flannery account in the accounts receivable subsidiary ledger. The diagonal line is entered in the Posting Reference column when the journal entry is made.

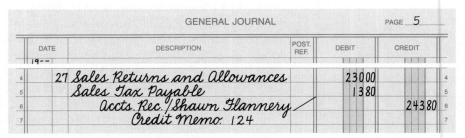

Figure 15-2 Recording a Sales Returns and Allowances Transaction in the General Journal

R E M E M B E R

Always record the title of the controlling account before you record the title of the subsidiary ledger account.

Sometimes a merchant will give a customer a cash refund instead of a credit for a sales return or allowance. Champion's policy is to give a cash refund only if the original sale was a cash sale. When a cash refund is given, the Cash in Bank account is affected instead of Accounts Receivable. The entry for a cash refund is recorded in the cash payments journal.

Posting Sales Returns and Allowances Transactions

After a sales returns and allowances transaction has been recorded in the general journal, it is posted to the appropriate accounts in the general ledger and the accounts receivable subsidiary ledger.

Figure 15-3 shows how the December 27 transaction is posted. Notice how the credit part of the transaction was posted. The $243.80 credit amount, remember, is posted to two accounts—the general ledger controlling account and a particular subsidiary ledger account. After the amount is posted to the general ledger account, the account number of Accounts Receivable is entered to the *left* of the diagonal in the Posting Reference column. After the amount is posted to the customer's account, a check mark (✔) is entered to the *right* of the diagonal line.

UNIT 3   The Accounting Cycle for a Merchandising Business

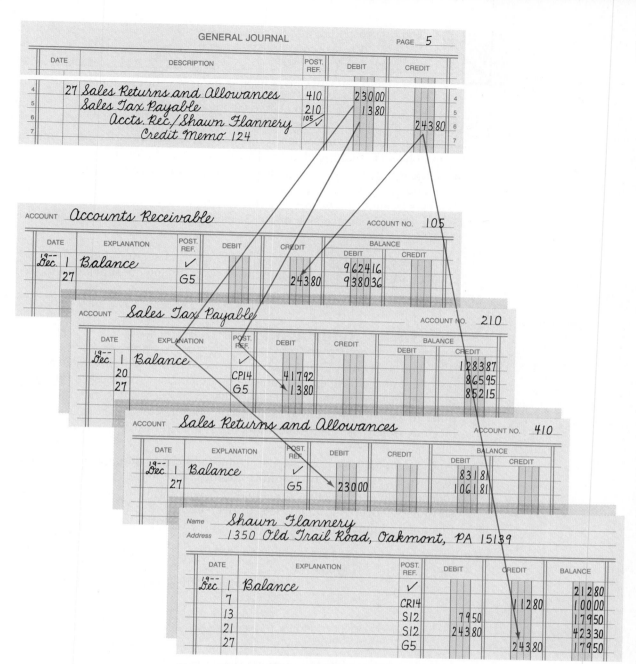

Figure 15-3 Posting a Sales Returns and Allowances Transaction

Before you go any further, complete the activity on page 324 to check your understanding of the material you have just read.

R — E — M — E — M — B — E — R

Be sure to post the total amount of a sales return or allowance transaction to both Accounts Receivable and the customer's account in the subsidiary ledger.

Check Your Learning

On notebook paper, complete each statement with the appropriate term.

1. When a business allows a charge customer to return merchandise for full credit, that transaction is called a(n) __?__ .
2. A(n) __?__ occurs when a business reduces the price for damaged merchandise that the charge customer chooses to keep.
3. The form that lists the details of a sales return or sales allowance transaction is called a(n) __?__ .
4. Sales Returns and Allowances reduces the balance of __?__ .
5. The normal balance side of the Sales Returns and Allowances account is the __?__ side.

Compare your answers to those in the answers section. Re-read the preceding part of the chapter to find the answers to any questions you missed.

Purchases Returns and Allowances

As you learned in Chapter 13, businesses buy many items for use in the operation of the business. In addition, merchandising businesses buy goods to resell to their customers. Occasionally, a business buys merchandise or other items on account that, upon inspection, turn out to be unacceptable. Like any other customer, a business may either return the items or take an allowance on them.

The form a business uses to notify its supplier (creditor) of a return or allowance is called a **debit memorandum,** or debit memo. A "debit" memo indicates the amount that the supplier's account in the accounts payable subsidiary ledger will be *debited,* or decreased. A debit memo prepared by Champion Building Products is shown in Figure 15-4. As you can see, the

	DEBIT MEMORANDUM	No. 51 Date: December 28, 19-- Invoice No.: 4681

CHAMPION BUILDING PRODUCTS, INC.
601 Mt. Lebanon Road
Pittsburgh, PA 15230

To: Wilson Electric, Inc.
1401 Delta Drive
Jackson, MS 39205

This day we have debited your account as follows:

Quantity	Description	Unit Price	Total
3	Electric garage door openers, stock number EG 31	$100.00	$300.00

Figure 15-4 Debit Memorandum

debit memo is prenumbered and has spaces to list the creditor's name, address, and invoice number. Champion prepares an original and one copy of each debit memo. The original is sent to the creditor. The copy becomes the source document for the journal entry.

A debit memo always results in a debit (decrease) to the Accounts Payable controlling account in the general ledger and to the creditor's account in the subsidiary ledger. The account credited depends on whether the debit memo is for merchandise or for some other asset bought on account.

Suppose that Champion prepared a debit memo for the return of a defective typewriter it had purchased on account. Since Champion no longer has the typewriter, the asset account Office Equipment is credited.

When Champion buys merchandise for resale to its customers, it debits the cost to the Purchases account. A return of that merchandise decreases the balance of Purchases. As for sales, however, a separate account is used to record the return of merchandise to a supplier: the Purchases Returns and Allowances account. A **purchases return,** then, occurs when a business returns merchandise bought on account to the supplier for full credit. A **purchases allowance** occurs when a business keeps unsatisfactory merchandise but pays less than its original purchase price.

Purchases Returns and Allowances appears in the cost of merchandise section of the chart of accounts. Like Purchases Discounts, it is a contra cost of merchandise account. Since the normal balance side of the Purchases account is the debit side, the normal balance side of Purchases Returns and Allowances is the credit side. This relationship is shown in the T accounts.

ACCOUNTING Notes
Using a separate account for purchases returns and allowances provides management with information for decision making. It can be very costly to return merchandise for credit. There are many costs that cannot be recovered, such as ordering costs, accounting costs, and freight costs. Sometimes there are lost sales resulting from poor ordering or unusable goods. Excessive returns may call for new purchasing procedures or new suppliers.

Purchases		Purchases Returns and Allowances	
Dr.	Cr.	Dr.	Cr.
+	−	−	+
Increase Side	Decrease Side	Decrease Side	Increase Side
Balance Side			Balance Side

Analyzing Purchases Returns and Allowances Transactions

On December 24, Champion Building Products purchased $5,680.04 in merchandise on account from Wilson Electric, Inc. On December 28, Champion returned some of that merchandise to Wilson Electric. Champion prepared and sent the debit memo shown in Figure 15-4.

December 28: Issued Debit Memo 51 for the return of merchandise purchased on account from Wilson Electric, Inc., $300.00.

Three accounts are affected by this transaction. The two general ledger accounts affected are Accounts Payable and Purchases Returns and Allowances. The accounts payable subsidiary ledger account affected is Wilson Electric, Inc.

Since Champion is returning merchandise purchased on account, it no longer owes money to the creditor for that merchandise. The liability account Accounts Payable, therefore, is debited for $300.00. Since the controlling account Accounts Payable is being debited, an account in the subsidiary ledger must also be debited. The Wilson Electric, Inc. account, therefore, is also debited for $300.00. Purchases Returns and Allowances is being increased since the amount of merchandise returned to suppliers has increased. It is credited for $300.00, the cost of the original merchandise purchased. This transaction is shown in T-account form.

GENERAL LEDGER		Purchases Returns and Allowances		**SUBSIDIARY LEDGER**	
Accounts Payable				Wilson Electric, Inc.	
Dr.	Cr.	Dr.	Cr.	Dr.	Cr.
–	+	–	+	–	+
$300.00			$300.00	$300.00	

Journalizing Purchases Returns and Allowances Transactions

A return of merchandise, or any other item, bought on account is recorded in the general journal. The journal entry for this transaction is shown in Figure 15-5. Look at the debit part of the entry. The amount will be posted to both the general ledger controlling account and a subsidiary ledger account. Both account titles, then, are written on the same line in the Description column, separated by a diagonal. A diagonal line is also entered in the Posting Reference column to remind the accounting clerk to post the $300.00 debit to two accounts.

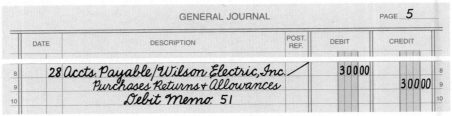

Figure 15-5 Recording a Purchases Returns and Allowances Transaction in the General Journal

R — E — M — E — M — B — E — R

A diagonal line in the Posting Reference column indicates that an amount is to be posted to two accounts.

Posting Purchases Returns and Allowances Transactions

Figure 15-6 shows how a purchases returns and allowances transaction is posted to the general and subsidiary ledger accounts. Notice again that the $300.00 debit is posted to two accounts. After the posting, the account number for the controlling account is placed to the left of the diagonal in the Posting Reference column. The check mark to the right of the diagonal indicates that the amount has been posted to the appropriate account in the subsidiary ledger.

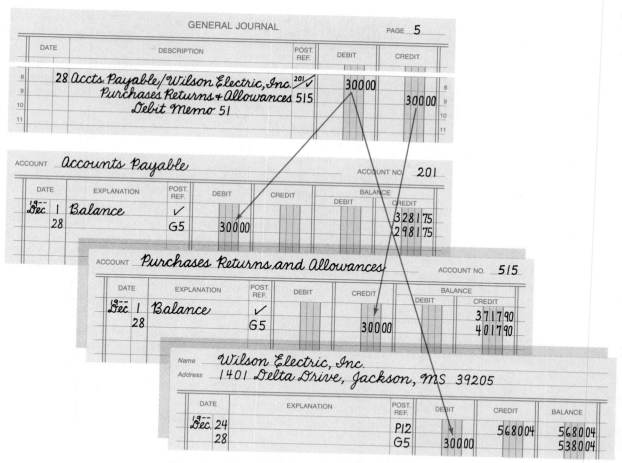

Figure 15-6 Posting a Purchases Returns and Allowances Transaction

Before reading further, complete the following activity to check your understanding of transactions involving purchases returns and allowances.

Check Your Learning

Write your answers to these questions on notebook paper.

1. What form is used to notify a creditor about the return of items bought on account and the decrease in the creditor's account?
2. How does a purchases return differ from a purchases allowance?
3. What type of account is Purchases Returns and Allowances?
4. What does a diagonal line in the Posting Reference column of the general journal indicate?
5. In what section of the chart of accounts does Purchases Returns and Allowances appear?

Compare your answers to those in the answers section. Re-read the preceding part of the chapter to find the correct answers to any questions you may have missed.

Correcting Entries

Unfortunately, errors are occasionally made when handling accounting records. Some ways to spot and correct errors were discussed in earlier chapters. One rule always applies to these and other corrections. *Never erase an error.*

Sometimes errors affect only subsidiary ledger accounts. For example, cash received on account from one customer may have been recorded in the cash receipts journal under another customer's name. The Accounts Receivable Credit column in the cash receipts journal is not affected by such an error. When the column total is posted, the balance of the Accounts Receivable account will match the total of the balances of all the customer accounts. The balances, however, in two customers' accounts in the accounts receivable subsidiary ledger will be incorrect.

This type of error is usually discovered in one of two ways. A customer often spots the error in a monthly statement. When auditing (examining) the business records, an accountant may also spot the error and inform the accounting clerk of it by memo. The accountant's memo becomes the source document for the correcting entry.

On December 15, Champion's accountant discovered an error affecting two customer accounts in the accounts receivable subsidiary ledger.

December 15: *Discovered that $75.00 received from the Gateway School District, a charge customer, on November 30 had been incorrectly credited to the Greensburg School District account, Memorandum 68.*

When the November 30 transaction was journalized and posted, Cash in Bank was debited for $75.00. Accounts Receivable and the Greensburg School District account were each credited for $75.00. The original journal entry is shown below in T-account form.

GENERAL LEDGER

Cash in Bank			Accounts Receivable		
Dr.		Cr.	Dr.		Cr.
+		–	+		–
$75.00					$75.00

SUBSIDIARY LEDGER

Greensburg School District	
Dr.	Cr.
+	–
	$75.00

The following T accounts show how the transaction *should* have been recorded:

GENERAL LEDGER

Cash in Bank			Accounts Receivable		
Dr.		Cr.	Dr.		Cr.
+		–	+		–
$75.00					$75.00

SUBSIDIARY LEDGER

Gateway School District	
Dr.	Cr.
+	–
	$75.00

As you can see, the only difference is the account that is credited in the accounts receivable subsidiary ledger. The Greensburg School District account was incorrectly credited. To correct the error, it must now be debited.

The Gateway School District account should have been credited. To correct the error, it must be credited now. The correcting entry, recorded in the general journal, is shown in Figure 15-7.

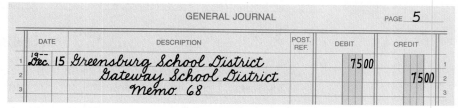

	DATE	DESCRIPTION	POST. REF.	DEBIT	CREDIT	
1	19-- Dec. 15	Greensburg School District		75 00		1
2		Gateway School District			75 00	2
3		Memo 68				3

Figure 15-7 Journalizing a Correcting Entry to Subsidiary Ledger Accounts

Summary of Key Points

1. A general journal is also needed in an accounting system using special journals. All transactions that cannot be recorded in the special journals are entered in the general journal.

2. A business may allow its customers to return unsatisfactory merchandise for full credit (a sales return) or to keep the merchandise at a lesser price (a sales allowance).

3. Sales returns and allowances are debited to the Sales Returns and Allowances account. This account is a contra revenue account and has a normal debit balance.

4. A credit memo is prepared by the seller to list the details of a sales return or sales allowance. It is the source document for the general journal entry.

5. A debit memo is prepared by the buyer to notify a creditor of a return or allowance. It is the source document for the general journal entry.

6. A merchandising business may not be satisfied with merchandise purchased on account. It too may return the merchandise for full credit (a purchases return) or keep the merchandise at a reduced cost (a purchases allowance).

7. Purchases returns and allowances are credited to the Purchases Returns and Allowances account. This account is a contra cost of merchandise account and has a normal credit balance.

8. A diagonal line in the Posting Reference column of the general journal means that the debit or credit amount is to be posted to the two accounts named in the Description column. One account is a general ledger controlling account and the other is a subsidiary ledger account.

9. Errors in the accounting records that are discovered after posting require a correcting entry in the general journal.

Review and Applications

Building Your Accounting Vocabulary

In your own words, write the definition of each of the following accounting terms. Use complete sentences for your definitions.

credit memorandum   purchases allowance   sales allowance
debit memorandum   purchases return   sales return

Reviewing Your Accounting Knowledge

1. Why is a general journal needed in an accounting system using special journals?
2. When special journals are used, what types of transactions are normally recorded in the general journal?
3. What is the difference between a sales return and a sales allowance?
4. What information is included on a credit memo?
5. Why is a separate general ledger account used to record sales returns and sales allowances?
6. To which subsidiary ledger is a sales return or allowance posted?
7. What form is prepared to notify a supplier that items purchased on account are being returned?
8. Which account is credited if a business returns an office calculator bought on account? Merchandise bought on account?
9. Classify these accounts: Sales Returns and Allowances and Purchases Returns and Allowances.
10. What does the Purchases Returns and Allowances account show?
11. How would you indicate that a purchases returns and allowances transaction has been posted to the subsidiary ledger account?

Improving Your Proofreading Skills

Reading carelessly when checking amounts of money and other figures often leads to problems. Compare each figure in Column A with the corresponding figure in Column B. On a separate sheet of paper, write the word "Different" if the two items *do not* agree. Write "Same" if the two items *do* agree.

	Column A	Column B
1.	$181,813	$181,831
2.	59874AX	58784AX
3.	10/11/51	10/11/52
4.	ECC-339	ECC-333
5.	306-54-6750	306-54-6750
6.	$160.36	$160.63
7.	998DIA	988DIA
8.	$5,622.40	$5,622.40

May 27   Purchased merchandise on account from Pro Golf Apparel, $3,200.00, Invoice PGA47, dated May 24, terms 2/10, n/30.

29   Discovered that an April purchase of $400.00 in office equipment had been journalized and posted to the Computer Equipment account, Memorandum 25.

29   Sold $150.00 in merchandise to Gayle Linwood on account, $9.00 sales tax, Sales Slip 334.

30   Purchased $420.00 in computer supplies from Mega Byte Corp., Invoice MB72, dated May 29, terms n/30.

31   Recorded cash sales of $3,540.00, plus $212.40 in sales taxes, Tape 40.

31   Recorded bank card sales for the period, $2,780.00, plus $166.80 sales taxes, Tape 40.

CHALLENGE

PROBLEM

Problem 15-4   Examining Correcting Entries

The following correcting entries were recorded in the general journal of the Pilgrim Gift Shop during September. The shop makes no sales on account.

Instructions: Give a brief description of the error that was made when each transaction was *originally* recorded. In other words, why is the correcting entry being prepared?

GENERAL JOURNAL   PAGE __14__

	DATE	DESCRIPTION	POST. REF.	DEBIT	CREDIT	
1	Sept. 8	Purchases		1 1 4 00		1
2		Transportation In			1 1 4 00	2
3		Memo. 209				3
4	12	Jonas Conlan Co.		8 2 4 50		4
5		Jonah Conway Corp.			8 2 4 50	5
6		Memo. 210				6
7	14	Office Equipment		4 8 3 90		7
8		Office Furniture			4 8 3 90	8
9		Memo. 211				9
10	20	Federal Income Tax Payable		6 2 4 00		10
11		Sales Tax Payable			6 2 4 00	11
12		Memo. 212				12
13	26	Bank Card Fees Expense		1 2 7 90		13
14		Miscellaneous Expense			1 2 7 90	14
15		Memo. 213				15
16						16

CHALLENGE

PROBLEM

Problem 15-5   Recording General Journal Transactions

You are an accounting clerk for Bayside Jewelers. The transactions that follow require journal entries. Record these entries on page 12 of the general journal.

Transactions:

Oct. 4   Received a letter from Imperial Gemstones stating that a 3% discount we took on its $4,200.00 invoice was disallowed because the payment was received after the end of the discount period, Memorandum 112.

Oct. 8 A journal entry was recorded and posted for a payment of $1,176.00 made to the Berenson Corp. for its invoice of $1,200.00 dated September 26 with terms of 2/10, n/30. During a routine check, the accounting supervisor discovered an invoice from Berenson dated September 10 that has not yet been paid. Berenson will not allow discounts if there are earlier, unpaid invoices, Memorandum 113.

9 John Schmidt returned damaged merchandise purchased on account, $114.50, plus sales tax of 4%, Credit Memo 96.

10 Bayside returned a shipment of defective merchandise to Harkness Corporation. The invoice from Harkness for $998.40 has been recorded and posted, Debit Memo 94.

11 Received a notice from the Weber Co. stating that we had taken a discount of 3% on an invoice of $6,340.00 with terms of 2/10, n/30. The invoice was paid within the discount period, Memorandum 114.

*A*rresting Facts
About Computer Crime

When the computer was first invented, *computer crime* referred to the theft or sabotage of computers. Today, the term means the unauthorized use of computer systems for unlawful purposes. The increasing use and importance of computers have given rise to a new breed of criminal.

Indeed, computer crime has become such a problem that laws in almost every state make it a risky business, resulting in convictions and serious sentences.

Computer-abetted crime is particularly troublesome because

• The crime is usually committed by someone who is authorized to use the system—a programmer, a clerk, or a bank teller, for example.

• It's difficult, though not impossible, to track down the culprit because, if the thief is clever enough, the records look tamper-free.

• Businesses don't like to reveal that they have been victims of computer crimes for fear of shaking the public's confidence in them.

Usually young, skilled, and male, computer criminals steal funds electronically. The electronic funds transfer system (EFTS) is particularly vulnerable. One embezzler who knew the bank's system transferred $10.8 million to a Swiss bank account before he was caught.

Some methods of computer crime are difficult to detect. Two unique methods are salami slicing and the Trojan horse.

• *Salami slicing.* An embezzler modifies a program to round down fractions of a penny in transactions such as salary calculations. These fractions are then added to the criminal's computer account. With several thousand employees, these fractions of a cent can add up.

No one knows for sure, but it is estimated that billions of dollars are lost to computer crime each year.

• *Trojan horse.* A hidden "criminal" program is used to scan data and steal passwords, which it then uses to enter and pillage accounts.

Computer crime can cost its victims millions of dollars. No matter how tempting it is for a computer thief to crack a system, however, there's always someone just as clever who can find the glitch and catch the thief.

Mini Practice Set

Application Activity 3

Recording Business Transactions in Special Journals

In Chapters 11 through 15, you have learned how to record the business transactions of a merchandising business in special journals. Now you will have the opportunity to review and apply what you have learned by working as an accounting clerk for The Apple Tree Boutique. The accounting stationery needed to complete this activity is included in the working papers accompanying this textbook.

When you have completed this activity, you will have done the following:

1. Analyzed business transactions.
2. Journalized business transactions in the four special journals and in the general journal.
3. Posted journal entries to the general ledger and to the accounts receivable and accounts payable subsidiary ledgers.
4. Posted the totals of the special journals to the general ledger.
5. Proved cash.
6. Prepared a schedule of accounts receivable and a schedule of accounts payable.

The Apple Tree Boutique

Todd and Toni Thomas own a merchandising business organized as a corporation called The Apple Tree Boutique. The retail store is a small, fashionable specialty shop for women's clothing. This husband-and-wife team has been operating successfully for five years.

Chart of Accounts

The chart of accounts for The Apple Tree Boutique appears on the next page. It includes the accounts receivable subsidiary ledger accounts and the accounts payable subsidiary ledger accounts.

Keeping the Accounting Records for

The Apple Tree Boutique

Since The Apple Tree Boutique has a large volume of business transactions, the business uses special journals and a general journal.

The previous accounting clerk, Dani Trio, has journalized and posted the business transactions for June 1 through June 15. Those transactions are included in the accounting stationery accompanying this textbook. The transactions that follow took place between June 16 and June 30.

Instructions: The forms for completing this activity are included in the working papers accompanying this textbook.

THE APPLE TREE BOUTIQUE
Chart of Accounts

ASSETS	101	Cash in Bank
	105	Accounts Receivable
	110	Merchandise Inventory
	115	Supplies
	120	Prepaid Insurance
	150	Store Equipment
	155	Office Equipment
LIABILITIES	201	Accounts Payable
	205	Sales Tax Payable
STOCKHOLDERS' EQUITY	301	Capital Stock
	305	Retained Earnings
	310	Income Summary
REVENUE	401	Sales
	405	Sales Discounts
	410	Sales Returns and Allowances
COST OF MERCHANDISE	501	Purchases
	505	Transportation In
	510	Purchases Discounts
	515	Purchases Returns and Allowances
EXPENSES	605	Advertising Expense
	610	Bank Card Fees Expense
	615	Miscellaneous Expense
	620	Rent Expense
	625	Salaries Expense
	630	Utilities Expense

ACCOUNTS RECEIVABLE SUBSIDIARY LEDGER

815	Sarah Locke
818	Allison McKensey
825	Marti Mitchell
870	Della Starr
880	Elena Trevino

ACCOUNTS PAYABLE SUBSIDIARY LEDGER

905	Ebony Creations
920	Jay-Jax Jeans
930	Montini Fashions
960	Store & Office Suppliers
980	Vanity Designers

(1) Record the remaining June transactions in the sales journal (page 18), cash receipts journal (page 15), purchases journal (page 12), cash payments journal (page 21), and general journal (page 7).

(2) Post the individual amounts from the five journals to the accounts receivable and accounts payable subsidiary ledgers on a daily basis.

(3) Post the individual amounts from the General columns of the cash receipts, purchases, cash payments, and general journals on a daily basis.

(4) Foot, prove, total, and rule the special journals.

(5) Post the column totals of the special journals to the general ledger accounts. Use the following order for posting: sales journal, cash receipts journal, purchases journal, cash payments journal.

(6) Prove cash. The balance shown on check stub 216 is $11,269.34.

(7) Prepare a schedule of accounts receivable and a schedule of accounts payable.

Transactions:

June 16   Sold $115.00 worth of merchandise on account to Marti Mitchell, plus $6.90 sales tax, Sales Slip 407.

     17   Issued Check 210 for $1,315.27 to Montini Fashions in payment of Invoice M131.

     18   Purchased $1,270.00 in merchandise on account from Jay-Jax Jeans, Invoice JJ215.

     18   Sold merchandise on account to Sarah Locke, $80.00 plus $4.80 sales tax, Sales Slip 408.

     18   Received a check for $95.40 from Della Starr to apply on account, Receipt 157.

     19   Wrote Check 211 for $565.30 to Store & Office Suppliers in full payment of our account.

     19   Paid Ebony Creations' Invoice EC462 for $425.73, less a 2% cash discount of $8.51, by issuing Check 212 for $417.22.

     21   Discovered that a $680.00 cash purchase of merchandise in May had been journalized and posted incorrectly as a debit to Merchandise Inventory, Memorandum 21.

     21   Sold on account to Elena Trevino $350.00 of merchandise plus sales tax of $21.00, Sales Slip 409.

     22   Prepared Receipt 158 for a $79.50 check received on account from Allison McKensey.

     23   Wrote Check 213 for $346.08 to Vanity Designers in payment of Invoice V340 for $353.14, less a $7.06 cash discount.

     24   Issued Debit Memo 42 for $150.00 to Jay-Jax Jeans for damaged merchandise returned to them.

     24   Received Invoice EC475 for $542.95 of merchandise purchased on account from Ebony Creations.

     25   Recorded the $4.00 bank service charge from the June bank statement.

     25   Recorded the bank card fee of $125.00 from the June bank statement.

     25   Purchased $664.31 in merchandise from Vanity Designers on account, Invoice V372.

     25   Bought a $1,200.00 cash register (store equipment) on account from Store & Office Suppliers, Invoice AB601.

     26   Sold merchandise to Allison McKensey on account totaling $130.00, plus sales tax $7.80, Sales Slip 410.

     26   Received $200.00 from Sarah Locke on account, Receipt 159.

     27   Prepared Receipt 160 for a $150.00 check received from Elena Trevino on account.

     28   Sold an old calculator (office equipment) for $40.00, Receipt 161.

     30   Issued Check 214 for $2,412.00 for the salaries for the month.

     30   Paid the annual insurance premium of $300.00 by issuing Check 215 to Reliable Insurance Agency.

     30   Recorded cash sales of $1,700.00, $102.00 sales taxes, Tape 32.

     30   Recorded bank card sales of $950.00, plus sales taxes of $57.00, Tape 32.

Chapter 16

PREPARING A TEN-COLUMN WORK SHEET

Learning Objectives

When you have completed Chapter 16, you should be able to do the following:

1. Describe the parts of a ten-column work sheet.
2. Determine which general ledger accounts must be adjusted and calculate the amounts of the adjustments needed.
3. Prepare a ten-column work sheet.
4. Define the accounting terms introduced in this chapter.

The work sheet you learned how to prepare in Chapter 7 had six amount columns. The work sheet you will learn to prepare in this chapter has *ten* amount columns. The four "new" columns are the debit and credit columns of the Adjustments and Adjusted Trial Balance sections.

These columns are used to calculate "adjustments" for account balances that are not up to date at the end of the fiscal period. For example, employees use supplies such as letterhead stationery and envelopes every day, but the Supplies account is not credited daily to record the cost of those supplies. Instead, at the end of the accounting period, the amount of supplies consumed is calculated and the Supplies account is "adjusted" by this amount.

In this chapter, you will learn which account balances must be adjusted at the end of the fiscal period. You will also learn how to calculate the needed adjustments and enter them on a ten-column work sheet.

New Terms

adjustment
beginning inventory
ending inventory
physical inventory
cost of merchandise sold
gross profit

Completing End-of-Fiscal-Period Work

The balances of the general ledger accounts summarize the effects of business transactions for an accounting period. They cannot, however, summarize the overall performance of a company. To evaluate performance, managers, stockholders, and creditors need more than a list of account totals. They need to know net income, the value of stockholders' (owners') equity, and the company's financial strength. Sound business decisions cannot be made without this vital information.

It is the purpose of all end-of-period reports to provide essential information that shows the financial position of a business organization. In Chapters 7 and 8, you learned about the steps taken at the end of every fiscal period to determine and report the financial condition of a sole proprietorship service business. The first step was to prepare a work sheet. In this chapter, you will prepare a work sheet typical of those used by merchandising businesses. This work sheet will be the basis for preparing end-of-period financial statements and journal entries.

The Ten-Column Work Sheet

The six-column work sheet in Chapter 7 had a heading and three amount sections: the Trial Balance section, the Income Statement section, and the Balance Sheet section. Each of these sections had a debit and a credit column. The Trial Balance section, remember, included all accounts listed in the chart of accounts, even those with zero balances. Each account was classified and its balance extended to the Balance Sheet or Income Statement section. Asset, liability, and owner's equity balances were extended to the Balance Sheet section. Revenue and expense balances were extended to the Income Statement section. The net income (or loss) was then determined.

The ten-column work sheet is prepared in much the same way. The ten-column work sheet, however, has five amount sections to complete instead of three. These five sections are (1) Trial Balance, (2) Adjustments, (3) Adjusted Trial Balance, (4) Income Statement, and (5) Balance Sheet.

Completing the Trial Balance Section

A trial balance is prepared to prove the equality of debits and credits in the general ledger. A trial balance may be prepared at any time during the fiscal period—provided that all amounts have been posted to the general ledger. Champion Building Products prepares its trial balance at the end of the fiscal period, using the first two columns of the work sheet.

To prepare the trial balance, the number and title of each account in the general ledger is entered on the work sheet in the Account Name section. The accounts are listed in the same order as they appear in the general ledger. The balance of each account is entered in either the Debit or the Credit column. After all balances have been entered, the Debit and Credit columns are ruled, totaled, and proved. A double rule is drawn across both columns once they are proved.

The Trial Balance section of Champion's work sheet is shown in Figure 16-1. Notice that every general ledger account is listed, even those with zero balances.

Today many businesses use computers to prepare their trial balances. Those trial balances are often printed out on extra-wide paper. The wide paper provides enough space so that the work sheet can be completed right on the printout. If the paper is not wide enough to complete the work sheet, the Trial Balance data must be copied onto multicolumn accounting paper before the work sheet can be completed.

	ACCT. NO.	ACCOUNT NAME	TRIAL BALANCE	
			DEBIT	CREDIT
1	101	Cash in Bank	21 284 42	
2	105	Accounts Receivable	6 364 35	
3	110	Merch. Inventory	84 921 10	
4	115	Supplies	5 549 50	
5	120	Prepaid Insurance	1 500 00	
6	150	Delivery Equipment	19 143 90	
7	155	Store Equipment	26 353 40	
8	201	Accounts Payable		12 316 95
9	205	Fed. Inc. Tax Payable		
10	210	Sales Tax Payable		1 983 60
11	301	Capital Stock		75 000 00
12	305	Retained Earnings		2 762 545
13	310	Income Summary		
14	401	Sales		377 385 00
15	405	Sales Discounts	3 550 42	
16	410	Sales Returns & Allow.	1 061 81	
17	501	Purchases	209 464 32	
18	505	Transportation In	4 215 80	
19	510	Purchases Discounts		9 808 54
20	515	Purchases Ret. & Allow.		4 017 90
21	601	Advertising Expense	2 864 50	
22	605	Bank Card Fees Expense	3 292 30	
23	610	Delivery Expense	2 693 96	
24	615	Insurance Expense		
25	620	Maintenance Expense	3 321 90	
26	625	Miscellaneous Expense	647 05	
27	630	Rent Expense	15 000 00	
28	635	Salaries Expense	84 000 00	
29	640	Supplies Expense		
30	645	Utilities Expense	3 158 71	
31	650	Fed. Inc. Tax Expense	9 750 00	
32			508 137 44	508 137 44
33				

Figure 16-1   The Trial Balance Section of the Work Sheet

R E M E M B E R

The debit and credit columns of the Trial Balance section must be equal. If they are not, you must find and correct any errors before continuing.

Calculating Adjustments

Not all changes in account balances are the result of daily business transactions. Some changes result from the passage of time or from the internal operations of the business. For example, insurance premiums are paid for a certain period of time and expire during that time period. Office supplies such as paper, pens, and pencils are bought for use by the business's employees. These supplies are used gradually during the accounting period. Supplies such as shopping bags and sales slips are also gradually used as sales are made. At the end of the period, the balances in accounts such as Prepaid Insurance and Supplies must be brought up to date.

Up to this point, the general ledger account balances have been changed through journal entries that are posted to the accounts. Those journal entries were made to record transactions that were supported by source documents. There are no source documents, however, for the changes in account balances caused by the passage of time or a business's internal operations. Such changes must be recorded through an adjustment to the account balance made at the end of the fiscal period. An **adjustment** is an amount that is added to or subtracted from an account balance to bring that balance up to date. For example, suppose that supplies costing $500 have been purchased during an accounting period. At the end of the period, $200 of these supplies are still on hand. The account balance for Supplies must be adjusted to show that the business has used $300 of supplies.

Every adjustment affects one permanent account and one temporary account. Items that are purchased for use in the operation of the business are recorded as assets (permanent accounts). As these assets are used up during business operations, they become expenses (temporary accounts) to the business. Accountants say that these assets are "expensed" because the costs of consumed assets are expenses of doing business. At the end of the fiscal period, therefore, an adjustment must be made to transfer the costs of the assets consumed to the appropriate expense accounts. As you recall, the expenses for a given fiscal period must be matched against the revenue for that period before net income (or net loss) can be determined.

The Adjustments section of the work sheet is used to calculate the amounts of the adjustments that must be made at the end of the fiscal period to bring various account balances up to date. After the work sheet has been completed and the financial reports prepared, the adjustments written on the work sheet will be recorded as journal entries. These journal entries will then be posted to the appropriate general ledger accounts. The balances in those accounts are thus brought up to date with the balances calculated on the work sheet. You will learn how to journalize adjustments in Chapter 18.

Determining the Adjustments Needed

How do you know which accounts must be adjusted at the end of the fiscal period? The account balances reported on the financial statements must reflect the actual balance for each account at the end of the fiscal period. If the balance shown for each account on the work sheet is not up to date *as of the last day of the fiscal period,* then that account balance must be adjusted.

Look at the trial balance for Champion Building Products shown in Figure 16-1. The first account listed is Cash in Bank. Since all cash received or paid out during the period has been journalized and then posted to the Cash in Bank account, the balance in this account is up to date. The balance in the controlling account Accounts Receivable is also up to date since all amounts owed or paid by charge customers have been journalized and posted.

The next account on the trial balance is Merchandise Inventory. In Chapter 11, you learned that Merchandise Inventory is the account merchandising businesses use to report the cost of merchandise on hand to sell to customers. The balance reported in the Trial Balance section ($84,921.10) is the merchandise on hand at the *beginning* of the fiscal period.

The amount of merchandise on hand is constantly changing during the fiscal period. The changes are not recorded in the Merchandise Inventory account. During the period, Champion recorded the cost of additional merchandise purchased in the Purchases account. As inventory was reduced by the sale of merchandise, the amount of each sale was recorded in the Sales account. No entries were posted to Merchandise Inventory. At the end of the fiscal period, therefore, the balance in Merchandise Inventory does *not* reflect the amount of merchandise on hand as of the last day of the fiscal period. This account balance must be adjusted.

Adjusting the Merchandise Inventory Account

Merchandise Inventory is an asset account that is found only in a merchandising business. At the beginning of each fiscal period, the balance in Merchandise Inventory represents the amount of merchandise on hand and available for sale. This balance is the beginning inventory. **Beginning inventory** is the merchandise a business has on hand at the *beginning* of a fiscal period. The merchandise a business has on hand at the *end* of a fiscal period is its **ending inventory.** The ending inventory for one fiscal period is the beginning inventory for the next fiscal period.

During a fiscal period, the balance of Merchandise Inventory usually is not changed. The balance of Merchandise Inventory is changed only when a physical inventory is taken. A **physical inventory** is an actual count of all the merchandise on hand and available for sale. A physical inventory can be taken at any time. One is always taken, however, at the end of a fiscal period.

Once the actual number of items on hand is known, the cost of the ending inventory can be calculated. This is done by multiplying the quantity of each different item by its unit cost. The cost of the ending inventory is the total cost of all the items on hand. Knowing the ending inventory cost is very important. With it, the Merchandise Inventory account can be brought up to date, and the cost of merchandise sold can be determined. The **cost of merchandise sold** is just what the words indicate. It is the actual cost to the business of the merchandise sold to customers. The cost of merchandise sold is reported on the income statement. At the end of a fiscal period, the total cost of merchandise sold during the period is calculated and used to determine the gross profit. **Gross profit** is the difference between the revenue earned from sales and the total cost of the merchandise sold.

Let's use an example to show the importance of the beginning and ending inventory amounts. Suppose two students decide to sell school buttons at a

It is important for a business to take an actual count of the merchandise it has on hand at least once a year.

sports event. They have 14 buttons left from their last sale. These buttons cost them 45¢ each. The cost of their beginning inventory is thus $6.30 ($0.45 × 14). The students purchased 100 more buttons at 45¢ each, for a total cost of $45.00.

The two students sold their buttons at the sports event for 75¢ each. Since they were so busy, they did not keep track of each sale. After the sports event was over, the students totaled their money and found that they had sold $77.25 worth of buttons. But how much of that $77.25 was profit and how much was the cost of the buttons?

To find this out, the students first counted the remaining buttons. They had 11 left. These 11 buttons cost 45¢ each, so the cost of their ending inventory was $4.95 ($0.45 × 11).

Next, to determine their profit, the students needed to know the cost of the buttons they had sold. The students originally had 14 buttons costing $6.30. They had purchased 100 buttons costing $45.00. The total cost of all the buttons they had available for sale was $51.30 ($6.30 + $45.00). To find the cost of the buttons sold, the students subtracted the cost of the buttons they still had ($4.95) from the cost of all the buttons that they had available for sale ($51.30). The cost of the buttons they had sold was $46.35. Next, the students subtracted the cost of the buttons sold from their total sales amount ($77.25). The difference was their gross profit of $30.90 ($77.25 − $46.35). This calculation is shown below.

Sales		$77.25
Beginning Inventory (14 @ 45¢)	$ 6.30	
Plus Purchases (100 @ 45¢)	+45.00	
Cost of Merchandise Available for Sale	$51.30	
Less Ending Inventory (11 @ 45¢)	− 4.95	
Cost of Merchandise Sold		−46.35
Gross Profit		$30.90

At the end of a fiscal period, businesses calculate their gross profit the same way the two students did. As you can see from the calculations, both beginning and ending inventory amounts are needed to determine gross profit.

The purpose of the end-of-fiscal-period work is to report the results of the merchandising operation (the net income or net loss) for the period and to prepare the general ledger accounts for the next period. The ending inventory for one fiscal period, remember, becomes the beginning inventory for the next period. At the end of each period, therefore, the beginning inventory amount recorded in Merchandise Inventory must be replaced by the ending inventory amount. This is accomplished by an adjustment to Merchandise Inventory.

R E M E M B E R

Every adjustment affects one permanent account and one temporary account.

▲ Calculating the Adjustment for Merchandise Inventory

When the Trial Balance section of Champion's work sheet was prepared, the Merchandise Inventory account had a debit balance of $84,921.10. This was the amount of merchandise on hand at the beginning of the fiscal period. At the end of the period, a physical inventory (an actual count) was made of the merchandise still on hand. The cost of the ending inventory was calculated to be $81,385.70. This difference is the result of all the purchases and sales of merchandise during the period. The $81,385.70 amount must replace the beginning inventory amount to bring the Merchandise Inventory account up to date for the next fiscal period.

To bring the balance of Merchandise Inventory up to date, it must be decreased by $3,535.40 ($84,921.10 − $81,385.70). Merchandise Inventory has a normal debit balance. To decrease the balance, Merchandise Inventory is credited for $3,535.40.

In double-entry accounting, every credit must have an equal debit. Remember too that each adjustment affects one permanent account and one temporary account. If Merchandise Inventory (a permanent account) is being credited, a temporary account must be debited. In this adjustment, the Income Summary account is debited for $3,535.40. Why is Income Summary debited?

In Chapter 9, you learned that Income Summary is a temporary equity account used as a sort of clearinghouse. Income Summary does not have a normal balance since it is used only at the end of the fiscal period to summarize information from other accounts. In Chapter 9, you used Income Summary to summarize the total revenue and total expenses for the period. The difference between these two amounts (the net income or net loss) was then closed into the capital account.

Income Summary is also used to make the adjustment to the Merchandise Inventory account. The debit side of Income Summary is used to record total expenses for the period. The cost of merchandise sold is an expense for a merchandising business. Since the inventory has decreased, this means that

Champion sold $3,535.40 of merchandise in addition to the merchandise purchased during the period. The cost of merchandise sold is increased by this amount. A reduction in merchandise inventory is, therefore, debited to Income Summary and credited to Merchandise Inventory.

The adjustment for Champion's Merchandise Inventory account is illustrated in the T accounts.

Merchandise Inventory		Income Summary	
Dr.	Cr.	Dr.	Cr.
+	−		
Bal. $84,921.10	Adj. $3,535.40	Adj. $3,535.40	

If the cost of the ending inventory is greater than the cost of the beginning inventory, Merchandise Inventory would be debited and Income Summary would be credited. For example, suppose that the beginning inventory was $84,921.10 and the ending inventory was $87,371.50. Since the inventory has increased by $2,450.40 ($87,371.50 − $84,921.10), Merchandise Inventory must be debited for that amount. Income Summary, then, would be credited for $2,450.40. This adjustment is illustrated in the T accounts.

Merchandise Inventory		Income Summary	
Dr.	Cr.	Dr.	Cr.
+	−		
Bal. $84,921.10			
Adj. 2,450.40			Adj. $2,450.40

R — E — M — E — M — B — E — R

If the ending inventory is less than the beginning inventory, Merchandise Inventory is credited for the amount of the difference. If the ending inventory is greater than the beginning inventory, Merchandise Inventory is debited for the amount of the difference.

▲ **Entering the Adjustment for Merchandise Inventory on the Work Sheet** The T accounts used to analyze the adjustment to Merchandise Inventory will serve as a guide to entering the adjustment on the work sheet. Look at the partial work sheet in Figure 16-2. To record the adjustment for Merchandise Inventory

1. Enter the credit amount of the adjustment in the Adjustments Credit column on the Merchandise Inventory line. Label this amount (a).

   The work sheet adjustments are the source of the information for the journal entries that will be made later to record the amount of each adjustment. To help in locating amounts on the work sheet, the debit and credit parts of each adjustment are labeled. A small letter in parentheses is placed just above and to the left of the amounts. The first adjustment is labeled (a); the second, (b); the third, (c); and so on.

2. Enter the debit amount of the adjustment in the Adjustments Debit column on the Income Summary line. Label this amount (a) also.

UNIT 3   The Accounting Cycle for a Merchandising Business

	ACCT. NO.	ACCOUNT NAME	TRIAL BALANCE		ADJUSTMENTS	
			DEBIT	CREDIT	DEBIT	CREDIT
1	101	Cash in Bank	2128442			
2	105	Accounts Receivable	636435			
3	110	Merch. Inventory	8492110			(a) 353540
13	310	Income Summary			(a) 353540	

Figure 16-2 Recording the Adjustment for Merchandise Inventory on the Work Sheet

R E M E M B E R

The two parts of an adjustment are labeled with small letters in parentheses.

This adjustment, when journalized, will bring the balance in Merchandise Inventory up to date.

Before you go any further, do the following activity to see if you understand the adjustment for Merchandise Inventory.

Check Your Learning

Answer these questions on a sheet of notebook paper.

1. Why must the Merchandise Inventory account be adjusted at the end of a fiscal period?
2. When is a physical inventory taken?
3. If the ending inventory is greater than the beginning inventory, which account is debited in the adjustment? credited?
4. If the ending inventory is less than the beginning inventory, which account is debited in the adjustment? credited?

Compare your answers to those in the answers section. Re-read the preceding part of the chapter to find the correct answers to any questions you may have missed.

Adjusting the Supplies Account

A merchandising business buys various supplies to be used by employees in the everyday operations of the business. Among these supplies are pencils and pens, typing paper, shopping bags, sales slips, price tags, and cash register tapes. As these supplies are purchased, their cost is debited to Supplies.

Some supplies are used up every day. As they are consumed, they become expenses of the business. It's impossible to keep daily records of each item as it is used. The Supplies account, therefore, is not updated until the end of the fiscal period.

On the work sheet, the balance of the Supplies account is $5,549.50. This amount is the value of the supplies on hand on January 1 *plus* the additional supplies bought during the year.

At the end of December, Champion Building Products took an inventory and found that there were actually $1,839.60 of supplies on hand. This means that $3,709.90 of supplies had been used during the year ($5,549.50 − $1,839.60 = $3,709.90).

The amount of supplies on hand has decreased by $3,709.90. Supplies (a permanent account) must be credited, therefore, for that amount. Supplies Expense (a temporary account) is used to record the cost of supplies used during the period. To update the account, Supplies Expense is debited for $3,709.90.

Supplies		Supplies Expense	
Dr.	Cr.	Dr.	Cr.
+	−	+	−
Bal. $5,549.50	Adj. $3,709.90	Adj. $3,709.90	

The adjustment to Supplies is shown in Figure 16-3, on lines 4 and 29. To enter the adjustment on the work sheet, follow the steps at the top of the next page.

	ACCT. NO.	ACCOUNT NAME	TRIAL BALANCE		ADJUSTMENTS	
			DEBIT	CREDIT	DEBIT	CREDIT
1	101	Cash in Bank	2128442			
2	105	Accounts Receivable	636435			(a) 353540
3	110	Merch. Inventory	8492110			(b) 370990
4	115	Supplies	554950			(c) 25000
5	120	Prepaid Insurance	150000			
6	150	Delivery Equipment	1914390			
7	155	Store Equipment	2635340			
8	201	Accounts Payable		1231695		
9	205	Fed. Inc. Tax Payable				(d) 14500
10	210	Sales Tax Payable		198360		
11	301	Capital Stock		7500000		
12	305	Retained Earnings		2762545		
13	310	Income Summary			(a) 353540	
14	401	Sales		37738500		
15	405	Sales Discounts	355042			
16	410	Sales Returns & Allow.	106181			
17	501	Purchases	20946432			
18	505	Transportation In	421580			
19	510	Purchases Discounts		980854		
20	515	Purchases Ret. & Allow.		401790		
21	601	Advertising Expense	286450			
22	605	Bank Card Fees Expense	329230			
23	610	Delivery Expense	269396			
24	615	Insurance Expense			(c) 25000	
25	620	Maintenance Expense	332190			
26	625	Miscellaneous Expense	64705			
27	630	Rent Expense	1500000			
28	635	Salaries Expense	8400000			
29	640	Supplies Expense			(b) 370990	
30	645	Utilities Expense	315871			
31	650	Fed. Inc. Tax Expense	975000		(d) 14500	
32			50813744	50813744	764030	764030

Figure 16-3 Recording Adjustments on the Work Sheet

UNIT 3   The Accounting Cycle for a Merchandising Business

1. Enter the credit amount of the adjustment (the supplies consumed) in the Adjustments Credit column on the Supplies line. Since this is the second adjustment, label it (b).
2. Enter the debit amount of the adjustment in the Adjustments Debit column on the Supplies Expense line. Label it (b).

Adjusting the Prepaid Insurance Account

On December 1, Champion purchased an insurance policy to protect the business from loss. The insurance coverage was for the six months December through May. The premium of $1,500.00 (or $250.00 per month) was debited to Prepaid Insurance.

The balance of the Prepaid Insurance account reported on Champion's work sheet is $1,500.00. This reflects the purchase of the insurance on December 1.

By the end of December, however, one month of the premium ($250.00) has expired. In other words, the amount of prepaid insurance has decreased by $250.00. Prepaid Insurance (a permanent account) must be credited for $250.00 to bring its balance up to date. That part of the premium that has expired is an expense of the business. The amount of the expired premium $250.00, therefore, is debited to Insurance Expense (a temporary account).

Prepaid Insurance		Insurance Expense	
Dr.	Cr.	Dr.	Cr.
+	–	+	–
Bal. $1,500.00	Adj. $250.00	Adj. $250.00	

The adjustment for Prepaid Insurance is shown on the partial work sheet in Figure 16-3, lines 5 and 24. To enter this adjustment on the work sheet, follow these steps:

1. Enter the credit amount of the adjustment in the Adjustments Credit column on the Prepaid Insurance line. Since this is the third adjustment, label it (c).
2. Enter the debit amount of the adjustment in the Adjustments Debit column on the Insurance Expense line. Label the amount (c).

Adjusting the Income Tax Expense Account

Champion Building Products is organized as a corporation. A corporation is considered to be a separate legal entity. Champion may own assets, must pay its own debts, and may enter into legal contracts. Under the law, a corporation is considered separate from its owners.

As a result, a corporation is required to pay federal income taxes on its net income. (Many states and cities also tax corporate income. For now, we will discuss only federal income taxes.) A corporation is put on a pay-as-you-go basis. That is, the corporation is required to estimate in advance its federal income taxes for the year. The corporation pays that estimated amount to the federal government in quarterly installments during the year. At the end of the fiscal year, the exact amount of net income and the tax on that income are determined. If the corporation owes additional taxes (as is usually the case), they are paid when the corporate income tax return is filed.

At the beginning of the fiscal period, Champion estimated that its income taxes would be $9,750.00. The business made quarterly payments of $2,437.50 in April, June, September, and December. These payments were recorded in the cash payments journal as debits to Federal Income Tax Expense and credits to Cash in Bank.

At the end of the fiscal period, Champion's accountant determined that Champion's federal income tax for the year was $9,895.00. Since Champion had already paid $9,750.00 in taxes, it only owes an additional $145.00.

The balance in the Federal Income Tax Expense account must be adjusted to show the additional tax expense for the period. To adjust Federal Income Tax Expense (a temporary account), that account is debited (increased) for $145.00. This amount is entered in the Adjustments Debit column on the Federal Income Tax Expense line. Since this is the fourth adjustment, the label (d) is used.

The $145.00 also represents an increase in Champion's liabilities. The additional tax will be paid in the future when the company files its income tax return. The balance in Federal Income Tax Payable (a permanent account) must, therefore, be adjusted. It is credited for $145.00. The $145.00 is entered in the adjustments Credit column on the Federal Income Tax Payable line. This entry is also labeled (d). This adjustment is shown on lines 9 and 31 on the work sheet in Figure 16-3 on page 350.

Federal Income Tax Expense		Federal Income Tax Payable	
Dr.	Cr.	Dr.	Cr.
+	−	−	+
Bal. $9,750.00			
Adj. 145.00			Adj. $145.00

Totaling and Ruling the Adjustments Section

After all adjustments have been entered, the Adjustments section of the work sheet is totaled and ruled. Each adjustment has an equal debit and credit, so the total of the Adjustments Debit and Credit columns must be the same. When the Adjustments section is proved, a double rule is drawn under the totals and across both columns, as shown in Figure 16-3 on page 350.

R — E — M — E — M — B — E — R

The Adjustments section of the work sheet, like the Trial Balance section, must be proved before the work sheet can be continued.

Completing the Adjusted Trial Balance Section

After all the adjustments are made, the Adjusted Trial Balance section is completed. This section shows the updated balances of all the general ledger accounts. To complete this section of the work sheet, the balance of each account in the Trial Balance section is combined with the adjustment, if any, in the Adjustments section. The new balance is then entered in the appropriate Adjusted Trial Balance column.

	ACCT. NO.	ACCOUNT NAME	TRIAL BALANCE DEBIT	TRIAL BALANCE CREDIT	ADJUSTMENTS DEBIT	ADJUSTMENTS CREDIT	ADJUSTED TRIAL BALANCE DEBIT	ADJUSTED TRIAL BALANCE CREDIT
1	101	Cash in Bank	2128442				2128442	
2	105	Accounts Receivable	636435				636435	
3	110	Merch. Inventory	8492110			(a) 353540	8138570	
4	115	Supplies	554950			(b) 370990	183960	
5	120	Prepaid Insurance	150000			(c) 25000	125000	
6	150	Delivery Equipment	1914390				1914390	
7	155	Store Equipment	2635340				2635340	
8	201	Accounts Payable		1231695				1231695
9	205	Fed. Inc. Tax Payable				(d) 14500		14500
10	210	Sales Tax Payable		198360				198360
11	301	Capital Stock		7500000				7500000
12	305	Retained Earnings		2762545				2762545
13	310	Income Summary			(a) 353540		353540	
14	401	Sales		37738500				37738500
15	405	Sales Discounts	355042				355042	
16	410	Sales Returns & Allow.	106181				106181	
17	501	Purchases	20946432				20946432	
18	505	Transportation In	421580				421580	
19	510	Purchases Discounts		980854				980854
20	515	Purchases Ret. & Allow.		401790				401790
21	601	Advertising Expense	286450				286450	
22	605	Bank Card Fees Expense	329230				329230	
23	610	Delivery Expense	269396				269396	
24	615	Insurance Expense			(c) 25000		25000	
25	620	Maintenance Expense	332190				332190	
26	625	Miscellaneous Expense	64705				64705	
27	630	Rent Expense	1500000				1500000	
28	635	Salaries Expense	8400000				8400000	
29	640	Supplies Expense			(b) 370990		370990	
30	645	Utilities Expense	315871				315871	
31	650	Fed. Inc. Tax Expense	975000		(d) 14500		989500	
32			50813744	50813744	764030	764030	50828244	50828244

Figure 16-4 Extending Balances to the Adjusted Trial Balance Section of the Work Sheet

ACCOUNTING **Tips**

When extending balances on the work sheet to other sections, be careful to transfer each debit balance to the appropriate debit column and each credit balance to the appropriate credit column. Start at line 1 and extend each balance in order.

Let's take a look at how new balances are computed. If an account balance has *not* been adjusted, it is simply extended to the same column (Debit or Credit) in the Adjusted Trial Balance section. Look at Figure 16-4. The balances of the first two accounts — Cash in Bank and Accounts Receivable — were not adjusted. Since both accounts have debit balances, those balances are extended to the Adjusted Trial Balance Debit column.

If the account balance in the Trial Balance section has been adjusted, the new balance must be calculated. The amount of the adjustment (from the Adjustments section) must be added to or subtracted from the amount in the Trial Balance section. The first adjusted balance is that for Merchandise Inventory.

Before being adjusted, Merchandise Inventory had a debit balance of $84,921.10. Adjustment (a) is a credit of $3,535.40. To determine the updated balance, the credit adjustment is subtracted from the debit balance. The adjusted balance of $81,385.70 ($84,921.10 − $3,535.40) is extended to the Adjusted Trial Balance Debit column.

The adjusted balances for Supplies, Prepaid Insurance, and Federal Income Tax Expense are calculated in the same way.

If an account has a zero balance in the Trial Balance section, the amount listed in the Adjustments section is extended to the same column in the Adjusted Trial Balance section. Federal Income Tax Payable, for example, has a zero balance in the Trial Balance section. Adjustment (d) is a credit of $145.00. This amount is extended to the Adjusted Trial Balance Credit column.

After all account balances have been extended to the Adjusted Trial Balance section, both columns are totaled. If total debits equal total credits, this section has been proved. A double rule is drawn under the totals and across both columns. If total debits do not equal total credits, an error has been made. Re-add each column. If the error is not found, check the amounts extended from the Trial Balance and Adjustments sections. The error must be found and corrected before the work sheet can be completed.

Before you read any further, do the following activity.

Check Your Learning

Write your answers to these questions on notebook paper.

1. If the Trial Balance shows a balance of $3,357.45 for Supplies and the amount of supplies on hand is actually $853.75, what is the amount of the adjustment? What account is debited? What account is credited?
2. If a company paid an annual insurance premium on November 1 of $1,740.00 and the fiscal period ended on December 31, what is the amount of the adjustment? What account is debited? credited?
3. If the Income Summary account is credited in the Adjustments section of the work sheet, is the ending inventory greater or less than the beginning inventory?
4. If a business has made quarterly federal income tax payments of $945.00 and its tax has been calculated at the end of the year to be $3,895.00, what is the amount of the adjustment? This adjustment is entered as a debit to the _____?_____ account and as a credit to the _____?_____ account.

Compare your answers to those in the answers section. Re-read the preceding part of the chapter to find the answers to any questions you missed.

Extending Amounts to the Balance Sheet and Income Statement Sections

Beginning with line 1, each account balance in the Adjusted Trial Balance section is extended either to the Balance Sheet section or to the Income Statement section. These extensions are shown in Figure 16-5.

The Balance Sheet section contains the balances of all the permanent general ledger accounts. Here you will find all asset, liability, and stockholders' equity accounts (in this case, Capital Stock and Retained Earnings).

The Income Statement section contains the balances of all the temporary general ledger accounts. This section includes all revenue, cost of merchandise, and expense accounts as well as Income Summary.

ACCT. NO.	ACCOUNT NAME	ADJUSTED TRIAL BALANCE DEBIT	CREDIT	INCOME STATEMENT DEBIT	CREDIT	BALANCE SHEET DEBIT	CREDIT	
101	Cash in Bank	21284 42				21284 42		1
105	Accounts Receivable	6364 35				6364 35		2
110	Merch. Inventory	81385 70				81385 70		3
115	Supplies	1839 60				1839 60		4
120	Prepaid Insurance	1250 00				1250 00		5
150	Delivery Equipment	19143 90				19143 90		6
155	Store Equipment	26353 40				26353 40		7
201	Accounts Payable		12316 95				12316 95	8
205	Fed. Inc. Tax Payable		145 00				145 00	9
210	Sales Tax Payable		1983 60				1983 60	10
301	Capital Stock		75000 00				75000 00	11
305	Retained Earnings		27625 45				27625 45	12
310	Income Summary	3535 40		3535 40				13
401	Sales		377385 00		377385 00			14
405	Sales Discounts	3550 42		3550 42				15
410	Sales Returns & Allow.	1061 81		1061 81				16
501	Purchases	209464 32		209464 32				17
505	Transportation In	4215 80		4215 80				18
510	Purchases Discounts		9808 54		9808 54			19
515	Purchases Ret. & Allow.		4017 90		4017 90			20
601	Advertising Expense	2864 50		2864 50				21
605	Bank Card Fees Expense	3292 30		3292 30				22
610	Delivery Expense	2693 96		2693 96				23
615	Insurance Expense	250 00		250 00				24
620	Maintenance Expense	3321 90		3321 90				25
625	Miscellaneous Expense	647 05		647 05				26
630	Rent Expense	15000 00		15000 00				27
635	Salaries Expense	84000 00		84000 00				28
640	Supplies Expense	3709 90		3709 90				29
645	Utilities Expense	3158 71		3158 71				30
650	Fed. Inc. Tax Expense	9895 00		9895 00				31
		508282 44	508282 44	350661 07	391211 44	157621 37	117071 00	32

Figure 16-5 Extending Adjusted Trial Balance Amounts to the Balance Sheet and Income Statement Sections

Completing the Work Sheet

ACCOUNTING *Tips*

When extending amounts on the work sheet (or on any other wide accounting form), use a ruler or a sheet of paper to help you keep track of the line you are working on.

After all amounts have been extended to the Balance Sheet and Income Statement sections, a single rule is drawn across these last four columns. All four columns are then totaled. As you learned in Chapter 7, at this point the totals of the debit and credit columns in the Balance Sheet and Income Statement sections are not equal. The difference between the two column totals in each section is the amount of net income (or net loss) for the period.

After the net income (or net loss) is recorded, the last four columns are ruled and totaled as shown in Figure 16-6 on page 356. Notice that the words "Net Income" are written in the Account Name column on the same line as the net income amount.

If the totals of the two Income Statement columns are equal, and the totals of the two Balance Sheet columns are equal, a double rule is drawn across all four columns. The double rule indicates that these sections of the work sheet have been proved. The complete ten-column work sheet for Champion Building Products is shown in Figure 16-6.

Champion Building Products, Inc.
Work Sheet
For the Year Ended December 31, 19 --

ACCT. NO.	ACCOUNT NAME	TRIAL BALANCE DEBIT	TRIAL BALANCE CREDIT	ADJUSTMENTS DEBIT	ADJUSTMENTS CREDIT	ADJUSTED TRIAL BALANCE DEBIT	ADJUSTED TRIAL BALANCE CREDIT	INCOME STATEMENT DEBIT	INCOME STATEMENT CREDIT	BALANCE SHEET DEBIT	BALANCE SHEET CREDIT
101	Cash in Bank	2128442				2128442				2128442	
105	Accounts Receivable	636435				636435				636435	
110	Merch. Inventory	8492110			(a) 353540	8138570				8138570	
115	Supplies	554950			(b) 370990	183960				183960	
120	Prepaid Insurance	150000			(c) 25000	125000				125000	
150	Delivery Equipment	1914390				1914390				1914390	
155	Store Equipment	2635340				2635340				2635340	
201	Accounts Payable		1231695				1231695				1231695
205	Fed. Inc. Tax Payable				(d) 14500		14500				14500
210	Sales Tax Payable		198360				198360				198360
301	Capital Stock		7500000				7500000				7500000
305	Retained Earnings		2762545				2762545				2762545
310	Income Summary			(a) 353540		353540		353540			
401	Sales		37738500				37738500		37738500		
405	Sales Discounts	355042				355042		355042			
410	Sales Returns & Allow.	106181				106181		106181			
501	Purchases	20946432				20946432		20946432			
505	Transportation In	421580				421580		421580			
510	Purchases Discounts		980854				980854		980854		
515	Purchases Ret. & Allow.		401790				401790		401790		
601	Advertising Expense	286450				286450		286450			
605	Bank Card Fees Expense	329230				329230		329230			
610	Delivery Expense	269396				269396		269396			
615	Insurance Expense			(c) 25000		25000		25000			
620	Maintenance Expense	332190				332190		332190			
625	Miscellaneous Expense	64705				64705		64705			
630	Rent Expense	1500000				1500000		1500000			
635	Salaries Expense	8400000				8400000		8400000			
640	Supplies Expense			(b) 370990		370990		370990			
645	Utilities Expense	315871				315871		315871			
650	Fed. Inc. Tax Expense	975000		(d) 14500		989500		989500			
		50813744	50813744	764030	764030	50828244	50828244	35066107	39121144	15762137	11707100
	Net Income							4055037			4055037
								39121144	39121144	15762137	15762137

Figure 16-6 Champion Building Products' Completed Work Sheet

Complete the following activity to check your understanding of the ten-column work sheet.

Check Your Learning

Use Figure 16-6 on page 356 to answer these questions. Write your answers on a sheet of notebook paper.

1. How many adjustments did Champion Building Products make at the end of the fiscal period?
2. What is the adjusted balance of Merchandise Inventory? How was that balance calculated?
3. What amount was extended to the Income Statement section for Federal Income Tax Expense?
4. To what section of the work sheet was the balance of Prepaid Insurance extended? Why?
5. What was the balance of Federal Income Tax Payable reported on the Trial Balance section?
6. How was the net income for the period calculated?

Compare your answers to those in the answers section. Re-read the preceding parts of the chapter to determine the correct answers to any questions you may have missed.

Summary of Key Points

1. The work sheet is prepared to organize all the data needed to update the accounts and to prepare the financial statements and end-of-period journal entries. The work sheet lists all accounts and their updated balances and shows the net income (or net loss) for the period.
2. The Trial Balance section of the work sheet includes all accounts listed in the chart of accounts, even those with zero balances.
3. Changes in some accounts are not reflected by the recording of the daily business transactions. Some accounts, therefore, must be updated at the end of a fiscal period. The end-of-period changes to such accounts are called adjustments.
4. Every adjustment requires a debit and a credit of equal amount. Every adjustment will affect one permanent general ledger account and one temporary general ledger account.
5. The beginning inventory is the amount of merchandise a business has on hand at the beginning of a fiscal period. The ending inventory is the amount of merchandise on hand at the end of a fiscal period. The balance of Merchandise Inventory changes only when it is adjusted to reflect the actual amount of merchandise on hand.
6. A corporation must pay income taxes on its net income for the year.

Review and Applications

Building Your Accounting Vocabulary

In your own words, write the definition of each of the following accounting terms. Use complete sentences for your definitions.

adjustment
beginning inventory

cost of merchandise
   sold
ending inventory

gross profit
physical inventory

Reviewing Your Accounting Knowledge

1. Why is a work sheet prepared before the financial statements?
2. What are the titles of the five sections of the ten-column work sheet?
3. Why are general ledger accounts that have zero balances entered in the Trial Balance section of the work sheet?
4. Why are certain general ledger accounts updated at the end of the fiscal period?
5. Name four accounts of a merchandising corporation that are typically adjusted at the end of the fiscal period.
6. What is meant by "expensing" an asset?
7. Why does the balance of the Merchandise Inventory account not change during the fiscal period?
8. Why is a physical inventory always taken at the end of the fiscal period?
9. Why is the merchandise inventory adjustment recorded in the Income Summary account?
10. What does the Adjusted Trial Balance section of the work sheet contain?

Improving Your Human Relations Skills

Ray Boyd is an accounting clerk at Masterson's, a small variety store. Lisa Jung, the company accountant, orally gave Ray the data for the adjustments at the end of the fiscal period. Ray wrote the amounts down, but made a mistake in one of the figures. Ray recorded the adjustments on the work sheet, extended the amounts, and completed the work sheet. When Lisa received the work sheet, she immediately recognized that an error had been made. Lisa redid the work sheet, then reported Ray's sloppy work to his supervisor. Was this situation handled properly? Why or why not?

Applying Accounting Procedures

Exercise 16-1   Calculating Adjustments

Several accounts that must be adjusted at the end of the fiscal period are listed on the next page. The current account balance (before any adjustment) is given for each account. The ending inventories of merchandise and supplies are also given, along with the amount of insurance that has expired and the federal income tax expense for the period.

Account Title	Current Balance	Adjustments Needed
Merchandise Inventory	$73,640	Ending inventory is $71,890.
Office Supplies	5,980	Office supplies on hand total $1,936.
Prepaid Insurance	1,980	Six months of premium ($165 per month) have expired.
Federal Income Tax Payable		
Income Summary		
Insurance Expense		
Office Supplies Expense		
Federal Income Tax Expense	5,800	Tax for the year is $5,994.

Instructions: Use a form similar to the one that follows.

(1) Determine the amount of the adjustment for each account.

(2) Enter the adjustment in the Adjustments Debit or Credit column. Label each adjustment (a), (b), (c), and so on.

(3) Calculate each new account balance and enter that amount in the Adjusted Trial Balance Debit or Credit column.

Account Title	Trial Balance Dr.	Trial Balance Cr.	Adjustments Dr.	Adjustments Cr.	Adjusted Trial Balance Dr.	Adjusted Trial Balance Cr.
Merchandise Inventory	$73,640					

Exercise 16-2 Reporting Amounts on the Work Sheet

Instructions: Use a form similar to the one below. For each amount, place a check in each section of the work sheet in which it would appear.

1. Balance of Supplies on January 1 plus purchases during the period
2. Beginning merchandise inventory
3. Quarterly federal income tax installments paid
4. Expired portion of insurance premium
5. Supplies consumed during the period
6. Ending merchandise inventory
7. Value of Prepaid Insurance on January 1
8. Additional federal income taxes owed
9. Supplies inventory on December 31
10. Value of Prepaid Insurance on December 31
11. Total federal income tax expense for the period

Number of Item	Trial Balance	Adjustments	Adjusted Trial Balance	Income Statement	Balance Sheet
1	✔				

SPREADSHEET

PROBLEM

Problem 16-1 Completing a Ten-Column Work Sheet

The December 31 trial balance for the Hillard Supply Corporation is listed on page 360. Also listed is the data needed for the adjustments (ending merchandise inventory, supplies used during the period, expired insurance premium, and the additional federal income taxes owed).

Instructions: Complete the ten-column work sheet for the Hillard Supply Corporation for the year ended December 31. The trial balance has already been entered on the work sheet.

	Trial Balance	
	Debit	Credit
Cash in Bank	$ 14,975.56	
Accounts Receivable	3,773.64	
Merchandise Inventory	86,865.10	
Supplies	2,940.60	
Prepaid Insurance	1,975.00	
Office Equipment	10,762.80	
Accounts Payable		$ 8,740.08
Federal Income Tax Payable		0.00
Sales Tax Payable		1,369.34
Capital Stock		45,000.00
Retained Earnings		30,928.42
Income Summary		
Sales		145,967.20
Purchases	93,874.75	
Insurance Expense	0.00	
Miscellaneous Expense	3,662.59	
Rent Expense	9,225.00	
Supplies Expense	0.00	
Federal Income Tax Expense	3,950.00	
	$232,005.04	$232,005.04

Data for Adjustments

Merchandise Inventory, December 31	$ 77,872.13
Supplies consumed during the period	2,171.15
Insurance premium expired during the period	489.00
Additional federal income taxes owed	318.00

Problem 16-2   Completing a Ten-Column Work Sheet

The December 31 trial balance for the J. J. Laine Corporation is listed below. Also listed is the data needed for the adjustments.

Instructions: Complete the ten-column work sheet for the J. J. Laine Corporation for the year ended December 31.

	Trial Balance	
	Debit	Credit
Cash in Bank	$13,865.69	
Accounts Receivable	4,385.03	
Merchandise Inventory	82,933.70	
Supplies	2,395.59	
Prepaid Insurance	1,350.00	
Store Equipment	30,756.69	
Accounts Payable		$ 8,489.48
Federal Income Tax Payable		0.00
Sales Tax Payable		1,590.58
Capital Stock		80,000.00
Retained Earnings		28,565.16
Income Summary		
Sales		71,487.20
Sales Returns and Allowances	945.59	
Purchases	39,495.69	
Transportation In	2,038.34	

Purchases Discounts		856.49
Insurance Expense	0.00	
Miscellaneous Expense	2,952.59	
Rent Expense	9,000.00	
Supplies Expense	0.00	
Federal Income Tax Expense	870.00	

Data for Adjustments

Merchandise Inventory, December 31	$78,672.13
Supplies on hand, December 31	394.45
Insurance premium expired during the period	490.00
Additional federal income taxes owed	210.00

Problem 16-3 Completing a Ten-Column Work Sheet

The balances of the general ledger accounts of Cropp Sound Shop, Inc., as of December 31 are listed below. Also listed are the adjustment data.

Instructions: Prepare a ten-column work sheet for the Cropp Sound Shop, Inc., for the year ended December 31.

Cash in Bank	$ 12,328.72
Accounts Receivable	1,734.84
Merchandise Inventory	23,648.50
Supplies	3,976.34
Prepaid Insurance	1,800.00
Store Equipment	14,395.38
Display Equipment	15,224.80
Accounts Payable	11,028.36
Federal Income Tax Payable	0.00
Sales Tax Payable	1,271.14
Capital Stock	25,000.00
Retained Earnings	9,408.24
Income Summary	
Sales	138,992.06
Sales Returns and Allowances	1,273.49
Purchases	87,118.33
Transportation In	1,174.30
Purchases Discounts	810.91
Purchases Returns and Allowances	325.48
Advertising Expense	2,438.56
Insurance Expense	0.00
Miscellaneous Expense	3,927.25
Rent Expense	9,750.00
Supplies Expense	0.00
Utilities Expense	4,395.68
Federal Income Tax Expense	3,650.00

Data for Adjustments

Ending merchandise inventory	$ 24,185.45
Ending supplies inventory	1,045.39
Insurance premium expired	675.00
Federal income tax expense for the year	3,924.00

Problem 16-4 Completing a Ten-Column Work Sheet

The balances of the general ledger accounts of the Springtime Floral Shop, Inc., as of December 31 are listed below.

Instructions: Prepare a ten-column work sheet for the Springtime Floral Shop, Inc., for the year ended December 31. The account titles have already been entered on the work sheet. The data for the adjustments is as follows.
(1) The cost of the ending merchandise inventory is $47,349.92.

(2) The cost of the supplies on hand on December 31 is $619.35.

(3) The one-year insurance premium of $1,656.00 was paid on April 1.

(4) The total federal income taxes owed for the year are $7,835.00.

Cash in Bank	$ 15,382.72
Accounts Receivable	2,853.94
Merchandise Inventory	49,208.50
Supplies	3,026.34
Prepaid Insurance	1,656.00
Store Equipment	19,406.68
Display Equipment	25,504.20
Computer Equipment	5,496.00
Accounts Payable	13,378.36
Federal Income Tax Payable	0.00
Sales Tax Payable	2,043.14
Capital Stock	50,000.00
Retained Earnings	22,425.36
Income Summary	
Sales	144,939.66
Sales Discounts	203.85
Sales Returns and Allowances	1,385.49
Purchases	79,318.73
Transportation In	1,192.30
Purchases Discounts	295.81
Purchases Returns and Allowances	491.48
Advertising Expense	3,148.56
Bank Card Fees Expense	288.40
Insurance Expense	0.00
Maintenance Expense	1,381.03
Miscellaneous Expense	3,775.39
Rent Expense	10,350.00
Supplies Expense	0.00
Utilities Expense	2,595.68
Federal Income Tax Expense	7,400.00

CHALLENGE **Problem 16-5   Locating Errors on the Work Sheet**

PROBLEM

The Hispino Card Shop began business as a corporation on December 1. It is now December 31, the end of the first fiscal period, and the work sheet for the corporation is being prepared.

Information for the Trial Balance and Adjustments sections has been recorded on the work sheet, which is included in the working papers. It is apparent from the totals on the work sheet that errors have been made in preparing these portions of the work sheet.

The accounting records show that

1. The merchandise on hand at the end of the month is valued at $13,350.00.
2. The supplies on hand on December 31 are valued at $419.75.
3. The insurance premium was paid on December 1. The premium was $980.00 and covers the period from December 1 to March 31.
4. The total federal income tax owed for the period is $243.00.

Instructions:

(1) Find and correct the error(s) in the Trial Balance section.

(2) On the line provided on the work sheet, write in the corrected totals for the Trial Balance section.

(3) Find and correct the error(s) in the Adjustments section.

(4) Write in the corrected totals for the Adjustments columns.

*D*ata Access vs. Privacy: A Delicate Balance

*S*cenario #1: It's 10:00 p.m. on a Friday evening. Early the next morning, Sandy is going camping with some friends. "Oh, no! I forgot to go to the bank."

No problem. The automatic teller machine (ATM) is always up and running. Sandy drives to the nearest bank, slips in her card, keys in her secret code number and the amount she wants, and—presto!—instant money. This machine knew who Sandy was, how much money she had in her account, and the new balance in her account after the transaction—in seconds.

Scenario #2: Company's coming for dinner in one hour. The carpet is covered with dog hairs. Your mother heads for the broom closet. "Oh, no! The vacuum cleaner isn't here. I forgot to pick it up at the repair shop."

No problem. You offer to go get it. Your mother gives you her credit card and you drive into town. The vacuum cleaner is ready. You hand your mother's credit card to the repair person, who validates it by sliding it through a little machine. The digital readout gives its approval in seconds. You get home just in time to race the cleaner across the rug.

In this fast-paced world, time is of the essence, and computers help us accomplish many time-consuming tasks efficiently. In order for organizations, businesses, and government agencies to accomplish their objectives, however, they must have access to a lot of personal data. To some, that is a threat to our right of privacy.

Information about our credit, health, and employment history could be embarrassing. It could even be harmful if confidentiality is not respected, if the information is incorrect, or if those who use it don't exercise good judgment and fairness.

Computers have dramatically increased the amount of data that can be collected, processed, and stored.

So while accessible databases save hours and dollars, they must be carefully guarded so they're used with our approval and with the right to review and to challenge incorrect facts.

There will probably be many debates on the issue of accessibility versus privacy. Can we have it both ways?

Chapter 17

PREPARING FINANCIAL STATEMENTS FOR A CORPORATION

In Chapter 16, you learned that some accounts in the general ledger are not up to date at the end of the fiscal period. You learned how to determine which accounts had to be adjusted, how to calculate the amount of each adjustment, and how to enter adjustments on a ten-column work sheet.

The work sheet is a working paper. It organizes all the accounting data needed to prepare the financial statements and the end-of-period journal entries. In this chapter, you will use the information on the work sheet to prepare the financial statements for a merchandising corporation. You will learn what information is included on each statement and why the statements are important to stockholders, creditors, and managers. You'll also learn how the equity accounts of a corporation differ from those of a sole proprietorship.

Learning Objectives

When you have completed Chapter 17, you should be able to do the following:

1. Explain how the ownership for a corporation is recorded in comparison to that for a sole proprietorship.

2. Explain the relationship between the work sheet and the financial statements for a merchandising business organized as a corporation.

3. Explain how the financial statements for a corporation differ from those for a sole proprietorship.

4. Prepare an income statement for a merchandising corporation.

5. Prepare a statement of retained earnings for a merchandising corporation.

6. Prepare a balance sheet for a merchandising corporation.

7. Define the accounting terms introduced in this chapter.

New Terms

capital stock
stockholders' equity
retained earnings
net sales
net purchases
gross profit on sales
operating expenses
operating income
statement of retained earnings

Accounting for a Corporation

A sole proprietorship is owned by one person. A corporation may be owned by one person or by hundreds of people. The ownership of a corporation is represented by shares of stock.

Recording the Ownership of a Corporation

As you recall, investments made by the owner of a sole proprietorship are recorded in the owner's capital account; for example, Jan Harter, Capital. An owner's investment of $25,000 in the sole proprietorship would be recorded as shown in the T accounts below. Cash in Bank is debited for $25,000 and Jan Harter, Capital is credited for the same amount.

Cash in Bank			Jan Harter, Capital	
Dr.	Cr.		Dr.	Cr.
+	−		−	+
$25,000				$25,000

An investment of this same amount in a corporation would be recorded by the corporation as shown in the following T accounts. Cash in Bank again is debited since the corporation is receiving cash. The account credited for the amount of the investment, however, is Capital Stock. **Capital stock** represents the total amount of investment in the corporation by its stockholders (owners).

Cash in Bank			Capital Stock	
Dr.	Cr.		Dr.	Cr.
+	−		−	+
$25,000				$25,000

Capital Stock is classified as a stockholders' equity account. **Stockholders' equity** is the value of the stockholders' claims to the assets of the corporation. The Capital Stock account is to a corporation what the owner's capital account is to a sole proprietorship. Capital Stock, then, has the same rules of debit and credit as an owner's capital account.

Capital Stock	
Dr.	Cr.
−	+
Decrease Side	Increase Side
	Balance Side

Reporting Stockholders' Equity in the Corporation

The form of business organization does not affect the amount of equity in the business. That is, one person may have an ownership interest in a sole proprietorship worth $20,000, or ten people may have shares of stock in a corporation worth $20,000. The difference between the two is in the way these two amounts are reported on the balance sheet.

The balance sheet of the sole proprietorship reports the balance of the owner's capital account. This amount is reported in the owner's equity section of the balance sheet. For a corporation, the owner's equity section of the balance sheet is called stockholders' equity. The law requires that stockholders' equity be reported in two parts: (1) equity contributed by stockholders and (2) equity earned through business profits.

▲ Equity Contributed by Stockholders

The first part of stockholders' equity is the amount of money invested by the stockholders. Stockholders contribute to equity in the corporation by buying shares of stock issued by the corporation. As you just learned, stockholders' investments are recorded in the account Capital Stock.

▲ Equity Earned Through Business Profits

The second part of stockholders' equity is the amount of net income earned during the fiscal period and retained by the corporation. In a sole proprietorship, this is the amount of net income less any withdrawals by the owner. In a corporation, this amount represents the increase in stockholders' equity from net income held by the corporation and not distributed to the stockholders as a return on their investment. This amount is called **retained earnings.**

Retained Earnings	
Dr.	Cr.
−	+
Decrease Side	Increase Side
	Balance Side

Earnings retained by a corporation are recorded in the account Retained Earnings. Retained Earnings is classified as a stockholders' equity account. Like the Capital Stock account, it is increased by credits and decreased by debits. Retained Earnings has a normal credit balance.

In a sole proprietorship, net income is recorded as an increase in capital. This increase in capital represents an increase in the assets of the business. In a corporation, retained earnings represent the growth, or increase, in the assets of the corporation.

Before learning about the financial statements prepared by a merchandising corporation, complete the following activity to check your understanding of the material you have just studied.

Check Your Learning

Write your answers to these questions on a sheet of notebook paper.

1. An investment of $40,000 by Jane Settles in a sole proprietorship is recorded as a credit to the __?__ account.
2. The sale of 50 shares of stock, for $2,500, by the Sims Corporation is recorded as a credit to the account __?__ .
3. The value of stockholders' claims to the assets of the business is called __?__ .
4. Stockholders' equity consists of two accounts: __?__ and __?__ .

Compare your answers to those in the answers section. Re-read the preceding part of the chapter to find the answers to any questions you may have missed.

Preparing End-of-Period Financial Statements

At the end of a fiscal period, a business prepares various financial statements. These statements summarize the changes that have taken place during the fiscal period and report the financial condition of the business at the end of the fiscal period. Managers use the information in these statements to evaluate past decisions and to help them make future decisions. Stockholders are interested in the business's performance and in its potential. Creditors want to know whether the business can pay its debts. Government agencies, employees, consumers, and the general public are also interested in the financial position of the business.

For these financial reports to be useful, the data must be presented in such a way that users can recognize similarities, differences, and trends from one period to another. The same types of statements, therefore, are prepared at the end of each fiscal period. The time period covered by the financial statements is the same from one period to another (for example, one month, one year, and so on).

Champion Building Products, a merchandising corporation, prepares three financial statements. These statements are the income statement, the statement of retained earnings, and the balance sheet. The first two statements report the changes that have taken place over the fiscal period. The balance sheet shows the financial position of the business on a specific date—the last day of the fiscal period. The data needed to complete all three statements are taken from the work sheet.

The Income Statement

As you know, the income statement reports the net income or net loss earned by a business in a fiscal period. In Chapter 8, you prepared an income statement for Global Travel Agency, a service business organized as a sole proprietorship. On that statement, Global Travel's total expenses were subtracted from its revenue to determine the net income or loss for the fiscal period.

A merchandising business, however, has an additional cost—the cost of the merchandise that was purchased and then resold to customers. That cost must be included when determining net income or loss. The income statement for a merchandising business, then, must be expanded. An income statement for a merchandising business has five sections: (1) Revenue, (2) Cost of Merchandise Sold, (3) Gross Profit on Sales, (4) Operating Expenses, and (5) Net Income (or Loss).

Financial statements are a central feature of accounting because they are the primary means of communicating important financial information to users.

The accounting stationery used for Champion's income statement has four amount columns. The far right column is used to enter totals. The other columns are used to enter balances that must be added or subtracted.

All of the information needed to prepare the income statement is taken from the work sheet, particularly the Income Statement section. As with all other financial statements, the income statement begins with a three-line heading. As you can see in Figure 17-1, the income statement for Champion Building Products has been prepared for the year ended December 31. After the heading has been written, the next information to be entered on the income statement is the revenue for the period.

Champion Building Products, Inc. Income Statement For the Year Ended December 31, 19--				
Revenue:				
Sales			377 385 00	
Less: Sales Discounts		3 550 42		
Sales Ret. & Allow.		1 061 81	4 612 23	
Net Sales				372 772 77

Figure 17-1 The Heading and Revenue Section of the Income Statement

The Revenue Section

The first section on the income statement is the revenue section. This section reports the net sales for the period. Look at Figure 17-1 again. The balances of the revenue account Sales and the contra revenue accounts Sales Discounts and Sales Returns and Allowances are reported in this section. As

UNIT 3   The Accounting Cycle for a Merchandising Business

you learned earlier, contra revenue accounts decrease the amount of revenue Champion receives from its sales transactions. **Net sales,** therefore, is the amount of sales for the period less any sales discounts, returns, or allowances. Refer to Figure 17-1 as you learn how to complete the revenue section.

1. On the first line, write the classification "Revenue:" at the left edge of the stationery.
2. On the second line, enter the title of the revenue account Sales, indented about one-half inch. Enter the balance of the account in the *third* amount column.
3. On the next lines, enter the deductions from Sales. Write the word "Less:" followed by the titles and balances of the two contra revenue accounts. (You may have to abbreviate the account titles.) Enter the balances of the accounts ($3,550.42 and $1,061.81) in the *second* amount column.
4. To find the total deduction from Sales, add the balances of the two contra revenue accounts. Write the total, on line 4, below the Sales balance in the *third* amount column.
5. On the next line, enter the words "Net Sales," indented about an inch. Subtract the total of the two contra accounts from the balance of the Sales account. Enter the amount in the *fourth* amount column. As you can see in Figure 17-1, Champion's net sales for the year are $372,772.77.

$3,550.42
+1,061.81
$4,612.23

$377,385.00
− 4,612.23
$372,772.77

The Cost of Merchandise Sold Section

Before a merchandising business can determine its net income or net loss, it must calculate the cost of the merchandise that was sold during the period. The cost of merchandise sold is calculated as follows:

$$
\begin{array}{l}
 \text{Beginning merchandise inventory} \\
+ \text{ Net purchases during the period} \\
\hline
= \text{Cost of merchandise available for sale} \\
- \text{ Ending merchandise inventory} \\
\hline
= \text{Cost of merchandise sold}
\end{array}
$$

As you can see from this equation, there are two steps involved in calculating the cost of merchandise sold. The first step is to determine the cost of all the merchandise that was available for sale. This is done by adding net purchases to the beginning inventory amount recorded in the Merchandise Inventory account. **Net purchases** is the amount of all costs related to merchandise purchased during the period. To calculate net purchases, the balance of Transportation In (the transportation charges for the period) is added to the balance of the Purchases account. The balances of Purchases Discounts and Purchases Returns and Allowances are then subtracted from that amount, leaving the net purchases.

$$
\begin{array}{l}
 \text{Purchases} \\
+ \text{ Transportation In} \\
\hline
= \text{Cost of Delivered Merchandise} \\
- \text{ Purchases Discounts} \\
- \text{ Purchases Returns and Allowances} \\
\hline
= \text{Net Purchases}
\end{array}
$$

Transportation charges increase the cost of merchandise. The contra cost of merchandise accounts—Purchases Discounts and Purchases Returns and Allowances—decrease the cost of the merchandise bought for resale.

The second step in calculating the cost of merchandise sold is to subtract the ending merchandise inventory amount from the cost of merchandise available for sale. The cost of merchandise sold section of the income statement is shown in Figure 17-2. Refer to this illustration as you read the following steps:

Champion Building Products, Inc.
Income Statement
For the Year Ended December 31, 19--

Revenue:				
Sales			377385 00	
Less: Sales Discounts		3550 42		
Sales Ret. & Allow.		1061 81	4612 23	
Net Sales				372772 77
Cost of Merchandise Sold:				
Merch. Inv., Jan. 1, 19--			84921 10	
Purchases	209464 32			
Plus: Transportation In	4215 80			
Cost of Delivered Merch.		213680 12		
Less: Purch. Discounts	9808 54			
Purch. Ret. & Allow.	4017 90	13826 44		
Net Purchases			199853 68	
Cost of Merch. Avail.			284774 78	
Merch. Inv., Dec. 31, 19--			81385 70	
Cost of Merch. Sold				203389 08
Gross Profit on Sales				169383 69

Figure 17-2 Income Statement Through Gross Profit on Sales

ACCOUNTING **Tips**

When adding a column of figures, start at the top of the column and add down. To verify that your total is correct, add the figures from the bottom up. When subtracting, first subtract in the normal manner. To verify your answer, add the answer to the number that was subtracted; the result should be the number that you subtracted from. This method of verifying works equally well manually or with a calculator.

1. On the line below net sales, write the words "Cost of Merchandise Sold:" at the left edge.
2. Next, write "Merchandise Inventory, January 1, 19—," indented about half an inch. Enter the amount of the beginning inventory in the *third* amount column. (The beginning inventory is found on the Merchandise Inventory line of the work sheet in the Trial Balance Debit column.)
3. Next, enter the title and balance of the Purchases account. Enter the balance amount in the *first* amount column.
4. On the next line, write the word "Plus:" followed by the title and balance of Transportation In. Enter the balance in the *first* amount column, below the Purchases amount.

$209,464.32
+ 4,215.80
$213,680.12

5. Add the balances of the Purchases and Transportation In accounts. The result is the *Cost of Delivered Merchandise.* Enter the amount in the *second* amount column.
6. On the next line, enter the deductions from Purchases. Write the word "Less:" and the titles and balances of the two contra cost of merchandise accounts. Enter the balances in the *first* amount column.

$ 9,808.54	
+ 4,017.90	
$13,826.44	
$213,680.12	
− 13,826.44	
$199,853.68	

7. To find the total deduction from Purchases, add the balances of the two contra cost accounts. Enter the total, on the same line, in the *second* amount column.

8. Subtract the total of the two contra cost accounts from the cost of delivered merchandise amount. The difference is the net purchases for the period. Enter the amount in the *third* amount column.

$ 84,921.10	
+199,853.68	
$284,774.78	

9. Now, add the net purchases amount to the beginning inventory amount. The total is the *Cost of Merchandise Available for Sale.* Enter the total in the *third* amount column.

10. On the next line, write "Merchandise Inventory, December 31, 19—." Enter the amount of the ending inventory in the *third* amount column. (The ending inventory is found on the Merchandise Inventory line of the work sheet in the Balance Sheet Debit column.)

$284,774.78	
− 81,385.70	
$203,389.08	

11. Subtract the ending inventory amount from the cost of merchandise available for sale. The difference is the *Cost of Merchandise Sold* during the period. Enter the amount in the *fourth* amount column.

As you can see in Figure 17-2, Champion sold merchandise costing $203,389.08 during the fiscal period.

The Gross Profit on Sales Section

In Chapter 16, you learned that the total amount received for all sales during the period actually represents two different amounts. The net, or total, sales amount includes the cost of the merchandise sold and the profit made from selling that merchandise. Once the cost of merchandise sold has been determined, the gross profit on sales can be calculated. The **gross profit on sales** is the amount of profit made during the period before expenses are deducted. Gross profit on sales is found by subtracting the cost of merchandise sold from net sales. In Figure 17-2, you can see that Champion had net sales of $372,772.77 and a cost of merchandise sold of $203,389.08. Champion's gross profit on sales is, therefore, $169,383.69.

$372,772.77	
−203,389.08	
$169,383.69	

The Operating Expenses Section

The next section of the income statement shows the operating expenses for the period. **Operating expenses** are the cash spent or the assets consumed to earn revenue for the business. Look at Figure 17-3 on page 372. The titles and balances of all expense accounts *except* Federal Income Tax Expense are listed in the same order as on the work sheet. While it is a normal expense for a corporation, Federal Income Tax Expense is not considered to be an operating expense. Rather than cash spent to *earn* revenue, the account represents cash paid out as a *result* of the revenue earned.

Notice that the balances of the expense accounts are entered in the *third* amount column. The balances are then totaled. This total, $118,938.32, is entered in the *fourth* amount column.

The Net Income Section

The final section of the income statement reports the net income (or net loss) for the period, both before and after federal income taxes. It is customary to list the federal income tax amount separately on the income statement. This is done so that the amount of the operating income is more easily

Champion Building Products, Inc.							
Income Statement							
For the Year Ended December 31, 19--							

Revenue:				
Sales			377385 00	
Less: Sales Discounts		3550 42		
Sales Ret. & Allow.		1061 81	4612 23	
Net Sales				372772 77
Cost of Merchandise Sold:				
Merch. Inv., Jan. 1, 19--			84921 10	
Purchases	209464 32			
Plus: Transportation In	4215 80			
Cost of Delivered Merch.		213680 12		
Less: Purch. Discounts	9808 54			
Purch. Ret. & Allow.	4017 90	13826 44		
Net Purchases			199853 68	
Cost of Merch. Avail.			284774 78	
Merch. Inv., Dec. 31, 19--			81385 70	
Cost of Merch. Sold				203389 08
Gross Profit on Sales				169383 69
Operating Expenses:				
Advertising Expense			2864 50	
Bank Card Fees Expense			3292 30	
Delivery Expense			2693 96	
Insurance Expense			250 00	
Maintenance Expense			3321 90	
Miscellaneous Expense			647 05	
Rent Expense			15000 00	
Salaries Expense			84000 00	
Supplies Expense			3709 90	
Utilities Expense			3158 71	
Total Oper. Expenses				118938 32
Operating Income				50445 37
Less: Fed. Income Taxes				9895 00
Net Income				40550 37

Figure 17-3 Champion's Completed Income Statement

seen on the business's income statement. **Operating income** is the taxable income of a corporation, or the amount of income earned before federal income taxes.

Look at Figure 17-3 again. To determine the operating income, the total operating expenses are subtracted from the gross profit on sales. As you can see, Champion's operating income for the period is $50,445.37. "Less: Federal Income Taxes" is written on the next line, indented one-half inch. The amount of income taxes, $9,895.00, is taken from the Income Statement Debit column of the work sheet. The amount of federal income taxes is subtracted from the operating income. The difference, $40,550.37, is the net income for the period. This amount must agree with the amount shown on the work sheet. If it does, a double rule is drawn under the amount to show that the income statement is proved and complete.

Before you go any further, do the following activity to see if you understand how the income statement is prepared.

$169,383.69
−118,938.32
$ 50,445.37

$50,445.37
− 9,895.00
$40,550.37

Check Your Learning

Answer these questions on a sheet of notebook paper.

1. If the net purchases of a business are $17,347.90 and the beginning inventory is $61,350.50, what is the cost of merchandise available for sale?
2. If the gross profit on sales is $22,913.86 and total expenses are $15,164.19, what is the operating income?
3. What is the cost of merchandise sold if the beginning inventory is $14,947.00, net purchases are $83,611.50, and the ending inventory is $15,669.14?
4. If net sales are $137,412.00 and the cost of merchandise sold is $63,010.27, what is the gross profit on sales?
5. How is the net income calculated?

Compare your answers to those in the answers section. Re-read the preceding part of the chapter to find the correct answers to any questions you may have missed.

The Statement of Retained Earnings

In a corporation, there are two stockholders' equity accounts: Capital Stock and Retained Earnings. The Capital Stock account represents the stockholders' investment in the corporation. The balance of this account changes only when additional shares of stock are issued by the corporation. The Retained Earnings account summarizes the profits accumulated and kept by a corporation less any amounts paid to stockholders as a return on their investment.

In Chapter 8, you learned how to prepare a statement of changes in owner's equity. That statement showed the changes that had occurred in the owner's capital account during the fiscal period. A similar statement — the statement of retained earnings — is prepared for a corporation. A **statement of retained earnings** reports the changes that have taken place in the Retained Earnings account during the period. Changes result from business operations (net income or loss) and the distribution of earnings. A net income increases the balance of the Retained Earnings account. A net loss and any distribution of earnings decrease the balance of the account.

Like the statement of changes in owner's equity, the statement of retained earnings is prepared as a supporting document for the balance sheet. The balance of the Retained Earnings account calculated on this statement is used when preparing the balance sheet. The information needed to prepare this report is found on the work sheet.

The statement of retained earnings for Champion Building Products is shown in Figure 17-4 on page 374.

The first line of this statement shows the balance of the Retained Earnings account at the beginning of the fiscal period. This balance, $27,625.45, is taken from the Balance Sheet Credit column of the work sheet. Champion

Champion Building Products, Inc.
Statement of Retained Earnings
For the Year Ended December 31, 19—

Retained Earnings, January 1, 19—	27625 45
Net Income	40550 37
Retained Earnings, December 31, 19—	68175 82

Figure 17-4 Statement of Retained Earnings

earned a net income of $40,550.37 for the period. This amount is added to the balance of the Retained Earnings account. There are no deductions from Retained Earnings. The new balance of the Retained Earnings account, then, is $68,175.82.

The Balance Sheet

The balance sheet reports the final, updated balances of all asset, liability, and stockholders' equity accounts as of a specific date. It is prepared from the information in the Balance Sheet section of the work sheet and from the statement of retained earnings.

Champion's balance sheet is shown in Figure 17-5. This balance sheet has been prepared in report form. In the report form, as you will recall, the classifications are shown one under the other.

Champion Building Products, Inc.
Balance Sheet
December 31, 19—

Assets		
Cash in Bank	21284 42	
Accounts Receivable	6364 35	
Merchandise Inventory	81385 70	
Supplies	1839 60	
Prepaid Insurance	1250 00	
Delivery Equipment	19143 90	
Store Equipment	26353 40	
Total Assets		157621 37
Liabilities		
Accounts Payable	12316 95	
Federal Income Tax Payable	145 00	
Sales Tax Payable	1983 60	
Total Liabilities		14445 55
Stockholders' Equity		
Capital Stock	75000 00	
Retained Earnings	68175 82	
Total Stockholders' Equity		143175 82
Total Liabilities and Stockholders' Equity		157621 37

Figure 17-5 Champion's Balance Sheet

The assets are listed first. The classification "Assets" is centered on the first line. The account titles and balances are then listed in the same order as they appear on the work sheet. The individual balances are entered in the first amount column. The total assets amount is entered in the second amount column. The double rule, however, is not entered until the Liabilities and Stockholders' Equity sections have been completed and are shown to be equal to total assets.

The Liabilities section is begun one blank line below the total assets amount. Again, the account titles and balances are listed as they appear on the work sheet. The individual balances are entered in the first amount column, and the total liabilities amount is entered in the second amount column.

$ 14,445.55
143,175.82
$157,621.37

Next, the Stockholders' Equity section is completed. Stockholders' equity consists of two accounts: Capital Stock and Retained Earnings. The balance of the Capital Stock account is taken from the Balance Sheet section of the work sheet. The balance of the Retained Earnings account is taken from the statement of retained earnings. Again, the individual balances are listed in the first amount column and the total in the second column.

Once these amounts have been entered, the total of the Liabilities section and the total of the Stockholders' Equity section are added. This total must agree with the total assets amount. If it does, the balance sheet is double ruled.

Financial Statements Prepared by Computer

Today most businesses rely on automated equipment or computers to maintain the general and subsidiary ledgers and to prepare the end-of-period financial statements. Computers offer businesses the advantages of speed and accuracy. Even small businesses can now afford the microcomputers specifically designed for the smaller business operation. There is a variety of accounting software available for microcomputers. Some businesses may prefer to have an outside computer company maintain their accounting records and prepare the statements.

If Champion's balance sheet had been prepared on a computer, the printout might look like that in Figure 17-6 on page 376. Other financial statements prepared by computer would look similar to this balance sheet.

Computer know-how can increase an executive's access to information for decision making, as well as improve the speed with which decisions can be made.

```
                    CHAMPION BUILDING PRODUCTS, INC.
                           BALANCE SHEET
                         DECEMBER 31, 19--

              ASSETS
Cash in Bank                              21284.42
Accounts Receivable                        6364.35
Merchandise Inventory                     81385.70
Supplies                                   1839.60
Prepaid Insurance                          1250.00
Delivery Equipment                        19143.90
Store Equipment                           26353.40
                                          --------
     Total Assets                                       157621.37
                                                        =========


              LIABILITIES
Accounts Payable                          12316.95
Federal Income Tax Payable                  145.00
Sales Tax Payable                          1983.60
                                          --------
     Total Liabilities                                   14445.55

          STOCKHOLDERS' EQUITY
Capital Stock                             75000.00
Retained Earnings                         68175.82
                                          --------
     Total Stockholders' Equity                         143175.82
                                                        ---------
     Total Liabilities and Stockholders' Equity         157621.37
                                                        =========
```

Figure 17-6 A Computer-Generated Balance Sheet

Summary of Key Points

1. Accounting for corporations differs from other forms of business only in reporting owner's equity on the balance sheet. Capital Stock replaces the individual owner's capital account. The Retained Earnings account is used to record the net income from business operations.
2. Three financial statements prepared by a merchandising corporation are the income statement, the statement of retained earnings, and the balance sheet.
3. The income statement for a merchandising business contains a section showing the cost of merchandise sold.
4. Net sales is the amount of total sales less deductions for sales discounts, returns, and allowances. Net purchases is the total cost of merchandise bought plus transportation charges less deductions for purchases discounts, returns, and allowances.
5. Gross profit on sales is the amount of net sales minus the cost of merchandise sold.
6. The federal income taxes paid by a corporation are listed separately on the income statement.
7. The statement of retained earnings reports the changes in the Retained Earnings account during the period.
8. The net income for the period is added to the balance of the Retained Earnings account.

17 Review and Applications

Building Your Accounting Vocabulary

In your own words, write the definition of each of the following accounting terms. Use complete sentences for your definitions.

capital stock
gross profit on sales
net purchases
net sales

operating expenses
operating income
retained earnings

statement of retained
earnings
stockholders' equity

Reviewing Your Accounting Knowledge

1. How does stockholders' equity differ from owner's equity?
2. What three financial statements are usually prepared by a merchandising corporation?
3. How does an income statement for a merchandising business differ from that for a service business?
4. How is net sales calculated? net purchases?
5. What is the difference between the cost of merchandise available for sale and the cost of merchandise sold?
6. How is the cost of merchandise sold calculated?
7. Why are the income taxes paid by a corporation listed separately on the income statement?
8. What is the difference between operating income and net income?
9. Why is the net income for the period added to Retained Earnings rather than to Capital Stock?
10. When does the balance of the Capital Stock account change?
11. Why is the income statement prepared before the statement of retained earnings and the statement of retained earnings prepared before the balance sheet?
12. What are the two stockholders' equity accounts included on the balance sheet?

Improving Your Analysis Skills

Joan Corrales is thinking of buying the Midtown Video Center. She has been given Midtown's financial statements for the past twelve months. What should Joan look for in these statements to help her make a decision about buying Midtown Video Center? Name as many items as you can.

Applying Accounting Procedures

Exercise 17-1 Determining the Cost of Merchandise Sold

The account balances at the top of page 378 were taken from the Income Statement section of the work sheet.

| | Income Statement | |
	Debit	Credit
Purchases	$121,390.00	
Transportation In	1,406.00	
Purchases Discounts		$4,920.00
Purchases Returns and Allowances		1,641.00

The beginning merchandise inventory was $36,819.40 and the ending merchandise inventory was $41,641.00.

Instructions:

(1) Determine the amount of net purchases for the period.

(2) Determine the cost of merchandise sold.

Exercise 17-2   Calculating Amounts on the Income Statement

Instructions: For each group of figures that follows, determine the missing amount.

1. Beginning merchandise inventory $81,269.40
   Net purchases   14,739.80
   Cost of merchandise available for sale   ?

2. Net sales $51,674.90
   Cost of merchandise sold   36,059.21
   Gross profit on sales   ?

3. Purchases $26,340.95
   Transportation In   1,438.21
   Cost of delivered merchandise   ?

4. Cost of merchandise available for sale $49,816.42
   Ending merchandise inventory   32,684.17
   Cost of merchandise sold   ?

5. Gross profit on sales $17,029.63
   Operating expenses   12,691.77
   Operating income   ?

6. Operating income $24,072.39
   Federal income taxes   6,419.00
   Net income   ?

SPREADSHEET Problem 17-1   Preparing an Income Statement

The work sheet for the Kardos Corporation for the year ended December 31 is shown on the following page.

Instructions: Prepare an income statement. Refer to Figure 17-3 on
PROBLEM page 372 if you need help in setting up the income statement.

Problem 17-2   Preparing a Statement of Retained Earnings

Instructions: Use the work sheet and the income statement from Problem 17-1 to prepare a statement of retained earnings for the Kardos Corporation.

Kardos Corporation
Work Sheet
For the Year Ended December 31, 19--

ACCT. NO.	ACCOUNT NAME	TRIAL BALANCE DEBIT	TRIAL BALANCE CREDIT	ADJUSTMENTS DEBIT	ADJUSTMENTS CREDIT	ADJUSTED TRIAL BALANCE DEBIT	ADJUSTED TRIAL BALANCE CREDIT	INCOME STATEMENT DEBIT	INCOME STATEMENT CREDIT	BALANCE SHEET DEBIT	BALANCE SHEET CREDIT
101	Cash in Bank	1926184				1926184				1926184	
105	Accounts Receivable	780419				780419				780419	
110	Merchandise Inventory	8923624			(a) 510890	8412734				8412734	
115	Supplies	601990			(b) 491640	110350				110350	
120	Prepaid Insurance	235200			(c) 98000	137200				137200	
140	Store Equipment	1968725				1968725				1968725	
150	Computer Equipment	738940				738940				738940	
201	Accounts Payable		1463247				1463247				1463247
205	Fed. Inc. Tax Payable				(d) 62100		62100				62100
210	Sales Tax Payable		138006				138006				138006
301	Capital Stock		7000000				7000000				7000000
305	Retained Earnings		1631552				1631552				1631552
310	Income Summary			(a) 510890		510890		510890			
401	Sales		35487191				35487191		35487191		
405	Sales Discounts	410645				410645		410645			
410	Sales Returns & Allow.	141982				141982		141982			
501	Purchases	19384192				19384192		19384192			
505	Transportation In	479041				479041		479041			
510	Purchases Discounts		890947				890947		890947		
515	Purchases Ret. & Allow.		576291				576291		576291		
601	Advertising Expense	310640				310640		310640			
605	Bank Card Fees Expense	283109				283109		283109			
610	Insurance Expense			(c) 98000		98000		98000			
615	Maintenance Expense	340591				340591		340591			
620	Miscellaneous Expense	78362				78362		78362			
625	Rent Expense	1200000				1200000		1200000			
630	Salaries Expense	7956490				7956490		7956490			
635	Supplies Expense			(b) 491640		491640		491640			
640	Utilities Expense	398000				398000		398000			
645	Fed. Inc. Tax Expense	1029100		(d) 62100		1091200		1091200			
		47187234	47187234	1162630	1162630	47249334	47249334	33174782	36954429	14074552	10294905
	Net Income							3779647			3779647
								36954429	36954429	14074552	14074552

379

Problem 17-3 Preparing a Balance Sheet

Instructions: Use the work sheet from Problem 17-1 and the statement of retained earnings you prepared in Problem 17-2 to prepare a balance sheet for the Kardos Corporation.

Problem 17-4 Preparing Financial Statements

Instructions: The partially completed work sheet for Ocean Bluffs Marine, Inc., is included in the working papers.
(1) Complete the work sheet.
(2) Prepare an income statement.
(3) Prepare a statement of retained earnings.
(4) Prepare a balance sheet.

COMPUTER

PROBLEM

Problem 17-5 Completing a Work Sheet and Financial Statements

The trial balance for the R & L Corporation has been prepared on a ten-column work sheet that is included in the working papers accompanying this textbook.

Instructions:
(1) Complete the work sheet for the fiscal year ended March 31. Use the following information to make the adjustments.

Ending merchandise inventory	$46,821.00
Ending supplies inventory	1,084.00
Expired insurance	1,250.00
Total federal income taxes for the year	546.00

(2) Prepare an income statement.
(3) Prepare a statement of retained earnings.
(4) Prepare a balance sheet.

CHALLENGE

PROBLEM

Problem 17-6 Evaluating the Effect of an Error on the Income Statement

The accounting clerk for Lakeside Camera Shop prepared the income statement that follows for the year ended December 31. The accounting supervisor at Lakeside noticed that the balance of the Transportation In account was omitted from this statement in error. That account has a balance of $519.40.

Instructions: Use the income statement shown on page 381 to answer these questions.
(1) In which section of the income statement should the account Transportation In have been shown?
(2) How is net purchases affected by this omission (understated or overstated)? By what amount?
(3) How does the omission of the Transportation In balance affect gross profit on sales? By what amount?
(4) What is the correct amount for the cost of merchandise sold for the period?
(5) What is the correct amount for net income?

Lakeside Camera Shop
Income Statement
For the Year Ended December 31, 19--

Revenue:				
Sales			11577645	
Less: Sales Discounts		37461		
Sales Ret. & Allow.		108691	146152	
Net Sales				11431493
Cost of Merchandise Sold:				
Merch. Inv., Jan. 1, 19--			5122926	
Purchases		3362490		
Less: Purch. Discounts	41073			
Purch. Ret. & Allow.	120486	161559		
Net Purchases			3200931	
Cost of Merch. Avail.			8323857	
Merch. Inv., Dec. 31, 19--			4471470	
Cost of Merch. Sold				3852387
Gross Profit on Sales				7579106
Operating Expenses:				
Advertising Expense			92980	
Bank Card Fees Expense			132464	
Miscellaneous Expense			163921	
Rent Expense			620000	
Salaries Expense			2960929	
Supplies Expense			276418	
Total Oper. Expenses				4246712
Operating Income				3332394
Less: Fed. Income Taxes				279000
Net Income				3053394

CHALLENGE PROBLEM

Problem 17-7   Calculating Income Statement Amounts

Instructions: Look at the following balances. Determine the missing amount for each of the question marks. Use the form in your working papers or plain paper.

	Net Sales	Beginning Inventory	Net Purchases	Ending Inventory	Cost of Merchandise Sold	Gross Profit
1.	$246,000	?	$126,400	$ 48,300	$130,900	$115,100
2.	85,000	$20,000	?	10,000	45,000	40,000
3.	?	34,200	58,800	?	66,600	85,400
4.	26,295	36,887	12,199	39,895	?	?
5.	48,683	?	18,321	25,249	?	28,262
6.	?	29,246	?	35,896	58,055	74,907
7.	41,160	38,443	29,526	?	?	28,880
8.	?	40,976	607,379	38,503	?	269,644
9.	289,656	64,813	?	60,042	181,635	?
10.	519,078	?	214,122	156,753	229,872	?

*I*s the Boss Always Right?

Would you do exactly what your boss told you to do even if it went against your conscience? Many people who believe they would follow their own conscience above their bosses' find that if an actual questionable situation arises, their conscience often loses. Studies have shown that the power an employee attributes to his or her employer can lead an employee to act unethically if the boss requests it. Sometimes the thought of losing a job can cause people to act in ways that they normally would never think of acting.

For instance, suppose you found yourself in the following situation. While working on an accounting degree at your local community college, you found a position as a night auditor in a local hotel which is part of a national chain, but is owned and managed locally. After several months on the job, you have become very familiar with the system and the books. As you reviewed the previous year's books, you noticed discrepancies. Once you checked the books carefully, you realized that over time a large sum of money had been embezzled. Alarmed at what you had discovered, you took the books to the hotel manager. Much to your surprise, he only laughed and told you not to worry about it. He recommended that you continue auditing the books by following the pattern of the previous night auditor.

What is your ethical dilemma? Your boss has, in effect, asked you to continue embezzling money. If you refuse to comply, you will almost certainly lose your job, and it is a well-paying one. If you are fired or even if you quit, who would believe that it happened because you caught your boss embezzling? You could report your boss to the management of the national hotel chain, but would they believe you? Would they do anything about it?

Discovering that someone you work with has done something unethical can place you in a difficult situation.

Could they even be in on the scheme?

Often an ethical situation can arise when you stumble upon the unethical actions of someone else. When this occurs, you have to be prepared to evaluate the situation, take a stand, and follow through. Such a situation can be even more difficult when the person you are up against is your boss. As in all ethical dilemmas, it is helpful to consider all your options before choosing what path you will take. Such a procedure ensures that you will have definite reasons for your actions that you can rely on should the going get tough.

Chapter  18

RECORDING ADJUSTING AND CLOSING ENTRIES

In Chapter 17, you learned how to prepare three financial statements for a merchandising business organized as a corporation. The income statement and the statement of retained earnings reported the changes that occurred as a result of business operations during the fiscal period. The balance sheet reported the financial position of the business as of the last day of the fiscal period.

In this chapter, you will complete the accounting cycle for a merchandising business. You will learn how to journalize and post the adjusting entries that were calculated on the work sheet in Chapter 16. You will also journalize and post the closing entries for Champion Building Products, Inc. After journalizing and posting the closing entries, you will prepare a post-closing trial balance.

Learning Objectives

When you have completed Chapter 18, you should be able to do the following:

1. Record adjusting entries in the general journal.
2. Post adjusting entries to the general ledger.
3. Record closing entries for a merchandising corporation.
4. Post closing entries to the general ledger accounts.
5. Prepare a post-closing trial balance.
6. Describe the steps in the accounting cycle.
7. Define the accounting terms introduced in this chapter.

New Terms

adjusting entries
software
hardware

Updating the General Ledger Accounts

In Chapter 16, you learned that some general ledger account balances are not completely up to date at the end of the fiscal period. For example, the balance of Merchandise Inventory reported in the Trial Balance section of the work sheet represents the beginning inventory rather than the ending inventory. The balance of the Supplies account does not reflect the supplies used up during the period. The Prepaid Insurance balance does not show that a part of the premium has expired. In addition, the amount recorded in Federal Income Tax Expense reflects the estimated taxes paid, not the actual amount that must be paid.

All of these accounts must be adjusted so that their balances are current as of the last day of the fiscal period. As you recall, the adjustments are made to bring account balances up to date and to expense the assets that have been consumed during business operations. These adjustments are planned, calculated, and recorded in the Adjustments section of the work sheet. The work sheet adjustments, however, do not update the general ledger accounts. Changes can be made to accounts only through journal entries.

Journalizing Adjustments

The journal entries that update the general ledger accounts at the end of a fiscal period are called **adjusting entries.** The source of the information for the adjusting entries is the Adjustments section of the work sheet. Figure 18-1 indicates that there are four adjustments entered in the Adjustments section of Champion Building Products' work sheet. Each of the adjustments shown on the work sheet affects two general ledger accounts: one

ACCT. NO.	ACCOUNT NAME	TRIAL BALANCE DEBIT	TRIAL BALANCE CREDIT	ADJUSTMENTS DEBIT	ADJUSTMENTS CREDIT
110	Merch. Inventory	8 4 9 2 1 10			(a) 3 5 3 5 40
115	Supplies	5 5 4 9 50			(b) 3 7 0 9 90
120	Prepaid Insurance	1 5 0 0 00			(c) 2 5 0 00
205	Fed. Inc. Tax Payable				(d) 1 4 5 00
310	Income Summary			(a) 3 5 3 5 40	
615	Insurance Expense			(c) 2 5 0 00	
620	Maintenance Expense	3 3 2 1 90			
625	Miscellaneous Expense	6 4 7 05			
630	Rent Expense	1 5 0 0 0 00			
635	Salaries Expense	8 4 0 0 0 00			
640	Supplies Expense			(b) 3 7 0 9 90	
645	Utilities Expense	3 1 5 8 71			
650	Fed. Inc. Tax Expense	9 7 5 0 00		(d) 1 4 5 00	
		50 8 1 3 7 44	50 8 1 3 7 44	7 6 4 0 30	7 6 4 0 30

Figure 18-1 Partial Work Sheet with Adjustments for Champion Building Products

UNIT 3   The Accounting Cycle for a Merchandising Business

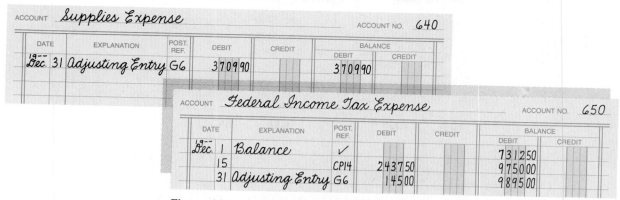

Figure 18-4 Adjusting Entries Posted to the General Ledger (Concluded)

Journalizing Closing Entries

In Chapter 9, you learned how to journalize and post the closing entries for a service business operated as a sole proprietorship. In the chapters in this unit, you have been studying the accounting records for a merchandising business organized as a corporation. Regardless of how a business is organized or whether it sells goods or services, the procedures for journalizing closing entries are the same. In other words, all closing entries transfer the balances of the temporary accounts to a permanent account. After the closing entries have been posted, all of the temporary accounts will have zero balances. The general ledger will then be ready for use during the next accounting period.

All the information needed for the closing entries is found in the Income Statement section of the work sheet. As you recall, the Income Statement columns of the work sheet contain the balances of all the temporary accounts.

Steps for Closing the Ledger

In Chapter 9, you journalized four entries to close the temporary general ledger accounts of a sole proprietorship. Only three closing entries are required to close the temporary accounts for a merchandising business organized as a corporation. A business organized as a corporation does not have a withdrawals account. No closing entry, therefore, is needed for this account, reducing the number of closing entries to three.

The account balances that must be closed for Champion Building Products are shown in Figure 18-5 on page 390. The first closing entry is made to close the accounts that have balances in the Income Statement *Credit* column of the work sheet. These accounts are the revenue and contra cost of merchandise accounts. In this first closing entry, then, the revenue and contra cost of merchandise accounts are closed into Income Summary. The second closing entry is made to close into Income Summary the balances of the cost of merchandise, contra revenue, and expense accounts listed in the Income Statement *Debit* column. The third closing entry is made to close the balance of Income Summary into Retained Earnings. The amount of this third entry is the net income or net loss for the fiscal period.

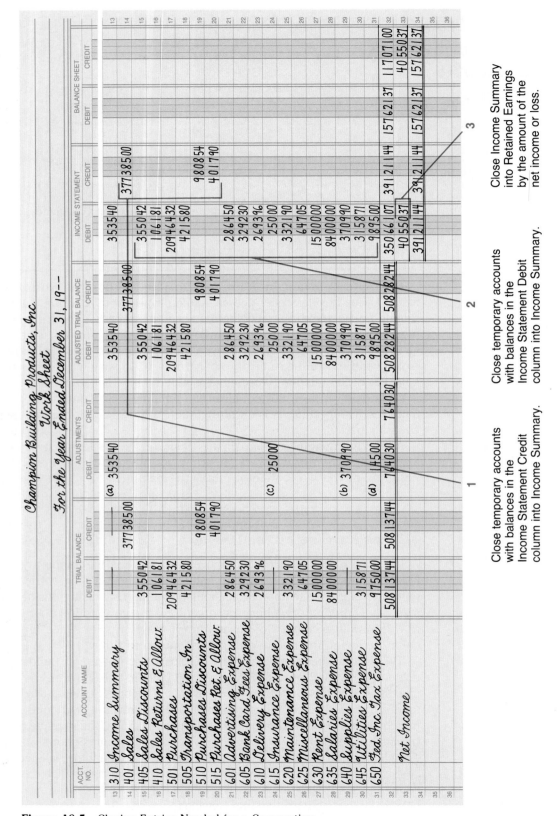

Figure 18-5 Closing Entries Needed for a Corporation

The worksheet shown contains the following:

Champion Building Products, Inc.
Work Sheet
For the Year Ended December 31, 19—

ACCT. NO.	ACCOUNT NAME	TRIAL BALANCE DEBIT	TRIAL BALANCE CREDIT	ADJUSTMENTS DEBIT	ADJUSTMENTS CREDIT	ADJUSTED TRIAL BALANCE DEBIT	ADJUSTED TRIAL BALANCE CREDIT	INCOME STATEMENT DEBIT	INCOME STATEMENT CREDIT	BALANCE SHEET DEBIT	BALANCE SHEET CREDIT
310	Income Summary			(a) 3535 40		3535 40		3535 40			
401	Sales		377385 00				377385 00		377385 00		
405	Sales Discounts	3550 42				3550 42		3550 42			
410	Sales Returns & Allow.	1061 81				1061 81		1061 81			
501	Purchases	209464 32				209464 32		209464 32			
505	Transportation In	4215 80				4215 80		4215 80			
510	Purchases Discounts		9808 54				9808 54		9808 54		
515	Purchases Ret. & Allow.		4017 90				4017 90		4017 90		
601	Advertising Expense	2864 50				2864 50		2864 50			
605	Bank Card Fees Expense	3292 30				3292 30		3292 30			
610	Delivery Expense	2693 96				2693 96		2693 96			
615	Insurance Expense			(c) 250 00		250 00		250 00			
620	Maintenance Expense	3321 90				3321 90		3321 90			
625	Miscellaneous Expense	647 05				647 05		647 05			
630	Rent Expense	15000 00				15000 00		15000 00			
635	Salaries Expense	84000 00				84000 00		84000 00			
640	Supplies Expense			(b) 3709 90		3709 90		3709 90			
645	Utilities Expense	3158 71				3158 71		3158 71			
650	Fed. Inc. Tax Expense	9750 00		(d) 145 00		9895 00		9895 00			
		508137 44	508137 44	7640 30	7640 30	508282 44	508282 44	350661 07	391211 44	157162 37	117071 00
	Net Income							40550 37			40550 37
								391211 44	391211 44	157162 37	157162 37

1. Close temporary accounts with balances in the Income Statement Credit column into Income Summary.

2. Close temporary accounts with balances in the Income Statement Debit column into Income Summary.

3. Close Income Summary into Retained Earnings by the amount of the net income or loss.

390 UNIT 3 The Accounting Cycle for a Merchandising Business

Let's now look more closely at each of these closing entries.

1. Close the temporary revenue and contra cost of merchandise accounts with credit balances into Income Summary. The first closing entry affects the following accounts: Sales, Purchases Discounts, Purchases Returns and Allowances, and Income Summary. When closing accounts with credit balances, each account is debited for the amount of its balance. Income Summary is credited for the total. To analyze this closing entry, look at the T accounts that follow.

Sales	
Dr.	Cr.
−	+
Clos. $377,385.00	Bal. $377,385.00

Income Summary	
Dr.	Cr.
Adj. $3,535.40	Clos. $391,211.44

Purchases Discounts	
Dr.	Cr.
−	+
Clos. $9,808.54	Bal. $9,808.54

Purchases Returns and Allowances	
Dr.	Cr.
−	+
Clos. $4,017.90	Bal. $4,017.90

After this closing entry is journalized and posted, the three temporary accounts — Sales, Purchases Discounts, and Purchases Returns and Allowances — will have zero balances. Income Summary will have a credit balance of $387,676.04.

R E M E M B E R

The sum of all the *credit* balances of the revenue and contra cost of merchandise accounts is the amount *credited* to Income Summary.

2. Close the contra revenue, cost of merchandise, and expense accounts with debit balances into Income Summary. When closing temporary accounts with debit balances, each account is credited for the amount of its balance. Crediting these accounts decreases each account balance to zero. The total of the balances is debited to Income Summary. To analyze this closing entry, look at the T accounts on page 392.

R E M E M B E R

The sum of all the *debit* balances of the contra revenue, cost of merchandise, and expense accounts is the amount *debited* to Income Summary.

Income Summary

Dr.	Cr.
Adj. $ 3,535.40	Clos. $391,211.44
Clos. 347,125.67	

Sales Discounts

Dr. +	Cr. −
Bal. $3,550.42	Clos. $3,550.42

Sales Returns and Allowances

Dr. +	Cr. −
Bal. $1,061.81	Clos. $1,061.81

Purchases

Dr. +	Cr. −
Bal. $209,464.32	Clos. $209,464.32

Transportation In

Dr. +	Cr. −
Bal. $4,215.80	Clos. $4,215.80

Advertising Expense

Dr. +	Cr. −
Bal. $2,864.50	Clos. $2,864.50

Bank Card Fees Expense

Dr. +	Cr. −
Bal. $3,292.30	Clos. $3,292.30

Delivery Expense

Dr. +	Cr. −
Bal. $2,693.96	Clos. $2,693.96

Insurance Expense

Dr. +	Cr. −
Adj. $250.00	Clos. $250.00

Maintenance Expense

Dr. +	Cr. −
Bal. $3,321.90	Clos. $3,321.90

Miscellaneous Expense

Dr. +	Cr. −
Bal. $647.05	Clos. $647.05

Rent Expense

Dr. +	Cr. −
Bal. $15,000.00	Clos. $15,000.00

Salaries Expense

Dr. +	Cr. −
Bal. $84,000.00	Clos. $84,000.00

Supplies Expense

Dr. +	Cr. −
Adj. $3,709.90	Clos. $3,709.90

Utilities Expense

Dr. +	Cr. −
Bal. $3,158.71	Clos. $3,158.71

Federal Income Tax Expense

Dr. +	Cr. −
Bal. $9,895.00	Clos. $9,895.00

After this closing entry has been journalized and posted, these temporary accounts will have zero balances. Income Summary will have a credit balance of $40,550.37.

3. Close Income Summary into Retained Earnings. After the second closing entry, Income Summary has a credit balance of $40,550.37. This balance represents the net income for the fiscal period. To close Income Summary, it must be debited for $40,550.37. Retained Earnings is credited for $40,550.37. This amount represents the increase in stockholders' equity from net income earned for the fiscal period.

Income Summary		Retained Earnings	
Dr.	Cr.	Dr.	Cr.
		−	+
Adj. $ 3,535.40	Clos. $391,211.44		
Clos. 347,125.67			Bal. $27,625.45
Clos. 40,550.37			Clos. 40,550.37

After the entry to close Income Summary into Retained Earnings has been posted, Income Summary will have a zero balance. The balance of Retained Earnings will be increased to $68,175.82.

The closing entries for Champion Building Products are shown in Figure 18-6. Notice that the words "Closing Entries" were written above the first entry to avoid having to write an explanation for each entry.

Figure 18-6
Closing Entries Recorded in the General Journal

	DATE	DESCRIPTION	POST. REF.	DEBIT	CREDIT	
11	19--	*Closing Entries*				11
12	Dec. 31	Sales		37738500		12
13		Purchases Discounts		980854		13
14		Purchases Returns and Allowances		401790		14
15		Income Summary			39121144	15
16	31	Income Summary		34712567		16
17		Sales Discounts			355042	17
18		Sales Returns and Allowances			106181	18
19		Purchases			20946432	19
20		Transportation In			421580	20
21		Advertising Expense			286450	21
22		Bank Card Fees Expense			329230	22
23		Delivery Expense			269396	23
24		Insurance Expense			25000	24
25		Maintenance Expense			332190	25
26		Miscellaneous Expense			64705	26
27		Rent Expense			150000	27
28		Salaries Expense			840000	28
29		Supplies Expense			370990	29
30		Utilities Expense			315871	30
31		Federal Income Tax Expense			989500	31
32	31	Income Summary		4055037		32
33		Retained Earnings			4055037	33

Closing Entry to Transfer a Net Loss

At the end of an accounting period, it is possible for a business to have a net loss. The amount of the net loss would first be calculated on the work sheet. For example, suppose a business has a net loss of $5,000.00 for the period. To analyze the closing entry for this loss, look at the T accounts.

Income Summary	
Dr.	Cr.
Adj. $ 3,612.00	Clos. $63,790.00
Clos. 65,178.00	Clos. 5,000.00

Retained Earnings	
Dr.	Cr.
−	+
Clos. $5,000.00	Bal. $25,480.00

To close Income Summary, it must be credited for $5,000.00. Retained Earnings is *debited* for $5,000.00 because the earnings retained by the business have *decreased* by the amount of the net loss. The closing entry made is a debit to Retained Earnings and a credit to Income Summary.

Check Your Learning

Use notebook paper to write your answers to these questions.

1. The source of information for the closing entries is the __?__ section of the work sheet.
2. To close temporary accounts having debit balances, __?__ each account for the amount of its __?__ .
3. The last closing entry is made to close the Income Summary account. For a corporation, the balance of Income Summary is closed into __?__ .
4. If, before the last closing entry, Income Summary has a debit balance, that debit balance represents a __?__ for the fiscal period.
5. If the balances of the revenue and contra cost of merchandise accounts in the Income Statement Credit column of the work sheet total $20,460.00, what closing entry is made to record this total?
6. If Income Summary has total debits of $145,700.00 and total credits of $160,200.00, what is its balance and what does it represent?

Compare your answers to those in the answers section. Re-read the preceding part of the chapter to find the answers to any questions you missed.

Posting Closing Entries

After closing entries are recorded in the general journal, they must be posted to the general ledger. For each entry posted, the words "Closing Entry" are written in the Explanation column of the general ledger account. A portion of Champion's general ledger showing the posted closing entries is shown in Figure 18-7 on pages 395-397.

R — E — M — E — M — B — E — R

Use a systematic procedure when posting. Begin with the date of the transaction. Continue posting by moving from the left of the account to the right. Remember to enter the account number in the Posting Reference column of the journal after you have posted a transaction.

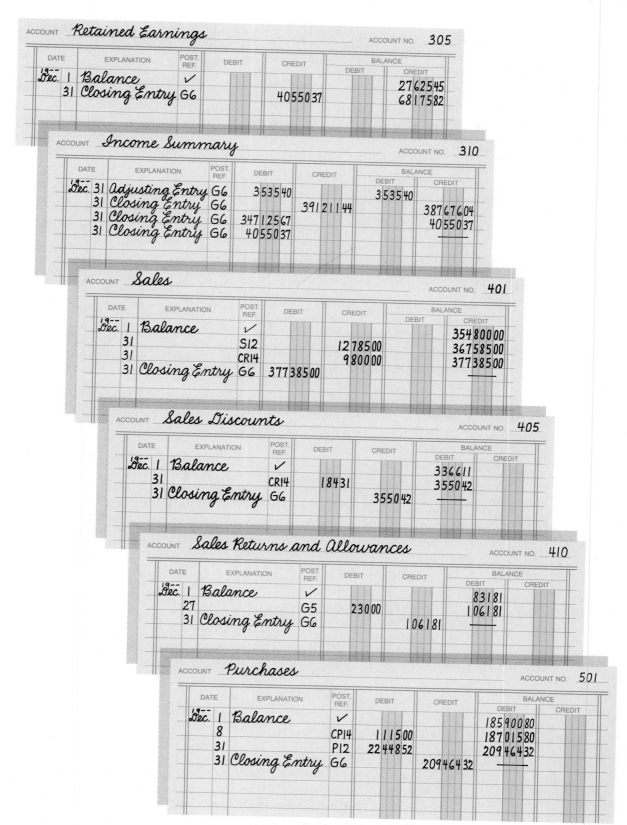

Figure 18-7 Partial General Ledger at the End of the Fiscal Period

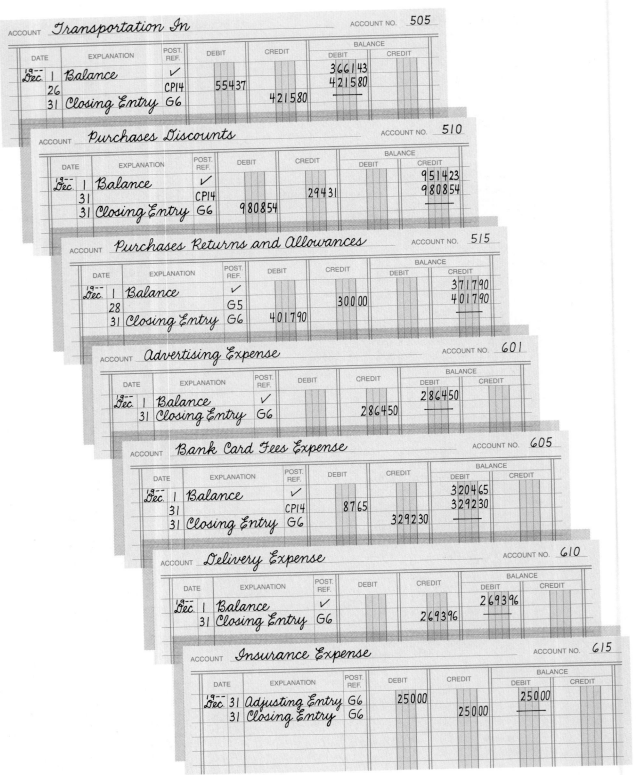

Figure 18-7 Partial General Ledger at the End of the Fiscal Period (Continued)

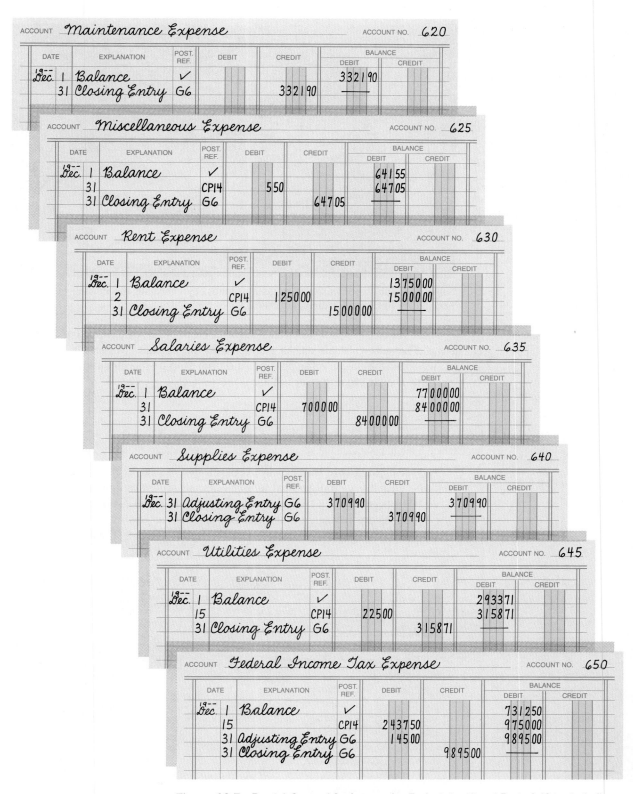

Figure 18-7 Partial General Ledger at the End of the Fiscal Period (Concluded)

Some accounting software programs automatically calculate the closing entries and update the Retained Earnings account.

After all closing journal entries have been posted, all temporary accounts should have zero balances. As a check that the permanent general ledger accounts are in balance after posting, the final step in the closing process is to prepare a post-closing trial balance.

Preparing a Post-Closing Trial Balance

A post-closing trial balance is prepared at the end of the fiscal period to test the equality of the general ledger after all adjusting and closing entries have been posted. This trial balance proves that the permanent general ledger accounts are in balance at the close of the accounting period.

The post-closing trial balance for Champion Building Products is shown in Figure 18-8.

Champion Building Products, Inc. Post-Closing Trial Balance December 31, 19--		
Cash in Bank	2128442	
Accounts Receivable	636435	
Merchandise Inventory	8138570	
Supplies	183960	
Prepaid Insurance	125000	
Delivery Equipment	1914390	
Store Equipment	2635340	
Accounts Payable		1231695
Federal Income Tax Payable		14500
Sales Tax Payable		198360
Capital Stock		7500000
Retained Earnings		6817582
Totals	15762137	15762137

Figure 18-8 Post-Closing Trial Balance

R E M E M B E R

The account balances that appear on the post-closing trial balance are the same as those on the balance sheet.

Before continuing, complete the following activity to check your understanding of the material you have just studied.

Check Your Learning

Use Figures 18-7 and 18-8 to answer the following questions. Write your answers on a sheet of notebook paper.

1. What was the balance of the Retained Earnings account before closing?
2. What is the balance of the Retained Earnings account after closing?
3. Does the $40,550.37 credit to Retained Earnings represent a net income or a net loss?
4. How many transactions affected Income Summary on December 31?
5. Name three expense accounts affected by both an adjusting entry and a closing entry.
6. The accounts that appear on the post-closing trial balance are the same as those on what financial statement?

Compare your answers to those in the answers section. Re-read the preceding part of the chapter to find the answers to any questions you may have missed.

An Accounting Cycle for a Merchandising Business

You have just completed the study of an accounting cycle for a merchandising business organized as a corporation. The accounting cycle for a merchandising business follows the same steps as for a service business. Sole proprietorships, corporations, and partnerships will all have similar accounting cycles. The basic steps in the accounting cycle, listed below, are the same regardless of the type of ownership.

1. Collect and verify data from business transactions.
2. Analyze business transactions.
3. Journalize.
4. Post to the general ledger and to the accounts receivable and accounts payable subsidiary ledgers.
5. Prepare a trial balance.
6. Complete the work sheet.
7. Prepare the financial statements—income statement, statement of retained earnings, and balance sheet.
8. Journalize and post the adjusting entries.
9. Journalize and post the closing entries.
10. Prepare a post-closing trial balance.

The steps in the accounting cycle are not affected by the type of accounting system used: manual or computerized. In a computerized accounting system, therefore, many of the routine procedures—such as posting—are performed by the computer. Let's look at the steps in the accounting cycle and see how those steps might be performed in a computerized accounting system.

A Computerized Accounting System

There are many different computerized accounting systems available to businesses today. Some businesses may need only a microcomputer, while others may need several large computers to store their accounting information. Whether large or small, all computers operate from computer programs that direct the operations of the computer. These computer programs are called **software.** The computers themselves and their related equipment, such as disk drives and printers, are called **hardware.**

A comparison of the steps in the accounting cycle for manual and computerized accounting systems appears in Figure 18-9.

Look again at the steps in the accounting cycle. The first two steps—collecting, verifying, and analyzing business transactions data—must be performed by an accounting clerk. Likewise, journal entries are made by an accounting clerk. In a computerized accounting system, the accounting clerk makes journal entries by inputting transaction data to the computer rather than writing it in a journal. Even in a computerized accounting system, the accounting clerk must still analyze transactions to determine the data to be entered into the computer.

The transaction data entered into the computer are maintained in a permanent file in the computer's memory. All the accounts used by a business are also stored in computer memory by account number. In a computerized accounting system, therefore, both the general ledger accounts and the subsidiary ledger accounts have account numbers.

When journal entries are made, the accounting clerk must identify for the computer the account numbers of the accounts involved. There is no need to enter account titles since that information is already stored in computer memory. After an account number is identified, the specific data for a transaction—the date, the amount debited or credited, and the source document reference—are entered into the computer.

When data for business transactions have been input, the accounting clerk instructs the computer to post those transactions to the ledger accounts stored in its memory. Computerized posting not only takes much less time than manual posting, but it also eliminates the errors that may be made in posting manually.

After the journal entries have been posted, the computer may be instructed to prepare a trial balance. The computer searches its ledger account files and prepares that trial balance using the current balance in each account. As in a manual accounting system, if transactions have not been posted or if errors have been made in entering information, the trial balance will not balance. Any errors must be found and corrected before continuing the work in the accounting cycle.

After the trial balance is proved, the information needed to prepare financial reports and to make adjusting and closing entries must be calculated. In some computerized systems, the trial balance is printed out on extra-wide paper and the work sheet is then completed manually on that paper. In other systems, adjustments are calculated manually and then entered into the computer. The computer calculates the new, end-of-period account balances and uses those account balances to prepare the financial statements. Notice that in a computerized accounting system, the adjusting entries are journalized and posted *before* the financial statements are prepared.

Steps	Manual	Computerized
1. Collect and verify data from business transactions	Same	Same
2. Analyze transactions	Same	Same
3. Journalize	Transaction data entered into journals	Transaction data input into computer
4. Post to general and subsidiary ledgers	Posted manually by accounting clerk	Posted by computer upon demand to ledger accounts stored in memory
5. Prepare trial balance	Account balances collected manually and trial balance prepared manually	Stored data used by computer to prepare trial balance upon demand
6. Complete the work sheet	Adjustments calculated manually; work sheet completed manually	Adjustments calculated manually, then entered into computer; work sheet not needed since computer stores data in its files for preparing financial statements
7. Prepare financial statements	Statements prepared manually in typed or handwritten form	Statements prepared by computer upon demand
8. Journalize and post adjusting entries	Entered into journal and posted after financial statements are prepared	Data entered and stored during adjustment of trial balance
9. Journalize and post closing entries	Entered into journal and posted to general ledger	Either entered into computer or program will close general ledger upon demand
10. Prepare post-closing trial balance	Prepared manually after general ledger is closed	Prepared by computer upon demand

Figure 18-9 Comparing Manual and Computerized Accounting Systems

In some accounting systems, information for closing entries must be entered into the computer, which will then post the closing entries and prepare a post-closing trial balance. In other systems, the computer is programmed to calculate, at the operator's command, the closing entries needed and to close the temporary accounts automatically.

Summary of Key Points

1. Adjusting entries are prepared at the end of the accounting period to bring the general ledger accounts up to date.
2. The Adjustments section of the work sheet provides the information for journalizing adjusting entries.
3. After adjusting entries are recorded in the general journal, they are posted to the general ledger accounts.
4. Closing entries are made to transfer the balances of the temporary accounts into a permanent account. Three closing entries are required for a corporation.
5. The information for journalizing closing entries is taken from the Income Statement section of the work sheet.
6. After closing entries are posted, the general ledger accounts are then ready for use in the next accounting period.
7. After closing entries have been posted to the general ledger accounts, a post-closing trial balance is prepared. The account balances that appear on the post-closing trial balance are the same as those on the balance sheet.
8. The basic steps in the accounting cycle are the same for all businesses, regardless of how they are organized or whether they use a manual or a computerized accounting system.

Review and Applications

Building Your Accounting Vocabulary

In your own words, write the definition of each of the following accounting terms. Use complete sentences for your definitions.

adjusting entries   hardware   software

Reviewing Your Accounting Knowledge

1. What is the purpose of adjusting entries?
2. Where would you find the information for journalizing the adjusting entries?
3. What is the purpose of closing entries?
4. Where can you find the information needed for journalizing the closing entries?
5. What are the three closing entries for a business organized as a corporation?
6. Why is Retained Earnings credited when the business earns a net income?
7. Why is Retained Earnings debited when the business has a net loss for an accounting period?
8. What type of general ledger accounts appear on the post-closing trial balance? On what financial statement will you find these same accounts?
9. Name the ten steps in the accounting cycle.
10. In what ways does a computerized accounting system differ from a manual accounting system?

Improving Your Math Skills

Accountants and other people who work with numbers often estimate answers before they find the actual answer. Grocery shoppers sometimes keep a running estimate in their heads of their purchases to avoid exceeding a pre-set dollar amount. Estimating an amount helps you know whether you've made a math error and need to double-check your answer. The easiest way to estimate is to round all numbers to whole numbers, either to the nearest ten or the nearest hundred. For example, to add 678, 792, 312, and 419 quickly, round to 700, 800, 300, and 400; then add to get 2,200. The actual answer is 2,201. Practice your estimating skills on the following problems. Then find the actual answers.

1. Add 315, 680, 234, 256, and 761.
2. Subtract 420, 336, and 790 from 2,140.
3. Divide 2,176 by 312.
4. Add 16, 78, 61, 92, 45, and 37.
5. Add 112, 90, 360, 47, and 163; then divide by 67.

Applying Accounting Procedures

Exercise 18-1 Identifying Accounts Affected by Adjusting and Closing Entries

The following account titles appear in the chart of accounts of Larkin's Department Store.

Accounts Payable
Accounts Receivable
Bank Card Fees Expense
Capital Stock
Cash in Bank
Equipment
Federal Income Tax Expense
Federal Income Tax Payable
Income Summary
Insurance Expense
Merchandise Inventory
Miscellaneous Expense

Prepaid Insurance
Purchases
Purchases Discounts
Purchases Returns & Allowances
Retained Earnings
Sales
Sales Returns & Allowances
Sales Tax Payable
Supplies
Supplies Expense
Transportation In
Utilities Expense

Instructions: Use a form similar to the one that follows to answer these questions about each account.
(1) Is the account affected by an adjusting entry?
(2) Is the account affected by a closing entry?
(3) Does the account appear on the post-closing trial balance?

Account Title	Is the account affected by an adjusting entry?	Is the account affected by a closing entry?	Does the account appear on the post-closing trial balance?
Accounts Payable	No	No	Yes

Exercise 18-2 Organizing the Steps in the Accounting Cycle

Instructions: Place the following steps of the accounting cycle in their proper order.

Analyzing transactions
Collecting/verifying transaction data
Completing the work sheet
Journalizing
Journalizing/posting adjusting entries
Journalizing/posting closing entries
Posting
Preparing financial statements
Preparing a post-closing trial balance
Preparing a trial balance

Problem 18-1 Journalizing Adjusting Entries

The following adjustments, shown at the top of page 405, appeared on the work sheet of Bayside Shoes.

Instructions: Record the adjusting entries for the year ended September 30. Use general journal page 4.

ACCT. NO.	ACCOUNT NAME	TRIAL BALANCE		ADJUSTMENTS	
		DEBIT	CREDIT	DEBIT	CREDIT
3	110 Merchandise Inventory	14 035 00		(a) 9 000 00	
4	115 Supplies	607 50			(b) 300 00
5	120 Prepaid Insurance	3 600 00			(c) 1 200 00
8	205 Federal Income Tax Pay.				(d) 500 00
12	310 Income Summary				(a) 9 000 00
22	615 Insurance Expense			(c) 1 200 00	
27	640 Supplies Expense			(b) 300 00	
28	645 Utilities Expense	3 160 00			
29	650 Federal Income Tax Exp.	2 350 00		(d) 500 00	

SPREADSHEET

PROBLEM

Problem 18-2 Journalizing Closing Entries

The following amounts appeared in the Income Statement section of the work sheet of Broadway Rugs. Inc.

Instructions: Record the necessary closing entries for the year ended June 30. Use general journal page 13.

ACCT. NO.	ACCOUNT NAME	INCOME STATEMENT	
		DEBIT	CREDIT
13	310 Income Summary		7 000 00
14	401 Sales		90 000 00
15	405 Sales Discounts	1 000 00	
16	410 Sales Ret. & Allow.	2 400 00	
17	501 Purchases	25 000 00	
18	505 Transportation In	3 000 00	
19	510 Purchases Discounts		500 00
20	515 Purchases Ret. & Allow.		1 500 00
21	610 Insurance Expense	300 00	
22	620 Miscellaneous Expense	600 00	
23	630 Rent Expense	1 200 00	
24	640 Supplies Expense	450 00	
25	650 Utilities Expense	1 400 00	
26	660 Federal Income Tax Exp.	5 532 00	
27		69 682 00	99 000 00
28	Net Income	29 318 00	
29		99 000 00	99 000 00

Problem 18-3 Journalizing and Posting Adjusting Entries

The following adjustments are from the Adjustments section of the work sheet of The Fabric Barn.

Instructions:

(1) Using the adjustment information, journalize the adjusting entries on page 17 of a general journal. Use September 30 as the date for the adjusting entries.

(2) Post the adjusting entries to the general ledger accounts, which are included in the working papers accompanying this textbook.

	Adjustments			
	Debit		Credit	
Merchandise Inventory			(a)	9,000.00
Prepaid Insurance			(b)	120.00
Supplies			(c)	1,480.00
Federal Income Tax Payable			(d)	962.00
Income Summary	(a)	9,000.00		
Insurance Expense	(b)	120.00		
Supplies Expense	(c)	1,480.00		
Federal Income Tax Expense	(d)	962.00		
		11,562.00		11,562.00

Problem 18-4   Journalizing and Posting Closing Entries

The following account balances appeared in the Income Statement section of the work sheet of the Sandwich Glass Shoppe.

Instructions:

(1) Journalize the closing entries for the year ended June 30. Use page 14 of a general journal.

(2) Post the closing entries to the general ledger accounts, which are included in your working papers.

	Income Statement	
	Debit	Credit
Income Summary	4,000.00	
Sales		150,000.00
Sales Returns and Allowances	5,000.00	
Purchases	90,000.00	
Transportation In	5,000.00	
Purchases Discounts		1,000.00
Purchases Returns and Allowances		1,500.00
Miscellaneous Expense	300.00	
Rent Expense	6,000.00	
Supplies Expense	1,630.00	
Utilities Expense	3,000.00	
Federal Income Tax Expense	4,700.00	
	119,630.00	152,500.00
Net Income	32,870.00	
	152,500.00	152,500.00

COMPUTER   Problem 18-5   Completing End-of-Period Activities

The general ledger accounts for Better Entertainment, Inc., as of December 31, the end of the fiscal period, appear in the working papers.

Instructions:

(1) Prepare a trial balance on a ten-column work sheet.

(2) Complete the work sheet. Use the following adjustment information.

PROBLEM

Merchandise inventory, December 31	$20,000.00
Supplies inventory, December 31	900.00
Unexpired insurance, December 31	1,800.00
Total federal income taxes for the year	2,965.00

(3) Prepare an income statement from the work sheet information.

(4) Prepare a statement of retained earnings.

(5) Prepare a balance sheet.

(6) Journalize and post the adjusting entries. Begin on general journal page 14.

(7) Journalize and post the closing entries.

(8) Prepare a post-closing trial balance.

CHALLENGE PROBLEM

Problem 18-6   Preparing Adjusting and Closing Entries

In the middle of the end-of-period activities, the accountant for the Leather Goods Shop was called away because of a death in the family. Before leaving, the accountant had prepared the work sheet and the financial statements. However, the business manager can only locate a trial balance and the income statement.

Instructions:

(1) Journalize the adjusting and closing entries on page 16 of a general journal.

(2) Using the information provided, prepare a post-closing trial balance.

Leather Goods Shop
Income Statement
For the Year Ended December 31, 19--

Revenue:			
Sales		$299,156	
Less: Sales Ret. & Allowances		9,500	
Net Sales			$289,656
Cost of Merchandise Sold:			
Merchandise Inventory, 1/1/--		$ 64,800	
Purchases	$168,624		
Plus: Transportation In	8,236		
Cost of Delivered Merchandise		$176,860	
Less: Purchases Discounts	$ 2,950		
Purchases Ret. & Allow.	2,108	5,058	
Net Purchases		171,802	
Cost of Merchandise Available		$236,602	
Merchandise Inventory, 12/31/--		60,400	
Cost of Merchandise Sold			176,202
Gross Profit on Sales			$113,454
Operating Expenses:			
Advertising Expense		$ 4,000	
Insurance Expense		1,800	
Miscellaneous Expense		1,600	
Salaries Expense		26,900	
Supplies Expense		2,744	
Utilities Expense		4,200	
Total Operating Expenses			41,244
Operating Income			$ 72,210
Less: Income Taxes			14,913
Net Income			$ 57,297

Leather Goods Shop
Trial Balance
December 31, 19--

Cash in Bank	$ 12,035	
Accounts Receivable	6,106	
Merchandise Inventory	64,800	
Supplies	3,916	
Prepaid Insurance	5,400	
Equipment	46,106	
Accounts Payable		$ 4,690
Federal Income Tax Payable		—
Sales Tax Payable		416
Capital Stock		40,000
Retained Earnings		24,603
Income Summary	—	—
Sales		299,156
Sales Returns and Allowances	9,500	
Purchases	168,624	
Transportation In	8,236	
Purchases Discounts		2,950
Purchases Returns and Allowances		2,108
Advertising Expense	4,000	
Insurance Expense	—	
Miscellaneous Expense	1,600	
Salaries Expense	26,900	
Supplies Expense	—	
Utilities Expense	4,200	
Federal Income Tax Expense	12,500	
	$373,923	$373,923

IRS: A Fertile Field of Career Opportunities

When you think of accounting, it's hard not to think of taxes. When you think of taxes, it's hard not to think of the Internal Revenue Service (IRS). If you're considering a career in accounting, you might want to consider what the IRS has to offer.

A four-year degree with 15 credit hours of accounting and 9 credit hours of business-related subjects will qualify you for a position as a special agent. For those who wish to follow this career path, the IRS provides one year of paid, intensive training after college. After the training period, agents work alone and with other agencies, such as the FBI or drug enforcement agencies. This law enforcement position usually involves criminal investigations. Special agents investigate tax fraud and illegal gains made by mobsters, drug traffickers, and racketeers.

Accounting majors with 15 credit hours of accounting and 6 credit hours of business law could become revenue agents. Revenue agents go out in the field to businesses to ensure that their staff accountants are maintaining proper records. Experienced revenue agents who choose not to pursue management positions can become international corporate accountants or computer audit specialists.

If you wish to delay college, you could find a position as a clerk or typist. You can then work your way up, picking up college accounting credits at night. The IRS encourages continuing education and promotion from within.

If you're in college, apply for an internship, a summer job, or a cooperative position. Cooperative positions pay college students salaries and benefits, and when you graduate, there's a job waiting for you.

The Internal Revenue Service offers many opportunities for persons with a background in accounting.

The IRS employs more accountants than any corporation. Many accountants in the private sector who specialize in taxes or auditing began their careers by working for the IRS. It just may be the best training ground for your future in accounting. Why not investigate it!

Mini Practice Set

APPLICATION ACTIVITY 4

A Complete Accounting Cycle for a Merchandising Corporation

In Unit 3, you studied the complete accounting cycle for a merchandising corporation that uses special journals. Now you will have the opportunity to review and apply what you have learned as you work through the accounting cycle for The Lighthouse Gallery, Inc.

When you have completed this activity, you will have done the following:

1. Analyzed business transactions.
2. Journalized business transactions in the four special journals and in the general journal.
3. Posted journal entries to the general ledger and to the accounts receivable and accounts payable subsidiary ledgers.
4. Posted the totals of the special journals to the general ledger.
5. Proved cash.
6. Prepared a schedule of accounts receivable and a schedule of accounts payable.
7. Prepared a trial balance and a work sheet.
8. Prepared financial statements.
9. Journalized and posted adjusting and closing entries.
10. Prepared a post-closing trial balance.

The Lighthouse Gallery, Inc.

The Dempsey family owns and operates a wholesale merchandising business organized as a corporation. The business, called The Lighthouse Gallery, Inc., sells a wide variety of lamps and lighting fixtures to service and retail businesses.

Chart of Accounts

The chart of accounts for The Lighthouse Gallery is shown on the following page. The accounts receivable subsidiary ledger accounts and the accounts payable subsidiary ledger accounts are also listed.

Keeping the Accounting Records for The Lighthouse Gallery, Inc.

The Lighthouse Gallery, Inc., has a large volume of business transactions. The business, therefore, uses special journals and a general journal to record its business activity.

Susan Scott, The Lighthouse Gallery's previous accounting clerk, has already journalized and posted the business transactions for December 1 through December 15. The transactions recorded thus far are included in the accounting stationery accompanying this textbook. The transactions for December 16 through December 31 are shown on the following pages.

THE LIGHTHOUSE GALLERY, INC.
Chart of Accounts

ASSETS

101	Cash in Bank
105	Accounts Receivable
110	Merchandise Inventory
115	Supplies
120	Prepaid Insurance
125	Office Equipment
130	Store Equipment

LIABILITIES

201	Accounts Payable
205	Federal Income Tax Payable
210	Sales Tax Payable

STOCKHOLDERS' EQUITY

301	Capital Stock
305	Retained Earnings
310	Income Summary

REVENUE

401	Sales
405	Sales Discounts
410	Sales Returns and Allowances

COST OF MERCHANDISE

501	Purchases
505	Transportation In
510	Purchases Discounts
515	Purchases Returns and Allowances

EXPENSES

605	Advertising Expense
610	Bank Card Fees Expense
615	Insurance Expense
620	Miscellaneous Expense
625	Rent Expense
630	Salaries Expense
635	Supplies Expense
640	Utilities Expense
650	Federal Income Tax Expense

ACCOUNTS RECEIVABLE SUBSIDIARY LEDGER

805	Bulb-Tronics Suppliers
830	Lumination Outlet
860	Serendipity Shop
865	Sparky Electrical Contractors
870	The Kilowatt House

ACCOUNTS PAYABLE SUBSIDIARY LEDGER

910	Brass Lamps, Ltd.
920	Creative Lamps, Inc.
930	Electrical Reflector Co.
940	Reddi-Bright Manufacturing
950	Stained Glass Outlet
960	Taylor Office Suppliers

Instructions: The forms for completing this activity are included in the working papers accompanying this textbook.

(1) Record the remaining December transactions in the sales, cash receipts, purchases, cash payments, and general journals.

(2) Post the individual amounts from the five journals to the accounts receivable and accounts payable subsidiary ledgers daily.

(3) Post the individual amounts from the General columns of the cash receipts, purchases, cash payments, and general journals daily.

(4) Foot, prove, total, and rule the special journals at the end of the month.

(5) Post the column totals of the special journals to the general ledger. Use this order for posting: sales, cash receipts, purchases, and cash payments.

(6) Prove cash. The balance shown on check stub 619 is $22,752.83.

(7) Prepare a schedule of accounts receivable and a schedule of accounts payable.

(8) Prepare a trial balance on a ten-column work sheet for the year ended December 31.

(9) Complete the work sheet. Use the following adjustment information.

Merchandise inventory, December 31	$24,850.43
Supplies inventory, December 31	120.00
Unexpired insurance, December 31	660.00
Total federal income taxes	4,500.00

(10) Prepare an income statement from the work sheet information.

(11) Prepare a statement of retained earnings.

(12) Prepare a balance sheet.

(13) Journalize and post the adjusting entries.

(14) Journalize and post the closing entries.

(15) Prepare a post-closing trial balance.

Transactions:

Dec. 16   Received Invoice 410 from Reddi-Bright Manufacturing for merchandise purchased on account, $1,475.00.

16   Paid the quarterly federal income tax installment of $1,050.00, Check 610.

16   Issued Check 611 for $2,548.00 to Brass Lamps, Ltd., in payment of Invoice 112 for $2,600.00 less a discount of $52.00.

17   Paid the monthly salaries by issuing Check 612 for $4,750.00.

17   Purchased $80.00 of supplies from Taylor Office Suppliers on account, Invoice 830.

17   Received a check for $1,965.60 from Bulb-Tronics Suppliers in payment of Sales Slip 479 for $2,003.40 less a cash discount of $37.80, Receipt 358.

19   Sold merchandise on account to Bulb-Tronics Suppliers, $2,600.00 plus $156.00 sales tax, Sales Slip 484.

19   Prepared Receipt 359 for a $1,716.00 check received from Lumination Outlet in payment of Sales Slip 480 for $1,749.00 less a $33.00 cash discount.

20   Purchased merchandise on account from Brass Lamps, Ltd., Invoice 215, $1,560.00.

20   Wrote Check 613 to Creative Lamps, Inc., to apply on account, $375.00.

21   Prepared Credit Memo 44 for $106.00 for the return of $100.00 in merchandise by Bulb-Tronics Suppliers, plus sales tax of $6.00.

23   Sold merchandise to Lumination Outlet on account, $1,580.00 plus sales tax of $94.80, Sales Slip 485.

Dec. 23 Received a check from Serendipity Shop to apply on account, Receipt 360 for $300.00.

23 Paid Electrical Reflector Co. for Invoice 326 for $1,890.00 less a $37.80 discount, Check 614 for $1,852.20.

25 Received from The Kilowatt House a check for $1,102.40 in payment of Sales Slip 483 for $1,123.60 less a cash discount of $21.20, Receipt 361.

26 Returned defective merchandise purchased on account from Brass Lamps, Ltd., $150.00, Debit Memo 28.

26 Received Invoice 335 from Electrical Reflector Co. for merchandise purchased on account totaling $1,630.00.

28 Wrote Check 615 for $120.00 to the *Daily Examiner* for a monthly advertisement.

28 Sparky Electrical Contractors sent a check for $450.00 to apply on account, Receipt 362.

29 Paid Stained Glass Outlet $1,625.00 on account, Check 616.

29 Sold to The Kilowatt House $1,990.00 of merchandise on account, plus $119.40 sales tax, Sales Slip 486.

30 Issued Check 617 to Reddi-Bright Manufacturing for $700.00 to apply on account.

30 Sold merchandise totaling $560.00 plus $33.60 sales tax to the Serendipity Shop on account, Sales Slip 487.

31 Recorded the bank service charge of $10.00 and the bank card fee of $150.00, December bank statement.

31 Paid transportation charges of $51.60 for merchandise shipped from Electrical Reflector Co., Check 618.

31 Recorded cash sales of $3,995.10 plus $239.71 in sales tax, Tape 41.

31 Recorded bank card sales of $1,736.27 plus sales tax of $104.18, Tape 41.

UNIT 4

ACCOUNTING FOR A PAYROLL SYSTEM

You have now learned how to record business transactions for businesses that provide services and for those that sell merchandise. Regardless of the type of business, all businesses that employ people must also keep records on the money paid to their employees and on the taxes paid to local, state, and federal governments. In this unit, you will learn how to keep records on employee earnings and how to record the payment of wages in the accounting records of the business.

Chapter

PAYROLL ACCOUNTING

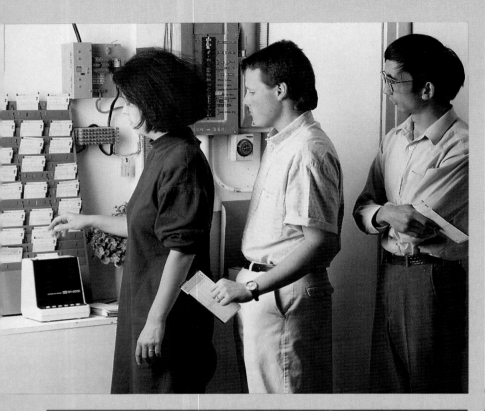

Most businesses have employees who help keep the business operating. In a private enterprise economy, people are free to work for any business they choose so long as they meet the requirements for employment. Businesses in turn must follow certain guidelines in paying their employees for the services they perform. For example, both federal and state laws require businesses to keep accurate payroll records and to prepare various reports on those earnings.

Most companies set up a system to ensure that their employees are paid on time and that their employees' paychecks are accurate. In this chapter, you will learn about such a system. You will learn how employee earnings and deductions from those earnings are calculated, as well as how paychecks are prepared. You will also learn about the earnings records kept for each employee.

Learning Objectives

When you have completed Chapter 19, you should be able to do the following:

1. Explain the importance of accurate payroll records.
2. Calculate gross earnings and net pay.
3. Explain the types of deductions from employees' gross earnings.
4. Prepare a payroll register.
5. Prepare an employee's earnings record.
6. Define the accounting terms introduced in this chapter.

New Terms

payroll
pay period
payroll clerk
gross earnings
salary
wage
time card
electronic badge readers
piece rate
commission
overtime rate
deduction
exemption
payroll register
net pay
direct deposit
employee's earnings record
accumulated earnings

The Importance of Payroll Records

A **payroll** is a list of a business's employees and the payments due to each employee for a specific pay period. A **pay period** is the amount of time for which an employee is paid. Most businesses use weekly, biweekly, semimonthly, or monthly pay periods.

The employee payroll is a major expense for most companies. To ensure that they have accurate records of their payroll costs, most businesses set up a payroll system for use in recording and reporting employee earnings information. A payroll system should accomplish two basic goals: (1) the collection and processing of all the information needed to prepare and issue payroll checks, and (2) the production of the necessary payroll records for accounting purposes and for reporting to government agencies, management, and others.

Businesses with many employees often hire a person who is responsible for preparing the payroll. This person is called a **payroll clerk.** The payroll clerk makes sure that employees are paid on time, employees are paid the correct amounts, payroll records are completed, payroll reports are filed, and payroll taxes are paid.

All payroll systems have certain tasks in common. Each payroll system includes (1) the calculation of earnings, (2) the calculation of deductions, (3) the recording of these amounts in the employer's payroll and accounting records, (4) the preparation of payroll checks, and (5) the reporting of employee earnings information to federal and state governments. In this and the next chapter, you will learn about these common payroll tasks.

Calculating Gross Earnings

Most employees are paid for the specific amount of time they have worked during a pay period. The total amount of money earned by an employee in a pay period is the employee's **gross earnings.** Gross earnings can be calculated in several ways. Some employees are paid on a salary basis; others are paid hourly wages, piece rates, or commissions. Employees may also be paid on a salary-plus-commission basis. In addition, if employees work extra hours during a pay period, the amount of overtime pay must be included in the calculation of gross earnings. Let's look at each of these ways of calculating gross earnings.

Salary

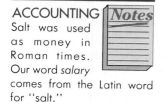

ACCOUNTING *Notes*
Salt was used as money in Roman times. Our word *salary* comes from the Latin word for "salt."

One common method of paying employees, especially those who are managers or supervisors, is by salary. A **salary** is a fixed amount of money paid to an employee for each pay period. In other words, an employee who is paid a salary is paid a fixed amount regardless of the number of hours worked during the pay period. The amount of the salary is the same as gross earnings, so no additional computations are needed. For example, Paula is paid a salary of $2,000 a month. Her gross earnings are thus $2,000 for each monthly pay period. Paula may work 160 hours one month and 180 hours the next, but her gross earnings will remain at $2,000 a month.

The hourly wage paid to some employees may be governed by a contract between the employer and a union.

Hourly Wage

$$
\begin{array}{r}
\$ \ \ 4.45 \\
\times \ \ \ \ 36 \\
\hline
26.70 \\
133.5 \ \ \\
\hline
\$160.20
\end{array}
$$

Another common way of determining gross earnings is the hourly wage. A **wage** is an amount of money paid to an employee at a specified rate per hour worked. The number of hours worked multiplied by the hourly wage equals the gross earnings for the pay period. For example, Karen Nielson is paid $4.45 per hour. Last week she worked 36 hours. Karen's gross earnings were thus $160.20 (see the calculations in the margin).

R — E — M — E — M — B — E — R

Gross earnings are calculated by multiplying the hourly rate by the total hours worked.

No. 11						
Name _Karen Nielson_						
Soc. Sec. No. _045-68-5733_						
Week Ending _6/30/--_						
DAY	IN	OUT	IN	OUT	IN	OUT	TOTAL
M	7:58	12:25	1:32	4:18			7¼
T	8:00	12:00	12:45	4:00			7¼
W	7:56	12:01	1:10	4:15			7
Th	8:01	11:55	1:02	4:16			7¼
F	7:45	12:02	1:05	3:58			7¼
S							
S							

		TOTAL HOURS	36
	Hours	Rate	Amount
REGULAR	36	$4.45	$160.20
OVERTIME	0		
		TOTAL EARNINGS	$160.20

Figure 19-1 A Time Card Completed by an Employee

To keep accurate records of the number of hours worked during each pay period, many businesses have their employees complete time cards. A **time card** is a record of the time an employee arrives at work each day, the time the employee leaves, and the total number of hours worked each day. The times may be recorded manually or by a time clock that registers each employee's arrival and departure times. For example, look at the time card Karen Nielson completed, shown in Figure 19-1.

Employee arrival and departure times are seldom exactly on the hour. As a result, most companies compute arrival and departure times to the nearest quarter hour (15 minutes). A quarter hour begins or ends on the hour, 15 minutes after the hour, 30 minutes after the hour, and 45 minutes after the hour. With this system, employees are paid for working to the nearest quarter hour, regardless of the time they enter and leave work. For example, on Monday Karen arrived for work at 7:58, left for lunch at 12:25, returned from lunch at 1:32, and left work at 4:18. Karen will be paid for working from 8:00 to 12:30 and from 1:30 to 4:15.

R E M E M B E R

When determining the number of hours worked, round arrival and departure times to the nearest quarter hour.

Some businesses are using computer technology at the point where employees enter and leave. This is done by **electronic badge readers.** Each employee's time card or identification badge has a magnetic strip on which is encoded certain employee information. When the time card is entered, the badge reader scans the magnetic strip. The identity of the employee, the department or area in which the employee works, and the arrival or departure time are entered directly into the computer. This electronic equipment enables a business to prepare a daily printout on employee work hours.

Regardless of how records on employee work hours are prepared, most companies have supervisors check the accuracy of the labor costs.

Piece Rate

In many factories and manufacturing plants, employees are paid a specific amount of money for each item, or piece, they produce during a pay period. The amount paid for each piece produced is called the **piece rate.** Most companies also pay an hourly wage in addition to the piece rate. For example, Leon is paid an hourly rate of $4.60 plus 12¢ for each piece he produces. Leon worked 40 hours last week and produced 535 items. His gross earnings for the week were $248.20 (see the calculations in the margin).

$$\begin{array}{r} \$\ 4.60 \\ \times\ \ \ \ 40 \\ \hline \$184.00 \end{array} \qquad \begin{array}{r} \$\ \ 535 \\ \times\ \ \ .12 \\ \hline \$64.20 \end{array}$$

$$\begin{array}{r} \$184.00 \\ +\ 64.20 \\ \hline \$248.20 \end{array}$$

Commission

A **commission** is an amount paid to an employee based on a percentage of the employee's sales. Many companies pay their sales employees a commission to encourage them to increase their sales. For example, Kate is paid a 5% commission on all her sales. Last week Kate's total sales were $7,184.00. Kate's gross earnings for the week were $359.20.

$$\begin{array}{r} \$\ 7,184 \\ \times\ \ \ \ .05 \\ \hline \$359.20 \end{array}$$

Salary Plus Commission or Bonus

Some companies pay their salespeople a base salary plus a commission or a bonus on the amount of their sales. For example, Jerry is paid a salary of $200.00 per week plus a commission of 3% of his sales. Jerry's sales were $4,640.00 last week. His gross earnings were $339.20.

$$\begin{array}{r} \$\ 4,640 \\ \times\ \ \ \ .03 \\ \hline \$139.20 \\ +200.00 \\ \hline \$339.20 \end{array}$$

Overtime Pay

$ 4.60
× 40
——————
$184.00

$ 6.90
× 3
——————
$ 20.70
+184.00
——————
$204.70

The number of hours an employee may work in a weekly pay period is regulated by state and federal laws. Generally, these laws require employers to pay overtime for all hours over 40 per work week. The **overtime rate,** set by the Fair Labor Standards Act of 1938, is $1\frac{1}{2}$ times the employee's regular hourly rate of pay. For example, Ben worked 43 hours last week; his hourly rate of pay is $4.60. Ben was paid for 40 hours at his regular rate of $4.60. He was also paid for the additional 3 hours at a rate of $6.90 ($4.60 × 1.5). Ben's gross earnings for the week were thus $204.70.

Employees who are paid a salary may also be entitled to overtime pay. If a salaried employee is to be paid overtime, the employee's hourly rate of pay must be determined. For example, Ellen's salary is $600.00 per week for a 40-hour week. Her hourly rate is determined by dividing $600.00 by 40 ($600.00 ÷ 40 = $15.00 per hour). Ellen's gross earnings for a 44-hour week would be $600.00 plus $90.00 for the 4 overtime hours at $22.50 per hour ($15.00 × 1.5), for a total of $690.00.

R — E — M — E — M — B — E — R

Employees who work more than 40 hours per work week must be paid overtime. The overtime rate is $1\frac{1}{2}$ times the employee's regular hourly rate of pay.

Before continuing, complete the following activity to check your understanding of the material you have just studied.

Check Your Learning

Use notebook paper to calculate the answers to these questions.

1. If an employee is paid $4.68 per hour and is paid overtime for all hours worked over 40, what is the gross pay for each of the following?
   a. 37 hours   **b.** 42 hours   **c.** 49 hours
2. Tom is paid a salary of $200.00 per week plus a commission of 7% on sales. Tom's total sales last week were $3,450.00. What were his gross earnings?
3. Clare earns $4.75 per hour plus 10¢ for each item she produces. If Clare produced 371 items last week and worked 40 hours, what were her gross earnings?

Compare your answers to those in the answers section. Re-read the preceding part of the chapter to find the correct answers to any questions you may have missed.

Determining Deductions from Gross Earnings

The first time you received a paycheck, you may have been surprised to see that the amount of the check was not the same as the amount of your gross earnings. Various amounts are taken out of all employees' gross earnings. An amount that is subtracted from gross earnings is called a **deduction.** Deductions include those required by law and those an employee voluntarily wishes to have withheld from earnings.

Deductions Required by Law

An employer is required by law to withhold payroll taxes on its employees' gross earnings. These taxes include the federal income tax and the social security tax. In addition, many cities and states require employers to withhold city or state income taxes.

 **Federal Income Tax**   Most people who work must pay the federal government a tax based on their annual incomes. To ensure that taxpayers have the funds to pay their taxes, employers are required to withhold a certain amount of money from each employee's earnings. In other words, the employer acts as a collection agent for the federal government. The employer periodically sends the money that has been withheld from all employees' earnings to the Internal Revenue Service (IRS).

The amount of taxes withheld from each employee's paycheck is an estimate of the amount the employee will owe in taxes at the end of the tax year. The exact amount of taxes is determined when the employee prepares a tax return. If too much money has been withheld, the IRS will refund the amount of the overpayment. If too little money has been withheld, the employee is required to pay the additional amount when the income tax return is filed. Generally, to avoid penalties, an employee must pay in at least 90% of the actual taxes owed.

The amount withheld for federal income taxes each pay period depends on three things: (1) the employee's marital status, (2) the number of exemptions claimed by the employee, and (3) the employee's gross earnings. The first two items of information are found on each employee's Form W-4. This

Employees who earn a stated amount of money for each item sold or a percent of the total value of their sales are paid a "straight" commission.

form, called the Employee's Withholding Allowance Certificate, must be filled out by each employee upon starting a job. A new W-4 form should also be filed if the employee's marital status or exemptions change. Employers are required to keep a current Form W-4 on file for each employee.

Karen Nielson's completed Form W-4 is shown in Figure 19-2. As you can see, an employee must include her or his name, address, social security number, and marital status. In addition, the employee must list the number of exemptions claimed (see line 4 on the form). An **exemption** is an allowance claimed by a taxpayer that reduces the amount of taxes that must be paid. Usually, a taxpayer is allowed one personal exemption and one exemption for each person the taxpayer supports, such as a child or an elderly parent. The greater the number of exemptions claimed by a taxpayer, the lower the amount deducted from earnings for federal income taxes.

Figure 19-2 Employee's Withholding Allowance Certificate

A few employees may not be required to pay federal or state income taxes in a given year. To qualify as an "exempt" employee, a person must have paid no federal income tax the previous year and state that no tax is expected to be paid in the current year. A person cannot claim to be exempt if he or she is claimed as a dependent by another person, has any nonwage income, or expects to have more than $500 in income. If a person writes "Exempt" on Form W-4, the employer will not withhold amounts for federal or state income taxes.

An employee's gross earnings also affect the amount withheld for federal income taxes. Once gross earnings have been calculated, most employers use tax tables supplied by the IRS each year to calculate the amount of federal tax to withhold from each employee's earnings. The partial tax tables shown in Figure 19-3 (pages 424-425) are for use with single and married persons who are paid weekly. Other tax tables are also available.

Let's look at an example of how tax tables are used to calculate the amount of tax to be withheld. Karen Nielson is single and claims no exemptions. One week she earned $160.20. This amount falls between $160 and $165 on the tax table for single persons. Reading across this line to the column for zero withholding allowances, you find that $17.00 is to be withheld from Karen's gross earnings for the week for federal taxes.

▲ **Social Security Tax** In addition to withholding employees' federal income taxes, employers must also collect social security taxes for the federal government. The present social security system was established by the Federal Insurance Contributions Act (FICA) in 1935. This tax is often referred to as FICA tax.

The social security system finances programs that provide income to certain individuals:

1. The old-age and disability insurance programs provide income to retired and disabled persons and their dependent children.
2. The survivors benefits program provides income to the spouse and dependent children of a deceased worker.
3. The medicare program provides certain health insurance benefits for the elderly.

The social security tax is an exact tax, not an estimated tax. The FICA tax rate is a percentage of the gross earnings of the employee. The rate is set by Congress, which has the power to change the rate at any time. Most employees must pay social security taxes, even those who claim to be exempt from federal income taxes. The present rate is 7.65% and is expected to remain at this rate through 1999.

Beginning in 1991, the FICA tax is divided into two parts and each must be recorded on payroll documents. The total FICA tax rate is 7.65%. This must now be separated to include 6.2% for social security and 1.45% for medicare. The social security part covers old age, survivors, and disability insurance. The medicare part covers hospital and medical insurance.

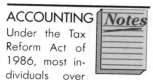

ACCOUNTING *Notes*
Under the Tax Reform Act of 1986, most individuals over the age of five should have a social security number. A person has the same social security number for life. This number is used when reporting an employee's earnings to state and federal governments. The employee's lifetime earnings—as well as all social security taxes paid—are also recorded by this number.

6.2%	Social Security Tax
1.45%	Medicare Tax
7.65%	Total FICA Tax

The FICA tax is deducted from each employee's earnings each pay period until the maximum taxable amount for the year is reached. This maximum amount is changed each year based on the average level of the nation. For 1994 the maximum amount that may be taxed for the social security tax is $60,600. There is no maximum for the medicare tax. The maximum amount of social security tax that, therefore, may be withheld is $3,757.20.

$60,600.00
×   .062
$3,757.20

▲ **State and Local Income Taxes** Most states also have an income tax on earnings to provide funds for the state. Many cities tax the incomes of the people who live or work in the city. In some areas, state and/or city tax rates are set as a percentage of gross earnings. In other areas, the tax amounts to be deducted are calculated using tax tables similar to the ones used by the federal government.

Voluntary Deductions

Most employers agree to deduct other amounts from their employees' paychecks. Once the employee asks that deductions be made, they are withheld from each paycheck until the employee notifies the employer to stop.

SINGLE Persons - **WEEKLY** Payroll Period

If the wages are -		And the number of withholding allowances claimed is -										
At least	But less than	0	1	2	3	4	5	6	7	8	9	10
		The amount of income tax to be withheld is -										
145	150	15	8	1	0	0	0	0	0	0	0	0
150	155	16	9	2	0	0	0	0	0	0	0	0
155	160	16	10	3	0	0	0	0	0	0	0	0
160	165	17	10	4	0	0	0	0	0	0	0	0
165	170	18	11	4	0	0	0	0	0	0	0	0
170	175	19	12	5	0	0	0	0	0	0	0	0
175	180	19	13	6	0	0	0	0	0	0	0	0
180	185	20	13	7	0	0	0	0	0	0	0	0
185	190	21	14	7	1	0	0	0	0	0	0	0
190	195	22	15	8	1	0	0	0	0	0	0	0
195	200	22	16	9	2	0	0	0	0	0	0	0
200	210	23	17	10	3	0	0	0	0	0	0	0
210	220	25	18	11	5	0	0	0	0	0	0	0
220	230	26	20	13	6	0	0	0	0	0	0	0
230	240	28	21	14	8	1	0	0	0	0	0	0
240	250	29	23	16	9	2	0	0	0	0	0	0
250	260	31	24	17	11	4	0	0	0	0	0	0
260	270	32	26	19	12	5	0	0	0	0	0	0
270	280	34	27	20	14	7	0	0	0	0	0	0
280	290	35	29	22	15	8	2	0	0	0	0	0
290	300	37	30	23	17	10	3	0	0	0	0	0
300	310	38	32	25	18	11	5	0	0	0	0	0
310	320	40	33	26	20	13	6	0	0	0	0	0
320	330	41	35	28	21	14	8	1	0	0	0	0
330	340	43	36	29	23	16	9	2	0	0	0	0
340	350	44	38	31	24	17	11	4	0	0	0	0
350	360	46	39	32	26	19	12	5	0	0	0	0
360	370	47	41	34	27	20	14	7	0	0	0	0
370	380	49	42	35	29	22	15	8	2	0	0	0
380	390	50	44	37	30	23	17	10	3	0	0	0
390	400	52	45	38	32	25	18	11	5	0	0	0
400	410	53	47	40	33	26	20	13	6	0	0	0
410	420	55	48	41	35	28	21	14	8	1	0	0
420	430	56	50	43	36	29	23	16	9	2	0	0
430	440	58	51	44	38	31	24	17	11	4	0	0
440	450	59	53	46	39	32	26	19	12	5	0	0
450	460	61	54	47	41	34	27	20	14	7	0	0
460	470	64	56	49	42	35	29	22	15	8	1	0
470	480	67	57	50	44	37	30	23	17	10	3	0
480	490	70	59	52	45	38	32	25	18	11	4	0
490	500	73	60	53	47	40	33	26	20	13	6	0
500	510	75	63	55	48	41	35	28	21	14	7	1
510	520	78	66	56	50	43	36	29	23	16	9	2
520	530	81	68	58	51	44	38	31	24	17	10	4
530	540	84	71	59	53	46	39	32	26	19	12	5
540	550	87	74	61	54	47	41	34	27	20	13	7
550	560	89	77	64	56	49	42	35	29	22	15	8
560	570	92	80	67	57	50	44	37	30	23	16	10
570	580	95	82	70	59	52	45	38	32	25	18	11
580	590	98	85	73	60	53	47	40	33	26	19	13
590	600	101	88	75	63	55	48	41	35	28	21	14
600	610	103	91	78	66	56	50	43	36	29	22	16
610	620	106	94	81	68	58	51	44	38	31	24	17
620	630	109	96	84	71	59	53	46	39	32	25	19
630	640	112	99	87	74	61	54	47	41	34	27	20
640	650	115	102	89	77	64	56	49	42	35	28	22
650	660	117	105	92	80	67	57	50	44	37	30	23
660	670	120	108	95	82	70	59	52	45	38	31	25
670	680	123	110	98	85	72	60	53	47	40	33	26
680	690	126	113	101	88	75	63	55	48	41	34	28
690	700	129	116	103	91	78	65	56	50	43	36	29
700	710	131	119	106	94	81	68	58	51	44	37	31
710	720	134	122	109	96	84	71	59	53	46	39	32
720	730	137	124	112	99	86	74	61	54	47	40	34
730	740	140	127	115	102	89	77	64	56	49	42	35
740	750	143	130	117	105	92	79	67	57	50	43	37
750	760	145	133	120	108	95	82	70	59	52	45	38
760	770	148	136	123	110	98	85	72	60	53	46	40
770	780	151	138	126	113	100	88	75	63	55	48	41
780	790	154	141	129	116	103	91	78	65	56	49	43
790	800	157	144	131	119	106	93	81	68	58	51	44
800	810	159	147	134	122	109	96	84	71	59	52	46
810	820	162	150	137	124	112	99	86	74	61	54	47
820	830	165	152	140	127	114	102	89	77	64	55	49
830	840	168	155	143	130	117	105	92	79	67	57	50
840	850	171	158	145	133	120	107	95	82	69	58	52
850	860	173	161	148	136	123	110	98	85	72	60	53
860	870	176	164	151	138	126	113	100	88	75	62	55
870	880	179	166	154	141	128	116	103	91	78	65	56
880	890	182	169	157	144	131	119	106	93	81	68	58
890	900	185	172	159	147	134	121	109	96	83	71	59
900	910	187	175	162	150	137	124	112	99	86	74	61
910	920	190	178	165	152	140	127	114	102	89	76	64
920	930	193	180	168	155	142	130	117	105	92	79	67
930	940	196	183	171	158	145	133	120	107	95	82	69

Figure 19-3 IRS Tax Tables

UNIT 4 Accounting for a Payroll System

MARRIED Persons - WEEKLY Payroll Period

If the wages are -		And the number of withholding allowances claimed is -										
At least	But less than	0	1	2	3	4	5	6	7	8	9	10
		The amount of income tax to be withheld is -										
145	150	4	0	0	0	0	0	0	0	0	0	0
150	155	5	0	0	0	0	0	0	0	0	0	0
155	160	6	0	0	0	0	0	0	0	0	0	0
160	165	6	0	0	0	0	0	0	0	0	0	0
165	170	7	0	0	0	0	0	0	0	0	0	0
170	175	8	1	0	0	0	0	0	0	0	0	0
175	180	9	2	0	0	0	0	0	0	0	0	0
180	185	9	3	0	0	0	0	0	0	0	0	0
185	190	10	3	0	0	0	0	0	0	0	0	0
190	195	11	4	0	0	0	0	0	0	0	0	0
195	200	12	5	0	0	0	0	0	0	0	0	0
200	210	13	6	0	0	0	0	0	0	0	0	0
210	220	14	8	1	0	0	0	0	0	0	0	0
220	230	16	9	2	0	0	0	0	0	0	0	0
230	240	17	11	4	0	0	0	0	0	0	0	0
240	250	19	12	5	0	0	0	0	0	0	0	0
250	260	20	14	7	0	0	0	0	0	0	0	0
260	270	22	15	8	2	0	0	0	0	0	0	0
270	280	23	17	10	3	0	0	0	0	0	0	0
280	290	25	18	11	5	0	0	0	0	0	0	0
290	300	26	20	13	6	0	0	0	0	0	0	0
300	310	28	21	14	8	1	0	0	0	0	0	0
310	320	29	23	16	9	2	0	0	0	0	0	0
320	330	31	24	17	11	4	0	0	0	0	0	0
330	340	32	26	19	12	5	0	0	0	0	0	0
340	350	34	27	20	14	7	0	0	0	0	0	0
350	360	35	29	22	15	8	1	0	0	0	0	0
360	370	37	30	23	17	10	3	0	0	0	0	0
370	380	38	32	25	18	11	4	0	0	0	0	0
380	390	40	33	26	20	13	6	0	0	0	0	0
390	400	41	35	28	21	14	7	1	0	0	0	0
400	410	43	36	29	23	16	9	2	0	0	0	0
410	420	44	38	31	24	17	10	4	0	0	0	0
420	430	46	39	32	26	19	12	5	0	0	0	0
430	440	47	41	34	27	20	13	7	0	0	0	0
540	550	64	57	50	44	37	30	23	16	10	3	0
550	560	65	59	52	45	38	31	25	18	11	4	0
560	570	67	60	53	47	40	33	26	19	13	6	0
570	580	68	62	55	48	41	34	28	21	14	7	1
580	590	70	63	56	50	43	36	29	22	16	9	2
590	600	71	65	58	51	44	37	31	24	17	10	4
600	610	73	66	59	53	46	39	32	25	19	12	5
610	620	74	68	61	54	47	40	34	27	20	13	7
620	630	76	69	62	56	49	42	35	28	22	15	8
630	640	77	71	64	57	50	43	37	30	23	16	10
890	900	131	118	106	96	89	82	76	69	62	55	49
900	910	134	121	108	98	91	84	77	70	64	57	50
910	920	136	124	111	99	92	85	79	72	65	58	52
920	930	139	127	114	101	94	87	80	73	67	60	53
930	940	142	129	117	104	95	88	82	75	68	61	55
940	950	145	132	120	107	97	90	83	76	70	63	56
950	960	148	135	122	110	98	91	85	78	71	64	58
960	970	150	138	125	112	100	93	86	79	73	66	59
970	980	153	141	128	115	103	94	88	81	74	67	61
980	990	156	143	131	118	105	96	89	82	76	69	62
990	1,000	159	146	134	121	108	97	91	84	77	70	64
1,000	1,010	162	149	136	124	111	99	92	85	79	72	65
1,010	1,020	164	152	139	126	114	101	94	87	80	73	67
1,020	1,030	167	155	142	129	117	104	95	88	82	75	68
1,030	1,040	170	157	145	132	119	107	97	90	83	76	70
1,040	1,050	173	160	148	135	122	110	98	91	85	78	71
1,050	1,060	176	163	150	138	125	112	100	93	86	79	73
1,060	1,070	178	166	153	140	128	115	103	94	88	81	74
1,070	1,080	181	169	156	143	131	118	105	96	89	82	76
1,080	1,090	184	171	159	146	133	121	108	97	91	84	77
1,090	1,100	187	174	162	149	136	124	111	99	92	85	79
1,100	1,110	190	177	164	152	139	126	114	101	94	87	80
1,110	1,120	192	180	167	154	142	129	117	104	95	88	82
1,120	1,130	195	183	170	157	145	132	119	107	97	90	83
1,130	1,140	198	185	173	160	147	135	122	109	98	91	85
1,140	1,150	201	188	176	163	150	138	125	112	100	93	86
1,150	1,160	204	191	178	166	153	140	128	115	102	94	88
1,160	1,170	206	194	181	168	156	143	131	118	105	96	89
1,170	1,180	209	197	184	171	159	146	133	121	108	97	91
1,180	1,190	212	199	187	174	161	149	136	123	111	99	92

Figure 19-3   IRS Tax Tables (Concluded)

CHAPTER 19   Payroll Accounting

Some common voluntary deductions include those for union dues, health insurance payments, life insurance payments, pension fund contributions, credit union deposits and payments, and charitable contributions.

Before continuing, complete the following activity to check your understanding of deductions from gross earnings.

Check Your Learning

Use notebook paper to write the answers to these questions.

1. List three deductions from employee earnings that are required by law.
2. What two items of information for computing federal income taxes are recorded on an employee's Form W-4?
3. Using the tax tables on pages 424-425, find the amount of taxes for these employees.
   a. Employee 1: Married; claims 2 exemptions; gross weekly earnings, $224.
   b. Employee 2: Single; claims 1 exemption; gross weekly earnings, $162.
4. Calculate the amount of social security tax that each employee in Question 3 must pay.

Compare your answers to those in the answers section. Re-read the preceding part of the chapter to find the correct answers to any questions you may have missed.

Completing the Payroll Register

We mentioned earlier that federal and state laws require businesses to keep accurate records of the amounts paid to employees. A payroll register is one form that is used. The **payroll register** is a form that summarizes information about employees' earnings for each pay period. The payroll clerk is usually responsible for preparing the payroll register.

The payroll register shown in Figure 19-4 is used by Lenker Consulting Service. As you can see, each employee's I.D. number and name are listed along with her or his marital status and the number of exemptions claimed. Refer to this illustration as you read the following descriptions of the other columns in the payroll register:

1. Total Hours Column. The information in this column is taken from each employee's time card. Regular and overtime hours are added together and the total number of hours entered in this column.
2. Rate Column. The employee's current rate of pay is written in this column. The employee's earnings record is the source of information for each employee's rate of pay.
3. Earnings Columns. The earnings section of the payroll register is divided into three columns: regular earnings, overtime earnings, and total earnings. To complete these columns, the payroll clerk must multiply the employee's total hours worked by the employee's hourly rate.

PAYROLL REGISTER

PAY PERIOD ENDING _June 30_ 19 --   DATE OF PAYMENT _June 30, 19--_

EMPLOYEE NUMBER	NAME	MAR. STATUS	EXEMP.	TOTAL HOURS	RATE	EARNINGS			DEDUCTIONS							NET PAY	CK. NO.
						REGULAR	OVERTIME	TOTAL	SOC. SEC. TAX	MEDICARE TAX	FED. INC. TAX	STATE INC. TAX	HOSP. INS.	OTHER	TOTAL		
012	Cropp, B.	M	0	39	4.25	165 75		165 75	10 28	2 40	7 00	4 97	3 20	(B) 5 00	32 85	132 90	183
014	Lee, V.	S	0	43	4.10	164 00	18 45	182 45	11 31	2 65	20 00	6 57	—	—	40 53	141 92	184
017	Moore, L.	S	1	41	4.45	178 00	6 67	184 67	11 45	2 68	13 00	6 65	2 10	—	35 88	148 79	185
011	Nielson, K.	S	0	36	4.45	160 20		160 20	9 93	2 33	17 00	4 77	3 20	—	37 23	122 97	186
018	Thorton, S.	M	1	31	4.25	131 75		131 75	8 17	1 91	3 00	2 74	3 20	(B) 5 00	24 02	107 73	187
					TOTALS	799 70	25 12	824 82	51 14	11 97	60 00	25 70	11 70	(B) 10 00	170 51	654 31	

Other Deductions: Write the appropriate code letter to the left of the amount: B—U.S. Savings Bonds; C—Credit Union; UD—Union Dues; UW—United Way.

Figure 19-4 Payroll Register

$ 4.25
× 39
$165.75

$164.00
+ 18.45
$182.45

$10.28
2.40
9.00
4.97
3.20
+ 5.00
$34.85

$165.75
− 34.85
$130.90

For example, Employee 12 worked 39 hours during the week ended June 30. Employee 12, whose hourly rate is $4.25, earned $165.75 for the week. Since no overtime hours were worked, regular earnings and total earnings are the same.

If an employee works overtime, the overtime earnings are entered in the middle column. Employee 14, for example, worked 3 overtime hours, earning $18.45. That employee's regular and overtime earnings are added and entered in the total earnings column.

4. Deductions Columns. On this payroll register, the deductions section is divided into seven columns. (The number of columns in this section varies from company to company.) Look at the deductions recorded for Employee 12. The deductions include those required by law—social security tax, medicare tax, federal income tax, and state income tax—and voluntary deductions for hospital insurance and U.S. savings bonds. After the amount of each deduction is calculated for an employee, the amounts are added and the total is entered in the total deductions column.

5. Net Pay Column. **Net pay** is the amount of money left after all deductions are subtracted from gross earnings. For example, Employee 12's net pay is $130.90.

6. Check Number Column. Most employees are paid by check. After the payroll checks have been prepared, the check numbers are recorded in this column.

Notice also that each amount column is totaled and the totals entered on the last line of the payroll register. The totals recorded for earnings, deductions, and net pay should be cross-checked to verify the amounts.

R — E — M — E — M — B — E — R

Gross (total) earnings minus deductions equals net pay.

Preparing Payroll Checks

Once the payroll register has been checked for accuracy, a paycheck is prepared for each employee. Most businesses prefer to pay their employees by check as a means of cash control. When a company has only a few employees, paychecks are often written on the company's regular checking account. Companies with several employees, however, generally have a separate checking account for payroll.

When a separate payroll account is used, funds must be put into this payroll account each pay period. This is usually done by writing a check on the company's regular checking account for the amount of the total net pay. This check is then deposited in the payroll checking account.

The payroll register is the source of information for preparing the paychecks. Along with the paycheck, each employee must be given a written explanation showing how the employee's net pay was calculated. A payroll check has an additional stub that is used for this purpose. A typical payroll check and stub are shown in Figure 19-5. Notice that the amounts recorded on the stub are the same as the amounts recorded in the payroll register for that employee. After each paycheck is written, its number is recorded in the payroll register.

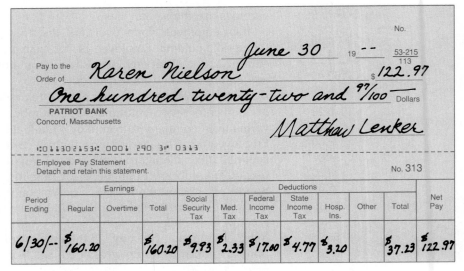

Figure 19-5 Completed Payroll Check and Stub

Some companies offer their employees the option of direct deposit of their paychecks. With **direct deposit,** the employee's net pay is deposited in her or his personal bank account. No paycheck is prepared. The employee does receive a record of the amount of money deposited and the amounts withheld for taxes and other deductions. Direct deposits are usually made through electronic funds transfer. With this system, the employer provides the employee's bank with a computer tape or card showing the wages that should be added to the employee's account. When the tape or card is run through the bank's computer system, the balance in the employee's account is automatically increased.

The Employee's Earnings Record

In addition to the payroll register, the employer must keep an individual payroll record for each employee. This payroll record is kept on a form called an **employee's earnings record.** An example of an employee's earnings record appears in Figure 19-6. The same amount columns that appear on the payroll register appear on the earnings record. In addition, there is a column on the earnings record for the employee's accumulated earnings. **Accumulated earnings** are each employee's year-to-date gross earnings, the employee's gross earnings from the beginning of the year through each pay period. For example, Karen Nielson's accumulated earnings as of June 30 are determined by adding her gross earnings for this pay period ($160.20) to her accumulated earnings for the previous pay period ($4,423.41).

$4,423.41
+ 160.20
$4,583.61

The earnings records are kept on a quarterly basis. This makes it easier for a business to complete government reports that are often required each quarter. At the end of each quarter, the amount columns on the earnings record are totaled. The final amount in the accumulated earnings column is carried forward to the top of the employee's earnings record for the next quarter, as shown in Figure 19-6.

EMPLOYEE'S EARNINGS RECORD FOR QUARTER ENDING June 30, 19--

Nielson, Karen L.
Last Name First Initial
419 East Main Street
Address Kingston, UT 84743

EMPLOYEE NO. 11 MARITAL STATUS S EXEMPTIONS Ø
POSITION Office Clerk
RATE OF PAY $4.45 SOC. SEC. NO. 045-68-5733

PAY PERIOD		EARNINGS			DEDUCTIONS							NET PAY	ACCUMULATED EARNINGS
NO.	ENDED	REGULAR	OVERTIME	TOTAL	SOCIAL SECURITY	MEDICARE	FED. INC. TAX	STATE INC. TAX	HOSP. INS.	OTHER	TOTAL		
													2309 14
1	4/7/--	178 00		178 00	11 04	2 58	19 00	5 16	3 20		40 98	137 02	2487 14
2	4/14/--	175 77		175 77	10 90	2 55	19 00	5 10	3 20		40 75	135 02	2662 91
3	4/21/--	178 00		178 00	11 04	2 58	19 00	5 16	3 20	(B) 5 00	45 98	132 02	2840 91
4	4/28/--	178 00	13 34	191 34	11 86	2 78	22 00	5 55	3 20		45 39	145 95	3032 25
5	5/5/--	166 87		166 87	10 35	2 42	18 00	4 84	3 20		38 81	128 06	3199 12
6	5/12/--	178 00		178 00	11 04	2 58	19 00	5 16	3 20		40 98	137 02	3377 12
7	5/19/--	175 77		175 77	10 90	2 55	19 00	5 10	3 20	(B) 5 00	45 75	130 02	3552 89
8	5/26/--	178 00		178 00	11 04	2 58	19 00	5 16	3 20		40 98	137 02	3730 89
9	6/2/--	178 00	11 67	189 67	11 76	2 75	21 00	5 50	3 20		44 21	145 46	3920 56
10	6/9/--	151 30		151 30	9 38	2 19	16 00	4 39	3 20		35 16	116 14	4071 86
11	6/16/--	178 00		178 00	11 04	2 58	19 00	5 16	3 20	(B) 5 00	45 98	132 02	4249 86
12	6/23/--	173 55		173 55	10 76	2 52	19 00	5 03	3 20		40 51	133 04	4423 41
13	6/30/--	160 20		160 20	9 93	2 33	17 00	4 77	3 20		37 23	122 97	4583 61
QUARTERLY TOTALS		2249 46	25 01	2274 47	141 04	32 99	246 00	66 08	41 60	(B) 15 00	542 71	1731 76	

Other Deductions: B – U.S. Savings Bonds; C – Credit Union; UD – Union Dues; UW – United Way.

EMPLOYEE'S EARNINGS RECORD FOR QUARTER ENDING September 30, 19--

Nielson, Karen L.
Last Name First Initial
419 East Main Street
Address Kingston, UT 84743

EMPLOYEE NO. 11 MARITAL STATUS S EXEMPTIONS Ø
POSITION Office Clerk
RATE OF PAY $4.45 SOC. SEC. NO. 045-68-5733

PAY PERIOD		EARNINGS			DEDUCTIONS							NET PAY	ACCUMULATED EARNINGS
NO.	ENDED	REGULAR	OVERTIME	TOTAL	SOCIAL SECURITY	MEDICARE	FED. INC. TAX	STATE INC. TAX	HOSP. INS.	OTHER	TOTAL		
													4583 61
1													

Figure 19-6 Employee's Earnings Record

A Computerized Payroll System

In recent years, computers have become an important part of payroll preparation and reporting for many businesses. Computers can process large quantities of payroll information quickly and accurately, thus helping to ensure that employees are paid on time and that their paychecks are accurate. Many businesses purchase their own computers, while others hire outside firms to process their payrolls for them.

When a company uses a computerized payroll system, basic information about each employee is stored in the computer's files. This information includes the employee's identification number, name, social security number, and method of calculating gross earnings. A payroll clerk normally inputs each employee's I.D. number and the number of hours worked during the pay period. The computer uses this information, along with the stored data on each employee's deductions and exemptions, to compute gross earnings, deductions, and net pay. The computer then prepares the payroll register.

The computer will also print the paychecks and the earnings information on the check stubs. If the employee is paid by direct deposit, the computer prepares the tape listing the amount of each employee's wages. The computer also prints the written record of earnings that each employee receives. The computer then prepares the employee's earnings records.

Many companies have their payrolls prepared by banks that use computerized payroll systems. When the payroll is prepared by a bank, information about each employee is stored in the bank's computers. When it is time for the payroll to be prepared, the number of hours worked by each employee must be communicated to the bank. The bank prepares the paychecks and sends the company a record of its employees' earnings for use in recording payroll information in the accounting system.

Summary of Key Points

1. Most employers have a payroll system to ensure that employees are paid on time and that their paychecks and payroll records are accurate. Employers are required to keep accurate records of all payroll information.
2. Gross earnings may be calculated by various methods: salary, hourly wage, piece rate, commission, or a combination of these methods.
3. An employee who works more than 40 hours per work week must be paid overtime. The overtime rate is $1\frac{1}{2}$ times the regular rate of pay.
4. Deductions from gross earnings are those required by law—such as federal income taxes, social security tax, medicare tax, and city or state income taxes—and those requested by the employee—such as union dues, insurance payments, and charitable contributions.
5. A payroll register is prepared for each pay period to summarize the payroll information for all employees. In addition, an individual earnings record is kept for each employee and updated each pay period.
6. Computers are used in many businesses for payroll preparation. In a computerized payroll system, the computer does all the calculations and prints the payroll register, the employee paychecks and stubs, and the employee's earnings records.

Review and Applications

Building Your Accounting Vocabulary

In your own words, write the definition of each of the following accounting terms. Use complete sentences for your definitions.

accumulated earnings
commission
deduction
direct deposit
electronic badge reader

employee's earnings record
exemption
gross earnings
net pay
overtime rate
pay period

payroll
payroll clerk
payroll register
piece rate
salary
time card
wage

Reviewing Your Accounting Knowledge

1. What are the two goals of a payroll system?
2. What five tasks are included in a payroll system?
3. What is the difference between a salary and a wage?
4. Why do some businesses pay their employees on a commission basis?
5. What three federal taxes are businesses required to withhold from employees' wages?
6. List three things that determine the amount withheld from employee earnings each pay period for federal income taxes.
7. What is a Form W-4?
8. Describe the programs that are financed by the social security system.
9. Explain the statement "the social security tax is an exact tax."
10. Name some common voluntary deductions that are withheld from employee paychecks.

Improving Your Human Relations Skills

Lenny Alvarez has a part-time job at a local department store. One of his classmates, Paul Tuan, also works at the same store after school and on weekends. One day Paul found Lenny between classes and told him that he would be half an hour late for work that evening. Paul asked Lenny to take his time card and punch in for him so that he would not lose pay for being late. Lenny believes that it is dishonest to punch in for Paul but he wants to remain friendly with him. What should Lenny say to Paul?

Applying Accounting Principles

Exercise 19-1   Calculating Total Hours Worked

Instructions: Part of a time card appears on page 432. Determine the total number of hours worked for the week. Use the form provided in the working papers.

431

DAY	IN	OUT	IN	OUT
M	8:03	12:30	1:30	5:10
T	7:49	12:07	12:59	5:05
W	7:58	12:15	12:45	4:30
TH	8:30	12:02	12:35	5:15
F	7:59	12:04	1:04	5:30

SPREADSHEET

PROBLEM

Exercise 19-2   Calculating Gross Earnings

Heywood Music Center has five employees. They are paid on a weekly basis with overtime for all hours worked over 40 per week. The overtime rate is $1\frac{1}{2}$ times the regular rate of pay. Employee names and other payroll information are given below.

David Brown: Single; 1 exemption; rate per hour, $4.95
Tonya Lutz: Single; 1 exemption; rate per hour, $5.25
Pat Lynch: Single; 2 exemptions; rate per hour, $4.80
Betty Quinn: Married; 2 exemptions; rate per hour, $4.90
Richard Sell: Married; 3 exemptions; rate per hour, $4.90

The time cards show that the total hours worked by each employee the week ending July 17 are listed here.

Brown: $33\frac{1}{2}$ hours   Quinn: $44\frac{1}{4}$ hours
Lutz: 38 hours   Sell: $39\frac{1}{2}$ hours
Lynch: 43 hours

Instructions: Use a form similar to the one that follows. Calculate the amount of regular earnings, overtime earnings, and gross earnings for each employee. The first employee's earnings have been completed as an example.

Employee	Total Hours	Pay Rate	Regular Earnings	Overtime Earnings	Gross Earnings
Brown, David	$33\frac{1}{2}$	$4.95	$165.83	—	$165.83

Exercise 19-3   Determining Taxes on Gross Earnings

Use the gross earnings computed in Exercise 19-2 to complete this exercise.

Instructions: Determine the amounts to be withheld from each employee's gross earnings for FICA and income taxes. Use the tax charts on pages 424-425 for the federal income tax. The state income tax is 1.5% of gross earnings. The rate for social security tax is 6.2%, and the medicare tax is 1.45%. Use the formula provided in the working papers.

SPREADSHEET

Problem 19-1   Preparing a Payroll Register

Win's Sport Shop has four employees. They are paid on a weekly basis with overtime paid for all hours over 38. The overtime rate is $1\frac{1}{2}$ times the

PROBLEM

432

regular rate of pay. The employee names and other information needed to prepare the payroll are as follows.

Megan Berg: Single; 0 exemptions; rate per hour, $4.95; employee no. 108
Don Holt: Married; 1 exemption; rate per hour, $5.25; employee no. 112; union member
Lisa Roberts: Married; 2 exemptions; rate per hour, $5.70; employee no. 102; union member
Steven Varga: Single; 1 exemption; rate per hour, $4.80; employee no. 109; union member

During the week ended July 7, Berg worked 39 hours, Holt worked 41 hours, and Varga and Roberts each worked 35 hours.

Instructions:

(1) Prepare a payroll register. List employees in alphabetical order by *last* name. Use the tax charts on pages 424-425 to determine the federal income taxes. There is no state income tax. Compute FICA taxes at 6.2% for social security and 1.45% for medicare. Union members pay weekly dues of $3.80.

(2) After the payroll data is entered in the payroll register, total the columns and check the accuracy of the totals. Date of payment, July 7, 19--.

Problem 19-2   Preparing Payroll Checks and Employee's Earnings Records

Use the payroll register from Problem 19-1 to complete this problem.

Instructions:

(1) Prepare a paycheck and stub for each employee. Record the paycheck numbers in the payroll register.

(2) Record the payroll information in the employee's earnings records.

COMPUTER

PROBLEM

Problem 19-3   Preparing the Payroll

Dan's Audio Center has a total of six employees and pays its employees on a weekly basis. Hourly employees are paid overtime for all hours over 40. The overtime rate is $1\frac{1}{2}$ times the regular rate of pay.

Dan's Audio Center pays its employees by one of three methods: hourly rate, salary, or salary plus a 5% commission on total sales. The following table lists the employees and the method by which their wages are computed.

Employee	Method of Computing Earnings		
	Hourly	Salary	Salary Plus Commission
Chris Carroll		$270.00	
Pat Cashin	$4.95		
Tyler Davis			$160.00 plus 5%
Debbie Strong			$140.00 plus 5%
Jason Witty	$4.65		
Steven Wong			$140.00 plus 5%

Employee deductions include federal income taxes (use the charts on pages 424-425), FICA taxes at 6.2% for social security and 1.45% for medicare, state income taxes of 1.5% of earnings, and a hospital insurance premium of $2.43 for single employees and $4.37 for married employees. Also, Steven Wong and Tyler Davis have $6.00 withheld each week for the purchase of U.S. savings bonds.

During the pay period ended October 14, the salespeople at Dan's Audio Center sold the following amounts of merchandise: Debbie Strong, $1,925.80; Steven Wong, $2,135.65; and Tyler Davis, $1,204.76. The hourly employees completed the following time cards.

No. **73**

Name **Jason Witty**

Soc. Sec. No. **093-48-7423**

Week Ending **10/14/--**

DAY	IN	OUT	IN	OUT	IN	OUT	TO
M	8:58	12:03	12:55	5:09			
T	8:55	11:55	1:00	4:00			
W	9:30	12:10	1:04	3:30			
Th	8:57	12:03	12:59	6:00			
F	8:58	12:00	1:00	6:05			
S	9:00	12:00					
S							

TOTAL HOURS

	Hours	Rate	Amo
REGULAR			
OVERTIME			

TOTAL EARNINGS

No. **92**

Name **Pat Cashin**

Soc. Sec. No. **087-46-3875**

Week Ending **10/14/--**

DAY	IN	OUT	IN	OUT	IN	OUT	TOTAL
M	8:55	12:06	1:01	5:35			
T	7:58	11:01	12:03	6:38			
W	9:03	1:10	2:00	6:00			
Th	7:59	11:55	1:10	4:51			
F	9:01	12:06	1:05	3:47			
S	9:00	12:03					
S							

TOTAL HOURS

	Hours	Rate	Amount
REGULAR			
OVERTIME			

TOTAL EARNINGS

Instructions:

(1) Prepare a payroll register for the week ended October 14. The date of payment is also October 14. Each employee's I.D. number, marital status, and number of exemptions claimed is listed on her or his employee's earnings record.

(2) Prepare a payroll check and stub for each employee.

(3) Record the payroll information for each employee on her or his employee's earnings record.

CHALLENGE

PROBLEM

Problem 19-4   Preparing the Payroll Register

North Shore Office Products has seven employees who are paid weekly. The hourly employees are paid overtime for all hours worked over 40, at a rate $1\frac{1}{2}$ times their regular rate of pay. The payroll information for each employee is listed below.

Lynn Ferchi:	Married; 2 exemptions; employee no. 105
Judy Fox:	Married; 2 exemptions; employee no. 137
John French:	Single; 1 exemption; employee no. 135
Sonya Knox:	Married; 4 exemptions; employee no. 141
David Kovic:	Single; 0 exemptions; employee no. 139
Pat Printer:	Single; 1 exemption; employee no. 113
Guy Whitten:	Married; 3 exemptions; employee no. 129

Lynn Ferchi is the store manager and is paid a salary of $300.00 per week plus 1% of all sales made in the store. Judy Fox and John French are salespeople who are paid a salary of $200.00 per week plus a 6% commission on all sales over $500.00 per week. Sonya Knox and David Kovic are office workers and are paid an hourly wage of $5.20. Pat Printer is the assistant manager of the store and is paid a weekly salary of $295.00. Guy Whitten is a stock person who is paid $4.40 per hour.

The payroll deductions include federal income tax, social security tax of 6.2%, medicare tax of 1.45%, and state income tax of 1.8%. Sonya Knox and Guy Whitten have $12.50 deducted each week for hospital insurance.

During the week ended March 24, Judy Fox had sales of $2,184.90 and John French had sales of $2,341.70. During the week, Sonya Knox worked 41 hours, David Kovic worked 38½ hours, and Guy Whitten worked 34 hours.

Instructions: Prepare a payroll register for the week ended March 24. Use the tax tables provided in the chapter.

CHALLENGE

PROBLEM

Problem 19-5   Preparing the Payroll Register

Belco Products, Inc., is a small manufacturer of plastic products. The company has 10 employees, all of whom are paid weekly. Overtime is paid at a rate of 1½ times the regular rate of pay for all hours worked over 40. Production employees are paid an hourly rate plus 20¢ for each piece over 300 produced per week. The payroll information for each employee appears below.

	Emp. No.	Marital Status	No. of Exemp.	Method of Payment
Lee Chan	108	M	1	Salary $52,520 a year
Rita Cortez	116	S	0	$5.75 per hour
Stanley Garfield	137	S	2	$6.00 per hour plus piece rate
Jan Hunt	144	M	3	$5.90 per hour plus piece rate
John McGarrell	156	S	1	$5.50 per hour
Pat Ritzmann	173	M	6	Salary $59,800 a year
Sarah Schoenle	178	M	1	$6.20 per hour plus piece rate
Peggy Sellers	186	M	4	$6.20 per hour plus piece rate
Carol Stack	189	S	2	Salary $500 a week
Gary Wright	192	M	3	Salary $275 a week plus 3% of sales

Additional information needed to complete the payroll for the week ended December 21 is shown here.

	Hours Worked	Pieces Produced	Sales	Accumulated Earnings
Lee Chan				
Rita Cortez	43			$50,500.00
Stanley Garfield	40	356		12,750.00
Jan Hunt	35	269		13,016.75
John McGarrell	41			8,610.90
Pat Ritzmann				11,350.50
Sarah Schoenle	42	402		57,500.00
Peggy Sellers	40	325		16,400.50
Carol Stack				14,982.19
Gary Wright			$21,025.00	25,000.00
				44,394.25

The payroll deductions include federal income tax, social security tax of 6.2%, medicare tax of 1.45%, and state income tax of 1.5%. The maximum taxable earnings for social security are $60,600. All employees have hospital insurance deductions of $5.25 for single employees and $7.50 for married employees.

Instructions: Prepare a payroll register for the week ended December 21.

Computers in Government

Imagine what it's like for the federal government to keep track of all its citizens, property, services, and legislation; enforce its laws; monitor its businesses; and protect its borders.

While it's not known exactly how much information the federal government maintains, here's one statistic that will help to put things in perspective. The computer archives of government agencies keep an average of 18 files on every living citizen. Without the aid of computers, the paperwork and people needed to process it would be out of control.

The United States government is the biggest computer user in the world. Here are some examples of how computers help various agencies within our federal government function.

The *Internal Revenue Service* processes over 95 million tax returns a year. They're sorted at the rate of 30,000 an hour, thanks to high-speed bar code readers; checked by computers; and stored on magnetic tape.

In 1890 Herman Hollerith's tabulating machine helped the *U.S. Census Bureau* count the population. It took six weeks to tabulate a population of 62,622,250. Today, computers keep a running count of our population, deaths, and births.

The *Securities and Exchange Commission* processes 6 million pages of documents every year to regulate the transactions of public corporations. It can retrieve instantly any data filed by the 10,000 corporations it regulates.

The *Social Security Administration* keeps records on 100 million workers and issues monthly checks to 36 million people. Without the help of computers, these tasks would require the efforts of thousands of clerks.

The *Federal Bureau of Investigation (FBI)* stores a database of over 8 million records. These

Computers can perform calculations quickly and accurately. The Cray Supercomputer, shown here, can perform 600 million calculations per second.

records are accessed by local police at the rate of 540,000 calls every day.

The *U.S. Forestry Service* operates in a shared information environment. All full-time personnel are computer literate. They use electronic mail, manage fires and supplies, and prepare environmental impact statements on computers.

Computers help our government manage a mountain of data.

Chapter 20

PAYROLL AND TAX RECORDS

In Chapter 19, you learned that employers use a payroll system to ensure that their employees are paid on time and that the amounts they are paid are accurate. Many businesses hire a payroll clerk whose sole responsibility is to prepare the payroll.

You also learned in Chapter 19 that various amounts are withheld from employees' earnings for taxes and other voluntary deductions. Employers are also required to pay taxes on their employees' earnings. You will learn about those taxes in this chapter. You'll also learn how to record the various journal entries affecting payroll in the business's accounting records.

Learning Objectives

When you have completed Chapter 20, you should be able to do the following:

1. Record payroll information in the cash payments journal.
2. Describe and calculate the employer's payroll taxes.
3. Record the employer's payroll taxes in the general journal.
4. Identify tax reports that are prepared regularly by the employer.
5. Define the accounting terms introduced in this chapter.

New Terms

unemployment taxes
federal tax deposit coupon
Form 941
Form W-2
Form W-3
Form 940

Journalizing and Posting the Payroll

In Chapter 19, you learned that a check is writtent to transfer the total net pay amount from the business's regular checking account to the business's payroll checking account. For Lenker Consulting Service, the check written on June 30 was for $654.31. The check is deposited in the payroll account, and all paychecks for the period are drawn on this payroll account. When that check is recorded in the cash payments journal, the payroll transaction amounts are entered into the employer's accounting system. The payroll register contains all the information needed to make the journal entry to record the payroll.

Analyzing the Payroll Transaction

Let's analyze the effect of the payment of the payroll on the employer's accounting system. Each pay period, the business pays out a certain amount of money to its employees in the form of wages. Employee wages are a normal operating expense of a business. The expense account used to record employees' earnings is often called Salaries Expense.

Salaries Expense	
Dr.	Cr.
+	−
$824.82	

The payment of the payroll increases the expenses of the business. To increase the amount in Salaries Expense, the account is debited for the total gross earnings for the pay period. For example, the total amount of gross earnings shown on Lenker's payroll register for the week ended June 30 is $824.82 (see Figure 20-1 on page 440). This amount is recorded as a debit to Salaries Expense.

R E M E M B E R

The total gross earnings each pay period is debited to Salaries Expense.

Various deductions, such as those for income and FICA taxes, are withheld from employees' gross earnings each pay period. The employer holds the amounts deducted from gross earnings until the specified times for paying them to the appropriate government agencies and businesses. These amounts are, therefore, *liabilities* of the employer since they are to be paid some time in the future.

Each type of payroll liability is recorded in a separate account. For example, total employees' federal income taxes withheld are recorded in Employees' Federal Income Tax Payable, employees' FICA taxes are recorded in Social Security Tax Payable and Medicare Tax Payable, and so on. The liability accounts used by Lenker Consulting Service to record payroll deductions are

Employees' Federal Income Tax Payable
Employees' State Income Tax Payable
Social Security Tax Payable
Medicare Tax Payable
Hospital Insurance Premiums Payable
U.S. Savings Bonds Payable

Amounts deducted from employees' earnings and held for payment by the employer are recorded as liabilities in the accounting records.

Let's look now at the credit part of the journal entry needed to record the payment of the payroll. The credit part of the journal entry is made up of several items. The largest item is for the amount of net pay. This is the amount actually paid out in cash by the employer to the employees. Cash in Bank, therefore, is credited for the total amount of net pay.

The difference between gross earnings and net pay equals the employer's payroll liabilities. Each payroll liability account is credited for its total amount shown on the payroll register. The following T accounts illustrate the effect of the payroll transaction. You can see that the credit part of the entry for Lenker Consulting Service is made up of seven parts.

Cash in Bank		Employees' Federal Income Tax Payable		Employees' State Income Tax Payable	
Dr.	Cr.	Dr.	Cr.	Dr.	Cr.
+	−	−	+	−	+
	$654.31		$60.00		$25.70

Social Security Tax Payable		Medicare Tax Payable		Hospital Insurance Premiums Payable		U.S. Savings Bonds Payable	
Dr.	Cr.	Dr.	Cr.	Dr.	Cr.	Dr.	Cr.
−	+	−	+	−	+	−	+
	$51.14		$11.97		$11.70		$10.00

$654.31
60.00
51.14
11.97
25.70
11.70
+ 10.00
$824.82

As you can see from these T accounts, the business has paid out $654.31 in cash (the total net pay). The business owes the federal government $60.00 for employees' federal income taxes, $51.14 for the employees' social security taxes, and $11.97 for the employees' medicare taxes. The business also owes employees' state income taxes of $25.70. The insurance company is owed $11.70. Finally, the federal government is owed $10.00 toward the purchase of U.S. savings bonds by the employees. The total of *all* these amounts is equal to the total gross earnings debited to Salaries Expense: $824.82.

Recording the Payroll in the Cash Payments Journal

The totals line of the payroll register is the source of information for recording the payroll transaction in the cash payments journal. Figure 20-1 on page 440 illustrates this entry. The amount of total gross earnings is debited to Salaries Expense. Each of the payroll liability accounts is credited for its individual column total. (Several different types of deductions may be recorded in the Other Deductions column of the payroll register. If so, the total for each *type* of deduction is determined and credited to the liability account.) Cash in Bank is credited for the amount of net pay.

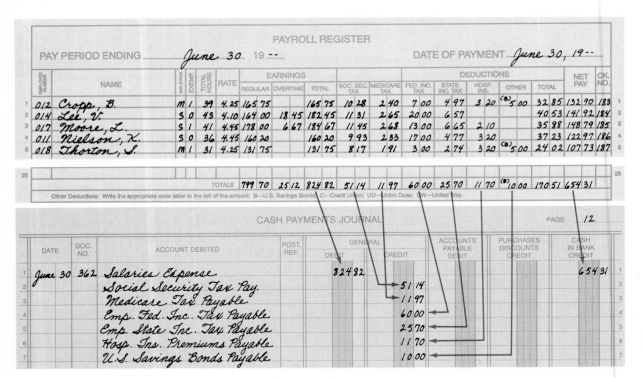

Figure 20-1 Recording the Entry for Payroll in the Cash Payments Journal

This entry could also be recorded in a general journal. As you can see in Figure 20-2, the journal entry is basically the same as the entry recorded in the cash payments journal. The only difference is that Cash in Bank is listed separately instead of being recorded in a special amount column.

	DATE	DESCRIPTION	POST. REF.	DEBIT	CREDIT	
1	19-- June 30	Salaries Expense		824 82		1
2		Social Security Tax Payable			51 14	2
3		Medicare Tax Payable			11 97	3
4		Emp. Fed. Inc. Tax Payable			60 00	4
5		Emp. State Inc. Tax Payable			25 70	5
6		Hosp. Ins. Prem. Payable			11 70	6
7		U.S. Savings Bonds Payable			10 00	7
8		Cash in Bank			654 31	8
9		Payroll Reg. 6/30, Check 362				9

GENERAL JOURNAL   PAGE 12

Figure 20-2 Recording the Entry for Payroll in a General Journal

Posting the Payroll Entry to the General Ledger

As you remember, amounts entered in the General columns of the cash payments journal are posted to the general ledger accounts individually.

Amounts entered in the special amount columns of the cash payments journal are posted as totals at the end of the month. The credit to Cash in Bank on June 30 is included in the Cash in Bank Credit column total that is posted at the end of the month. The posting of the journal entry for the payroll is shown in Figure 20-3.

Figure 20-3 Posting the Payroll Entry to the General Ledger

Before reading any further, do the following activity to check your understanding of the journal entry made to record the payroll.

Check Your Learning

Write your answers to these questions on notebook paper.

1. The amount recorded and posted to the Salaries Expense account is the total ___?___ for the pay period.
2. The amounts deducted from the gross earnings of the employees are considered ___?___ of the business until they are paid.
3. Cash in Bank is credited for the total ___?___ for the period.
4. If a business uses special journals, the payment of wages is recorded in the ___?___ journal.

Compare your answers to those in the answers section. Re-read the preceding part of the chapter to find the correct answers to any questions you may have missed.

Computing the Employer's Payroll Taxes

In addition to withholding money for taxes from employees' wages, the employer must also *pay* taxes on its employees' wages. The employer's taxes are considered operating expenses of the business. They usually consist of the employer's FICA taxes, the federal unemployment tax, and the state unemployment tax.

Payroll records are frequently the first of a business's accounting records to be computerized.

The Employer's FICA Taxes

Under the Federal Insurance Contributions Act, the employee and the employer must both pay the FICA taxes on the employee's earnings. As you recall, an employee pays set percentages of her or his gross earnings for social security tax and medicare tax. The employer likewise pays the same set percentages on the employee's total gross earnings as taxes. The current rates are 6.2% for social security tax and 1.45% for medicare tax.

At Lenker Consulting Service for the week ended June 30, the employees' total social security taxes were $51.14 and the total medicare taxes were $11.97. The employer's taxes on the employees' earnings are $51.14 and $11.96 (6.2% of $824.82 and 1.45% of $824.82). Occasionally, a difference of a few cents results because the employer's taxes are calculated on the total gross earnings of all employees while employees' taxes are calculated individually. This is why the employees' contribution to the medicare tax is $11.97 and the employer's contribution is $11.96.

The social security taxes are paid on an employee's gross earnings up to $60,600. The medicare taxes are paid on all gross earnings. After an employee has earned $60,600, both the employee and the employer are exempt from paying social security taxes for the remainder of the year. The payroll clerk must check the accumulated earnings on each employee's earnings record to determine when that employee has reached one of these maximum taxable amounts. If the payroll is prepared by computer, the maximum taxable amount is entered into the computer memory at the beginning of the year. When an employee reaches the limit, the computer automatically drops that tax for the employee.

R E M E M B E R

Both employees and employers pay FICA taxes on employees' gross earnings. The same percentage rates are used for both calculations.

Federal and State Unemployment Taxes

The Federal Unemployment Tax Act (FUTA) requires employers to pay unemployment taxes, which are based on a percentage of their employees' gross earnings. **Unemployment taxes** are collected to provide funds for workers who are temporarily out of work. For example, workers who lose their jobs during an economic recession are paid unemployment compensation to help them live until they can find other jobs.

The employer must pay both a federal unemployment tax and a state unemployment tax. The maximum federal unemployment tax is 6.2% on the first $7,000 of an employee's annual wages. The percentage rates for state unemployment taxes vary among states, as do maximum taxable amounts. Employers are allowed to deduct up to 5.4% of their state unemployment taxes from federal unemployment taxes. Most employers then pay a federal tax of .8% (6.2% − 5.4%).

$824.82
× .008
$ 6.60
$824.82
× .054
$ 44.54

For Lenker Consulting Service, the federal unemployment tax for the week ended June 30 is found by multiplying the total gross earnings of $824.82 by .8%. Lenker's federal unemployment taxes are $6.60.

The state unemployment tax for the week ended June 30 is determined by multiplying the total gross earnings by 5.4%. Lenker's state unemployment taxes are $44.54.

In a few states, employees are required to pay unemployment taxes. The percentage amounts vary from one state to another.

Journalizing the Employer's Payroll Taxes

The payroll taxes that are paid by the employer are considered to be expenses of doing business. The total payroll taxes are, therefore, recorded in the expense account Payroll Tax Expense. Like the taxes and other deductions withheld from employees' earnings, the employer's taxes are collected and held until they are required to be paid. The employer's payroll taxes thus represent *liabilities* of the business.

$ 51.14
11.96
6.60
+ 44.54
$114.24

The Social Security Tax Payable account and the Medicare Tax Payable account are used to record both the employees' FICA taxes and the employer's FICA taxes. The employer's unemployment taxes are recorded in the accounts Federal Unemployment Tax Payable and State Unemployment Tax Payable.

T accounts can be used to analyze the debit and credit parts of the entry for payroll taxes. The following T accounts illustrate the entry for Lenker Consulting Service's payroll taxes.

Payroll Tax Expense		Social Security Tax Pay		Medicare Tax Payable	
Dr.	Cr.	Dr.	Cr.	Dr.	Cr.
+	-	-	+	-	+
$114.24			$51.14		$11.96

Federal Unemployment Tax Payable		State Unemployment Tax Payable	
Dr.	Cr.	Dr.	Cr.
-	+	-	+
	$6.60		$44.54

Since no check is being written at this time, the employer's payroll tax liabilities are recorded in the general journal. The source document for the journal entry is the payroll register. This general journal entry is shown in Figure 20-4.

	GENERAL JOURNAL			PAGE 9	
DATE	DESCRIPTION	POST. REF.	DEBIT	CREDIT	
19-- June 30	Payroll Tax Expense		114 24		1
	Social Security Tax Payable			51 14	2
	Medicare Tax Payable			11 96	3
	Fed. Unemployment Tax Pay.			6 60	4
	State Unemployment Tax Pay.			44 54	5
	Payroll Register 6/30				6

Figure 20-4 Recording the Entry for the Employer's Payroll Taxes

UNIT 4   Accounting for a Payroll System

The date used for this journal entry is the same as the ending date of the pay period. The Payroll Tax Expense account is debited for the total amount of the employer's taxes. The individual payroll tax liability accounts are credited for the amount of each tax.

Posting Payroll Taxes to the General Ledger

After the journal entry has been made to record the payroll tax amounts, these amounts are posted to the appropriate general ledger accounts. The posting of the employer's payroll taxes is shown in Figure 20-5.

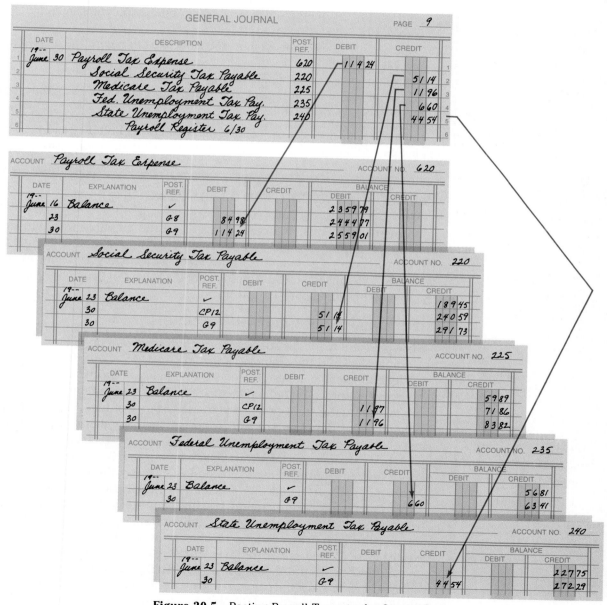

Figure 20-5 Posting Payroll Taxes to the General Ledger

Notice that the Social Security Tax Payable and the Medicare Tax Payable accounts have two entries for the June 30 payroll. The first entry in each account was posted from the cash payments journal. It is the amount of taxes withheld from the *employees'* earnings. The second entry is the amount of taxes paid by the *employer* on the employees' total gross earnings for the pay period.

Check Your Learning

Use notebook paper to write your answers to the following questions.

1. If the federal unemployment tax rate is .8%, how much has the employer paid in federal unemployment taxes on one employee's accumulated earnings of $14,264.91?
2. What are the titles of the liability accounts used to record the employer's payroll taxes?
3. Payroll taxes are usually paid only by the ___?___ .
4. What is the amount of the employer's social security taxes on employees' gross earnings of $33,468.92?

Compare your answers to those in the answers section. Re-read the preceding part of the chapter to find the answers to any questions you missed.

Paying the Payroll Tax Liabilities

At regular intervals, the payroll taxes and the amounts withheld from employees' earnings are paid by the employer. These amounts include (1) FICA and employees' federal income taxes, (2) employees' state income taxes, (3) federal and state unemployment taxes, and (4) amounts voluntarily withheld from employees' earnings.

FICA and Federal Income Taxes

The payment made for social security and medicare taxes includes both the employees' and the employer's tax amounts. The payment for employees' federal income taxes is the total amount of taxes withheld from employees' earnings for federal income tax. These two amounts are sent in one payment to the appropriate government agency or to a bank designated by the Internal Revenue Service to receive such payments. The payment must be made when the total of the two taxes owed is $500.00 or more. The business writes one check for the total amount owed. For Lenker Consulting Service, this is monthly. Larger businesses may pay these taxes weekly.

After recording the June 30 payroll and the employer's payroll taxes, Lenker Consulting Service found that its employees' federal income tax, social security tax, and medicare tax liabilities totaled $571.16. This amount included the employees' federal income taxes of $195.61, social security taxes of $291.73, and medicare taxes of $83.82.

A **federal tax deposit coupon** (Form 8109) is also prepared and sent with the check to show the amount of taxes being sent to the federal government. The Form 8109 prepared by Lenker Consulting Service is shown in Figure 20-6. Notice the ovals on the right side of the form. One oval is filled in

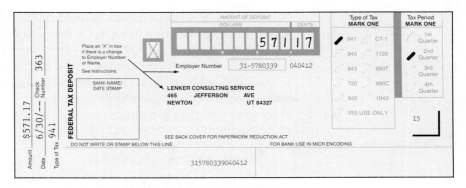

Figure 20-6   Federal Tax Deposit Coupon (Form 8109)

to indicate which tax is being paid, and one oval is filled in to indicate the tax period covered. The oval for the FICA and federal income tax payment is the one labeled "941."

The check written to pay social security, medicare, and employees' federal income taxes is recorded in the cash payments journal. The entry is shown on lines 10, 11, and 12 in Figure 20-7. Since the liability accounts Employees' Federal Income Tax Payable, Social Security Tax Payable, and Medicare Tax Payable are being decreased by the payment, those accounts are debited. Employees' Federal Income Tax Payable is debited for $195.61, Social Security Tax Payable is debited for $291.73, and Medicare Tax Payable is debited for $83.82. Cash in Bank is also being decreased by the payment, so that account is credited for the total amount being paid out, $571.16.

	DATE	DOC. NO.	ACCOUNT TITLE	POST. REF.	GENERAL DEBIT	GENERAL CREDIT	ACCOUNTS PAYABLE DEBIT	PURCHASES DISCOUNTS CREDIT	CASH IN BANK CREDIT	
10	June 30	363	Emp. Fed. Inc. Tax Payable		195 61				571 16	10
11			Social Security Tax Payable		291 73					11
12			Medicare Tax Payable		83 82					12
13	30	364	Emp. State Inc. Tax. Pay.		319 98				319 98	13
14	30	365	Fed. Unemploy. Tax Pay.		63 41				63 41	14
15	30	366	State Unemploy. Tax Pay.		272 29				272 29	15
16	30	367	Hosp. Ins. Premiums Pay.		46 80				46 80	16
17	30	368	U. S. Savings Bonds Pay.		50 00				50 00	17
18										18

CASH PAYMENTS JOURNAL — PAGE *12*

Figure 20-7   Recording the Journal Entries for the Payment of Payroll Liabilities

State Income Taxes

The amounts withheld by the employer for employees' state income taxes are also paid regularly. The entry to record the payment of a state income tax liability is shown on line 12 in Figure 20-7.

Federal and State Unemployment Taxes

Most businesses pay the federal unemployment tax quarterly. If a business has accumulated federal unemployment taxes of less than $100 for the year, only one annual payment is necessary. A federal tax deposit coupon

(Form 8109) is also prepared and sent with the check for federal unemployment taxes. The oval filled in for this payment is labeled "940," which is the number assigned to FUTA taxes. The journal entry made to record the payment of federal unemployment taxes is shown on line 13 in Figure 20-7.

State unemployment taxes are also paid on a quarterly basis. The requirements for paying unemployment taxes vary from state to state. The journal entry to record the payment of the state employment taxes is shown on line 14 in Figure 20-7.

Other Liability Amounts

In addition to the payments for taxes, an employer is also responsible for making payments to appropriate organizations for all voluntary deductions from employees' earnings. For Lenker Consulting Service, these deductions are for insurance premiums and U.S. savings bonds. Other companies may withhold amounts from employees' earnings for union dues, charitable contributions, and so on.

On June 30, Lenker Consulting Service prepared checks to pay the amounts withheld for employees' insurance premiums ($46.80) and the amounts withheld for the employees' purchase of U.S. savings bonds ($50.00). The journal entries for these two cash payments are shown on lines 15 and 16 in Figure 20-7.

Posting the Journal Entries for Payment of Payroll Liabilities

After all the payments for the employer's payroll liabilities have been recorded, the entries are posted to the appropriate general ledger accounts. The postings made to Lenker Consulting Service's general ledger accounts are shown in Figure 20-8 on pages 449-450.

Check Your Learning

Use Figure 20-8 on page 449 to answer these questions.

1. How many different entries were made on June 30 to record the checks written by Lenker Consulting Service to pay its payroll liabilities?
2. Why wasn't just one check written to pay all the payroll liabilities?
3. What was the amount of the check written to pay the FICA and employees' federal income taxes?
4. What was the total liability for unemployment taxes for the June 30 payroll?
5. How much cash did Lenker Consulting Service pay out on June 30 for its payroll liabilities?
6. What is the balance of Hospital Insurance Premiums Payable after all entries have been posted for June 30?

Compare your answers with those in the answers section. Re-read the preceding part of the chapter to find the correct answers to any questions you may have missed.

Figure 20-8 Posting the Payments of Payroll Liabilities to the General Ledger

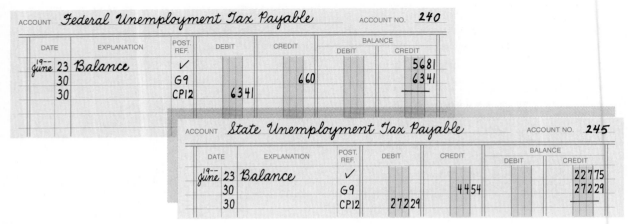

Figure 20-8 Posting the Payments of Payroll Liabilities to the General Ledger (Concluded)

Filing the Employer's Quarterly Federal Tax Return

Each employer must file a **Form 941,** the employer's quarterly federal tax return. This document reports the accumulated amounts of federal income taxes and FICA taxes withheld from employees' earnings for the quarter. The data for completing Form 941 is obtained from the employees' earnings records and from the tax payments made during the quarter. The employer's quarterly federal tax return prepared by Lenker Consulting Service for the quarter ended June 30 is shown in Figure 20-9 on page 451.

Filing the Employer's Annual Tax Reports

Each employer must complete certain other forms on an annual basis. These forms report payroll information to employees and to various government agencies. The most common forms prepared are the wage and tax statement, the transmittal of income and tax statements, and the employer's federal and state unemployment tax returns.

Wage and Tax Statement

The wage and tax statement is also called Form W-2. **Form W-2** summarizes an employee's earnings and tax deductions for the previous calendar year. This information includes: (1) gross earnings for the year, (2) federal income tax withheld, (3) FICA tax withheld, and (4) state and local income taxes withheld. The form must be prepared and given to each employee by January 31 of the following year. If an employee ends employment before December 31 and requests Form W-2, it must be furnished to the employee within 30 days. A copy of Karen Nielson's Form W-2 from Lenker Consulting Service is shown in Figure 20-10 on page 452.

The number of Form W-2 copies prepared depends on whether state and local income taxes are withheld from employees' earnings. When state and local income taxes are *not* withheld, four copies (A through D) are prepared. The employer sends Copy A to the Internal Revenue Service and gives

UNIT 4   Accounting for a Payroll System

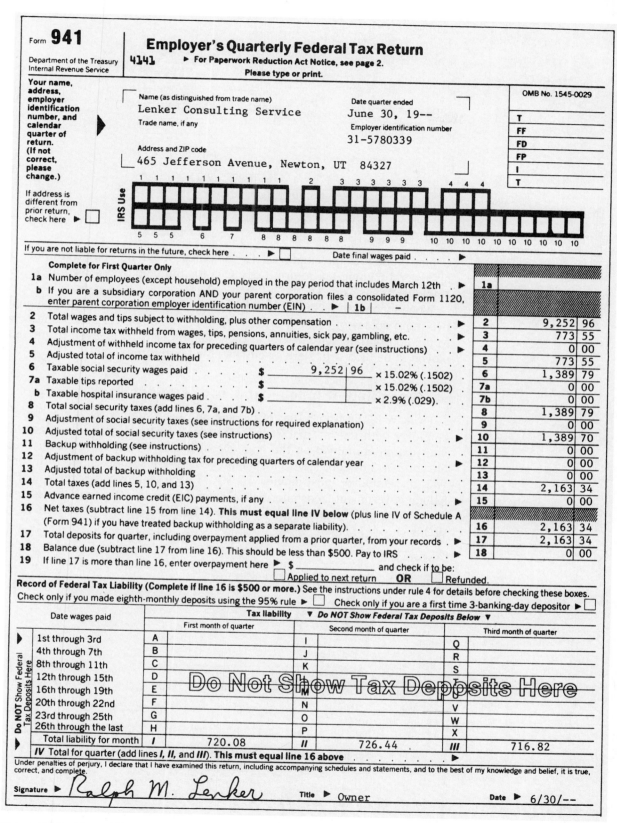

Figure 20-9 Form 941, Employer's Quarterly Federal Tax Return

Figure 20-10 Form W-2,
Wage and Tax Statement

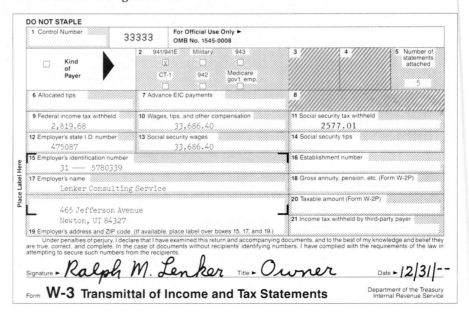

a Control number	22222	Void ☐	For Official Use Only ►		
b Employer's identification number 31-5780339			1 Wages, tips, other compensation 7394.40	2 Federal income tax withheld 358.80	
c Employer's name, address, and ZIP code Lenker Consulting Service 465 Jefferson Avenue Newton, UT 84327			3 Social security wages 7394.40	4 Social security tax withheld 458.45	
			5 Medicare wages and tips 7394.40	6 Medicare tax withheld 107.22	
			7 Social security tips	8 Allocated tips	
d Employee's social security number 045-68-5733			9 Advance EIC payment	10 Dependent care benefits	
e Employee's name (first, middle, last) Karen L. Nielson			11 Nonqualified plans	12 Benefits included in Box 1	
			13 See Instr. for Box 13	14 Other	
419 East Main Street Kingston, UT 84743					
			15 Statutory employee ☐ Deceased ☐ Pension plan ☐ Legal rep. ☐ 942 emp. ☐ Subtotal ☐ Deferred compensation ☐		
f Employee's address and ZIP code					
16 State UT	Employer's state I.D. No. 475087	17 State wages, tips, etc. 7,394.40	18 State income tax 233.48	19 Locality name	20 Local wages, tips etc.	21 Local income tax

Cat. No. 10134D   Department of the Treasury-Internal Revenue Service

Form **W-2** Wage and Tax Statement **1993**

For Paperwork Reduction Act Notice, see separate instructions.
OMB No. 1545-0008

Copies B and C to the employee. The employee must file Copy B with her or his federal income tax return; Copy C is for the employee's own files. The employer keeps Copy D.

When income taxes are withheld for either the state or local government, two more copies of Form W-2 are prepared. The employer sends one copy to the appropriate state or city agency. The other copy is given to the employee to be filed with state or city income tax returns.

Transmittal of Income and Tax Statements

Form W-3, the transmittal of income and tax statements, is filed by the employer with the Internal Revenue Service. **Form W-3** summarizes the information contained on the employees' Forms W-2. The employer must file Form W-3 by February 28 for the preceding year's taxes. Along with Form W-3, the employer must include Copy A of each employee's Form W-2. The federal government feeds information from the forms into computers for use in checking individual income tax returns. Lenker Consulting Service's Form W-3 is shown in Figure 20-11.

DO NOT STAPLE

1 Control Number 33333	For Official Use Only ► OMB No. 1545-0008			
☐ Kind of Payer ►	2 941/941E ☐ Military ☐ 943 ☐ CT-1 ☐ 942 ☐ Medicare gov't. emp. ☐ (941/941E checked X)	3	4	5 Number of statements attached 5
6 Allocated tips	7 Advance EIC payments	8		
9 Federal income tax withheld 2,819.68	10 Wages, tips, and other compensation 33,686.40	11 Social security tax withheld 2577.01		
12 Employer's state I.D. number 475087	13 Social security wages 33,686.40	14 Social security tips		
15 Employer's identification number 31 — 5780339		16 Establishment number		
17 Employer's name Lenker Consulting Service		18 Gross annuity, pension, etc. (Form W-2P)		
465 Jefferson Avenue Newton, UT 84327		20 Taxable amount (Form W-2P)		
		21 Income tax withheld by third-party payer		
19 Employer's address and ZIP code (If available, place label over boxes 15, 17, and 19.)				

Place Label Here

Under penalties of perjury, I declare that I have examined this return and accompanying documents, and to the best of my knowledge and belief they are true, correct, and complete. In the case of documents without recipients' identifying numbers, I have complied with the requirements of the law in attempting to secure such numbers from the recipients.

Signature ► *Ralph M. Lenker*   Title ► *Owner*   Date ► 12/31/--

Form **W-3** Transmittal of Income and Tax Statements   Department of the Treasury Internal Revenue Service

Figure 20-11 Form W-3,
Transmittal of Income
and Tax Statements

Employer's Federal and State Unemployment Tax Returns

Each employer is also responsible for filing **Form 940,** an employer's annual unemployment tax return. The information on this return includes both federal and state unemployment taxes paid during the year. This form must be filed by January 31 for the preceding calendar year. The requirements for filing state unemployment tax returns vary from state to state.

Summary of Key Points

1. The payroll register is the source of information for preparing the entry to record the payment of the payroll. This entry is recorded in the cash payments journal.
2. Employees' wages are considered to be a normal operating expense for the business. The amount of the total gross earnings is debited to the Salaries Expense account.
3. Amounts deducted from employees' earnings and held by the employer are liabilities of the business. The employer must make regular payments of the amounts withheld to the appropriate government agencies or to other businesses or organizations.
4. Employers are required to pay taxes on the total amount of their employees' gross earnings. These amounts are operating expenses of the business. Employer's payroll taxes include social security and medicare taxes, federal unemployment taxes, and state unemployment taxes.
5. FICA taxes are paid by both the employee and the employer. The same percentages used to calculate employees' deductions are used to determine the employer's FICA taxes. The employer's FICA taxes are calculated on the total gross earnings amount.
6. The entry to record the employer's payroll taxes is made in the general journal.
7. Employers must report earnings and tax information to employees once a year on Form W-2.
8. Each employer is required to file quarterly and annual tax reports on employee earnings and on taxes paid by the employee and the employer.

Review and Applications

Building Your Accounting Vocabulary

In your own words, write the definition of each of the following accounting terms. Use complete sentences for your definitions.

federal tax deposit
  coupon
Form W-2

Form W-3
Form 940
Form 941

unemployment
  taxes

Reviewing Your Accounting Knowledge

1. Why is the amount of the total gross earnings rather than total net pay charged to the Salaries Expense account?
2. Why are the amounts withheld from employees' paychecks liabilities of the employer?
3. What account is credited for the total amount of the employees' net pay?
4. How is the amount owed by the employer for FICA taxes determined?
5. Why do few employers pay the full 6.2% federal unemployment taxes?
6. Why is the employer's share of payroll taxes recorded in Payroll Tax Expense?
7. In what journal is the entry for the employer's payroll taxes recorded?
8. What is the source of information for preparing Form 941?
9. When do employees receive Form W-2 from their employers?
10. Explain how an employee uses the different copies of Form W-2.
11. Why does the federal government require the employer to submit copies of the employees' Forms W-2 with Form W-3?

Improving Your Communications Skills

In business communications, courtesy makes a good impression on people and encourages them to respond favorably. Courteous messages are stated in polite, positive words and use the "you" approach whenever possible. Rewrite the following sentences, changing them to courteous statements.

1. Give us more information if you want us to act on your complaint.
2. You will not get the discount unless you pay the bill in 10 days.
3. We cannot extend to you more than a $200 line of credit just now.
4. Send us your check or we can't ship your order.
5. We cannot deliver your order because our plant is closed until July 15.

Applying Accounting Procedures

Exercise 20-1   Calculating Employee Tax Deductions

Instructions: Use the form provided in the working papers. For each of the following gross earnings amounts, determine: (1) employees' federal income tax to be withheld (use the tax tables on pages 424-425 of the textbook); (2) FICA taxes to be withheld (the rate for social security tax is 6.2% and the rate for medicare tax is 1.45%); (3) state income tax to be withheld (the state tax rate is 1.5%).

	Marital Status	Exemptions	Gross Earnings
1.	M	2	$183.74
2.	S	0	$216.48
3.	S	1	$243.84
4.	M	1	$162.80
5.	S	1	$149.99

Exercise 20-2 Calculating Employer's Payroll Taxes

Instructions: Use the form provided in the working papers. For each of the following total gross earnings amounts, determine the employer's FICA taxes (social security 6.2%, medicare 1.45%), the federal unemployment tax (.8%), and the state unemployment tax (5.4%).

1.	$ 914.80
2.	$1,113.73
3.	$2,201.38
4.	$ 791.02
5.	$1,245.75

Exercise 20-3 Identifying Entries for Payroll Liabilities

The following list includes several common payroll-related items. These items are included either in the entry to record the payment of the payroll or the entry to record the employer's payroll taxes.

Employees' federal income taxes
State unemployment tax
U.S. savings bonds
Employer's FICA taxes
Federal unemployment tax

Employees' state income taxes
Union dues
Employees' FICA taxes
Life insurance premiums

Instructions: Use the form provided in the workbook. Place a check mark in the column that describes the entry in which the item is recorded.

Problem 20-1 Recording the Payment of the Payroll

The totals of the payroll register for Aurora Garden Shop are shown below. On November 30, the accountant wrote Check 731 to pay the payroll.

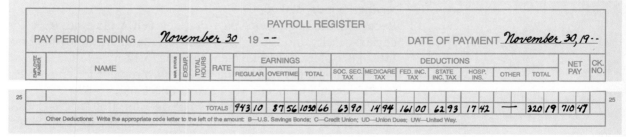

PAYROLL REGISTER

PAY PERIOD ENDING _November 30_ 19 --   DATE OF PAYMENT _November 30, 19--_

EMPLOYEE NUMBER	NAME	MAR. STATUS	EXEMP.	TOTAL HOURS	RATE	EARNINGS			DEDUCTIONS							NET PAY	CK. NO.
						REGULAR	OVERTIME	TOTAL	SOC. SEC. TAX	MEDICARE TAX	FED. INC. TAX	STATE INC. TAX	HOSP. INS.	OTHER	TOTAL	
	TOTALS					943 10	87 56	1030 66	63 90	14 94	161 00	62 93	17 42	—	320 19	710 47

Other Deductions: Write the appropriate code letter to the left of the amount: B—U.S. Savings Bonds; C—Credit Union; UD—Union Dues; UW—United Way.

Instructions:

(1) Record the payroll entry in the cash payments journal.

(2) Post the entry to the general ledger accounts.

SPREADSHEET

PROBLEM

Problem 20-2 Journalizing Payroll Transactions

The Potter Company's payroll register for the week ended June 28 appears on the next page.

PAYROLL REGISTER

PAY PERIOD ENDING June 28   19____   DATE OF PAYMENT June 28, 19--

EMPLOYEE NUMBER	NAME	MAR STATUS	EXEMP	TOTAL HOURS	RATE	EARNINGS			DEDUCTIONS							NET PAY	CK. NO.
						REGULAR	OVERTIME	TOTAL	SOC. SEC. TAX	MED. TAX	FED. INC. TAX	STATE INC. TAX	HOSP. INS.	OTHER	TOTAL		
12	Blondi, M.	M	1	38	4.95	188 10		188 10	11 66	2 73	3 00	3 76		(UD) 4 65	25 80	162 30	1
14	Dilloway, S.	S	1	41	4.90	196 00	7 35	203 35	12 61	2 95	17 00	4 07			36 63	166 72	2
19	Lake, M.	S	0	42½	5.60	224 00	21 00	245 00	15 19	3 55	29 00	4 90		(UD) 4 65	57 29	187 71	3
13	Lapolla, J.	M	2	36	5.25	189 00		189 00	11 72	2 74	—	3 78		(UD) 4 65	22 89	166 11	4
18	Zeoli, N.	S	1	26	5.40	140 40		140 40	8 70	2 04	7 00	2 81		(UD) 4 65	25 20	115 20	5
					TOTALS	937 50	28 35	965 85	59 88	14 01	56 00	19 32	—	18 60	167 81	798 04	

Other Deductions: Write the appropriate code letter to the left of the amount: B—U.S. Savings Bonds; C—Credit Union; UD—Union Dues; UW—United Way.

(1) Record the entry for the payment of the payroll on page 15 of the cash payments journal. Check 573 was written on June 28 to pay the payroll.

(2) Use the information in the payroll register to compute the employer's payroll taxes. These include FICA taxes (6.2% for social security, 1.45% for medicare) and federal (.8%) and state (5.4%) unemployment taxes.

(3) Record the entry for the employer's payroll taxes on page 7 of the general journal.

Problem 20-3   Recording and Posting Payroll Transactions

The Clune Marina completed the following payroll transactions during the first two weeks of May. Clune's pays its employees on a biweekly basis.

Instructions:

(1) Record the May 13 transactions in the cash payments journal (page 12) and in the general journal (page 14).

(2) Post both payroll entries to the appropriate general ledger accounts.

(3) Journalize and post the May 16 transactions.

Transactions:

May 13   Wrote Check 636 to pay the payroll of $3,840.58 (gross earnings) for the pay period ended May 13. The following amounts were withheld: FICA taxes, $238.12 for social security and $55.69 for medicare; employees' federal income taxes, $639.00; employees' state income taxes, $96.02; insurance premium, $21.00; U.S. savings bonds, $20.00.

13   Recorded the employer's payroll taxes (FICA tax rate, 6.2% for social security and 1.45% for medicare; federal unemployment tax rate, 0.8%; state unemployment tax rate, 5.4%).

16   Paid the amounts owed to the federal government for employees' federal income taxes and FICA taxes, Check 637.

16   Purchased U.S. savings bonds for employees for $100.00, Check 638.

16   Paid $148.00 to the American Insurance Company for employees' insurance, Check 639.

COMPUTER PROBLEM

Problem 20-4   Recording and Posting Payroll Transactions

The Book Worm pays its employees twice a month. Employee earnings and tax amounts for the pay period ended March 31 are listed below.

Gross Earnings	Soc. Sec. Tax	Medicare Tax	Emp. Fed. Inc. Tax	Emp. State Inc. Tax
$12,183.40	$755.37	$176.66	$679.00	$239.20

(1) Prepare Check 713 (payable to "Book Worm Payroll Account") to transfer the net pay amount to the payroll checking account.

(2) Journalize and post the payroll transaction.

(3) Journalize and post the entry to record the employer's payroll taxes. Use general journal page 19. The social security tax rate is 6.2%, and the medicare tax rate is 1.45%; the state unemployment tax rate is 5.4%; and the federal unemployment tax rate is .8%.

(4) Prepare checks dated March 31 to pay the following payroll liabilities:

  (a) Federal unemployment taxes, payable to First City Bank (Check 714).

  (b) State unemployment taxes, payable to the State of Missouri (Check 715).

  (c) Employee's federal income taxes and FICA taxes, payable to First City Bank (Check 716).

(5) Journalize and post the entries for the payment of the payroll liabilities.

(6) Prepare Forms 8109 for the two federal tax deposits made in #4.

CHALLENGE

PROBLEM

Problem 20-5 Recording Payroll Transactions

The Wiesel Company pays its employees each week. The payroll register for the week ended September 16 is shown below.

PAYROLL REGISTER

PAY PERIOD ENDING *September 16* 19 - -   DATE OF PAYMENT *September 16, 19--*

EMPLOYEE NUMBER	NAME	MAR. STATUS	EXEMP.	TOTAL HOURS	RATE	REGULAR	OVERTIME	TOTAL	SOC. SEC. TAX	MED. TAX	FED. INC. TAX	STATE INC. TAX	HOSP. INS.	OTHER	TOTAL	NET PAY	CK. NO.
102	Abbott, D.	M	2	39	5.20	202 80		202 80	12 57	2 94	—	4 06	3 80	(C) 5 00	28 37	174 43	1
116	Concannon, A.	S	0	42	4.80	192 00	14 40	206 40	12 80	2 99	23 00	4 13	2 45	(B) 5 00	50 37	156 03	2
109	Flowers, B.	M	1	41	5.35	214 00	8 03	222 03	13 77	3 22	9 00	4 44	3 80		34 23	187 80	3
121	Jackson, P.	S	1	36	4.95	178 20		178 20	11 05	2 58	13 00	3 56	2 45	(C) 10 00	42 64	135 56	4
117	Oller, W.	S	0	31	5.10	158 10		158 10	9 80	2 29	16 00	3 16	2 45	(B) 5 00	38 70	119 40	5
123	Repicky, J.	S	1	40	5.10	204 00		204 00	12 65	2 96	17 00	4 08	2 45	(C) 15 00	54 14	149 86	6
141	Toomey, B.	M	2	33	5.35	176 55		176 55	10 95	2 56	—	3 53	3 80		20 84	155 71	7
139	Welsh, T.	S	0	41	5.10	204 00		204 00	13 12	3 07	18 00	4 23	2 45	(UW) 3 00	43 87	167 78	8
	TOTALS					1,529 65	30 08	1,559 73	96 71	22 61	96 00	31 19	23 65	UW 3 00 / B 10 00 / C 10 00	313 16	1,246 57	25

Other Deductions: Write the appropriate code letter to the left of the amount: B—U.S. Savings Bonds; C—Credit Union; UD—Union Dues; UW—United Way.

Instructions:

(1) Record the payment of the payroll on page 16 of the cash payments journal. Check 831 was written on September 16 to pay the payroll.

(2) Compute the employer's payroll taxes (FICA tax rates, 6.2% social security, 1.45% medicare; state unemployment tax rate, 5.4%; federal unemployment tax rate, 0.8%). The following employees have accumulated earnings of $7,000 or more: Abbott, Concannon, Flowers, Repicky, and Welsh. Record the entry for the employer's payroll taxes on page 8 of the general journal.

(3) Record the payment of all FICA and employees' federal income taxes, Check 832. The previous account balances were: Employees' Federal Income Tax Payable, $189.00, and Social Security Tax Payable, $191.48, and Medicare Tax Payable, $44.92.

(4) Record the income tax payment to the state, Check 833. The balance in the account Employees' State Income Tax Payable before the September 16 payroll was $178.40.

(5) Record the payments for amounts withheld from employees:

  (a) Check 834 to Tri-County Credit Union (previous balance, $270.00).

  (b) Check 835 for hospital insurance (previous balance, $260.15).

*M*oney Shuffling

Ask the average taxpayer how he or she feels about the IRS, and you will garner few positive responses. Paying taxes, however, is part of living in the United States. Most employees expect to see money withheld from their paychecks, assuming in good faith that the money will be passed along to the IRS. With some planning, perhaps some money will be refunded when the returns are filed.

What if, however, your money was not going to the government? What if, instead, the money withheld from your check was being used to pay off company debts, to pacify threatening creditors, or to buy into a high-risk investment? Such a situation might occur more often than you think. For example, a business owner who is losing money may feel that she could get her business under control by temporarily directing her employee's withholding funds into other channels, such as using the money to pay off some pressing debts. "After all," her rationalization might go, "the IRS does not need this money right now, but I do. Things will ease up soon, and by that time I will have the money to pay the taxes."

What is the ethical dilemma in this situation? If you were an accounting clerk managing payroll for this particular business, what course of action would you take? Would you go along with the owner's plan? One way to decide might be to ask yourself the question, to whom does the money belong? Legally, it belongs to the government; it is only being held by the employer. In essence, the employer transferred the money to the employee in the form of a salary; the employee transferred the money to the government by designating that a certain amount be withheld from his or her salary. If the employer "borrows" the money from

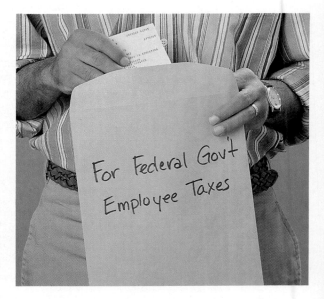

Looking at all the available options can help you resolve ethical questions.

the government, but returns it before the taxes are due, however, who is to know?

Before making a decision, it is wise to consider the other options. For example, if the unpaid debts are a result of bad business practices, the owner could seek financial counseling to determine the best solution to the problem. If the situation is really just a cash flow problem, and money is expected soon, a loan could be taken to pay off the most pressing debts, and then the loan could be repaid when the cash comes in. Perhaps the time span of repayment could be renegotiated with the creditors. Often, receiving a payment, even if it is less than the amount due, will assure a creditor that efforts are being made to repay, and the creditor may be willing to rework the terms.

Mini Practice Set

APPLICATION ACTIVITY 5

Payroll Accounting

In Unit 4, you studied the procedures involved in a payroll system—from determining and recording employees' earnings to preparing employers' tax reports. Now you will have the opportunity to review and apply what you have learned as you prepare the payroll and maintain payroll records for a business called The Greens.

When you have completed this activity, you will have done the following:

1. Calculated employees' gross earnings.
2. Determined deductions from employees' gross earnings.
3. Calculated employees' net pay.
4. Prepared a payroll register.
5. Written payroll checks and stubs for employees.
6. Recorded payroll information on employees' earnings records.
7. Journalized and posted the payroll transaction.
8. Calculated the employer's payroll taxes.
9. Journalized and posted the employer's payroll tax transaction.
10. Journalized and posted the payment of FICA taxes and federal income taxes.
11. Prepared Form 8109.
12. Journalized and posted the payment of a monthly insurance premium.

The Greens

The Greens is a golf shop located in Concord, Massachusetts. It is a merchandising business, organized as a corporation, owned and operated by the Jackson family. The store has been in operation for almost five years. During that time, its sales have increased each year, and the business is now showing a good profit.

Payroll Information

The store presently employs eight people. A Form W-4 is on file for each employee. The list that follows summarizes the data on those documents.

Chris Carroll:	Single; claims 1 exemption
Ralph DeLuca:	Single; claims 1 exemption
Christina Frei:	Single; claims 1 exemption
Gary Gula:	Single; claims 0 exemptions
Anne Holland:	Married; claims 2 exemptions
Marcy Jackson:	Married; claims 2 exemptions
Betty Quinn:	Married; claims 3 exemptions
Yourself:	Single; claims 1 exemption

The business pays its employees on a weekly basis. Overtime is paid at the rate of $1\frac{1}{2}$ times the regular rate of pay for all hours worked over 40. The weekly pay period runs from Monday through Saturday, with employees being paid on Saturday for that week's work. The store is closed for business on Sunday.

The employees are paid by one of three methods: hourly rate, salary, or salary plus a 10% commission on the amount of merchandise sold. The following table lists the employees, the method by which their wages are computed, and other pertinent information.

Employee	Emp. No.	Position	Employee Status	Rate of Pay
Marcy Jackson	010	Manager	Full-time	$500.00/week
Anne Holland	011	Salesperson	Full-time	$175.00/week plus 10% commission
Christina Frei	012	Accounting clerk	Part-time	$200.00/week
Gary Gula	013	Stock clerk	Full-time	$4.95/hour
Betty Quinn	016	Salesclerk	Full-time	$5.15/hour
Ralph DeLuca	018	Salesclerk	Full-time	$5.15/hour
Chris Carroll	019	Stock clerk	Part-time	$4.90/hour
Yourself	022	Accounting clerk	Part-time	$200.00/week

Federal and state tax tables are used to determine income taxes to be withheld. These tables are included in the working papers that accompany this textbook. The current rates for other taxes are as follows.

FICA: Employee and employer contributions:
　　　　Social Security: 6.2%
　　　　Medicare: 1.45%
State unemployment tax: 5.4%
Federal unemployment tax: 0.8%

Preparing the Payroll for The Greens

The business entered the third quarter of its fiscal year at the beginning of July. It is presently the last week of July. Christina Frei, the accounting clerk, is on vacation. In her absence, you are to prepare this week's payroll.

Today is Saturday, July 29. The time cards for the employees who are paid on an hourly basis are included in the working papers accompanying this textbook. The hours worked by those employees are listed below and on the following page.

Chris Carroll

	IN	OUT	IN	OUT
M	2:00	5:00		
T	2:00	6:00		
W	3:00	5:00		
TH	2:00	6:00		
F	2:00	6:00		
S	9:00	2:00		

Ralph DeLuca

	IN	OUT	IN	OUT
M	9:00	12:00	12:30	5:00
T	9:00	11:30	12:00	5:00
W	9:00	1:00		
TH	9:00	12:00	12:30	4:00
F	8:30	1:00	1:30	3:00
S	9:00	1:30		

Gary Gula

	IN	OUT	IN	OUT
M	9:00	12:00	1:00	3:00
T	9:00	12:00	1:00	5:00
W	8:00	12:00	1:00	5:00
TH	9:00	12:00	1:00	3:30
F	9:00	12:00	1:00	4:00
S	9:00	12:00		

Betty Quinn

	IN	OUT	IN	OUT
M	9:00	12:00	12:30	5:00
T	9:00	12:30	1:00	6:00
W	9:00	12:00	1:00	4:30
TH	8:30	12:30	1:00	5:00
F	9:00	11:30	12:00	5:00
S	9:00	1:00		

Instructions:

(1) Complete the timecards for the four hourly employees. Enter the total hours worked at the bottom of each card.

(2) Anne Holland recorded sales this week of $1,241.00. Calculate her commission and add it to her salary to determine her gross earnings.

(3) Enter the payroll information for all employees in the payroll register. Each employee was recently assigned an employee number because Marcy Jackson is planning to computerize the payroll system. Since this payroll is being prepared manually, list the employees in the payroll register in alphabetical order by *last name*.

(4) Use the following information to complete the payroll register:

    (a) Use the federal and state tax charts to determine income tax amounts to be withheld.

    (b) Chris Carroll, Ralph DeLuca, Gary Gula, and Anne Holland each have a $5.00 deduction for the purchase of U.S. savings bonds.

    (c) Christina Frei, Marcy Jackson, and Betty Quinn each have $3.00 deducted for donations to the United Way.

    (d) All employees pay an insurance premium each week. Married employees pay $4.55 and single employees pay $2.75.

    (e) None of The Greens' employees has reached the maximum taxable amount for the FICA taxes.

(5) Calculate the net pay for each employee.

(6) Total all amount columns in the payroll register. Prove the accuracy of the totals.

(7) Write Check 972 on the business's regular checking account for the amount of the total net pay. Make the check payable to The Greens Payroll Account. In Christina's absence, Marcy Jackson will sign the check for you. Complete the deposit slip for the payroll account.

(8) Record the payroll transaction in the cash payments journal, page 19. Use information contained in the payroll register and Check 972 as the source documents. Post the transaction to the general ledger accounts.

(9) Write the paychecks for the employees. Use the information in the payroll register to complete the check stubs. After a check has been written for an employee, enter the check number in the payroll register.

(10) Enter this week's payroll information on the employee's earnings records for Chris Carroll and Anne Holland only. Be sure to add the current gross earnings amount to the accumulated total.

(11) Calculate and record the employer's taxes for this pay period in the general journal, page 15. The source of information is the payroll register.

(12) Make a deposit for the taxes owed to the federal government. The total includes the amounts withheld for employees' federal income tax, social security tax, and medicare tax. Complete Form 8109 by entering the amount owed. Write Check 973, payable to the First Federal Bank of Boston, for the taxes.

(13) Enter the transaction in the cash payments journal.

(14) Pay the monthly insurance premium by writing Check 974 to Yankee Insurance Company for $164.40. Record the payment in the cash payments journal.

(15) Complete the posting from the cash payments journal.

UNIT 5

ACCOUNTING FOR SPECIAL PROCEDURES

In addition to accounting for everyday business transactions, many businesses must also account for financial events that occur less frequently. Among these financial events are accounting for cash funds, accounting for the depreciation of certain assets, accounting for accounts receivable that cannot be collected, accounting for the cost of inventories, and accounting for money that is borrowed or loaned by the business.

Chapter

ACCOUNTING FOR CASH FUNDS

In earlier chapters, you learned that businesses use a checking account for depositing cash receipts and making cash payments. The use of a checking account is an important internal control for any business. Merchandising businesses, however, need to have some cash on hand to make change for customers who pay cash for their purchases. In addition, most businesses find it easier to use cash for small, incidental cash payments rather than writing a large number of checks for very small amounts.

In this chapter, you will learn about two cash funds businesses use to handle these situations: a change fund and a petty cash fund. Since errors in making change do occur in merchandising businesses, you will also learn how to record the amounts of those errors in the accounting records for the business.

Learning Objectives

When you have completed Chapter 21, you should be able to do the following:

1. Record the entry to establish a change fund.
2. Prove the cash in the cash register drawer at the end of each business day.
3. Record the entry to establish a petty cash fund.
4. Prepare a petty cash requisition to replenish the petty cash fund.
5. Use a petty cash register to record petty cash disbursements.
6. Record the journal entry to replenish the petty cash fund.
7. Determine whether cash is short or over and record the amount of the shortage or overage.
8. Define the accounting terms introduced in this chapter.

New Terms

change fund
petty cash fund
petty cash disbursement
petty cashier
petty cash voucher
petty cash requisition
petty cash register

The Change Fund

Many businesses, including such retail stores as drugstores and supermarkets, need change funds. A **change fund** is an amount of money, consisting of varying denominations of bills and coins, that is used to make change in cash transactions. For example, a customer who pays for a $13.80 purchase with a $20.00 bill must be given change of $6.20.

Establishing a Change Fund

When a business first establishes a change fund, the amount of change needed for the fund is estimated. The size of the fund does not change unless the business finds that it needs more or less change than its original estimate. The change fund is established by writing a check for the amount of the fund. The check is made payable to the person who will be in charge of the change fund. That person cashes the check and places the bills and coins in the cash register drawer. Let's look at an example.

All merchandising businesses need to have cash on hand in order to make change for customers.

December 1: *The accountant for East Side Book Store wrote Check 150 for $100.00 to establish a change fund.*

When a check is written to establish a change fund, a new asset account is needed to record the amount of the fund. This asset account is usually called Change Fund. The Change Fund account appears immediately after Cash in Bank in the chart of accounts.

Look at the T accounts that follow. The asset account Change Fund is debited for the amount of the check written to establish the fund ($100.00). As you already know, any check written by the business decreases Cash in Bank, so that account is credited for the amount of the check.

Change Fund		Cash in Bank	
Dr.	Cr.	Dr.	Cr.
+	−	+	−
$100.00			$100.00

East Side Book Store uses special journals to record its business transactions. All checks written by the business are recorded in its cash payments journal. The journal entry made to record the establishment of the change fund for East Side Book Store is shown in Figure 21-1.

Figure 21-1 Recording the Journal Entry To Establish a Change Fund

The Change Fund account is usually debited only once — when the business first establishes its change fund. If the business needs to increase the size of the change fund later, a check is written for the amount of the cash increase. For example, suppose that East Side Book Store finds that it needs a change fund of $125.00. A check would be written for $25.00. In the journal entry, Change Fund would be debited for $25.00, bringing the account balance to $125.00. Cash in Bank would be credited for $25.00.

Using the Change Fund

The amount of cash in the change fund is put in the cash register drawer at the beginning of the day. When a cash sale occurs, the salesclerk rings up the sale on the cash register, which automatically records the transaction on the cash register tape. At the end of the day, the cash in the cash register drawer is counted. The amount of cash in the change fund is set aside for use as change for the next day. The balance of the cash from the drawer is deposited in the business's checking account. Let's look at an example.

Suppose East Side Book Store has $470.00 in its cash register drawer at the end of the day on May 15. The cash sales, and the taxes on those sales, shown on the cash register tape total $370.00. A cash proof is prepared to verify that the amount of cash in the drawer is equal to the total cash sales for the day plus the change fund cash. Look at the cash proof shown in Figure 21-2. As you can see, the amount of cash in the drawer at the end of the day minus the amount of cash in the change fund equals the total sales shown on the cash register tape.

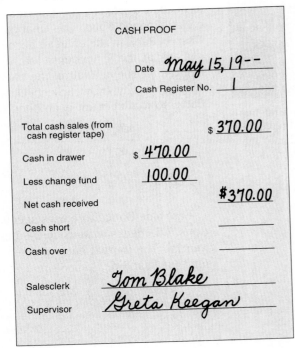

Figure 21-2   Cash Proof Form

Most businesses require that salesclerks sign the cash proof to indicate that they have counted the cash in the drawer and verified its accuracy. The supervisor also checks these amounts and signs the cash proof. The cash proof form is attached to the cash register tape, which is the source document for journalizing the cash sales for the day in the cash receipts journal.

UNIT 5   Accounting for Special Procedures

Recording Cash Short and Over

Many cash transactions occur during each business day. Occasionally, a salesclerk makes an error and gives the incorrect amount of change to a customer. When this happens, the amount of cash in the cash register drawer, less the beginning change fund, will not agree with the cash sales amount recorded on the cash register tape. If the salesclerk gives a customer too much change, the amount of cash in the drawer at the end of the day will be *short*. If the salesclerk gives a customer too little change, the cash amount will be *over*.

The amounts of cash either gained or lost through errors made in giving change to customers must be recorded in the business's accounting records. The account used to record these amounts is Cash Short and Over. Cash Short and Over is a temporary owner's equity account. Cash shortages result in losses or expenses to the business; they are recorded as debits to Cash Short and Over. Cash overages are gains or revenue for the business; they are recorded as credits to Cash Short and Over. Note that Cash Short and Over does not have a normal balance side. If cash overages occur more often than cash shortages, Cash Short and Over will have a credit balance. If there are more cash shortages (as usually happens), it will have a debit balance. At the end of the fiscal period, the balance of Cash Short and Over is closed into Income Summary.

Cash Short and Over	
Dr.	Cr.
Cash	Cash
Shortages	Overages

Cash shortages or overages are recorded in the cash receipts journal when the cash sales for the day are recorded. Look at the journal entry in Figure 21-3. In this transaction, the cash register tape showed that cash sales were $520.00 and the sales taxes were $26.00—for a total of $546.00. The actual cash in the cash register drawer, after the amount of the change fund was subtracted, was $545.00. In the journal entry, Sales is credited for $520.00, the total selling price of the merchandise sold. Sales Tax Payable is credited for $26.00. Cash in Bank is debited for $545.00. Since the amount of the debit must equal the amount of the credit, Cash Short and Over is debited for $1.00, the amount of the shortage.

$546.00 sales
−545.00 cash
$ 1.00 short

	DATE	DOC. NO.	ACCOUNT TITLE	POST. REF.	GENERAL DEBIT	GENERAL CREDIT	SALES CREDIT	SALES TAX PAYABLE CREDIT	ACCOUNTS RECEIVABLE CREDIT	CASH IN BANK DEBIT	
22	31	T30	Cash Short and Over		1 00		520 00	26 00		545 00	22
23											23

CASH RECEIPTS JOURNAL PAGE 15

Figure 21-3 Recording a Cash Shortage in the Cash Receipts Journal

$547.00 cash
−546.00 sales
$ 1.00 over

The journal entry to record a cash overage is similar to that for a cash shortage, except that Cash Short and Over is *credited* for the amount of the overage. For example, suppose, in the previous example, that the amount of cash in the drawer had been $547.00 after the amount of the change fund had been subtracted. In the journal entry, Cash in Bank would be debited for $547.00 and Cash Short and Over would be credited for $1.00. The credits to Sales and Sales Tax Payable would be the same.

When amounts are entered in the General columns of the cash receipts journal, the title of the account being debited or credited must be written in the Account Title column.

Before you read any further, do the following activity to check your understanding of accounting for change funds and cash shortages and overages.

Check Your Learning

Write your answers to these questions on notebook paper.

1. What kinds of businesses need change funds?
2. If a business has a change fund of $75 and wants to increase the amount of the fund to $100, which accounts are debited and credited in the cash payments journal? For what amounts?
3. Hingham Convenience Store has a change fund of $150.00. Cash sales and the sales taxes for one day totaled $982.00. At the end of the day, the cash in the cash register drawer totaled $1,127.00. Is cash short or over? By what amount?
4. Describe the debits and credits made to record the following transaction in the cash receipts journal: Sales, $375.00; sales taxes, $18.75; net cash, $390.75.
5. Describe the debits and credits made to record the following transaction in the cash receipts journal: Sales, $620.00; sales taxes, $24.80; net cash, $647.10.

Compare your answers to those in the answers section. Re-read the preceding part of the chapter to find the correct answers to any questions you may have missed.

The Petty Cash Fund

In earlier chapters, you learned that most businesses control cash by writing checks for all payments made. Writing checks for very small payments, however, is costly, time consuming, and impractical for many businesses. Many businesses keep some cash on hand for making small, incidental cash payments. This cash on hand is called a **petty cash fund.** Typical cash payments made from a petty cash fund are for purchases of postage stamps and small amounts of supplies and for such expenses as small delivery bills and taxi or bus fare for employees on business errands.

The word "petty" indicates that only small amounts of cash are paid out of this fund. When setting up a petty cash fund, each business determines the maximum amount that will be paid out by a petty cash disbursement. A **petty cash disbursement** is any payment made from the petty cash fund. All payments over the maximum amount are paid by check. The person responsible for maintaining the petty cash fund and for making cash disbursements is called the **petty cashier.**

Establishing the Petty Cash Fund

Before a petty cash fund is established, a business must determine the amount of cash needed in the fund. The business estimates the amount of cash that will be needed for a certain period of time, usually a month. This estimate is based on the company's past experiences in making cash payments of small amounts. Let's look at an example of how a petty cash fund is established.

On May 1, East Side Book Store decided to establish a petty cash fund. Crystal Casteel, an office clerk, was appointed petty cashier. The business decided that the petty cash fund would contain $100.00 and that any amounts over $10.00 would be paid by check. The company accountant, Greta Keegan, wrote Check 151 for $100.00, payable to "Petty Cashier— Crystal Casteel," to establish the fund. Crystal Casteel cashed the check and placed the money, consisting of small denominations of bills and coins, in a petty cash box. For better internal control over the fund, the petty cash box is kept in an office safe or a locked desk drawer. Crystal is now responsible for the $100.00 in the petty cash fund. She will make all petty cash disbursements.

When a petty cash fund is established, a new asset account—Petty Cash Fund—is created. Petty Cash Fund appears in the chart of accounts after the Cash in Bank and Change Fund accounts.

The establishment of East Side's petty cash fund is illustrated in the T accounts. Petty Cash Fund is debited for $100.00, the amount of the fund. Cash in Bank is credited for $100.00, the amount of the check. The Petty Cash Fund account usually is debited only once: when the petty cash fund is established.

Petty Cash Fund		Cash in Bank	
Dr.	Cr.	Dr.	Cr.
+	−	+	−
$100.00			$100.00

The cash payments journal entry to establish a petty cash fund is shown in Figure 21-4.

CASH PAYMENTS JOURNAL   PAGE _12_

DATE	DOC. NO.	ACCOUNT TITLE	POST. REF.	GENERAL DEBIT	GENERAL CREDIT	ACCOUNTS PAYABLE DEBIT	PURCHASES DISCOUNTS CREDIT	CASH IN BANK CREDIT	
19-- May 1	Ck150	Change Fund		100 00				100 00	1
1	Ck151	Petty Cash Fund		100 00				100 00	2

Figure 21-4 Recording the Journal Entry To Establish a Petty Cash Fund

When petty cash disbursements occur more often than expected and the petty cash fund is used up before the end of the specified time period, the company may decide to increase the dollar size of the petty cash fund. The journal entry to record the increase is similar to the entry to establish the petty cash fund shown in Figure 21-4. When the petty cash fund is increased, Petty Cash Fund is debited and Cash in Bank is credited for the amount of the increase.

Making Petty Cash Payments

The petty cashier is responsible for making payments from the petty cash fund. Whenever a cash payment is made, a petty cash voucher is completed. A **petty cash voucher** is a proof of payment from the petty cash fund.

An example of a petty cash voucher is shown in Figure 21-5. Petty cash vouchers are usually prenumbered. If they are not, the petty cashier numbers them as they are issued. The petty cash voucher includes the following information: (1) the date of the payment, (2) the person or business to whom the payment is made, (3) the amount of the payment, (4) the reason for the payment, (5) the account to be debited, (6) the signature of the person approving the payment (usually the petty cashier), and (7) the signature of the person receiving the payment. After the petty cash disbursement is made, the paid voucher is usually filed in the petty cash box until the fund is reimbursed.

```
                    PETTY CASH VOUCHER

  No. 001                      Date  May 2, 19--

  Paid to  Premier Office Supply Co.        $ 7.10
  For  Ream of typing paper
  Account  Supplies

  Approved by                   Payment received by
  Crystal Casteel               John Marks
```

Figure 21-5   Petty Cash Voucher

Replenishing the Petty Cash Fund

As payments are made out of the petty cash fund, the amount of cash in the petty cash box decreases. Some businesses set a minimum amount that must be kept in the petty cash box. When the amount of cash in the fund reaches that minimum amount, petty cash is replenished. Replenishing the petty cash fund restores the fund to its original cash balance.

The petty cash fund is usually replenished once a month or when its balance reaches the minimum amount. The petty cash fund is also replenished at the end of the business's fiscal period, even if the minimum balance has not been reached. At the end of a fiscal period, the business's financial statements must report the financial condition of the business at that time. The petty cash fund, therefore, is replenished to update the balances of the accounts affected by petty cash payments. The petty cash fund is then at its original amount for the start of the next fiscal period.

The first step in replenishing the petty cash fund is to reconcile the cash balance in the fund.

▲ **Reconciling the Petty Cash Fund**   The petty cash fund is reconciled to determine whether the fund is in balance. To reconcile the fund, the petty cashier first adds all the paid petty cash vouchers. This total is then subtracted from the original cash balance of the fund. The difference is the *reconciled petty cash balance,* or the amount of money that *should be* in the petty cash box. If a count of the cash in the petty cash box agrees with the reconciled balance, the fund is in balance. If the two amounts do not agree, the petty cash fund is either short or over.

On May 1, Crystal Casteel, the petty cashier for East Side Book Store, totaled all the petty cash vouchers. The total petty cash disbursements for the month were $87.75. As you recall, the original amount of money established for East Side's petty cash fund was $100.00. The reconciled petty cash balance was then calculated as follows:

Original balance	$100.00
Total of paid petty cash vouchers	− 87.75
Reconciled petty cash balance	$ 12.25

When Crystal counted the actual amount of cash in the petty cash box, she found that there was $12.25. The petty cash fund, therefore, is in balance.

▲ **Preparing a Petty Cash Requisition Form**   When the petty cash fund is replenished, the amounts paid out of petty cash must be recorded in the appropriate general ledger accounts.

After the petty cash fund has been reconciled, the petty cashier prepares a petty cash requisition. A **petty cash requisition** is a form requesting money to replenish the petty cash fund. A typical petty cash requisition is illustrated in Figure 21-6 below. This form serves as the source of information for the check written to replenish the petty cash fund. The check stub then serves as the source document for the entry recorded in the cash payments journal.

PETTY CASH REQUISITION

Accounts for which payments were made:	Amount
Supplies	$24.45
Advertising Expense	14.80
Delivery Expense	19.00
Miscellaneous Expense	11.75
Travel Expense	17.75
TOTAL CASH NEEDED TO REPLENISH FUND	$87.75

Requested by: *Crystal Casteel*   Date **5/31/--**
Petty Cashier

Approved by: *Greta Keegan*   Date **5/31/--**
Accountant

Check No. **168**

Figure 21-6   Petty Cash Requisition

To prepare the petty cash requisition, the petty cashier first sorts the paid petty cash vouchers according to the accounts to be debited. The vouchers for each account are totaled. The account title and the total amount to be debited to that account are then recorded on the petty cash requisition. Look at Figure 21-6 on page 271 again. During May, East Side Book Store made petty cash disbursements affecting the general ledger accounts Supplies, Advertising Expense, Delivery Expense, Miscellaneous Expense, and Travel Expense.

The total of all the paid petty cash vouchers is the amount of cash needed to replenish the petty cash fund. When the accountant receives the petty cash requisition from the petty cashier, a check is written for the total of the paid vouchers. The check is made payable to the petty cashier, who cashes the check and places the money in the petty cash box.

R E M E M B E R

The *only* time Petty Cash Fund is debited is when the fund is initially established or when the amount of money in the fund is increased.

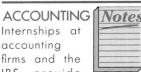
Using a Petty Cash Register

Some businesses like to have a written record of all the paid petty cash vouchers. A **petty cash register** is a record of all disbursements made from the petty cash fund. The petty cash register is a supplemental record used to summarize the types of petty cash disbursements. It is not an accounting journal because no amounts are posted from this register to general ledger accounts.

▲ **Recording Petty Cash Vouchers in a Petty Cash Register** Not all businesses having a petty cash fund use a petty cash register. Those who do might use a form similar to that shown in Figure 21-7. This illustration shows how East Side Book Store's petty cash vouchers would be recorded.

Notice that the establishment of the petty cash fund on May 1 is noted on line 1 of the register. Each petty cash payment is identified by date, voucher number, and a brief explanation. The amount of each disbursement is entered in the Payments column *and* in the appropriate Distribution of Payments column. There are three special amount columns: Supplies, Delivery Expense, and Miscellaneous Expense. The General Amount column is used for petty cash payments that cannot be entered in one of the three special amount columns.

▲ **Totaling and Proving the Petty Cash Register** When the petty cash fund is replenished, the petty cash register is totaled and proved. Refer to Figure 21-7 as you read the following steps on totaling and proving a petty cash register:

1. Enter the date the fund is being replenished in the Date column. Also enter the word "Totals" in the Explanation column.
2. Single rule the amount columns.

	DATE	VOU. NO.	EXPLANATION	PAYMENTS	SUPPLIES	DELIVERY EXPENSE	MISC. EXPENSE	GENERAL ACCOUNT TITLE	AMOUNT	
1	19-- May 1	—	Est. Petty Cash Fund, Ck 151, $100							1
2	2	1	Ream typing paper	7 10	7 10					2
3	3	2	Postage on incoming mail	2 50			2 50			3
4	4	3	Newspaper Ad	9 80				Advertising Expense	9 80	4
5	5	4	Buying trip-gas & parking	9 50				Travel Expense	9 50	5
6	7	5	Daily newspaper	3 50			3 50			6
7	8	6	Collect telegram	1 25			1 25			7
8	10	7	Pens and pencils	2 50	2 50					8
9	12	8	Dara's Delivery Service	9 50		9 50				9
10	16	9	Daily newspaper	3 50			3 50			10
11	18	10	Memo pads	8 45	8 45					11
12	20	11	Postage stamps	1 00			1 00			12
13	22	12	Ad in high school yearbk.	5 00				Advertising Expense	5 00	13
14	26	13	File folders	6 40	6 40					14
15	29	14	Dara's Delivery Service	9 50		9 50				15
16	30	15	Buying trip-gas & tolls	8 25				Travel Expense	8 25	16
17	31		Totals	8 7 75 / 87 75	2 4 45 / 24 45	1 9 00 / 19 00	1 1 75 / 11 75		3 2 55 / 32 55	17
18										18
19			Reconciled balance $12.25							19
20			Replenishment check +87.75							20
21			Total $100.00							21

Figure 21-7   A Typical Petty Cash Register

3. Foot each amount column.
4. Verify that the total of the Payments column is equal to the total of the Distribution of Payments columns. In this example, total payments equal $87.75. The total of the Supplies, Delivery Expense, Miscellaneous Expense, and General columns also equals $87.75 ($24.45 + $19.00 + $11.75 + $32.55). Once verified, the totals are then recorded below the footings.
5. Draw a double rule under the amount columns to show that the totals have been proved.
6. Next, enter the petty cash fund replenishment information. Skip one line. Then write the reconciled petty cash balance (the amount of cash that should be in the petty cash box before it is replenished). For East Side Book Store, that amount is $12.25.
7. On the next line, write the amount of the check written to replenish the petty cash fund.
8. Add the balance in the petty cash fund and the amount of the check. The sum should equal the original amount of the petty cash fund.

As you can see, the petty cash register helps the petty cashier keep track of the petty cash disbursements by account. When the petty cash fund is replenished, the totals of the special columns and the amounts recorded in the General column would be listed on the petty cash requisition form.

Using a Petty Cash Envelope

Small businesses sometimes use a petty cash envelope for recording petty cash disbursements. A form very similar to the petty cash register is printed on the front of the petty cash envelope. Entries to record cash disbursements are the same as for a petty cash register.

The paid petty cash vouchers are placed in the petty cash envelope. When the petty cash fund is replenished, the petty cash envelope— containing all the paid vouchers for the period—is sealed and filed. A new envelope is used to record the next period's petty cash disbursements.

Journalizing the Check
To Replenish the Petty Cash Fund

When the check is written to replenish the petty cash fund, it must be recorded in the cash payments journal. The check stub is the source document for recording the journal entry. Look at the cash payments journal shown in Figure 21-8.

	DATE	DOC. NO.	ACCOUNT TITLE	POST. REF.	GENERAL DEBIT	GENERAL CREDIT	ACCOUNTS PAYABLE DEBIT	PURCHASES DISCOUNTS CREDIT	CASH IN BANK CREDIT	
1	19-- May 1	Ck150	Change Fund		100 00				100 00	1
2	1	Ck151	Petty Cash Fund		100 00				100 00	2
19	31	Ck168	Supplies		24 45				87 75	19
20			Advertising Expense		14 80					20
21			Delivery Expense		19 00					21
22			Miscellaneous Expense		11 75					22
23			Travel Expense		17 75					23

CASH PAYMENTS JOURNAL   PAGE 12

Figure 21-8 Recording the Replenishment of the Petty Cash Fund in the Cash Payments Journal

The date of the transaction is the date of the check. As you can see, Cash in Bank is credited for $87.75, the amount of the check. The individual accounts are debited for the amount of the paid petty cash vouchers as listed on the petty cash requisition. For example, the Supplies account is debited for $24.45.

The petty cashier is the only person who has access to the petty cash fund and the only person authorized to disburse cash from the fund.

R—E—M—E—M—B—E—R

When replenishing the petty cash fund, always credit Cash in Bank and debit the accounts for which petty cash payments have been made. The Petty Cash Fund account is not affected by this transaction.

Before you read any further, do the following activity to check your understanding of how to establish and replenish a petty cash fund.

Check Your Learning

Use notebook paper to write your answers to these questions.

1. The Shutter Bug, a retail camera shop, established a petty cash fund of $80.00. The petty cashier had paid vouchers totaling $73.00. What is the reconciled amount of the petty cash fund?
2. Lovell's Flower Shop wrote a check for $60.00 to establish a petty cash fund. Which account is debited and which account is credited in the journal entry to record this transaction?
3. During January, Lovell's paid the following petty cash vouchers: Supplies, $16.00; Advertising Expense, $9.00; Delivery Expense, $15.90; and Miscellaneous Expense, $8.75. When the petty cash fund is reconciled, how much money should be in the petty cash box?
4. Using the information given in Question 3, which accounts are debited and credited to record the replenishment of the petty cash fund? What are the amounts of each debit and credit?
5. What is the purpose of a petty cash requisition?

Compare your answers to those in the answers section. Re-read the preceding part of the chapter to find the answers to any questions you missed.

Handling Cash Short and Over in the Petty Cash Fund

The petty cashier may occasionally make an error when paying out cash from the petty cash fund. When this happens, the amount of cash in the petty cash box will not agree with the reconciled petty cash balance.

As with the change fund, any amounts of cash gained or lost through errors made by the petty cashier must be recorded in the business's accounting records. As you remember, cash shortages represent expenses for the business, while cash overages represent revenues. The Cash Short and Over account is used to record these cash shortages and overages.

Let's look at an example. At the end of June, Crystal Casteel, the petty cashier at East Side Book Store, classified and totaled the petty cash vouchers. The accounts affected by the petty cash disbursements were as follows:

Supplies	$15.75
Advertising Expense	25.00
Delivery Expense	20.45
Miscellaneous Expense	12.30
Travel Expense	9.50

The total petty cash disbursements for June were $83.00. Crystal then reconciled the petty cash fund.

Original balance	$100.00
Total of paid petty cash vouchers	− 83.00
Reconciled petty cash balance	$ 17.00

When Crystal counted the actual cash left in the petty cash box, however, she found that there was only $15.50. The petty cash fund was short $1.50. Instead of needing $83.00 to bring the petty cash fund up to the original $100.00, $84.50 is needed ($83.00 + $1.50). The $1.50 cash shortage is considered to be an expense and will be debited to Cash Short and Over.

When Crystal prepared the petty cash requisition form, she listed the accounts to be debited for the petty cash disbursements. She also indicated that the Cash Short and Over account was to be debited for $1.50. The cash payments journal entry to record the replenishment is shown in Figure 21-9.

CASH PAYMENTS JOURNAL   PAGE 13

	DATE	DOC. NO.	ACCOUNT TITLE	POST. REF.	GENERAL DEBIT	GENERAL CREDIT	ACCOUNTS PAYABLE DEBIT	PURCHASES DISCOUNTS CREDIT	CASH IN BANK CREDIT	
19	30	CKI87	Supplies		15 75				84 50	19
20			Advertising Expense		25 00					20
21			Delivery Expense		20 45					21
22			Miscellaneous Expense		12 30					22
23			Travel Expense		9 50					23
24			Cash Short and Over		1 50					24

Figure 21-9   Recording a Petty Cash Fund Shortage in the Cash Payments Journal

A petty cash overage would be recorded in a similar manner. If, for example, the actual cash in the petty cash box had been $17.75, there would have been a cash overage of $0.75. Cash Short and Over would have been credited for that amount in the journal entry. Instead of needing $83.00 to replenish the fund, only $82.25 would have been requested.

If a business uses a petty cash register, the cash shortage or overage is also reported in that record. Look at Figure 21-10 to see how the June cash shortage of $1.50 was recorded on the petty cash register page.

PETTY CASH REGISTER   PAGE 2

	DATE	VOU. NO.	EXPLANATION	PAYMENTS	OFFICE SUPPLIES	DELIVERY EXPENSE	MISC. EXPENSE	GENERAL ACCOUNT TITLE	GENERAL AMOUNT	
1	June 1	16	Postage stamps	5 00			5 00			1
14	30	29	Cab fare	1 25				Travel Expense	1 25	14
15	30		Totals	83 00 / 83 00	15 75 / 15 75	20 45 / 20 45	12 30 / 12 30		34 50 / 34 50	15
16										16
17			Reconciled balance $17.00							17
18			Cash short (1.50)							18
19			Replenishment ck. 84.50							19
20			Total $100.00							20

Figure 21-10   Recording a Cash Shortage in the Petty Cash Register

Summary of Key Points

1. A change fund is an amount of money, consisting of various denominations of bills and coins, that is used to make change for cash transactions.
2. The asset account Change Fund is usually debited only once—when the change fund is established.
3. A cash proof is prepared at the end of each business day to determine whether the cash in the cash register drawer, less the amount of the change fund, is equal to the cash sales shown on the cash register tape.
4. A petty cash fund is the cash a business has on hand for making small, incidental cash payments.
5. The asset account Petty Cash Fund is usually debited only once—when the petty cash fund is established.
6. A petty cash voucher is prepared by the petty cashier when a disbursement is made from the petty cash fund.
7. The petty cashier prepares a petty cash requisition to request that the petty cash fund be replenished.
8. Some companies want a record of all petty cash disbursements on one form. Such companies may use a petty cash register or a petty cash envelope to record all petty cash disbursements.
9. When errors are made in making change for cash customers or paying out cash from the petty cash fund, cash is said to be short or over. Shortages and overages are recorded in the account Cash Short and Over.

Review and Applications

Building Your Accounting Vocabulary

In your own words, write the definition of each of the following accounting terms. Use complete sentences for your definitions.

change fund
petty cash fund
petty cash
   disbursement

petty cash register
petty cash requisition

petty cash voucher
petty cashier

Reviewing Your Accounting Knowledge

1. Which accounts are debited and credited when a change fund is established?
2. When does a cash shortage occur?
3. Explain why a cash shortage is treated like an expense.
4. What type of account is Cash Short and Over?
5. Why would a business want to set up a petty cash fund?
6. List three payments that might be made from a petty cash fund.
7. Which accounts are debited and credited to establish a petty cash fund?
8. How often is the Petty Cash Fund account debited?
9. Why should the petty cash fund be replenished at the end of the fiscal period?
10. What is meant by reconciling the petty cash fund?
11. Explain the procedure for replenishing the petty cash fund.
12. Why is the petty cash register not considered a journal?

Improving Your Decision-Making Skills

Alec Grey was recently appointed petty cashier for the Jerez Company. Alec is concerned because some employees have asked him to cash small personal checks for them from the petty cash fund. Other employees have asked to borrow money from the fund until payday. Alec believes he would be wrong to cash personal checks or lend money from the petty cash fund. How can he handle this situation without creating hard feelings among the employees?

Applying Accounting Procedures

Exercise 21-1 Preparing a Cash Proof

The change fund for Messina's Grocery Store is $200.00. On March 31, total cash sales from cash register 6 are $964.00 and sales taxes are $57.84. A count of cash shows $1,216.84 in the cash register drawer.

Instructions: Use the form in your working papers to prepare a cash proof. Sign your name as salesclerk.

Exercise 21-2   Calculating Cash Short and Over

Buddie's Gift Shop has a change fund of $125.00. The cash sales, sales tax, and amount of cash in the cash register drawer for the week of February 11-16 are shown below.

Instructions: Determine the total sales amount, net amount of cash received, and any cash shortage or overage. Use notebook paper or the form provided in your working papers.

Date	Cash Sales	Sales Tax	Cash in Drawer
Feb. 11	$183.50	$ 7.34	$315.84
12	199.75	7.99	332.49
13	206.10	8.24	338.34
14	223.15	8.93	358.18
15	234.30	9.37	366.62
16	288.90	11.56	435.46

Exercise 21-3   Preparing a Petty Cash Voucher

Riddle's Card Shop has a petty cash fund of $75.00. On October 3, the store ran out of tape for the cash register. Paul Howard, an employee, went to Adco Office Supplies to buy the cash register tape (office supplies). The total cost was $2.67.

Instructions: Reimburse Paul Howard by completing petty cash voucher 13 in your workbook. Sign your name as petty cashier.

Exercise 21-4   Replenishing a Petty Cash Fund

Arts and Crafts, Inc., has a petty cash fund of $80.00. During the first six months of the period, the business had the petty cash disbursements below.

Instructions: Use notebook paper or the form in your workbook.
(1) For each period, determine the total petty cash payments, the reconciled petty cash balance, the amount of cash short or over (if any), and the amount of the check needed to replenish the fund.
(2) Determine the balance of Cash Short and Over at the end of the six months. Is this balance revenue or an expense for Arts and Crafts?

Date	Supplies	Delivery Expense	Miscellaneous Expense	Advertising Expense	Actual Cash in Petty Cash Box
Jan. 31	$29.15	$ 9.42	$16.40	$10.00	$15.03
Feb. 28	14.62	11.09	19.63	13.95	20.70
Mar. 31	20.65	12.16	14.10	17.00	14.31
Apr. 30	15.63	8.73	12.98	19.67	24.89
May 31	9.95	4.05	26.07	23.95	14.48 `
June 30	19.46	13.60	18.42	17.41	10.11

Problem 21-1   Establishing a Change Fund

On April 1, Chang Nee opened Nee's Chinese Restaurant. He wrote Check 115 to establish a change fund of $150.00. At the end of the business day on April 1, the shop's cash register tape (T1) showed cash sales of $340.00, plus sales taxes of $17.00. An actual cash count of the money indicated that $505.00 was in the cash register drawer.

Instructions:

(1) Record the entry to establish the change fund on page 1 of the cash payments journal.

(2) Prepare a cash proof for April 1. Sign your name on the Salesclerk line.

(3) Record the cash sales for April 1 in the cash receipts journal, page 1.

Problem 21-2 Establishing and Replenishing a Petty Cash Fund

Medical Health Services established a petty cash fund for payments of $10.00 or less. The following transactions involve the fund.

(1) Record the entry to establish the petty cash fund on page 6 of the cash payments journal.

(2) Record the entry for replenishing the petty cash fund in the cash payments journal.

Transactions:

June 1 Wrote Check 501 for $100.00 to establish a petty cash fund.

30 The accountant wrote Check 549 to replenish the petty cash fund. Paid petty cash vouchers included: Medical Supplies, $40.00; Delivery Expense, $27.00; Miscellaneous Expense, $12.00; and Office Expense, $16.00.

Problem 21-3 Establishing and Replenishing a Petty Cash Fund

Gateway Studios, a film producing company, decided to establish a petty cash fund. On September 1, the accountant, Al Rosen, wrote Check 418 for $70.00 to establish the fund. The following disbursements were made.

Instructions:

(1) Record the entry to establish the petty cash fund in the cash payments journal, page 9.

(2) Make a list of the paid petty cash vouchers.

(3) Classify the petty cash disbursements by account. Calculate the total amount paid out for each account.

(4) Prepare a petty cash requisition, signing your name on the Petty Cashier line. On September 30, an actual count of the cash in the petty cash box indicated a balance of $1.50.

(5) Record the entry in the cash payments journal to replenish the petty cash fund on September 30. Use Check 441.

Transactions:

Sept. 1 Purchased memo pads for the office, $2.75, Voucher 101 (Office Supplies).

3 Prepared Voucher 102 for a $7.50 newspaper ad (Advertising Expense).

5 Wrote Voucher 103 for the postage on an outgoing package, $1.75 (Miscellaneous Expense).

8 Paid Dandy Delivery Service $5.65, Voucher 104 (Delivery Expense).

10 Issued Voucher 105 for pens and pencils, $3.75 (Office Supplies).

12 Paid $2.20 for postage stamps, Voucher 106 (Miscellaneous Expense).

15 Wrote Voucher 107 to Dandy Delivery Service, $6.75 (Delivery Expense).

Sept. 20 Paid the news carrier $4.25 for delivery of the daily newspaper, Voucher 108 (Miscellaneous Expense).
   22 Bought typing paper for $7.50, Voucher 109 (Office Supplies).
   25 Paid $4.50 to Dandy Delivery Service, Voucher 110 (Delivery Expense).
   27 Prepared Voucher 111 for a $10.00 ad (Advertising Expense).
   28 Bought $4.40 in postage stamps, Voucher 112 (Miscellaneous Expense).
   30 Prepared Voucher 113 for a $7.50 ad (Advertising Expense).

Problem 21-4   Using a Petty Cash Register

Use the information in Problem 21-3 to complete this problem.

Instructions:

(1) Enter the information about the establishment of the petty cash fund on line 1 of a petty cash register, page 1.
(2) Record the petty cash disbursements in the petty cash register.
(3) Total and prove the petty cash register on September 30.
(4) Check 441 was issued to replenish the petty cash fund. Record the replenishment information in the petty cash register.

Problem 21-5   Handling a Petty Cash Fund

Copy World, a duplicating service business, is owned and operated by Kathleen Houser. A petty cash fund was established on December 1 when the accountant wrote Check 563 for $100.00. The accounts for which petty cash disbursements are likely to be made include: Office Supplies, Photo Supplies, Advertising Expense, Delivery Expense, and Miscellaneous Expense.

Instructions:

(1) Record the entry to establish the petty cash fund on page 12 of a cash payments journal.
(2) Record the establishment of the fund on the first line of the petty cash register, page 1.
(3) Record each petty cash disbursement in the petty cash register.
(4) Foot, prove, total, and rule the petty cash register on December 31.
(5) Reconcile the petty cash fund. An actual cash count of the fund shows a balance of $1.50.
(6) Prepare a petty cash requisition. Sign your name as Petty Cashier.
(7) Record the cash payments journal entry to replenish the petty cash fund by issuing Check 580.
(8) Record the replenishment information in the petty cash register.
(9) The accountant believes the petty cash fund should be increased by $25.00. Record the issuance of Check 581 on December 31.

Transactions:

Dec. 1 Bought an $8.00 ad in the local newspaper, Voucher 101.
   2 Prepared Voucher 102 for $7.50 to pay Mercury Messenger for packages delivered.
   3 Bought adding machine tape for 75¢, Voucher 103.
   5 Paid $9.50 for flowers for an employee's birthday, Voucher 104.
   7 Prepared Voucher 105, $5.25, for a typewriter ribbon.
   9 Paid $4.40 for postage stamps, Voucher 106.

Dec. 12 Bought photo supplies for $9.00, Voucher 107.
15 Paid $8.50 to have the shop's windows washed, Voucher 108.
18 Bought memo pads, pencils, and pens for office use, $6.30, issuing Voucher 109.
20 Prepared Voucher 110 for $7.50 to pay Mercury Messenger for packages delivered.
23 Prepared Voucher 111 incorrectly and voided it.
23 Bought stationery for $8.00, Voucher 112.
27 Paid the news carrier $4.75 for the daily newspaper, Voucher 113.
29 Issued Voucher 114 to Mercury Messenger for packages delivered, $7.50.
30 Bought photo supplies, $5.80, issuing Voucher 115.
31 Issued Voucher 116 for a newspaper ad, $5.00.

CHALLENGE   **Problem 21-6   Locating Errors in a Petty Cash Register**

PROBLEM

The Decorating Den is owned and operated by Lou Montgomery. On July 1, a petty cash fund of $125.00 was established with Check 411. The store prepares a petty cash voucher for each petty cash disbursement. The vouchers are then entered in a petty cash register, which is included in the working papers. When the petty cash register was totaled on July 31, the accounting clerk discovered that the footings of the distribution of payments columns did not equal total payments.

Instructions:

(1) Compare the following petty cash disbursement information with the entries in the petty cash register.

(2) Correct any errors you find in the petty cash register by drawing a line through the incorrect item and writing the correction above it.

(3) Total all columns after corrections have been made.

(4) Record the replenishment information on the register. The amount in the petty cash box on July 31 is $15.75.

Date	Vou. No.	Paid to	For	Account	Amount
July 2	1	Paperama	Shopping bags	Store Supplies	$9.45
3	2	Windsor's	ZIP Code book	Miscellaneous Expense	5.20
5	3	Post Office	Stamps	Miscellaneous Expense	6.25
6	4	Prater Delivery	Delivery charge	Delivery Expense	3.50
8	5	Howard Mfg.	Wallpaper book	Samples Expense	8.10
10	6	Windsor's	Typing paper	Office Supplies	6.30
10	7	Daily Examiner	Newspaper ad	Advertising Expense	7.50
11	8	Paperama	Coffee filters	Miscellaneous Expense	2.10
13	9	May Stationers	Writing tablets	Office Supplies	8.93
14	10	Swift Carriers	Delivery charge	Delivery Expense	5.85
19	11	Void			
19	12	Post Office	Postage due	Miscellaneous Expense	2.10
21	13	Prater Delivery	Delivery charge	Delivery Expense	3.50
24	14	Town Taxi	Delivery charge	Delivery Expense	7.35
26	15	Windsor's	Pens/pencils	Office Supplies	6.14
29	16	Daily Examiner	Newspaper ad	Advertising Expense	8.00
30	17	Windsor's	Typing ribbons	Office Supplies	9.13
31	18	M&M Supply	Order booklets	Store Supplies	7.65

Code Words for a Cashless Society

While a cashless society still seems straight out of science fiction, the symptoms have already invaded our way of life.

Electronic funds transfer systems (EFTS) use computers, telephone lines, and satellites to process financial transactions. Using an EFTS,

• Your employer can deposit your paychecks directly to your personal bank account.

• You can pay loans or make investments by transferring funds directly from your bank account to another bank or financial institution.

According to one survey, more funds are now transferred *every month* than all transactions done by traditional means before the EFTS was introduced.

Automated teller machines (ATMs) are interactive systems that let you access your bank account simply by entering a bank card, an identification number, and transaction codes. At an ATM, you can get account updates, withdraw or deposit funds, or transfer funds from one account to another.

In major cities across the country, networks, such as CIRRUS, link local banks to national computer systems. With a card and an identification code, you can withdraw cash instantly from your bank in Boston while you're vacationing in Los Angeles.

It's been estimated that in half of all United States households, at least one person uses an ATM.

Point-of-sale (POS) *systems* have not caught on quite so fast. Like ATMs, but located in retail stores, POS terminals connect your account with the store's account. You simply present your debit card to the clerk, who enters it into the terminal. The cost of your purchase is transferred from your account to the store's account.

Whenever you use an automatic teller machine, you are using an input device connected to a mainframe computer.

Unlike with credit cards, there's no time lag between purchase and payment. You don't have to write a check (and half a dozen people won't need to process it). The store is paid instantly, with no exchange of cash. POS terminals are expensive, so retailers banking on a cashless operating system may have to wait a bit.

Living in a cashless society might be in your not-too-distant future.

Chapter  22

ACCOUNTING FOR THE DEPRECIATION OF PLANT AND EQUIPMENT

Businesses own many different types of assets used to earn revenue for the business. Cash is one asset, as are office supplies, equipment, buildings, land, and merchandise. One type of asset requires special treatment in a business's accounting records. The assets in this group—such as office equipment, store equipment, delivery equipment, and buildings—all have two things in common. First, they are long-term assets that are expected to produce benefits for the business for more than one year. Second, they are purchased for use in operating the business rather than for resale.

When assets are used by a business for several years, the costs of those assets must be allocated, or spread, over the number of years of the assets' productive lives. In this chapter, you will learn how that is done.

Learning Objectives

When you have completed Chapter 22, you should be able to do the following:

1. Identify plant assets.
2. Explain the need to depreciate plant assets.
3. Calculate the annual estimated depreciation expense of a plant asset.
4. Calculate depreciation for a partial year.
5. Determine the book value of a plant asset.
6. Record adjusting entries in the general journal for depreciation.
7. Define the accounting terms introduced in this chapter.

New | Terms

current assets
plant and equipment
depreciation
disposal value
straightline depreciation
accumulated depreciation
book value

Plant and Equipment

Throughout this textbook, you have learned about various assets that are used in the operation of a business. These assets can be classified as either current assets or plant and equipment. **Current assets** are assets that are either used up or converted to cash during the normal operating cycle of the business, usually one year. Cash is a current asset. Accounts receivable is also a current asset because the business expects to collect cash from charge customers within a short period of time, usually 30-60 days. Merchandise is a current asset because it is sold within a short period of time, increasing cash or accounts receivable when sold.

Plant and equipment, or simply *plant assets,* are long-lived assets that are used in the production or sale of other assets or services over several accounting periods. Plant assets include land, buildings, delivery equipment, store equipment, and office equipment.

R E M E M B E R

Plant assets are used for more than one accounting period. Current assets are consumed or converted to cash in one accounting period.

You learned in Chapter 16 that assets such as supplies and prepaid insurance are consumed in the operation of a business. The costs of those assets are converted to expenses at the end of the period. Like other expenses, they must be matched with the revenue earned during the same period (the matching principle of accounting). Since current assets are used or consumed during one accounting period, the costs of those assets are easily matched to the revenue for the period. Plant assets, however, are used for a number of accounting periods. A business, then, must have a method of spreading, or allocating, the cost of a plant asset over the number of accounting periods during which the asset will be used to produce revenue. The method most businesses use is called depreciation.

Allocating the Cost of Plant Assets

The number of years a plant asset can be used—its useful life—varies from one asset to another. A delivery truck, for example, might have a useful life of six years. A microcomputer might have a useful life of only three years, since it might become obsolete within that period.

Allocating the cost of a plant asset over that asset's useful life is called **depreciation.** For accounting purposes, all plant assets except land depreciate, or decrease in value. The cost of land is not depreciated, since land is considered to have an unlimited useful life.

When a plant asset is depreciated, its cost is spread out over its useful life. For example, suppose that a plant asset costs $40,000 and has a useful life of ten years. The cost of the asset will be depreciated over those ten years. A portion of the $40,000 will be transferred to an expense account each year. At the end of ten years, most of the total cost of the plant asset will have been expensed.

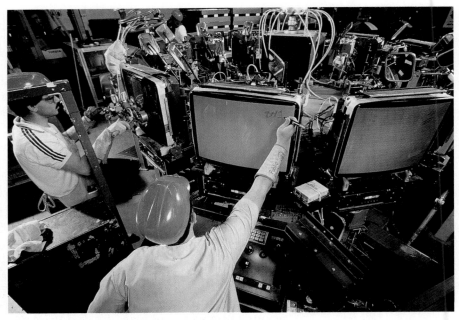

Plant assets are long-term tangible assets that are used for more than one accounting period. These assets are purchased for use in the business rather than for resale.

Estimating Depreciation of a Plant Asset

It is important to remember that depreciation is a way of *estimating* how fast an asset is used up or loses value. No one can predict such amounts with certainty. Depreciation amounts are estimates of the decrease in value or usefulness of a plant asset over a period of time. There are four factors that affect the estimate of depreciation. Two are based on certainty and two are estimates based on past experience. The four are (1) the cost of the plant asset, (2) the estimated useful life of the asset, (3) the estimated disposal value of the asset, and (4) the depreciation method used.

Plant Asset Cost

The cost of a plant asset is the price paid for the asset plus any sales taxes, delivery charges, and installation charges. The total cost is the amount debited to the plant asset account—for example, Delivery Equipment—at the time of purchase.

Estimated Useful Life of a Plant Asset

The *estimated useful life* of a plant asset is the number of years the asset is expected to be used before it wears out, becomes outdated, or is no longer needed by the business. In determining the estimated useful life of a plant asset, the accountant may consider past experiences with the same type of asset. The Internal Revenue Service (IRS) also publishes guidelines on the estimated useful service lives for many assets.

Disposal Value of a Plant Asset

At some point, a plant asset will need to be replaced, sold, or discarded. Usually this occurs while the asset still has some monetary value. For example, if a business needs to buy a new delivery truck, the old delivery truck can often be traded in on the new truck. The estimated value of a plant asset at its replacement time is called **disposal value.** Disposal value is also called trade-in value or salvage value.

The disposal value assigned to a plant asset is an estimate that is based on previous, actual disposal values of similar assets. In addition, the IRS publishes guidelines on disposal values that many businesses use.

Depreciation Method

There are several methods that can be used in accounting for the depreciation of a plant asset. In this first-year accounting course, you will learn about a simple and widely used accounting method for estimating the amount of depreciation called the straight-line method. **Straight-line depreciation** is a method of equally distributing the depreciation expense on a plant asset over its estimated useful life.

Other methods of computing depreciation include units-of-production and accelerated methods. Units-of-production estimates useful life measured in units of use rather than units of time. Accelerated depreciation methods are based on the theory that an asset loses more value in the early years of its useful life than in the later years. Under the sum-of-the-years'-digits method, the depreciable cost of an asset is multiplied each year by a fraction to calculate the depreciation expense. The declining-balance method uses a depreciation rate that is usually either 1½ or 2 times the straight-line depreciation rate. If the rate used is twice the straight-line depreciation rate, the method is called "double-declining-balance."

Before going further, do the following activity to check your understanding of depreciation.

Check Your Learning

Use a sheet of notebook paper to answer these questions.
1. What is a current asset? Give two examples of current assets.
2. What is a plant asset? Give two examples of plant assets.
3. Explain what depreciation is.
4. Why do businesses use depreciation? What accounting principle is involved?
5. What are the four factors that affect the estimate of depreciation?
6. Which two factors in question 5 do you think are estimates? Which two are certain?

Compare your answers to those in the answers section. Re-read the preceding part of the chapter to find the correct answers to any questions you may have missed.

Calculating Estimated Depreciation

Superior Appliance Center purchased a delivery truck on January 5 for $16,500.00 cash. The truck has an estimated disposal value of $1,500.00 and an estimated useful life of five years. The purchase of the truck is recorded in Superior's cash payments journal as a debit of $16,500.00 to Delivery Equipment and a credit for the same amount to Cash in Bank.

The cost of the truck will be depreciated over each year of the truck's useful life. To estimate the amount of depreciation for each year, the amount to be depreciated must first be determined. This amount is calculated by subtracting the estimated disposal value from the original cost of the asset. The estimated amount to be depreciated for Superior's new delivery truck is calculated as follows:

Original Cost	–	Estimated Disposal Value	=	Estimated Amount To Be Depreciated
$16,500.00	–	$1,500.00	=	$15,000.00

Superior must subtract the estimated disposal value because that amount represents a part of the cost of the asset that the business expects to recover. That amount, therefore, cannot be treated as an expense.

The next step is to calculate the annual depreciation expense. Superior uses the straight-line method of calculating depreciation. In that method, remember, the depreciation expense is distributed equally over the asset's useful life. To determine the annual expense, the estimated amount to be depreciated is divided by the number of years of the asset's estimated useful life. As you recall, the delivery truck has an estimated useful life of five years.

Estimated Amount To Be Depreciated	÷	Estimated Useful Life	=	Estimated Annual Depreciation Expense
$15,000.00	÷	5	=	$3,000.00

As you can see from this calculation, the estimated annual depreciation expense for the delivery truck is $3,000.00.

Calculating Depreciation Expense for Part of a Fiscal Year

The $3,000.00 depreciation expense we just calculated was for a full year. Suppose that Superior had purchased the delivery truck in April instead of in January. In that case, Superior would have owned the delivery truck for only 9 months of the year. The amount of the depreciation expense for the first year, therefore, must be calculated for 9 months instead of 12 months. Depreciation expense for a partial year is calculated as follows:

Estimated Annual Depreciation Expense	×	Fraction of Year	=	Estimated Depreciation Expense for Partial Year
$3,000.00	×	$\frac{9}{12}$	=	$2,250.00

Check Your Learning

Handy Home Improvements bought a truck on January 4 at a cost of $23,000.00. The truck has an estimated disposal value of $5,000.00 and an estimated useful life of five years. Use a sheet of notebook paper to calculate the answers to the following questions.

1. What is the estimated amount to be depreciated on this truck?
2. What is the estimated annual depreciation expense?
3. What is the estimated monthly depreciation expense?
4. If the truck had been bought on May 3, instead of on January 4, what would the estimated depreciation expense be for the partial year?

Compare your answers to those in the answers section. Re-read the preceding part of the chapter to find the correct answers to any questions you may have missed.

Plant Asset Records

Most businesses maintain a record of each plant asset and the depreciation that has been recorded for that asset. Figure 22-1 shows the plant asset record for the delivery truck purchased by Superior Appliance Center. As you can see, this record provides detailed information about the delivery

PLANT ASSET RECORD

ITEM __Delivery Truck__ GENERAL LEDGER ACCOUNT __Delivery Equipment__

SERIAL NUMBER __2911-50041__ MANUFACTURER __VanPower__

PURCHASED FROM __Lake City Trucks__ EST. DISPOSAL VALUE __$1,500.00__

ESTIMATED LIFE __5 years__ LOCATION __Company Garage__

DEPRECIATION METHOD __Straight-line__ DEPRECIATION PER YEAR __$3,000.00__ RATE OF DEPRECIATION __20%__

DATE	EXPLANATION	ASSET			ACCUMULATED DEPRECIATION			BOOK VALUE
		DEBIT	CREDIT	BALANCE	DEBIT	CREDIT	BALANCE	
1/5/93	Purchased	16,500		16,500				16,500
12/31/93						3,000	3,000	13,500
12/31/94						3,000	6,000	10,500
12/31/95						3,000	9,000	7,500
12/31/96						3,000	12,000	4,500
12/31/97						3,000	15,000	1,500

Figure 22-1 Plant Asset Record

truck. The plant asset record also includes: (1) the date of purchase, (2) the original cost, (3) the estimated useful life, (4) annual depreciation, (5) accumulated depreciation, and (6) book value at the end of each year.

Each year a plant asset is used by a business, its value is decreased through the recording of depreciation expense. The amount of depreciation expense accumulates from one year to the next. **Accumulated depreciation** is the total amount of depreciation for a plant asset that has been recorded up to a specific point in time. The bottom of the plant asset record in Figure 22-1 on page 489 contains a depreciation schedule. At the end of the third year, for example, the accumulated depreciation that has been recorded for the delivery truck is $9,000.00.

The far right column of the depreciation schedule shows the book value of the plant asset. **Book value** is the original cost of a plant asset less its accumulated depreciation. For example, at the end of the third year, the book value of the delivery truck is $7,500.00 ($16,500.00 − $9,000.00). Notice too that the book value of the delivery truck at the end of five years is $1,500.00, which is the truck's estimated disposal value. With the straight-line method, the truck will not be depreciated beyond its estimated disposal value.

R E M E M B E R

After a plant asset is purchased, its cost is allocated over its estimated useful life.

Accounting for Depreciation Expense at the End of a Fiscal Year

During a fiscal period, a business may buy several plant assets. The costs of these assets are recorded as debits to the appropriate asset account. When a plant asset is purchased, the accountant sets up a depreciation schedule for the asset such as the one shown in Figure 22-1 on page 489. The amount of depreciation taken for the plant asset, however, is usually not recorded in the accounting records until the end of the fiscal period. At that time, an adjusting entry is made to record the depreciation expense for each plant asset.

The information for calculating the adjustments for depreciation is taken from the plant asset records. Many businesses prepare a summary of total depreciation expense for each type of plant asset. For example, a business may have ten delivery trucks, with each truck having its own plant asset record. At the end of the fiscal period, the depreciation expense for all the trucks will be totaled. The total will then be entered on a summary form under the title of the asset account, in this case, Delivery Equipment. Superior Appliance Center's depreciation summary form is shown in Figure 22-2.

Businesses that use computerized accounting systems store plant asset information in the computer. When a summary of total depreciation is

```
           1993 SUMMARY OF ESTIMATED DEPRECIATION EXPENSE
                        December 31, 1993

                                       Estimated
                                      Depreciation    Depreciation
          Asset              Cost       Expense         To Date

   Building               50000.00      2500.00         8125.00
   Delivery Equipment     16500.00      3000.00         9000.00
   Office Equipment       10000.00      1000.00         3000.00
   Store Equipment       250000.00     25000.00        75000.00

     Totals              326500.00     31500.00        95125.00
```

Figure 22-2 Depreciation Summary Form

needed, the computer calculates the totals and prints them out for use in making adjustments for depreciation expense.

Look again at the summary in Figure 22-2. As you can see, Superior's total depreciation expense for the year is $31,500.00. This amount is the total of all depreciation expense for all plant assets. The total accumulated depreciation for all of Superior's plant assets is $95,125.00.

Adjusting for Depreciation Expense

At the end of a fiscal period, adjusting entries are recorded to show the amount of depreciation expense for each plant asset for the period. The adjusting entry for depreciation affects two accounts for each type of plant asset: Depreciation Expense and Accumulated Depreciation.

▲ **Depreciation Expense**   Depreciation Expense is, of course, classified as an expense account. During a fiscal period, the account has a zero balance because the adjustment for depreciation is recorded only at the end of the fiscal period. Like other expense accounts, Depreciation Expense is reported on the income statement. It is a temporary account whose balance is transferred into Income Summary through a closing entry.

A business having many different types of plant assets needs several accounts for depreciation expense. Each depreciation expense account, therefore, is labeled with the title of the plant asset that is being depreciated. For example, the title of the depreciation expense account for delivery trucks and equipment would be Depreciation Expense—Delivery Equipment.

▲ **Accumulated Depreciation**   The Accumulated Depreciation account summarizes the total amount of depreciation that has been allocated to a plant asset since the original purchase. Examples of the titles of accumulated depreciation accounts are Accumulated Depreciation—Delivery Equipment and Accumulated Depreciation—Building.

Accumulated Depreciation is classified as a contra plant asset account. As you recall, the balance of a contra account reduces the balance of its related account. In the case of an accumulated depreciation account, the related account is a plant asset account. For example, Accumulated Depreciation—Delivery Equipment is a contra account to the asset account Delivery Equipment.

Accumulated Depreciation	
Dr.	Cr.
−	+
Decrease Side	Increase Side
	Balance Side

The balance of an accumulated depreciation account represents the cost of an asset that has been allocated as depreciation expense over a period of time. As a contra asset account, the rules of debit and credit for an accumulated depreciation account are opposite those for asset accounts. An accumulated depreciation account is increased on the credit side and decreased on the debit side. It has a normal credit balance. The balance of an accumulated depreciation account is reported on the balance sheet as a decrease to its related plant asset account.

R E M E M B E R

The normal balance of an asset account, such as Delivery Equipment, is a debit. The normal balance of a contra asset account, such as Accumulated Depreciation—Delivery Equipment, is a credit.

▲ Analyzing the Adjustment for Depreciation Expense

Let's use these accounts now to analyze the adjustment needed at the end of a fiscal period for Superior's delivery truck.

Looking at the depreciation schedule in Figure 22-1 on page 489, you can see that the annual depreciation expense for the delivery truck is $3,000.00. The two accounts affected by the adjustment for depreciation of the delivery truck are Depreciation Expense—Delivery Equipment and Accumulated Depreciation—Delivery Equipment. Depreciation Expense—Delivery Equipment is debited for $3,000.00, which is the portion of the original cost of the delivery truck that is being allocated as an expense for this fiscal period. The contra asset account Accumulated Depreciation—Delivery Equipment is credited for $3,000.00 because that account is increased by the amount of the cost allocated to this fiscal year.

Depreciation Expense—Delivery Equipment			Accumulated Depreciation—Delivery Equipment	
Dr.	Cr.		Dr.	Cr.
+	−		−	+
$3,000.00				$3,000.00

Suppose this is the third year of the estimated useful life of Superior's delivery truck. At the end of the third year, the adjustment made to record the depreciation of the delivery truck is again a debit of $3,000.00 to Depreciation Expense—Delivery Equipment and a credit of $3,000.00 to Accumulated Depreciation—Delivery Equipment. This is the same adjustment that has been made each year. Look at the T accounts below. Before recording the depreciation amount, the Depreciation Expense account has a zero balance. As you recall, the balances of all expense accounts are closed at the end of each fiscal period. The Accumulated Depreciation account, however, shows the total amount of the asset's cost that has been allocated to date — that is, since the asset was purchased. As you can see, at the end of the third year, this total is $9,000.00.

Depreciation Expense— Delivery Equipment		Accumulated Depreciation— Delivery Equipment	
Dr.	Cr.	Dr.	Cr.
+	−	−	+
$3,000.00			1st Yr. $3,000.00
			2nd Yr. 3,000.00
			3rd Yr. 3,000.00
			Bal. $9,000.00

The adjustments for the depreciation of other plant assets — such as buildings, office equipment, and so on — are calculated the same way as the adjustment for the delivery equipment. Now that you know how to analyze depreciation adjustments using T accounts, let's look at how these adjustments are entered on a work sheet.

Recording Depreciation Adjustments on a Work Sheet

After the adjusting entries for depreciation are analyzed, they are entered in the Adjustments section of the work sheet. The placement of these adjustments is shown on the partial work sheet in Figure 22-3 on pages 494-495.

The balances of the Accumulated Depreciation accounts before adjustments appear on lines 9 and 11 in the Trial Balance Credit column. The depreciation expense accounts (lines 24 and 25) do not have balances in the Trial Balance section. Adjustments (e) and (f) are entered in the Adjustments section to show the depreciation expense and the increases in accumulated depreciation for this fiscal year. Note that the depreciation expense accounts are debited and the accumulated depreciation accounts are credited.

After the adjustments for depreciation are entered in the Adjustments section, each amount is extended to the other work sheet columns. The amounts for the asset accounts Delivery Equipment and Building are extended to the Adjusted Trial Balance Debit column and, eventually, to the Balance Sheet Debit column. Notice that these account balances are not affected by the adjustments for depreciation.

The balances of the accumulated depreciation accounts in the Trial Balance section are added to the amounts in the Adjustments Credit column. The total is then extended first to the Adjusted Trial Balance Credit column and then to the Balance Sheet Credit column.

The balances of the depreciation expense accounts are extended to the Adjusted Trial Balance Debit column and to the Income Statement Debit column.

Superior
Work
For the Year Ended

	ACCT. NO.	ACCOUNT NAME	TRIAL BALANCE DEBIT	TRIAL BALANCE CREDIT	ADJUSTMENTS DEBIT	ADJUSTMENTS CREDIT
8	150	Delivery Equipment	16500 00			
9	155	Accum. Depr.-Del. Equip.		6000 00		(e) 3000 00
10	160	Building	50000 00			
11	165	Accum. Depr.-Building		5625 00		(f) 2500 00
23	601	Advertising Expense	1600 00			
24	605	Depr. Exp.-Del. Equip.	—		(e) 3000 00	
25	610	Depr. Exp.-Building	—		(f) 2500 00	

Figure 22-3 Recording the Adjustments for Accumulated Depreciation and Depreciation Expense on the Work Sheet (Left Side)

Before you read any further, do the following activity to check your understanding of the calculation of depreciation.

Check Your Learning

On January 5, the Lavalle Corporation bought office equipment for $34,000.00. The equipment has an estimated useful life of five years and a disposal value of $4,000.00. The following depreciation schedule has been set up for this equipment.

Year	Cost	Annual Depreciation	Accumulated Depreciation	Book Value
Date of purchase	$34,000.00	—	—	$34,000.00
First year		$6,000.00	$ 6,000.00	28,000.00
Second year		6,000.00	12,000.00	?
Third year		6,000.00	18,000.00	16,000.00
Fourth year		6,000.00	?	10,000.00
Fifth year		6,000.00	30,000.00	4,000.00

Using this depreciation schedule, answer the questions that follow.

1. Accumulated Depreciation has a normal ___?___ balance and is classified as a ___?___ account.
2. The adjusting entry made to record depreciation at the end of the first year is:
   a. a debit of $ ___?___ to the ___?___ account.
   b. a credit of $ ___?___ to the ___?___ account.
3. What is the book value at the end of the second year?
4. What is the accumulated depreciation at the end of the fourth year?

Compare your answers to those in the answers section. Re-read the preceding part of the chapter to find the correct answers to any questions you may have missed.

Appliance Center
Sheet
December 31, 19--

ADJUSTED TRIAL BALANCE		INCOME STATEMENT		BALANCE SHEET		
DEBIT	CREDIT	DEBIT	CREDIT	DEBIT	CREDIT	
1650000				1650000		8
	900000				900000	9
5000000				5000000		10
	812500				812500	11
160000		160000				23
300000		300000				24
250000		250000				25

(Right Side)

Reporting Depreciation Expense and Accumulated Depreciation on Financial Statements

The depreciation expense accounts appear on the income statement as expenses. The placement of the depreciation expense accounts is shown on the partial income statement of Superior Appliance Center shown in Figure 22-4.

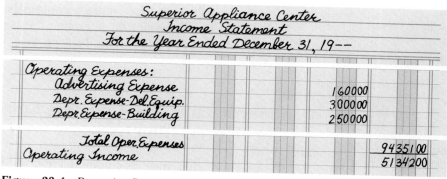

Superior Appliance Center
Income Statement
For the Year Ended December 31, 19--

Operating Expenses:		
Advertising Expense	160000	
Depr. Expense-Del. Equip.	300000	
Depr. Expense-Building	250000	
Total Oper. Expenses		9435100
Operating Income		5134200

Figure 22-4   Reporting Depreciation Expense on the Income Statement

On the balance sheet, the accumulated depreciation accounts are listed immediately below their related plant asset accounts in the Assets section. Their placement is illustrated on the partial balance sheet for Superior Appliance Center shown in Figure 22-5.

Superior Appliance Center
Balance Sheet
December 31, 19--

Assets

Delivery Equipment	1650000	
Less: Accumulated Depreciation-Delivery Equip.	900000	750000
Building	5000000	
Less: Accumulated Depreciation- Building	812500	4187500

Figure 22-5   Reporting Accumulated Depreciation on the Balance Sheet

Depreciation does not represent the physical deterioration of a plant asset or the decrease in its market value. It is simply a means of allocating the *cost* of the asset over the years in which it is used.

The balances of $7,500.00 for Delivery Equipment and $41,875.00 for Building entered in the second amount column represent the book value of those assets. As you can see, the contra account balance is subtracted from its related plant asset account to determine the book value. The book value of each plant asset reported on the balance sheet is the same as that shown on the plant asset record.

Journalizing the Adjusting Entries for Depreciation Expense

After the work sheet is completed and the financial statements are prepared, the adjustments for depreciation expense are recorded in the general journal.

The information for the journal entries is taken directly from the Adjustments section of the work sheet. The adjusting entries for depreciation shown in Figure 22-6 are made using the partial work sheet in Figure 22-3 on pages 494-495.

	DATE	DESCRIPTION	POST. REF.	DEBIT	CREDIT	
1		*Adjusting Entries*				1
10	Dec. 31	Depreciation Expense—Delivery Equip.		3 000 00		10
11		Accum. Depr.—Delivery Equip.			3 000 00	11
12		31	Depreciation Expense—Building		2 500 00		12
13		Accum. Depr.—Building			2 500 00	13

GENERAL JOURNAL   PAGE 29

Figure 22-6 Recording Adjusting Entries for Depreciation Expense

As with all journal entries, adjusting entries for depreciation must be posted to the general ledger. A partial general ledger showing the posting of the two depreciation adjusting entries is shown in Figure 22-7.

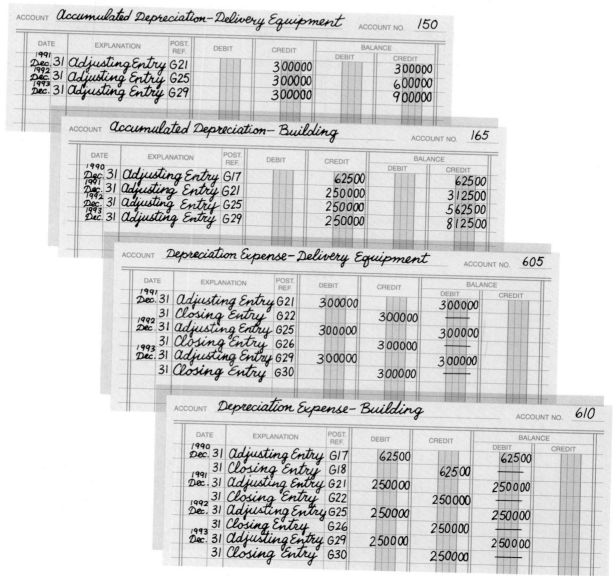

Figure 22-7 Posting Adjusting and Closing Entries for Depreciation Expense to the General Ledger

Journalizing Closing Entries for Depreciation Expense

After adjusting entries are journalized and posted, the next step in the accounting cycle is to close the ledger. In the second closing entry, you'll remember, those accounts with debit balances in the Income Statement Debit column of the work sheet are closed into Income Summary. This closing entry includes the depreciation expense accounts. A part of that closing entry is shown in Figure 22-8.

	DATE	DESCRIPTION	POST. REF.	DEBIT	CREDIT	
		GENERAL JOURNAL			PAGE 30	
1		Closing Entries				1
5	Dec. 31	Income Summary		16250900		5
8		Advertising Expense			160000	8
9		Depr. Expense–Delivery Equip.			300000	9
10		Depr. Expense–Building			250000	10

Figure 22-8   Recording the Closing Entries

When this closing entry is posted to the general ledger, the balances of the Depreciation Expense accounts will be reduced to zero as shown in Figure 22-7 on page 497.

Summary of Key Points

1. Assets that will be used in the production or sale of other assets or services for more than one accounting period are called plant and equipment, or plant assets.
2. The useful life of a plant asset is limited because it wears out from normal use, becomes outdated, or is no longer needed by the business.
3. The original cost of a plant asset, less its disposal value, is allocated as an expense over its estimated useful life.
4. The portion of a plant asset's cost allocated as an expense during a fiscal year is called depreciation.
5. Before depreciation can be estimated, four things must be known: (a) the cost of the asset, (b) its estimated useful life in years, (c) its disposal value, and (d) the depreciation method being used.
6. The straight-line method of calculating depreciation distributes the cost of a plant asset equally over its estimated useful life. It is a widely used method for financial accounting purposes.
7. Annual depreciation is calculated by the straight-line method using the following formula:

Original Cost	−	Estimated Disposal Value	=	Estimated Amount To Be Depreciated	÷	Years of Estimated Useful Life	=	Estimated Annual Depreciation

8. A plant asset record is kept for each plant asset that is depreciated. The plant asset record usually includes a depreciation schedule that also shows the accumulated depreciation and the book value of the plant asset.
9. Accumulated depreciation is the total amount of depreciation allocated to an asset as of a certain date. Book value is the original cost of a plant asset less the accumulated depreciation.
10. An adjusting entry for depreciation is made at the end of each fiscal year.

Review and Applications

Building Your Accounting Vocabulary

In your own words, write the definition of each of the following accounting terms. Use complete sentences for your definitions.

accumulated
  depreciation
book value

current asset
depreciation
disposal value

plant and equipment
straight-line
  depreciation

Reviewing Your Accounting Knowledge

1. What distinguishes a plant asset from a current asset?
2. Why is the useful life of a plant asset limited?
3. What is meant by "allocating the cost" of a plant asset?
4. Why is the cost of land not depreciated?
5. What four factors affect the estimated depreciation?
6. How is the annual depreciation expense for a plant asset calculated under the straight-line method?
7. What is the purpose of a plant asset record?
8. When is the depreciation on a plant asset recorded?
9. Which two accounts are affected by an adjusting entry for depreciation?
10. What type of account is Accumulated Depreciation?
11. Into which account are the depreciation expense accounts closed at the end of the fiscal period?

Improving Your Analysis Skills

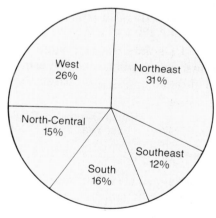

In business, graphs are often used to illustrate facts and figures in a form that is easy to "see" and understand. The three most common types of graphs are the line graph, the bar graph, and the circle graph (often called a pie chart). Being able to interpret the information presented in a graph is an important business skill.

At the left is a circle graph that illustrates the sales, by region, of the Wesley Corporation. Use the graph to answer the questions that follow.

1. Which region had the highest sales?
2. Which region had the lowest sales?
3. If total sales were $547,500, what were each region's sales?
4. How much greater than the South's sales were the sales of the Northeast region (in dollars)?

Applying Accounting Procedures

Exercise 22-1 Classifying Asset Accounts

Listed below are the assets of New England Sports Equipment, Inc.

Accounts Receivable
Building
Cash in Bank
Change Fund
Delivery Equipment
Land
Merchandise Inventory
Office Equipment
Office Furniture
Petty Cash Fund
Prepaid Insurance
Store Equipment
Supplies

Instructions: Use a form similar to the one that follows. For each asset, indicate whether it is a current asset or plant and equipment by placing a check mark in the correct column.

Asset	Current Asset	Plant and Equipment
Accounts Receivable	✔	

Exercise 22-2 Calculating Estimated Annual Depreciation

Instructions: Determine the estimated amount to be depreciated and the estimated annual depreciation for each of the following plant assets. Use the straight-line method of depreciation.

	Plant Asset	Original Cost	Estimated Disposal Value	Estimated Useful Life
1.	Building	$385,000	$15,000	25 yrs.
2.	Calculator	150	0	3 yrs.
3.	Chair	360	20	5 yrs.
4.	Computer	4,800	200	10 yrs.
5.	Typewriter	1,600	100	12 yrs.

SPREADSHEET

PROBLEM

Exercise 22-3 Calculating Depreciation Expense for Part of a Year

Instructions: Calculate the estimated amount to be depreciated, the estimated annual depreciation, and the estimated depreciation for the first year for each of the following plant assets.

	Plant Asset	Months Owned First Year	Original Cost	Estimated Disposal Value	Estimated Useful Life
1.	Cash register	8	$ 450	$ 30	7 yrs.
2.	Computer	2	6,500	1,500	10 yrs.
3.	Conference table	6	1,900	100	25 yrs.
4.	Delivery truck	3	36,400	6,400	5 yrs.
5.	Desk	11	3,180	300	20 yrs.

Exercise 22-4 Preparing a Depreciation Schedule

The Quade Corporation bought a copy machine on January 7 of the current year at a cost of $2,360. The copy machine has an estimated useful life of 5 years and an estimated disposal value of $100.

Instructions: Prepare a depreciation schedule for this machine using the straight-line method of depreciation. Use a form similar to the one that follows.

Date	Cost	Annual Depreciation	Accumulated Depreciation	Book Value
January 7	$2,360	—	—	$2,360

Problem 22-1   Opening a Plant Asset Record

On July 10, Brookside Laundry purchased an Apex commercial dryer from Taunton Bros. Appliances for $1,500. Taunton Bros. charged Brookside $200 to install the dryer. The dryer has an estimated useful life of 4 years and an estimated disposal value of $260.

Instructions: Prepare a plant asset record, including the depreciation schedule, for Brookside's new dryer. Use the form provided in your working papers. Other necessary information is as follows.

> Serial number: TMC46312
> General ledger account: Laundry Equipment
> Location: Main Street store
> Depreciation method: Straight-line
> Rate of depreciation: 25%

Problem 22-2   Recording Adjusting Entries for Depreciation

The following adjustments for depreciation were entered on the work sheet for the Bushnell Company for the year ended April 30.

	Adjustments	
	Debit	Credit
Delivery Equipment		
Accumulated Depreciation — Delivery Equipment		(e) 3,800
Office Equipment		
Accumulated Depreciation — Office Equipment		(f) 1,400
Depreciation Expense — Delivery Equipment	(e) 3,800	
Depreciation Expense — Office Equipment	(f) 1,400	

Instructions: Record the adjusting entries on general journal page 11.

Problem 22-3   Reporting Depreciation Expense
on the Work Sheet

The trial balance of the Cagle Company appears on the work sheet included in the working papers. All adjustments except those for depreciation have already been recorded on the work sheet.

Instructions:

(1) Record the following adjustments for depreciation expense on the work sheet.

(d) Estimated annual depreciation for office equipment is $2,500.00.
(e) Estimated annual depreciation for store equipment is $1,200.00.

(2) Complete the work sheet.

Problem 22-4 Reporting Depreciation on the Financial Statements

Use the work sheet you prepared in Problem 22-3 to complete this problem.

Instructions: Prepare an income statement, statement of changes in owner's equity, and balance sheet for the Cagle Company for the year ended June 30.

Problem 22-5 Calculating and Recording Depreciation Expense

The National Box Company purchased manufacturing equipment on August 1 at a total cost of $410,000. The equipment has an estimated useful life of 25 years and an estimated disposal value of $20,000. The partial depreciation schedule that follows was set up for the equipment.

Instructions:

(1) Calculate annual depreciation, accumulated depreciation, and book value for each of the first two years. The fiscal year ends December 31. Use the form provided in the workbook.

(2) Calculate the depreciation adjustment to be entered on the work sheet at the end of the first year. Use T accounts to show the accounts debited and credited.

(3) Journalize the adjustment for depreciation at the end of the first year.

(4) Post the adjusting entry to the general ledger accounts.

Date	Cost	Annual Depreciation	Accumulated Depreciation	Book Value
Purchased Aug. 1	$410,000	—	—	$410,000

COMPUTER Problem 22-6 Calculating and Recording Adjustments
PROBLEM

The December 31 trial balance of the Olson Laundry Service is included in the working papers accompanying this textbook.

Instructions:

(1) Calculate and record the end-of-period adjustments on the work sheet.
  (a) Laundry supplies on hand total $1,200.00.
  (b) Office supplies on hand total $250.00.
  (c) The amount of the expired insurance premium is $5,000.00.
  (d) Use the following information to calculate the estimated annual depreciation expense.

Plant Asset	Cost	Estimated Disposal Value	Estimated Useful Life
Laundry Equipment	$ 13,000	$ 1,000	10 years
Dry Cleaning Equipment	32,000	2,000	10 years
Building	160,000	10,000	25 years

  (e) The total federal income tax expense for the year is $4,250.00.

(2) Complete the work sheet.

(3) Journalize and post the adjusting entries. Begin on general journal page 16.

(4) Journalize and post the closing entries.

Problem 22-7   Examining Depreciation Adjustments

The University Book Store sells both hardcover and paperback books. On May 2, the store purchased a new book-listing machine from Yong Manufacturing Co. The cost of the machine was $2,700. It has an estimated disposal value of $100 and an estimated useful life of 8 years.

On December 31, the adjustment for depreciation for the first year was entered on the work sheet. Accumulated Depreciation—Store Equipment was credited for $325 in the Adjustments section of the work sheet. Depreciation Expense—Store Equipment was debited for the same amount.

Instructions: Answer the following questions regarding this adjustment.

(1) What is wrong with the adjustment for depreciation made on December 31?

(2) What must be changed to make the entry correct?

(3) If this error is not corrected, what effect will it have on the total expenses for the period?

(4) If the error is not corrected, will the net income for the period be understated or overstated?

(5) If the error is not corrected, what effect will it have on the balances reported on the balance sheet?

(6) One year from now, another adjustment for this machine will be entered on the work sheet. Calculate the following:

    (a) Amount entered in the Adjustments section for annual depreciation.

    (b) Amount extended to the Adjusted Trial Balance section for Accumulated Depreciation—Store Equipment.

    (c) Amount extended to the Adjusted Trial Balance section for Depreciation Expense—Store Equipment.

    (d) Amount extended to the Balance Sheet section for Store Equipment.

*P*laying a Supporting Role:
The Theatrical Accountant

*W*hen you think of a Broadway play, who do you think of? Actors. Director. Producer. Set designer. Stage manager. After all, theater is art, and these are the artists. There's another cast of characters, however, behind the scenes who contribute to the success of any theatrical production. Producers need the specialized talents of an attorney, a manager, and a theatrical accountant—because behind all the glitter, theater is also a business.

The theatrical accountant's work begins long before opening night. Preparations for a production often take from one to five years. During this period, the accountant helps the attorney prepare the prospectus for potential financial investors. The prospectus includes budgets, profit-sharing formulas, and royalty arrangements. The accountant's expertise enables her or him to answer tax and accounting questions and to predict the backers' return on investment in the show. The accountant also helps the business manager project operating expenses and prepare a budget. The accountant works with the attorney to prepare financial reports required by the state.

Before the show is in rehearsal, the accountant is involved with the preparation of contracts and the federal and state registrations needed for payroll deductions. The accountant reviews contracts for the show's major stars that outline payment arrangements.

When rehearsals start, the accountant keeps closely detailed records and prepares weekly profit and loss statements to determine whether the production is within budget. By the time the curtain goes up, the accountant will have interacted

Theatrical accountants make sure that the business end of show business is in order so that the show can go on.

with just about all of the creative and business staff.

The next time you go to the theater, reserve some applause for the hard-working accountant. Maybe one day, that person will be *you.*

Chapter 23

ACCOUNTING FOR UNCOLLECTIBLE ACCOUNTS RECEIVABLE

In previous chapters, you learned that many businesses sell goods or services on account. These businesses have developed various procedures to choose the customers to whom they will extend credit. Credit checks help businesses determine the prospective customers' ability to make payments. They also help businesses decide the maximum amount of credit to extend to each customer.

Regardless of these procedures, some charge customers cannot or will not pay the amounts they owe. These unpaid accounts must eventually be removed from the accounting records as uncollectible. In this chapter, you will learn about two methods of accounting for charge customers who fail to pay the amounts owed.

Learning Objectives

When you have completed Chapter 23, you should be able to do the following:

1. Explain the difference between the direct write-off method and the allowance method of accounting for uncollectible accounts.
2. Journalize the entry to record the direct write-off of an uncollectible account receivable.
3. Explain how the adjustment for uncollectible accounts using the allowance method is recorded on the work sheet.
4. Journalize the adjusting entry for estimated uncollectible accounts.
5. Journalize the entry to write off an uncollectible account using the allowance method.
6. Journalize the entry to record the collection of a written-off account.
7. Describe two methods that can be used to estimate bad debts expense.
8. Define the accounting terms introduced in this chapter.

New   Terms

uncollectible account
direct write-off method
allowance method
book value of accounts receivable
percentage of net sales method
aging of accounts receivable method

Extending Credit

Selling goods and services on credit is now standard practice for businesses of all sizes and types: retailers, wholesalers, manufacturers, sole proprietorships, and corporations. Businesses sell on credit because they expect to sell more than if they accepted only cash. The additional sales result in higher profit.

Before a business extends credit, it carefully checks each prospective customer's credit rating. This credit check helps the business determine the customer's ability to pay her or his debts. Retail stores may ask potential customers to complete an application for credit. They also rely on reports from personal references, credit card companies, and local retail credit bureaus. When wholesalers and manufacturers consider extending credit to customers, they use reports from national credit-rating organizations such as Dun and Bradstreet, reports from wholesale credit bureaus, and customers' financial statements.

No matter how thorough a business's credit checks are, there will be some charge customers who cannot or will not pay the amounts they owe. Those accounts receivable accounts that cannot be collected are called **uncollectible accounts,** or bad debts. An account that is uncollectible becomes an expense to the business because it decreases owner's or stockholders' equity. It must be removed from the accounting records as an account receivable and recorded as an expense.

In this chapter, we will look at two methods of accounting for uncollectible accounts: the direct write-off method and the allowance method.

The Direct Write-Off Method

One method of accounting for uncollectible accounts is the direct write-off method. With the **direct write-off method,** the uncollectible amount is removed from the accounts receivable subsidiary ledger and the controlling account in the general ledger when the business determines that the amount owed is not going to be paid. A journal entry is made crediting Accounts Receivable and the customer's account and debiting an expense account called Bad Debts Expense. The direct write-off method is used mainly by small businesses and businesses with few charge customers. Let's look at an example of how this method is used.

Writing Off an Uncollectible Account

On June 4, Quinn's Bicycle Shop sold a bicycle on account to Mark Hamada for $250.00 plus $15.00 sales tax. When this transaction was journalized, Accounts Receivable and the Mark Hamada account were debited for $265.00, Sales was credited for $250.00, and Sales Tax Payable was credited for $15.00.

After trying for over a year to collect the amount owed, Quinn's decided that Mark Hamada was not going to pay the $265.00.

August 25: *Wrote off Mark Hamada's account as uncollectible, $265.00, Memorandum 48.*

In this transaction, Bad Debts Expense is debited for $265.00 because the uncollectible account has now become an expense to the business. Since the charge customer is not going to pay, the amount is no longer an account receivable. Accounts Receivable and the account Mark Hamada are, therefore, credited for $265.00.

GENERAL LEDGER

Bad Debts Expense		Accounts Receivable		Mark Hamada	
Dr.	Cr.	Dr.	Cr.	Dr.	Cr.
+	−	+	−	+	−
$265.00			$265.00		$265.00

SUBSIDIARY LEDGER

Figure 23-1 shows how this transaction is recorded in the general journal and posted to the general ledger and accounts receivable subsidiary ledger accounts.

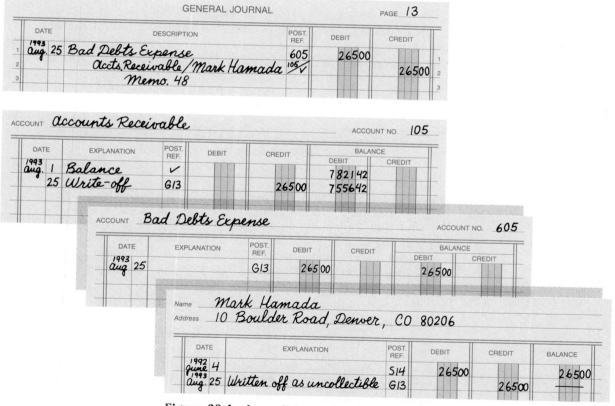

Figure 23-1 Journalizing and Posting the Direct Write-Off of an Uncollectible Account

Notice the explanation entered in Mark Hamada's account. When an account is written off as uncollectible, it is important to note this in the account. Anyone looking at the account must be able to see that it was written off, not paid off.

When using the direct write-off method, **Accounts Receivable** is credited because it has been determined that the charge customer is not going to pay. The amount, therefore, is no longer an account receivable. The loss of the uncollectible amount is charged to **Bad Debts Expense**, which is debited for the amount of the loss.

Collecting a Written-Off Account

Occasionally, a charge customer whose account was written off as uncollectible will later pay the amount owed. When this happens, the customer's account must first be reinstated, or returned to the accounting records. The cash receipt can then be journalized and posted.

September 5: *Received $265.00 from Mark Hamada, whose account was written off as uncollectible on August 25, Memorandum 51 and Receipt 309.*

This transaction requires *two* journal entries. The first journal entry, shown in Figure 23-2, reverses the August 25 entry to write off the account. The memo is the source document for this entry.

	DATE	DESCRIPTION	POST. REF.	DEBIT	CREDIT	
	GENERAL JOURNAL				PAGE 14	
1	1993 Sept. 5	Accounts Receivable/Mark Hamada	105 ✓	265 00		1
2		Bad Debts Expense	605		265 00	2
3		Memo. 51				3

Figure 23-2   Journal Entry To Reinstate a Written-Off Account

After this transaction is posted, the cash receipt is journalized and posted. The cash receipt transaction is recorded in the cash receipts journal. Cash in Bank is debited for $265.00 and Accounts Receivable and the Mark Hamada account are credited for $265.00. The receipt is the source document for this entry.

When both of the September 5 journal entries are posted, Mark Hamada's account in the subsidiary ledger will contain all of the information about the series of transactions. Figure 23-3 shows that subsidiary ledger account.

Name   **Mark Hamada**
Address   **10 Boulder Road, Denver, CO 80206**

DATE	EXPLANATION	POST. REF.	DEBIT	CREDIT	BALANCE
1992 June 4		S14	265 00		265 00
1993 Aug. 25	Written off as uncollectible	G13		265 00	
Sept. 5	Reinstated	G14	265 00		265 00
5		CR25		265 00	

Figure 23-3   Mark Hamada Account

Businesses that sell on credit believe that the increase in sales revenue will offset the amount of uncollectible accounts.

The Tax Reform Act of 1986 made the direct write-off method the only method that a business can use for income tax purposes. The direct write-off method is an accepted accounting procedure for businesses that have few uncollectible accounts. A business that often sells on credit, however, should use a method of accounting for uncollectible accounts that will match revenue with the expenses incurred to earn that revenue.

Before learning about that method, complete the following activity to check your understanding of the direct write-off method.

Check Your Learning

Record the following transactions, in general journal form, on a sheet of notebook paper.

Apr. 10 *Sold merchandise on account to Sonya Dickson, $600.00 plus $30.00 sales tax, Sales Slip 928.*

Nov. 30 *Wrote off Sonya Dickson's account as uncollectible, $630.00, Memorandum 78.*

Dec. 30 *Received $630.00 from Sonya Dickson in full payment of her account, which was written off on November 30, Memorandum 89 and Receipt 277.*

Compare your answers to those in the answers section. Re-read the preceding part of the chapter to find the correct answers to any questions you may have missed.

Matching Bad Debts Expense with Revenue

When the direct write-off method of accounting for uncollectible accounts is used, an unpaid account is written off when the business determines that it will not be paid. Frequently, a year or more may pass before the business decides that an account is uncollectible. Under the direct write-off method, the bad debts expense is recorded as an expense in the period in which the account was written off, not during the period when the sale was made.

When measuring business income, one of the most fundamental principles of accounting is that *revenue must be matched with the expenses incurred in generating that revenue.* This means that expenses incurred to earn revenue should be deducted in the same fiscal period that the revenue is earned. For example, a bad debts expense is caused by selling goods on account to a customer who fails to pay. This expense, therefore, is really incurred in the year in which the sale takes place, even though the amount owed is determined to be uncollectible in some future period. That is, a 1992 credit sale that is determined to be uncollectible some time during 1993 represents an expense for 1992. In order to charge the bad debts expense against 1992 revenues, the business must estimate how much of the 1992 revenues will become uncollectible.

This advance provision for bad debts is made by an adjusting entry at the end of the fiscal period. The adjusting entry meets two objectives: (1) Accounts Receivable is reduced to the amount the business can reasonably expect to receive, and (2) the estimated potential bad debts expense is charged to the current fiscal period. Let's now look at the method of accounting for uncollectible accounts that uses this procedure.

The Allowance Method

The **allowance method** of accounting for uncollectible accounts matches potential bad debts expenses with sales made during the same fiscal period. At the end of the fiscal period, an estimate is made of the amount of uncollectible accounts that will result from the sales made during the period. The estimated uncollectible amount is then recorded as an adjustment on the work sheet. The adjusting entry shows that the estimated uncollectible amount has been entered into the accounting records of the business. The two accounts affected by this adjustment for uncollectible accounts are Bad Debts Expense and Allowance for Uncollectible Accounts.

As in the direct write-off method, the account Bad Debts Expense is used to summarize the uncollectible accounts receivable for a fiscal period. Under the allowance method, however, the amount recorded is an *estimate,* not the actual amount that proved to be uncollectible. In addition, in the allowance method, Bad Debts Expense is used only at the end of the fiscal period — when an adjustment for the estimated uncollectible amount is debited to the account.

When the adjustment is being made, it is impossible for the business to know exactly which charge customers will fail to pay the amounts they owe.

As a result, the estimated uncollectible amount cannot be credited to Accounts Receivable. Remember, the balance of the Accounts Receivable controlling account must always equal the total of the accounts in the accounts receivable subsidiary ledger. If a specific customer account cannot be credited, neither can Accounts Receivable. Since Accounts Receivable cannot be used to record the estimated uncollectible amount, another account must be opened. This account is Allowance for Uncollectible Accounts.

Allowance for Uncollectible Accounts	
Dr.	Cr.
−	+
Decrease Side	Increase Side
	Balance Side

Allowance for Uncollectible Accounts is used to summarize the estimated uncollectible accounts receivable of the business. It is classified as a contra asset account and appears on the balance sheet as a deduction from Accounts Receivable. By using this contra asset account, the balance of Accounts Receivable still equals the total of the customer accounts in the subsidiary ledger. The balance of Allowance for Uncollectible Accounts represents the amount the business estimates to be uncollectible. The difference between the two accounts represents the book value of accounts receivable. **Book value of accounts receivable** is the amount the business can reasonably expect to receive from all its charge customers. Let's look at the adjustment for estimated uncollectible accounts.

Adjusting for Uncollectible Accounts

Sonaguard, a company that sells burglar and fire alarm systems, uses the allowance method of accounting for uncollectible accounts. On December 31, Sonaguard estimated that its bad debts expense for the fiscal year ended December 31 was $1,350.00. (There are various methods that can be used to estimate bad debts expense. You will learn more about two frequently used methods later in the chapter.)

In this adjustment, Bad Debts Expense is being debited for $1,350.00, the estimated uncollectible amount for the year. Allowance for Uncollectible Accounts is being increased. It is credited for $1,350.00, the amount of current Accounts Receivable that Sonaguard estimates to be uncollectible.

Bad Debts Expense			Allowance for Uncollectible Accounts	
Dr.	Cr.		Dr.	Cr.
+	−		−	+
Adj. $1,350.00				Bal. $ 125.00
				Adj. 1,350.00

Figure 23-4, at the top of pages 512-513, shows how this adjustment is recorded and extended on the work sheet.

Notice that, on line 3, Allowance for Uncollectible Accounts has a $125.00 balance in the Trial Balance Credit column. This balance has been carried over from previous years. If the previous years' uncollectible accounts had exactly equaled the estimated amounts, Allowance for Uncollectible Accounts would have a zero balance. This seldom happens.

	ACCT. NO.	ACCOUNT NAME	TRIAL BALANCE		ADJUSTMENTS	
			DEBIT	CREDIT	DEBIT	CREDIT
1	101	Cash in Bank	1265000			
2	105	Accounts Receivable	4489300			
3	110	Allow. for Uncoll. Accts.		12500		(a) 135000
22	605	Advertising Expense	60000			
23	610	Bad Debts Expense			(a) 135000	

Figure 23-4 Recording the Adjustment for Uncollectible Accounts on the Work Sheet (Left Side)

Notice too that the new balance is determined and extended first to the Adjusted Trial Balance Credit column and then to the Balance Sheet Credit column. The new balance of the Bad Debts Expense account is extended first to the Adjusted Trial Balance Debit column and then to the Income Statement Debit column.

Reporting Estimated Uncollectible Amounts on the Financial Statements

The Bad Debts Expense account appears on Sonaguard's income statement as an expense. The placement of the Bad Debts Expense account is shown in the partial income statement in Figure 23-5.

Sonaguard
Income Statement
For the Year Ended December 31, 19– –

Operating Expenses:						
Advertising Expense					60000	
Bad Debts Expense					147500	
Total Oper. Expenses						3834500
Operating Income						2469800

Figure 23-5 Reporting Bad Debts Expense on the Income Statement

On the balance sheet, Allowance for Uncollectible Accounts is listed immediately below Accounts Receivable in the Assets section. The partial balance sheet of Sonaguard is shown in Figure 23-6.

Sonaguard
Balance Sheet
December 31, 19– –

Assets			
Cash in Bank			1265000
Accounts Receivable		4489300	
Less: Allowance for Uncollectible Accts.		147500	4341800

Figure 23-6 Reporting the Allowance for Uncollectible Accounts on the Balance Sheet

UNIT 5   Accounting for Special Procedures

	ADJUSTED TRIAL BALANCE		INCOME STATEMENT		BALANCE SHEET		
	DEBIT	CREDIT	DEBIT	CREDIT	DEBIT	CREDIT	
guard Sheet December 31, 19--	12 650 00				12 650 00		1
	44 893 00				44 893 00		2
		1 475 00				1 475 00	3
	6 000 00		6 000 00				22
	1 350 00		1 350 00				23

(Right Side)

Notice that the balances of Accounts Receivable and Allowance for Uncollectible Accounts are entered in the first amount column. The difference between the two balances—the book value of accounts receivable—is entered in the second amount column.

R—E—M—E—M—B—E—R

Allowance for Uncollectible Accounts is a contra asset account. It is listed on the balance sheet just below Accounts Receivable. The balance of Allowance for Uncollectible Accounts reduces the balance of Accounts Receivable.

Before continuing, complete the following activity.

Check Your Learning

Use Figures 23-4, 23-5, and 23-6 on page 512 and this page to answer these questions. Write your answers on a sheet of notebook paper.

1. What was the balance of Allowance for Uncollectible Accounts before the adjustment?
2. What is the estimated bad debts expense for this fiscal period?
3. Was the Accounts Receivable account affected by the adjustment?
4. On what financial statement is Bad Debts Expense reported?
5. What is the book value of accounts receivable on December 31?

Compare your answers to those in the answers section. Re-read the preceding part of the chapter to find the correct answers to any questions you may have missed.

Journalizing the Adjusting Entry for Uncollectible Accounts

After the work sheet is completed and the financial statements are prepared, the adjusting entries are journalized. The information for the adjusting entries, as you know, is found in the Adjustments section of the work sheet as shown in Figure 23-4.

Figure 23-7 shows how the adjusting entry for the estimated uncollectible amount is recorded in the general journal and posted to the appropriate general ledger accounts.

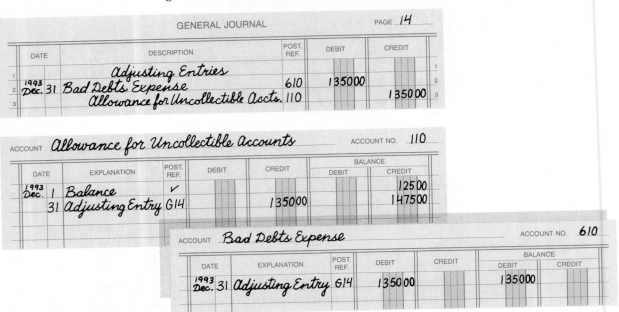

Figure 23-7 Journalizing and Posting the Adjusting Entry for Uncollectible Accounts

At the end of the fiscal period, the balance of the Bad Debts Expense account is closed, along with the balances of the other expense accounts, into Income Summary. It will have a zero balance at the beginning of the next fiscal period. The balance of Allowance for Uncollectible Accounts is not affected by the closing entries. Its balance at the beginning of the next fiscal period is $1,475.00.

R E M E M B E R

When using the allowance method of accounting for uncollectible accounts, an estimate is made at the end of the fiscal period of the amount owed by charge customers that will not be paid. The use of an estimate for bad debts expense allows a company to match expenses and revenue for a fiscal period.

Writing Off Uncollectible Accounts Receivable

When it becomes clear that a charge customer is not going to pay the amount owed, the uncollectible account must be removed from the accounting records. With the direct write-off method, Bad Debts Expense is debited and Accounts Receivable and the customer's account in the subsidiary ledger are credited.

Most businesses require potential charge customers to complete an application for credit.

Under the allowance method, however, the expense incurred has already been provided for by the adjusting entry debiting Bad Debts Expense and crediting Allowance for Uncollectible Accounts. In the previous section, you learned that Allowance for Uncollectible Accounts is not closed at the end of the fiscal period. It acts as a reservoir: At the end of the fiscal period, it is "filled up" by the adjusting entry. The account balance is saved until it is needed some time in the future. When a charge customer's account finally proves uncollectible, the business can dip into that reservoir to write off the account. Let's look at an example.

After many attempts to collect the amount owed, Sonaguard decided to write off the account of the Sullivan Company.

April 18: Wrote off the account of the Sullivan Company as uncollectible, $150.00, Memorandum 136.

In this transaction, Allowance for Uncollectible Accounts is debited for $150.00. That account is decreased because the $150.00 is no longer part of an estimate; it is an actual amount. Accounts Receivable and the Sullivan Company account in the accounts receivable subsidiary ledger are credited for $150.00 since Sonaguard no longer expects to receive a payment from Sullivan.

GENERAL LEDGER

SUBSIDIARY LEDGER

Allowance for Uncollectible Accounts		Accounts Receivable		Sullivan Company	
Dr.	Cr.	Dr.	Cr.	Dr.	Cr.
−	+	+	−	+	−
$150	Bal. $1,415		$150	Bal. $150	$150

Figure 23-8 shows how the journal entry to write off the account is journalized and posted. Notice that, with the allowance method, an expense account is not affected by the write-off. The expense was recorded as part of the adjusting entry in a previous year.

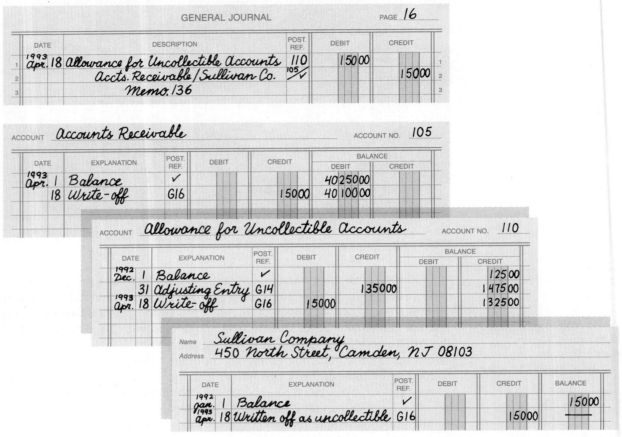

Figure 23-8 Journalizing and Posting the Write-Off of an Uncollectible Account under the Allowance Method

Collecting an Account Written Off by the Allowance Method

A charge customer whose account was written off as uncollectible by the allowance method may later pay the amount owed. When this happens, the customer's account must first be reinstated by an entry that is the exact opposite of the write-off entry.

November 19: *Received a check for $150.00 from the Sullivan Company, whose account was written off April 18, Memorandum 154 and Receipt 1243.*

The general journal entry to reinstate the account receivable and reverse the original write-off transaction is shown in Figure 23-9.

GENERAL JOURNAL

	DATE	DESCRIPTION	POST. REF.	DEBIT	CREDIT	
1	1993 Nov. 19	Accounts Receivable/Sullivan Co.	105 ✓	1500 00		1
2		Allowance for Uncollectible Accts.	110		1500 00	2
3		Memo. 154				3

Figure 23-9 Journalizing the Entry To Reinstate a Written-Off Account Under the Allowance Method

After this transaction is posted, the cash receipt transaction can be journalized and posted. (The entry is recorded as a normal cash receipt in the cash receipts journal.) Figure 23-10 shows the Sullivan Company's account after the cash receipt transaction has been posted. Notice that the account shows that (1) the account was declared uncollectible and was written off, (2) the account was later reinstated, and (3) the amount previously written off was collected in full.

Name   Sullivan Company
Address   450 North Street, Camden, NJ 08103

DATE	EXPLANATION	POST. REF.	DEBIT	CREDIT	BALANCE
1992 Jan. 1	Balance	✓			1500 00
1993 Apr. 18	Written off as uncollectible	G16		1500 00	
Nov. 19	Reinstated	G18	1500 00		1500 00
19		CR29		1500 00	

Figure 23-10 Sullivan Company Account

Before you read about how to estimate the amount of the bad debts expense, do the following activity to check your understanding of the material you have just learned.

Check Your Learning

Record the following transactions in general journal form on a sheet of notebook paper.

Dec. 31 The adjusting entry for the estimated bad debts expense for the fiscal year ended December 31 was $1,850.00.

May 4 Using the allowance method, wrote off the account of Jack Bowers as uncollectible, $1,050.00, Memorandum 241.

Nov. 18 Received $1,050.00 from Jack Bowers in full payment of his account, which was written off May 4, Memorandum 321 and Receipt 1078.

Compare your answers to those in the answers section. Re-read the preceding part of the chapter to find the correct answers to any questions you may have missed.

Estimating Bad Debts Expense

When a company uses the allowance method, it must carefully estimate the amount of uncollectible accounts. Estimates are usually based on judgment and past experience. In addition, there are various methods that can be used to estimate bad debts expense. Two common methods that are used are the percentage of net sales method and the aging of accounts receivable method.

Percentage of Net Sales Method

In the **percentage of net sales method** of estimating bad debts expense, the business assumes that a certain percentage of each year's net sales will be uncollectible. Net sales, remember, is Sales less Sales Discounts and Sales Returns and Allowances. The amount of the adjustment for bad debts is found by multiplying the amount of the current year's net sales by a certain percentage.

Sonaguard uses the percentage of net sales method to estimate its bad debts expense. Let's see how this method works. In recent years, Sonaguard's actual losses from bad debts have been approximately 2% of its net sales. On this basis, Sonaguard's accountant believes that the 2% figure should continue to be used to estimate bad debts expense. (The percentage may be changed if actual losses for several years show that it is an unreasonable figure.)

Year	Net Sales	Losses from Bad Debts
1	$ 59,000	$1,062 (1.8%)
2	65,000	1,430 (2.2%)
3	67,000	1,273 (1.9%)
Totals	$191,000	$3,765 (2.0%)

To calculate the current year's estimate of bad debts expense, Sonaguard must first determine the amount of its net sales. As shown, net sales can be found by subtracting the end-of-period balances of Sales Discounts and Sales Returns and Allowances from the end-of-period balance of Sales.

Sales		$74,500.00
Less: Sales Discounts	$3,000.00	
Sales Returns and Allowances	4,000.00	− 7,000.00
Net Sales		$67,500.00

$67,500.00
× .02
$ 1,350.00

The bad debts expense for the current year is then determined by multiplying the net sales amount ($67,500.00) by the set percentage of 2%. Sonaguard's bad debts expense for the fiscal period is, therefore, estimated to be $1,350.00.

When this method of estimating bad debts expense is used, the estimated amount is the amount recorded as the adjustment on the work sheet, regardless of any balance in Allowance for Uncollectible Accounts. The $1,350.00 amount is based on the current year's net sales. The balance in Allowance for Uncollectible Accounts represents estimates based on previous years' net sales amounts. This adjustment is shown in the T accounts on page 511.

The adjustment is first entered on the work sheet and later entered into the accounting records by journalizing the adjusting entry. At the beginning of the next fiscal period, Allowance for Uncollectible Accounts will have a credit balance of $1,475.00.

The Aging of Accounts Receivable Method

With the **aging of accounts receivable method,** each customer's account is examined and "aged," or classified according to its due date. The accounts are then separated into age groups: not yet due, 1-30 days past due, 31-60 days past due, and so on. Based on past experience, a business can estimate what percentage of each age group will be uncollectible. The total amount for each age group is multiplied by the percentage considered to be uncollectible for that group. The resulting amounts are the estimated uncollectible amounts for each age group. The total of all the estimated uncollectible amounts by age groups represents the *end-of-period balance* of Allowance for Uncollectible Accounts.

Let's look at an example. The Ink Spot, a printing business, uses the aging of accounts receivable method to estimate its bad debts expense. At the end of the fiscal period, the company examined its accounts receivable. The computer printout in Figure 23-11 is an analysis of the Ink Spot's accounts receivable accounts. As you can see, each customer's account was placed in a certain age group.

```
                         THE INK SPOT
                 Analysis of Accounts Receivable
                       December 31, 19--

                      Total                    Days Past Due
Account  Customer's   Amount    Not Yet   ---------------------------------
Number     Name       Owed       Due      1-30   31-60   61-90   Over 90

  800  James Allgood  $  300.00 $ 300.00
  805  Kathy Bell         50.00          $ 50.00
  810  J. W. Boyet       800.00                                  $800.00
  815  Eric Conner       200.00   200.00
  820  Ray DeVall        175.00                  $175.00
  825  Steve Grey      1,000.00 1,000.00
  830  Anna Jackson       40.00                          $40.00
  835  Jan Parker        225.00   225.00
  840  Lynn Stevens      306.50          306.50
  845  Betty Walsh       750.00   750.00

       TOTALS        $3,846.50 $2,475.00 $356.50 $175.00 $40.00 $800.00
```

Figure 23-11 Computer-Generated Analysis of Accounts Receivable

The computer printout in Figure 23-12 on page 520 illustrates how the estimated uncollectible amount is determined from the accounts receivable analysis in Figure 23-11. As you can see, the Ink Spot estimates that a total of $729.26 of its accounts receivable will be uncollectible.

An adjustment must now be made to bring the balance of Allowance for Uncollectible Accounts up to the estimated figure of $729.26. The balance of Allowance for Uncollectible Accounts reported in the Trial Balance Credit column is $49.80. The amount of the adjustment for bad debts expense must

```
                    THE INK SPOT
              Aging of Accounts Receivable
            Estimated Uncollectible Amount
                  December 31, 19--

                                    Estimated      Estimated
                                    Percentage    Uncollectible
         Age Group        Amount   Uncollectible     Amount

  Not yet due           $2,475.00       2%         $ 49.50
  1-30 days past due       356.50       4%           14.26
  31-60 days past due      175.00      10%           17.50
  61-90 days past due       40.00      20%            8.00
  Over 90 days past due    800.00      80%          640.00

  Total                 $3,846.50                  $729.26
```

Figure 23-12   Accounts Receivable Aging Schedule

take this balance into consideration. To determine the adjustment for bad debts expense based on the aging of accounts receivable method, the balance of Allowance for Uncollectible Accounts ($49.80) is subtracted from the total estimated uncollectible amount ($729.26). The adjustment amount is, therefore, $679.46.

Bad Debts Expense			Allowance for Uncollectible Accounts	
Dr.	Cr.		Dr.	Cr.
+	–		–	+
Adj. $679.46				Bal. $ 49.80
				Adj. 679.46
				Bal. $729.26

After the adjusting entry is journalized and posted, the balance of Allowance for Uncollectible Accounts will be $729.26, the balance as determined by the aging schedule.

Summary of Key Points

1. Even though each prospective charge customer's ability to pay is carefully checked before credit is granted, some charge customers will not or cannot pay the amounts they owe. Charge customers' accounts that are declared uncollectible become an expense to the business.

2. In the direct write-off method of accounting for uncollectible accounts, Bad Debts Expense is debited and Accounts Receivable is credited when a customer's account is determined to be uncollectible.

3. The allowance method of accounting for uncollectible accounts enables the business to match bad debt expenses with sales for the same fiscal period. An adjustment is made at the end of the period debiting Bad Debts Expense and crediting Allowance for Uncollectible Accounts.

4. Allowance for Uncollectible Accounts is a contra asset account and is shown on the balance sheet as a deduction from Accounts Receivable.

5. The book value of accounts receivable is the difference between the balance of Accounts Receivable and the balance of Allowance for Uncollectible Accounts. It is the amount the business can reasonably expect to receive from its charge customers.

6. When it is clear that a charge customer's account is uncollectible, it must be written off. Under the allowance method, Allowance for Uncollectible Accounts is debited and Accounts Receivable is credited.

7. When a charge customer whose account has been written off pays the amount owed, the account must first be reinstated before the cash receipt can be journalized.

8. Two common methods used to estimate bad debts expense are the percentage of net sales method and the aging of accounts receivable method.

Review and Applications

Building Your Accounting Vocabulary

In your own words, write the definition of each of the following accounting terms. Use complete sentences for your definitions.

aging of accounts
   receivable method
allowance method

book value of
   accounts
   receivable
direct write-off
   method

percentage of net
   sales method
uncollectible account

Reviewing Your Accounting Knowledge

1. Name two methods of accounting for uncollectible accounts. Which method is likely to be used by a large business with many charge customers? By a business that sells mainly on a cash basis?
2. Why should an explanation be included in the Explanation column of a charge customer's account when it is written off?
3. Why does the collection of an accounts receivable account previously written off require two journal entries?
4. Which accounting principle is violated when the direct write-off method of accounting for uncollectible accounts is used? How?
5. With the allowance method, which two general ledger accounts are affected by the adjusting entry to record the estimated uncollectible amount for the period?
6. Why is Allowance for Uncollectible Accounts classified as a contra asset account?
7. How is the book value of accounts receivable determined?
8. How does the entry to write off a charge customer's account using the direct write-off method differ from the allowance method?
9. Name two methods that can be used to estimate the bad debts expense for the fiscal period.
10. If a company had net sales of $630,000 and estimates that its bad debt losses will be 2% of net sales, what is the amount of the adjustment?
11. Which method of estimating uncollectible accounts analyzes each accounts receivable account?

Improving Your Decision-Making Skills

Andrus Jewelers, Inc., has been using the direct write-off method of accounting for uncollectible accounts. For the current fiscal year, credit sales are more than double cash sales for the first time. The Accounts Receivable account has also doubled in amount. Bad debt losses are increasing.

Should the company make a change in the way it accounts for uncollectible accounts? If so, what should it do and why? Should the credit department be notified of the increasing bad debt losses? What suggestions would you give the credit department concerning extending credit?

Applying Accounting Procedures

Exercise 23-1 Comparing the Direct Write-Off and Allowance Methods

Listed below is a partial chart of accounts for Baker Kitchenware.

101 Cash in Bank
105 Accounts Receivable
107 Allowance for Uncollectible Accounts

310 Income Summary
401 Sales
610 Bad Debts Expense

Instructions: Use a form similar to the one shown. The first transaction has been completed as an example. For each of the following transactions,

(1) In the direct write-off method section, identify by account number the accounts that would be debited and credited. If the transaction would not be recorded, enter "NA" in the debit and credit columns.

(2) In the allowance method section, identify by account number the accounts that would be debited and credited. If the transaction would not be recorded, enter "NA" in the debit and credit columns.

Date	Direct Write-Off Method		Allowance Method	
	Debit	Credit	Debit	Credit
December 1	105	401	105	401

Transactions:

Dec. 1 Sold a shirt on account to a charge customer.
   3 Wrote off a charge customer's account as uncollectible.
  17 Reinstated a charge customer's account that had been written off in October.
  17 Collected cash from the charge customer whose account was reinstated.
  31 Recorded the adjusting entry for uncollectible accounts for the period.
  31 Recorded the closing entry for Bad Debts Expense.

SPREADSHEET

PROBLEM

Exercise 23-2 Estimating Bad Debts Expense by the Percentage of Net Sales Method

Listed below are the end-of-period account balances for several companies. Each company uses the percentage of net sales method to estimate its uncollectible accounts. The percentage used by each company is also listed below.

Instructions: Calculate the amount of the adjustment for bad debts expense using the percentage of net sales method. Use the form provided in your working papers.

	Sales	Sales Discounts	Sales Returns and Allowances	Percentage of Net Sales
Andrews Co.	$142,360	$1,423	$ 936	2%
The Book Nook	209,100	3,180	1,139	1%
Cable, Inc.	173,270	1,730	1,540	$1\frac{1}{2}\%$
Davis, Inc.	65,460	650	690	2%
Ever-Sharp Co.	95,085	900	1,035	$1\frac{1}{4}\%$

Exercise 23-3 Completing an Aging Schedule

The Gibson Company uses the aging of accounts receivable method to estimate its uncollectible amount. The aging schedule is shown below.

Instructions: Complete the schedule, using the form in the workbook.

Age Group	Amount	Estimated Percentage Uncollectible	Estimated Uncollectible Amount
Not yet due	$14,320	2%	
1-30 days past due	3,640	5%	
31-60 days past due	3,752	10%	
61-90 days past due	2,280	20%	
91-180 days past due	1,920	25%	
Over 180 days past due	634	60%	
Totals	$26,546		

Problem 23-1 Using the Direct Write-Off Method

The Parker Supply Company uses the direct write-off method of accounting for uncollectible accounts.

Instructions:

(1) Record the following transactions in the general journal, page 14.

(2) Post the transactions to the appropriate accounts.

Transactions:

May 7 Wrote off the $288.75 account of Edward Cobb as uncollectible, Memorandum 223.

June 4 Wrote off the account of Joan Schmidt as uncollectible, $243.60, Memorandum 249.

29 Wrote off the $57.75 account of Albert Olson as uncollectible, Memorandum 255.

Sept. 12 Received $288.75 from Edward Cobb in full payment of his account, which was written off in May, Memorandum 298 and Receipt 944.

Dec. 19 Wrote off Anna Waybright's account as uncollectible, $100.80, Memorandum 329.

Problem 23-2 Calculating and Recording Estimated Bad Debts Expense

Plato Tire Company uses the allowance method of accounting for uncollectible accounts. At the end of the fiscal period, the following accounts appeared on Plato's trial balance.

Accounts Receivable	$110,000.00	
Allowance for Uncollectible Accounts		$ 4,000.00
Sales		900,000.00
Sales Discounts	10,000.00	
Sales Returns and Allowances	50,000.00	
Bad Debts Expense	0.00	

Instructions:

(1) Determine the amount of the adjustment for bad debts for the fiscal period ended December 31. Management estimates that uncollectible accounts will be 1% of net sales.

(2) Journalize the adjusting entry in the general journal, page 8.

(3) Post the adjusting entry to the general ledger accounts.

(4) Determine the book value of accounts receivable.

Problem 23-3 Writing Off Accounts under the Allowance Method

Taylor Furniture Company, Inc., uses the allowance method of accounting for uncollectible accounts.

Instructions:

(1) Record the following transactions in the general journal, page 9.

(2) Post the transactions to the appropriate accounts. (The opened general ledger and accounts receivable subsidiary ledger are included in the working papers.)

(3) Prepare the Assets section of the balance sheet for Taylor Furniture Company, Inc., using the partial general ledger in the working papers. The balances of other asset accounts needed are Merchandise Inventory, $33,000.00; Supplies, $2,000.00; and Prepaid Insurance, $1,200.00.

Transactions:

Apr. 2   Wrote off the $593.25 account of Tom Pernell as uncollectible, Memorandum 29.

May 17   Wrote off Roger Nagel's $262.50 account as uncollectible, Memorandum 32.

July 9   Wrote off the account of the King Company as uncollectible, $840.00, Memorandum 43.

    31   Received $131.25 from the Zeron Company in full payment of its account, which had been written off on November 10, Memorandum 49 and Receipt 399.

Dec. 28   Wrote off the account of Stull, Inc., as uncollectible, $945.00, Memorandum 74.

    31   Recorded the adjusting entry for estimated uncollectible accounts for the period. The bad debts expense estimate is based on 2% of the net sales of $150,000.00.

    31   Recorded the closing entry for Bad Debts Expense.

Problem 23-4 Estimating Bad Debts Expense by the Aging of Accounts Receivable Method

Pilgrim Appliance Company uses the allowance method of accounting for uncollectible accounts. The company estimates the uncollectible amount by aging its accounts receivable accounts.

Instructions:

(1) Complete the analysis of accounts receivable that is included in the working papers accompanying this textbook.

(2) Calculate the estimated uncollectible amount. Use the form provided in the working papers.

(3) Journalize the December 31 adjusting entry for bad debts expense on general journal page 11. Allowance for Uncollectible Accounts has a credit balance of $142.00.

(4) Post the adjusting entry to the general ledger accounts.

(5) Calculate the book value of accounts receivable.

**Problem 23-5   Reporting Uncollectible Amounts
on the Financial Statements**

The work sheet for Anderson Paper Products, Inc., is included in the working papers accompanying this textbook. The trial balance has been completed on the work sheet, along with all adjustments except that for bad debts.

Instructions:

(1) Record the adjustment for bad debt losses in the Adjustments section of the work sheet. Bad debt losses are estimated to be 1.5% of net sales. Label the adjustment (a).
(2) Complete the work sheet.
(3) Prepare an income statement, a statement of retained earnings, and a balance sheet.
(4) Record the adjusting entries on page 18 of the general journal.
(5) Post the adjusting entries to the general ledger accounts.
(6) Record the closing entries in the general journal.
(7) Post the closing entries to the general ledger accounts.

CHALLENGE **Problem 23-6   Handling Write-Offs in the Allowance Method**

McCloud's Department Store uses the allowance method to account for uncollectible accounts.

Instructions: Journalize the following transactions on page 13 of the general journal. Post the transactions to Terry Mahady's account, provided in the working papers.

Transactions:

Jan. 14   Wrote off the account of Terry Mahady as uncollectible, $194.50, Memorandum 398.
June 25   Received a check for $30.00 from Terry Mahady on account, Memorandum 467 and Receipt 1298.
Dec. 10   Received notice that Terry Mahady had been declared bankrupt. Received 40% of the balance due and wrote off the remainder of his account, Receipt 1588 and Memorandum 541.

*C*omputer Viruses:
The Enemy Within

*C*omputer viruses are small computer programs that appear harmless but, as part of their operation, "reproduce" and insert themselves into previously uninfected programs. Like a biological virus, a computer virus spreads quickly. It can cause havoc by slowing entire systems or, worse, destroying stored data. Some viruses even lie dormant, scheduled to go off months or even years in the future.

A computer virus often starts at a personal computer and winds its way through a computer network. Its victim can be anyone: governments, businesses, universities, research facilities, private citizens.

It is estimated that thousands of computers a year are attacked—from laptops to the most powerful networks. One computer virus can turn into an epidemic, affecting many computer systems. New strains surface every week.

Some viruses (called "worms") are pretty harmless, like the Cookie Monster that interrupted users with the message, "I want a cookie." Others are more destructive. In 1988 a disgruntled former employee of an insurance and brokerage company was convicted of electronically destroying over 150,000 payroll records and planting a "time bomb" virus intended to erase computer records every month.

A computer virus is often difficult to detect and usually expensive to cure. As computer viruses have increased, so too have the number of protection programs created to ward off the enemy. Disk Defender, Data Physician, and Vaccinate are just some of the many "virus busters" now on the market.

Who commits these acts of vandalism? It could be a hostile employee, but a pattern seems to be emerging. The culprits are, more often than not,

Increased security measures are needed to prevent the spread of computer viruses.

young people in their late teens or early 20s who have spent a lot of time with computers. Perhaps they're trying to prove they can beat the system. They've learned computer use, but not computer ethics.

What may have started as a prank has now mushroomed into an epidemic that is disruptive, destructive, and deeply disturbing to computer users everywhere. There's an enemy within—but where?

Chapter 24

ACCOUNTING FOR INVENTORIES

In earlier chapters, you learned how important it is for a business to maintain control over its cash. Improper control of cash can result in poor management decisions. It can also mean a lack of cash for other needs and, in some cases, business failure.

For a merchandising business, it is equally important to control merchandise. Merchandising businesses spend a great deal of time and money purchasing, storing, and selling merchandise. To exercise control over its merchandise, a merchandising business establishes a system of inventory procedures.

In this chapter, you will learn how businesses count their inventories, how they account for increases and decreases in quantities of merchandise in inventory, and how they assign a cost value to merchandise remaining in inventory.

Learning Objectives

When you have completed Chapter 24, you should be able to do the following:

1. Explain the importance of maintaining consistent inventory records.
2. Explain the difference between a periodic and a perpetual inventory system.
3. Determine the cost of a merchandise inventory using the following methods: specific identification; first in, first out; last in, first out; and weighted average cost.
4. Assign a value to merchandise inventory using the lower-of-cost-or-market rule.
5. Define the accounting terms introduced in this chapter.

New Terms

periodic inventory system
perpetual inventory system
online
specific identification method
first in, first out method
last in, first out method
weighted average cost method
market value
conservatism

Merchandise Inventory

Earlier you learned that goods purchased by a business for resale to customers are called merchandise. The cost of all those goods still on hand at the end of a fiscal period is recorded in the Merchandise Inventory account.

Merchandise plays a very important role in any merchandising business. It is one of the business's largest asset accounts. This is because much of the business's cash is used to purchase merchandise. Like cash, merchandise must be subject to a control system that helps the business keep track of its merchandise. Businesses need to know not only how much merchandise is sold but also which items of merchandise have been sold. The business also needs to know if a certain item of merchandise is not selling. The business may stop buying that item and find some means—through sales or promotions, for example—to eliminate that item from its inventory.

In a merchandising business, the quantity and cost value of merchandise on hand are important in presenting a realistic picture of the company's financial position. Merchandise Inventory is the only account reported on both the balance sheet and the income statement. The balance of the Merchandise Inventory account at the end of the fiscal period (the ending inventory) is reported on the balance sheet because it is classified as an asset account. The beginning and ending inventory balances are reported on the income statement because they are used to determine the cost of merchandise sold.

An inventory control system requires certain information to function efficiently. That information includes the quantity of merchandise on hand at a given time and the cost of that merchandise.

Determining the Quantity of Inventories

The quantity of merchandise on hand must be determined before the cost of this merchandise can be calculated and reported on the financial statements. There are two systems businesses use to determine the quantity of merchandise on hand: a periodic inventory system and a perpetual inventory system.

The Periodic Inventory System

One of the most commonly used systems of determining the quantity of merchandise on hand is a periodic inventory system. A **periodic inventory system** requires a physical count of all merchandise on hand. With this system, each inventory item is counted. The total number of a particular item on hand is recorded on an inventory card or sheet. A typical inventory sheet is shown in Figure 24-1 on page 530. As you can see, the sheet lists the stock number of the item, a description of the item, the quantity on hand, the unit cost, and the total value of the inventory item on hand.

For businesses having many items in inventory, the process of identifying and counting all items of merchandise can be very time-consuming. For this reason, inventory should be counted when it is at its lowest level. Many seasonal businesses take their inventories at the end of their peak selling periods when much of their merchandise has been sold. Most businesses take a periodic inventory of their merchandise at least once a year.

INVENTORY SHEET

DATE *Jan. 5, 19--*   CLERK *Brian Cropp*   PAGE *1*

STOCK NO.	ITEM	UNIT	QUANTITY	UNIT COST	TOTAL VALUE
1901	Needles	Pkg	24	1 14	27 36
2132	Thread	Spool	12	65	7 80
2136	Thread	Spool	18	55	9 90
3245	Zipper	Each	18	1 50	27 00
1917	Pins	Box	24	79	18 96
4971	Buttons	Pkg	12	89	10 68
4993	Tape Measure	Each	15	1 49	22 35
				TOTAL FOR THIS SHEET	789 14

Figure 24-1   Inventory Sheet Used in a Periodic Inventory System

Some businesses use automated equipment to assist them in taking inventories. When automated equipment is used, the user merely enters the stock number of the item and the amount still on hand into a small handheld computer. After the physical count of all items in stock is taken, a complete printout can be obtained from the computer. An example of a stock-on-hand printout is shown in Figure 24-2.

```
               Abbott's Department Store
                   Physical Inventory
                     Department 34
                    June 30, 19--

                                       Unit       Total
    Stock                              Cost        Value
     No.          Item       Unit  Qty

    012844   Patton Desk Lamp   Each    8    32.40    259.20
    012846   Captain's Lamp     Each    4    39.95    159.80
    012852   Doon Table Lamp    Each    7    46.55    325.85
    012857   18-Inch Table Lamp Each    3    43.80    131.40
    012859   Floor Lamp         Each    9    63.60    572.40
    012862   Kline Floor Lamp   Each    3    72.69    218.07
    012864   Warnen Night Lamp  Pair    6    39.45    236.70
    012867   10-Inch Night Lamp Each    0    42.59
    012868   Patton Bulbs       Each   28     2.35     65.80
    012873   10-Inch Lamp Shade Each   12    19.50    234.00
    012875   12-Inch Lamp Shade Each   16    22.86    365.76
    012876   14-Inch Lamp Shade Each    5    27.95    139.75
    012883   Lamp Dimmer        Each    7     9.45     66.15
                                                    -------
                                                   2774.88
                                                   =======
```

Figure 24-2   Computer Printout of Inventory

UNIT 5   Accounting for Special Procedures

The Perpetual Inventory System

Another system that can be used to account for inventories is the perpetual inventory system. A **perpetual inventory system** requires that a constant, up-to-date record of merchandise on hand be kept. With this inventory system, a business can determine the balance of the Merchandise Inventory account at any time since all purchases and sales are recorded immediately. In addition, the cost of merchandise sold can be determined easily since the accounting records indicate merchandise purchases and balances on hand.

Businesses using a perpetual inventory system may use stock record sheets or cards. A stock card used in a perpetual inventory system is shown in Figure 24-3. Each time the level of stock is increased or decreased, the amount of the increase or decrease is recorded on the stock card. For example, when an incoming order of merchandise is received, the quantity is recorded in the In column of the stock card. Sales of the item are recorded in the Out column.

Computers have enabled many businesses to maintain perpetual inventory systems.

STOCK CARD

STOCK NO.	ITEM			
C 1297	Altmore Disk Player			

SUPPLIER	SUPPLIER'S CATALOGUE NO.
Star Electric	91246

UNIT	MINIMUM	MAXIMUM
Each	15	60

DATE	EXPLANATION	IN	OUT	BALANCE
7/1/--	Balance on Hand			48
7/8/--	Shipping Order 21928		6	42
7/12/--	Shipping Order 22201		10	32
7/20/--	Shipping Order 22456		8	24
7/24/--	Shipping Order 22719		12	12
7/24/--	Purchase Requisition 19426			
7/31/--	Receiving Report 21563	48		60

Figure 24-3   Stock Card Used in a Perpetual Inventory System

Manual perpetual inventory systems are generally used by businesses that sell large items. For example, a television dealer would probably find it convenient to maintain a separate stock card for every type of item in stock. Each time a new inventory item is purchased, a new card is prepared and inserted in the file. If the item is discontinued, the card is pulled from the inventory file.

Computerized Inventory Systems

With the increased use of computers, many businesses maintain computerized perpetual inventory systems. This is done through terminals or cash registers that are online to a central computer system. **Online** means that a terminal or cash register is linked directly to the computer and feeds data into the appropriate files controlled by the computer. For example, when a sale is made by a business using a computerized inventory system, the item number, the quantity, and the price of the item being sold are entered into the cash register by the salesperson. The cash register is online to a computer, which updates the inventory cost records immediately. With this information stored in the computer, management may obtain inventory quantities and values at any time. An example of a computer printout for a perpetual inventory system is shown in Figure 24-4.

```
              CENTER SPORTS SHOP
              PERPETUAL INVENTORY
                 DEPARTMENT 28
                 SEPTEMBER 30,   19--

                                        UNIT      TOTAL
  STOCK                                 COST      VALUE
  NO.        ITEM           UNIT  QTY

  2305   Warner Rods        Each    7   27.45     192.15
  2319   Tanner Rods        Each    9   31.48     283.32
  2320   Paterson Rods      Each   13   34.95     454.35
  2325   Junior Rods        Each   10   22.50     225.00
  2337   Weber Reel         Each   13   29.45     382.85
  2339   Art Reel           Each    8   25.85     206.80
  2345   Pro Reel # 4       Each    4   38.50     154.00
  2353   # 9 Hooks          Box    16    8.75     140.00
  2356   # 6 Hooks          Box    13    7.95     103.35
                                                 -------
                                                 2141.82
                                                 =======
```

Figure 24-4 Computer Printout from a Perpetual Inventory System

In a perpetual inventory system, the Merchandise Inventory account always shows the balance of merchandise on hand. A physical count should be taken at least once a year, usually at the year's end, to verify the balance reported in the Merchandise Inventory account.

Before you learn how to determine the cost of inventory on hand, do the following activity to check your understanding of periodic and perpetual inventory systems.

Check Your Learning

Write the answers to these questions on notebook paper.

1. The ___?___ inventory system requires a physical count of the merchandise on hand.
2. The ___?___ inventory system provides constant inventory data.
3. Which type of inventory system might be used by a small stereo store?
4. Which type of inventory system might be used by a large supermarket?
5. Why do companies that use a perpetual inventory system still take a periodic inventory at the end of the year?

Compare your answers to those in the answers section. Re-read the preceding part of the chapter to find the correct answers to any questions you may have missed.

Determining the Cost of Inventories

Once the quantity of merchandise on hand has been determined, the cost of the merchandise must be calculated. If a perpetual inventory system is used, it is easy for the business to determine the cost of the inventory because the actual cost of each item is recorded on the stock card or in the computer.

If a periodic inventory system is used, however, the cost of the inventory is more difficult to determine. Calculating the cost of each item in inventory is not always easy because businesses may buy the same item many times within a single inventory period. The cost of an item may change from one purchase to another. To simplify matters, businesses using the periodic inventory system assign costs to the items in inventory. The inventory costs may be assigned using one of four commonly accepted inventory costing methods. These four methods are specific identification; first in, first out; last in, first out; and weighted average cost.

The Specific Identification Costing Method

When the **specific identification method** is used, the exact cost of each item on the inventory sheet must be determined and assigned to that item. The actual cost of each item is usually obtained from the purchase invoice. Unfortunately, the task of looking up the actual cost of each item is very time-consuming unless you are dealing with a small number of items.

The specific identification method is most often used by businesses that have a low unit volume of merchandise with, usually, high unit prices. For example, appliance stores, automobile dealerships, and furniture stores often use this method. Specific identification is the most realistic costing method because it assigns the actual cost to each item in inventory. Let's look at an example.

The Triangle Video Store started the fiscal year with a beginning inventory of 15 video cassette recorders. The VCRs had been purchased for $250.00 each. During the period, the store purchased an additional 50 VCRs. When a periodic inventory was taken on May 31, there were 12 VCRs still on hand. The costs of the VCRs are as follows:

Beginning inventory	15 units @ $250.00 each	=	$ 3,750.00
Purchased August 4	20 units @ $250.00 each	=	5,000.00
Purchased December 8	10 units @ $253.00 each	=	2,530.00
Purchased February 27	10 units @ $258.00 each	=	2,580.00
Purchased May 1	10 units @ $260.00 each	=	2,600.00
Total Available	65		$16,460.00

Using the specific identification method, Triangle must check its purchase invoices to find the actual cost of each of the 12 VCRs still on hand at the end of May. After checking its invoices, Triangle found that

4 VCRs were purchased @ $253.00 each	=	$1,012.00
5 VCRs were purchased @ $258.00 each	=	1,290.00
3 VCRs were purchased @ $260.00 each	=	780.00
12 VCRs (ending inventory)		$3,082.00

In this example, the actual cost of each VCR was determined. The total cost of the ending inventory was determined by adding the purchase costs of the 12 VCRs: $3,082.00. With this figure, the cost of merchandise sold can be calculated by subtracting the cost of the ending inventory from the cost of the merchandise available for sale. For example,

Total VCRs available for sale (65 units)	$16,460.00
Less ending inventory (12 units)	− 3,082.00
Cost of merchandise sold (53 units)	$13,378.00

The First In, First Out Costing Method

The **first in, first out method** (fifo) of assigning cost assumes that the first items purchased (first in) were the first sold (first out). When assigning costs to inventory, therefore, the fifo method assumes that the last items purchased are the ones on hand at the end of the fiscal period. For example, think about milk that is stocked by a supermarket. Since milk is perishable, the supermarket puts the milk it purchased first at the front of the shelf. As that milk is sold, later purchases of milk are added at the back of the shelves.

Let's apply the fifo costing method to our VCR example. During the period, 65 VCRs were available for sale.

Beginning inventory	15 units @ $250.00 each =	$ 3,750.00
Purchased August 4	20 units @ $250.00 each =	5,000.00
Purchased December 8	10 units @ $253.00 each =	2,530.00
Purchased February 27	10 units @ $258.00 each =	2,580.00
Purchased May 1	10 units @ $260.00 each =	2,600.00
	65 units	$16,460.00

Under the fifo method, the first items purchased are assumed to be the first items sold. In other words, the 53 VCRs sold are assumed to be the 15 VCRs in the beginning inventory plus the 20 VCRs purchased on August 4, plus the 10 VCRs purchased on December 8, plus 8 of the 10 VCRs purchased on February 27. The items remaining in inventory are the last ones purchased: 2 VCRs purchased on February 27 and 10 VCRs purchased on May 1. The cost of the ending inventory is calculated as follows:

10 units @ $260.00 each =	$2,600.00
2 units @ $258.00 each =	516.00
12 units	$3,116.00

The cost of merchandise sold using the fifo method is as follows:

Total VCRs available for sale (65 units)	$16,460.00
Less ending inventory (12 units)	3,116.00
Cost of merchandise sold (53 units)	$13,344.00

The Last In, First Out Costing Method

The **last in, first out method** (lifo) of assigning inventory cost assumes that the last items purchased (last in) are the first items sold (first out). When the lifo method is used, the business assumes that the first items purchased are still on hand at the end of the fiscal period. The earliest costs, therefore, are the ones used to assign a cost to the inventory.

If the Triangle Video Store uses the lifo method rather than the fifo method of assigning costs to the ending inventory, the value of the ending inventory will be different. Let's return to the VCR example.

Beginning inventory	15 units @ $250.00 each	=	$ 3,750.00
Purchased August 4	20 units @ $250.00 each	=	5,000.00
Purchased December 8	10 units @ $253.00 each	=	2,530.00
Purchased February 27	10 units @ $258.00 each	=	2,580.00
Purchased May 1	10 units @ $260.00 each	=	2,600.00
	65 units		$16,460.00

Using the lifo method, the business would assume that the 12 VCRs remaining in stock are from the beginning inventory of 15 units. The cost of the ending inventory is calculated as follows:

$$12 \text{ units } @ \ \$250.00 \text{ each } = \ \$3,000.00$$

The cost of merchandise sold using the lifo method is as follows:

Total VCRs available for sale (65 units)	$16,460.00
Less ending inventory (12 units)	− 3,000.00
Cost of merchandise sold (53 units)	$13,460.00

Before you learn about the weighted average cost method of assigning costs to ending inventory, do the following activity to check your understanding of the specific identification, lifo, and fifo methods.

Check Your Learning

The following items were purchased by Reid Leather Goods during the month of April:

April 2	36 wallets @ $7.92 each
April 8	24 wallets @ $7.84 each
April 18	18 wallets @ $7.98 each
April 26	30 wallets @ $8.06 each

1. If 46 wallets remain on hand at the end of the accounting period, find the cost of the ending inventory using the specific identification method. Of the 46 wallets in inventory, 12 were purchased on April 2; 20 were purchased on April 8; 3 were purchased on April 18; and 11 were purchased on April 26.
2. Using the ending inventory of 46 wallets, find the cost of the ending inventory using the lifo and the fifo methods.

Compare your answers to those in the answers section. Re-read the preceding part of the chapter to find the correct answers to any questions you may have missed.

The Weighted Average Cost Method

Another method that may be used to assign costs to an inventory is the weighted average cost method. The **weighted average cost method** is a means of calculating cost by adding all the purchases of an item (units and cost) to the beginning inventory (units and cost) of that item. The total cost is then divided by the total units to obtain the average cost per unit. The average cost per unit is used to determine the cost of the ending inventory. Again, we will use the Triangle Video Store example. Purchases were as follows:

Beginning inventory	15 units @ $250.00 each =	$ 3,750.00
Purchased August 4	20 units @ $250.00 each =	5,000.00
Purchased December 8	10 units @ $253.00 each =	2,530.00
Purchased February 27	10 units @ $258.00 each =	2,580.00
Purchased May 1	10 units @ $260.00 each =	2,600.00
	65 units	$16,460.00

To determine the cost of the ending inventory, Triangle needs to know the average cost per VCR. This cost is calculated by dividing the total cost of the VCRs available for sale ($16,460.00) by the total units available for sale (65).

$$\$16,460.00 \div 65 = \$253.23 \text{ (average cost per unit)}$$

The number of items remaining in the ending inventory (12) is multiplied by the average cost per unit ($253.23). The answer is the cost of the ending merchandise inventory.

$$12 \times \$253.23 = \$3,038.76$$

The cost of merchandise sold is again calculated as follows:

Total VCRs available for sale (65 units)	$16,460.00
Less ending inventory (12 units)	− 3,038.76
Cost of merchandise sold (53 units)	$13,421.24

This method is called the weighted average cost method because the average cost per unit is calculated on total units available for sale during the period. The more units purchased at a certain price, the more effect—or weight—that purchase price has on the average. For example, the purchase of 20 VCRs on August 4 has a greater effect than does the purchase of the 10 VCRs on May 1.

Choosing an Inventory Costing Method

A business may use any one of the four methods of assigning costs to ending inventory: specific identification, fifo, lifo, or weighted average cost. Once a company has chosen a method, however, it must use that method consistently. The consistent use of an inventory costing method helps owners and creditors compare financial reports from one period to another. The Internal Revenue Service does allow a business to change methods, but

Quick access to inventory data should produce better management decisions and an advantage over competition.

 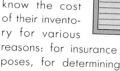
the business must first get permission from the IRS. This restriction helps to ensure that the proper amount of taxes are paid to state and federal governments.

When making a decision about the inventory costing method to use, the owner or manager compares the four methods and selects the one that is likely to be the most beneficial to the company. The owner or manager should also consider both the present economic conditions and the future economic outlook. For example, the present economic condition could be a period of inflation or perhaps a recession. The outlook for the future might be higher prices for new merchandise, caused by inflation or strong demand for that particular type of merchandise. On the other hand, the outlook could be for stable prices, prices that remain the same as at the present time. Business owners and managers must consider all these factors when making decisions that will affect the profitability of the business.

To illustrate what a company may do, let's compare the four methods to see the effect that each would have on the inventory cost reported on financial statements.

Comparing the Four Methods of Determining Inventory Cost

The specific identification method requires that the actual cost be determined for each item remaining in inventory at the end of the fiscal period. This process is normally too time-consuming for all but small businesses that have few items in inventory. For this reason, few businesses use the specific identification method.

The fifo and lifo methods are based on certain assumptions about the items remaining in inventory. Fifo assumes that the items in inventory are the last ones purchased and so assigns a cost to inventory based on the last purchase price of an item. Lifo assumes that the first items purchased are the ones remaining in inventory and assigns a cost based on the first purchase price.

The weighted average cost method takes into account the costs of all the merchandise available for sale during the period. With this method, an average cost per item is determined for each type of merchandise in inventory. The average cost per item is assigned to all items remaining in inventory.

Look at the following table, which compares the gross profit calculated using the four different costing methods. For this illustration, we have assumed that the VCRs were all sold for $320.00 each for total sales of $16,960.00 (53 × $320.00).

	Specific Identification	First In, First Out	Last In, First Out	Weighted Average
Sales	$16,960.00	$16,960.00	$16,960.00	$16,960.00
Less: Cost of merchandise sold	13,378.00	13,344.00	13,460.00	13,421.24
Gross profit	$ 3,582.00	$ 3,616.00	$ 3,500.00	$ 3,538.76

The cost of the ending inventory affects the gross profit for the period, which in turn affects the operating income for the period. As you recall, operating income is calculated by subtracting operating expenses from the gross profit. Businesses pay income taxes on the operating income earned. The inventory costing method used by a business, therefore, can raise or lower its taxes. Businesses generally select the inventory costing method that will result in the lowest income taxes given current and projected future economic conditions.

Reporting Inventory Cost Using the Lower-of-Cost-or-Market Method

Once the cost of the inventory has been calculated, it is reported on the income statement and the balance sheet. When reporting the cost of the ending inventory, a business may value the inventory at the cost calculated by one of the four inventory costing methods or at market value, whichever is lower. **Market value** is the current price that is being charged for similar items of merchandise in the market. Market value is the cost at which the inventory items could be replaced at the time the inventory is taken.

Let's look at an example. Assume that Triangle Video Store determines that the current market value of the 12 VCRs it has in inventory is $248.00 each. Using the market value, the total cost of the VCRs is $2,976.00. Assume also that Triangle determines its inventory cost using the fifo method. Under this method, the cost of the ending inventory was determined as $3,116.00. Following the lower-of-cost-or-market rule, Triangle would report the value of its inventory at $2,976.00.

Cost is usually the most appropriate basis for assigning a value to the inventory, but occasionally an inventory may be valued at less than its cost. For example, some merchandise items may deteriorate or become obsolete.

If the market value of such items is less than the cost, the difference is a loss to the business. In such a case, it is more conservative to report inventory at market value.

Conservatism is one of the fundamental guidelines of accounting. To be conservative is to take the safe route. In reporting the financial position of a business, it is best to present amounts that are least likely to result in an overstatement of income or property values. The lower-of-cost-or-market basis for inventory valuation is thought to be a conservative approach for two reasons: (1) losses, or decreases, in inventory value are recognized when they occur and increases in market value are never recorded; (2) inventory values reported on the balance sheet are never greater, but may be less, than the actual cost of the inventory.

Summary of Key Points

1. It is important for a business to keep accurate inventory records. Information about inventory is needed for inventory control and to help a business present a realistic picture of its financial position on its financial statements.
2. A periodic inventory system requires a physical count of the merchandise still on hand at the end of a fiscal period. Most businesses take a periodic inventory at least once a year.
3. A perpetual inventory system is one in which the business keeps a current record of all merchandise on hand. This system provides continuous merchandise inventory information to management.
4. The specific identification method of costing ending inventory assigns the exact cost to each item still on hand.
5. The first in, first out method (fifo) assumes that the first items purchased were the first items sold. The items still on hand at the end of the fiscal period are assumed to be the last items purchased. Inventory cost is assigned using the cost of the last items purchased.
6. The last in, first out method (lifo) assumes that the last items purchased were the first items sold. The items still on hand at the end of the period are assumed to be the first ones purchased. Inventory cost is assigned using the cost of the first items purchased.
7. The weighted average cost method uses the average cost of all items available for sale during the period to assign a cost to the ending inventory.
8. A company's gross profit on sales and net income are affected by its method of estimating inventory cost.
9. The lower-of-cost-or-market rule for reporting inventory value allows a business to follow a conservative approach in valuing its inventory.

Review and Applications

Building Your Accounting Vocabulary

In your own words, write the definition of each of the following accounting terms. Use complete sentences for your definitions.

conservatism
first in, first out
  method
last in, first out
  method
market value

online
periodic inventory
  system
perpetual inventory
  system

specific identification
  method
weighted average
  cost method

Reviewing Your Accounting Knowledge

1. Why should a company have a control system for its merchandise inventory?
2. What must be determined before the cost of merchandise sold can be calculated?
3. What is the difference between a periodic inventory system and a perpetual inventory system?
4. Why must a periodic inventory be completed at least once a year?
5. Why is it difficult for some businesses to use a perpetual inventory system?
6. What advantage is there in using a perpetual inventory system?
7. Why is the specific identification method the most realistic method for determining inventory cost?
8. What is meant by the phrase "with the fifo method, the inventory is based on the most recent costs"?
9. What does the term "weighted" mean in relation to the weighted average cost method?
10. How does the inventory costing method affect a business's gross profit on sales and net income?
11. What is the lower-of-cost-or-market rule and why is it used?

Improving Your Human Relations Skills

Virginia Lacey and Carl White were assigned the task of taking the annual inventory. One person was to count the items, and the other would write the information on the inventory form. As they were taking the inventory, the following situations occurred. If you were Carl, what would you have done in each situation?

1. As they began work, Virginia said, "I'll do the counting since I don't like to sit and write." Carl doesn't like to sit and write either.
2. Virginia suggested that they estimate some of the inventory items.

Applying Accounting Procedures

Exercise 24-1 Costing Inventory by the Specific Identification Method

The Home and Garden Center made the following purchases of lawn mowers during the year.

March 24	10 mowers @ $93.00 each
April 19	12 mowers @ $94.95 each
May 16	8 mowers @ $96.00 each
June 20	15 mowers @ $97.00 each
July 18	18 mowers @ $98.50 each

Instructions: Calculate the cost of the ending inventory using the specific identification method. Of the 12 mowers on hand, 3 were purchased on April 19, 4 on May 16, 2 on June 20, and 3 on July 18. Use the form provided in the working papers.

Exercise 24-2 Costing Inventory by the Fifo Method

During the first six months of the year, the Linen Loft had the following 60″ round tablecloths available for sale.

Beginning inventory	24 tablecloths @ $7.14 each
Purchased March 1	18 tablecloths @ $7.49 each
Purchased April 10	12 tablecloths @ $7.95 each
Purchased May 12	24 tablecloths @ $8.09 each
Purchased June 6	24 tablecloths @ $8.24 each

Instructions: Calculate the cost of the ending inventory of 29 tablecloths using the fifo method. Use the form provided in the workbook.

Exercise 24-3 Costing Inventory by the Lifo Method

Noble Tire Company had the following beginning inventory and purchases of 22-inch whitewall tires during the year.

Beginning inventory	12 tires @ $19.85 each
Purchased April 18	24 tires @ $21.10 each
Purchased July 6	36 tires @ $22.00 each
Purchased September 14	18 tires @ $22.25 each
Purchased November 28	18 tires @ $24.00 each

Instructions: Calculate the cost of the ending inventory of 38 tires using the lifo method. Use the form provided in the workbook.

Exercise 24-4 Costing Inventory by the Weighted Average Cost Method

Peterson's Hardware Store began the year with 16 smoke detectors on hand, at a cost of $1.98. During the year, the business made the following purchases of smoke detectors.

January 9	48 smoke detectors @ $2.25 each
April 4	60 smoke detectors @ $2.45 each
June 30	24 smoke detectors @ $2.69 each
September 15	36 smoke detectors @ $2.62 each
December 20	72 smoke detectors @ $2.66 each

Instructions: Calculate the cost of the ending inventory of 27 smoke detectors using the weighted average cost method. Use the form provided in the workbook.

Problem 24-1   Calculating the Cost of Ending Inventory

The Morehouse Film Shop sells inexpensive cameras. On January 2, the beginning inventory was 80 cameras. The total cost of the 80 cameras was $1,426.40. During the fiscal period, the shop bought additional cameras. The costs of the cameras available for sale during the period are as follows.

Beginning inventory	80 units @ $17.83 each	=	$1,426.40
Purchased January 3	10 units @ $17.95 each	=	179.50
Purchased March 15	25 units @ $18.15 each	=	453.75
Purchased July 27	20 units @ $18.25 each	=	365.00
Purchased September 27	15 units @ $18.30 each	=	274.50
Purchased November 29	20 units @ $18.33 each	=	366.60
	170		$3,065.75

At the end of the fiscal year, there were 32 cameras remaining in the ending inventory.

Instructions:

(1) Assign a cost to the ending inventory using the specific identification method. Of the 32 cameras on hand, 9 were purchased on July 27, 8 were purchased on September 27, and 15 were purchased on November 29.

(2) Assign a cost to the ending inventory using the fifo, lifo, and weighted average cost methods.

Problem 24-2   Calculating the Cost of Merchandise Sold

Use the inventory information of the Morehouse Film Shop in Problem 24-1 to complete this problem.

Instructions: Determine the cost of merchandise sold under each of the four costing methods. Use the form provided in the working papers accompanying this textbook.

Problem 24-3   Completing an Inventory Sheet

Tom's Bike Shop assigns a value to its inventory using the lower-of-cost-or-market rule. A partial inventory record is shown below. The first line of the inventory record has been completed as an example. The complete inventory record is included in the working papers accompanying this textbook.

			INVENTORY RECORD			
ITEM NO.	ITEM	ENDING INVENTORY	COST PER UNIT	CURRENT MARKET VALUE	PRICE TO BE USED	TOTAL COST
1	2	3	4	5	6	7
0247	Tubes 24"	24	2.67	2.83	2.67	64.08
0391	Tubes 25"	36	2.80	2.74		

Instructions: Complete the inventory record. To do so,

(1) Select the lower-of-cost-or-market value. Enter that amount in Column 6.

(2) Calculate the total cost of each item by multiplying the total number of each item in inventory (from Column 3) by the amount entered in Column 6.

(3) Add all the amounts in Column 7 to determine the total cost of the ending inventory.

SPREADSHEET

PROBLEM

Problem 24-4   Calculating Gross Profit on Sales

Using the four inventory costing methods, Matt Lake summarized the cost of his bookstore's ending inventory as follows.

Specific Identification	First In, First Out	Last In, First Out	Weighted Average Cost
$1,476.00	$1,581.40	$1,410.93	$1,447.36

Matt's Bookstore also reported the following amounts.

Net Sales	$2,674.92
Beginning Inventory	2,246.80
Net Purchases	374.51

Instructions: Using the above information, determine the cost of merchandise sold and the gross profit on sales using each of the four inventory costing methods.

Problem 24-5   Reporting Ending Inventory on the Income Statement

Jen's Card Shop uses a fiscal year beginning January 1. At the beginning of the fiscal period, the shop had a beginning inventory of cards valued at $2,700.00 (6,000 cards @ 45¢ each). During the year, the business made the following purchases.

January 20	700 cards @ 47¢ each	=	$ 329.00
March 5	2,500 cards @ 45¢ each	=	1,125.00
April 23	2,000 cards @ 48¢ each	=	960.00
August 14	1,500 cards @ 47¢ each	=	705.00
October 3	1,200 cards @ 50¢ each	=	600.00
November 17	3,500 cards @ 52¢ each	=	1,820.00
Total Purchases	11,400		$5,539.00

During the year, the cards were sold for 95¢ each. There were 4,525 cards in inventory at the end of the period.

Instructions:

(1) Calculate the cost of the ending inventory using the fifo, lifo, and weighted average cost methods.

(2) Using the costs obtained in Step 1, determine the cost of merchandise sold for each method.

(3) Prepare a partial income statement for each method showing sales and the calculation of gross profit on sales. Assume that the sales and purchases amounts are net amounts.

Problem 24-6   Reporting Ending Inventory
on the Income Statement

The Spoke and Wheel Bicycle Shop started its fiscal year on January 1 with the following inventory of bicycles.

Stock No.	Description	Units on Hand	Unit Cost	Selling Price
2-3780	28″ bicycle	6	$188.00	$399.00
3-412X	26″ bicycle	11	159.00	325.00
3-406Y	24″ bicycle	7	136.00	299.00

During the fiscal period, the Spoke and Wheel Bicycle Shop made the following purchases.

March 9	10	28″ bicycles @ $194.00 each
	5	24″ bicycles @ $139.00 each
June 24	10	26″ bicycles @ $165.00 each
November 6	12	28″ bicycles @ $199.00 each
	12	26″ bicycles @ $168.00 each

The inventory for the fiscal period ended December 31 showed the following items in stock.

8	28″ bicycles
9	26″ bicycles
6	24″ bicycles

Instructions:

(1) Calculate the total cost of merchandise available for sale for each size of bicycle. To calculate this cost, first determine the cost of the beginning inventory for each bicycle size. Then add the cost of purchases for the period. As an example, the calculation on the cost of the 28″ bicycles available for sale is shown below.

Beginning inventory	6	28″ bicycles @ $188.00 each	=	$1,128.00
Purchased March 9	10	28″ bicycles @ $194.00 each	=	1,940.00
Purchased November 6	12	28″ bicycles @ $199.00 each	=	2,388.00
	28	28″ bicycles		$5,456.00

Do the same type of calculation on the cost of merchandise available for sale for the 26″ and the 24″ bicycles.

(2) Using the lifo method, assign a cost to the ending inventory for each size of bicycle.

(3) Calculate the cost of merchandise sold for each bicycle size. Total the costs for the three sizes of bicycles.

(4) Prepare a partial income statement showing sales and the calculation of the gross profit on sales.

CHALLENGE   **Problem 24-7   Calculating Cost of Merchandise Sold**
and Gross Profit on Sales

Lisa Moore owns and operates Encore Audio Center. The store started its fiscal period on May 1 with the following inventory of phone answering

PROBLEM   machines.

Stock No.	Brand	Units on Hand	Unit Cost
3845	Lenox	4	$57.00
4931	Lancaster	6	65.00
9265	Paterson	3	48.00
4850	McMahon	5	72.00

The transactions that follow took place during May.

The Encore Audio Center uses the fifo method to calculate the value of its merchandise inventory. The May 31 inventory indicated that the following machines were still on hand:

#3845	4 machines	#9265	7 machines
#4931	5 machines	#4850	3 machines

Although the purchase price of the answering machines varied, the selling price remained the same throughout May. The selling prices are as follows:

#3845	$89.00	#9265	$72.00
#4931	$93.00	#4850	$99.00

Instructions:

(1) Determine how many units of each of the four answering machines were sold during May.

(2) Calculate the gross profit on sales for each type of answering machine using the chart provided in the working papers.

Transactions:

May 2   Purchased 10 #4931 machines at $66.00 each.
     4   Bought 5 units of #4850 machines for $75.00 a unit.
     9   Purchased 6 machines, stock no. 3845, for $58.00 per unit plus a $12.00 transportation charge.
    14   Purchased 5 #9265 machines at a cost of $50.00 each.
    17   Purchased 8 machines at $67.00 per unit, stock no. 4931.
    19   Purchased 4 #3845 machines at $59.00 per unit plus transportation charges of $8.00.
    22   Returned 2 of the machines that had been purchased on May 17 for full credit.
    27   Bought 8 machines, stock number 9265, at a cost of $52.00 per unit.
    29   Purchased 4 #4931 machines at a cost of $68.00 each.
    30   Returned 2 of the machines purchased on May 4 for full credit.

*H*ome Is Where the Office Is

The alarm jolts Meg out of a sound sleep at 5:30 a.m. She rolls out of bed, heads for the shower, dresses, gulps down breakfast, races for the car, makes her way to the highway, and then drives 28 miles in bumper-to-bumper traffic to the office. When she finally arrives, there are 12 phone messages stuck to her phone. The staff meeting is already underway. Back at home, Meg's husband, Jim, is already at work—and he hasn't left the house. He slept until 7:00, jogged three miles, had a hearty breakfast, skimmed *The Wall Street Journal*, and made five phone calls. Then he hooked up a modem to his personal computer and started work.

Jim is a "telecommuter," one of a new breed of home-based workers. Advances in computer technology have enabled workers to use home computers and modems to receive and deliver information and assignments via telephone lines. Within the last ten years, home offices have grown over 50%. The Department of Labor predicts that half of the American work force will be doing the same in the next 10 to 15 years.

The likely candidates for telecommuting are people who do not require much space or staff, such as tax and financial consultants and freelance designers, reporters, or writers. The at-home worker may also be a parent who wants to stay home to care for children.

What are the benefits? With fewer meetings and memos, telecommuters experience a lower stress level, greater productivity, and improved creativity. If they are self-employed, overhead and operating costs are usually lower. Telecommuters also have more control over their lives and greater flexibility.

There are also disadvantages. At-home workers

Advances in technology have enabled millions of Americans to work at home.

often need to "escape" for relaxation and lack peer interaction. If they are self-employed, their insurance costs are higher while their pay may be less.

What's best: an office in the home or outside the home? It depends on the quality of life that a worker strives for and what he or she is willing to sacrifice for it. Waiting for the bus in a Monday morning rainstorm could make working at home sound awfully sweet!

ACCOUNTING FOR NOTES PAYABLE AND RECEIVABLE

When businesses buy on credit, current liabilities called accounts payable are created. When businesses sell on credit to charge customers, current assets called accounts receivable are created. Credit is granted on the assumption that the debt will be paid in the near future. That is, payment is expected within 30 to 60 days. These debts exist in the form of open accounts, which represent a general agreement to pay.

In this chapter, you will learn how to record formal loan agreements—both payable and receivable—in the accounting records of a business.

Learning Objectives

When you have completed Chapter 25, you should be able to do the following:

1. Explain how promissory notes are used by businesses.
2. Determine the due date, interest expense, and maturity value of a promissory note.
3. Explain the difference between interest-bearing and non-interest-bearing notes.
4. Record journal entries for notes payable and notes receivable.
5. Define the accounting terms introduced in this chapter.

New Terms

promissory note
issue date
term
payee
principal
face value
interest
interest rate
maturity date
maker
maturity value
note payable
interest-bearing note payable
non-interest-bearing note payable
bank discount
proceeds
other expense
note receivable
other revenue

Promissory Notes

A **promissory note** is a written promise to pay a certain amount of money at a specific time. "Promissory note" is often shortened to simply the word "note." Promissory notes are formal documents that are evidence of credit granted or received. For example, a business may ask for a promissory note from a customer who wants more time to pay an account receivable. A business may issue a promissory note to obtain a loan from a bank.

To be upheld in a court of law, a promissory note must contain certain information. That information is shown in Figure 25-1.

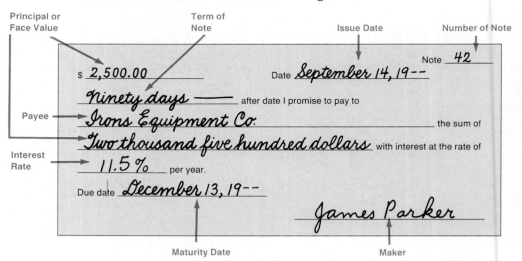

Figure 25-1
Promissory Note

The date on which a note is written is called its **issue date.** The **term** of the note is the amount of time the borrower has to repay the note, such as 90 days. The **payee** is the person or business to whom the note is payable. The **principal** of the note is the amount being borrowed. The **face value** is the amount written on the "face" of the note. The principal and the face value are usually, but not always, the same.

Interest is the fee charged for the use of money. The **interest rate** is the amount of interest to be charged stated as a percentage of the principal. The **maturity date** is the due date of the note, that is, the date on which the note must be paid. The **maker** of the note is the person or business promising to repay the principal and interest.

Determining the Maturity Date of a Note

When a note is signed, the maker agrees to repay the note within a certain period of time, usually expressed in days or months. This period of time is the term of the note. Both the term and the issue date are needed to determine the maturity date of a note.

Let's use the promissory note in Figure 25-1 as our example. In signing this note, James Parker agreed to pay Irons Equipment Co. the principal plus interest 90 days from September 14. To determine the maturity date,

1. Determine the number of days left in the month in which the note is issued. No interest is charged for the issue date, so subtract the date of the

30	September
−14	Issue date
16	Days left in September
90	Days in term
−16	Days in September
74	
74	
−31	Days in October
43	
43	
−30	Days in November
13	

note from the number of days in the month. In our example, you would subtract 14 from 30 days, leaving 16 days in September.

Remember that January, March, May, July, August, October, and December have 31 days; February has 28 days (29 days in a leap year); and April, June, September, and November have 30 days.

2. Determine the number of days the note has left after the first month. To do this, subtract the days calculated in Step 1 from the term of the note.

3. Subtract the number of days in the next month (October) from the number of days left after Step 2. In our example, the 31 days in October are subtracted from 74.

4. Subtract the number of days in the third month (November) from the days left after Step 3. The 30 days in November are subtracted from 43.

5. Since there are 13 days left after subtracting the 30 days in November, the due date will be 13 days into the next month. In other words, the due date for this particular note is December 13.

Businesses and banks use time calendars to calculate the maturity date of a note. An example of a time calendar is shown in Figure 25-2. The time calendar has two sets of days: (1) the day of the month (left and right sides), and (2) the day of the year by month.

Day of month	Jan.	Feb.	Mar.	Apr.	May	June	July	Aug.	Sept.	Oct.	Nov.	Dec.	Day of month
1	1	32	60	91	121	152	182	213	244	274	305	335	1
2	2	33	61	92	122	153	183	214	245	275	306	336	2
3	3	34	62	93	123	154	184	215	246	276	307	337	3
4	4	35	63	94	124	155	185	216	247	277	308	338	4
5	5	36	64	95	125	156	186	217	248	278	309	339	5
6	6	37	65	96	126	157	187	218	249	279	310	340	6
7	7	38	66	97	127	158	188	219	250	280	311	341	7
8	8	39	67	98	128	159	189	220	251	281	312	342	8
9	9	40	68	99	129	160	190	221	252	282	313	343	9
10	10	41	69	100	130	161	191	222	253	283	314	344	10
11	11	42	70	101	131	162	192	223	254	284	315	345	11
12	12	43	71	102	132	163	193	224	255	285	316	346	12
13	13	44	72	103	133	164	194	225	256	286	317	347	13
14	14	45	73	104	134	165	195	226	257	287	318	348	14
15	15	46	74	105	135	166	196	227	258	288	319	349	15
16	16	47	75	106	136	167	197	228	259	289	320	350	16
17	17	48	76	107	137	168	198	229	260	290	321	351	17
18	18	49	77	108	138	169	199	230	261	291	322	352	18
19	19	50	78	109	139	170	200	231	262	292	323	353	19
20	20	51	79	110	140	171	201	232	263	293	324	354	20
21	21	52	80	111	141	172	202	233	264	294	325	355	21
22	22	53	81	112	142	173	203	234	265	295	326	356	22
23	23	54	82	113	143	174	204	235	266	296	327	357	23
24	24	55	83	114	144	175	205	236	267	297	328	358	24
25	25	56	84	115	145	176	206	237	268	298	329	359	25
26	26	57	85	116	146	177	207	238	269	299	330	360	26
27	27	58	86	117	147	178	208	239	270	300	331	361	27
28	28	59	87	118	148	179	209	240	271	301	332	362	28
29	29	...	88	119	149	180	210	241	272	302	333	363	29
30	30	...	89	120	150	181	211	242	273	303	334	364	30
31	31	...	90	...	151	...	212	243	...	304	...	365	31

NOTE: For leap years, after February 28, the number of the day is one greater than that given in the table.

Figure 25-2
Time Calendar

CHAPTER 25 Accounting for Notes Payable and Receivable

To calculate a maturity date using the time calendar, follow these steps:

1. Locate the issue day of the note (for example, 14) in the Day of Month column. Move across the day of the year columns until you come to the issue month (September). In our example, September 14 is the 257th day of the year.

257
+90
347

2. Add the number of days in the term of the note (90) to the day of the year. The sum of the two numbers is 347.
3. Find the number 347 in the day of the year columns. The date for the 347th day of the year is the due date of the note, or December 13.

Before reading further, do the following activity to check your understanding of how to calculate the maturity date of a note.

Check Your Learning

Find the maturity date for each of the following notes. Use the manual method first and check your answer by the time calendar method.

	Issue Date	Term
1.	August 18	60 days
2.	October 3	90 days
3.	July 21	120 days
4.	January 14	60 days (leap year)
5.	September 9	120 days
6.	December 19	180 days

Compare your answers to those in the answers section. Re-read the preceding part of the chapter to find the correct answers to any questions you may have missed.

Calculating Interest on a Note

The interest on a promissory note is based on three factors: the principal, the interest rate, and the term of the note. The equation that is used to compute interest is

$$\text{Interest} = \text{Principal} \times \text{Interest Rate} \times \text{Time} \qquad (I = PRT)$$

Interest rates are usually stated on an annual basis; that is, they are usually based on a borrowing period of one year. To find the interest on a promissory note for one year, multiply the principal by the interest rate. For example, the interest on an 11.5%, $2,500 promissory note for one year is $287.50 ($2,500.00 × .115 = $287.50).

If the term of a promissory note is less than a year, the time used in the calculations must be expressed as a fraction of one year. The fraction may be stated in days or months. For example, on September 14, James Parker signed a note for $2,500 at 11.5% interest for 90 days. Since the term of the note is expressed in days, 365 days are used as the denominator of the time fraction. The interest is calculated as follows:

UNIT 5   Accounting for Special Procedures

Principal	×	Interest Rate	×	Time	=	Interest
$2,500.00	×	.115	×	$\frac{90}{365}$	=	$70.89

$2,500.00 Principal
+   70.89 Interest
$2,570.89 Maturity value

The interest on the note shown in Figure 25-1 is $70.89. On the maturity date, James Parker must repay the maturity value of the note. **Maturity value** is the principal plus the interest. In our example, the maturity value is $2,570.89.

If the term of this note had been three months instead of 90 days, the denominator of the time fraction would be 12. The interest would be calculated as follows:

Principal	×	Interest Rate	×	Time	=	Interest
$2,500.00	×	.115	×	$\frac{3}{12}$	=	$71.88

R E M E M B E R

Interest rates are based on a borrowing period of one year. To calculate interest on a note signed for a shorter time period, express the term of the note as a fraction of one year.

Calculating Interest Using an Interest Table

To calculate interest, businesses and banks often use an interest table similar to the one shown in Figure 25-3.

To calculate interest using an interest table, first find the term of the note in the Day column. We will use James Parker's note again for this example. The term of that note is 90 days. Next, follow the row across until you reach the column for the interest rate (11.5%). As you can see, the factor where the two meet is 2.835616.

The interest table is for interest on $100.00. The amount of the principal ($2,500.00) must, therefore, be divided by $100.00. Multiply this number (25) by the factor of 2.835616 to find the total interest. The interest calculated using the interest table is also $70.89. Factors in an interest table are rounded

SIMPLE INTEREST ON $100, 365 DAY BASIS

DAY	11.50 % INTEREST	DAY	11.75 % INTEREST	DAY	12.00 % INTEREST	DAY	12.25 % INTEREST	DAY	12.50 % INTEREST	DAY	12.75 % INTEREST
30	0.945205	30	0.965753	30	0.986301	30	1.006849	30	1.027397	30	1.047945
60	1.890411	60	1.931507	60	1.972603	60	2.013699	60	2.054795	60	2.095890
90	2.835616	90	2.897260	90	2.958904	90	3.020548	90	3.082192	90	3.143836
120	3.780822	120	3.863014	120	3.945205	120	4.027397	120	4.109589	120	4.191781
150	4.726027	150	4.828767	150	4.931507	150	5.034247	150	5.136986	150	5.239726
180	5.671233	180	5.794521	180	5.917808	180	6.041096	180	6.164384	180	6.287671
210	6.616438	210	6.760274	210	6.904110	210	7.047945	210	7.191781	210	7.335616
240	7.561644	240	7.726027	240	7.890411	240	8.054795	240	8.219178	240	8.383562
270	8.506849	270	8.691781	270	8.876712	270	9.061644	270	9.246575	270	9.431507
300	9.452055	300	9.657534	300	9.863014	300	10.068493	300	10.273973	300	10.479452
330	10.397260	330	10.623288	330	10.849315	330	11.075342	330	11.301370	330	11.527397
360	11.342466	360	11.589041	360	11.835616	360	12.082192	360	12.328767	360	12.575342
365	11.500000	365	11.750000	365	12.000000	365	12.250000	365	12.500000	365	12.750000
366	11.531507	366	11.782192	366	12.032877	366	12.283562	366	12.534247	366	12.784932

Figure 25-3 Interest Table

Businesses often issue notes when borrowing money from banks to cover short-term cash needs.

off so there may be a few cents difference from the interest calculated manually.

Using the Computer To Calculate Interest

A computer is often used to calculate the interest and maturity value of a note. With a computer program that is designed to calculate interest, a business simply enters the principal, interest rate, and term of the note. The computer calculates the interest and the maturity value. The use of a computer saves much time for businesses that issue or receive many notes.

Now that you know how to determine the maturity value of a promissory note, let's look at how businesses use such notes.

Now complete the following activity to check your understanding of how to calculate interest.

Check Your Learning

Find the interest and the maturity values for each of the following notes. First find the interest manually and then use the interest table to check your answer.

	Principal	Interest Rate	Term
1.	$ 4,000.00	11.5%	60 days
2.	10,000.00	11.75%	90 days
3.	6,500.00	12.75%	60 days
4.	900.00	12.25%	120 days
5.	2,400.00	12%	180 days

Compare your answers to those in the answers section. Re-read the preceding part of the chapter to find the correct answers to any questions you may have missed.

Notes Payable

A **note payable** is a promissory note issued to a creditor. A note payable may also be issued by a business to borrow money from a bank. A note payable is a liability of the business issuing the note. Notes issued by a business, therefore, are summarized in the Notes Payable account. Notes Payable is a liability account and has a normal credit balance.

Two types of notes that are frequently issued by businesses are interest-bearing notes payable and non-interest-bearing notes payable.

Interest-Bearing Notes Payable

A note that requires that the face value plus interest be paid on the maturity date is called an **interest-bearing note payable.** On an interest-bearing note, the face value and the principal are the same. The note we used in earlier examples (issued by James Parker) is an interest-bearing note. Its maturity value is $2,570.89 ($2,500.00 face value plus interest of $70.89).

Now let's look at how an interest-bearing note payable is recorded in a business's accounting records.

▲ Recording the Issuance of an Interest-Bearing Note Payable
On April 3, the Eastwick Office Equipment Co. had the following transaction.

April 3: Borrowed $7,000.00 from the State Street Bank and issued a 90-day, 12% note payable to the bank, Note 6.

The accounts affected by this transaction are Cash in Bank and Notes Payable. In this transaction, Cash in Bank is debited for $7,000.00 because the money borrowed from the bank is increasing the business's cash. Notes Payable is credited for $7,000.00 because the transaction increases the business's liability.

Cash in Bank			Notes Payable	
Dr.	Cr.		Dr.	Cr.
+	−		−	+
$7,000.00				$7,000.00

This transaction is recorded in Eastwick's cash receipts journal as shown in Figure 25-4. The interest on the note is not recorded until it is actually paid on the maturity date.

	DATE	DOC. NO.	ACCOUNT TITLE	POST. REF.	GENERAL DEBIT	GENERAL CREDIT	SALES CREDIT	SALES TAX PAYABLE CREDIT	ACCOUNTS RECEIVABLE CREDIT	CASH IN BANK DEBIT	
1	19-- Apr. 3	N6	Notes Payable			7 000 00				7 000 00	1

CASH RECEIPTS JOURNAL   PAGE 16

Figure 25-4   Recording the Issuance of an Interest-Bearing Note Payable

▲ Recording the Issuance of an Interest-Bearing Note Payable
On April 3, the Eastwick Office Equipment Co. had the following transaction:

July 2: Eastwick Office Equipment Co. issued Check 892 for $7,207.12 payable to State Street Bank in payment of the note payable issued April 3.

The check that is prepared to repay the bank loan is written for the maturity value of the note (principal plus interest). Using the interest equation, the interest on Eastwick's note is calculated as follows:

$7,000.00 Principal
+ 207.12 Interest
$7,207.12 Maturity value

Principal	×	Interest Rate	×	Time	=	Interest
$7,000.00	×	.12	×	$\frac{90}{365}$	=	$207.12

The maturity value of the note is found by adding the interest to the principal. In this case, the maturity value is $7,207.12.

The payment of the note is recorded in the accounting records to show the decrease in the company's liability. Notes Payable is debited for $7,000.00, reducing its balance to zero. The interest charged by the bank for the use of the money is now recognized as an expense. Interest Expense is debited for $207.12. Cash in Bank is credited for $7,207.12, the total amount being paid.

Notes Payable		Interest Expense		Cash in Bank	
Dr.	Cr.	Dr.	Cr.	Dr.	Cr.
–	+	+	–	+	–
$7,000.00	Bal. $7,000.00	$207.12			$7,207.12

The entry made in the cash payments journal to record this transaction is shown in Figure 25-5.

					GENERAL		ACCOUNTS PAYABLE	PURCHASES DISCOUNTS	CASH IN BANK	
	DATE	DOC. NO.	ACCOUNT TITLE	POST. REF.	DEBIT	CREDIT	DEBIT	CREDIT	CREDIT	
1	July 2	CK892	Notes Payable		7 000 00				7 207 12	1
2			Interest Expense		207 12					2

CASH PAYMENTS JOURNAL — PAGE 19

Figure 25-5 Recording the Payment of an Interest-Bearing Note Payable

Before reading further, do the following activity to check your understanding of notes payable.

Check Your Learning

Use a sheet of notebook paper to answer these questions.

1. On June 12, Frank's Lobster Pound issued a $9,000.00, 120-day, 12% note payable to the American Bank of Commerce.
   a. What is the title of the account debited? For what amount?
   b. What is the title of the account credited? For what amount?
   c. What is the classification of each account?
   d. What is the maturity value of the note?
2. On October 10, Brighton Tree Service issued Check 498 in payment of a $12,500.00, 90-day, 12.25% note payable.
   a. What is the maturity date of the note?
   b. What is the face value of the note? The maturity value?
   c. To record this transaction, which accounts are debited and credited? For what amounts?

Compare your answers to those in the answers section. Re-read the preceding section of the chapter to find the answers to any questions you may have missed.

Non-Interest-Bearing Notes Payable

Sometimes a bank requires a borrower to pay the interest on a note payable in advance. The bank deducts the interest charge from the face value of the note, in effect "discounting" the amount of money received by the borrower on the issue date. A note from which the interest has been deducted in advance is called a **non-interest-bearing note payable.** The note is referred to as "non-interest-bearing" because there is no interest rate stated on the note itself. The interest deducted in advance is called the **bank discount.** The cash actually received by the borrower is called the **proceeds.** The proceeds equal the face value minus the bank discount.

Since interest on a non-interest-bearing note payable is deducted at the time the money is borrowed, the maturity value of the note is the same as the face value amount. An example of a non-interest-bearing note payable is shown in Figure 25-6.

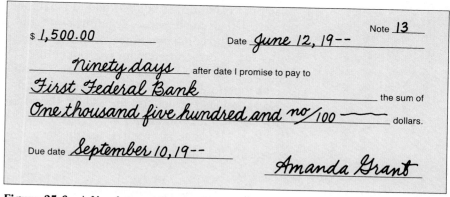

$ 1,500.00   Date June 12, 19--   Note 13

_____Ninety days_____ after date I promise to pay to
First Federal Bank _____ the sum of
One thousand five hundred and no/100 ————— dollars.

Due date September 10, 19--
                                                    Amanda Grant

Figure 25-6   A Non-Interest-Bearing Note Payable

Let's look at how the proceeds of a non-interest-bearing note payable are calculated. The note shown in Figure 25-6 is the source document for the following transaction.

June 12: Amanda Grant, owner of Amanda's Shoes, signed a $1,500.00, 90-day non-interest-bearing note payable that the First Federal Bank discounted at a rate of 12%, Note 13.

The first step is to calculate the bank discount, which is the interest on the note. The bank discount is calculated the same way as the interest on an interest-bearing note. The face value of the note ($1,500.00) is multiplied by the discount rate (12%) and by the term (90 days). As you recall, the term is always expressed in years or as a fraction of a year.

Face Value	×	Discount Rate (Interest Rate)	×	Time	=	Bank Discount
$1,500.00	×	.12	×	$\frac{90}{365}$	=	$44.38

$1,500.00	Face value
− 44.38	Bank discount
$1,455.62	Proceeds

The amount of the bank discount is subtracted from the face value of the note to determine the proceeds. The proceeds, the amount Amanda Grant actually receives, are $1,455.62.

▲ Recording the Issuance of a Non-Interest-Bearing Note

Payable The T accounts that follow show the three accounts affected by this transaction: Cash in Bank, Discount on Notes Payable, and Notes Payable. In this transaction, Cash in Bank is debited for $1,455.62, the proceeds of the note—or the amount of cash actually received.

The face value of a non-interest-bearing note includes two amounts: (1) the amount actually borrowed ($1,455.62) and (2) the future interest charge ($44.38). The future interest charge (the bank discount) has already been paid and is not a liability at the time the note is issued. The bank discount amount cannot then be recorded in a liability account. The $44.38 could be recorded in an expense account, since the bank discount is an interest charge. The company, however, has not yet incurred the expense. Instead, the $44.38 is recorded in an account entitled Discount on Notes Payable. The Discount on Notes Payable account is classified as a contra liability account and therefore has a normal debit balance. In this transaction, Discount on Notes Payable is debited for $44.38, the future interest charge included in the face value of the note.

Notes Payable is credited for the face value of the note, $1,500.00, increasing the business's liability.

Cash in Bank		Discount on Notes Payable		Notes Payable	
Dr.	Cr.	Dr.	Cr.	Dr.	Cr.
+	−	+	−	−	+
$1,455.62		$44.38			$1,500.00

This entry is recorded in the cash receipts journal, as shown in Figure 25-7.

	DATE	DOC. NO.	ACCOUNT TITLE	POST. REF.	GENERAL DEBIT	GENERAL CREDIT	SALES CREDIT	SALES TAX PAYABLE CREDIT	ACCOUNTS RECEIVABLE CREDIT	CASH IN BANK DEBIT	
1	June 12	N13	Notes Payable			1500 00				1455 62	1
2			Discount on Notes Pay		44 38						2

CASH RECEIPTS JOURNAL   PAGE 8

Figure 25-7 Recording the Issuance of a Non-Interest-Bearing Note Payable

Discount on Notes Payable would be reported on the balance sheet as a deduction from Notes Payable. If a balance sheet were prepared for Amanda's Shoes on June 30, the accounts would appear as shown in Figure 25-8 at the top of page 557. The $1,455.62 amount represents the book value of notes payable.

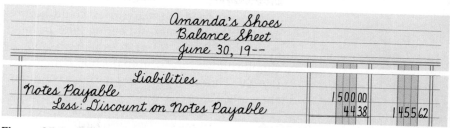

Figure 25-8   Reporting Non-Interest-Bearing Notes Payable on the Balance Sheet

R E M E M B E R

On interest-bearing notes, the face value is equal to the principal, or the amount borrowed. On non-interest-bearing notes, the face value equals the maturity value of the note.

▲ **Recording the Payment of a Non-Interest-Bearing Note Payable**   When the non-interest-bearing note payable is due, Amanda Grant will pay First Federal Bank the face value of the note, which is also the note's maturity value.

September 10: Amanda's Shoes issued Check 1241 for $1,500.00 to the First Federal Bank in payment of the June 12 non-interest-bearing note payable.

As you can see from the T accounts, Notes Payable is debited for $1,500.00 to show the decrease in the liability. Cash in Bank is credited for $1,500.00, the amount of the check written to pay the maturity value of the note. This transaction removes the note payable from the accounting records.

Notes Payable			Cash in Bank	
Dr.	Cr.		Dr.	Cr.
−	+		+	−
$1,500.00	Bal. $1,500.00			$1,500.00

When a non-interest-bearing note payable matures, the amount of the bank discount must be recognized as an expense. It is transferred from the Discount on Notes Payable account to the Interest Expense account. As you can see from the T accounts, Interest Expense is debited for $44.38 and Discount on Notes Payable is credited for $44.38. This transaction shows that the bank discount has now become an expense.

Interest Expense			Discount on Notes Payable	
Dr.	Cr.		Dr.	Cr.
+	−		+	−
$44.38			Bal. $44.38	$44.38

Two separate journal entries could be prepared to record (1) the payment of the non-interest-bearing note payable (in the cash payments journal) and (2) the interest expense (in the general journal). It is much simpler, however, to prepare one compound entry in the cash payments journal. The entry recorded in the accounting records of Amanda's Shoes is shown in Figure 25-9.

CASH PAYMENTS JOURNAL   PAGE 12

DATE	DOC. NO.	ACCOUNT TITLE	POST. REF.	GENERAL DEBIT	GENERAL CREDIT	ACCOUNTS PAYABLE DEBIT	PURCHASES DISCOUNTS CREDIT	CASH IN BANK CREDIT	
19-- Sept. 10	C1241	Notes Payable		1 500 00				1 500 00	1
		Interest Expense		44 38					2
		Discount on Notes Payable			44 38				3

Figure 25-9   Recording the Payment of a Non-Interest-Bearing Note Payable

The Interest Expense account is classified as an other expense account. An **other expense** is a non-operating expense—an expense that does not result from the normal operations of the business. A separate section for other expenses appears on the income statement, as a deduction from operating income.

Before continuing, complete the following activity to check your understanding of non-interest-bearing notes.

Check Your Learning

Use a sheet of notebook paper to answer these questions.

1. On October 14, Canton Car Care Center issued a $10,000.00, 60-day, 12% non-interest-bearing note payable to the Canton National Bank.
   a. Which accounts are debited and credited? For what amounts?
   b. What is the amount of the bank discount? The proceeds?
2. On December 13, Canton Car Care Center issued Check 146 to the Canton National Bank in payment of the $10,000.00 non-interest-bearing note payable issued October 14. One entry is recorded in the business's cash payments journal.
   a. What is the maturity value of this note? The face value?
   b. Which accounts are debited and credited? For what amounts?

Compare your answers to those in the answers section. Re-read the preceding part of the chapter to find the answers to any questions you may have missed.

Notes Receivable

On occasion, a business may grant a customer additional time to pay a debt. The customer may be asked to sign a promissory note. Promissory notes that a business accepts from customers are called **notes receivable.**

Notes Receivable is an asset account and has a normal debit balance. Like a note payable, a note receivable is due on a specific future date and carries an interest charge for the term of the note.

Recording the Receipt of a Note Receivable

On March 1, Eastwick Office Equipment Co. sold $1,750.00 of merchandise on account to Peter Johnson. That transaction was recorded in Eastwick's sales journal. On April 6, Eastwick had the following transaction.

April 6: *Eastwick Office Equipment Co. received a 60-day, 12.5% note from Peter Johnson for $1,750.00 to pay the account receivable, Note 4.*

In this transaction, Eastwick agreed to accept a note receivable in payment of the amount owed by Peter Johnson. When a customer signs a promissory note as payment of an amount owed on an account receivable, the amount owed to the business becomes a note receivable. Notes Receivable is being increased, so that account is debited for $1,750.00. Accounts Receivable is credited for the same amount to decrease its balance. Peter Johnson's account in the accounts receivable subsidiary ledger is also credited for $1,750.00, decreasing the amount he owes as an account receivable.

GENERAL LEDGER

Notes Receivable	
Dr.	Cr.
+	−
$1,750.00	

Accounts Receivable	
Dr.	Cr.
+	−
Bal. $1,750.00	$1,750.00

SUBSIDIARY LEDGER

Peter Johnson	
Dr.	Cr.
+	−
Bal. $1,750.00	$1,750.00

The general journal entry for this transaction is shown in Figure 25-10.

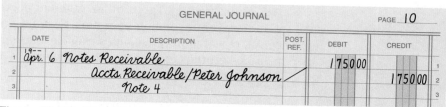

Figure 25-10 Journalizing the Receipt of a Note Receivable

Recording the Receipt of Cash for a Note Receivable

On June 5, Eastwick should receive a check from Peter Johnson in payment of the note accepted on April 6. Since the note is an interest-bearing note, the check should be for the maturity value of the note (principal plus interest). The maturity value is calculated as follows:

Principal	×	Interest Rate	×	Time	=	Interest
$1,750.00	×	.125	×	$\frac{60}{365}$	=	$35.96

$1,750.00 Principal
+   35.96 Interest
$1,785.96 Maturity value

The maturity value is, therefore, $1,785.96.

Notes offer several advantages to businesses: they are legal evidence of a debt, they earn interest, and they can be used as security for a loan.

June 5: *Received a check for $1,785.96 from Peter Johnson in payment of the $1,750.00 note accepted on April 6 plus interest of $35.96, Receipt 496.*

In this transaction, cash is being received so Cash in Bank is debited for $1,785.96. The collection of the note receivable reduces the balance in Notes Receivable. That account is credited for the principal, or face value, of the note, $1,750.00.

The interest received for extending the time for payment on an account receivable is revenue for the payee of the note. The amount received, $35.96, is credited to an other revenue account called Interest Income. **Other revenue** is non-operating revenue—revenue that a business receives or earns from activities outside the normal operations of the business. Like other expenses, other revenue is reported separately on the income statement.

Cash in Bank		Notes Receivable		Interest Income	
Dr.	Cr.	Dr.	Cr.	Dr.	Cr.
+	–	+	–	–	+
$1,785.96		Bal. $1,750.00	$1,750.00		$35.96

The cash receipts journal entry to record the collection of a note receivable is shown in Figure 25-11.

	DATE	DOC. NO.	ACCOUNT TITLE	POST. REF.	GENERAL DEBIT	GENERAL CREDIT	SALES CREDIT	SALES TAX PAYABLE CREDIT	ACCOUNTS RECEIVABLE CREDIT	CASH IN BANK DEBIT	
1	19-- June 5	R496	Notes Receivable			1750 00				1785 96	1
2			Interest Income			35 96					2

Figure 25-11 Journalizing the Collection of a Note Receivable

Before reading further, do the following activity to check your understanding of notes receivable.

Check Your Learning

Use a sheet of notebook paper to answer these questions.

1. On May 30, BioTech Computers accepted a 90-day, 9%, $6,000.00 note receivable from Amy Andrus, a charge customer.
   a. Which accounts are debited and credited? For how much?
   b. Is this an interest-bearing or a non-interest-bearing note?
2. On August 28, BioTech received a check from Amy Andrus in payment of the $6,000.00 note dated May 30.
   a. What was the amount of Amy Andrus's check?
   b. Which accounts are debited and credited? For how much?

Compare your answers to those in the answers section. Re-read the preceding section of the chapter to find the answers to any questions you may have missed.

Summary of Key Points

1. A promissory note is a written promise to pay a certain amount of money at a specific future time.
2. Promissory notes issued by businesses to creditors or to banks to obtain a loan are called notes payable. Notes Payable is a liability account.
3. Interest is the fee charged to the maker of a promissory note for the use of money. Interest is calculated as a percentage of the face value of the note, based on a borrowing period of one year. Borrowing periods of less than one year are expressed as fractions of a year.
4. The equation for calculating interest on a promissory note is $I = PRT$, or Interest = Principal × Rate × Time.
5. Interest on interest-bearing notes is paid on the maturity date of the note. The maturity value of an interest-bearing note equals the face value plus the interest charge.
6. A non-interest-bearing note payable is a note from which the interest has been deducted in advance. The interest deducted from the note's face value in advance is called the bank discount. The amount of cash actually received by the maker after the interest has been deducted is called the proceeds. The maturity value of a non-interest-bearing note payable is the same as its face value.
7. When the issuance of a non-interest-bearing note payable is journalized, the amount of the bank discount is debited to the Discount on Notes Payable account. Discount on Notes Payable is a contra liability account.
8. When a non-interest-bearing note payable is paid, the interest charge is transferred from Discount on Notes Payable to Interest Expense.
9. Promissory notes accepted by businesses from charge customers are called notes receivable. Notes Receivable is an asset account.

Review and Applications

Building Your Accounting Vocabulary

In your own words, write the definition of each of the following accounting terms. Use complete sentences for your definitions.

bank discount	maker	other expense
face value	maturity date	other revenue
interest	maturity value	payee
interest rate	non-interest-bearing	principal
interest-bearing note	note payable	proceeds
payable	note payable	promissory note
issue date	note receivable	term

Reviewing Your Accounting Knowledge

1. Name the two parties to a promissory note.
   a. Which party issues the note?
   b. Which party receives the note?
2. Describe a situation in which a business might (a) receive a promissory note and (b) issue a promissory note.
3. What is the basic equation for the calculation of interest?
4. How is the interest on a note calculated if the term is less than a year?
5. How is the maturity value of an interest-bearing note determined?
6. Name two types of notes a business may issue. What is the major difference between the two?
7. What is the difference between interest and a bank discount?
8. When a non-interest-bearing note payable is issued, how are the proceeds calculated?
9. How is the Discount on Notes Payable account classified? What is its normal balance?
10. Why are Interest Income and Interest Expense reported separately on the income statement?

Improving Your Math Skills

Many businesses today borrow money for capital expansion or to meet operating expenses during periods when earnings are below expectations. The interest formula can be used to calculate the cost of borrowing money. Use the formula to complete the following problems.

1. With an interest rate of 9.5%, what is the cost of borrowing $42,400 for one year?
2. What is the cost of borrowing $20,000 at 13% for one year? for six months?
3. If the amount of interest charged on a one-year, $8,400 loan is $820, what is the interest rate?

4. What is the interest rate on a $22,000 loan costing $990 for six months?

5. What is the amount borrowed when interest is $725, the rate is 10.5%, and the time is six months?

Applying Accounting Procedures

Exercise 25-1 Determining the Maturity Date of Notes

Instructions: Determine the maturity date for each of the following notes.

	Issue Date	Term
1.	November 18	60 days
2.	August 3	90 days
3.	July 22	120 days
4.	February 5	3 months
5.	April 28	9 months

Exercise 25-2 Calculating Interest

Instructions: Calculate the interest charge for each of the following notes.

	Principal	Interest Rate	Term
1.	$ 600	15%	90 days
2.	3,500	12%	60 days
3.	9,600	9%	4 months
4.	2,500	10%	180 days
5.	1,500	11.5%	6 months

Exercise 25-3 Determining the Maturity Value

Instructions: Determine the interest and the maturity value of each of the following notes.

	Principal	Interest Rate	Term
1.	$ 900	9%	80 days
2.	1,200	12%	60 days
3.	3,250	10%	90 days
4.	2,430	15%	2 months
5.	210	8%	3 months

SPREADSHEET

PROBLEM

Exercise 25-4 Calculating the Bank Discount and Proceeds

Instructions: Calculate the amount of the bank discount and the proceeds for each of the following non-interest-bearing notes.

	Face Value	Term	Discount Rate
1.	$ 300	60 days	12%
2.	3,840	90 days	9%
3.	2,100	4 months	11%
4.	5,000	7 months	7%
5.	800	5 months	8%

Problem 25-1 Recording Transactions for Interest-Bearing Notes Payable

Instructions: Record the following transactions in a cash receipts journal and a cash payments journal.

Transactions:

Jan. 14 Borrowed $1,500.00 from the Beaumont Bank by issuing a 90-day, 12% interest-bearing note payable (Note 78).

Apr. 14 Issued Check 1468 for $1,544.38 to the Beaumont Bank in payment of the $1,500.00 note issued on January 14, plus interest of $44.38.

May 31 Borrowed $12,400.00 from the Merchant's Bank and Trust on a 90-day, 12.5% interest-bearing note, Note 79.

Aug. 29 Paid the Merchant's Bank and Trust the maturity value of the note issued on May 31, Check 8842 for $12,782.19.

Problem 25-2 Recording Transactions for Non-Interest-Bearing Notes Payable

Instructions: Record the following transactions in a cash receipts journal and a cash payments journal.

Transactions:

June 10 Borrowed $6,000.00 from Lincoln County National Bank by issuing a 60-day, non-interest-bearing note payable (proceeds, $5,901.37) that the bank discounted at 10% (Note 67).

Aug. 9 Issued Check 74285 for $6,000.00 in payment of the note issued June 10; recorded the interest expense.

30 Borrowed $16,000.00 from Citizen's Bank, issuing a 120-day non-interest-bearing note payable (Note 68), less the 10.5% bank discount of $552.33.

Dec. 28 Issued Check 84298 in payment of the note issued on August 30; recorded the interest expense.

Problem 25-3 Recording Transactions for Notes Receivable

Instructions: Journalize the following transactions.

Transactions:

June 4 Received a 90-day, 8.5%, $1,450.00 note receivable from Bill Jackson for an extension on his account. The note was dated June 2 (Note 461).

Aug. 14 Accepted a 60-day, 9% note receivable for $1,800.00 from Susan Keys for an extension on her account receivable, Note 69 dated August 13.

31 Received a $1,480.39 check from Bill Jackson in payment of the note dated June 2, Receipt 888.

Oct. 12 Received from Susan Keys a check for the maturity value of the note dated August 13, Receipt 984.

Problem 25-4 Recording Notes Payable and Notes Receivable

Instructions: Record the following transactions in a cash receipts journal (page 47), cash payments journal (page 56), and general journal (page 19).

Transactions:

Mar. 19 Borrowed $9,000.00 from the Hornbeck National Bank by issuing a 90-day, 12% interest-bearing note payable, Note 87.

June 4 Received a 120-day, 13% note receivable for $1,900.00 from Lee Hebert as a time extension on his account receivable, Note 6 dated June 1.

17 Paid the Hornbeck National Bank the maturity value of the note issued on March 19, Check 2784.

Sept. 29 Received a check from Lee Hebert for the maturity value of the note dated June 1, Receipt 4428.

Oct. 6 Borrowed $2,700.00 from Jonesboro Bank and Trust, signing a 60-day non-interest-bearing note payable (Note 878), discounted at 11.5%.

Dec. 5 Prepared a check for the note issued on October 6 (Check 2954) and recorded the interest expense.

COMPUTER **Problem 25-5 Recording Notes Payable and Notes Receivable**

The following is a partial list of accounts used by the McMahon Company.

PROBLEM

101	Cash in Bank	205	Discount on Notes Payable
105	Notes Receivable	210	Accounts Payable
110	Accounts Receivable	710	Interest Income
201	Notes Payable	750	Interest Expense

Instructions: Record the following transactions in a cash receipts journal (page 67), cash payments journal (page 73), and general journal (page 27).

Transactions:

May 7 Borrowed $4,000.00 from the Jefferson State Bank by signing a 60-day, 9.5% non-interest-bearing note, Note 284.

15 Issued a $3,000.00, 90-day, 9% interest-bearing note (Note 283) to the Hicks Company in place of the amount owed on account.

21 Received a 120-day, 10% note for $1,200.00 from Jane Sinclair for an extension of time on her account, Note 94 dated May 20.

July 6 Issued Check 4711 in payment of the non-interest-bearing note given to the Jefferson State Bank on May 7.

Aug. 13 Issued Check 5044 for the maturity value of the note issued to the Hicks Company on May 15.

Sept. 17 Received a check from Jane Sinclair for the maturity value of the note dated May 20, Receipt 5921.

CHALLENGE **Problem 25-6 Calculating Current and Future Interest**

Frequently, notes that are issued or received in one fiscal period do not mature until the next fiscal period. As a result, the interest expense paid or the interest income received applies to two different fiscal periods. Listed on
PROBLEM page 566 is the information for ten different notes.

Instructions: For each note,

(1) Determine the maturity date. Assume February has 28 days.

(2) Determine what portion of the interest applies to the current year and what portion of the interest applies to the following year. December 31 is the end of the fiscal period.

Amount	Issue Date	Interest Rate	Term
1. $ 1,100	December 10	9%	30 days
2. 700	November 21	12%	60 days
3. 17,100	October 10	10%	90 days
4. 4,000	December 5	15%	60 days
5. 15,000	November 10	6.5%	120 days
6. 3,000	September 8	7%	180 days
7. 6,600	November 17	10%	70 days
8. 840	October 1	9.5%	6 months
9. 1,200	December 1	10%	3 months
10. 2,700	August 1	8%	9 months

CHALLENGE

PROBLEM

Problem 25-7   Renewing a Note Receivable

Occasionally, a note may be renewed on its maturity date instead of being paid off. When this occurs, the interest on the first note is paid, the first note is canceled, and a new note for the same principal amount is issued—usually at a higher interest rate. The Donne Company had the following transactions.

Instructions: Record the following transactions on general journal page 24.

Transactions:

Mar. 14 Sold merchandise on account to Lynn Reid for $1,800.00, plus sales tax of $90.00, terms 30 days, Sales Slip 688.

Apr. 13 Accepted a 60-day, 9% note for $1,890.00 from Lynn Reid in place of the accounts receivable amount, Note 416.

June 12 Received the interest due from Lynn Reid for the note dated April 13 and agreed to renew the note at 10% for 90 days, Receipt 2444 and Note 417.

Sept. 10 Received a check from Lynn Reid for the maturity value of the note issued June 12, Receipt 3555.

Computer Graphics

Without the help of models or trick photography, computers can create three-dimensional images that are shaded and can move. The most famous of these computer-generated special effects are those seen in movies such as *Star Wars* and *Terminator 3*. Moviemakers, however, aren't the only ones using computer graphics.

The business manager captures management's attention by using computer-generated charts and graphs to emphasize critical spreadsheet data. With an integrated business software program, colorful graphs and charts are created in minutes.

By manipulating stored data on the computer, the cartographer, a map maker, creates numerous configurations with awesome speed and accuracy.

Using state-of-the-art computer-aided design (CAD) software, the architect sits at the keyboard instead of the drawing board to create renderings of design concepts.

Before trying them out on an actual machine, the industrial engineer works at a computer to create simulated sequences of his company's spot-welding operations. The process is quick and reliable.

The salesperson needs to highlight a product feature for an important sales presentation the next day. With the help of her new presentation software, a microcomputer, and laser printer, she creates an impressive overhead visual in less than an hour. Her startled competition has no time to respond. She closes the sale.

You've all seen video games, which use animated computer graphics. More sophisticated graphics programs are now used to create simulations that help train pilots and astronauts, test new engineering designs, develop new drugs or chemicals to fight disease, or "see" the area around a black hole.

The computer gives this architect the opportunity to try out many designs before committing the ideas to costly and time-consuming models.

Thanks to the advent of computer graphics, presentations and reports are more persuasive; spreadsheets are clear and memorable; and designs are created with greater accuracy, in less time, and for less money.

Computer graphics has enabled skilled professionals to spend more time on creative tasks, less on tedious ones. Everybody wins!

UNIT 6

ACCOUNTING FOR OTHER FORMS OF BUSINESS ORGANIZATION

In this last unit of the textbook, you will learn how accounting for a partnership differs from accounting for a sole proprietorship or a corporation. You will also learn about accounting for a publicly held corporation. Publicly held corporations publish their operating results in annual reports. These reports are studied and analyzed by many people, both inside and outside the corporation. People who own stock in the corporation study annual reports to analyze how well the corporation is operating. Other people may be interested in purchasing stock and want to determine whether the stock is a good investment.

Wen

OLD FA

HAMB

31

BASKIN-ROBB

ICE CRE

POPEY

FAMOUS FR

CHICKE

& BISCUI

Featuring GH

HO

APPLE D

1

DRIVE-UP WIND

LUNCH CHICKEN S D

SM FRI N DRINK 9

2 TACO SM DRINK 4

SKIPPER'S

u.s. army   u.s. marine orps

ARMED FORCES
RECRUITING STAT ON

u.s. navy   u.s. a force

mi it-lube

NO
APPOINTME
NECESSARY

TAKE OUT
CALL 4673781

Wendy's

→

PICK UP
WINDO

Chapter  26

ACCOUNTING FOR PARTNERSHIPS

The accounting procedures that you have learned up to now have been applied to businesses organized as sole proprietorships or as closely held corporations. Most of these procedures can also be applied to businesses organized as partnerships. For example, the purchase of supplies for cash is handled in the same manner by all forms of business organizations.

You'll remember, however, that transactions involving ownership equity for a sole proprietorship and a closely held corporation were handled differently. There are also differences in accounting for the ownership equity of a partnership.

In this chapter, you will examine briefly some of the characteristics of a partnership. You will learn the procedures involved in accounting for partners' equity and in dividing the net income or loss among the partners.

Learning Objectives

When you have completed Chapter 26, you should be able to do the following:

1. List the major characteristics, advantages, and disadvantages of the partnership form of business organization.
2. Journalize transactions involving partners' equity for a partnership.
3. Use two different methods to distribute the earnings of a partnership among the partners.
4. Prepare the financial statements for a partnership.
5. Define the accounting terms introduced in this chapter.

New Terms

partnership
mutual agency
partnership agreement
statement of changes in partners' equity

Accounting for a Partnership

As you learned in Chapter 1, a **partnership** is an association of two or more persons to operate, as co-owners, a business for profit. Any type of business may be organized as a partnership. Partnerships, however, are more common in the professions or in businesses that provide professional services. For example, accounting and legal firms are often organized as partnerships. Each partner can have her or his own clients, yet share with the other partners the expenses of operating an office.

Characteristics of a Partnership

The partnership form of business organization has certain unique features. Let's look at some of them.

Ease of Formation

Like a sole proprietorship, there are no special legal requirements that must be met to form a partnership. A partnership is automatically formed when two or more persons agree to operate as partners. A partnership is a voluntary arrangement. No one can be forced into a partnership or required to continue as a partner.

Unlimited Liability

Each partner is personally liable for the debts of the partnership. That means that if the partnership's creditors cannot be paid out of the assets of the partnership, a partner's personal assets may be used to pay the partnership's debts. As you recall, the owner of a sole proprietorship also has unlimited liability.

Limited Life

A partnership may be ended for a number of reasons. These reasons may include death, withdrawal, bankruptcy, or incapacity of any partner. A partnership may also be ended when the project for which the partnership was formed is completed or when the time period set by the partners has expired. For example, two architects may agree to combine their talents to design and oversee the construction of a building. When the building has been completed, the partnership is dissolved.

Mutual Agency

Each partner is an agent of the partnership. In other words, any partner can, in the name of the firm, enter into agreements that are binding on all other partners. This relationship is known as **mutual agency.**

Co-ownership of Partnership Property

When a partner invests assets in the partnership, he or she gives up all personal rights of ownership. All of the partnership assets are co-owned by the partners.

Partnerships are the least common form of business organization.

Advantages and Disadvantages of a Partnership

One of the most important advantages of a partnership is that it provides the opportunity to bring together the abilities, experiences, and resources of two or more individuals. A partnership is easy to form, the only requirement being the agreement of the partners. Members of a partnership are usually able to make decisions without having to hold a formal meeting of the partners. Although a partnership must have a legal purpose, there are few other legal restrictions. Finally, federal and state income taxes are not levied against the partnership. Each partner must pay personal income taxes on her or his share of the business's net income.

There are, of course, disadvantages to the partnership form. As discussed earlier, a partnership has a limited life, each partner is personally liable for the debts of the partnership, and all partners may be held responsible for the decision of one partner. In addition, a partner cannot transfer her or his interest in the partnership without the consent of the other partners. The ability to work together without major disagreements, however, may be the greatest test of the partnership form of organization.

The Partnership Agreement

A partnership may be formed when two or more individuals orally agree to operate a business as co-owners. However, it is advisable to have a written partnership agreement. A **partnership agreement** is a written document that sets out the terms under which the partnership will operate. There is no standard form for a partnership agreement. It should, however, include the following types of information:

1. The name and address of each partner.
2. The name, location, and nature of the partnership.
3. The date of the agreement and the length of time the partnership is to run.
4. The investment of each partner.
5. The duties, rights, and responsibilities of each partner.
6. The amount of withdrawals allowed each partner.
7. The procedures for sharing profits and losses.
8. The procedure for distributing assets when the partnership is dissolved.

Each partner should, of course, sign the agreement.

Accounting for Partners' Equity

Accounting for owners' equity for a partnership is basically the same as for a sole proprietorship. A sole proprietorship has only one capital account; a partnership has two or more capital accounts. A separate capital account is set up for each partner to record that partner's investment in the business. Each partner also has a separate withdrawals account in which to record the amount of cash or other assets the partner withdraws from the business for personal use.

In a partnership, separate capital and withdrawals accounts are set up for each partner.

Recording the Partners' Investments

When the partnership is formed, the value of cash and other assets invested by each partner is listed in the partnership agreement. Separate entries are then made to record each partner's investment in the business. Let's look at an example.

On January 1, Pat Donald and Harold Thompson agreed to form a partnership to operate an accounting firm. The name of the firm was to be Donald & Thompson, CPAs. Each partner agreed to invest the following assets in the new business (Memorandum 1):

	Donald	Thompson
Cash	$12,000	
Office supplies	1,000	
Office equipment (market value)	12,000	
Building (market value)		$30,000
Land		15,000
Total assets invested	$25,000	$45,000

The journal entries made to record the partners' initial investments are shown in Figure 26-1. Notice that the asset accounts Office Equipment and Building are debited for their current market value. Each partner's capital account is then credited for the total amount of the assets that partner invested.

GENERAL JOURNAL   PAGE 1

DATE	DESCRIPTION	POST. REF.	DEBIT	CREDIT
19-- Jan. 1	Cash in Bank		12 000 00	
	Office Supplies		1 000 00	
	Office Equipment		12 000 00	
	Pat Donald, Capital			25 000 00
	Memo. 1			
1	Building		30 000 00	
	Land		15 000 00	
	Harold Thompson, Capital			45 000 00
	Memo. 1			

Figure 26-1 Recording the Partners' Investments in the Business

R — E — M — E — M — B — E — R

When a partner invests noncash assets in the business, they are recorded in the partnership records at their current market value.

Recording Additional Investments

Any additional investments by the partners are recorded in a similar manner. For example, in April each partner agreed to invest an additional $5,000.00 cash in the business.

April 4: *Recorded the additional investment of $5,000.00 by each partner, Memorandum 42.*

The general journal entry to record this transaction is shown in Figure 26-2.

	DATE	DESCRIPTION	POST. REF.	DEBIT	CREDIT	
	GENERAL JOURNAL				PAGE 10	
1	19-- apr. 4	Cash in Bank		10 000 00		1
2		Pat Donald, Capital			5 000 00	2
3		Harold Thompson, Capital			5 000 00	3
4		Memo 42				4

Figure 26-2 Journalizing an Additional Investment by the Partners

Recording Withdrawals by the Partners

During the fiscal period, the partners may withdraw cash or other assets for personal use, according to the terms of the partnership agreement. Partners' withdrawals are recorded in the same way as are the withdrawals of the owner of a sole proprietorship. The amount of the withdrawal is debited to the partner's withdrawals account and credited to the appropriate asset account. The amounts withdrawn by the partners do not have to be equal.

May 12: *Pat Donald withdrew $1,200.00 cash for personal use (Check 123) and Harold Thompson withdrew $1,800.00 cash for personal use (Check 124).*

Figure 26-3 shows how these withdrawals are recorded in general-journal form.

	DATE	DESCRIPTION	POST. REF.	DEBIT	CREDIT	
	GENERAL JOURNAL				PAGE 12	
1	19-- May 12	Pat Donald, Withdrawals		1 200 00		1
2		Cash in Bank			1 200 00	2
3		Check 123				3
4	12	Harold Thompson, Withdrawals		1 800 00		4
5		Cash in Bank			1 800 00	5
6		Check 124				6

Figure 26-3 Journalizing Withdrawals by the Partners

Before continuing, complete the following activity to check your understanding of the material you have just studied.

UNIT 6 Accounting for Other Forms of Business Organization

On a sheet of notebook paper, indicate whether each of the following statements is true or false.

1. A separate capital account is set up for each partner.
2. A partnership has an unlimited life.
3. A partnership pays income taxes just like a corporation.
4. The duties, rights, and responsibilities of each partner should be listed in a partnership agreement.

Compare your answers with those in the answers section. Re-read the preceding part of the chapter to find the correct answers to any questions you may have missed.

Division of Partnership Income or Loss

At the end of each accounting period, the net income or net loss from partnership operations is divided among the partners. Partners may divide the net income or loss among themselves in any way they choose. The specific method should be set out in the partnership agreement. If it is not, the law provides that net income or net loss be divided equally among the partners.

There are many ways for partners to divide profits and losses. The division is generally based on the services and capital contributed by the partners to the partnership. For example, if the partners share equally in the work of the business but one partner has invested more capital, it seems only fair that the one who has invested more should stand to gain more. When the profits of the accounting period are divided, each partner's capital account is increased. If the business incurs a net loss for the accounting period, the capital account of each partner is decreased.

Let's look now at two methods that can be used to distribute partnership profits or losses. To illustrate the two methods, we'll use two examples for each method. In the first example, the partnership has a net income of $24,000. In the second example, the partnership has a net loss of $12,000.

R E M E M B E R

If the partnership agreement does not set out how net income or loss is to be distributed, the net income or loss is shared equally among the partners.

Dividing Profits and Losses Equally

The easiest way to divide a partnership's net income or loss is equally. This method is often used when all partners invest equal amounts of capital and share equally in the work of the business.

ACCOUNTING *Notes*
A partnership rewards partners in the form of partnership profits. Partners, therefore, do not have take-home pay as do the employees of the partnership business. Instead, active partners commonly withdraw regular amounts of money on a weekly or monthly basis in anticipation of their share of annual profits.

▲ **Net Income of $24,000**   During the first fiscal year of operations, the Donald & Thompson, CPAs partnership earned a net income of $24,000. The partnership agreement states that the profits or losses are to be divided between the two partners equally. Each partner's share of the net income is calculated as shown here.

Donald's share: $24,000 ÷ 2 = $12,000
Thompson's share: $24,000 ÷ 2 = $12,000

On December 31, the closing entry for a $24,000 net income divided equally between the two partners would be journalized as shown in Figure 26-4.

	DATE	DESCRIPTION	POST. REF.	DEBIT	CREDIT	
		GENERAL JOURNAL			PAGE 25	
1	19--	*Closing Entries*				1
15	Dec. 31	*Income Summary*		24 00 00		15
16		*Pat Donald, Capital*			12 00 00	16
17		*Harold Thompson, Capital*			12 00 00	17

Figure 26-4   Closing Entry To Divide Net Income Equally

The effect of this division of net income on the partners' capital accounts is illustrated below.

Pat Donald, Capital			Harold Thompson, Capital	
Dr.	Cr.		Dr.	Cr.
–	+		–	+
	Bal. $30,000			Bal. $50,000
	Clos. 12,000			Clos. 12,000

▲ **Net Loss of $12,000**   If the partnership had incurred a net loss of $12,000 for the fiscal period, each partner's share would be calculated as shown here.

Donald's share: $12,000 ÷ 2 = $6,000
Thompson's share: $12,000 ÷ 2 = $6,000

The closing entry on December 31 to distribute the $12,000 net loss equally between the two partners would appear as in Figure 26-5.

	DATE	DESCRIPTION	POST. REF.	DEBIT	CREDIT	
		GENERAL JOURNAL			PAGE 25	
1	19--	*Closing Entries*				1
15	Dec. 31	*Pat Donald, Capital*		6 00 00		15
16		*Harold Thompson, Capital*		6 00 00		16
17		*Income Summary*			12 00 00	17

Figure 26-5   Closing Entry To Divide Net Loss Equally

The net loss amount is debited to each partner's capital account as shown in the following T accounts.

Pat Donald, Capital			Harold Thompson, Capital	
Dr.	Cr.		Dr.	Cr.
–	+		–	+
Clos. $6,000	Bal. $30,000		Clos. $6,000	Bal. $50,000

Dividing Profits and Losses on a Fractional-Share Basis

The second simplest way to divide net income or loss is to assign each partner a stated fraction of the total. The size of the fraction usually takes into consideration: (1) the amount of each partner's investment and (2) the value of each partner's services to the business.

Let's suppose that the Donald & Thompson, CPAs partnership agreement states that the profits or losses are to be divided between the two partners on this basis: Thompson, $\frac{2}{3}$, and Donald, $\frac{1}{3}$.

When partners share net income or loss on a fractional-share basis, the basis is often stated as a ratio. Thompson's $\frac{2}{3}$ and Donald's $\frac{1}{3}$ could be expressed as a 2:1 ratio (2 to 1). To turn a ratio into a fraction, add the figures and use the total as the denominator of the fraction. For example,

$$2:1 \qquad 2 + 1 = 3 \qquad \tfrac{2}{3} \text{ and } \tfrac{1}{3}$$

▲ **Net Income of $24,000** The division of the net income based on the partners' capital investments would be calculated as follows:

Donald's share:	$24,000 $\times \frac{1}{3}$ = $ 8,000
Thompson's share:	$24,000 $\times \frac{2}{3}$ = $16,000

The December 31 closing entry would appear as shown in Figure 26-6.

	GENERAL JOURNAL			PAGE 25
DATE	DESCRIPTION	POST. REF.	DEBIT	CREDIT
19--	*Closing Entries*			
Dec. 31	Income Summary		24 000 00	
	Pat Donald, Capital			8 000 00
	Harold Thompson, Capital			16 000 00

Figure 26-6 Closing Entry To Divide Net Income on a Fractional-Share Basis

The effect of this method of dividing partnership earnings on the partners' capital accounts is illustrated below.

Pat Donald, Capital			Harold Thompson, Capital	
Dr.	Cr.		Dr.	Cr.
–	+		–	+
	Bal. $30,000			Bal. $50,000
	Clos. 8,000			Clos. 16,000

While a partnership does not pay income taxes, it is required to file an informational tax return with the IRS on Form 1065.

▲ **Net Loss of $12,000**   If the partnership had incurred a net loss of $12,000 for the fiscal period, the December 31 distribution would be computed as shown here.

Donald's share:	$12,000 \times \frac{1}{3} = \$4,000$
Thompson's share:	$12,000 \times \frac{2}{3} = \$8,000$

On December 31, the closing entry would be prepared as shown in Figure 26-7.

	DATE	DESCRIPTION	POST. REF.	DEBIT	CREDIT	
1		*Closing Entries*				1
	19--					
15	Dec. 31	Pat Donald, Capital		4 000 00		15
16		Harold Thompson, Capital		8 000 00		16
17		Income Summary			12 000 00	17

GENERAL JOURNAL   PAGE 25

Figure 26-7   Closing Entry To Divide Net Loss on a Fractional-Share Basis

The effect of this division of net loss on the partners' capital accounts is shown in the following T accounts:

Pat Donald, Capital	
Dr.	Cr.
−	+
Clos. $4,000	Bal. $30,000

Harold Thompson, Capital	
Dr.	Cr.
−	+
Clos. $8,000	Bal. $50,000

Before continuing, complete the following activity to check your understanding of how to distribute partnership earnings.

Check Your Learning

Answer these questions on a sheet of notebook paper.

Norton and Player are partners in a law firm. They share profits and losses on a fractional-share basis: Norton, $\frac{3}{8}$; Player, $\frac{5}{8}$. On December 31 (the end of the fiscal period), the partnership had a net income of $36,000.

1. What is each partner's share of the net income?
2. The ending capital balances were as follows: Norton, $32,000; Player, $40,000. What is the balance of each partner's capital account after the closing entry dividing the net income is posted?

Compare your answers to those in the answers section. Re-read the preceding part of the chapter to find the answers to any questions you missed.

Preparing Financial Statements for a Partnership

At the end of the fiscal period, a work sheet is prepared for the partnership and the financial statements are completed. The firm of Donald & Thompson, CPAs prepares an income statement, a statement of changes in partners' equity, and a balance sheet.

The Income Statement

The income statement is prepared in the same way as for any service business. Total expenses are subtracted from total revenue to determine the amount of the net income or net loss. The net income or net loss is divided among the partners and may be entered on the income statement.

The partnership agreement of Donald & Thompson, CPAs states that net income or net loss will be divided equally. At the end of the fiscal period, the firm had a net income of $24,000.00. According to the terms of the partnership agreement, each partner receives $12,000.00. If this division were included on Donald & Thompson's income statement, it would appear as shown in Figure 26-8.

Donald & Thompson, CPAs Income Statement For the Year Ended December 31, 19--		
Net Income		24 000 00
Division of Net Income:		
Pat Donald	12 000 00	
Harold Thompson	12 000 00	
Net Income		24 000 00

Figure 26-8 Reporting the Division of Net Income on the Income Statement

The Statement of Changes in Partners' Equity

The **statement of changes in partners' equity** reports the changes in each partner's capital account resulting from the business operations. It is very similar to the statement of changes in owner's equity for a sole proprietorship. The only difference between the two is that the statement of partners' equity for the partnership contains a separate column for each partner. Figure 26-9 shows the statement of changes in partners' equity for the firm of Donald & Thompson, CPAs.

Notice that the net income has been divided between the partners as set forth on the income statement.

Donald & Thompson, CPAs Statement of Changes in Partners' Equity For the Year Ended December 31, 19--	Donald	Thompson	Totals
Beginning Capital, January 1, 19--			
Add: Investments	30 000 00	50 000 00	80 000 00
Net Income	12 000 00	12 000 00	24 000 00
Subtotal	42 000 00	62 000 00	104 000 00
Less: Withdrawals	3 000 00	5 000 00	8 000 00
Ending Capital, December 31, 19--	39 000 00	57 000 00	96 000 00

Figure 26-9 Statement of Changes in Partners' Equity

The Balance Sheet

For a partnership, the owners' equity section of the balance sheet is referred to as the Partners' Equity section. Each partner's capital account is listed separately in the Partners' Equity section, as shown in Figure 26-10. The capital account amounts reported on the balance sheet are taken from the statement of changes in partners' equity.

Donald & Thompson, CPAs Balance Sheet December 31, 19--		
Partners' Equity		
Pat Donald, Capital	39 000 00	
Harold Thompson, Capital	57 000 00	
Total Partners' Equity		96 000 00
Total Liabilities and Partners' Equity		101 250 00

Figure 26-10 The Partners' Equity Section of the Balance Sheet of a Partnership

Recording the Closing Entries for a Partnership

As you remember, the four closing entries made for a sole proprietorship at the end of the period are as follows:

1. Close the revenue accounts into Income Summary.
2. Close the expense accounts into Income Summary.

3. Close Income Summary into the owner's capital account by the amount of the net income or net loss.
4. Close the withdrawals account into the capital account.

The first two closing entries for a partnership are the same as those listed above. In the third closing entry, Income Summary is closed into the partners' capital accounts. The amount of the net income or net loss is divided among the partners as shown on the income statement. Finally, each partner's withdrawals account is closed into that partner's capital account.

The closing entries involving the capital accounts for the partnership of Donald & Thompson, CPAs are shown in Figure 26-11. Notice that each partner's withdrawals account is closed separately.

	DATE	DESCRIPTION	POST. REF.	DEBIT	CREDIT	
1	19--	Closing Entries				1
15	Dec. 31	Income Summary		2400000		15
16		Pat Donald, Capital			1200000	16
17		Harold Thompson, Capital			1200000	17
18	31	Pat Donald, Capital		300000		18
19		Pat Donald, Withdrawals			300000	19
20	31	Harold Thompson, Capital		500000		20
21		Harold Thompson, Withdr.			500000	21

GENERAL JOURNAL   PAGE 25

Figure 26-11   Partial Closing Entries for a Partnership

Summary of Key Points

1. A partnership is an association of two or more persons to carry on, as co-owners, a business for profit.
2. The actions of one partner acting on behalf of the partnership are binding on all partners. This is known as mutual agency.
3. In a partnership, a capital account and a withdrawals account are set up for each partner.
4. The net income or loss of a partnership is divided among the partners according to the terms set forth in the partnership agreement.
5. Division of partnership profits and losses is generally based on the contribution of services and capital by the partners.

Review and Applications

Building Your Accounting Vocabulary

In your own words, write the definition of each of the following accounting terms. Use complete sentences for your definitions.

mutual agency
partnership

partnership
agreement

statement of changes
in partners' equity

Reviewing Your Accounting Knowledge

1. What are five characteristics of a partnership?
2. List three advantages and three disadvantages of the partnership form of business organization.
3. Why is a written partnership agreement important?
4. What information is usually included in a partnership agreement?
5. What do partners usually consider when deciding on how the profits and losses of the partnership will be divided?
6. When assets other than cash are invested in a partnership, at what value are these assets recorded?
7. Name two methods partners might use to divide profits and losses.
8. What three financial statements are prepared for a partnership at the end of a fiscal period?
9. How does the balance sheet for a partnership differ from that for a sole proprietorship?
10. How do the closing entries of a partnership differ from those of a sole proprietorship?

Improving Your Decision-Making Skills

Amy Palaski is the owner of a small retail business organized as a sole proprietorship. She is thinking about forming a partnership with Gene Hogan, whom she considers friendly and trustworthy. What things should Amy consider before deciding whether to form a partnership with Gene?

Applying Accounting Procedures

Exercise 26-1   Determining Partners' Fractional Shares

The ratios used by several partnerships to divide partnership earnings appear below.

Instructions: Determine the fractions that would be used to calculate each partner's share of net income or loss. Use the form provided in the working papers.

1. 3:1
2. 5:3:1
3. 3:2:1:1
4. 2:2:1
5. 3:2

Exercise 26-2 Dividing Partnership Earnings

Listed below are the net income and the method of dividing net income or loss for several different partnerships.

Instructions: Use the form provided in the working papers to determine each partner's share of the net income.

	Net Income	Method of Dividing Partnership Earnings
1.	$45,000	Equally: 2 partners
2.	$89,700	Fractional share: $\frac{2}{3}, \frac{1}{3}$
3.	$22,000	Fractional share: 3:1
4.	$32,000	Fractional share: $\frac{2}{5}, \frac{2}{5}, \frac{1}{5}$
5.	$92,700	Equally: 3 partners

Problem 26-1 Recording Partners' Investments

On June 1, Jennifer Thiry and Matthew Deck agreed to combine their individual sole proprietorships into a new business organized as a partnership. The partnership would take over all the assets of the two proprietorships. The assets invested by Thiry and Deck are listed below.

Instructions: Prepare the entries required to record the investment by each partner. Use page 1 of a general journal. The source document is Memorandum 1.

	Thiry	Deck
Cash	$ 2,300	$1,200
Accounts receivable	7,000	2,000
Merchandise	5,000	8,000
Equipment	12,000	5,000

Problem 26-2 Dividing Partnership Earnings Equally

On January 3, May Allrite and John Waters formed a partnership to be known as Allrite-Waters Products. The partnership agreement stated that net income or loss would be divided equally between Allrite and Waters.

Instructions:

(1) Determine each partner's share of the net income of $28,743.

(2) Record the December 31 entry, on page 4 of the general journal, to close the Income Summary account into the partners' capital accounts.

Problem 26-3 Preparing Closing Entries for a Partnership

Barbara Scott and Martin Towers are partners in the firm of Office Interiors. Their partnership agreement states that Scott and Towers respectively share net income or loss in a 3:2 ratio.

At the end of the fiscal period (December 31), the business had a net loss of $9,700. During the period, Scott had withdrawals of $6,600 and Towers had withdrawals of $5,400.

Instructions:

(1) Journalize the closing entries to divide the net loss between the partners and to close the withdrawals accounts. Use general journal page 14.

(2) Post the closing entries to the general ledger accounts.

Problem 26-4   Preparing a Statement of Changes in Partners' Equity

On January 1, Jack Hires and Carol Buckley formed a partnership called Research Consultants. Each partner invested $50,000 in cash on that date. The partnership agreement stated that the net income or loss would be shared equally.

During the year, Hires invested an additional $1,500 and withdrew $8,500 for personal use. Buckley invested an additional $2,000 and withdrew a total of $7,500. Net income for the year was $33,176.

Instructions: Prepare a statement of changes in partners' equity for the year ended December 31.

COMPUTER   **Problem 26-5   Completing End-of-Period Activities for a Partnership**

PROBLEM

Richard Lions and Carrie Castle are partners in the firm of R & C Roofing. They have agreed to divide net income or loss on the following basis: Lions, $\frac{3}{4}$; Castle, $\frac{1}{4}$.

The completed worksheet for R & C Roofing for the year ended December 31 appears in the working papers accompanying this textbook.

Instructions:

(1) Prepare an income statement for the partnership.
(2) Prepare a statement of changes in partners' equity. During the year, the partners made the following additional investments in the business: Lions, $3,500; Castle, $200.
(3) Prepare a balance sheet.
(4) Journalize the adjusting and closing entries, beginning on page 27 of the general journal.

CHALLENGE   **Problem 26-6   Evaluating Methods of Dividing Partnership Earnings**

PROBLEM

Maureen O'Riley, David White, and Jo Garrity have decided to form a partnership to operate a restaurant. The partners plan to invest the following assets in the business:

	O'Riley	White	Garrity
Cash	$22,000	$40,000	
Supplies	5,000	2,000	
Equipment	7,500	4,000	
Building			$50,000
Land			15,000

They are considering the following plans for the division of net income or loss:

1. Equally.
2. O'Riley, 40%; White, 40%; Garrity, 20%.
3. In the same ratio as the beginning balances of their capital accounts.

Instructions: Assume that the business had a net income of $17,500. Calculate the division of net income under each of the three plans.

*F*orensic Accountants: Fraud Sleuths

Auditors are independent accountants who are hired to check a business's accounting records. In a corporation's annual report, the auditor's statement assures stockholders that the financial information is true, accurate, and consistent with generally accepted accounting principles.

Ideally, these audits should reveal incidents of illegal tampering. In standard audits, accountants review samples of inventory, accounts receivable, and accounts payable; check bank balances; and verify the authenticity of contracts with outside vendors. Routine audits usually end there. When fraud is suspected or when an accounting firm is sued for malpractice because it did not report accounting irregularities, it's time to call in the "fraud sleuths," officially called "forensic accountants."

Often members of small accounting firms, these specialists go beyond the routine evaluation. They delve deeply into the financial records and personnel profiles of a business in ways that an accountant performing a standard audit would not.

Like detectives, they probe relentlessly into contracts, memos, liens, property records, and banking records. They look for collusion, kickbacks, and secret bank accounts; prepare profiles of key people involved with a company, including officers, employees, and vendors; investigate computer databases to uncover suspicious or irregular activities, such as a corporate officer buying property with unaccounted income. They might use computers with special software designed to track distribution of funds and find out if checks made out to different payees eventually ended up in the same bank account.

With an increase in the incidence of fraud and malpractice suits, there's an increase in demand

Some accountants specialize in auditing business records to uncover fraud.

for these investigative accountants. As a result, forensic accounting is a well-paying field.

If this sounds like an exciting career, get your CPA and auditing experience. You may even want to curl up with a Sherlock Holmes mystery whenever you have a chance!

Chapter 27

ACCOUNTING FOR CORPORATIONS

Up to this point in your study of accounting, you have learned about the accounting procedures for the sole proprietorship and partnership forms of business organization. In Unit 3, you recorded the business transactions for a family-owned corporation. Most business transactions are recorded in the same manner regardless of how the business is organized. The major difference lies in accounting for ownership equity.

In this chapter, you will learn how to account for the ownership equity of the publicly held corporation. You will also learn how a corporation distributes its earnings to stockholders and how to prepare the financial statements for a publicly held corporation.

Learning Objectives

When you have completed Chapter 27, you should be able to do the following:

1. List the major characteristics, advantages, and disadvantages of the corporate form of business organization.
2. Journalize transactions involving the issuance of stock.
3. Journalize transactions involving cash dividends.
4. Prepare financial statements for a publicly held corporation.
5. Define the accounting terms introduced in this chapter.

New Terms

closely held corporation
publicly held corporation
board of directors
authorized capital stock
par value
common stock
proxy
preferred stock
paid-in capital in excess of par
dividend
statement of stockholders' equity

Publicly Held Corporations

In the United States, there are more sole proprietorships and partnerships than there are corporations. Corporations, however, account for more business activity than the other two combined.

There are different types of corporations. In Unit 3, you learned how to record the business transactions for a family-owned, closely held corporation. **Closely held corporations** are corporations owned by a few persons or by a family. The stock of a closely held corporation is not sold to the general public.

In this chapter, you will learn about another type of corporation: the publicly held corporation. A **publicly held corporation** is one whose stock is widely held, has a large market, and is usually traded on a stock exchange. You're probably familiar with many corporations whose stock is traded on stock exchanges like the New York Stock Exchange or the American Stock Exchange. The stockholders of such publicly held corporations as IBM, General Motors, Polaroid, and McDonalds number in the millions.

Characteristics of a Corporation

The corporate form of business organization has several unique features. Let's look at some of them.

Legal Permission To Operate

To operate a business as a corporation, the incorporators (organizers) must file an application with state officials for permission to operate. Once the application is approved, it becomes the corporation's charter. As you learned in Chapter 1, the charter indicates the purpose of the business and spells out the rules under which the business must operate. The charter also states the type and amount of stock a corporation is authorized to issue.

Separate Legal Entity

A corporation is a separate legal entity that is created and exists only by law. A corporation may enter into contracts, borrow money, and conduct business in the same manner as a person. It may acquire, own, and sell property in its name. It can also sue and be sued in the courts.

Stockholders

The owners of a corporation are called stockholders. Ownership is divided into units called shares of stock. Each stockholder receives a *stock certificate* as proof of ownership. The stock certificate lists the name of the stockholder, the number of shares issued, and the date they were issued.

Professional Management

Stockholders own the corporation, but they do not manage it. The stockholders elect a **board of directors,** who govern and are responsible for the affairs of the corporation. One of the first duties of the board of directors is to hire professional managers to operate the business.

ACCOUNTING *Notes*
How do you get to be the president of a large corporation in the United States? Probably by beginning your career as an accountant. Statistically, more accountants have risen to be presidents of large U.S. corporations than people with any other background.

Altogether, about 30 million Americans (or one person out of eight) own shares in corporations.

Organization Costs

Forming a corporation is a much more costly process than forming a sole proprietorship or a partnership. To get started, corporations incur various *organization costs*. Organization costs include incorporation fees paid to the state, attorneys' fees for legal services, payments to promoters to sell stock, the cost of printing stock certificates, and other costs to bring the corporation into existence.

Advantages and Disadvantages of a Corporation

One of the most important advantages of a corporation is the *limited liability* of its owners. A corporation is a separate legal entity; it is responsible for its own actions and liabilities. The risk of an individual stockholder is limited to the amount he or she has invested. As mentioned earlier, shares of stock may be sold by one stockholder to another without disrupting the activities of the business or requiring the approval of other stockholders. Another advantage is that a corporation has a continuous existence even though the ownership may change.

There are, of course, disadvantages to the corporate form of business organization. First, corporations are more closely regulated by state and federal governments and are required to file numerous reports. Second, since stock is publicly held, corporations are required to disclose their operations more fully to the public. Third, corporate income is subject to federal and state income taxes. If the earnings of the corporation are distributed to stockholders, they too must pay taxes on that same income. This disadvantage is sometimes called *double taxation*.

Stockholders' Equity

Stockholders' equity, as you know, is the value of the stockholders' claims to the assets of the corporation. As you learned in Chapter 17, corporations must report stockholders' equity in two parts: (1) the equity that has been paid into the corporation by stockholders, and (2) the equity earned by the corporation and retained in the business. Let's look now at how transactions affecting stockholders' equity are handled.

Capital Stock

Capital stock refers to the shares of ownership in the corporation, the amount invested by the stockholders. When a corporation receives permission from the state to operate, it is authorized to sell a certain number of shares of stock to investors. The maximum number of shares a corporation may issue is called its **authorized capital stock.** The authorized capital stock of a corporation is usually much greater than the number of shares the corporation plans to sell right away. This allows the corporation to sell additional shares at a later time without having to ask the state to increase the authorized amount.

State laws may require that an amount or value be assigned to each share of stock before it is sold to the public. The amount assigned to each share is referred to as par value. **Par value** is simply the dollar amount printed on the stock certificates. The par value is used to determine the amount credited to the capital stock account. A corporation is free to select any par value; par values of $1, $5, and $25 are common. Most corporations set the par value low because state laws do not allow the corporation to sell the stock below its par value when it is first issued for sale to the public.

The corporate charter specifies the types of capital stock that a corporation may issue. The two main types of stock are common and preferred.

Common Stock

If the corporation issues only one class of capital stock, it is called **common stock.** The ownership of common stock usually carries certain basic rights. Common stockholders have the right to vote and elect the board of directors and, in effect, exercise control over the operations of the corporation. Each share of stock is entitled to one vote. Stockholders' meetings are usually held once a year. If a stockholder cannot attend the meeting, he or she may send in a **proxy,** which gives the stockholder's voting rights to someone else. Common stockholders have the right to share in the earnings of the corporation by receiving dividends. Common stockholders are also entitled to share in the assets of the corporation if it ceases operations.

Preferred Stock

In order to appeal to as many potential investors as possible, a corporation may issue preferred stock. **Preferred stock** has certain privileges (or preferences) over common stock. Preferred stockholders are entitled to receive dividends before common stockholders. The preferred stock dividend is stated in specific dollars, such as $6, or as a percentage of the stock's par value, such as 6%. The stock itself is then referred to as "$6 preferred stock" or "6% preferred stock."

Preferred stockholders are also given preference to the assets of the corporation should it cease operations. In return for these special privileges, the preferred stockholder gives up the right to vote and, in turn, the right to participate in the control of the corporation.

A separate account is set up by the corporation for each class of stock.

Before continuing, complete the following activity to check your understanding of the material you have just studied.

Check Your Learning

Record your answers to these questions on notebook paper.

1. A(n) ___?___ corporation is one whose stock is traded on a stock exchange.
2. ___?___ is the amount assigned to a share of stock. It is the amount used to record entries in the capital stock account.
3. Two types of stock issued by corporations are ___?___ and ___?___ .
4. Stock with a stated dividend per share is called ___?___ .

Compare your answers to those in the answers section. Re-read the preceding part of the chapter to find the correct answers to any questions you may have missed.

Issuing Common Stock

When common stock is issued, the Common Stock account is credited for the par value of the stock. The amount of money received for the stock may not always be the par value. Let's look at some examples.

▲ **Issuing Common Stock at Par Value**   On January 1, the Sender Corporation was incorporated and authorized to sell 20,000 shares of common stock with a par value of $10. On January 3, the company had the following transaction.

January 3: Issued 10,000 shares of $10 par common stock at $10 per share, Memorandum 3.

$ 10,000 shares
× $10
$100,000

In this transaction, the Sender Corporation received $100,000 cash in return for the 10,000 shares. Whenever shares of stock are sold at par value, the amount credited to the Common Stock account is determined by multiplying the number of shares issued by the par value. In this transaction, therefore, Cash in Bank is debited for $100,000 and Common Stock is credited for $100,000. This transaction is shown in general journal form in Figure 27-1.

	GENERAL JOURNAL			PAGE 1
DATE	DESCRIPTION	POST. REF.	DEBIT	CREDIT
19-- Jan. 3	Cash in Bank		1 00 00 0 00	
	Common Stock			100 00 0 00
	Memo. 3			

Figure 27-1 Journalizing the Sale of Common Stock at Par Value

▲ **Issuing Common Stock in Excess of Par Value** Investors are often willing to pay more than par value for the stock of a corporation. When stock sells at a price above par, the excess over par is credited to a separate stockholders' equity account called **paid-in capital in excess of par.** Paid-in Capital in Excess of Par appears in the chart of accounts immediately below the Common Stock account. The amounts recorded in this account are not profits to the corporation. Rather, they represent part of the stockholders' investment in the corporation.

Paid-in Capital
in Excess of Par

Dr.	Cr.
–	+
Decrease Side	Increase Side
	Balance Side

One year after the Sender Corporation was incorporated, it had the following transaction.

June 15: Issued 5,000 shares of $10 par common stock at $11.50 per share, Memorandum 147.

5,000 shares
×$11.50
$57,500

In this transaction, the Sender Corporation received $57,500 in exchange for 5,000 shares of its common stock. Before the transaction can be journalized, the corporation must determine how much of the $57,500 is to be credited to Common Stock and how much is to be credited to Paid-in Capital in Excess of Par. Remember, the amount credited to the Common Stock account is the par value of the shares issued.

Total cash received	$57,500
Common stock, 5,000 shares @ $10 par value	−50,000
Excess, 5,000 shares @ $1.50 per share	$ 7,500

In the transaction, Cash in Bank is debited for $57,500.00, the total amount of cash received. Common Stock is credited for $50,000.00, the total par value of the shares issued. Paid-in Capital in Excess of Par is credited for $7,500.00, the excess over par paid for the shares. The transaction is shown in general journal form in Figure 27-2 on page 592.

	DATE	DESCRIPTION	POST. REF.	DEBIT	CREDIT	
1	19-- June 15	Cash in Bank		5750000		1
2		Common Stock			5000000	2
3		Paid-in Capital in Excess of Par			750000	3
4		Memo. 147				4

Figure 27-2   Journalizing the Sale of Common Stock at a Price in Excess of Par

R E M E M B E R

When common stock is issued by a corporation, the Common Stock account is credited for the par value of the stock. Any excess over par received for the sale of the stock is credited to the Paid-in Capital in Excess of Par account.

Issuing Preferred Stock

When preferred stock is issued, the Preferred Stock account is credited for the par value of the stock. Investors buy preferred stock to receive the stated dividend that it pays. Unlike common stock, preferred stock is almost always issued at its par value.

When the Sender Corporation was incorporated on January 2, it was also authorized to issue 1,000 shares of preferred stock with a par value of $100 and a stated dividend of $6. On January 4, the company had the following transaction.

January 4: Issued 250 shares of $6 preferred stock, $100 par, at $100 per share, Memorandum 6.

250 shares
× $100
$25,000

In this transaction, the Sender Corporation received $25,000 cash in return for the 250 shares of preferred stock. Whenever preferred stock is sold at par value, the amount to be credited to the $6 Preferred Stock account is determined by multiplying the number of shares issued by the par value of the stock.

In this transaction, therefore, Cash in Bank is debited for $25,000, the total amount of cash received. The $6 Preferred Stock account is credited for $25,000, the total par value of the shares issued. This transaction is shown in general journal form in Figure 27-3.

GENERAL JOURNAL   PAGE 1

	DATE	DESCRIPTION	POST. REF.	DEBIT	CREDIT	
9	Jan. 4	Cash in Bank		2500000		9
10		$6 Preferred Stock			2500000	10
11		Memo. 6				11

Figure 27-3   Journalizing the Sale of Preferred Stock at Par Value

Before continuing, complete the following activity to check your understanding of the issuance of stock.

Check Your Learning

Write your answers to these questions on notebook paper.

1. What accounts are debited and credited when a corporation issues common stock at its par value?
2. What amount is used to determine the amount credited to the capital stock account?
3. Is Paid-in Capital in Excess of Par debited or credited when stock is sold above its par value?
4. The Gillis Corporation issued 1,500 shares of common stock, $5 par value, at $7.50. What accounts are debited and credited? For what amounts?

Compare your answers to those in the answers section. Re-read the preceding part of the chapter to find the correct answers to any questions you may have missed.

Distributing the Earnings of a Corporation

When the owner of a sole proprietorship or a partnership that has earned sufficient profits wishes to take money out of the business, a check is written on the business's checking account. The amount of the check is recorded in the owner's withdrawals account.

Owners (stockholders) of a publicly held corporation cannot withdraw cash whenever they want. Publicly held corporations distribute cash to stockholders in the form of dividends. **Dividends** are a return on the money invested by the stockholder. In other words, a corporation distributes a part of the corporation's retained earnings to its stockholders as a return on their investment. Most dividends are paid in cash and are expressed as a specific amount per share; for example, $1.25 per share. A person who owned 100 shares of stock would then receive $125.00 (100 shares × $1.25). Most publicly held corporations pay dividends on a quarterly basis.

Dividends may be declared, or authorized, only by the corporation's board of directors. Of course, before a cash dividend can be authorized, the corporation should have a sufficient amount of cash available to pay the dividend. In addition, since dividends decrease Retained Earnings, there must be an adequate balance in that account. Retained Earnings, remember, summarizes the net income earned and retained by the corporation.

Once a dividend has been declared, the board of directors must arrange to pay the dividends to stockholders on a certain date. There are three dates that are important in the dividend process.

1. *Date of declaration:* The date on which the board of directors declares, or votes to pay, a dividend. Once a dividend is declared, a liability is created for the amount of the total cash dividends to be paid.
2. *Date of record:* The date on which the ownership of shares is set. Persons who own stock on this date, called stockholders of record, are entitled to the dividend. The date of record is usually one or two weeks after the date of declaration.
3. *Date of payment:* The date on which the dividend is paid.

Journal entries must be recorded on the date of declaration and on the date of payment. No journal entry is required on the date of record. Let's look at the transactions involved when dividends were declared by the board of directors of the Sender Corporation during its second year of incorporation.

Preferred Stock Dividends

As mentioned earlier, preferred stockholders have certain preferences over common stockholders. The most common preference is the right to receive dividends before they are paid to common stockholders.

November 15: The board of directors of the Sender Corporation declared an annual cash dividend on the 250 shares of $6 preferred stock issued, Memorandum 215. The dividend is payable to preferred stockholders of record as of November 29 with payment due on December 15.

▲ **Date of Declaration** When a dividend is declared, the total amount of the dividend is debited to an account entitled Dividends. The Dividends account is a temporary contra stockholders' equity account. It is used to summarize the dividends declared by the corporation during the fiscal period. At the end of the fiscal period, the total of the Dividends account is debited to (closed into) the Retained Earnings account. In this way, it is very similar to the sole proprietor's or partner's withdrawals account.

Dividends	
Dr.	Cr.
+	−
Increase Side	Decrease Side
Balance Side	

The amount of the dividend could be debited directly to the Retained Earnings account. Most corporations, however, prefer to use a separate account so that the dividend amounts can be easily determined.

If a corporation is authorized to issue two types of stock, a separate dividends account is set up for each type of stock. The Sender Corporation, therefore, has a Dividends—Preferred account and a Dividends—Common account.

The total amount of the preferred stock dividend declared by the Sender Corporation on November 15 is $1,500 (250 shares × $6 stated dividend). This amount is then debited to the Dividends—Preferred account. On November 15, a liability is created and the corporation has a legal obligation, or debt, to its preferred stockholders. As a result, the amount of the dividend is credited to a liability account entitled Dividends Payable—Preferred.

The general journal entry for the November 15 transaction is shown in Figure 27-4.

Figure 27-4 Journalizing the Declaration of a Preferred Stock Cash Dividend

▲ **Date of Record** On November 29, the corporation checks its records and prepares a list of preferred stockholders entitled to receive the dividend. No journal entry is required on this date.

▲ **Date of Payment** On December 15, the Sender Corporation's accountant wrote one check for the total amount of the preferred stock dividend payable. This check was deposited in a special dividends checking account, from which separate checks made payable to each individual stockholder of record were drawn.

December 15: *Issued Check 373 for $1,500.00 in payment of the preferred stock dividend declared November 15.*

In this transaction, Dividends Payable—Preferred is debited for $1,500.00 since the liability is now being decreased. Cash in Bank is credited for $1,500.00, the total amount being paid out. This transaction is shown in general journal form in Figure 27-5.

Figure 27-5 Journalizing the Payment of a Preferred Stock Cash Dividend

The stated dividend rate for preferred stock is an *annual* rate. That is, the stated dividend indicates the dividend that will be paid to preferred stockholders per year. If the board of directors pays dividends annually, the preferred stockholders will receive the entire stated dividend at one time.

If the corporation pays dividends on a quarterly basis, for example, the stated dividend is paid to stockholders in four equal installments. For example, suppose that the Sender Corporation pays quarterly dividends on its $100 par $6 preferred stock. The quarterly dividend would be $1.50 ($6.00 ÷ 4). If the dividend were paid semiannually, the semiannual dividend would be $3.00 ($6.00 ÷ 2).

Common Stock Dividends

Dividends are also paid to common stockholders.

November 15: *The board of directors declared a quarterly cash dividend on common stock of 50¢ per share (on 15,000 shares of common stock issued) to all stockholders of record as of December 1, payable on December 26 (Memorandum 215).*

▲ **Date of Declaration**   The total amount of the common stock dividend is $7,500.00 (15,000 shares × $0.50). This amount is debited to the Dividends—Common account. Another liability has been created by the declaration of the common stock dividend. The total amount of the dividend ($7,500.00) is credited to the liability account Dividends Payable—Common. The entry is shown in general journal form in Figure 27-6.

	GENERAL JOURNAL			PAGE 35
DATE	DESCRIPTION	POST. REF.	DEBIT	CREDIT
19--				
Nov 15	Dividends – Common		7500 00	
	Dividends Payable – Common			7500 00
	Memo. 215			

Figure 27-6   Journalizing the Declaration of a Common Stock Cash Dividend

▲ **Date of Record**   On December 1, the corporation checks its records and prepares a list of common stockholders entitled to receive the dividend. No journal entry is required on this date.

▲ **Date of Payment**   On December 26, the Sender Corporation's accountant wrote a check for the total amount of the common stock dividend payable. The check was deposited in the dividends checking account and a separate check was prepared for each common stockholder.

December 26: *Issued Check 389 for $7,500.00 in payment of the common stock dividend declared November 15.*

In this transaction, Dividends Payable—Common is debited for $7,500.00 since the liability is being decreased. Cash in Bank is credited for $7,500.00. This transaction is shown in general journal form in Figure 27-7.

	GENERAL JOURNAL			PAGE 39
DATE	DESCRIPTION	POST. REF.	DEBIT	CREDIT
19--				
Dec. 26	Dividends Payable – Common		7500 00	
	Cash in Bank			7500 00
	Check 389			

Figure 27-7   Journalizing the Payment of a Common Stock Cash Dividend

The total amount available for a common stock dividend may depend upon the amount paid to preferred stockholders. For example, suppose that on November 15, the board of directors of the Sender Corporation had declared a total cash dividend of $3,000. Preferred stockholders receive dividends before common stockholders, and they receive these dividends at a stated amount. The dividend for preferred stockholders, you'll remember, totaled $1,500 ($6 stated dividend × 250 shares). The amount available for dividends to common stockholders would then be only $1,500, or 10¢ per share.

Before going on, complete the following activity to check your understanding of the dividend process.

Check Your Learning

Record your answers to the following questions on notebook paper.

1. The date on which the board of directors votes to pay a dividend is called the date of ___?___ .
2. The date on which ownership of shares for dividend payment is set is called the date of ___?___ .
3. The date a dividend is paid is called the ___?___ date.
4. Journal entries for dividends are recorded on the date of ___?___ and the date of ___?___ .
5. The Engstrom Corporation has issued 2,500 shares of $5 preferred stock. If the board of directors declares an annual dividend on its preferred stock, what is the total amount of the cash dividend?

Compare your answers to those in the answers section. Re-read the preceding part of the chapter to find the answers to any questions you may have missed.

Financial Statements for the Corporation

The income statement of a publicly held corporation is similar to that prepared by a closely held corporation. As you remember, the federal income taxes paid by the corporation are reported separately on the income statement.

While publicly held corporations can prepare a statement of retained earnings, many corporations now prepare a statement of stockholders' equity. In this section, we'll examine the information reported on that statement and how it is prepared. We'll also see how stockholders' equity is reported on the corporation's balance sheet.

Statement of Stockholders' Equity

In Chapter 17, you learned how to prepare a statement of retained earnings for a closely held corporation. That statement reported the changes that had taken place in the Retained Earnings account during the period.

Today, most corporations use computers to maintain up-to-date lists of their stockholders.

The statement of retained earnings you prepared was very simple. It showed the beginning balance of Retained Earnings, the net income earned by the corporation for the period, and the ending balance of Retained Earnings.

Many corporations now prepare a statement of stockholders' equity rather than the statement of retained earnings. The **statement of stockholders' equity** reports the changes that have taken place in *all* of the stockholders' equity accounts during the fiscal period. Companies are increasingly using this statement because it reveals much more about the transactions affecting stockholders' equity during the period. The types of information reported on a statement of stockholders' equity include

1. The number of any shares of stock issued and the total amount received for those shares.
2. Net income for the period.
3. Any dividends declared during the period.

The statement of stockholders' equity prepared by the Sender Corporation at the end of its second year of incorporation appears in Figure 27-8. The information needed to prepare the statement is taken from the work sheet and from the general ledger accounts. Notice that the titles of the four stockholders' equity accounts appear at the top of the form. There is also a Total column at the far right. The first line shows the balance in the accounts at the beginning of the fiscal period. Transactions affecting the stockholders' equity accounts are then described in the wide column. The increase or decrease amounts are recorded in the individual account columns and in the total column. For example, the second line on the statement indicates that the company issued 5,000 shares of common stock during the period. The issuance of the 5,000 shares increased the balance of the Common Stock account by $50,000. Since the shares were issued at a price above par value, the Paid-in Capital in Excess of Par account was increased by $7,500.

As you know, the net income earned by a corporation increases Retained Earnings. Any dividends declared by the corporation decrease Retained Earnings. Amounts that decrease account balances are enclosed in parentheses on the statement. Notice that the dividends declared on the preferred and common stock are listed separately. Also notice that the Retained Earnings column of the statement of stockholders' equity contains the same information that would be reported on a statement of retained earnings.

	$100 Par $6 Preferred Stock	$10 Par Common Stock	Paid-in Capital in Excess of Par	Retained Earnings	Total
	Sender Corporation				
	Statement of Stockholders' Equity				
	For the Year Ended December 31, 19--				
Balance, January 1, 19--	25 000 00	100 000 00		27 600 00	152 600 00
Issuance of 5,000 shares of common stock		50 000 00	7 500 00		57 500 00
Net Income				13 525 00	13 525 00
Cash Dividends:					
Preferred Stock				⟨1 500 00⟩	⟨1 500 00⟩
Common Stock				⟨7 500 00⟩	⟨7 500 00⟩
Balance, December 31, 19--	25 000 00	150 000 00	7 500 00	32 125 00	214 625 00

Figure 27-8 Statement of Stockholders' Equity

As with the statement of retained earnings, the balance calculated on the statement of stockholders' equity for Retained Earnings is used to prepare the corporation's balance sheet.

Balance Sheet

The balance sheet of a publicly held corporation is similar to that for a closely held corporation.

The Dividends Payable accounts are reported in the liabilities section. Since the Sender Corporation paid the dividend liabilities before the end of the fiscal period, zero balances are reported for these accounts, as shown in Figure 27-9.

Sender Corporation		
Balance Sheet		
December 31, 19--		
Liabilities		
Accounts Payable	14 562 10	
Dividends Payable—Preferred	—	
Dividends Payable—Common	—	
Total Liabilities		27 016 00

Figure 27-9 Reporting the Balances of the Dividends Payable Accounts on the Balance Sheet

The stockholders' equity section of the balance sheet of a publicly held corporation is more detailed than that of a closely held corporation. As you can see in Figure 27-10, each capital stock account is listed separately under the heading "Paid-in Capital." Each listing describes the par value, the number of shares authorized, and the number of shares issued. Preferred stock is always listed before common stock. Notice also that the Dividends accounts are *not* listed in the stockholders' equity section. The Dividends accounts, remember, are closed into Retained Earnings at the end of the fiscal period. The balance of Retained Earnings shown on the balance sheet reflects the dividends declared during the period.

Sender Corporation
Balance Sheet
December 31, 19--

Stockholders' Equity				
Paid-in Capital:				
$6 Preferred Stock, $100 par, 1,000 shares authorized, 250 shares issued	25 000 00			
Common Stock, $10 par, 20,000 shares authorized, 15,000 shares issued	150 000 00			
Paid-in Capital in Excess of Par	7 500 00			
Total Paid-in Capital		182 500 00		
Retained Earnings		32 125 00		
Total Stockholders' Equity			214 625 00	
Total Liab. & Stockholders' Equity			241 641 00	

Figure 27-10   The Stockholders' Equity Section of the Balance Sheet

R — E — M — E — M — B — E — R

The total value of all stockholders' equity is reported on the balance sheet. This total includes the total paid-in capital — the balances of $6 Preferred Stock, Common Stock, and Paid-in Capital in Excess of Par — and the balance of the Retained Earnings account.

Summary of Key Points

1. A closely held corporation is one that is owned by a few persons or by a family. A publicly held corporation is one whose stock is widely held, has a wide market, and is usually traded on a stock exchange.
2. A corporation must have permission from the state to operate, is considered to be a separate legal entity, is owned by its stockholders, and is usually run by professional managers.
3. Two types of stock a corporation may issue are common and preferred.
4. The par value of stock is the dollar amount or value assigned to each share of stock. Par value is used to determine the amount credited to the capital stock account when stock is issued.

5. Common stockholders have the right to vote and elect the board of directors of the corporation, to share in the earnings of the corporation, and to share in the assets of the corporation should it cease operations.

6. Preferred stockholders do not have the right to vote but are entitled to receive dividends before the common stockholders.

7. If stock is issued at a price higher than its par value, the amount received over par is credited to an account called Paid-in Capital in Excess of Par.

8. Corporations distribute a part of their earnings to stockholders in the form of dividends.

9. The total amount of a cash dividend is debited to the Dividends account. Dividends is a temporary contra stockholders' equity account. At the end of the fiscal period, the balance of the Dividends account is debited to (closed into) Retained Earnings. A separate Dividends account is set up for each type of stock.

10. Corporations may prepare a statement of stockholders' equity, which reports the changes that have occurred in all of the stockholders' equity accounts during the fiscal period.

Review and Applications

Building Your Accounting Vocabulary

In your own words, write the definition of each of the following accounting terms. Use complete sentences for your definitions.

authorized capital
  stock
board of directors
closely held
  corporation
common stock

dividend
paid-in capital in
  excess of par
par value
preferred stock
proxy

publicly held
  corporation
statement of
  stockholders'
  equity

Reviewing Your Accounting Knowledge

1. What is the difference between a closely held corporation and a publicly held corporation?
2. Name five characteristics of a corporation.
3. List three advantages and three disadvantages of the corporate form of business organization.
4. What are some of the rights of common stockholders?
5. What are the differences between common and preferred stock?
6. When stock is sold at a price above its par value, what amount is credited to the capital stock account?
7. What is the classification of the Paid-in Capital in Excess of Par account? What is its normal balance?
8. Name and explain the three dates important to the dividend process.
9. What type of account is Dividends?
10. When a dividend is declared, what accounts are debited and credited?
11. At what date does a dividend become a liability to the corporation? Explain.
12. What type of information is reported on the statement of stockholders' equity?

Improving Your Communications Skills

Using simple, concise wording will make your messages easier to read and understand. There are many wordy expressions that can be replaced with one or two simple words. For example, the wordy expression "in the event that" can be replaced with the word "if."

Change each of the following wordy expressions to make them more concise. Refer to a dictionary if necessary.

1. at the present time
2. in a satisfactory manner
3. bring to a conclusion
4. make an effort
5. due to the fact that
6. it would appear that
7. in the amount of
8. herewith enclosed please find
9. in view of the fact that

Applying Accounting Procedures

Exercise 27-1 Examining Capital Stock Transactions

The Dublin Corporation was organized and authorized to issue 10,000 shares of $100 par, 8% preferred stock and 500,000 shares of $10 par common stock. The transactions illustrated in the following T accounts took place during the first month of operations.

Instructions: Describe each transaction.

Cash in Bank	
Dr.	Cr.
+	−
(1) $300,000	
(2) 200,000	
(3) 700,000	

8% Preferred Stock	
Dr.	Cr.
−	+
	(2) $200,000

Common Stock	
Dr.	Cr.
−	+
	(1) $300,000
	(3) 500,000

Paid-in Capital in Excess of Par	
Dr.	Cr.
−	+
	(3) $200,000

Exercise 27-2 Distributing Corporate Earnings

During its first year of operations, the Long-Horn Corporation issued 17,500 shares of $10 par common stock. At the end of the fiscal period, the corporation had a net income of $350,000. The board of directors declared a cash dividend of $5 per share.

Instructions: Answer the following questions.

(1) How much of the net income earned for the year was paid out to the stockholders?

(2) How much of the net income was retained by the corporation?

Exercise 27-3 Examining the Statement of Stockholders' Equity

The following transactions took place during the fiscal period of Victor Jewelry Corporation.

Instructions: Use the form provided in the working papers to indicate which of the transactions would be reported on the statement of stockholders' equity.

Transactions:

1. Paid accounts payable of $50,000.
2. Issued 2,000 shares of $10 par common stock, receiving $15 per share.
3. The board of directors declared a cash dividend of $12,000 for all common stockholders.
4. Bought equipment on account at a total cost of $125,000.
5. Paid the cash dividend declared in Transaction #3.
6. Issued 500 shares of $100 par, $7 preferred stock.
7. Paid the federal income tax installment of $5,000.
8. Earned a net income of $150,000 for the fiscal period.

Exercise 27-4   Determining Stockholders' Equity

The balance sheet of the Speedy Transport Company, Inc., included the following amounts.

$6 Preferred Stock, $100 Par	$ 90,000
Common Stock, $10 Par	150,000
Paid-in Capital in Excess of Par	40,000
Retained Earnings	55,000

Instructions: Answer the following questions.

(1) How many shares of $6 preferred stock have been issued by Speedy Transport Company, Inc.?

(2) How many shares of common stock have been issued?

(3) What is the total stockholders' equity?

Problem 27-1   Journalizing the Issue of Stock

On June 1, the Hadley Corporation was incorporated and authorized to issue 1,000 shares of $100 par, 9% preferred stock and 10,000 shares of $25 par common stock.

Instructions: Record the following transactions on page 1 of the general journal.

Transactions:

June 1   Issued 200 shares of 9% preferred stock at $100 per share, Memorandum 3.

     2   Issued 3,000 shares of common stock at $25 per share, Memorandum 7.

     6   Received $31 per share for 2,000 shares of common stock issued, Memorandum 10.

     7   Issued 50 shares of 9% preferred stock at par, Memorandum 11.

Problem 27-2   Journalizing Common and Preferred Stock Dividend Transactions

The Maple Corporation has issued 8,000 shares of $80 par, 7% preferred stock and 35,000 shares of $25 par common stock.

Instructions:

(1) Record the following transactions on general journal page 14.

(2) Post the transactions to the general ledger accounts provided in the working papers.

Transactions:

Oct. 15   The board of directors declared an annual cash dividend on the 7% preferred stock, payable on December 1, Memorandum 407.

Nov. 5   Declared an annual cash dividend of $1.25 on 35,000 shares of common stock, payable on December 17, Memorandum 415.

Dec. 1   Paid the preferred stock cash dividend declared on October 15, Check 1163.

     17   Paid the common stock dividend declared on November 5, Check 1201.

     31   Closed Income Summary into Retained Earnings for the amount of the net income of $135,000.

     31   Closed the two Dividends accounts into Retained Earnings.

Problem 27-3 Journalizing Stockholders' Equity Transactions

The Walters Clothing Company, Inc., has issued 10,000 shares of $100 par, 9% preferred stock and 100,000 shares of $20 par common stock.

Instructions: Record the following selected transactions on general journal page 27.

Transactions:

Mar. 1 Declared the semiannual cash dividend on the preferred stock issued, payable April 15, Memorandum 1064.

  1 Declared a semiannual cash dividend of $2 per share on the common stock issued, payable April 15, Memorandum 1065.

Apr. 15 Paid the preferred stock cash dividend, Check 3614.

  15 Paid the common stock cash dividend, Check 3615.

May 12 Issued 1,000 shares of preferred stock at $100 per share, Memorandum 1203.

Aug. 1 Issued 25,000 shares of common stock at $22.50 per share, Memorandum 1369.

Sept. 1 Declared the semiannual cash dividend on the preferred stock issued, payable October 1, Memorandum 1568.

  1 Declared a semiannual cash dividend of $1 per share on the common stock issued, payable October 15, Memorandum 1569.

Dec. 31 Closed the net income for the period of $767,400 from Income Summary into Retained Earnings.

  31 Closed the two Dividends accounts into Retained Earnings.

Problem 27-4 Preparing a Statement of Stockholders' Equity

The following balances appeared in the general ledger accounts of Walters Clothing Company, Inc., on January 1, the beginning of the fiscal period.

9% Preferred Stock ($100 par)	$1,000,000
Common Stock ($20 par)	2,000,000
Paid-in Capital in Excess of Par	87,500
Retained Earnings	1,155,000
Dividends — Preferred	0
Dividends — Common	0

Instructions: Use the above information and the transactions from Problem 27-3 to prepare a statement of stockholders' equity for Walters Clothing Company, Inc.

Problem 27-5 Preparing Corporate Financial Statements

The Silverplate Corporation is authorized to issue 10,000 shares of $100 par, 9% preferred stock and 500,000 shares of $5 par common stock. The balances on page 606 appeared in the Balance Sheet section of the company's work sheet for the year ended December 31.

Instructions:

(1) Prepare the statement of stockholders' equity.

   (a) During the period, the corporation issued 500 shares of 9% preferred stock at par and 25,000 shares of common stock at $9.

   (b) The net income for the fiscal period was $425,000.

(2) Prepare the balance sheet.

Accounts Payable	$ 62,412
Accounts Receivable (net)	150,680
Building (net)	639,298
Cash in Bank	406,010
Common Stock	750,000
Dividends — Common	262,500
Dividends — Preferred	45,000
Dividends Payable — Common	150,000
Dividends Payable — Preferred	22,500
Equipment (net)	363,009
Federal Income Tax Payable	20,000
Land	772,500
Merchandise Inventory	316,315
Paid-in Capital in Excess of Par	300,000
9% Preferred Stock	500,000
Prepaid Insurance	3,600
Retained Earnings	735,000
Sales Tax Payable	4,500
Supplies	10,500

CHALLENGE Problem 27-6 Recording Stockholders' Equity Transactions

Fitness for Health, Inc., is authorized to issue 100,000 shares of $5 par common stock and 5,000 shares of $100 par, 8% preferred stock. On January 1, the beginning of the fiscal period, the stockholders' equity accounts had the following balances:

8% Preferred Stock	$150,000
Paid-in Capital in Excess of Par — Preferred	11,250
Common Stock	225,000
Paid-in Capital in Excess of Par — Common	112,500
Retained Earnings	366,800
Dividends — Preferred	0
Dividends — Common	0

Instructions:
(1) Record the following transactions on general journal page 42.
(2) Prepare the stockholders' equity section of the balance sheet.

Transactions:

Mar. 15 The board of directors approved a semiannual cash dividend of $62,250 for preferred and common stockholders. The dividend is payable to stockholders of record as of April 15 with payment on May 1, Memorandum 635.

Apr. 19 Issued 500 shares of preferred stock at $108, Memorandum 651.

May 1 Paid the dividend declared on March 15, Check 2956.

Aug. 10 Issued 12,000 shares of common stock in exchange for land valued at $15,000 and a building valued at $55,000, Memorandum 793.

Sept. 1 The board of directors approved a semiannual cash dividend of $79,250 for preferred and common stockholders. The dividend is payable to stockholders of record as of October 1 with payment on November 1, Memorandum 828.

Nov. 1 Paid the dividend declared on September 1, Check 4837.

Dec. 31 Closed Income Summary into Retained Earnings in the amount of the net income of $296,490.

31 Closed the Dividends accounts into Retained Earnings.

*T*elecommunications

*N*o need for you to worry about mail or messages being misplaced or delayed or sent to the wrong address. Thanks to *electronic mail systems.*

• Letters, memos, and reports can be sent in a fraction of the time mail or messenger services take.

• A salesperson can send the day's orders to the home office to be processed the next day.

• You can post or read messages on a computer bulletin board.

No need to spend hours at the card catalog and library stacks. Thanks to *information utilities,*

• A researcher can search vast databases for the specific information needed.

• An investor can get instant access to financial and stock information.

• A writer can search months of news stories for articles on a specific topic.

Forget overnight delivery. Thanks to *facsimile transmission* (FAX), exact duplicates of documents can be sent across the country as fast as you can telephone your mother.

And that's just how it's done. Using telephone lines, computers can "talk" to computers. To accomplish this marvel, all communicators need are

• Access to the telephone system.

• A computer (screen, keyboard, disk drives) to process information.

• Two modems (short for *modulator-demo*dulator) to convert the computer's digital signals into audio signals that can be sent over telephone lines and then converted back into digital signals on the receiving end.

• Communications software—either written by the user or, in most cases, commercially prepared—that enables the computer, the modem, and the telephone to work together smoothly.

"Telecomputing" refers to sending data from one computer to another via telephone lines.

• A printer to produce "hard copy" if the receiver wishes.

Computer communications is playing an increasingly important role not only in businesses but also in schools, hospitals, libraries, and homes. More and more people are using computers to obtain information and to send it. You might say that they're "letting their fingers do the talking."

Chapter 28

ANALYZING AND INTERPRETING FINANCIAL STATEMENTS

In preceding chapters, you learned about the development of an accounting system and how to prepare the system's end product: financial statements. Financial statements are issued to provide information about an organization to aid users in making decisions about that organization.

In this chapter, you will learn about the methods used to analyze and interpret financial statements. During statement analysis, relationships between dollar amounts may be discovered and used to make more fully informed decisions.

New Terms

relevance
reliability
comparability
full disclosure
materiality
investments
current liabilities
long-term liabilities
selling expenses
administrative expenses
horizontal analysis
base year
vertical analysis
working capital
ratio analysis
liquidity ratio
current ratio
quick ratio
profitability ratios

Learning Objectives

When you have completed Chapter 28, you should be able to do the following:

1. List the qualitative characteristics and general accounting guidelines for accounting information.
2. Prepare a classified balance sheet and income statement.
3. Prepare horizontal and vertical analyses of financial statements.
4. Calculate commonly used liquidity and profitability ratios.
5. Use liquidity and profitability ratios to analyze a business's performance.
6. Define the accounting terms introduced in this chapter.

Evaluating Financial Statements

The financial statements issued by a business are used by many different people to evaluate the business's financial performance. The managers of a business analyze its financial statements to help them evaluate past performance and make more informed predictions and decisions that will affect the future operations of the business. Investors (owners), creditors, and unions are also interested in the financial performance of a business. Investors and creditors want to protect their equity. Unions want to obtain fair wages for the efforts of the business's employees.

If accounting information is to be useful, it must be understandable. Qualitative characteristics and other general accounting guidelines help accountants make the financial information more understandable.

Qualitative Characteristics

In accounting, *qualitative characteristics* are those characteristics that make information provided by accountants more trustworthy and useful. Three of these characteristics are relevance, reliability, and comparability.

▲ **Relevance**   In accounting, **relevance** means that the information "makes a difference" to a user in reaching a decision about a business. Investors, creditors, and other users of a business's financial information need relevant information to make informed decisions. Not all information is relevant.

> **EXAMPLE:** *On January 30, a business reported that its sales for the preceding year were $500,000, which was an increase of 14% over sales two years ago. This information is relevant because it is useful in evaluating previous net income and in predicting future sales.*

▲ **Reliability**   Users of accounting data must be able to assume that the data is reliable. **Reliability** relates to the confidence users have in the financial information. In other words, people who are making decisions based on financial data want to know that the information is free of mistakes and biased opinions of what should or should not be reported. Reliable information is based on facts, not hopes for the future.

> **EXAMPLE:** *A business reported a net income of $150,000 after taxes. This information is reliable because the management of the business, the accountant, and the auditor (a person who checks all of the business's accounting records) are required to agree on the amount of the company's net income before it can be publicly reported.*

▲ **Comparability** **Comparability** refers to accounting information that can be compared from one fiscal period to another or from one business to another. For example, an investor may want to compare the net income made by two similar businesses to determine which business is the better investment. Accounting reports are based on certain rules so that users can make intelligent comparisons. In other words, users need to know that they are comparing apples to apples and not apples to potatoes.

> **EXAMPLE:** *A business reported that its after-tax net income was $300,000 in one year and $275,000 in the previous year. Since both amounts are reported on an after-tax basis, they are comparable.*

General Accounting Guidelines

Accounting is the "common language" of business. Accountants want to ensure that users understand that language by making sure financial reports are clear and consistent. To do this, accountants follow certain general guidelines. Two of these guidelines are full disclosure and materiality.

▲ **Full Disclosure** "To disclose" means "to uncover or to make known." The guideline of **full disclosure** requires that anyone preparing a financial report include enough information so that the report is complete. Relevant information left out of a report or half truths are not acceptable. Information in the report must not lead the reader to wrong conclusions.

> **EXAMPLE:** *At the end of its report, a business included a footnote about a lawsuit it was involved in. It also stated that the case had not been settled and no financial claim had yet been made against the company. This note prepares readers for a possible financial claim the company may have to pay. The report would not meet the requirement of full disclosure if it had failed to mention the lawsuit and the possible claim.*

▲ **Materiality** If something is "material," it carries weight. The guideline of **materiality** states that relatively important data are included in financial reports. Important data are material; unimportant data are immaterial. Accounting workers deal with many different kinds of financial transactions involving small dollar amounts. Such transactions are of little concern except to recordkeepers. When preparing financial reports—as opposed to keeping records—information is material if it is likely to influence the conclusions or decisions made by a user of the report.

> **EXAMPLE:** *In an annual report of a business reporting net income of $10 million a year, the understatement of profit by $5,000 may be immaterial. The same $5,000 understatement by a business reporting a net income of $20,000 would be material.*

Classified Financial Statements

The analysis of financial statements is made easier when the information reported is separated into related categories, or classifications.

Classifying the Balance Sheet

You have learned that there are three major categories of accounts reported on the balance sheet: assets, liabilities, and owner's equity. Information related to these accounts becomes more useful when assets and liabilities are classified into groups. For example, assets may be classified as current assets; investments; property, plant, and equipment; and other assets. Liabilities are classified as current liabilities or long-term liabilities.

An example of a classified balance sheet is shown in Figure 28-1 on page 612. Refer to this illustration as you read the paragraphs that follow.

▲ **Current Assets** Current assets are cash or other assets intended to be converted to cash, sold, or consumed generally within the next accounting period. Accounts such as Cash in Bank, Accounts Receivable, and Merchandise Inventory are classified as current assets. These assets are reported on the balance sheet in their order of liquidity. That is, the most liquid asset is reported first; the next most liquid asset, second; and so on.

▲ **Investments** Investments are assets, generally long term in nature, that are not intended to be converted to cash or to be used in the normal operations of the business within the next accounting period. Examples of investments include land held for some future purpose of the business, stocks of other companies, and bonds of government agencies or other businesses. Companies often purchase such assets expecting to earn a return on their investment.

▲ **Property, Plant, and Equipment** Property, plant, and equipment are the long-lived physical assets used in the normal operations of the business. These long-lived assets are used in the production and sale of goods, the performance of services, and other requirements of the business. Plant and equipment are referred to as plant assets. You were first introduced to plant assets in Chapter 22 when you learned about the depreciation of plant and equipment assets.

▲ **Other Assets** Other assets are any assets that do not fit within any of the preceding categories. Examples of other assets are deposits for utilities and the book value of trademarks, copyrights, and patents.

▲ **Current Liabilities** Current liabilities are debts of the business that must be paid within the next accounting period. Examples of current liabilities are notes payable due within the upcoming accounting period, amounts owed to creditors, and federal income taxes payable.

▲ **Long-Term Liabilities** Long-term liabilities are debts that are not required to be paid within the next accounting period. Examples of long-term liabilities include mortgages and notes payable that have maturity dates longer than one year.

▲ **Stockholders' Equity** Capital invested or contributed by stockholders of the corporation includes amounts reported in the capital stock and paid-in capital accounts. Equity earned and retained by the corporation is reported as retained earnings. These accounts are classified on the balance sheet as stockholders' equity.

Fitness Forever, Inc.
Balance Sheet
December 31, 1993

Assets

Current Assets:

Cash in Bank	$ 17,200	
Accounts Receivable	48,030	
Merchandise Inventory	53,000	
Store Supplies	4,210	
Prepaid Insurance	780	
Total Current Assets		$123,220

Investments:

A-Z Technologies, Inc. (stock)		21,000

Property, Plant, and Equipment:

Equipment (net)	31,000	
Building (net)	110,000	
Land	15,000	
Total Property, Plant, and Equipment		156,000
Total Assets		**$300,220**

Liabilities

Current Liabilities:

Notes Payable	$ 15,000	
Accounts Payable	39,000	
Sales Tax Payable	1,765	
Total Current Liabilities		$ 55,765

Long-Term Liabilities:

Mortgage Payable		28,000
Total Liabilities		83,765

Stockholders' Equity

Common Stock, $90 par, 4,000 shares authorized, 800 shares issued	72,000	
Retained Earnings	144,455	
Total Stockholders' Equity		216,455
Total Liabilities and Stockholders' Equity		**$300,220**

Figure 28-1 Classified Balance Sheet

Classifying the Income Statement

Like the balance sheet, an income statement is more useful if the information reported there is classified. The information reported on an income statement for a merchandising business is commonly divided into four categories: revenue, cost of merchandise sold, operating expenses, and other revenue and expenses. There is no cost of merchandise sold section on the income statement of a service business.

An example of a classified income statement is shown in Figure 28-2.

▲ **Revenue**   As you recall, revenue is earned by providing services or selling merchandise to customers. Sales discounts and returns reduce the net sales revenue earned by a merchandising business.

UNIT 6 Accounting for Other Forms of Business Organization

Fitness Forever, Inc.
Income Statement
For the Year Ended December 31, 1993

Revenue:

Sales	$578,000	
Less: Sales Returns	3,000	
Net Sales		$575,000
Cost of Merchandise Sold:		
Merchandise Inventory, Jan. 1, 1993	49,000	
Net Purchases	385,000	
Merchandise Available for Sale	434,000	
Merchandise Inventory, Dec. 31, 1993	53,000	
Cost of Merchandise Sold		381,000
Gross Profit on Sales		194,000
Operating Expenses:		
Selling Expenses:		

Advertising Expense	$10,000		
Depr. Exp. — Store Equip.	4,000		
Sales Salaries Expense	50,000		
Store Supplies Expense	10,350		
Total Selling Expenses		74,350	
Administrative Expenses:			
Depr. Exp. — Office Equip.	2,800		
Insurance Expense	900		
Miscellaneous Expense	750		
Office Salaries Expense	69,000		
Total Administrative Expenses		73,450	
Total Operating Expenses			147,800
Operating Income			46,200
Other Expenses:			
Interest Expense			3,400
Net Income			$ 42,800

Figure 28-2 Classified Income Statement

▲ **Cost of Merchandise Sold**   Merchandising businesses buy merchandise to resell to their customers. The cost of merchandise sold is the net amount paid by the business for merchandise sold to customers.

▲ **Operating Expenses**   Operating expenses are the cash spent, assets consumed, or liabilities incurred to earn revenue for the business. To compare the separate operating expenses of a business from one period to the next, expenses are usually classified by function. Two common ways to classify operating expenses are as selling expenses and administrative expenses. **Selling expenses** are incurred to sell or market the merchandise or services sold by the business. Examples of selling expenses are the costs of advertising and the salaries of salespeople.

Administrative expenses are costs related to the management of the business. Examples of administrative expenses are office expenses and salaries of management personnel.

CHAPTER 28   Analyzing and Interpreting Financial Statements

Today's computer programs can quickly and accurately produce classified financial statements from information stored in the computer's memory.

▲ **Other Revenue and Expenses**   As you learned in Chapter 25, other revenue and other expenses are non-operating revenue or expenses. That is, other revenue and expenses do not result from the normal operations of the business. Examples of other revenue or expenses are the interest paid and interest earned on notes.

R—E—M—E—M—B—E—R

The financial statements issued by public corporations may be analyzed by many people. Classifying the accounts reported on the financial statement makes analysis easier because the accounts of the corporation are separated into related groups.

Before you read about how to analyze financial statements, complete the following activity to check your understanding of classified financial statements.

Check Your Learning

Match the account in Column A with the proper classification in Column B. Write your answers on notebook paper.

Column A	Column B
1. Accounts Payable	**A.** Administrative Expense
2. Cash in Bank	**B.** Cost of Merchandise Sold
3. Equipment	**C.** Current Asset
4. Interest Income	**D.** Current Liability
5. Land	**E.** Investments
6. Merchandise Inventory	**F.** Long-Term Liability
7. Mortgage Payable	**G.** Selling Expense
8. Office Salaries Expense	**H.** Other Revenue and Expenses
9. Purchases	**I.** Property, Plant, and Equipment
10. Retained Earnings	**J.** Stockholders' Equity
11. Store Supplies Expense	
12. TBS, Inc. (stock)	

Compare your answers to those in the answers section. Re-read the preceding part of the chapter to find the correct answers to any questions you may have missed.

The Analysis of Financial Statements

As mentioned earlier, many people analyze financial statements to evaluate the financial performance of a business. The information reported on financial statements is expressed primarily in dollar amounts. Although dollar amounts are useful for many purposes, amounts by themselves generally don't mean very much. The analysis of financial statements is more meaningful when the dollar relationships within the financial statements are converted to percentages. These percentages enable readers to more easily clarify and compare changes from one accounting period to another, as well as changes within one accounting period.

Three types of analyses using percentages are horizontal analysis, vertical analysis, and ratio analysis.

Horizontal Analysis

The comparison of the same items on financial statements for two or more accounting periods and the analysis of changes from one period to the next is called **horizontal analysis.** The comparison of financial statements normally begins with the comparison of the current and past year's statements. The current balance of one item is compared with the balance of the same item on the previous year's statement. Look at the comparative balance sheet shown in Figure 28-3 on page 616.

With horizontal analysis, each amount on the current statement (the first column) is compared with its corresponding amount on the previous statement (the second column). The dollar increase or decrease is calculated and reported in the third column. The percentage of the increase or decrease is also reported (fourth column). Decreases are reported by enclosing the amount and the percentage in parentheses.

Let's look at an example. On the comparative balance sheet, the ending balance of Cash in Bank for 1992 was $7,453. For the following year, 1993, the balance of Cash in Bank was $17,200. By subtracting the 1992 balance from the 1993 balance, you find that cash for the current year increased by $9,747. To calculate the percentage of the increase, divide the amount of the increase ($9,747) by the base year amount and multiply by 100. A **base year** is a year that is used for comparison, in this case, 1992.

$$\frac{\$9,747}{\$7,453} = 1.3078 \times 100 = 130.78\%$$

As you can see, both dollar amounts and percentages may be compared. Although dollar comparisons are easier to compute, percentage changes are more revealing. For example, look again at the increase in Cash in Bank of $9,747. The percentage increase more clearly shows how substantial the increase was from 1992 to 1993. The firm's cash position improved greatly. Notice also that Fitness Forever almost doubled its investment in the stock of A-Z Technologies during 1993.

R — E — M — E — M — B — E — R

To calculate the percentage of increase or decrease, divide the dollar amount of the increase or decrease by the base year amount and multiply by 100.

Fitness Forever, Inc.
Comparative Balance Sheet
December 31, 1993 and 1992

	1993	1992	Increase (Decrease) (1993 over 1992) Dollars	Percentage
Assets				
Current Assets:				
Cash in Bank	$ 17,200	$ 7,453	$ 9,747	130.78%
Accounts Receivable	48,030	41,200	6,830	16.58%
Merchandise Inventory	53,000	49,000	4,000	8.16%
Store Supplies	4,210	4,120	90	2.18%
Prepaid Insurance	780	650	130	20.00%
Total Current Assets	123,220	102,423	20,797	20.31%
Investments:				
A-Z Technologies, Inc. (stock)	21,000	11,000	10,000	90.91%
Property, Plant, and Equipment:				
Equipment (net)	31,000	29,000	2,000	6.90%
Building (net)	110,000	115,000	(5,000)	(4.35%)
Land	15,000	15,000	0	0.00%
Total Property, Plant, and Equipment	156,000	159,000	(3,000)	(1.89%)
Total Assets	$300,220	$272,423	$27,797	10.20%
Liabilities				
Current Liabilities:				
Notes Payable	$ 15,000	$ 14,000	$ 1,000	7.14%
Accounts Payable	39,000	37,900	1,100	2.90%
Sales Tax Payable	1,765	1,345	420	31.23%
Total Current Liabilities	55,765	53,245	2,520	4.73%
Long-Term Liabilities:				
Mortgage Payable	28,000	33,000	(5,000)	(15.15%)
Total Liabilities	83,765	86,245	(2,480)	(2.88%)
Stockholders' Equity				
Common Stock, $90 par, 4,000 shares authorized, 800 shares issued	72,000	72,000	0	0.00%
Retained Earnings	144,455	114,178	30,277	26.52%
Total Stockholders' Equity	216,455	186,178	30,277	6.26%
Total Liabilities and Stockholders' Equity	$300,220	$272,423	$27,797	10.20%

Figure 28-3 Comparative Balance Sheet Showing Horizontal Analysis

Vertical Analysis

With **vertical analysis,** each dollar amount reported on a financial statement is also stated as a percentage of a base amount reported on the same statement. In other words, vertical analysis uses percentages to show the relationship of the different parts to the total on a particular financial statement. Each amount on the income statement, for example, is reported as a percentage of net sales. On the balance sheet, each individual asset is reported as a percentage of total assets. The individual liabilities and equities are reported as a percentage of total liabilities and stockholders' equity. Current year percentages may then be compared with percentages from past periods or with percentages from other businesses within the same industry. The percentages may also be used to construct future budgets.

Let's look at an example of vertical analysis. A comparative income statement showing vertical analysis appears in Figure 28-4. As you can see, the net sales amount for each year is assigned a percentage of 100%. Every other amount on the income statement is then compared to the net sales amount. (Amounts may not total exactly 100% because of rounding.)

Look at the amounts reported for sales. In 1992, sales were $556,000; in 1993, the amount had increased to $578,000. To calculate the percentages, each amount is divided by the net sales amount.

Fitness Forever, Inc.
Comparative Income Statement
For the Years Ended December 31, 1993 and 1992

	1993		1992	
	Dollars	Percentage	Dollars	Percentage
Revenue:				
Sales	$578,000	100.52%	$556,000	100.51%
Less: Sales Returns	3,000	0.52%	2,800	0.51%
Net Sales	575,000	100.00%	553,200	100.00%
Cost of Merchandise Sold:				
Merch. Inv., January 1	49,000	8.52%	46,000	8.32%
Net Purchases	385,000	66.96%	375,000	67.79%
Merchandise Available for Sale	434,000	75.48%	421,000	76.10%
Merch. Inv., December 31	53,000	9.22%	49,000	8.86%
Cost of Merchandise Sold	381,000	66.26%	372,000	67.25%
Gross Profit on Sales	194,000	33.74%	181,200	32.75%
Operating Expenses:				
Selling Expenses:				
Advertising Expense	10,000	1.74%	9,100	1.64%
Depr. Exp. — Store Equip.	4,000	0.70%	4,000	0.72%
Sales Salaries Expense	50,000	8.70%	47,000	8.50%
Store Supplies Expense	10,350	1.80%	9,240	1.67%
Total Selling Expenses	74,350	12.93%	69,340	12.53%
Administrative Expenses:				
Depr. Exp. — Office Equip.	2,800	0.49%	2,800	0.51%
Insurance Expense	900	0.16%	870	0.16%
Miscellaneous Expense	750	0.13%	810	0.15%
Office Salaries Expense	69,000	12.00%	66,000	11.93%
Total Administrative Exp.	73,450	12.77%	70,480	12.74%
Total Operating Expenses	147,800	25.70%	139,820	25.27%
Operating Income	46,200	8.03%	41,380	7.48%
Other Expenses:				
Interest Expense	3,400	0.59%	3,800	0.69%
Net Income	$ 42,800	7.44%	$ 37,580	6.79%

Figure 28-4 Comparative Income Statement Showing Vertical Analysis

	1993		1992	
Sales	$578,000		$556,000	
Net Sales	$575,000	= 100.52%	$553,200	= 100.51%

Look at another example. In dollar amounts, the gross profit on sales for 1992 and 1993 were different—$181,200 for 1992 and $194,000 for 1993. When converted to percentages of net sales, however, the results for the two years are almost exactly the same. In other words, gross profit on sales increased in 1993, but net sales also increased. As a result, the relationship of gross profit on sales to net sales remained the same.

R — E — M — E — M — B — E — R

On an income statement arranged for vertical analysis, each dollar amount is expressed as a percentage of net sales. On a balance sheet arranged for vertical analysis, each asset amount is expressed as a percentage of total assets and each liability or equity amount is expressed as a percentage of total liabilities and stockholders' equity.

Vertical analysis is useful for comparing the importance of certain components in the operation of the business. It is also useful for pointing out important changes in the components from one year to the next.

The income statement and the balance sheet may also be prepared to show both horizontal and vertical analysis on the same statement.

Now do the following activity to check your understanding of horizontal and vertical analyses.

Check Your Learning

Match the items in Column A with the proper statements in Column B. Write your answers on notebook paper.

Column A

1. Comparative statement
2. Horizontal analysis
3. Net sales
4. Total assets (or Total liabilities and stockholders' equity)
5. Vertical analysis

Column B

A. Expresses each item on the statement as a percentage of a base item on the same statement
B. The base used in vertical analysis of the balance sheet
C. Comparison of an amount on one statement with the same item on a preceding year's statement
D. The base used in vertical analysis of the income statement
E. A statement that reports amounts for two or more fiscal periods

Compare your answers to those in the answers section. Re-read the preceding part of the chapter to find the correct answers to any questions you may have missed.

Working Capital

The amount by which current assets exceed current liabilities is known as the company's **working capital.** Working capital is an important measure of a company's ability to meet its short-term liquidity needs. Because current liabilities are usually paid out of current assets, working capital represents the excess assets available to continue business operations. It represents the assets available to purchase inventory, obtain credit, and expand operations. Lack of working capital can lead to the failure of the business.

The working capital for Fitness Forever, Inc., for 1991 and 1992 is calculated as follows:

	1992	1991
Current Assets	$123,220	$102,423
– Current Liabilities	– 55,765	– 53,245
Working Capital	$ 67,455	$ 49,178

Working capital is useful when analyzing one company's financial statements. It is, however, difficult to compare one company's working capital with another company's. For example, working capital of $50,000 may be adequate for a small grocery store but totally inadequate for a large grocery store.

R E M E M B E R

Working capital is current assets less current liabilities.

Ratio Analysis

A ratio is a relationship between two numbers. **Ratio analysis** then is a comparison of two items on a financial statement, resulting in a percentage that is used to evaluate the relationship between the two items. Ratio analysis is generally used to determine a business's financial strength, activity, and the debt-paying ability. Two general measures of financial strength and debt-paying ability are liquidity ratios and profitability ratios.

All examples used in the following discussion are taken from the comparative financial statements shown in Figures 28-3 and 28-4.

Liquidity Ratios

As you recall from Chapter 5, liquidity refers to the ease with which an asset can be converted to cash. A **liquidity ratio** is a measure of a business's ability to pay its current debts as they become due and to provide for unexpected needs of cash. Two common ratios that are used to determine liquidity are the current ratio and the quick ratio.

Computer software can be used to calculate liquidity and profitability ratios, which can then be used for forecasting.

▲ **Current Ratio** The **current ratio** is the relationship between current assets and current liabilities. The current ratio is calculated by dividing the dollar amount of current assets by the dollar amount of current liabilities. On the comparative balance sheet in Figure 28-3 on page 616, current assets for 1993 are $123,220. Current liabilities are $55,765. The current ratio is calculated as follows:

$$\frac{\text{Current Assets}}{\text{Current Liabilities}} \quad \frac{\$123,220}{\$55,765} = 2.21 \text{ or } 2.21:1$$

Ratios are often written as $1:1$ (1 to 1) or $2:2$ (2 to 2).

The current ratio for one period may be compared to the current ratio for another period to determine whether the ratio is increasing or decreasing. For example, to find the current ratio for 1992, the current assets of $102,423 are divided by the current liabilities of $53,245.

$$\frac{\$102,423}{\$53,245} = 1.92:1$$

The current liabilities of a business must be paid within a year. These liabilities are paid from current assets. The current ratio indicates whether the business is in a good position to pay its current debts. A widely used rule-of-thumb is that the current ratio should be at least $2:1$. A current ratio of $2:1$ indicates that a business has current assets that are two times its current liabilities. In other words, the business has $2 of current assets for each $1 of current liabilities.

A ratio of $2:1$ or higher is considered favorable by creditors because it indicates that a business is able to pay its debts. A low ratio may indicate that a company could have trouble paying its current debts.

▲ **Quick Ratio**   One of the limitations of the current ratio is that it is based on total current assets. Current assets include merchandise inventory and prepaid items such as supplies and insurance. Inventory may take time to convert to cash, while prepaid items are consumed during business operations. A more rigorous measure of debt-paying ability is the quick ratio. The **quick ratio** is a measure of the relationship between short-term liquid assets and current liabilities. Short-term liquid assets—those that can be converted to cash quickly—are cash and net receivables. The quick ratio is calculated by dividing the total cash and receivables by current liabilities.

Let's look at an example. Again using the balance sheet in Figure 28-3 on page 616, cash and receivables for 1993 total $65,230. Current liabilities are $55,765. Dividing cash and receivables by current liabilities gives a ratio of 1.17:1.

$$\frac{\text{Cash and Receivables}}{\text{Current Liabilities}} \quad \frac{\$65,230}{\$55,765} = 1.17:1$$

Quick ratios may also be compared from one year to the next. For example, cash and receivables for 1992 were $48,653. Current liabilities were $53,245.

$$\frac{\$48,653}{\$53,245} = 0.91:1$$

A quick ratio of 1 to 1 is considered adequate. That is, if a business has a quick ratio of 1:1 or higher, the business has $1 in liquid assets for each $1 of its current liabilities. As you can see, Fitness Forever improved its liquidity position in 1992.

Before continuing, complete the following activity to check your understanding of the material you have just studied.

Check Your Learning

Use the following accounting data to answer the questions.

| Current Assets | $135,000 | Cash in Bank | $ 9,500 |
| Current Liabilities | 62,000 | Accounts Receivable | 18,250 |

1. What is the working capital?
2. What is the current ratio?
3. What is the quick ratio?

Compare your answers to those in the answers section. Re-read the preceding part of the chapter to find the correct answers to any questions you may have missed.

Profitability Ratios

Profitability ratios are used to evaluate the earnings performance of the business during the accounting period. A business's earning power is an important measure of its ability to grow and to continue to earn revenue. Two commonly used profitability ratios are the return on common stockholders' equity and the return on sales.

▲ **Return on Common Stockholders' Equity** Return on common stockholders' equity shows how well a business has used the resources provided by stockholders' investments. This ratio looks at profitability from the point of view of the investor. Investors commit their dollars to a business and want to receive a fair return on their investments. Investors also want to compare the return on an investment with other possible investments.

Fitness Forever, Inc., has only one class of capital stock. As a result, the return on common stockholders' equity is calculated by dividing net income by the average common stockholders' equity. Average common stockholders' equity is found by adding the beginning stockholders' equity amount and the ending stockholders' equity amount and dividing that total by 2. (If the company also had preferred stock, the preferred stock dividends for the period would have to be subtracted from the net income amount and the balances of the preferred stock accounts subtracted from the stockholders' equity amount.)

Look again at the comparative income statement in Figure 28-4. The net income for 1993 is $42,800. On the comparative balance sheet in Figure 28-3, the beginning common stockholders' equity amount for 1993 is $186,178 and the ending stockholders' equity amount is $216,455. (The ending amount reported for 1992 is the beginning amount for 1993.) The average common stockholders' equity amount is $201,317 ($186,178 + $216,455 = $402,633 ÷ 2). The return on common stockholders' equity for 1993 then is calculated as follows:

$$\frac{\text{Net Income}}{\text{Average Common Stockholders' Equity}} \quad \frac{\$42,800}{\$201,317} = 0.2126 \text{ or } 21.26\%$$

The return on common stockholders' equity shows that the business earned more than 21 cents for each dollar invested in the business by the common stockholders.

The return on common stockholders' equity ratio can be compared to the ratios for previous periods. For example, in 1992 Fitness Forever had a net income of $37,580. The beginning stockholders' equity amount (taken from a previous statement) was $142,598 and the ending stockholders' equity amount was $186,178. The return on owners' investment for 1992 is

$$\frac{\$37,580}{\$164,388} = 0.2286 \text{ or } 22.86\%$$

As you can see, the return on common stockholders' equity decreased slightly from 1992 to 1993.

▲ **Return on Sales**   The return on sales reflects the portion of each dollar of sales that represents profit. Return on sales is computed during vertical analysis of the income statement. To calculate the return on sales, divide the net income by the net sales for the period. In 1993, Fitness Forever had a net income of $42,800 and net sales of $575,000. The return on sales is calculated as follows:

$$\frac{\text{Net Income}}{\text{Net Sales}} \quad \frac{\$42,800}{\$575,000} = 0.0744 \text{ or } 7.44\%$$

This return on sales percentage indicates that each dollar of sales in 1993 produced 7.44 cents of profit. This percentage may be compared to other accounting periods to determine whether it is increasing or decreasing. For example, net income in 1992 was $37,580 and net sales were $553,200. The return on sales for 1992 is thus 6.79%.

$$\frac{\$37,580}{\$553,200} = 0.0679 \text{ or } 6.79\%$$

As you can see, profit per sales dollar increased in 1993 by 0.65 cents over 1992.

Now complete the following activity to check your understanding of profitability ratios.

Check Your Learning

Match the descriptions in Column A with the proper items in Column B.

Column A	Column B
1. Computed during vertical analysis of the income statement	**A.** Return on common stockholders' equity
2. Measures management's success with the use of investors' capital	**B.** Return on sales
3. Allows investors to compare the return on an investment with other potential investment opportunities	
4. Represents profit per dollar of sales	

Compare your answers to those in the answers section. Re-read the preceding part of the chapter to find the correct answers to any questions you may have missed.

Summary of Key Points

1. Qualitative characteristics are those characteristics that make accounting information useful and understandable. The three qualitative characteristics are relevance, reliability, and comparability.

2. Two guidelines accountants follow when preparing financial statements are full disclosure and materiality.

3. Classified balance sheets and income statements are usually prepared by accountants to help make these financial statements more useful and easier to analyze for the user.

4. Three types of analyses made of financial statements are horizontal analysis, vertical analysis, and ratio analysis.

5. The analysis of a change between two amounts on a financial statement from one accounting period to the next is called horizontal analysis.

6. Vertical analysis requires that each amount on a financial statement be restated as a percentage of a base figure on the same statement.

7. Liquidity ratios measure the ability of a business to meet its short-term debts. Common liquidity measures are the current ratio and the quick ratio.

8. Profitability ratios analyze the earning performance of the business. Two commonly used profitability ratios are return on common stockholders' equity and return on sales.

Review and Applications

Building Your Accounting Vocabulary

In your own words, write the definition of each of the following accounting terms. Use complete sentences for your definitions.

administrative expenses
base year
comparability
current liabilities
current ratio
full disclosure

horizontal analysis
investments
liquidity ratios
long-term liabilities
materiality
profitability ratios
quick ratio

ratio analysis
relevance
reliability
selling expenses
vertical analysis
working capital

Reviewing Your Accounting Knowledge

1. Identify the people or businesses that would be interested in analyzing the financial statements of a business.
2. What are the three qualitative characteristics of accounting?
3. Name two guidelines accountants follow to make sure financial statements are clear and consistent.
4. What is the purpose of classifying financial statements?
5. What is the difference between horizontal and vertical analysis?
6. What is the purpose of computing ratios from amounts on financial statements?
7. Why might a creditor be interested in the liquidity ratios of a business?
8. How are the current ratio and the quick ratio similar? different?
9. Who might be interested in the profitability ratios of a business?
10. Which ratios will help you to answer the following questions:
    a. How effective is the firm's use of credit?
    b. Are the resources (assets) of the firm being used effectively?

Improving Your Decision-Making Skills

The following information was taken from the accounting records of the Lorain Corporation:

Current assets	$238,000
Total stockholders' equity	85,680
Current liabilities	152,320

How would you evaluate this company's debt? If you were a creditor, would you extend additional credit to the company?

Applying Accounting Procedures

Exercise 28-1   Preparing a Horizontal Analysis

The following amounts appeared on the comparative balance sheet for the Sharp Hats Co.

Instructions: Determine the amount of increase or decrease and the percentage of increase or decrease for each amount listed. Use the form in the working papers and round percentages to two decimal places.

	1992	1991
Current Assets	$540,000	$510,000
Property, Plant, and Equipment	455,000	470,000
Total Assets	$995,000	$980,000
Liabilities	$410,000	$400,000
Stockholders' Equity	585,000	580,000
Total Liabilities and Stockholders' Equity	$995,000	$980,000

Exercise 28-2 Preparing a Vertical Analysis

The following amounts appeared on the comparative income statement of the Sharp Hats Co.

Instructions: Prepare a comparative income statement using vertical analysis. Round percentages to two decimal places.

	1992	1991
Net Sales	$700,000	$625,000
Cost of Merchandise Sold	450,000	380,000
Gross Profit on Sales	250,000	245,000
Operating Expenses	175,000	175,000
Net Income	$ 75,000	$ 70,000

Exercise 28-3 Calculating Liquidity Ratios

The following account balances were taken from the financial statements of the Times-Wright Corporation.

Instructions:

(1) Determine the company's working capital.

(2) Calculate the current ratio.

(3) Calculate the quick ratio.

Cash in Bank	$ 90,000	Accounts Payable	$185,000
Accounts Receivable	185,000	Federal Inc. Tax Payable	30,000
Merchandise Inventory	165,000	Sales Tax Payable	10,000
Prepaid Expenses	11,500		

Exercise 28-4 Calculating Profitability Ratios

The following data were taken from the financial statements of the Exact Fit Company.

Instructions: For each year,

(1) Calculate the return on common stockholders' equity. The beginning common stockholders' equity amount for 1991 was $751,500.

(2) Calculate the return on sales.

	1992	1991
Net Sales	$315,000	$265,000
Net Income	25,000	23,500
Capital Stock	500,000	500,000
Retained Earnings	300,000	275,000

Problem 28-1   Preparing a Classified Balance Sheet

The following account balances appeared on the December 31 work sheet for the Q-Tex Company. The corporation is authorized to issue 10,000 shares of $100 par common stock.

Instructions: Prepare a classified balance sheet for the Q-Tex Company.

Accounts Payable	$10,750	Merchandise Inventory	$14,800
Accounts Receivable (net)	6,700	Mortgage Payable	25,000
Building (net)	37,500	Notes Payable	5,700
Cash in Bank	7,500	Office Equipment (net)	18,000
Common Stock	50,000	Office Supplies	1,200
Edge It Corp. (stock)	23,000	Retained Earnings	38,500
Land	22,000	Sales Tax Payable	750

Problem 28-2   Using Horizontal Analysis

The following is a partial comparative income statement for Mini-Sports Shop, Inc.

Instructions: Complete the comparative income statement using horizontal analysis. Round all percentages to two decimal places. Use the form provided in the working papers.

Mini-Sports Shop, Inc.
Comparative Income Statement
For the Years Ended August 31, 1992 and 1991

	1992	1991
Revenue:		
Sales	$232,345	$208,578
Less: Sales Returns and Allowances	4,350	3,988
Net Sales	227,995	204,590
Cost of Merchandise Sold	135,678	122,345
Gross Profit on Sales	92,317	82,245
Operating Expenses:		
Selling Expenses:		
Advertising Expense	9,500	8,700
Delivery Expense	7,678	7,456
Depr. Exp. — Store Equipment	1,000	1,000
Sales Salaries Expense	21,500	19,899
Travel Expense	4,567	4,134
Total Selling Expenses	44,245	41,189
Administrative Expenses:		
Bad Debts Expense	2,350	2,200
Depr. Exp. — Office Equipment	2,000	2,000
Insurance Expense	2,500	2,400
Miscellaneous Expense	2,367	2,200
Office Salaries Expense	12,345	11,397
Rent Expense	5,000	4,500
Total Administrative Expenses	26,562	24,697
Total Operating Expenses	70,807	65,886
Operating Income	21,510	16,359
Other Revenue	4,500	1,550
Other Expenses	270	456
Net Income	$ 25,740	$ 17,453

Problem 28-3 Using Vertical Analysis

The following is a partial comparative balance sheet for the Mini-Sports Shop, Inc.

Instructions: Complete the comparative balance sheet using vertical analysis. Round the percentages to two decimal places. Use the form provided in the working papers.

Mini-Sports Shop, Inc.
Comparative Balance Sheet
August 31, 1993 and 1992

	1993	1992
Assets		
Current Assets:		
Cash in Bank	$ 11,900	$ 10,890
Accounts Receivable (net)	16,780	15,450
Merchandise Inventory	45,000	38,700
Prepaid Expenses	2,100	1,860
Total Current Assets	75,780	66,900
Investments:		
Runner, Inc. (stock)	10,500	8,500
Property, Plant, and Equipment:		
Equipment (net)	35,000	30,000
Building (net)	75,000	80,000
Land	15,000	15,000
Total Property, Plant, and Equip.	125,000	125,000
Total Assets	$211,280	$200,400
Liabilities		
Current Liabilities:		
Notes Payable	$ 22,500	$ 18,600
Accounts Payable	15,600	13,200
Sales Tax Payable	1,300	1,200
Total Current Liabilities	39,400	33,000
Long-Term Liabilities:		
Mortgage Payable	15,000	25,000
Total Liabilities	54,400	58,000
Stockholders' Equity		
Common Stock, $100 par, 5,000 shares authorized, 500 shares issued	50,000	50,000
Retained Earnings	106,880	92,400
Total Stockholders' Equity	156,880	142,400
Total Liabilities and Stockholders' Equity	$211,280	$200,400

SPREADSHEET

PROBLEM

Problem 28-4 Calculating Ratios

The following balances appeared on the financial statements of The Music Center, Inc.

Cash in Bank	$135,000	Notes Payable	$ 25,000
Accounts Receivable	195,000	Accounts Payable	210,000
Merchandise Inventory	387,000	Dividends Payable	0
Prepaid Insurance	20,000	Federal Inc. Tax Pay.	15,000
Supplies	13,000	Sales Tax Payable	10,000

Instructions:

(1) Use the account balances to compute the working capital, the current ratio, and the quick ratio.

(2) Compute the working capital, current ratio, and quick ratio after considering each of the following *independent* transactions. In other words, determine what effect each transaction would have on the three ratios.

Transactions:

1. Received cash on account, $100,000.
2. Paid accounts payable, $100,000.
3. Purchased merchandise on account, $75,000.
4. Borrowed $150,000, signing a long-term note payable.
5. Paid notes payable of $25,000.
6. Issued common stock at par, receiving $125,000.
7. Paid cash for supplies, $25,000.
8. Declared a cash dividend of $125,000.
9. Paid $50,000 on the long-term note payable.
10. Borrowed $75,000, signing a 30-day note payable.

CHALLENGE Problem 28-5 Determining Financial Statement Amounts

The abbreviated financial statements for the Eastway Metal Company appear below. The statements have several dollar amounts missing.

Instructions: Compute the missing amounts and complete the financial statements. Assume that stockholders' equity did not change. Additional information needed is given here.

Current ratio:	2:1
Quick ratio:	1.5:1
Gross profit percentage:	40%
Return on sales:	4%
Return on common stockholders' equity:	6%

Eastway Metal Company
Balance Sheet
December 31, 19—

Cash in Bank	$?	Current Liabilities	$?	
Merchandise Inventory	?	Long-Term Liabilities	225,000	
Property, Plant, and Equipment	?	Stockholders' Equity	?	
		Total Liabilities and		
Total Assets	$ 500,000	**Stockholders' Equity**	$ 500,000	

Eastway Metal Company
Income Statement
For the Year Ended December 31, 19—

Net Sales	$?
Cost of Merchandise Sold	?
Gross Profit on Sales	?
Total Operating Expenses	?
Net Income	$ 10,500

CHALLENGE Problem 28-6 Determining Financial Statement Amounts

An abbreviated comparative income statement for Bay State Lumber, Inc., is shown on page 629.

Instructions: Complete the statement by determining the missing amounts for each of the question marks. Determine percentages to the nearest tenth of a percent. Use plain paper or the form provided in the working papers.

Bay State Lumber, Inc.
Comparative Income Statement
For the Years Ended December 31, 1992 and 1991

	1992	1991	Increase (Decrease) 1992 over 1991 Dollars	Percentage
Net Sales	$690,106	?	$116,966	?
Cost of Merchandise Sold	?	$281,834	59,028	?
Gross Profit on Sales	349,244	?	?	19.9%
Total Operating Expenses	?	176,085	?	7.7%
Operating Income	159,612	115,221	?	?
Other Revenue	1,802	?	197	?
Other Expenses	?	1,403	?	(39.5%)
Net Income	?	?	?	?

*D*oes Friendship Always Come First?

*C*ould you confront a friend who had broken company policy, or even the law, and still maintain that friendship? Would you be willing to risk a friendship if you felt that your friend's code of ethics did not match yours? Before you answer, consider the following situation.

Devon and Jason have been best friends since high school. They both went to the same college, roomed together, and majored in accounting. During their senior year, a financial firm was on campus recruiting, and both young men landed a job. Within the firm, they both did well, but diverged in their responsibilities. Jason handled most of the customer accounts while Devon pursued managerial accounting.

One day, during Devon's routine auditing of the different departments, Devon found some numbers in Jason's records that had been deliberately falsified. Devon agonized over what to do. Since Jason was the only one with access to these records, he had to have been the one who set up the phony auditing trail. Should he confront Jason personally? Should he go directly to Jason's boss? In the end, Devon decided to go directly to Jason.

Jason admitted to Devon what he had done, and said that he had been too ashamed to tell Devon about it before. The problem was that Jason was not able to immediately pay back the money he had taken. He promised Devon that he would pay back the money, but asked Devon not to tell anyone.

What is the ethical dilemma that Devon faces? If Devon reports Jason, Jason would most likely lose his job, might have criminal charges brought against him, and would probably no longer call Devon his friend. The money Jason took also might be lost for good. If Devon agrees to shield Jason,

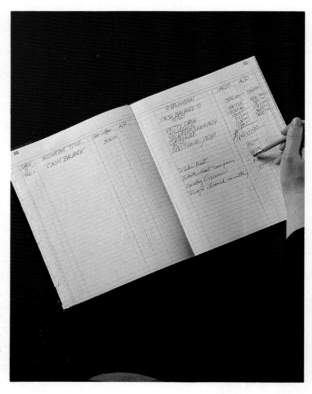

Friends often share common interests, ideas, and activities. Friendships can become very complicated, though, when a friend's code of ethics differs from yours.

the money belonging to the firm's customers might eventually be repaid, but if the theft were discovered, Devon would be implicated along with Jason. If you were in Devon's place, what would you do?

Additional Reinforcement Problems

Additional problems are not included for Chapter 1.

Chapter 2, Problem 2A Determining the Effects of Business Transactions on the Accounting Equation

Ashley Moore has set up a business for herself as an accountant.

Instructions: Use a form similar to the one below. For each of the following transactions,

(1) Identify the accounts affected.
(2) Write the amount of the increase or decrease in the space provided.
(3) Determine the new balance for each account.

	ASSETS					=	LIABILITIES	+	OWNER'S EQUITY
Trans.	Cash in Bank	Accts. Rec.	Office Supp.	Comp. Equip.	Office Equip.	=	Accounts Payable	+	A. Moore, Capital
1									

Transactions:

1. Ashley Moore, the owner, opened a checking account for the business by depositing $48,000 of her personal funds.
2. Paid the monthly rent of $1,500.
3. Bought office supplies on account for $1,000.
4. Ashley Moore invested $3,000 of office equipment in the business.
5. Paid cash for a new computer for the business, $5,000.
6. Paid for an advertisement in the local newspaper, $200.
7. Completed accounting services for a client and sent a bill for $800.
8. Paid $700 on account for the office supplies bought earlier.
9. Received $500 on account from a client.
10. Ashley Moore withdrew $1,000 from the business for personal use.

Chapter 3, Problem 3A Analyzing Transactions into Debit and Credit Parts

Paul Morales owns a cleaning service. The accounts he uses to record and report business transactions are listed on the following page.

Cash in Bank   Store Equipment
Accounts Receivable Van
Cleaning Supplies   Accounts Payable
Cleaning Equipment Paul Morales, Capital

Instructions:

(1) Prepare a T account for each account listed above.
(2) Analyze and record each of the following business transactions in the appropriate T accounts. Identify each transaction by number.
(3) After recording all transactions, compute and record the account balance on the normal balance side of each T account.
(4) Add the balances of those accounts with normal debit balances.
(5) Add the balances of those accounts with normal credit balances.
(6) Compare the two totals. Are they the same?

Transactions:

1. Paul Morales invested $30,000 from his savings into the business.
2. Invested cleaning equipment, valued at $650, in the business.
3. Bought a van on account from Westside Motors for $19,360.
4. Bought cleaning supplies for $550, Check 100.
5. Bought a new rug shampooer on account from Harris Equipment for $1,250.
6. As a favor, sold some cleaning supplies on credit to a neighboring business, $50.
7. Purchased storage shelves for the business for $650, Check 101.
8. Paid $500 on account to Harris Equipment, Check 102.
9. Bought cleaning supplies for $175, Check 103.
10. Paid $1,250 on account to Westside Motors, Check 104.

Chapter 4, Problem 4A   Analyzing Transactions

Jane Black owns the Arbor Landscaping Service. She plans to use the following accounts for recording and reporting business transactions.

Cash in Bank   Jane Black, Withdrawals
Accounts Receivable Landscaping Fees
Equipment   Maintenance Expense
Accounts Payable   Rent Expense
Jane Black, Capital Utilities Expense

Instructions:

(1) Prepare a T account for each account listed above.
(2) Analyze and record each of the following transactions, using the appropriate T accounts. Identify each transaction by number.
(3) After recording all transactions, compute a balance for each account.
(4) Test for the equality of debits and credits.

Transactions:

1. Jane Black invested $25,000 cash in the business.
2. Bought a new lawnmower on account from Mason Lawn Products, Inc., for $1,400.
3. Jane Black invested equipment valued at $125 in the business.
4. Paid the rent for the month of $350, Check 101.
5. Wrote Check 102 for $20 for minor repairs to the equipment.
6. Completed landscaping for a customer and sent a bill for $350.

7. Paid the utility bill of $75, Check 103.
8. Deposited the daily receipts for landscaping services, $175.
9. Sent Check 104 for $500 to Mason Lawn Products as a payment on account.
10. Received $150 from a charge customer on account.
11. Ms. Black withdrew $150 for her personal use, Check 105.
12. Paid the telephone bill of $35, Check 106.
13. Deposited the daily receipts of $600 for landscaping services.

Chapter 5, Problem 5A   Recording Transactions in the General Journal

Six months ago, Jack Wiley opened his own engineering company. He uses the following accounts to record the business's transactions.

Cash in Bank	Accounts Payable—Engineering Suppliers
Accounts Receivable—Hempfield Township	Accounts Payable—Mohawk Van Dealers
Accounts Receivable—Unity Township	Jack Wiley, Capital
Engineering Supplies	Jack Wiley, Withdrawals
Surveying Equipment	Professional Fees
Blueprint Equipment	Advertising Expense
Motor Vehicles	Rent Expense
	Utilities Expense

Instructions: Record the following transactions on page 6 of a general journal.

Transactions:

June 1 Jack Wiley invested surveying equipment valued at $800 in the business, Memorandum 202.
3 Wrote Check 150 to New Town Press for advertisements, $125.
6 Completed services for Hempfield Township and sent a bill for $750, Invoice 91.
8 Paid the $85 utility bill, Check 151.
15 Purchased $160 in engineering supplies from Engineering Suppliers on account, Invoice 1161.
18 Received a check for $375 from Hempfield Township to apply on account, Receipt 123.
20 Sent a bill for $900 to Unity Township for engineering services performed on account, Invoice 92.
22 Sent Check 152 for $160 to Engineering Suppliers on account.
25 Jack Wiley withdrew $15 in engineering supplies for personal use, Memorandum 203.
28 Received $500 from Unity Township on account, Receipt 124.
30 Purchased a $16,000 van from Mohawk Van Dealers on account, Invoice 553.

Chapter 6, Problem 6A   Posting Business Transactions

Bruno Ciani started a business to provide dental services to the community. The accounts used by the business, Bruno Ciani, D.D.S., have been opened and are included in the working papers accompanying this textbook. The general journal entries for the May business transactions are also included in the working papers.

Instructions:

(1) Post each journal entry to the appropriate accounts in the ledger.

(2) Prove the ledger by preparing a trial balance.

Chapter 7, Problem 7A Preparing a Six-Column Work Sheet

The final balances in the general ledger of the Bodyworks Fitness Center at the end of July are as follows.

101	Cash in Bank	$16,095.50
105	Accounts Receivable—R. D. Best	350.00
110	Supplies	612.00
115	Exercise Equipment	15,090.00
120	Office Equipment	2,600.00
125	Office Furniture	3,200.00
201	Accounts Payable—Lake Co.	688.00
205	Accounts Payable—Pro Equipment Co.	2,405.95
210	Accounts Payable—Walton Supply Co.	620.50
301	Lynn Foster, Capital	31,679.55
305	Lynn Foster, Withdrawals	1,500.00
310	Income Summary	0.00
401	Membership Fees	10,500.00
405	Class Fees	8,400.00
501	Advertising Expense	1,250.00
505	Maintenance Expense	1,619.00
510	Miscellaneous Expense	515.00
515	Rent Expense	1,900.00
520	Salaries Expense	6,100.00
525	Utilities Expense	3,462.50

Instructions: Prepare a work sheet for the month ended July 31.

Chapter 8, Problem 8A Preparing Financial Statements

The work sheet for the A-1 Driving School appears below.

A-1 Driving School
Work Sheet
For the Quarter Ended September 30, 19--

ACCT. NO.	ACCOUNT NAME	TRIAL BALANCE DEBIT	TRIAL BALANCE CREDIT	INCOME STATEMENT DEBIT	INCOME STATEMENT CREDIT	BALANCE SHEET DEBIT	BALANCE SHEET CREDIT	
101	Cash in Bank	6 107 00				6 107 00		1
105	Accts. Rec.—Andover Pub. Schools	450 00				450 00		2
110	Accts. Rec.—Taunton Pub. Schools	1 600 00				1 600 00		3
115	Office Equipment	2 510 00				2 510 00		4
120	Motor Vehicles	30 600 00				30 600 00		5
201	Accts. Pay.—Bay State Motors		15 423 00				15 423 00	6
205	Accts. Pay.—Tappley Co.		1 629 00				1 629 00	7
301	Mark O'Keefe, Capital		18 516 00				18 516 00	8
305	Mark O'Keefe, Withdrawals	3 600 00				3 600 00		9
310	Income Summary							10
401	Instruction Fees		15 960 00		15 960 00			11
501	Advertising Expense	2 000 00		2 000 00				12
505	Fuel Expense	1 656 00		1 656 00				13
510	Maintenance Expense	1 800 00		1 800 00				14
515	Rent Expense	900 00		900 00				15
520	Utilities Expense	305 00		305 00				16
		51 528 00	51 528 00	6 661 00	15 960 00	44 867 00	35 568 00	17
	Net Income			9 299 00			9 299 00	18
				15 960 00	15 960 00	44 867 00	44 867 00	19

Instructions:

(1) Prepare an income statement for the quarter ended September 30.

(2) Prepare a statement of changes in owner's equity. Mark O'Keefe made no additional investments during the period.

(3) Prepare a balance sheet in report form.

Chapter 9, Problem 9A   Preparing Closing Entries

The following information appeared on the work sheet of Young Air Conditioning Repair for the year ended June 30.

	Income Statement		Balance Sheet	
	Debit	Credit	Debit	Credit
Harold Young, Capital				38,000.00
Harold Young, Withdrawals			8,000.00	
Income Summary	—	—		
Repair Service Fees		37,000.00		
Advertising Expense	2,000.00			
Miscellaneous Expense	1,500.00			
Rent Expense	12,000.00			
Telephone Expense	1,200.00			
Utilities Expense	3,600.00			
	20,300.00	37,000.00	56,419.00	39,719.00
Net Income	16,700.00			16,700.00
	37,000.00	37,000.00	56,419.00	56,419.00

Instructions: Using the information above, prepare the four journal entries to close the temporary capital accounts. Use journal page 19.

Chapter 10, Problem 10A   Reconciling the Bank Statement

On April 30, the accounting clerk for Horizon Movers received the bank statement dated April 28. After comparing the company's checkbook with the bank statement, the accounting clerk found

1. The checkbook balance on April 30 was $13,462.96.

2. The ending bank statement balance was $13,883.80.

3. The bank statement showed a service charge of $17.50.

4. Deposits of $675.00 on April 28 and $925.00 on April 29 did not appear on the bank statement.

5. The following checks were outstanding:

Check 1266	$125.00	Check 1270	$1,462.19
Check 1268	69.42	Check 1271	381.73

Instructions:

(1) Record the bank service charge in the checkbook.

(2) Reconcile the bank statement for Horizon Movers.

(3) Record the entry for the bank service charge on general journal page 13.

(4) Post the bank service charge to the appropriate ledger accounts.

Chapter 11, Problem 11A   Recording Sales Transactions

The Home Furnishings Center is a retail furniture store. During June, it had the charge sales appearing on page 636.

Instructions:

(1) Record the charge sales for June on sales journal page 9.

(2) Foot, total, prove, and rule the sales journal at the end of the month.

Transactions:

June 2 Sold a chair to Elaine McGarrell for $245.00 plus sales tax of $12.25, Sales Slip 160.

      4 Sold to Larry Falzarano a set of end tables, $175.00 plus $8.75 sales tax, Sales Slip 161.

     10 Sold a magazine rack to Gail Buresh, $22.95 plus sales tax of $1.15, Sales Slip 162.

     11 Sold to Stan Garfield a $179.00 bentwood rocker, $8.95 sales tax, Sales Slip 163.

     15 Sold two earthenware lamps to Margaret Balzotti for $299.90 plus sales tax of $15.00, Sales Slip 164.

     17 Sold a sofa and love seat totaling $1,495.00, sales tax $74.75, to Elaine McGarrell, Sales Slip 165.

     20 Sold a telephone stand, $55.00 plus sales tax of $2.75, to Gail Buresh, Sales Slip 166.

     22 Sold a coffee table to Larry Falzarano for $259.95 plus $13.00 sales tax, Sales Slip 167.

     27 Sold to Elaine McGarrell for $55.00 plus a sales tax of $2.75 a set of three framed prints, Sales Slip 168.

     29 Sold a $69.96 side table to Margaret Balzotti, sales tax $3.50, Sales Slip 169.

Chapter 12, Problem 12A   Journalizing and Posting Cash Receipts Transactions

Hanover House, a retail store, uses special journals and an accounts receivable subsidiary ledger to record its business transactions. The accounts receivable subsidiary ledger is included in the working papers. During the month of August, the store had the cash receipts transactions that follow.

Instructions:

(1) Record the transactions in the cash receipts journal on page 17.

(2) Post the individual amounts from the Accounts Receivable Credit column to the customers' accounts in the accounts receivable subsidiary ledger.

(3) Foot, prove, total, and rule the cash receipts journal.

Transactions:

Aug. 2 Julie Murphy sent a check for $535.50 in payment of a sales slip totaling $546.00 less a $10.50 discount, Receipt 213.

      7 Received cash on account from Kathy Curley, $75.00, Receipt 214.

      8 Received a check for $200.00 from Richard Stratton on account, Receipt 215.

     10 Received a $96.90 check from Robert Gaudet as payment for merchandise totaling $98.80, less a $1.90 discount, Receipt 216.

     12 Recorded cash sales of $1,603.15, plus $64.13 in sales taxes, Tape 96.

     12 Bank card sales totaled $647.50 plus $25.90 sales taxes, Tape 96.

     15 Kathy Curley sent a $75.00 check on account, Receipt 217.

     18 Sold $25.00 of supplies, as a favor, to Arthur Moore, Receipt 218.

Aug. 24 Julie Murphy sent a check for $200.00 on account, Receipt 219.
  28 A $57.40 check was received on account from Robert Gaudet, Receipt 220.
  31 Recorded cash sales, $2,004.91 plus sales taxes of $80.20, Tape 97.
  31 Recorded $495.75 in bank card sales, sales tax $19.83, Tape 97.

Chapter 13, Problem 13A   Journalizing and Posting Purchases on Account

Highland Fashions uses a purchases journal to record its purchases on account. The opened general ledger accounts appear in the working papers.

Instructions:

(1) Record the following transactions on page 11 of a purchases journal.
(2) Post the amounts in the General Debit column to the general ledger.
(3) Foot, prove, total, and rule the purchases journal.
(4) Post the totals of the special amount columns to the general ledger accounts.

Transactions:

Oct. 2 Purchased merchandise on account, $1,263.59, from Liberty Sportswear, Invoice 1633.
  4 Bought supplies on account from Bowen Office Products, Invoice 4301 for $116.25.
  10 Received Invoice 7893 for merchandise purchased on account from Top Drawer Tops, $609.05.
  12 Bought $129.50 worth of merchandise on account from Liberty Sportswear, Invoice 1702.
  15 Davis, Inc., sent Invoice 4782 for merchandise purchased on account, $503.20.
  19 Purchased a new cash register (store equipment) on account from Purcell Equipment, $1,595.00, Invoice 0613.
  23 Received an invoice for merchandise bought on account from Top Drawer Tops, $352.00, Invoice 7909.
  26 Purchased $1,050.90 worth of merchandise on account from Davis, Inc., Invoice 4883.
  29 Received Invoice 4362 for $79.43 for supplies purchased on account from Bowen Office Products.

Chapter 14, Problem 14A   Recording Cash Payment Transactions

Arroyo Leather Goods uses special journals and subsidiary ledgers to record its business transactions. A portion of the company's accounts are included in the working papers.

Instructions:

(1) Record the following transactions in the cash payments journal, page 16.
(2) Post the transactions to the accounts payable subsidiary ledger daily.
(3) Foot, prove, total, and rule the cash payments journal at the end of the month.
(4) Post the total of the Accounts Payable Debit column only to the general ledger.
(5) Prepare a schedule of accounts payable.

Transactions:

Nov. 1 Wrote Check 815 to Mesa Realtors for the November rent of $1,200.00.

2 Paid Harris Luggage Co. $1,309.50 for Invoice 1642 totaling $1,350.00 less the 3% discount of $40.50, Check 816.

4 Purchased $300.00 worth of merchandise from Suede Unlimited for cash, Check 817.

8 Issued Check 818 for office supplies costing $136.95.

9 Paid the telephone bill of $214.92, Check 819.

11 Sent Check 820 to Kenwood Manufacturing, $1,225.00, for Invoice P613 for $1,250.00 less a 2% discount of $25.00.

12 Sent $500.00 to Curry Leather Co. on account, Check 821.

15 Issued Check 822 for $2,509.78 to Renaissance Leather in full payment of Invoice 4389 for $2,561.00 less a $51.22 discount.

16 Purchased a roll of stamps for $25.00 (Misc. Exp.), Check 823.

17 Paid Invoice 1427 from Bugatti Leather Works, $1,125.00 less a discount of $22.50, Check 824 for $1,102.50.

18 Paid the $305.00 electric bill by issuing Check 825.

22 Paid $1,200.00 for a one-year fire insurance policy, Check 826.

24 Purchased merchandise for $1,260.00 cash, Check 827.

25 Recorded the bank service charge of $25.00 from the November bank statement.

25 The bank card fee listed on the November bank statement was $176.60.

26 Sent Check 828 to Kenwood Manufacturing for $666.35, in payment of Invoice P668 for $679.95, less a 2% discount of $13.60.

29 Purchased office supplies for cash, Check 829 for $63.89.

30 Sent Check 830 for $450.00 to Harris Luggage Co. on account.

Chapter 15, Problem 15A Recording General Journal Transactions

Instructions: Record the following transactions of the Pottery Shoppe on page 9 of the general journal.

Transactions:

Jan. 5 Gave credit to Megan O'Hara for the return of $80.00 in merchandise sold on account, plus $4.80 sales tax, Credit Memo 36.

10 Discovered that a $320.00 payment on account from Jack Perkins had been incorrectly journalized and posted to John Parker's account, Memorandum 20.

15 Returned defective merchandise purchased on account from Phillips Corp., $270.00, Debit Memo 42.

20 Discovered that a $330.00 purchase of supplies on account from Holbrook Office Supplies had been incorrectly journalized and posted to the Purchases account, Memorandum 21.

Chapter 15, Problem 15B Analyzing Correcting Entries

The correcting entries on the following page were recorded in the general journal of the Merchandise Mart during July.

Instructions: Give a brief description of the error that was probably made when each transaction was originally recorded.

	DATE	DESCRIPTION	POST. REF.	DEBIT	CREDIT	
1	19-- July 5	Store Equipment		485 00		1
2		Office Equipment			485 00	2
3		Memo. 77				3
4	9	Purchases		1500 00		4
5		Merchandise Inventory			1500 00	5
6		Memo. 78				6
7	14	Steve Snider		90 00		7
8		Stan Snyder			90 00	8
9		Memo. 79				9
10	17	Sales Returns and Allowances		105 00		10
11		Sales			105 00	11
12		Memo. 80				12
13	19	Supplies		165 00		13
14		Purchases			165 00	14
15		Memo. 81				15

Chapter 16, Problem 16A   Completing a Ten-Column Work Sheet

The December 31 account balances for Allston Fabrics, Inc., are listed below. Also listed is the data needed for the adjustments.

	Debit	Credit
Cash in Bank	$ 8,971.14	
Accounts Receivable	5,623.80	
Merchandise Inventory	52,339.50	
Supplies	3,250.00	
Prepaid Insurance	1,800.00	
Office Equipment	8,675.00	
Store Equipment	26,114.25	
Accounts Payable		$ 6,446.90
Federal Income Tax Payable		
Sales Tax Payable		792.97
Capital Stock		30,000.00
Retained Earnings		26,022.38
Income Summary		
Sales		177,890.25
Sales Returns and Allowances	1,316.90	
Purchases	59,296.75	
Transportation In	3,557.80	
Purchases Discounts		1,008.04
Advertising Expense	1,500.00	
Insurance Expense		
Miscellaneous Expense	3,065.40	
Rent Expense	10,800.00	
Salaries Expense	47,600.00	
Supplies Expense		
Federal Income Tax Expense	8,250.00	

Data for Adjustments

Merchandise Inventory, December 31	$ 60,062.00
Supplies on hand, December 31	1,106.50
Insurance premium expired during the period	900.00
Additional federal income taxes owed	1,930.00

Instructions: Complete the ten-column work sheet for Allston Fabrics, Inc., for the year ended December 31. The account titles have already been entered on the work sheet.

Chapter 17, Problem 17A Preparing Financial Statements

The completed work sheet for the Darnell Hobby and Crafts Center appears in the working papers.

Instructions:

(1) Prepare the income statement for the fiscal year ended June 30.

(2) Prepare a statement of retained earnings.

(3) Prepare a balance sheet.

Chapter 18, Problem 18A Journalizing Adjusting Entries

The Bell City Fishing Supply Co. ended its fiscal period on March 31. The following appeared in the Adjustments section of the work sheet.

	Debit	Credit
Merchandise Inventory		(a) 7,000.00
Supplies		(b) 1,632.00
Prepaid Insurance		(c) 900.00
Federal Income Tax Payable		(d) 1,130.00
Income Summary	(a) 7,000.00	
Insurance Expense	(c) 900.00	
Supplies Expense	(b) 1,632.00	
Federal Income Tax Expense	(d) 1,130.00	

Instructions: Journalize the adjusting entries on general journal page 24.

Chapter 18, Problem 18B Journalizing Closing Entries

The following account balances appeared in the Income Statement section of the work sheet for the Merryville Corporation for the year ended June 30.

	Debit	Credit
Income Summary	3,462.00	
Sales		96,412.00
Sales Discounts	867.00	
Sales Returns and Allowances	1,735.00	
Purchases	35,000.00	
Transportation In	1,700.00	
Purchases Discounts		750.00
Purchases Returns and Allowances		455.00
Advertising Expense	900.00	
Bank Card Fees Expense	647.00	
Insurance Expense	1,200.00	
Miscellaneous Expense	369.00	
Rent Expense	18,000.00	
Supplies Expense	2,612.00	
Utilities Expense	4,200.00	
Federal Income Tax Expense	5,343.00	
	76,035.00	97,617.00
Net Income	21,582.00	
	97,617.00	97,617.00

Instructions: Journalize all the closing entries on general journal page 17.

Chapter 19, Problem 19A   Preparing a Payroll Register

Kelly's Supermarket has four employees. They are paid on a weekly basis with overtime paid for all hours worked over 40. The overtime rate is $1\frac{1}{2}$ times the regular rate of pay. The employee names and other information needed to prepare the payroll are as follows.

Don Bell: Married; 3 exemptions; rate per hour, $6.50; employee no. 106
Alice Kerr: Single; 1 exemption; rate per hour, $5.75; employee no. 112; union member
Eric Sullivan: Married; 2 exemptions, rate per hour, $5.25; employee no. 117; union member
Carol Vinton: Single; 0 exemptions; rate per hour, $5.90; employee no. 119; union member

During the week ended May 6, Bell worked 44 hours, Kerr and Vinton each worked 40 hours, and Sullivan worked 41 hours.

Instructions:
(1) Prepare a payroll register. The date of payment is May 6. List employees in alphabetical order by last name.
   (a) Compute FICA taxes at 6.2% for social security and 1.45% for medicare.
   (b) Use the tax charts on pages 424-425 to determine federal income taxes. There is no state income tax.
   (c) All four employees have deductions for hospital insurance: $3.70 for single employees and $5.10 for married employees.
   (d) Union members pay weekly dues of $2.50.
(2) After the payroll information is entered in the payroll register, total the columns and check the accuracy of the totals.

Chapter 20, Problem 20A   Recording Payroll Transactions

The payroll register of Star Bakery for the week ended March 31 appears below.

PAYROLL REGISTER

PAY PERIOD ENDING _____ 19 ____   DATE OF PAYMENT _____

Emp. No.	NAME	Mar. Status	Exemp.	Total Hours	RATE	Earnings Regular	Overtime	Total	Soc. Sec. Tax	Medicare Tax	Fed. Inc. Tax	State Inc. Tax	Hosp. Ins.	Other	Total	Net Pay	Ck. No.
13	Austin, Corrine	S	1	39	6.25	243 75		243 75	15 11	3 53	23 00	9 75	4 50		55 89	187 86	1
16	Fisher, Paul	M	4	40	7.00	280 00		280 00	17 36	4 06	—	11 20	5 25	UW 3 85	41 72	238 28	2
19	Lopez, Lisa	S	1	25	5.80	145 00		145 00	8 99	2 10	8 00	5 80	4 50		29 39	115 61	3
23	Rutherford, Amy	S	0	43	6.80	272 00	30 60	302 60	18 76	4 39	38 00	12 10	4 50	UW 3 00	80 75	221 85	4
26	Williams, Randy	S	2	35	6.50	227 50		227 50	14 11	3 30	13 00	9 10	4 50	e 5 00	49 01	178 49	5
27	Wong, Cynthia	M	3	43	5.90	236 00	26 55	262 55	16 28	3 81	2 00	10 50	5 25	UW 2 25	40 09	222 46	6
	TOTALS					1404 25	57 15	1461 40	90 61	21 19	84 00	58 45	28 50	14 10	296 85	1164 55	

Other Deductions: Write the appropriate code letter to the left of the amount: B—U.S. Savings Bonds; C—Credit Union; UD—Union Dues; UW—United Way.

Instructions: Record the following transactions in the cash payments journal (page 21) and in the general journal (page 11).

Transactions:

Mar. 31 Wrote Check 603 to pay the payroll for the period ended March 31.

     31 Recorded the employer's payroll taxes (FICA tax rates 6.2% for social security tax, 1.45% for medicare tax; federal unemployment tax rate, 0.8%; state unemployment tax rate, 5.4%).

     31 Issued Check 604 for the amounts owed to the federal government for employees' federal income taxes ($252.00) and FICA taxes ($435.04).

     31 Paid $114.00 to the Mutual Insurance Company for the employees' hospital insurance, Check 605.

Chapter 21, Problem 21A Maintaining a Petty Cash Register

Maureen Miller owns a financial consulting business. She established a petty cash fund on July 1 by writing Check 336 for $100.00. She also records all petty cash disbursements in a petty cash register. The accounts for which petty cash disbursements are usually made include Office Supplies, Delivery Expense, Miscellaneous Expense, and Advertising Expense.

Instructions:

(1) Record the establishment of the petty cash fund on the first line of the petty cash register, page 1.

(2) Record each of the following petty cash disbursements in the petty cash register.

(3) Foot, prove, total, and rule the petty cash register at the end of the month.

(4) Reconcile the petty cash fund. An actual cash count of the fund shows a balance of $5.68.

(5) Check 362 was issued to replenish the petty cash fund. Record the replenishment information in the petty cash register.

Transactions:

July 1 Paid $1.20 for postage due on a letter, Voucher 101.

     3 Purchased a $9.00 ad in the *Towne Sentinel* newspaper, Voucher 102.

     5 Bought a ream of typing paper for $4.75 and issued Voucher 103.

     6 Paid $6.00 for a mailgram, Voucher 104.

     8 Issued Voucher 105 for $9.90 to Express Couriers in payment for the delivery of packages.

    10 Paid the newscarrier $4.10 for daily newspapers and issued Voucher 106.

    13 Bought pens, pencils, and memo pads for $6.60, Voucher 107.

    15 Purchased a $9.50 advertisement in a local trade journal, Voucher 108.

    19 Issued Voucher 109 for $8.70 for office supplies.

    22 Express Couriers delivered financial data from a client, $9.90, Voucher 110.

    26 Issued Voucher 111 for $2.12 for additional postage due on mail.

    27 Bought an ad in the *Towne Sentinel* for $8.70 and issued Voucher 112.

    29 Purchased a typewriter ribbon for $5.50, issuing Voucher 113.

    30 Voided Voucher 114 due to an error.

    30 Issued Voucher 115 for $4.10 to the newscarrier.

Chapter 22, Problem 22A   Calculating and Recording
Depreciation Expense

The American Carpet Company purchased a delivery truck on October 12, 1991, at a total cost of $78,900. The delivery truck has an estimated useful life of 3 years and an estimated disposal value of $900.

Instructions:

(1) Prepare a depreciation schedule for the delivery truck using the straight-line method. Use the form provided in the working papers.

(2) Record the following transactions on general journal page 41. Post the transactions to the ledger accounts provided.

Transactions:

1991

Oct. 12   Purchased a delivery truck for $78,900 cash, Check 1436.

Dec. 31   Recorded the adjusting entry for the depreciation expense on the delivery truck.

1992

Dec. 31   Recorded the adjusting entry for the year's depreciation expense.

Chapter 23, Problem 23A   Calculating and Recording
Bad Debts Expense

Quality Rugs, Inc., uses the allowance method of accounting for uncollectible accounts. At the end of the fiscal period, the following accounts appeared on Quality's trial balance.

Accounts Receivable	$18,647.25	
Allowance for Uncollectible Accounts		$ 1,060.50
Sales		452,612.00
Sales Discounts	5,431.35	
Sales Returns and Allowances	13,578.36	
Bad Debts Expense	0.00	

Instructions:

(1) Determine the amount of the adjustment for bad debts for the fiscal period ended December 31. Management estimates that uncollectible accounts will be 1.25% of net sales.

(2) Journalize the adjusting entry in the general journal, page 10.

(3) Post the adjusting entry to the general ledger accounts.

(4) Determine the book value of accounts receivable.

Chapter 24, Problem 24A   Calculating the Cost of Merchandise
Sold

Harvey's Camera Shop uses a one-year fiscal period beginning January 1. At the beginning of the fiscal period, the shop had a beginning inventory of film valued at $785.23 (527 rolls of film at $1.49 each). During the year, the business made the following purchases.

January 15	500 rolls of film @ $1.49 each =	$ 745.00
March 4	1,200 rolls of film @ $1.53 each =	1,836.00
April 16	1,000 rolls of film @ $1.55 each =	1,550.00
August 24	1,500 rolls of film @ $1.54 each =	2,310.00
October 15	1,750 rolls of film @ $1.59 each =	2,782.50
November 12	2,500 rolls of film @ $1.62 each =	4,050.00
Total Purchases	8,450	$13,273.50

There were 363 rolls of film in inventory at the end of the period.

Instructions:

(1) Calculate the cost of the ending inventory using the specific identification, fifo, lifo, and weighted average cost methods. For the specific identification method, 350 of the rolls were purchased on November 12 and 13 rolls were purchased on October 15.

(2) Using the costs obtained in Step 1, determine the cost of merchandise sold for each method.

Chapter 25, Problem 25A   Recording Notes Payable and Notes Receivable Transactions

Instructions: Record the following transactions in a cash receipts journal (page 18), cash payments journal (page 25), and general journal (page 11).

Transactions:

Mar.   3   Borrowed $7,500.00 from the American State Bank by issuing a 120-day, 11% interest-bearing note payable, Note 7.

June 14   Received a 90-day, 12% note receivable for $1,800.00 from Marie Richards for an extension of time on her account receivable, Note 3 dated June 12.

July   1   Paid the American State Bank the maturity value of the note issued on March 3, Check 1748.

Sept. 10   Received a check from Marie Richards for the maturity value of the note receivable dated June 12, Receipt 2422.

16   Borrowed $2,500.00 from the Peoples National Bank, signing a 90-day non-interest-bearing note payable (Note 8), discounted at 11.5%.

Dec. 15   Prepared Check 2254 for the note issued on September 16 and recorded the interest expense.

Chapter 26, Problem 26A   Recording the Partners' Investment

On June 15, Walter Adams and Janice Lee agreed to combine their individual sole proprietorships into one firm organized as a partnership. The partners were to invest all the assets of their two former businesses. Those assets are listed below.

	W. Adams	J. Lee
Cash	$247,000	$517,500
Accounts Receivable	78,000	
Merchandise Inventory	123,000	
Equipment	154,500	

Instructions: Prepare the general journal entries (page 1) required to record the partners' investments. The source document is Memorandum 1.

Chapter 26, Problem 26B   Dividing Partnership Earnings

On January 1, Susan Keith and Mike Yonan formed a partnership organized under the name Ready-to-Serve Hot Foods. Mike and Susan each invested $75,000. Because Mike was going to operate the business, he was to receive 67% of the profits and losses. Susan, who was only investing capital, was to receive 33% of the profits and losses.

During the year, Mike Yonan invested an additional $10,000 in cash in the business and withdrew $4,800. Susan, who expected a profitable first year, withdrew $7,500. Net income for the year ended December 31 amounted to $27,500.

Instructions:

(1) Journalize the entries needed to close the Income Summary and withdrawals accounts. Use general journal page 12.

(2) Post the closing entries to the general ledger accounts.

(3) Prepare a statement of changes in partners' equity.

Chapter 27, Problem 27A   Recording Stockholders' Equity Transactions

The Maxwell Corporation was organized on September 1 and authorized to issue 10,000 shares of $100 par, $8 preferred stock and 25,000 shares of $50 par common stock.

Instructions: Record the following transactions in general journal form. Use general journal page 1.

Transactions:

1991

Sept. 1 Issued 4,000 shares of $8 preferred stock at $100.00 per share, Receipt 101.

12 Issued 12,000 shares of common stock at $50.00 per share, Receipt 102.

Nov. 15 Received $52.50 per share for 2,500 shares of common stock issued, Receipt 215.

Dec. 16 Received $5,000.00 for 50 shares of $8 preferred stock issued, Receipt 298.

1992

Mar. 24 Issued 1,000 shares of common stock at $55.00 per share, Receipt 389.

Aug. 15 Declared a dividend of $32,400 on 4,050 shares of $8 preferred stock outstanding, payable on September 15 to stockholders of record on September 1, Memorandum 316.

15 Declared a cash dividend of 25¢ per share on 15,500 shares of common stock outstanding, payable on September 30 to stockholders of record on September 1, Memorandum 317.

Sept. 15 Paid the preferred stock dividend declared on August 15, Check 1763.

30 Paid the common stock dividend declared on August 15, Check 1802.

Dec. 31 Prepared the closing entries in the general journal to close Income Summary for the net income of $102,600 and to close the two Dividends accounts.

Chapter 27, Problem 27B   Preparing a Statement of Stockholders' Equity

The account balances on page 646 appeared on the December 31 trial balance of Broughton Products, Inc.

$4 Preferred Stock ($50 Par)	$200,000
Common Stock ($10 Par)	400,000
Paid-in Capital in Excess of Par	200,000
Retained Earnings	275,000
Dividends — Preferred	16,000
Dividends — Common	80,000

Instructions: Prepare the statement of stockholders' equity for the year ended December 31. During the fiscal period, the corporation issued 5,000 shares of common stock at $22 per share. Net income for the period was $125,000.

Chapter 28, Problem 28A Using Horizontal Analysis

A partial comparative income statement for Wonderland Toys, Inc., is shown below.

Instructions: Complete the comparative income statement using horizontal analysis. Round all percentages to two decimal places. Use the form provided in the working papers.

Wonderland Toys, Inc.
Comparative Income Statement
For the Years Ended August 31, 1992 and 1991

	1992	1991
Revenue:		
Sales	$243,576	$219,326
Less: Sales Returns and Allowances	3,450	4,566
Net Sales	240,126	214,760
Cost of Merchandise Sold	143,579	126,784
Gross Profit on Sales	96,547	87,976
Operating Expenses:		
Selling Expenses:		
Advertising Expense	8,700	7,600
Delivery Expense	8,674	8,796
Depr. Expense — Store Equip.	1,500	1,200
Sales Salaries Expense	23,400	20,120
Travel Expense	5,342	4,123
Total Selling Expenses	47,616	41,839
Administrative Expenses:		
Bad Debts Expense	2,250	2,320
Depr. Expense — Office Equip.	1,550	1,575
Insurance Expense	1,500	2,355
Office Salaries Expense	13,635	12,345
Rent Expense	4,000	5,000
Supplies Expense	3,245	2,100
Total Administrative Expenses	26,180	25,695
Total Operating Expenses	73,796	67,534
Operating Income	22,751	20,442
Other Income	3,000	2,550
Other Expenses	280	355
Net Income	$ 25,471	$ 22,637

Chapter 28, Problem 28B Using Vertical Analysis

A partial comparative balance sheet for Wonderland Toys, Inc., is shown on the following page.

Additional Reinforcement Problems

Instructions: Complete the comparative balance sheet using vertical analysis. Round the percentages to two decimal places. Use the form provided in the working papers.

Wonderland Toys, Inc.
Comparative Balance Sheet
August 31, 1993 and 1992

	1993	1992
Assets		
Current Assets:		
Cash in Bank	$ 12,790	$ 11,900
Accounts Receivable (net)	14,567	16,890
Merchandise Inventory	38,500	35,000
Prepaid Expenses	2,300	1,900
Total Current Assets	68,157	65,690
Investments:		
Runner, Inc. (stock)	12,500	10,500
Property, Plant, and Equipment:		
Equipment (net)	40,000	45,000
Building (net)	80,000	85,000
Land	15,000	15,000
Total Property, Plant, and Equipment	135,000	145,000
Total Assets	$215,657	$221,190
Liabilities		
Current Liabilities:		
Notes Payable	$ 27,600	$ 22,600
Accounts Payable	24,500	15,000
Sales Tax Payable	1,200	890
Total Current Liabilities	53,300	38,490
Long-Term Liabilities:		
Mortgage Payable	20,000	30,000
Total Liabilities	73,300	68,490
Stockholders' Equity		
Common Stock, $10 Par, 25,000 shares authorized, 5,000 shares issued	50,000	50,000
Retained Earnings	92,357	102,700
Total Stockholders' Equity	142,357	152,700
Total Liabilities and Stockholders' Equity	$215,657	$221,190

Enrichment Chapter A

Recording Transactions in the Combination Journal

In earlier chapters you learned that businesses that have a large volume of financial transactions use special journals to record those transactions. Special journals, you'll remember, are designed for recording a "special" kind of business transaction. Therefore, similar entries are recorded in one journal. Each journal has several special amount columns, which speed up the journalizing and posting process. Finally, through the use of special journals, the workload can be distributed among a number of employees.

Although special journals are ideally used in large businesses, they are not very practical for small service and retail businesses with few employees. Such businesses usually have only one accounting clerk. It is impractical for one clerk to record transactions in five different journals. At the same time, using only a general journal is very time consuming. For many small businesses, these problems are solved by using one journal—a combination journal.

The Combination Journal

As its name implies, a *combination journal* is a multicolumn journal that combines the features of the general journal and the special journals into one book of original entry. Like the special journals, the combination journal has special amount columns that are used to record transactions that occur frequently. In addition, the combination journal has General Debit and Credit columns in which to record transactions for which there are no special amount columns. Therefore, all the transactions of a business can be recorded in a single, multicolumn journal.

| | | | | | GENERAL | | ACCOUNTS RECEIVABLE | | COMBINATION |
DATE	ACCOUNT TITLE	DOC. NO.	POST. REF.		DEBIT	CREDIT	DEBIT	CREDIT	
1									
2									
3									
4									

Figure 1 The Combination Journal (*Left Side*)

A business designs its combination journal to fit its own special needs. The number of columns, the selection of the special columns, and the arrangement of the columns will depend upon the type of business and the transactions that take place. Most businesses, however, use combination journals with between 10 and 13 columns. Care must be taken in determining how many columns to include. Too many columns will make the journal too large and difficult to use.

R E M E M B E R

Small businesses design their combination journal to meet their own special needs.

The arrangement of the columns varies from one business to another. The columns should be arranged to make recording and posting easy and accurate. For example, look at Hi-Tech Home Entertainment Center's combination journal in Figure 1. The Date, Account Title, Document Number, and Posting Reference columns are located at the far left. These columns are followed by the General Debit and Credit columns.

The General columns are followed by the special amount columns for Accounts Receivable, Sales, Sales Tax Payable, Accounts Payable, Purchases, and Cash in Bank.

Notice too the line numbers that appear to the left and right sides of each page of the journal. These line numbers help the accounting clerk avoid writing amounts on the wrong lines.

R E M E M B E R

When recording transactions, use the line numbers as a guide to avoid writing amounts on the wrong line.

Using the Combination Journal

A properly designed combination journal can be used efficiently for recording every possible business transaction. Receipts of cash are recorded in the Cash in Bank Debit column; cash payments are entered in the Cash in Bank Credit column. The purchase of merchandise, for cash or on account,

JOURNAL		PAGE					
SALES CREDIT	SALES TAX PAYABLE CREDIT	ACCOUNTS PAYABLE		PURCHASES DEBIT	CASH IN BANK		
		DEBIT	CREDIT		DEBIT	CREDIT	

COMBINATION

DATE	ACCOUNT TITLE	DOC. NO.	POST. REF.	GENERAL DEBIT	GENERAL CREDIT	ACCOUNTS RECEIVABLE DEBIT	ACCOUNTS RECEIVABLE CREDIT
19-- June 6	Cash Sales	T61	—				
8	Sales Discounts	R62	405	8 00			
	James Angelo		✓				424 00
10	Valley Hospital	375	✓			530 00	
13	Office Equipment	M11	135	650 00			
	Val Venturi, Capital		301		650 00		
14	Sales Returns & Allow.	CM5	410	90 00			
	Sales Tax Payable		220	5 40			
	Tracey Sands		✓				95 40
15	Clair Anderson	M12	✓			80 00	
	Carl Andersen		✓				80 00
16	Video Distributors	I003	✓				
18	Supplies	I214		100 00			
	Beste Office Suppliers		✓				
21	Tele Communications Sy	CK350	✓				
	Purchases Discounts		505		6 00		
23	Utilities Expense	CK351	630	175 00			
24	Purchases	CK352	—				
26	Salaries Expense	CK353	625	3200 00			
	Social Security Tax Pay.		205		198 40		
	Medicare Tax Pay.		206		46 40		
	Emp. Fed. Inc. Tax Pay.		210		480 00		
	Emp. State Inc. Tax Pay.		215		70 40		
26	Payroll Tax Expense	P.Reg.	620	456 00			
	Social Security Tax Pay.		205		198 40		
	Medicare Tax Pay.		206		46 40		
	Fed. Unemploy. Tax Pay.		225		25 60		
	State Unemploy. Tax Pay.		230		185 60		
27	Val Venturi Withdrawals	CK354	310	500 00			
28	Compact Discs. Mfg.	DM10	✓				
	Purchases Returns & Allow.		510		90 00		
29	Supplies	M13	110	125 00			
	Purchases		501		125 00		
30	Totals			5309 40 / 5309 40	2122 20 / 2122 20	610 00 / 610 00	599 40 / 599 40
				(✓)	(✓)	(103)	(103)

Figure 2   Recording Transactions in a Combination Journal (*Left Side*)

is recorded in the Purchases Debit column. Transactions affecting creditor accounts are written in the Accounts Payable Debit and Credit columns. The sale of merchandise is recorded in the Sales Credit and Sales Tax Payable Credit columns. Transactions affecting charge customer accounts are entered in the Accounts Receivable Debit and Credit columns. Finally, general ledger accounts for which there are no special columns are recorded in the General Debit and Credit columns. Adjusting and closing entries, for example, would be recorded in the General Debit and Credit columns.

R E M E M B E R

The General columns are used to record any amount for which no special columns are provided.

Recording Transactions in the Combination Journal

JOURNAL   PAGE __6__

	SALES CREDIT	SALES TAX PAYABLE CREDIT	ACCOUNTS PAYABLE DEBIT	ACCOUNTS PAYABLE CREDIT	PURCHASES DEBIT	CASH IN BANK DEBIT	CASH IN BANK CREDIT	
1	1250 00	75 00				1325 00		1
2						416 00		2
3								3
4	500 00	30 00						4
5								5
6								6
7								7
8								8
9								9
10								10
11								11
12				4200 00	4200 00			12
13								13
14				100 00				14
15			200 00					15
16							194 00	16
17							175 00	17
18					300 00		300 00	18
19								19
20								20
21								21
22								22
23							2404 80	23
24								24
25								25
26								26
27								27
28								28
29							500 00	29
30			90 00					30
31								31
32								32
33								33
34	1750 00	105 00	290 00	4300 00	4500 00	1741 00	3573 80	34
	(401)	(220)	(201)	(201)	(501)	(101)	(101)	

Hi-Tech Home Entertainment Center's business transactions for the month of June are recorded in the combination journal shown in Figure 2.

Proving and Posting the Journal

Like special journals, an important feature of the combination journal is that it saves time in both recording and posting transactions. The amounts entered in the General columns are posted on a daily basis to the appropriate general ledger accounts. Amounts entered in the Accounts Receivable and Accounts Payable columns are also posted on a daily basis to the appropriate charge customer or creditor accounts in the accounts receivable and accounts payable subsidiary ledgers. At the end of the month, the combination journal is footed, proved, totaled, and ruled. Totals of the special amount columns of the combination journal are then posted to the general ledger accounts named in the column headings. Figure B-2 shows how the combination journal will look at the end of the month after all postings have been made.

Exercise 1 Analyzing Transactions for Combination Journal Entries

John Dunn owns The Country Store, a small retail store. He uses a combination journal with the following columns.

General Debit   Accounts Payable Debit
General Credit   Accounts Payable Credit
Accounts Receivable Debit   Purchases Debit
Accounts Receivable Credit   Cash in Bank Debit
Sales Credit   Cash in Bank Credit
Sales Tax Payable Credit

Instructions: Use a form similar to the one that follows. For each of the following selected transactions, indicate in which column(s) of the combination journal the debit and credit parts of the entry would be recorded. The first transaction has been completed as an example.

Date	Trans.	General Dr.	General Cr.	Accounts Receivable Dr.	Accounts Receivable Cr.	Sales Cr.	Sales Tax Payable Cr.	Accounts Payable Dr.	Accounts Payable Cr.	Purchases Dr.	Cash in Bank Dr.	Cash in Bank Cr.
1	Debit	✔										
	Credit								✔			

Transactions:

Dec. 1 Purchased a microcomputer on account from King's Computer Outlet.
   2 John Dunn withdrew cash for personal use.
   5 Sold merchandise on account to Bernard Peterson, plus sales tax.
   8 Purchased merchandise on account from Cory Distributors.
  10 Issued Credit Memo 14 to Tom Tray, a charge customer, for the return of merchandise sold on account plus sales tax.
  13 Issued Debit Memo 20 to Cory Distributors for the return of merchandise purchased from them on account.
  15 Received a check from Bernard Peterson in full payment of his account.
  18 Issued a check to Cory Distributors in payment of our account less the purchases return and less a purchases discount.
  22 John Dunn invested a calculator in the business.
  25 Issued a check for the monthly payroll less deductions for FICA taxes, federal income tax, and state income tax.
  25 Recorded the employer's payroll tax liabilities for FICA taxes, federal unemployment tax, and state unemployment tax.
  30 Recorded cash sales plus sales tax.
  31 Recorded the adjusting entry for the office supplies consumed during the period.

Dec. 31 Recorded the closing entry to transfer the net income to the capital account.

Problem 1 Recording Transactions in the Combination Journal

Craig Glasser is a physician who operates a family medical practice. His practice, Glasser Family Medical Center, uses a combination journal with these amount columns.

General Debit
General Credit
Accounts Receivable Debit
Accounts Receivable Credit
Medical Fees Credit
Laboratory Fees Credit

Accounts Payable Debit
Accounts Payable Credit
Medical Supplies Debit
Cash in Bank Debit
Cash in Bank Credit

Instructions:

(1) Record the following transactions on page 17 of the combination journal.

(2) Total, prove, and rule the combination journal.

Transactions:

Oct. 1 Received $2,100.00 in medical fees from patients, Receipt 90.

2 Issued Check 414 for the cash purchase of $120.00 of office supplies.

4 Purchased medical supplies on account from Wharton Laboratories, Invoice 1406 for $1,950.00, terms n/60.

6 Craig Glasser invested medical equipment valued at $750.00 in the medical practice, Memorandum 30.

8 Billed a patient, Daniel O'Connell, $150.00 for his annual physical, Statement 40.

9 Completed lab services for Carl Fisher and billed him $160.00, Statement 41.

11 Purchased a new examination table (medical equipment) on account from Medical Suppliers, Invoice L163 for $1,452.50, terms n/45.

13 Billed Patricia Vallano $300.00 for medical services, Statement 42.

15 Issued Check 415 for $2,004.81 for the monthly salaries expense of $2,500.00 less deductions: social security tax, $155.00, medicare tax, $36.25; employees' federal income taxes, $209.00; employees' state income taxes, $94.94.

15 Recorded the employer's payroll tax liabilities: social security tax, $155.00, medicare tax, $36.25; federal unemployment taxes, $20.00; state unemployment taxes, $145.00, payroll register.

18 Issued Debit Memo 16 to Wharton Laboratories for $200.00 for the return of medical supplies purchased on account.

20 Paid the telephone bill, Check 416 for $110.00.

22 A check for $110.00 was received from John Marshall to apply on his account, Receipt 91.

25 Craig Glasser withdrew $1,250.00 cash from the business, Check 417.

28 Received $75.00 from Daniel O'Connell to apply on his account, Receipt 92.

31 Sent Statement 43 for $95.00 to Donna Gordon for lab services completed on account.

31 Issued Check 418 for the November rent of $900.00.

Recording Transactions in the Combination Journal

Problem 2 Recording Transactions in the Combination Journal

Jon James owns Candles 'n Things, a small merchandising business specializing in glass products, figurines, decorative candles, and other small gift items. Candles 'n Things uses a combination journal with these amount columns.

General Debit
General Credit
Accounts Receivable Debit
Accounts Receivable Credit
Sales Credit
Sales Tax Payable Credit

Accounts Payable Debit
Accounts Payable Credit
Purchases Debit
Cash in Bank Debit
Cash in Bank Credit

Instructions:

(1) Record the following transactions on page 12 of the combination journal.

(2) Total, prove, and rule the combination journal.

Transactions:

Dec. 1 Issued Check 151 for $700.00 to Pine Valley Realty for the monthly rent.

2 Received a check for $204.82 from Wilma Hutchins in payment of her account of $209.00 less a discount of $4.18, Receipt 303.

3 Purchased $400.00 of merchandise on account from the Stained Glass Outlet, Invoice 479 dated December 2, terms 2/10, n/30.

4 Issued Check 152 for $75.00 to The Knight Crier for advertisements.

5 Issued Check 153 for $230.30 to Phoenix Glass Co. in payment of their invoice for $235.00.

6 Sent Credit Memo 35 to Stan Kopak for damaged merchandise returned, $50.00 plus $2.25 sales tax.

8 Sold merchandise on account to Mindy Silvis, $100.00 plus sales tax of $4.50, Sales Slip 205.

10 Discovered that $95.00 received on account from Mindy Silvis on November 16 had been journalized and posted to Robert Sylvan's account, Memorandum 16.

11 Recorded the monthly salaries of $2,100.00 less deductions: social security tax, $130.20; medicare tax, $30.45; employees' federal income taxes, $326.00; and employees' state income taxes, $48.09; Check 154 for $1,565.26.

11 Recorded the employer's payroll tax liabilities: social security tax, $130.20; medicare tax, $30.45; federal unemployment tax, $16.80; state unemployment tax, $121.80; payroll register.

12 Sent Check 155 for $392.00 to the Stained Glass Outlet in payment of Invoice 479 less a discount of $8.00.

15 Received $150.00 from Al Holland to apply on his account, Receipt 304.

18 Issued Debit Memo 20 to Glazing Unlimited for $25.00 for the return of merchandise purchased on account.

20 The owner, Jon James, withdrew $500.00 for personal use, Check 156.

24 Sold $200.00 in merchandise on account to Rob Vesco plus sales tax of $9.00, Sales Slip 206.

Dec. 26   Purchased $300.00 of merchandise on account from Phoenix Glass Co., Invoice 601.

     28   Purchased store equipment on account, from Abbot Enterprises, $200.00, Invoice 609.

     29   Paid a $150.00 electric bill for the month by issuing Check 157 to Dukane Power Company.

     31   Recorded cash sales of $3,000.00, plus $135.00 sales taxes, Tape 52.

Problem 3   Recording Adjusting and Closing Entries in a Combination Journal

Shown below is part of the December 31 work sheet for Balloons & Gifts Boutique.

Instructions:

(1) Record the adjusting entries in the combination journal. Then total, prove, and rule the General columns of the journal.

(2) Record the closing entries in the combination journal. Then total, prove, and rule the General columns of the journal.

ACCT. NO.	ACCOUNT NAME	ADJUSTMENTS DEBIT	ADJUSTMENTS CREDIT	INCOME STATEMENT DEBIT	INCOME STATEMENT CREDIT	BALANCE SHEET DEBIT	BALANCE SHEET CREDIT
110	Merchandise Inventory	(a) 2000 00				26000 00	
115	Office Supplies		(b) 270 00			95 00	
120	Store Supplies		(c) 1840 00			327 00	
130	Prepaid Insurance		(d) 700 00			100 00	
301	Lisa Phillips, Capital						28400 00
305	Lisa Phillips, Withdrawals					1200 00	
310	Income Summary		(a) 2000 00		2000 00		
401	Sales				46000 00		
405	Sales Returns & Allow.			405 00			
501	Purchases			18000 00			
505	Purchases Discounts				225 00		
510	Purchases Returns & Allow.				150 00		
610	Insurance Expense	(d) 700 00		700 00			
620	Miscellaneous Expense			180 00			
630	Office Supplies Expense	(b) 270 00		270 00			
640	Rent Expense			6000 00			
650	Store Supplies Expense	(c) 1840 00		1840 00			

Enrichment Chapter B

The Accrual Basis of Accounting

Some small businesses keep their financial records on a cash basis. The *cash basis* of accounting recognizes revenue and expenses only when cash is received or paid out. Often, however, cash is received from charge customers and payments are made to creditors in an accounting period other than the fiscal period in which the original transaction occurred. When this happens, financial statements may not accurately report data. To overcome this, some businesses use the *accrual basis* of accounting, which recognizes revenue when it is actually earned and expenses when they are actually incurred.

R E M E M B E R

With the accrual basis of accounting, revenue is recorded when it is earned, and expenses are recorded when they are actually incurred.

Accruals and Deferrals

The word "accrue" means to accumulate or grow in size. In accounting, an *accrual* is the recognition of revenue or an expense that has accumulated over time but has not yet been recorded. Accruals are required when

1. *There are unrecorded revenues.* An example is interest earned on a note receivable in one accounting period but not collected until the next period.
2. *There are unrecorded expenses.* An example is wages earned by employees in one fiscal period but not paid until the next fiscal period.

The word "defer" means to delay or postpone. In accounting, a *deferral* is a delay in recognizing revenue for cash already received or an expense for a bill already paid. Deferrals are required when

1. *Already recorded revenues apply to two or more accounting periods.* An example is rent received in advance when some of the rental time is in one accounting period and the rest is in the next accounting period.
2. *Already recorded expenses must be spread out over two or more accounting periods.* An example is office supplies when some of the supplies are used in one accounting period and the remainder in the next accounting period.

Adjusting entries are used to recognize unrecorded revenue and expenses and to allocate already recorded revenue and expenses to the appropriate accounting periods.

R — E — M — E — M — B — E — R

Adjusting entries must be recorded when (1) there are unrecorded revenue and expenses at the end of the fiscal period, and (2) already recorded revenue and expenses must be allocated over two or more accounting periods.

Accruals

Accruals are revenue or expenses that are gradually earned or incurred over time. In order to report a company's financial position accurately, accruals should be recognized in the accounting period in which they occur.

Accrued Revenue

Accrued revenue is revenue that has been earned but not yet received and recorded. Examples of accrued revenue include interest earned on a note receivable and fees from advertising services earned but not yet received.

On December 5, the Circle Distributing Co. accepted a $5,000, 90-day, 9% note receivable from a charge customer, Paul Stanley. Stanley issued the note as an extension on his charge account. Circle Distributing Co. recorded the transaction as a debit of $5,000 to Notes Receivable and a credit of $5,000 to Accounts Receivable and Paul Stanley's account in the subsidiary ledger. On December 31, 26 days of interest had accrued (been earned) on the note receivable: $5,000.00 \times .09 \times \frac{26}{365} = $32.05. An adjusting entry must be made on December 31 to record the amount of interest income earned during the fiscal period.

Since the interest earned will not be received until the maturity date, the accrued interest is debited to an account called Interest Receivable. Interest Income is credited for $32.05.

December

S	M	T	W	T	F	S
1	2	3	4	5	6	7
8	9	10	11	12	13	14
15	16	17	18	19	20	21
22	23	24	25	26	27	28
29	30	31				

Interest Receivable		Interest Income	
Dr.	Cr.	Dr.	Cr.
+	−	−	+
Adj. $32.05			Adj. $32.05

The adjusting entry is shown in Figure 1.

GENERAL JOURNAL   PAGE 18

	DATE	DESCRIPTION	POST. REF.	DEBIT	CREDIT
1		*Adjusting Entries*			
2	19-- Dec. 31	Interest Receivable		32 05	
3		Interest Income			32 05

Figure 1 Recording the Adjusting Entry for Accrued Revenue

The Accrual Basis of Accounting

On March 5, Circle received a check from Paul Stanley for $5,110.96, the maturity value of the note ($5,000.00 principal + $110.96 interest). Of the total interest, $32.05 had been earned and reported in the previous accounting period. The remaining $78.91 should be recorded as income in the *current* fiscal period.

In the entry, Cash in Bank is debited for $5,110.96, the total amount of cash received. Notes Receivable is credited for $5,000.00. Interest Receivable is credited for $32.05 since this amount has now been received. Interest Income is credited for $78.91, the amount of the interest that applies to the current accounting period.

Cash in Bank			Notes Receivable	
Dr.	Cr.		Dr.	Cr.
+	–		+	–
$5,110.96			Bal. $5,000.00	$5,000.00

Interest Receivable			Interest Income	
Dr.	Cr.		Dr.	Cr.
+	–		–	+
Adj. $32.05	$32.05			$78.91

The entry for this transaction, shown in general journal form, appears in Figure 2.

GENERAL JOURNAL PAGE 26

DATE	DESCRIPTION	POST. REF.	DEBIT	CREDIT	
19-- Mar. 5	Cash in Bank		511096		1
	Notes Receivable			500000	2
	Interest Receivable			3205	3
	Interest Income			7891	4
	Receipt 416				5

Figure 2 Recording the Payment of a Note Receivable

Accrued Expenses

Most expenses are recorded when they are paid, or a liability is incurred. There are, however, some business expenses that build up daily but are not recorded until an adjusting entry is made at the end of the fiscal period. Some examples of these *accrued expenses* are salaries and wages earned by employees but not yet paid to them, interest incurred on unpaid notes, and property taxes owed but not yet paid.

To acquire cash with which to provide services, communities impose a tax on property. Owners usually pay the property tax twice a year, with each payment covering a six-month period and one-half of the annual tax.

Pike Department Store owns the building and land on which it operates. The value of the property is $300,000. The total annual property taxes are $7,800. Pike is located in a state where property taxes must be paid in May and November. The May payment covers the first six months of the calendar year, and the November payment covers the last six months of the calendar year.

The Accrual Basis of Accounting

Pike's fiscal period ends on March 31. As a result, at the end of its fiscal period, Pike owes property taxes of $1,950 ($7,800 × $\frac{3}{12}$) for the months of January, February, and March. These taxes, however, will not be paid until May. In order to show the correct amount of the property tax expense for the current fiscal period, an adjusting entry must be recorded on March 31. The adjusting entry would be recorded as shown in Figure C-3.

Property Tax Expense			Property Tax Payable	
Dr.	Cr.		Dr.	Cr.
+	−		−	+
Bal. $5,850.00				Adj. $1,950.00
Adj. $1,950.00				

	GENERAL JOURNAL			PAGE 57
DATE	DESCRIPTION	POST. REF.	DEBIT	CREDIT
	Adjusting Entries			
19-- Mar. 31	Property Tax Expense		1950 00	
	Property Tax Payable			1950 00

Figure 3   Recording the Adjusting Entry for Accrued Expenses

R E M E M B E R

An adjusting entry must be made at the end of the fiscal period for expenses that have accrued but have not yet been recorded.

On May 15, Pike wrote a check for the semiannual property tax payment of $3,900. Of this amount, $1,950 is an expense charged to the prior fiscal period and $1,950 is an expense charged to the current accounting period. The entry to record this payment is shown in Figure C-4.

Property Tax Expense			Property Tax Payable	
Dr.	Cr.		Dr.	Cr.
+	−		−	+
$1,950.00			$1,950.00	Bal. $1,950.00

Cash in Bank	
Dr.	Cr.
+	−
	$3,900.00

	GENERAL JOURNAL			PAGE 60
DATE	DESCRIPTION	POST. REF.	DEBIT	CREDIT
19-- May 15	Property Tax Expense		1950 00	
	Property Tax Payable		1950 00	
	Cash in Bank			3900 00
	Check 401			

Figure 4   Recording the Payment of Property Taxes

The Accrual Basis of Accounting

Deferrals

Sometimes a business receives cash or a receivable for revenue not yet earned. Cash is also paid out for expenses before those expenses are actually incurred. So that a business can more accurately show its financial condition, unearned revenue and prepaid expenses must be deferred (postponed) to the proper fiscal period.

Unearned Revenue

Unearned revenue is revenue received before it is actually earned. Examples of unearned revenue include cash received in advance for rental properties, for season tickets to various events, for insurance premiums, and for work to be done in the future. Because the business has an obligation to deliver the merchandise or perform the service for which it has already received payment, unearned revenue represents a current liability to the business.

As the business delivers the merchandise or performs the service, it earns a part of the advance payment. The earned portion must be transferred from a liability account to a revenue account through an adjusting entry made at the end of the fiscal period.

Let's look at an example. Randall Real Estate rents space in its building to a tax accountant. On November 1, the accountant paid Randall $1,200 in advance for rent for the months of November through April. The entry to record this transaction is shown in the T accounts below and in Figure 5.

Cash in Bank			Unearned Rental Income	
Dr.	Cr.		Dr.	Cr.
+	–		–	+
$1,200.00				$1,200.00

	GENERAL JOURNAL				PAGE 24
DATE	DESCRIPTION	POST. REF.	DEBIT	CREDIT	
19-- Nov. 1	Cash in Bank		1 200 00		
	Unearned Rental Income			1 200 00	
	Receipt 181				

Figure 5 Recording the Receipt of Unearned Revenue

When Randall's fiscal period ends on December 31, the company will have earned rental income of $400 for two of the six months paid in advance ($1,200 × $\frac{1}{3}$).

Unearned Rental Income			Rental Income	
Dr.	Cr.		Dr.	Cr.
–	+		–	+
Adj. $400.00	Bal. $1,200.00			Adj. $400.00

The adjusting entry to record the rental income earned through December 31 is shown in Figure 6.

The Accrual Basis of Accounting

GENERAL JOURNAL   PAGE _29_

DATE	DESCRIPTION	POST. REF.	DEBIT	CREDIT	
	Adjusting Entries				1
19-- Dec. 31	Unearned Rental Income		400 00		2
	Rental Income			400 00	3

Figure 6   Recording the Adjusting Entry for Unearned Revenue

R — E — M — E — M — B — E — R

Revenue received in advance is recorded in a liability account. That account must be adjusted at the end of the fiscal period to recognize the revenue earned during the period.

Prepaid Expenses

A *prepaid expense* is an expense paid in advance. Examples include the purchase of office supplies, premiums paid on insurance policies, rent paid in advance of the use of the rental property, and bank discounts on non-interest-bearing notes payable.

A prepaid expense is usually recorded initially in an asset account. The portion of the asset that is used up during the accounting period is an expense for that accounting period. The portion of the asset that is *not* used up is an asset that is deferred to the next accounting period. At the end of the accounting period, an adjusting entry is made to record the amount of the expense.

The Lampley Corporation records the purchase of office supplies in the Office Supplies account. At the end of the accounting period, the Office Supplies account had a balance of $2,570. On December 31, a physical inventory showed that only $570 of office supplies were still on hand. By subtracting the ending supplies inventory from the balance of the Office Supplies account ($2,570 balance − $570 on hand = $2,000 used), the amount of office supplies used during the fiscal period is determined.

Office Supplies Expense			Office Supplies	
Dr.	Cr.		Dr.	Cr.
+	−		+	−
Adj. $2,000.00			Bal. $2,570.00	Adj. $2,000.00

The adjusting entry to record the office supplies expense is shown in Figure 7.

GENERAL JOURNAL   PAGE _10_

DATE	DESCRIPTION	POST. REF.	DEBIT	CREDIT	
	Adjusting Entries				1
19-- Dec. 31	Office Supplies Expense		2 000 00		2
	Office Supplies			2 000 00	3

Figure 7   Recording the Adjusting Entry for a Prepaid Expense

Exercise 1   Identifying Accruals and Deferrals

Instructions: Use a form similar to the one that follows. For each item listed below, indicate whether the item is a prepaid expense, unearned revenue, an accrued expense, or accrued revenue by placing a check mark in the correct column. The first item has been completed as an example.

1. A two-year premium paid on a fire insurance policy.
2. Tuition collected in advance by a boarding school.
3. Interest on an interest-bearing note payable due in the next period.
4. Cash received for a three-year subscription to a magazine.
5. Fees due for the completed designs for three of five buildings.
6. Property taxes incurred for the last three months of the fiscal period.
7. Salaries owed but not yet paid.
8. Interest on an interest-bearing note receivable that matures in the next fiscal period.
9. Office supplies purchased.
10. Cash received for season tickets for home football games.

Item	Prepaid Expense	Unearned Revenue	Accrued Expense	Accrued Revenue
1	✔			

Problem 1   Recording Adjusting Entries

The Pinnacle Printing Company uses the accrual basis of accounting. Its fiscal period ends on June 30. The following account balances appear in the company's general ledger as of June 30.

Cash in Bank	$34,616	Office Supplies Expense	$ 0
Interest Receivable	0	Salaries Expense	76,500
Office Supplies	8,335	Rental Income	0
Salaries Payable	0	Interest Income	0
Unearned Rental Income	1,000		

Instructions: Record the adjusting entries on general journal page 14.
(1) The office supplies on hand on June 30 are valued at $935.
(2) Pinnacle's 5-day weekly payroll totals $1,500. Salaries have been earned, but not yet recorded, for June 28-30.
(3) On June 30, 30 days of interest had accrued on an $8,000, 90-day, 9% note receivable from a charge customer.
(4) Of the $1,000 recorded in the Unearned Rental Income account, $250 had been earned as of June 30.

Problem 2   Recording Transactions for Notes Payable

The Landry Corporation uses the accrual basis of accounting. Its fiscal period ends on December 31.

On November 15, the Landry Corporation borrowed $9,500 from the First Federal Savings Bank by issuing a 120-day, $9\frac{1}{2}\%$ interest-bearing note payable.

Instructions: Record the following transactions on general journal page 41.
(1) The issuance of the note payable (Note 7).
(2) The adjusting entry to record the amount of the accrued interest payable.
(3) The payment of the note on the maturity date (Check 411).

The Accrual Basis of Accounting

Answers to "Check Your Learning" Activities

Chapter 2, Page 19
1. a. $7,000; b. $1,500; c. $8,000
2. $40
3. $20
4. $14,000

Chapter 2, Page 21
1. $25,000
2. liabilities
3. $158,000

Chapter 2, Page 27
1. Cash in Bank, +$30,000; Jan Swift, Capital, +$30,000
2. Office Furniture, +$700; Jan Swift, Capital, +$700
3. Delivery Equipment, +$10,000; Cash in Bank, −$10,000
4. Office Furniture, +$5,000; Accounts Payable, +$5,000
5. Accounts Receivable, +$700; Office Furniture, −$700
6. Accounts Payable, −$2,000; Cash in Bank, −$2,000
   Ending Balances: Assets, $33,700 = Liabilities, $3,000 + Owner's Equity, $30,700

Chapter 2, Page 30
1. Jan Swift, Capital, −$50; Cash in Bank, −$50
2. Cash in Bank, +$1,000; Jan Swift, Capital, +$1,000
3. Jan Swift, Capital, −$600; Cash in Bank, −$600
4. Jan Swift, Capital, −$800; Cash in Bank, −$800
5. Cash in Bank, +$200; Accounts Receivable, −$200
   Ending Balances: Assets, $33,250 = Liabilities, $3,000 + Owner's Equity, $30,250

Chapter 3, Page 44
1. debit
2. credit
3. debit
4.

Office Equipment	
Debit	Credit
+	−
$2,000	$500
1,500	
Bal. $3,000	

The balance of $3,000 is recorded on the debit side.

Chapter 3, Page 46
1. right
2. left
3. credit
4.

Accounts Payable	
Debit	Credit
−	+
$600	$700
200	500
400	300
	Bal. $300

The balance of $300 is recorded on the credit side.

5.

Patrick Vance, Capital	
Debit	Credit
−	+
$1,500	$ 9,000
700	3,000
	1,500
	Bal. $11,300

The balance of $11,300 is recorded on the credit side.

Chapter 4, Page 66

1. The normal balance side of any account is the side on which increases are recorded in that account.
2. A debit increases an expense account.
3. The normal balance for a revenue account is a credit balance.
4. A credit increases a revenue account.
5. A debit balance is the normal balance for an expense account.
6. A credit decreases the withdrawals account.
7. A debit balance is the normal balance for a withdrawals account.

Chapter 4, Page 75

1. Cash in Bank; Rent Expense
2. Cash in Bank is an asset account; Rent Expense is an expense account.
3. Cash in Bank is decreased; Rent Expense is increased.
4. Rent Expense is debited for $2,000.
5. Cash in Bank is credited for $2,000.
6. Rent Expense is debited for $2,000 and Cash in Bank is credited for $2,000.

Rent Expense	
Debit	Credit
+	−
$2,000	

Cash in Bank	
Debit	Credit
+	−
	$2,000

Chapter 5, Page 88

1. fiscal period
2. cycle; fiscal period
3. source documents
4. general journal

Chapter 5, Page 91

1. September 12
2. Office Supplies, $125
3. Cash in Bank, $125
4. Check 424

Chapter 5, Page 97

1. Advertising Expense
2. 9
3. Memorandum 2

4. October 15
5. 2
6. Global Travel completed services for Burton Company and billed them $450, Invoice 1000.

Chapter 5, Page 100

1. a. assets; b. assets; c. owner's equity; d. expenses; e. revenue; f. liabilities; g. expenses
2. a. Cash in Bank; b. Accounts Receivable—Martinez Company; c. Accounts Payable—Podaski Co.; d. B. Watson, Capital; e. Membership Fees; f. Maintenance Expense; g. Miscellaneous Expense
3. a. 1; b. 1; c. 3; d. 5; e. 4; f. 2; g. 5

Chapter 6, Page 112

1. the date: June 6, 19—
2. Accounts Payable—Monroe Products
3. $250; credit balance
4. 101

Chapter 6, Page 117

1. the letter and page number of the journal entry
2. $4,200
3. a zero balance
4. to indicate that an amount is not being posted from a journal
5. Credit Balance column

Chapter 7, Page 135

1. heading
2. Accounts appear in the same order as they appear in the chart of accounts.
3. A dash is entered in the normal balance amount column.

Chapter 7, Page 140

1. Balance Sheet
2. net income or net loss
3. capital
4. Check to see that all debit and credit balances have been extended properly. If all balances have been extended, check the addition and subtraction.

Chapter 8, Page 154

1. Who? What? When?
2. For the Quarter Ended June 30, 19—
3. individual account balances; totals
4. net income; $236

Chapter 8, Page 157
1. capital account
2. income statement
3. $23,200
4. balance sheet

Chapter 8, Page 160
1. October 31, 19—
2. heading, assets section, and liabilities and owner's equity sections
3. in the same order as they appear in the Balance Sheet section of the work sheet
4. statement of changes in owner's equity

Chapter 9, Page 173
1. a. Ticket Revenue; b. Income Summary; c. $6,000; $6,000
2. a. June 30, 19—; b. Income Summary; c. $3,100; d. Gas and Oil Expense, Miscellaneous Expense, Utilities Expense; e. $700, $600, $1,800

Chapter 9, Page 176
1. work sheet
2. 4
3. Income Summary
4. increased
5. 3

Chapter 10, Page 194
1. Global Travel Agency
2. Hilda G. Burton; Patriot Bank
3. ABA
4. account

Chapter 10, Page 199
1. $2,938.95
2. $635.00
3. $782.00
4. $2,938.95
5. Yes

Chapter 11, Page 217
1. Sales
2. sales slip
3. liability
4. credit terms
5.

Accounts Receivable	
Dr.	Cr.
+	—
$53.00	

Sales	
Dr.	Cr.
—	+
	$50.00

Sales Tax Payable	
Dr.	Cr.
—	+
	$3.00

Chapter 11, Page 223
1. sales of merchandise on account
2. that the transaction has been posted to the accounts receivable ledger
3. daily
4. an account in the general ledger that summarizes a subsidiary ledger; its balance must equal the total of all the account balances in the subsidiary ledger
5. An accounts receivable subsidiary ledger account form has lines at the top for the name and address of the customer and it has only one Balance column.

Chapter 11, Page 228
1. 3
2. to test for the equality of debits and credits before entering the totals in ink
3. by placing the Sales account number, in parentheses, below the double rule in the Sales Credit column
4. Debit
5. a check mark

Chapter 12, Page 242
1. receipt; tape; tape
2. debit side; it is a contra account to Sales, an account which has a normal credit balance
3. $105; $3,395

Chapter 12, Page 247
1. R311
2. General Credit
3. $1,790.00
4. by placing a dash in the Posting Reference column
5. $923.44

Chapter 13, Page 270
1. May 24
2. July 2

3. August 7
4. October 2
5. November 6; $70; $3,430
6. December 13; $18; $582
7. March 20; $19.04; $932.96
8. September 3; $145.10; $7,109.90

Chapter 13, Page 274
1. Purchases
2. decrease
3. debits; credits
4. Purchases; Accounts Payable
5. Store Equipment; Accounts Payable
6. all purchases other than purchases of merchandise on account

Chapter 13, Page 280
1. December 15, 19—
2. Sung International Imports
3. Accounts Payable Credit; Purchases Debit
4. accounts payable
5. check mark
6. Accounts Payable Credit; Purchases Debit; general ledger accounts
7. account number

Chapter 14, Page 293
1. the premium
2. check stub
3. credit
4. because over time such discounts can add up to a sizable reduction in costs
5. decrease

Chapter 14, Page 301
1. 7
2. 0
3. $1,135.21
4. 1
5. $1,008.36
6. no
7. general journal
8. 7

Chapter 14, Page 307
1. Purchases Discounts
2. individual accounts in the general ledger periodically
3. Accounts Payable
4. Cash in Bank
5. Accounts Payable; general
6. $5,000; yes

Chapter 15, Page 324
1. sales return
2. sales allowance
3. credit memorandum
4. Sales
5. debit

Chapter 15, Page 327
1. debit memorandum
2. A purchases return occurs when a business returns to the supplier for full credit merchandise bought on account. A purchases allowance occurs when a business keeps unsatisfactory merchandise but pays less than its original cost.
3. a contra cost of merchandise account
4. that the amount is to be posted to both the general and the subsidiary ledgers
5. cost of merchandise

Chapter 16, Page 349
1. because the balance of the account does not reflect the amount of merchandise on hand at the end of the fiscal period
2. A physical inventory can be taken at any time. It is always taken at the end of the fiscal period.
3. Merchandise Inventory (debited); Income Summary (credited)
4. Income Summary (debited); Merchandise Inventory (credited)

Chapter 16, Page 354
1. $2,503.70; Supplies Expense; Supplies
2. $290.00; Insurance Expense; Prepaid Insurance
3. greater than
4. $115.00; Federal Income Tax Expense; Federal Income Tax Payable

Chapter 16, Page 357
1. 4
2. $81,385.70; the credit adjustment of $3,535.40 was subtracted from the Trial Balance amount of $84,921.10
3. $9,895.00
4. Prepaid Insurance is an asset account; asset accounts are extended to the Balance Sheet section of the work sheet.
5. $0
6. The total of the Income Statement Debit column was subtracted from the total of the Income Statement Credit column.

Answers to "Check Your Learning" Activities

Chapter 17, Page 366

1. Jane Settles, Capital
2. Capital Stock
3. stockholders' equity
4. Capital Stock and Retained Earnings

Chapter 17, Page 373

1. $78,698.40
2. $7,749.67
3. $82,889.36
4. $74,401.73
5. Net income is calculated by subtracting the federal income taxes from the operating income.

Chapter 18, Page 386

1. Income Summary; Merchandise Inventory; $2,000
2. Supplies Expense
3. Insurance Expense
4. consumed
5. $720.00

Chapter 18, Page 394

1. Income Statement
2. credit; balance
3. Retained Earnings
4. net loss
5. Each revenue and contra cost of merchandise account is debited for the amount of its balance. Income Summary is credited for $20,460.00.
6. The balance of $14,500.00 represents a net income for the period.

Chapter 18, Page 399

1. $27,625.45
2. $68,175.82
3. net income
4. 4
5. Insurance Expense, Supplies Expense, and Federal Income Tax Expense
6. balance sheet

Chapter 19, Page 420

1. a. $173.16; b. $201.24; c. $250.38
2. $441.50
3. $227.10

Chapter 19, Page 426

1. federal income tax; social security and medicare tax; city or state income tax
2. Marital status; number of exemptions
3. a. $2.00; b. $10.00

4. a. $13.89; b. $10.04

Chapter 20, Page 442

1. gross earnings
2. liabilities
3. net pay
4. cash payments

Chapter 20, Page 446

1. $56.00
2. Social Security Tax Payable; Medicare Tax Payable; Federal Unemployment Tax Payable; State Unemployment Tax Payable
3. employer
4. $2,075.07

Chapter 20, Page 448

1. 7
2. the payments were made to different government agencies and businesses
3. $571.16
4. $51.14
5. $1,323.64
6. $0

Chapter 21, Page 468

1. merchandising businesses, including such retail stores as supermarkets and drug stores
2. Change Fund is debited for $25.00; Cash in Bank is credited for $25.00.
3. short; $5
4. Cash in Bank Debit, $390.75; Cash Short and Over Debit, $3.00; Sales Credit, $375.00; Sales Tax Payable Credit, $18.75
5. Cash in Bank Debit, $647.10; Sales Credit, $620.00; Sales Tax Payable Credit, $24.80; Cash Short and Over Credit, $2.30

Chapter 21, Page 475

1. $7
2. Petty Cash Fund is debited and Cash in Bank is credited.
3. $10.35
4. Debits: Supplies, $16.00; Advertising Expense, $9.00; Delivery Expense, $15.90; and Miscellaneous Expense, $8.75. Credit: Cash in Bank, $49.65.
5. A petty cash requisition is prepared to request money to replenish the petty cash fund.

Chapter 22, Page 487

1. A current asset is an asset that is either used up or converted to cash during one accounting period. Examples include cash and accounts receivable.

2. A plant asset is a long-lived asset that is used in the production or sale of other assets or services over several accounting periods. Examples include equipment, machinery, and buildings.

3. Depreciation is the process of spreading the cost of a plant asset over the asset's useful life.

4. Businesses use depreciation to allocate the costs of their assets. The matching principle is involved. Like other expenses, the costs of assets consumed during a fiscal period must be matched with the revenue earned during the same period.

5. (a) the cost of the plant asset, (b) the estimated useful life of the asset, (c) the estimated disposal value of the asset, and (d) the depreciation method used

6. Based on estimates: b, c; based on certainty: a, d

Chapter 22, Page 489

1. $23,000 − $5,000 = $18,000
2. $18,000 ÷ 5 years = $3,600
3. $3,600 ÷ 12 months = $300
4. $3,600 × $\frac{8}{12}$ = $2,400

Chapter 22, Page 494

1. credit; contra asset
2. a. $6,000; Depreciation Expense — Office Equipment
    b. $6,000; Accumulated Depreciation — Office Equipment
3. $22,000
4. $24,000

Chapter 23, Page 509

19—			
Apr. 10	Accts. Rec./Sonya Dickson	630.00	
	Sales		600.00
	Sales Tax Payable		30.00
	Sales Slip 928		
Nov. 30	Bad Debts Expense	630.00	
	Accts. Rec./Sonya Dickson		630.00
	Memo. 78		
Dec. 30	Accts. Rec./Sonya Dickson	630.00	
	Bad Debts Expense		630.00
	Memo. 89		
30	Cash in Bank	630.00	
	Accts. Rec./Sonya Dickson		630.00
	Receipt 277		

Chapter 23, Page 513

1. $125.00
2. $1,350.00
3. no
4. income statement
5. $43,418.00

Chapter 23, Page 517

Adjusting Entry

19—			
Dec. 31	Bad Debts Expense	1,850.00	
	Allow. for Uncoll. Accts.		1,850.00
19—			
May 4	Allow. for Uncoll. Accts.	1,050.00	
	Accts. Rec./Jack Bowers		1,050.00
	Memo. 241		
Nov. 18	Accts. Rec./Jack Bowers	1,050.00	
	Allow. for Uncoll. Accts.		1,050.00
	Memo. 321		
18	Cash in Bank	1,050.00	
	Accts. Rec./Jack Bowers		1,050.00
	Receipt 1078		

Chapter 24, Page 532

1. periodic
2. perpetual
3. periodic inventory
4. computerized perpetual inventory
5. Companies that use a perpetual inventory system take a periodic inventory at the end of the period to verify the balance in Merchandise Inventory.

Chapter 24, Page 535

1. $364.44
2. lifo: $363.52; fifo: $369.48

Chapter 25, Page 550

1. October 17
2. January 1
3. November 18
4. March 14
5. January 7
6. June 17

Chapter 25, Page 552

1. $75.62; $4,075.62
2. $289.73; $10,289.73
3. $136.23; $6,636.23
4. $36.25; $936.25
5. $142.03; $2,542.03

Answers to "Check Your Learning" Activities

Chapter 25, Page 554

1. a. Cash in Bank, $9,000.00
   b. Notes Payable, $9,000.00
   c. Cash in Bank, asset; Notes Payable, liability
   d. $9,355.07
2. a. January 8
   b. $12,500.00; $12,877.57
   c. Notes Payable is debited for $12,500.00; Interest Expense is debited for $377.57; and Cash in Bank is credited for $12,877.57.

Chapter 25, Page 558

1. a. Cash in Bank is debited for $9,802.74; Discount on Notes Payable is debited for $197.26; and Notes Payable is credited for $10,000.00.
   b. $197.26; $9,802.74
2. a. Maturity value, $10,000; face value, $10,000
   b. Notes Payable is debited for $10,000.00; Interest Expense is debited for $197.26; Discount on Notes Payable is credited for $197.26, and Cash in Bank is credited for $10,000.00.

Chapter 25, Page 561

1. a. Notes Receivable is debited for $6,000.00; Accounts Receivable is credited for $6,000.00; and Amy Andrus's account is credited for $6,000.00.
   b. interest-bearing
2. a. $6,133.15
   b. Cash in Bank is debited for $6,133.15; Notes Receivable is credited for $6,000.00; and Interest Income is credited for $133.15.

Chapter 26, Page 575

1. true
2. false
3. false
4. true

Chapter 26, Page 579

1. Norton, $13,500; Player, $22,500
2. Norton, $45,500; Player, $62,500

Chapter 27, Page 590

1. publicly held corporation

2. par value
3. common stock; preferred stock
4. preferred stock

Chapter 27, Page 593

1. Cash in Bank is debited; Common Stock is credited.
2. par value
3. credited
4. Cash in Bank, $11,250 debit; Common Stock, $7,500 credit; Paid-in Capital in Excess of Par, $3,750 credit

Chapter 27, Page 597

1. declaration
2. record
3. payment
4. declaration; payment
5. $12,500

Chapter 28, Page 614

1. D
2. C
3. I
4. H
5. I
6. B and C
7. F
8. A
9. B
10. J
11. G
12. E

Chapter 28, Page 618

1. E
2. C
3. D
4. B
5. A

Chapter 28, Page 621

1. $73,000
2. 2.18:1
3. 0.45:1

Chapter 28, Page 623

1. B
2. A
3. A
4. B

Glossary

a

account subdivision under the three sections of the basic accounting equation used to summarize increases and decreases in assets, liabilities, and owner's equity

accountant a person who handles a broad range of jobs related to the making of choices and decisions about the design of a business's accounting system and the preparation and explanation of financial reports

accounting clerk entry-level job that can vary with the size of the company from specialization in one part of the system to a wide range of recordkeeping tasks

accounting cycle a full range of activities that help a business keep its accounting records in an orderly fashion

accounting system a systematic process of recording and reporting the financial information resulting from business transactions

accounts payable an amount owed to a creditor for goods or services bought on credit

accounts payable subsidiary ledger a separate ledger that contains accounts for all creditors; it is summarized in the Accounts Payable account in the general ledger

accounts receivable an amount to be received from a customer for goods or services sold on credit

accounts receivable subsidiary ledger a separate ledger that contains accounts for all charge customers; it is summarized in the Accounts Receivable account in the general ledger

accumulated depreciation the total amount of depreciation for a plant asset that has been recorded up to a specific point in time

accumulated earnings an employee's year-to-date gross earnings

adjusting entries journal entries that update the general ledger accounts at the end of the fiscal period

adjustment an amount that is added to or subtracted from an account balance to bring that balance up to date

administrative expenses costs related to the management of a business (for example, office expenses)

aging of accounts receivable method a method of estimating bad debts expense in which each customer's account is examined and classified by age, the age classifications are multiplied by certain percentages, and the total estimated uncollectible amounts are added to determine the end-of-period balance of Allowance for Uncollectible Accounts

allowance method a method of accounting for uncollectible accounts in which an estimate is made of the amount of sales on account for which payment will not be received

assets property or economic resources owned by a business or individual

authorized capital stock the maximum number of shares of stock a corporation may issue

b

balance sheet a report of the final balances in all asset, liability, and owner's equity accounts at a specific time

balance side the same side of an account as the side used to increase that account

bank card a credit card issued by a bank and honored by many businesses

bank card fee a fee charged by a bank for handling a business's bank card sales; it is stated as a percentage of the total bank card sales

bank discount the interest charge deducted in advance on a non-interest-bearing note payable

bank service charge a fee charged by the bank for maintaining bank records and processing bank statement items for the depositor

bank statement an itemized record of all transactions occurring in a depositor's account over a given period, usually a month

base year a year used for comparison

basic accounting equation assets = liabilities + owner's equity; shows the relationship between assets and total equities

beginning inventory the merchandise a business has on hand at the beginning of a fiscal period

board of directors a group of people, elected by the common stockholders, who are responsible for the affairs of a corporation

book value the value of an asset at a specific point in time; for a plant asset, it equals the initial cost of the plant asset minus the accumulated depreciation

book value of accounts receivable the amount a business can realistically receive from its charge customers

business entity an organization that exists independently of its owner's personal holdings

business transaction a business event, such as the buying, selling, or exchange of goods, that causes a change in the assets, liabilities, or owner's equity of a business

c

canceled checks checks paid by the bank and deducted from the depositor's account

capital the money invested in a business by an owner; the owner's equity in a business; the owner's claim or right to a business's assets

capital stock the total amount of investment in a corporation by its stockholders

cash discount the amount a charge customer can deduct if merchandise is paid for within a specified time

cash payments journal a special journal used to record all transactions in which cash is paid out or decreased

cash receipt cash received by a business

cash receipts journal a special journal used to record all transactions in which cash is received

cash sale a transaction in which a business receives full payment for the merchandise sold at the time of the sale

certified public accountant (CPA) a public accountant who has passed the licensing exam on accounting theory, practice, auditing, and business law

change fund an amount of money, consisting of varying denominations of bills and coins, that is used for making change in cash transactions

charge customer a customer to whom a sale on account is made

chart of accounts a list of all the accounts used in journalizing a business's transactions

charter a written permission to operate as a corporation; it spells out the rules under which a business must operate

check a written order from a depositor telling the bank to pay cash to the person or business named on the check

check stub the portion remaining after a check has been detached from a checkbook; the check stub contains details of the cash payment

checking account a bank account that allows a bank customer to deposit cash and to write checks against the account balance

closely held corporation a corporation, often owned by a few people or by a family, that does not offer its stock for sale to the general public

closing entries journal entries made to close out, or reduce to zero, the balances in the temporary capital accounts and to transfer the net income or loss for the period to the capital account

commission an amount paid to an employee based on a percentage of the employee's sales

common stock the stock issued by a corporation when it is authorized to issue only one class of stock

comparability the accounting principle that allows the financial information from one period to be compared to that of another period; also, the comparison of financial information of two or more businesses

compound entry a journal entry having two or more debits or credits

computerized accounting system a system in which financial information is recorded by entering it into a computer

conservatism accounting guideline requiring that accountants choose the "safer," or more conservative, method when there is a choice of procedures

contra account an account whose balance is a decrease to another account

controlling account an account that acts as a control on the accuracy of the accounts in a related subsidiary ledger; its balance must equal the total of all the account balances in the subsidiary ledger

corporation a business organization legally recognized to have a life of its own

correcting entry an entry made to correct an error in a journal entry discovered after posting

cost of merchandise the actual cost to the business of the merchandise to be resold to customers

cost of merchandise sold the actual cost to the business of the merchandise sold to customers

credit an agreement to pay for a purchase at a later time; an entry to the right side of a T account

credit card a card containing a customer's name and account number that is presented when buying merchandise on account

credit memorandum a form that lists the details of a sales return or sales allowance; the charge customer's account is credited for the amount of a return or allowance

credit terms terms for a sale on account that set out the time allowed for payment

creditor a person or business that has a claim to the assets of a business; a person or business to which money is owed

current assets those assets that are either used up, sold, or converted to cash during one accounting period

current liabilities debts of a business that must be paid within the next accounting period

current ratio the relationship between current assets and current liabilities; calculated by dividing the dollar amount of current assets by the dollar amount of current liabilities

d

debit an entry made to the left side of a T account

debit memorandum a form used by a business to notify a creditor of a return or allowance

deduction (payroll) an amount that is subtracted from an employee's gross earnings

deposit slip a bank form on which the currency (bills and coins) and checks to be deposited are listed

depositor a person or business that has cash on deposit in a bank

depreciation the allocation of the cost of a plant asset over its useful life

direct deposit the depositing of an employee's net pay directly into her or his personal bank account; usually made through electronic funds transfer

direct write-off method a procedure in which an uncollectible account is removed from the accounts receivable subsidiary ledger and the controlling account in the general ledger when a business determines that the amount owed is not going to be paid

discount period the period of time in which a cash discount is available

disposal value the estimated value of a plant asset at its replacement time; often called trade-in value or salvage value

dividends a return on the investments by the stockholders of a corporation;

charged against the corporation's retained earnings

double-entry accounting a financial recordkeeping system in which each transaction affects at least two accounts; for each debit there must be an equal credit

drawee the bank on which a check is written

drawer the person who signs a check

due date the date by which an invoice must be paid

e

electronic badge reader computerized equipment that reads a magnetic strip on an employee's time card and automatically records the employee's arrival or departure time

electronic funds transfer system a system that enables banks to transfer funds from the account of one depositor to the account of another without the immediate exchange of checks

employee's earnings record an individual payroll record prepared for each employee; includes data on earnings, deductions, net pay, and accumulated earnings

ending inventory the merchandise a business has on hand at the end of a fiscal period

endorsement an authorized signature written or stamped on the back of a check

equity the total financial claims to the assets, or property, of a business

exemption an allowance claimed by a taxpayer that reduces the amount of taxes that must be paid

expense the cost of the goods or services that are used to operate a business; expenses decrease owner's equity

external controls those controls provided outside a business (for example, controls maintained by banks to protect deposits)

f

face value the amount written on the "face" of a promissory note; usually the same as the principal

federal tax deposit coupon (Form 8109) a form sent with the payment for FICA and federal income taxes or federal unemployment taxes to indicate the total amount of taxes being paid

financial statements reports prepared to summarize the changes resulting from business transactions that have occurred during the fiscal period

first in, first out method (fifo) an inventory costing method that assumes the first items purchased (first in) were the first items sold (first out)

fiscal period the time covered by an accounting report (usually one year)

FOB destination shipping terms specifying that the supplier pays the shipping cost to the buyer's destination

FOB shipping point shipping terms specifying that the buyer pays the shipping charge from the supplier's shipping point

footing a column total written in pencil in small figures

Form 940 the employer's unemployment tax return; it includes both federal and state unemployment taxes paid during the year

Form 941 the employer's quarterly federal tax return; it reports the accumulated amounts of FICA and federal income tax withheld from employees' earnings for the quarter as well as FICA tax owed by the employer

Form W-2 a form that provides the employee with a summary of earnings and amounts withheld for federal, state, and local taxes; also called a wage and tax statement

Form W-3 a summary of the information contained on the employees' Forms W-2; also called a transmittal of income and tax statements

full disclosure accounting guideline requiring that a financial report include enough information so that it is complete

g

general bookkeeper one person who keeps all the accounting records, usually for a small- or medium-sized business

general journal an all-purpose journal in which all transactions may be recorded

general ledger the group of accounts used by a business

going concern the assumption that a business entity will continue to operate for an indefinite time

gross earnings the total amount of money earned by an employee during a pay period

gross profit the difference between the revenue earned from sales and the total cost of the merchandise sold

gross profit on sales the amount of profit made during the fiscal period before expenses are deducted; it is found by subtracting the cost of merchandise sold from net sales

h

hardware computers and related equipment, such as disk drives and printers

horizontal analysis the comparison of the same items on accounting statements for two or more accounting periods and the analysis of changes from one period to the next

i

income statement a report of the net income or net loss for a fiscal period; sometimes called a "profit and loss" statement

Income Summary account the account in the general ledger used to summarize the revenue and expenses for the fiscal period

interest the fee charged for the use of money

interest rate the fee charged for the use of the principal when a loan is made

interest-bearing note a note that requires the face value plus interest to be paid at maturity

internal controls steps a business takes to protect cash (for example, limiting the number of persons handling cash)

inventory the items of merchandise a business has in stock

investments those assets owned by a business but not used in the operation of the business

invoice a bill; a form that lists the quantity, description, unit price, and total cost of the items sold and shipped to a buyer

issue date the date on which a promissory note is written

j

journal a chronological record of a business's transactions

journalizing the process of recording business transactions in a journal

l

last in, first out method (lifo) an inventory costing method that assumes that the last items purchased are the first items sold

ledger a book or file containing a separate page for each business account; serves as a permanent record of financial transactions

ledger account form the accounting stationery used to record financial information about a specific account

liabilities amounts owed to creditors; the claims of creditors to the assets of the business

liquidity ease with which an asset can be converted to cash

liquidity ratios measures of a business's ability to meet current debts as they become due and to provide for unexpected needs for cash

long-term liabilities debts that are not required to be paid within the next accounting period

loss the result of a company's spending more than it receives in revenue

m

maker the person or business promising to repay the principal and interest when a loan is made

managerial accounting accounting within a business firm to provide financial information to management

manual accounting system a system in which accounting information is processed by hand

manufacturing business a business that transforms raw materials into finished products through the use of labor and machinery

market value the current "market" price that is being charged for a specific item; the price at which inventory items could be replaced at the time an inventory is taken

matching principle principle stating that expenses are compared to revenues for the same period

materiality an accounting guideline stating that relatively important data should be included in financial reports

maturity date the due date of a promissory note; the date on which the principal and interest must be paid

maturity value the principal plus interest on a note that must be paid on the maturity date

medicare a federal program that provides certain health insurance benefits to retired people.

merchandise goods bought for resale to customers

merchandising business a business that buys goods (for example, books or clothing) and then sells those goods for a profit

mutual agency the characteristic of partnerships under which any partner can enter into agreements for the business that are binding on all other partners

n

net income the amount left after expenses for the period have been subtracted from revenue for the same period

net loss the amount by which total expenses exceed total revenue

net pay the amount of money left after all deductions have been subtracted from gross earnings

net purchases the total cost of all merchandise purchased during a fiscal period, less any purchases discounts, returns, or allowances

net sales the amount of sales for the fiscal period, less any sales discounts, returns, or allowances

non-interest-bearing note a note from which the interest is deducted at the time the note is made; a promissory note that has no stated rate of interest on its face

normal balance the increase side of an account: assets, debit side; liabilities and capital, credit side

note payable a promissory note issued to a creditor

note receivable a promissory note that a business accepts from a customer or other person who owes the business money

not-for-profit organization an organization that does not operate for the purpose of making a profit

NSF check a check returned by the bank because there are not sufficient funds in the drawer's checking account to cover the amount of the check

o

on account buying on credit; agreeing to pay for an item later

online the direct link-up of a terminal or cash register to a centralized computer system

operating expenses the cash spent or assets consumed to earn revenue for a business; operating expenses do not include federal income tax expense

operating income the taxable income of a corporation

other expense a non-operating expense; an expense that does not result from the normal operations of the business

other revenue non-operating revenue; revenue earned for transactions outside the normal operations of the business

outstanding checks checks that have been written but not yet presented to the bank for payment

outstanding deposits deposits that have been made and recorded in the checkbook but that do not appear on the bank statement

overtime rate a rate of pay $1\frac{1}{2}$ times an employee's regular rate of pay; overtime is paid for all hours worked over 40 per week

owner's equity the owner's claims to or investment in the assets of the business

p

packing slip a form that lists the items included in a shipment

paid-in capital in excess of par the amount of cash received by a corporation over the stock's par value

par value the dollar amount assigned to each share of stock when the corporation's charter is approved; used to determine the amount credited to the capital stock account

partnership a type of business ownership in which two or more persons agree to operate the business as co-owners

partnership agreement a written document that sets out the terms under which a partnership will operate

pay period the amount of time for which an employee is paid

payee the person or business to whom a check is written; the person or business to whom a promissory note is payable

payroll a list of the employees of a business that shows the payments due to each employee for a specific pay period

payroll clerk a person whose responsibility is the preparation of the payroll

payroll register a form that summarizes information about employees' earnings for each pay period

percentage of net sales method a method of estimating bad debts expense in which a business assumes that a certain percentage of each year's net sales will be uncollectible

periodic inventory system an inventory system in which the number of items on hand is determined by a physical count

permanent accounts accounts that are continuous from one accounting period to the next; balances are carried forward to the next period (for example, assets, liabilities, and owner's capital accounts)

perpetual inventory system an inventory system in which a constant, up-to-date record of the amount of merchandise on hand is maintained

petty cash disbursement a payment made from the petty cash fund

petty cash fund cash kept on hand for making small, incidental cash payments

petty cash register a record of all disbursements made from the petty cash fund

petty cash requisition a form requesting money to replenish the petty cash fund

petty cash voucher a form that provides proof of payment from the petty cash fund

petty cashier the person responsible for maintaining the petty cash fund and for making petty cash disbursements

physical inventory an actual count of all the merchandise on hand and available for sale

piece rate the amount paid to an employee for each item, or piece, produced

plant and equipment long-lived assets that are used in the production or sale of other assets or services over several accounting periods; commonly called plant assets

post-closing trial balance the trial balance prepared after the closing entries have been journalized and posted

posting the process of transferring information in a journal entry to accounts in a ledger

preferred stock stock whose owners have certain privileges over common stockholders

premium the amount paid for insurance

principal the amount of money being borrowed on a promissory note

private enterprise economy an economy in which people are free to produce the goods and services they choose

proceeds the amount of cash actually received by a borrower on a non-interest-bearing note payable

processing stamp a stamp placed on a creditor's invoice that outlines the steps to be followed in processing the invoice for payment

profit the amount of revenue earned above the expenses incurred to operate the business

profitability ratios ratios used to evaluate the earnings performance of a business during the accounting period (for example, return on common stockholders' equity)

promissory note a written promise to pay a certain amount of money at a specific, future time

property items of value that are owned or controlled by a business; economic resources of a business

property rights creditors' and owners' financial claims to the assets of a business

proving cash the process of determining whether the amounts of cash recorded in a business's accounting records and in its checkbook agree

proving the ledger adding all debit balances and all credit balances of ledger accounts and then comparing the two totals to see whether they are equal

proxy a document that transfers a stockholder's voting rights to someone else

publicly held corporation a corporation whose stock is widely held, has a large market, and is usually traded on a stock exchange

purchase discount term used by the buyer to refer to a cash discount offered for early payment

purchase order a written offer to a supplier to buy certain items

purchase requisition a written request that a certain item or items be ordered

Purchases the account used to record the cost of merchandise purchased during a fiscal period

purchases allowance a price reduction given when a business keeps unsatisfactory merchandise it has bought

purchases journal a special journal used to record all transactions in which items are bought on account

purchases return the return to the supplier for full credit of merchandise bought on account

q

quick ratio a measure of the relationship between short-term liquid assets (cash and receivables) and current liabilities

r

ratio analysis a numerical comparison of two items on a financial statement that is used to evaluate the relationship of the two items

receipt a form that serves as a record of cash received

reconciling the bank statement the process of determining any differences between a bank statement balance and a checkbook balance

relevance a characteristic of accounting requiring that information "make a difference" in reaching a business decision

reliability a characteristic requiring that accounting information be reasonably free of bias and error

report form a format for preparing the balance sheet in which the classifications of accounts are one under another

restrictive endorsement a check endorsement that restricts or limits how a check may be handled (for example, "For Deposit Only")

retailer a business that sells to the final user (consumer)

retained earnings earnings held by a corporation and not paid to stockholders as a return on their investment

revenue income earned by a business from its operations; revenue increases owner's equity

revenue principle accounting principle that states that revenue is recognized and recorded on the date it is earned

ruling a single line drawn under a column of figures to signify that the entries above the rule are to be added or subtracted; a double rule under an amount signifies a total

s

salary a fixed amount of money paid to an employee for each pay period

sale on account the sale of goods that will be paid for later

sales allowance a price reduction granted by a business for damaged goods kept by the customer

sales discount a cash discount

sales journal a journal used only to record the sale of merchandise on account

sales return any merchandise returned for full credit or a cash refund

sales slip a form that lists the details of a sale

sales tax a tax levied by a city or state on the retail sale of merchandise

schedule of accounts payable a list of all creditors in the accounts payable ledger, the balance in each account, and the total amount owed to all creditors

schedule of accounts receivable a list of each charge customer, the balance in the customer's account, and the total amount due from all customers

selling expenses expenses incurred in selling or marketing the merchandise or services sold by a business

service business a business operated for profit that provides a needed service for a fee

signature card a card containing the signature(s) of the person(s) authorized to write checks on a checking account

slide accidental misplacement of a decimal point in an amount

software computer programs that direct the operation of the computer

sole proprietorship a business that has one owner

source document a paper prepared as evidence that a transaction occurred

special journals multicolumn journals with columns reserved for the recording of specific types of transactions

specific identification method an inventory costing method in which the exact cost of each item in inventory is determined and assigned; used most often by businesses that have a low unit volume of merchandise with high unit prices

statement of changes in owner's equity a financial statement prepared to summarize the effects of business transactions on the capital account

statement of changes in partners' equity a financial statement that reports the changes in each partner's capital account as a result of business operations

statement of retained earnings a statement that reports the changes that have taken place in the Retained Earnings account during the fiscal period; prepared as a supporting document for the balance sheet

statement of stockholders' equity a statement that reports the changes that have taken place in all of the stockholders' equity accounts during the period

stockholders' equity the value of the stockholders' claims to the assets of the corporation

stop payment order a demand by the depositor that a bank not honor a certain check

straight-line depreciation a method of equally distributing the cost of a plant asset over the asset's estimated useful life

subsidiary ledger a ledger that is summarized in a controlling account in the general ledger

t

T account an account shaped like a "T" that is used for analyzing transactions

temporary capital accounts accounts used to record information during the fiscal period that will be transferred to a permanent capital account at the end of the period

term the length of time the borrower has to repay a promissory note

tickler file a file that contains a folder for each day of the month; invoices are placed in the folders according to their due dates

timecard a record of the time an employee arrives at work, the time the employee leaves, and the total number of hours worked each day

transposition error the accidental reversal of two numbers

trial balance a proof of the equality of total debits and credits

u

uncollectible account an account receivable that cannot be collected

unemployment taxes taxes collected to provide funds for workers who are temporarily out of work; usually paid only by the employer

v

vertical analysis a method of analysis that requires the restating of each dollar amount reported on a financial statement as a percentage of a base amount reported on the same statement

voiding a check canceling a check by writing the word "Void" on the front of a check in ink

w

wage an amount of money paid to an employee at a specified rate per hour worked

weighted average cost method an inventory costing method in which all purchases of an item are added to the beginning inventory of that item; the total cost is then divided by the total units to obtain the average cost per unit

wholesaler a business that sells to retail businesses

withdrawal the removal of cash or another asset from the business by the owner for personal use

work sheet a working paper used to collect information from ledger accounts for use in completing end-of-fiscal-period work

working capital the amount by which current assets exceed current liabilities

Credits

Cover Photos © Marble background, Otto Rogge/The Stock Market
World Trade Center, Ben Simmons/The Stock Market

Index

posting transaction for, 440-441
system, 417
payroll clerk, 417
payroll register, 426 *def.*
completing, 426-427
deductions section of, 427
earnings section of, 426
net pay section of, 427
payroll taxes
computing, 443-444
journalizing, 444-445
paying, 446-448
posting, 445, 448
percentage of net sales method of
estimating uncollectible
accounts, 518-519
periodic inventory system, 529 *def.*
permanent accounts, 62 *def.*
perpetual inventory system, 531
def.
petty cash disbursement, 468
petty cash fund, 468
cash short and over in, 475-476
envelope, 473
establishing, 469
increasing, 469
making payments from, 468, 470
reconciling, 470-471, 475-476
recording transactions in petty
cash register, 472-473
replenishing, 470-472, 474
requisition form, 471-472
voucher for, 470
petty cash register, 472 *def.*
recording vouchers in, 472
totaling and proving, 472-473
petty cash requisition, 471 *def.*
petty cash voucher, 470 *def.*, 472
petty cashier, 468 *def.*
physical inventory, 345 *def.*
piece rate, 419 *def.*
plant and equipment asset, 485
book value of, 490
cost of, 486
depreciation of, 487-488
disposal value of, 487
record, 489-490
post-closing trial balance, 169 *def.*
for a merchandising
corporation, 398
preparing, 178-179
posting, 108 *def.*
to accounts payable ledger,
300-303
to accounts receivable ledger,
222-223
adjusting entries, 387-389
from the cash payments journal,
300-303, 305
from the cash receipts journal,
247-251, 252-254
closing entries, 175-178, 394-398

in a computerized system, 117,
229
frequency of, 111
to general ledger accounts, 109,
111-116, 225-227, 252-254
payroll transaction, 440-441
from purchases journal, 276-277,
278-279
reference, 111-112
from sales journal, 222-223,
225-227
posting reference, 111-112
preferred stock, 589-590 *def.*
dividends, 594-595
issuing, 592
premium, insurance, 290
prepaid expense, 661
prepaid insurance, 290, 351
principal, of promissory note, 548
private enterprise economy, 3-5
proceeds, 555 *def.*
processing stamp, on invoice, 269
profit, 3 *def.*
gross, 345 *def.*
profitability ratios, 621 *def.*
promissory note, 548 *def.*
bank discount, 555
calculating interest on, 550-552
determining maturity date of,
548-550
face value, 548
interest, 548, 550-552
interest-bearing, 552-554
interest rate, 548
issue date, 548
maker, 548
maturity date, 548-550
maturity value, 551
non-interest-bearing, 555-558
payee, 548
principal, 548
proceeds, 555
term, 548
See also notes payable; notes
receivable
property, 18 *def.*
rights, 18, 20-21
taxes, accrued, 658-659
property, plant, and equipment
asset, 611
proprietorship. *See* sole
proprietorship
proxy, 589
public accounting, 10
publicly held corporation, 587 *def.*
See also corporation
purchase allowance, 325 *def.*
purchase discount, 269 *def.*
purchase order, 267 *def.*
purchase requisition, 266 *def.*
purchase return, 325 *def.*
purchases, 271 *def.*

on account, 49-50, 266-271,
279-280
cash, 48, 290
in a computerized accounting
system, 279-280
discount, 269-270, 291-292,
296-297
journalizing, 272-274
source document for, 268
purchases journal, 271 *def.*
posting column totals, 278-279
posting the general column of,
277
posting to the accounts payable
subsidiary ledger, 276
recording transactions in,
272-274
totaling, proving, and ruling, 278
purchases returns and allowances
account, 325
journalizing, 326
posting, 326-327
purchasing procedures, 266-269

q

qualitative characteristics, of
accounting information,
609-610
quick ratio, 620 *def.*

r

ratio
analysis, 619-622
current, 619-620
liquidity, 619-621
profitability, 621-622
quick, 620-621
return on common stockholders'
equity, 621
return on sales, 622
receipt, 85 *def.*, 239
cash, 239
journalizing cash, 243-247,
294-296
kinds of, 239-241
reconciled petty cash balance,
470-471
reconciling
bank statements, 196-198
petty cash fund, 470-471
record of original entry. *See*
journal
reinstatement, of written-off
account receivable, 508,
516-517
relevance, 609
reliability, 609
report form, 157 *def.*
restrictive endorsement, 191 *def.*